Mastering
Digital Audio Production

Mastering™
Digital Audio Production
The Professional Music
Workflow with Mac OS® X

Cliff Truesdell

Wiley Publishing, Inc.

Acquisitions Editor: Pete Gaughan

Development Editor: Stef Maruch

Technical Editor: Scott Tusa

Production Editor: Rachel Meyers

Copy Editor: Sally Engelfried

Production Manager: Tim Tate

Vice President and Executive Group Publisher: Richard Swadley

Vice President and Executive Publisher: Joseph B. Wikert

Vice President and Publisher: Neil Edde

Media Project Supervisor: Laura Atkinson

Media Development Specialist: Angie Denny

Media Development Quality Assurance: Kit Malone

Book Designers: Maureen Forys, Happenstance Type-O-Rama; Judy Fung

Compositor: Craig Woods, Happenstance Type-O-Rama

Proofreader: Nancy Hanger

Indexer: Jack Lewis

Anniversary Logo Design: Richard Pacifico

Cover Designer: Ryan Sneed

Cover Image: © Pete Gardner / Digital Vision / gettyimages

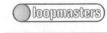

For general information on our other products and services or to obtain technical support, please contact our Customer Care Department within the U.S. at (800) 762-2974, outside the U.S. at (317) 572-3993 or fax (317) 572-4002.

Wiley also publishes its books in a variety of electronic formats. Some content that appears in print may not be available in electronic books.

Library of Congress Cataloging-in-Publication Data is available from the publisher.

Dear Reader,

Thank you for choosing *Mastering Digital Audio Production*. This book is part of a family of premium quality Sybex digital-arts books, all written by outstanding authors who combine practical experience with a gift for teaching.

Sybex was founded in 1976. More than 30 years later, we're still committed to producing consistently exceptional books. With each of our titles on graphics and audio, we're working hard to set a new standard for the industry. From the writers and artists we work with to the paper we print on, our goal is to bring you the best books available.

I hope you see all that reflected in these pages. I'd be very interested to hear your comments and get your feedback on how we're doing. Feel free to let me know what you think about this or any other Sybex book by sending me an e-mail at nedde@wiley.com, or if you think you've found an error in this book, please visit `http://wiley.custhelp.com`. Customer feedback is critical to our efforts at Sybex.

Best regards,

Neil Edde
Vice President and Publisher
Sybex, an Imprint of Wiley

Acknowledgments

First and foremost I want to thank Nate Perry, whose patience, guidance, and friendship have made this book and many other things possible.

I would also like to thank everyone who worked so hard to make this book a reality, Matt Wagner, Pete Gaughan, Stef Maruch, Scott Tusa, Rachel Meyers, and Sally Engelfried, for all of their excellent help and insight; the people who generously offered their time as interview subjects, Ralph Spight, Blake Robin, Matt Granz and Mark Pistel, Scott and Nate (again); and my great friends, Michael "Deal Machine" Dean, Lynne Hermann, Michael Scanland, Clint Blatchford, Robert Stratton, Ignacio Orellana-Garcia, Jen Satzger, and Michelle Honeck.

And, of course, my always interesting and inspiring family, Mom, Dad, Rose, Charlie, and especially my brothers, Daniel and Sam.

About the Author

Cliff Truesdell is a recording engineer, producer, and musician at Take Root Recording Studio in San Francisco. His credits on dozens of CDs include recording engineer, arranger, multi-instrumentalist, and songwriter. Cliff began playing guitar at age 13 and studied high-speed finger tapping techniques with shred-guitar masters Joe Stump and Toshi Iseda and also took some very memorable lessons from Mission of Burma's guitar player Roger Miller.

After studying music education at Berklee College of Music in Boston, Cliff moved to the Bay Area in 1998. Acquiring a used PC running Windows 95 from a friend, he began experimenting with Sonic Foundry's Acid program, creating loop-based electronic music. A trip to Seattle to work in a Pro Tools–based recording studio led to a solid conversion to the Mac operating system. Returning to San Francisco, he began an internship at Found Sound recording studio, learning advanced Pro Tools and recording techniques from studio owner Thom Canova. When Found Sound changed hands in 2002 and became Take Root Studio, the new owner, Nate Perry, eventually realized that Cliff hadn't left and hired him as assistant studio manager.

In 2003 Cliff co-founded the punk/rock & roll band Black Furies; signed to Gearhead Records in 2005, they have released three CDs to date and continue to record and tour extensively. Cliff's original music has appeared in a variety of media, including video games and professional skateboard videos. Recent credits include contributions the soundtrack for the independent film *DIY or Die!*, MTV's *Real World* and *Road Rules*, and Bravo's hit show *Queer Eye for the Straight Guy*.

Cliff resides in San Francisco's lovely, scenic Mission district; his current projects include a series of loop libraries and Reason ReFill collections to be released in fall 2007.

Contents at a Glance

Contents

Introduction

It's a little embarrassing to think about it now, but when I first bought a computer with the intention of using it to create music I was shocked to find out I'd need external devices such as an audio interface and a MIDI keyboard and interface, as well as a DAT machine or other tape device to record the computer's audio output. I just assumed that everything I wanted to do would take place in the computer, including the mixing and storing of my final songs and works-in-progress. I assumed that my computer would be the digital equivalent of my Tascam four-track recording unit. It was a big letdown to realize that I couldn't just plug my guitar and microphone directly in to the computer and start writing songs.

After the initial disappointment passed, I bit the bullet and began to work hard with what was available to me. At that point in time you really had to want things to work, and you really had to love the combination of technology and music, because if you didn't the frustrations involved in making music on computer would make any sane person quit altogether.

As time went by I began to upgrade my computer recording equipment. On my second computer, using the new and exciting looping technology that was becoming available, I was able to get considerably closer to creating and recording completely "in-the-box." Though there were still many limitations and frustrations, it was obvious that the technology was improving. I was able to see pretty clearly that even if what I had hoped for and expected from that first computer didn't exist yet, it was not too far in the future.

Today, not so many years later, digital recording (like digital everything else) has come a very long way in a relatively short time. What I had incorrectly assumed was possible less than a decade ago is standard procedure today for many recording engineers, musicians, and producers. Today you can see these advances put to good use by laptop performers and by other musicians using computers in just about every genre, as well as the sound designers and soundtrack composers who often work entirely in desktop and laptop environments. While many studios and artists today incorporate a combination of analog, live, and digital instrumentation, it's not uncommon for entire CDs, movies, recording projects, and even careers in music to take place "in-the-box."

While MP3 and AAC technology, along with digital stores such as iTunes and digital music players such as the iPod, have revolutionized how music is bought and sold, simultaneously the powerful combination of audio recording and digital music creation has led to a full-scale revolution in how music is created.

And that's what much of the focus of this book is—to introduce the reader to some of the incredible possibilities available today for creating music on your OS X Apple computer.

Another important concept covered in detail in this book relates to one of the most exciting developments in digital music production that has taken place over the last few years: the ability to work with multiple applications at once as plug-in virtual instruments and through ReWire technology.

Using ReWire (a protocol developed by the Propellerhead software company), a Mac or Windows user can connect programs like Reason, Live, and Logic together in a single session, all of the programs perfectly synced together, all of the audio output routed to a single host program. This allows the user to take advantage of the strengths of one program that may be deficient in another and vice versa—for example, having Reason's synths and samplers available in Ableton Live or Live's looping abilities available in a Pro Tools session.

Another result of the many advances in digital music technology is a leveling of the music software, and by extension the music creation, playing field. Today's home studio owners and amateur musicians have access to much of the same technology that used to be the sole territory of the professional recording engineer. Of the five main programs I'll cover in this book, one (GarageBand) is free and probably already installed on your Mac. Two others, Ableton Live and Propellerhead's Reason, are used by music professionals all over the world, yet their full versions remain affordable to the average consumer. The other two, Digidesign's Pro Tools and Apple's Logic, are considered industry-standard DAW (digital audio workstation) software, yet both are available in "light" versions (Pro Tools LE and Logic Express). These light versions are considerably less expensive than their full version counterparts, yet still contain many of the features needed to create incredibly high quality, professional sounding recordings.

Who Should Read This Book

This book is for anyone who wants to make music on an Apple computer in any capacity. Whether you are a high school student looking to make beats on an iMac, a soundtrack composer, a professional engineer recording rock and roll bands on a Pro Tools HD system in a high-powered studio, a guitar player with a home studio built around your MacBook, or someone who just started fooling around with GarageBand because it came installed on your new Mac, I'm sure there's something in these pages that will enhance the way you create music. My hope is that anyone who reads this book will be able to incorporate some of these programs, plug-ins, instruments, and concepts into their music and workflow.

What You Will Learn

Some of the things you will learn in this book include:

◆ How to get the best performance out of your OS X Mac

◆ How to use your primary recording and music creation software

◆ How to expand your primary recording software and use it conjunction with other programs

◆ How to locate, install, and use plug-in effects

◆ How to locate, install, and use plug-in virtual instruments

◆ How to work with and create Apple Loop files

◆ How to work with MIDI, simply and seamlessly

◆ How to set up a laptop studio

◆ How to create a master CD for duplication

◆ How to export your songs and create and share high-quality MP3 and AAC files

What You Need

In order to get the most out of this book I recommend that you use the following:

An Apple computer with Mac OS X 10.3 or higher   You may be able to get by with an earlier version of OS X, but most of the programs and plug-ins I'll be covering are frequently updated. The more up-to-date your version of OS X is, the less likely it is that you'll run into any compatibility issues with the software I'll be discussing.

A MIDI keyboard   Even if you already own a different type of MIDI controller or mixer, having a standard MIDI keyboard will be your best bet for working with many of the programs, demos, and tutorials covered in this book. If you need help deciding which MIDI keyboard is right for you, skip ahead to the section "MIDI Keyboards and Interfaces" in Chapter 11.

I also highly recommend that you acquire one or more of the host programs covered in Chapters 3 through 6. Each program has its advantages, depending on what kind of music you are creating and what your focus is.

Ableton Live   Live is very loop oriented but also capable of recording and working with complete audio tracks. Ableton's support of both the Audio Unit and VST plug-in format and its ability to act as both a ReWire Master and Slave make it one of the most expandable program's available.

Pro Tools   This has a number of advantages over other many digital audio programs. Pro Tools comes with its own hardware interface, plug-ins, and included third-party software, much of it ReWire-compatible. Pro Tools is available in multiple versions depending on your budget and studio size, from the inexpensive M-Powered and LE versions to the professional-level HD systems.

Logic   Apple's program is available in two versions: Logic Pro and the considerably less expensive Logic Express. Logic's included virtual instruments, deep MIDI functionality, and support for ReWire and Audio Units make for a very impressive music-making package.

GarageBand   This is the least expensive of these and may already be installed on your Mac. GarageBand's simple implementation of MIDI functionality, included loops and loop support, and included instruments make it one of the best deals going for entry level music creation software. GarageBand also supports ReWire and the Audio Units plug-in format, which means you can use it with many of the programs and plug-ins covered in this book.

No single program will work with all of the software, plug-ins, and virtual instruments that are covered in this book, but most of the software, plug-ins, and virtual instruments that are covered will work with multiple programs. No matter which host program you choose, you'll find a lot to work with in the following chapters.

The *Mastering* Series

The *Mastering* series from Sybex provides outstanding instruction for readers with intermediate and advanced skills, in the form of top-notch training and development for those already working in their field and clear, serious education for those aspiring to become pros. Every *Mastering* book features:

- The Sybex "by professionals for professionals" commitment. *Mastering* authors are themselves practitioners, with plenty of credentials in their areas of specialty.

- A practical perspective for a reader who already knows the basics—someone who needs solutions, not a primer.

◆ Real-World Scenarios, ranging from case studies to interviews, that show how the tool, technique, or knowledge presented is applied in actual practice.

◆ Skill-based instruction, with chapters organized around real tasks rather than abstract concepts or subjects.

◆ Self-review test "Master It" problems and questions, so you can be certain you're equipped to do the job right.

What Is Covered in This Book

Mastering Digital Audio Production: The Professional Music Workflow with Mac OS X is organized to reflect the creative and recording process, covering the tools you'll use to create and record music projects from beginning to end.

Chapter 1 contains the basic information you'll need to set up and optimize your OS X Mac for music production. Chapters 2 through 6 each cover, in detail, a specific DAW (digital audio workstation) program. Chapters 7 through 9 introduce you to many of the different programs, plug-in effects, and virtual instruments that can be used in conjunction with your primary recording software. Chapters 10 through 12 give you specific information about Apple Loops, using MIDI and building a laptop-based studio. Finally, Chapter 13 is about what steps to take when your recording sessions are over and it's time to create CDs and share your finished music projects with the world.

Chapter 1: Optimizing Your System   Introduces you to the Mac OS X options and settings that are most relevant to audio production work. It also lays out the possibilities and requirements for an efficient, high-quality digital studio hardware setup.

Chapter 2: Reason   Familiarizes you with Propellerhead's sequencing program, including Reason's interface and instruments, and as well as the program's looping, sampling, sequencing, and sound manipulation functionality.

Chapter 3: Ableton Live   Shows you the components that make up Live's interface and introduces you to the program's in-depth but easy to use looping, audio recording, and MIDI sequencing tools. It also shows you how to use Live in conjunction with Reason through Propellerhead's ReWire protocol.

Chapter 4: Pro Tools   Covers the basic functionality that is found in all versions of Pro Tools 7, as well as the included plug-ins and virtual instruments that are included with every copy of the program. You'll also learn how to integrate both Live and Reason into a Pro Tools session using ReWire.

Chapter 5: Logic   Demystifies one of the most complex DAW programs by showing you simple, clearly outlined ways to access the best of Logic's many features, including the program's included virtual instruments and plug-in effects. You'll also learn how to combine Live and Reason with Logic using ReWire.

Chapter 6: GarageBand   Covers everything you need to know about Apple's GarageBand program, from creating music with the included Apple Loops to using virtual instruments and plug-in effects to recording and editing your own audio tracks. Combining GarageBand with Live and Reason through ReWire is covered as well.

Chapter 7: More Really Useful Software   Introduces you to a range of excellent software, including audio editors, plug-in hosts, file converters, and organizational tools, many of them free or inexpensive. You'll learn ways to use these programs to enhance your music creation and recording abilities.

Chapter 8: Plug-ins   Covers the incredible world of plug-in effects available for OS X, including the free Audio Units already installed on your computer, the differences in plug-in file types, and the commercial and free plug-ins available for every DAW program.

Chapter 9: Virtual Instruments   Explores the many virtual samplers, synthesizers, drum machines, keyboards, and amplifiers currently available for OS X, giving you hands-on experience with free and demonstration versions of instruments in every category.

Chapter 10: Apple Loops   Covers the use of loop files in digital music making; the difference and different uses for ACID loops, REX loops, and Apple Loops; and creating and exporting loops from any program and using Apple's free Apple Loops Utility to turn any WAV or AIFF sound file into an Apple Loop.

Chapter 11: MIDI   Gives you the lowdown on what MIDI is and how easy OS X makes it to use MIDI with your DAW. Each program's MIDI functionality is covered as well as information on different kinds of MIDI interfaces and choosing the right MIDI interface for your needs.

Chapter 12: The Laptop Studio   Gives you all the information you need to create a laptop-based studio for portable recording and in-the-box composition. Including tips on selecting the right program, interface, and external gear as well as instructions and techniques for mobile recording.

Chapter 13: Post Production   Details everything you need to know once your songs are recorded and ready for the next stage. This chapter covers CD authoring, the mastering process, converting your files to MP3 and AAC, and how to get your music on iTunes and on the Internet.

The Appendix   Gathers together all the Master It problems from the chapters and provides a solution for each.

What's on the DVD

The companion DVD is home to all the demo files, samples, and bonus resources mentioned in the book.

But on top of this, we've assembled a huge, top-notch collection of third-party software to help you with your audio work and education. Many of the major applications featured in this book are included, as well as tons of smaller programs, plug-ins, demo and sample files, virtual instruments, and training tools:

Ableton Live 6   Is a complete digital audio solution, providing functionality from creation to production to performance.

Sibelius 4   Complete software for writing, playing, printing, and publishing music notation.

Finale Notepad   Compose, edit, arrange, listen to, and print your music with stunning, professional-quality results.

Battery 2   Is a drum sampler from Native Instruments with extensive sample editing and sound shaping functionality.

Reaktor 5   Is a set of music and sound creation tools from Native Instruments that includes synthesizers, effects, and drum modules.

Audacity 1.2.4   Is a free, open-source audio recording and editing program.

Peak Pro 5 and Peak LE   Is the sample editing and CD mastering solution that audio professionals depend on.

WireTap Pro 1.2   Can be used to record the audio output from any OS X application.

AudioFinder 3.9.8   Can be used to organize, edit, and convert any audio files on your OS X Mac.

iDrum   Is a straightforward yet powerful virtual drum machine that can be used as a plug-in or standalone unit.

Buzzer2 1.0.1   Is a fun and excellent sounding Audio Unit virtual synthesizer.

Zoyd   Is a freely available synthesizer study (not a finished product) capable of creating excellent industrial sounds.

Absynth 3   Is a virtual synthesizer from Native Instruments, well-suited for creating ambient sounds.

The following sections list many of the plug-ins, programs, and usable files that are included on the companion DVD, but even this is *not* an exhaustive list! Explore the disc to find all the fantastic stuff we've crammed in here.

Refills, Loops, and Samples

Reason Refills   Such as Reason Refills from Audio Warrior, Flatpack 2 from LapJockey, Sonic Flavours, and PowerFX Systems

Apple Loops   Sample tracks and loops of M Audio Pro Sessions

Gdrive Sample Collection   An intricately created synthesizer ReFill for Reason

BFD 1.5 and Guru 1.0   Drum modules from FXpansion. (Demo versions may not contain all the functionality that the book highlights.)

DOD Vol. 7 Previews   The latest high-quality realistic sounding drum loops from Drums on Demand

Rex2 Samples   Excerpts from Percussionism and Session Drums collections by Loopmasters

Plug-Ins

DigitalFishPhones   A set of three nice-sounding, easy to use VST plug-ins

Destroy FX   Interesting and unusual Audio Unit and VST sound-altering tools

Waves   Some of the most popular and well-crafted plug-ins for digital audio recording

Cycling '74 (Pluggo Junior)   Plug-in suites with interesting and unique effects and instruments

AVOX Antares Vocal Toolkit (THROAT, DUO, and CHOIR)   Vocal plug-ins that you can use to change, fix, or duplicate vocal tracks (10-day demo version)

SonicBirth 1.1.4   An application for designing and building your own original Audio Unit plug-ins

CamelSPACE, CamelPhat, Cameleon 5000, and CamelCrusher   Sound design and audio processing tools from Camel Audio

Sound Toys' TDM Effects   Expansion packs of presets for SoundToys' TDM plug-ins

PlugAdmin OS X 1.4   A program for organizing, backing up, activating, and deactivating your OS X plug-ins

Virtual Instruments and Tracks and Even More Software

Analog Factory   Combines the best of Arturia virtual synthesizers in one unit.

Guitar Pro 5   Tablature editing and creation software for guitar players

Universal UVI Player   Multiformat player from UltimateSoundBank.

NOTE   The DVD also includes a Links page that will take you to the web pages of just about every tool, sample, application, and plug-in maker mentioned in this book!

How to Contact the Author

I welcome feedback from you about this book or about books you'd like to see from me in the future. You can reach me by writing to cliff@clifftruesdell.com. For more information about my work, please visit my website at www.clifftruesdell.com.

Sybex strives to keep you supplied with the latest tools and information you need for your work. Please check their website at www.sybex.com, where we'll post additional content and updates that supplement this book if the need arises. Enter **digital audio** in the Search box (or type the book's ISBN—**9780470102596**), and click Go to get to the book's update page.

Chapter 1

Optimizing Your System

Apple computers have been at the forefront of music creation technology since Digidesign introduced Sound Tools for Macintosh (later known as "Pro Tools") in 1987. As computers have become more powerful, with increased processor speed and storage capacity, the software has in turn become much more complicated. The good news is that the process of setting up, installing, running, and maintaining recording hardware and software has become easier with each generation of the Mac operating system.

OS X is a quantum leap forward on this path. Along with its other ever-expanding list of features like Dashboard and Spotlight, OS X now makes the setting up and running of your music studio easier than ever.

The topics covered in this chapter are designed to help you get the most out of OS X and your music software, maximizing functionality and stability to ensure a powerful and consistent workflow in your studio environment.

In this chapter, you'll learn to

◆ Set your computer's preferences for optimal performance

◆ Disable the Dashboard utility

◆ Format and partition a hard drive

◆ Run OS X maintenance scripts

The Right Memory

Setting up your Mac for audio production is crucial if you want to get the most out of your software. While having a dedicated computer for your audio applications is suggested, it may not always be feasible. Even if you are doing most of your recording and music creation on a computer that is also being used for other tasks, the suggestions in the following sections will help you get the most out of your Mac.

One distinct advantage that Apple computers have over the average consumer PC is that they are essentially ready to go out of the box, without much setup needed (aside from installing and configuring your audio software and hardware, of course). However, whether you are buying a new Mac specifically for music production or adding on to your current system, it will be well worth your while to take these simple steps.

How Much RAM?

One of the first questions you should address is also one of the most commonly asked: "How much RAM do I need to run my audio production software?" The answer is simple: as much as your Mac can hold and as much as you can afford to buy. You really cannot have too much RAM installed in your system. Audio production and music software are big RAM hogs. Some music software will say that its minimum system requirement is 256MB of RAM, but any system with less than 512MB of RAM will reach its limit pretty quickly. This means that your computer will start freezing up, generating various error messages, and possibly crashing. Having more RAM will mean a faster response time, faster mix-downs and file conversions, more recording and MIDI tracks, more plug-ins, and more stability. Although you can add more RAM later, you'll save time, money, and stress by getting your Mac outfitted with a lot of memory up front. If you're planning on doing any intensive music production, especially using virtual synthesizers, samplers, and plug-ins, you should start out with a minimum of 1GB of installed RAM.

Adding More RAM

Adding RAM to a desktop G4 or G5 is a pretty simple matter, especially with the newer G5 models. Apple has made it easy to open the CPU to locate the available slots and install more memory. See the documentation that came with your Mac for the details specific to your Apple computer. You can buy more RAM from your local Apple store or a third-party retailer, but make sure you are clear about what model and processor type your computer is. You should be aware that Apple doesn't support third-party RAM and installing it yourself will void your AppleCare warranty.

TROUBLESHOOTING RAM

If your computer is crashing frequently and/or if you're having frequent kernel panics (the screen fades and a big gray box appears in the middle) you may have installed a bad RAM chip. This problem can often be diagnosed using the Hardware Test CD that came with your computer or by removing individual RAM chips and seeing if the computer still crashes and freezes.

Adding RAM to an iMac, Mac Mini, or Mac laptop is a somewhat more difficult proposition. Unless you really know your way around the inside of a computer, don't try to do this yourself. If you decide to add more RAM to one of these models, you should bring it to your local Apple Store or another professional to get the job done correctly. It's also much more expensive to add RAM to a laptop after purchase than it is to add it to a desktop computer.

When it comes to already installed RAM, most current Macs' standard configurations are not put together with professional music software in mind. Luckily, Apple allows you to customize any Mac you purchase from them, and adding RAM is always an available option. If you intend to run multiple programs, plug-ins, and virtual instruments in a single session, or if you expect to expand your recording system, you should consider buying your laptop, iMac, or Mac Mini with the maximum amount of RAM already installed.

Setting System Preferences

Under System Preferences you can access and change some basic settings that will greatly improve your Mac's overall performance (thereby improving the performance of your music software).

Access these settings by selecting System Preferences from the Apple drop-down menu at the top left of your screen. This will open the System Preferences window, which features several icons that you can click to set your preferences for each category. Once you make a change, click the Show All button at the top of the window to return to the main System Preferences window shown in Figure 1.1.

NICKELS AND DIMES: SAVING CPU CYCLES

Like many of the suggestions made in this chapter, disabling the Animate Opening Applications function of the Dock frees up a small amount of processor resources. So why bother? Well, by itself it's not that big a deal, but combine this with the elimination of three or four other "small" resource hogs and pretty soon you'll find that you are saving a good chunk of power. That's power that can be used to run that really important extra plug-in or to give you the push you need to mix down the 36-track song you just wrote without crashing!

FIGURE 1.1

OS X System Preferences

Dashboard & Exposé

Exposé allows you to set up Active Screen Corners, which cause a specific action to take place as you move your mouse to one corner of your screen, such as activating your screensaver or viewing the desktop. There are two good reasons to leave the Active Screen Corners turned off. The first is that having this setting activated will use up some of your processor's resources. The other is that most recording software is quite complicated, requiring you to make adjustments all over the screen and window. It can be annoying to be in the middle of a project and accidentally cause Dashboard to open or to have all your open windows disappear suddenly. Leave these four blank, or if one or more has already been assigned a function, reset it by selecting the dash (–) from its drop-down menu.

At the bottom half of the window you'll see the Keyboard Shortcuts section. Here you can assign keyboard shortcuts to the Exposé functions. By default, OS X assigns Dashboard and OS X keyboard shortcuts to keys F9 through F12. Many recording and audio production programs also assign sometimes important keyboard shortcuts to these keys, so you should change these settings. At the same time, being able to execute a simple keyboard shortcut to view the desktop or all open application windows is very useful. One solution is assigning a more complex keyboard shortcut to these functions that won't interfere with your recording software. To do this hold down the Shift, Option, Control, or Command keys, or any combination of keys while selecting the Keyboard Shortcuts drop-down menu. Figure 1.2 shows each function assigned a Control+Shift+F# keyboard shortcut.

Reassigning this keyboard shortcut is especially important if you are using any version of Pro Tools. The F12 command that Pro Tools uses to start recording will not work if you leave the Dashboard defaults on; it will open Dashboard instead. In general, however, your music software's keyboard shortcuts will be compatible with or will override the OS X keyboard shortcuts.

Desktop & Screen Saver

To set up your Desktop & Screen Saver preferences so that they use minimal processor resources, follow these steps:

1. Open the Desktop & Screensaver Preferences.

2. Under the Desktop tab make sure that the Change Picture check box at the bottom of the window is not selected.

3. Under the Screen Saver tab move the Start Screen Saver slider all the way to the right so that the setting is Never, as shown in Figure 1.3.

FIGURE 1.2
Dashboard & Exposé
preferences

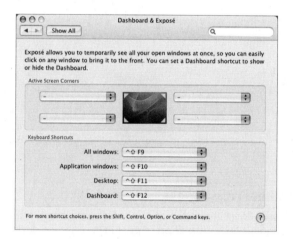

FIGURE 1.3
Desktop & Screen
Saver settings

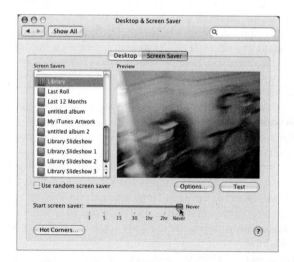

The Dock

The Dock acts as OS X's program shortcut menu, giving you quick access to your most frequently used programs, files, and folders, such as your favorite loop, sample collections, or session template files.

The Dock is an essential tool in OS X, but it has a downside: it can take up valuable real estate on your monitor window. And, depending on where you choose to place it, the Dock can pop up when you're in the middle of working on a session or editing a file (note to Apple: a keyboard shortcut that keeps the dock hidden would be helpful). Finally, some of the Dock's cooler visual functions can take up valuable processor power. To set the Dock preferences to work best for your system and software:

1. Open the Dock preferences and use the Dock Size slider to minimize the Dock to the smallest size that you can comfortably work with. At its absolute minimum you may not be able to make out which programs are which, so use your own judgment.

2. Turn the Magnification effect off by deselecting the box next to the Magnification slider.

3. Disable Animate Opening Applications and enable Automatically Hide and Show the Dock.

   Figure 1.4 shows your new settings in the Dock preferences window.

FIGURE 1.4
The Dock preferences

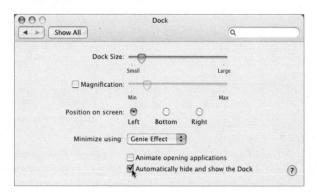

POSITIONING THE DOCK FOR AUDIO APPLICATIONS

Where you choose to place the Dock may depend on which program or programs you use most often. Since many music production programs place the transport controls (the Stop, Play, Record, Fast Forward and Rewind buttons at the bottom of the interface, for minimum intrusion you should position the Dock vertically on the left or right side of the screen. There are exceptions, however. For example, Pro Tools users may not want to place the Dock on the left side of the screen where many of the functions of the Pro Tools edit window reside.

Security

Unless you feel strongly that you have files you need to protect, it's a good idea to leave FileVault turned off under the Security preferences. FileVault's encryption process takes up a lot of extra space and resources. FileVault will be turned off by default. If you've previously activated FileVault you may want to consider deactivating it to free up the system resources it uses.

Spotlight

OS X's Spotlight automatically assigns keyboard shortcuts to some Spotlight functions. In particular, the Command+spacebar shortcut used to record tracks in Pro Tools will automatically open Spotlight instead of tracking your session. You can disable this keyboard shortcut by deselecting the Spotlight Menu Keyboard Shortcut check box, as shown in Figure 1.5.

FIGURE 1.5
Spotlight preferences

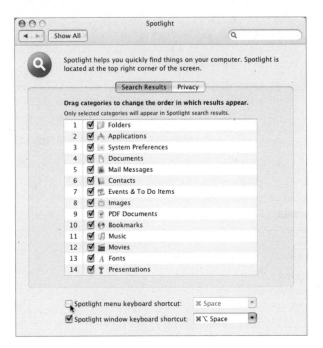

Disabling this shortcut does not mean you've disabled Spotlight. In fact, you can assign a different shortcut to Spotlight, either here or in the Keyboard & Mouse preferences window. However, I find that when I need to find something with Spotlight, it's just as easy to click the Spotlight icon on the top right of the screen.

Energy Saver

As the setup information for many recording programs will tell you, when you are using your computer for music-related applications, the Energy Saver settings should *always* be turned off. Under the Sleep tab, move the two sleep option sliders all the way to the right so their settings are Never, as shown in Figure 1.6.

Next, choose the Options tab and select Highest from the Processor Performance drop-down menu at the bottom of the window. Since your computer will not be going to sleep you don't have to worry about whether the Wake Options are selected or not.

Keyboard & Mouse

Generally you will want to leave the Keyboard & Mouse settings alone. However, if your mouse seems sluggish or if you are experiencing the "jumping mouse" syndrome (where your mouse seems to suddenly appear on the opposite side of the screen) you adjust its settings with the Tracking Speed slider under the Mouse tab.

Under the Keyboard Shortcuts tab you'll see more keyboard shortcuts, including the previously covered Spotlight shortcuts. As you can see in Figure 1.7, the Show Spotlight Search Field keyboard shortcut is currently disabled, as is the Dashboard F12 shortcut.

FIGURE 1.6

The Energy Saver's Sleep settings

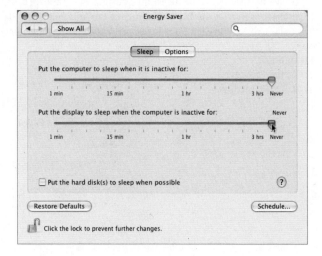

FIGURE 1.7

Disabled Dashboard and Spotlight keyboard shortcuts in the Keyboard Shortcuts preferences window

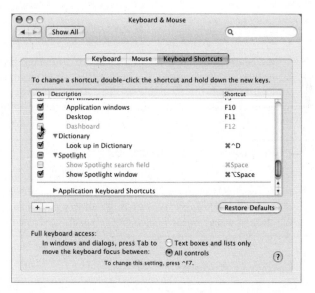

In general, your music software's keyboard shortcuts will override your system's keyboard shortcuts, Spotlight and Pro Tools being the obvious exception. If you find that this is not the case, you can return to the Keyboard Shortcuts tab in the Keyboard & Mouse preferences and disable or reassign any keyboard shortcuts you wish.

Sound

In the Sound preferences, under the Input and Output tabs, you'll choose the default input and output that your computer will use for recording and playing back audio. This will affect the default output for programs like iTunes and QuickTime. Regardless of what you choose in the Sound preferences window, in some programs you may have to set the output in the program's preferences. If you would like to route all incoming and outgoing audio through your third-party hardware interface, choose the Input or Output tab and select the device you wish to use from the list.

Figure 1.8 shows a Digidesign HW (002) interface selected as the default output.

FIGURE 1.8
Sound preferences
audio output settings.

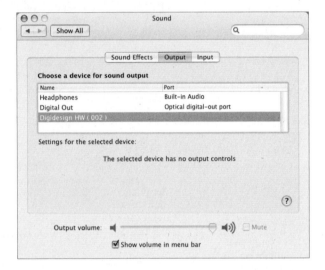

Make sure your hardware interfaces are connected properly and powered up before you try to set your Sound preferences. If your hardware interface is connected but not powered on, it may not show up in the list of available devices. Also, if you restart your computer with the device turned off, your computer will default to the built-in sound settings.

TROUBLESHOOTING MISSING SOUND

If you are not hearing any sound when recording into your Mac's built-in ⅛-inch line in or when playing music from iTunes or another audio application, the Sound Preferences window is the first place you should check. You can accidentally turn off the sound for your Mac in a number of ways. Under both the Input and Output tabs, make sure the volume slider is not all the way to the left and that the mute box is unchecked.

Software Update

Every Mac has a built-in Software Update feature that automatically checks for updates to OS X, your iLife programs, QuickTime, and so on. This is a great feature and should be used regularly. However, as you can probably guess, downloading and installing software can be a processor-intensive task and require your computer to restart. In order to avoid having your computer access this function while you are in the middle of an important project, click the Software Update icon and deselect the Check for Updates button, as shown in Figure 1.9. After you do this, make sure to perform your own checks for updates by regularly selecting Software Update from the Apple menu.

FIGURE 1.9
Deselect the Check for
Updates box.

Tips, Tricks, and Software

The suggestions in the following sections will help you get the best performance out of your OS X Mac and music software. The more of these you can implement, the better your performance will be.

Leave Room

Make sure that the hard disk you are running your operating system on has a significant amount of free space, at least 6GB if possible. OS X's performance relies heavily on virtual memory, which requires as much free space as possible. Filling your hard drive with unneeded files and software will drastically reduce you computer's performance. To see how much free space is left on your hard drive, select the drive icon on your Desktop and press Command+I to view the Get Info window. In the Get Info window under the General field, as shown in Figure 1.10, you'll see your hard drive's total capacity, how much is still available, and how much is currently being used.

If you're running low on space, here are some suggestions for cleaning up your hard drive:

Remove unneeded fonts A large collection of fonts can cause your system to slow down. If it's necessary for you to have a large font collection (for example, if you are using your Mac for design work as well as audio production), you can use an application such as OS X's Font Book to temporarily turn off less frequently used fonts.

FIGURE 1.10
View your hard drive's
Get Info window.

Remove unnecessary software   Everyone occasionally downloads and installs some piece of software that you ultimately don't need. Maybe it's a copy of Tetris, an MP3 player that iTunes has replaced, or some other application that you never use. Check out your Applications folder and see if there's some weeding that you can do. Remove a program by selecting it and moving it to the Trash and then search the program's name in Spotlight to find other files related to the program, such as preferences, extra files, and settings, and move those to the Trash as well. (Don't forget to empty the Trash to recover the space used by those files.)

Remove duplicate files   Duplicate files can be created any number of ways. Reinstalling a program after moving files around, accidentally copying a folder to a new location, or having multiple versions of the same MP3 files are some of the more common instances. Use a program like Hyperbolic's TidyUp! (available at www.hyperbolicsoftware.com) to locate and delete duplicate files.

Back up items and remove them from your hard drive   If your Mac has a SuperDrive, it's an easy matter to buy some recordable CDs or DVDs and store or archive any files you want to keep but don't necessarily need immediate access to. Single-sided recordable DVDs can hold up to 4.7GB of data. If you have one of the more recent MacBook Pro or G5 models, you can archive your files using double-sided DVDs which can hold twice as much data.

Disabling Dashboard

Dashboard is one of the cool new features included in Mac OS X 10.4. Dashboard allows you to download and install widgets, which are small applications that do all kinds of interesting things. From calculators to streaming audio radio stations and much more, Dashboard widgets are a lot of fun and can be very useful. The only problem is that all widgets take up some processor power, and some use an awful lot. Also, if Dashboard is running in the background while you are working in OS X, some active widgets may be accessing the Internet, creating a further drain on your system's resources.

OS X doesn't make it easy to turn Dashboard on and off. Probably the simplest way to accomplish this is the Disable Dashboard utility available at www.natal.be. This utility is actually two small applications, as shown in Figure 1.11, which you can drag to your desktop or Applications folder. Open the appropriate application to deactivate or reactivate Dashboard.

FIGURE 1.11
The Disable Dashboard utility's Disable and Enable Dashboard buttons

Activity Monitor

OS X comes with a built-in program for monitoring whatever programs are currently running on your system and exactly how many resources (RAM and virtual memory) each program is currently using. The Activity Monitor is located in your Applications/Utilities folder.

With the Activity Monitor you can clearly see which programs are resource hogs, how much real and virtual memory each program is using, and how much CPU and system memory is currently being used and is available. You can also use the Activity Monitor to quit active programs that you don't recognize or are not able to otherwise access. Select any program in the Activity Monitor window, as shown in Figure 1.12, and click the Quit Process button in the top left corner. Be careful with this though, especially if you are not sure exactly a currently running program is or is doing. Quitting the wrong program can sometimes cause your computer to freeze up or to shut down—not something you want to have happen in the middle of a session.

FIGURE 1.12
View active
programs in the
Activity Monitor.

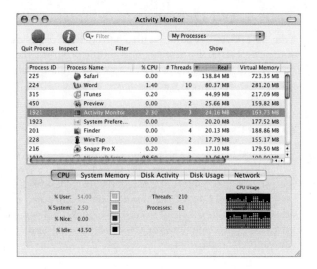

Universal Binary

Apple surprised the computing world in 2005 with the announcement that future Apple computers would be gradually making the switch to Intel processors from the current PowerPC processors. If you have one of the new Intel-based Macs, most of the software that you were using on PowerPC Macs will work fine, thanks to translation software called Rosetta (read more about it at www.apple.com/rosetta). However, some versions of certain programs may experience slight sluggishness, and there are some plug-ins and features of your music software that may not work altogether. To avoid any potential headaches and to get the most out of the new, faster Intel-based Macs, be sure that wherever possible you are using Universal Binary–compatible versions of your software. Programs that are compatible will have the Universal Binary logo shown here.

The following programs covered in this book are now available in Universal Binary–compatible versions:

- Reason 3.0.5
- Live 6
- Pro Tools 7.1
- Logic 7.2
- GarageBand 3.0.4

Your Hard Drives

Your Mac obviously comes with a hard drive. For basic operation of your DAW program this may suffice, especially if you are using a simple program like GarageBand or if you are doing basic songwriting and programming in a program like Reason which is effectively optimized for OS X. However, at the least you'll want to invest in one external hard drive for backing up your files.

BACKING UP

While this subject for is a no-brainer for many people, I am constantly amazed at the number of conversations I have with people who have lost all or part of a session due to crashing hard drives, spilled liquids, or any other number of mishaps that could be avoided or at least minimized by backing up your sessions on regular basis. The best plan for backing up is to have a separate, dedicated external hard drive that you plug in at least once a day to make copies of all of the files you are currently working on. When a session is complete, you can either store the hard drive or copy the files to DVD or another storage medium for archiving.

If it can be avoided, do not record to the same drive that is running your operating system and DAW software. Doing so will greatly compromise your recording abilities, especially when it comes to track and plug-in counts. Probably the most common configuration these days is to run your operating system and audio software from your internal hard drive while recording the audio tracks to *at least* one external drive.

Having more drives at your disposal means more power. Many programs incorporate this concept into their operating procedure. For example, Pro Tools' Round Robin allocation allows you to send your files to multiple drives to alleviate the strain on any one drive. This is covered in more detail in Chapter 4, "Pro Tools, " in the section "Pro Tools and OS X."

Another program that gives you this option is Apple's own Logic Pro, which automatically asks where you'd like the recorded file to reside when you arm a track for recording. Spreading different tracks among multiple hard drives enhances Logic's performance. This is especially important when you wish to take advantage of Logic's processor-intensive built-in synthesizers, samplers, and virtual amplifiers.

Researching the Best Hard Drive

When shopping for an external hard drive, two crucial elements are the speed and the size of the drive. Currently available FireWire drives generally range from 5400 to 7200RPM. Unless you are specifically buying a drive for portability, you will definitely want to get a 7200RPM drive. When it comes to size, 80GB may seem like a lot of space, but do a few sessions with multiple takes, remixes, and different versions of the same songs and you'll be surprised how quickly your hard drives fill up. Combine this with regular backing up or multiple sessions and you'll be out of space before you know it. Always assume you'll need more room.

It's a good idea to research a particular model as much as possible before buying an external drive. While it's possible to save a few dollars buying a lesser-known brand on eBay or at a discount store or website, you may end up regretting it later. A warranty can replace a crashed hard drive, but it can't replace the session you've just spent a week recording and mixing. You can check out user reviews for specific models on Amazon.com and Apple.com or by searching on Google for the brand name and model number of the hard drive you are considering. Also check out Internet forums such as those at www.TapeOp.com and the Digidesign Users Conference (duc.digidesign.com) or other groups related to your recording software and see what hard drives other people are using and what their experience has been. To get you started, try researching Seagate, LaCie, Western Digital, and Maxtor, which are all frequently recommended drives for audio recording.

USB 2 OR FIREWIRE?

On paper, the difference between a USB 2 and a FireWire drive may not look that huge. In reality, there is a noticeable difference in how fast information is transferred between the two types of drives. Tests show that FireWire drives are significantly faster across the board. Because USB 2 drives are generally less expensive than FireWire drives, they are a good choice for backing up your files or storage. However, for writing, recording, and sequencing music, where speed is crucial, it's best to go with FireWire.

Formatting Hard Drives

When you buy a new drive, you need to format it to optimize it for your Mac and for music production. While most drives are capable of reading and storing data as soon as you plug them in, they may not be optimized for your needs. If you are reformatting a drive that you have already used, make sure that any files you want to keep are backed up on another drive. Formatting and reformatting will completely erase any files currently residing on your drive. Use the following steps to format or reformat any hard drive:

1. Once your drive is powered up, plugged in, and appears on your desktop, go to your Applications/Utilities folder and start the Disk Utility program.

2. Select your disk from the available disks on the left side of the Disk Utility window.

3. Select the Erase tab and, from the Volume Format drop-down menu, choose Mac OS Extended (Journaled), as shown in Figure 1.13. (Journaling is a relatively new feature, introduced with OS X 10.2, that protects your hard drive from power failures and other hardware-related problems.)

4. Name your drive in the Name field.

5. If you think there's a possibility that you may need to use this drive to copy files from a computer running OS 9, select the Install Mac OS 9 Disk Driver check box.

6. Click Erase.

Your new drive is now optimized for music production and ready to go.

Partitioning

You might want to consider partitioning one or more of your hard drives if you have large enough drives. There are a number of reasons to do this such as that you may want a drive that is readable on both OS X and Windows XP. (On the new Intel-based Macs, it's possible to run both operating systems from different partitions on a single disk.) Or you may want to partition for the same reason I do: I use two-thirds of my partitioned drive for storage and one-third to keep a backup version of OS X and certain programs. This way if my system crashes, I can plug in the backup version and have immediate access to my other drives.

To partition a hard drive, follow these steps:

1. Start Disk Utility.

2. Select the drive you wish to partition from the list on the left side of the Disk Utility window.

3. Select the Partition tab.

4. From the Volume Scheme drop-down menu, choose the number of partitions you wish to divide your hard drive into. Figure 1.14 shows the Disk Utility separating a hard drive into three partitions.

FIGURE 1.13
Use the Disk Utility to format your new hard drive.

FIGURE 1.14
Creating three separate partitions on a single hard drive with the Disk Utility

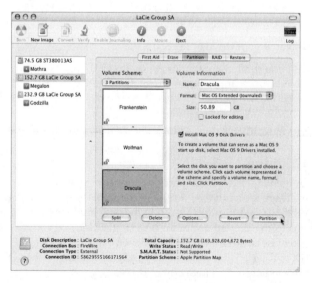

5. You can give each partition a separate name by selecting it and then entering a name in the Name field under Volume Information.

6. Change the size of the partition by entering a higher or lower number in the Size field.

7. If you think that there is a possibility that you may use this drive in conjunction with a Mac running OS 9, select the Install Mac OS 9 Disk Drivers check box.

To format your drive to contain a Windows XP operating system:

1. Click the Options button and choose Master Boot Record from the Partition Scheme window that appears (see Figure 1.15) and click OK to return to the Disk Utility window.

FIGURE 1.15
Select Master
Boot Record

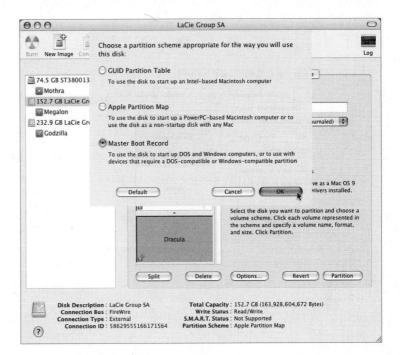

2. Select any one of the partitions in the Volume Scheme section and choose MS-DOS from the Format drop-down menu.

MULTIPLE OS X INSTALLATIONS

Another advantage to having multiple versions of OS X: Whenever Apple releases a new version of OS X or an upgrade to the current version, it can sometimes take a couple weeks or even longer before your music software is upgraded to be compatible. By having both the older and newer versions of OS X running on two separate hard drives (or partitions), you can take advantage of new features that come with a new operating system without having to wait for all of your music software to catch up.

Running OS X on an External Drive

If you have an older internal hard drive or your hard drive is nearly full, another possible way to increase your available power is to install OS X on an external drive and run your operating system and music software from there. This offers a number of benefits, especially for laptop users whose internal hard drives are often significantly slower than desktop internal drives.

For example, all of the current MacBooks have internal drives with a speed of 5400RPM. By installing OS X on a 7200RPM external drive you can increase your track count (number of audio and MIDI tracks in a single session) and the number of plug-ins you can use in a session.

To install OS X on an external drive:

1. Insert your OS X installation CD and restart your computer.

2. Follow the normal installation procedure.

3. When prompted, choose the external drive as the location where you would like to install OS X.

To start your computer from an external drive:

1. Open System Preferences and click the Startup Disk icon.

2. Under Select the System You Want to Use to Start Up Your Computer, choose which operating system you would like to use.

3. If you want to restart immediately click the Restart button.

Figure 1.16 shows the multiple instances of OS X on my computer.

FIGURE 1.16
Use the Startup Disk Preferences to choose which instance of OS X you want to use.

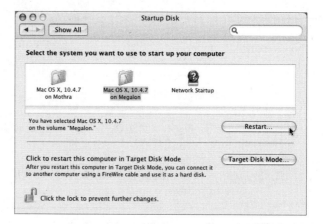

OS X Maintenance

You can keep your OS X Mac in the best possible working condition by keeping up with a few simple maintenance tasks. Aside from the immediate benefits of increased speed and efficiency, performing regular maintenance can help prevent crashes and freeze-ups.

🌐 Real World Scenario

CUSTOM INSTALLATION OF OS X 10.4 TIGER

When I'm setting up a new operating system for audio recording, I like to take advantage of OS X's custom installation options, which allow you to choose which fonts, printer drivers, and languages are included in your operating system. Choosing the custom installation option can save over 3GB of space on your computer.

To perform a custom installation:

1. Insert your OS X installation disc and restart your computer. Select your default language.

2. Continue past the introduction and License Agreement.

3. In the Choose Destination window, select your destination drive and click the Options button.

4. Choose the Erase and Install option and format the disk as Mac OS Extended (Journaled), then click OK.

5. Click Continue.

6. Click the Customize button on the lower left.

If you plan on using a printer, you can select and install the drivers for your model by opening the Printer Drivers list and choosing to install the drivers for one or more specific brands.

7. In the Customization window, deselect Printer Drivers, Additional Fonts, and Language Translation.

8. Click the Install button.

Maintenance Scripts

OS X runs a series of daily, weekly, and monthly maintenance scripts on your computer. These scripts clean up unnecessary files, delete and fix others, and are automatically scheduled to run during late night/early morning hours. If your Mac is turned off or asleep at these times, the scripts will not run.

There is also a variety of shareware and freeware programs that will run maintenance scripts and clean up your system. I recommend the easy-touse freeware program OnyX. You can download OnyX from:

www.macupdate.com/info.php/id/11582

Or you can find it by searching for it on Version Tracker (www.versiontracker.com).

Once you've installed OnyX:

1. Double-click the program icon to start the program. OnyX will ask you for your administrator password to make sure you are allowed access to its functions.

2. Choose the Maintenance tab and, in the Run Maintenance Scripts section, select the Daily Script, Weekly Script, and Monthly Script check boxes.

3. Click the Execute button to start the process, as shown in Figure 1.17.

FIGURE 1.17
Use OnyX to run
maintenance scripts.

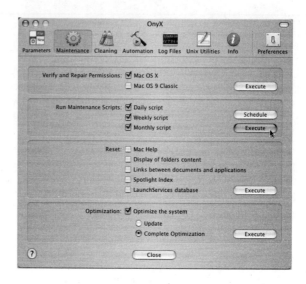

OTHER THIRD-PARTY SOFTWARE FOR MAINTENANCE

There are many other programs that you can use to optimize and maintain your computer. Some currently available freeware and shareware utilities include:

◆ TinkerTool (www.bresink.de)

◆ Cocktail (www.maintain.se/cocktail)

◆ System Optimizer X (www.mkd.cc/sox)

◆ AppleJack (applejack.sourceforge.net)

◆ Maintenance (www.destinyofshadow.com/blog)

◆ UltimateTask (www.jaanpatterson.com)

If you can't find these programs at the websites listed, check for them on www.versiontracker.com.

Repairing Permissions

Many crashes can be prevented, and systems that crash frequently can often be fixed simply by repairing permissions. Permissions are settings on your Mac that determine access to the programs, files, and folders on your computer. Sometimes these settings are altered by third-party software when you install new programs.

You can use OnyX to repair permissions. Under the same Maintenance tab that contains the previously mentioned maintenance scripts, you will also see the Verify and Repair Permissions section. Select Mac OS X and click the Execute button, as shown in Figure 1.18.

You can also use the Disk Utility to verify and repair permissions. I prefer to use OnyX to do this because it allows me to include verifying and repairing permissions as one of a number of maintenance tasks that I can take care of all at once.

FIGURE 1.18
Use OnyX to repair
permissions.

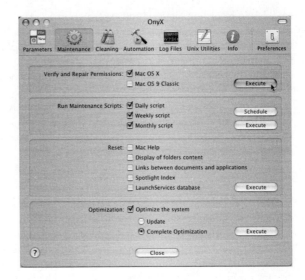

Surf Smart

When it comes to viruses and the Mac, there's really no comparison to the dangers faced by the average PC user. That said, viruses are a growing problem for Mac users. More viruses for OS X are popping up every day.

You may want to have web access for your workstation so you can download software updates for your primary programs, new programs, loops, plug-ins, and demos. Some users, especially those using their Macs for more than audio recording, will have even more things to do on the Web.

If at all possible, try to use a separate computer for downloading the necessary files, burn them to a disc, and use the disc to install the programs or updates to your primary music workstation. If this is not realistic for you, at least do the following to help keep your computer virus free:

- Avoid file-sharing programs such as LimeWire and Cabos.

- Invest in a virus protection program such as Symantec's Norton AntiVirus. You can also find a number of freeware and shareware virus protection utilities at www.versiontracker.com.

- Don't open e-mail attachments from unknown senders and be careful with unexpected e-mail attachments from known senders.

- Never, ever install an application unless you are 100 percent sure of its origin and creator.

Hardware Maintenance

Keeping all of your hardware (your CPU, external drives and audio/MIDI interfaces) clean and protected and keeping your drivers up-to-date can go a long way toward increasing both the lifespan and functionality of your equipment.

Smoke and Dust

It's hard to believe it now, but there was a time in the not-so-distant past when smoking was allowed in many recording studios. You've probably seen photos and movies of guys back in the '50s and '60s smoking in recording sessions and control rooms. I doubt there are many professional studios left in the world that would allow clients to blow smoke at a $3000 Neumann microphone (unless you're Keith Richards, maybe). Keeping your computer, microphones, and hardware interfaces in a smoke-free environment is just common sense these days.

Ultimately though, at least as far as your CPU is concerned, smoke particles are not nearly as much a threat as dust particles.

Desktop computers, like your G4 or G5, cool themselves with fans that can bring dust inside the CPU. This dust can build up over time and cause various problems. It's a good idea to keep a dust vacuum handy and use it regularly all around your recording area. At your local hardware or computer store you can also buy dust removal air spray cans, which you can use to keep your CPU as well as your keyboard, monitor, and audio interfaces as dust-free as possible.

Updating Hardware Drivers

Another way to make sure your audio interface hardware is functioning at its best is to keep your drivers and software up to date by regularly checking the manufacturer's website. The companies that make your recording hardware (M-Audio, Digidesign, and so on) and MIDI devices release occasional updates that, once installed, will allow your devices to work better. In many cases, new drivers are included automatically with software updates, but it's still a good idea to check the manufacturer's website to make sure your software is up to date.

The Bottom Line

Set your computer's preferences for optimal performance   Setting up your system's preferences correctly can serve two functions: it saves processor resources for your audio software and makes your interactions with OS X smoother when working in your DAW program.

Master It   Use System Preferences to turn off the screen saver, then resize and automatically and hide the dock when it's not in use.

Disable the Dashboard utility   Dashboard widgets can be fun and useful, but they can also drain your computer's resources by running in the background or connecting to the Internet when you're in the middle of some other task.

Master It   Use the Disable Dashboard utility to turn Dashboard off.

Format and partition a hard drive   Installing a new FireWire or USB hard drive is usually as simple as plugging it in. To optimize it for audio recording you may need to reformat it. You can also partition your drive for multiple uses.

Master It   Recreate the steps you would take to reformat or partition a hard drive (don't *actually* reformat or partition your hard drive unless you mean to).

Run OS X maintenance scripts   OS X performs regular maintenance of your computer at regular intervals. This maintenance can help to prevent crashes and keep your system running at its best. Many of these scripts run at times when your computer may be turned off. To work around this, you can download and install a maintenance program to run these scripts manually.

Master It   Download and install the OnyX program and use it to run all of the OS X maintenance scripts.

Chapter 2

Reason

Propellerhead's Reason 3 is an incredible music production program, offering nearly limitless possibilities for looping, sampling, sequencing, and creating original sounds. This chapter will familiarize you with Reason's interface, instruments, and functionalities.

In this chapter, you'll learn to:

◆ Create a new Reason song with a mixer, instruments, and effects

◆ Edit loops in the Dr. Rex Loop Player

◆ Add effects as inserts and sends

◆ Create and save your own patches with the Malström synthesizer

◆ Create Automation on a Reason Mixer 14:2

Overview of the Reason Program

While Reason was certainly created with the electronic musician in mind, it works incredibly well in any genre. And though Reason can do some intricate tasks, it doesn't necessarily have to perform complex functions; you can also create fairly simple configurations to come up with great sounds and sequences.

Some of the tasks you can perform with Reason include:

◆ Creating entire songs consisting of drum tracks, bass lines, synthesizer lines, and virtually any instrument you can think of

◆ Combining Reason's instruments and effects in infinite combinations

◆ Creating individual tracks or parts of songs

◆ Creating and exporting original loops from scratch or by altering existing loops

◆ Creating simple or complex samples from any sound source

◆ Using Reason's samplers to mimic acoustic instruments such as pianos, guitars, and even an entire orchestra

Introducing Reason's Instruments

The basic instruments contained within the Reason program are described next.

Dr. Rex Loop Player Plays RX2 format loop files, allowing you to time-stretch and pitch-shift loops to fit your songs and sessions.

Redrum drum machine   Performs basic or complicated drum programming using Reason's included drum kits, or you can build your own kits with WAV or AIFF samples.

NN19 sampler   A basic virtual sampler based on popular hardware samplers.

NN-XT advanced Sampler   A more intricate sampler with basic and complex sampling and sound editing features.

SubTractor Analog Synthesizer   A virtual synthesizer based on various analog hardware synthesizers. Great for creating bass lines and other melodies.

Malström Graintable Synthesizer   A virtual synthesizer with an amazing range of sounds and options.

Combinator   A new device that allows you to combine multiple instruments and effects into a single, recallable configuration.

Introducing Reason's Effects

Reason also comes with many effects, including:

- ◆   Two reverb units, for creating room sounds and distancing effects

- ◆   A distortion unit for adding analog tape–style saturation, creating lo-fi sounds, or overdriving a track to make it stand out in a mix

- ◆   A suite of mastering and EQ units to get the best possible sounds out of the included instruments and to create great-sounding final mixes

What Reason Doesn't Do

There are a few things Reason doesn't do:

- ◆   You can't record directly into it. For example, if you want to add your own vocals or a live guitar track, Reason doesn't have that capability.

- ◆   While it does contain an extremely powerful loop player and editor, Reason does not offer the same kind of time-stretching and pitch-shifting of WAV and AIFF loops that programs like Ableton Live or GarageBand do. However, Reason can be used in conjunction with these and other audio recording programs through ReWire, Propellerhead's software protocol that allows you to connect Reason's audio output directly to other music software.

- ◆   Unlike most music software, Reason is an entirely self-contained program. It does not take advantage of third-party plug-ins or instruments. Reason's uniqueness, versatility, and power make it especially useful in conjunction with other programs through ReWire, which I'll explain and cover in detail in relation to each DAW program in each of the next four chapters.

Tech Support and Resources

Reason users can access Reason tech support pages at `www.propellerheads.se`. These pages contain detailed instructions on how to solve many issues you may have related to Reason. If you cannot find the answer to your question in the support archives, you can access e-mail support from the same page. You can also find help by reading and posting in the Reason forums. You must be a registered Reason user to access these forums. Information on how to register your copy of Reason is included with the software.

Your main resource for Reason updates, tutorials, and tools is, of course, the Propellerhead website. Aside from `www.propellerheads.se` there are great Reason resources on the Web. For free Reason ReFills (see the "ReFills" sidebar), tutorials, and more, check out the following sites:

`www.peff.com`

`www.freewebz.com/dorumalaia`

`www.psylux.com/reason`

`www.reasonbanks.com`

`paranooyer.eigenstart.nl`

ReFills

ReFills are files that contain patches, loops, or instruments that you can use with Reason's instruments and effects. Some ReFills contain only one type of file. For example, a particular ReFill might contain only patches for the Malström Graintable Synthesizer or loops for the Dr. Rex Loop Player. Many ReFills, however, contain multiple files for different Reason instruments.

Reason's included Reason Factory Sound Bank ReFill has loops, synthesizer patches, sampler instruments, and effects patches for all of Reason's instruments and effects. Propellerhead offers free ReFill downloads to registered users of Reason; just log in to your account at www.propellerheads.se. Many other companies also make and sell ReFills: try a Google search for "Reason ReFills" to get an idea of what's available. Many ReFill creators will offer demo versions containing a few of the included files.

The Mastering Session Files

Included on this book's companion DVD is a folder called `MMA Audio Files`. Copy this folder to your desktop or another location where you will have easy access to its contents. Within this folder is a folder named `Reason` that contains the example sessions that you'll be using in this chapter.

Installation and Audio Setup

Before getting down to business, you need to install Reason and set up audio input and output.

Reason comes with three CDs, and all three are required to install and run the program. One CD contains the Reason program itself and the other two are ReFills that contain samples, loops, and instrument patches you will use to create music with Reason. Many of the tutorials in the following sections can be followed using the limited function demo version of Reason available from `www.propellerheads.se`.

Once you install Reason on your computer, you need to set the program's preferences. The first thing you'll want to do is set up Reason to work with your MIDI keyboard.

Basic MIDI Setup

It's highly recommended that you use a MIDI keyboard in conjunction with Reason to take full advantage of the program's instruments and effects.

You can find much more information on MIDI keyboards and Reason's more advanced MIDI capabilities in Chapter 11, "MIDI."

To set up Reason to work with your MIDI keyboard, follow these steps:

1. Select Reason ➤ Preferences and then choose Control Surfaces and Keyboards from the drop-down menu at the top.

2. Make sure your MIDI keyboard is attached and powered on, then click the Auto-detect Surfaces button (see Figure 2.1).

FIGURE 2.1
Add a control surface.

If your MIDI controller does not appear on the list, click the Add button and choose your manufacturer and model from the drop-down menus. If your MIDI keyboard is not on the drop-down menus, choose Other.

If your manufacturer and model are on the drop-down menu, be sure to read any special instructions Reason provides for your specific model. These instructions will be in the form of a short paragraph or two under the Model drop-down menu, as shown in Figure 2.2.

FIGURE 2.2
View information and instructions about your MIDI keyboard or control surface.

3. Next, in the MIDI Input field, choose your MIDI input. This may either be the name of your MIDI controller (as in Figure 2.2) or, if you have installed one, the name of your MIDI interface or possibly the name of any MIDI driver software you have installed.

4. Click the OK button to close this window.

5. Back in the Preferences window, put select the Use with Reason check box, as shown in Figure 2.3.

FIGURE 2.3
Select the Use with
Reason check box.

NO MIDI KEYBOARD?

If you do not have a MIDI keyboard, you can use the Matrix Pattern Sequencer or create notes in the Key lane to trigger the instruments in the following tutorials. If this is the case, before you move on to the instrument tutorials please read the section "The Matrix Pattern Sequencer" or the first part of "The Reason Sequencer" section through the subsection "The Key Lane."

1. Go to the Advanced MIDI tab and set Bus A through D and MIDI Clock Sync to match your MIDI input choice, as shown in Figure 2.4.

FIGURE 2.4
Set MIDI preferences.

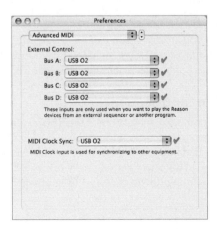

Reason is now configured for basic MIDI operations. For more in depth information on Reason's MIDI functions see the "Reason" section of Chapter 11.

Audio Output

Next, you'll want to select the Audio tab to check Reason's Audio preferences. Here you can decide which of your audio devices you want to use for Reason's output. Select the appropriate device from the Audio Card menu as shown in Figure 2.5. If you wish to use an external audio interface, make sure that device is attached and powered on, or it will not show up on the list.

FIGURE 2.5
Set Audio Output preferences.

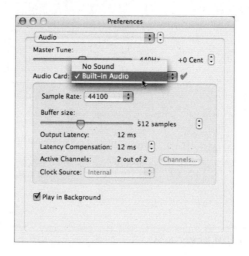

A First Look at Reason

Now you're ready to go hands-on. Follow the instructions in this section to get a look at Reason's basic setup.

When you installed Reason, a folder was created containing the program, sound banks, and other files. In this folder you'll find a file named Tutorial Song.rns. Open this file to get a look at Reason's Instruments and Sequencer windows. Use the scroll bar on the right side of the Reason window to get a look at the different instruments and effects that make up this song. Figure 2.6 shows the Reason tutorial session.

To give you an idea of some of the possibilities available when working in Reason, the programmers at Propellerhead have included lots of functionality in creating this default session. Don't worry if this seems overwhelming at first; it's not as hard as it seems.

Transport and Sequencer

The Transport bar at the bottom of the Reason screen contains the Record, Play, and Stop functions, looping functions, tempo settings, click track settings, and more.

Above the Transport bar is a portion of Sequencer window. To see more of the window, move your mouse to the top of Sequencer window. When it changes to two arrows, one pointing up and the other pointing down, click and drag upward to view more, as shown in Figure 2.7.

FIGURE 2.6

A Reason session

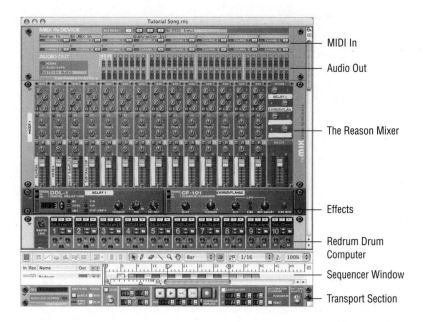

MIDI In

Audio Out

The Reason Mixer

Effects

Redrum Drum Computer

Sequencer Window

Transport Section

FIGURE 2.7

Expand the Sequencer window.

Edit Views   Tools   Quantization Functions

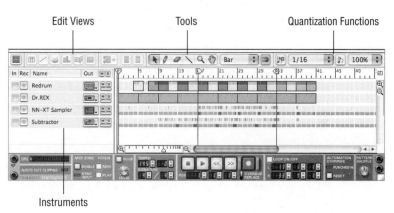

Instruments

You can use the same clicking and dragging method to hide the Sequencer window as well.

To get a clearer view of the Sequencer window, choose Window ➤ Detach Sequencer Window. You can now resize the detached Sequencer window by using your mouse to select and drag the bottom right corner. Choose Attach Sequencer window to bring it back into place when you are done.

Instruments and Effects

Reason comes with a variety of different instruments and effects, which can be used alone or in any combination. As I'll cover later, you can apply any effect to any instrument individually or use the send and return functions of Reason's Mixer 14:2 unit to apply the same effect to multiple instruments. You can see Mixer 14:2 and Reason's Digital Delay and Chorus/Flanger effects in Figure 2.6.

Reason Interface Basics

Each Reason instrument has its own functions and parameters. There are some similarities between all of the instruments and how they load and save files and interact with Reason's file browsing functions.

BROWSE AND SAVE BUTTONS

Most of the instruments and many of the effects will have the four buttons and file display window shown in Figure 2.8.

FIGURE 2.8
The Browse Patch and
Save buttons

The middle button (the folder icon) opens the Reason Browser window, allowing you to browse for loops, instruments, or effects patches, depending on which instrument or effects you are working with. Once you've loaded a patch or loop, the two arrows on the left will allow you to scroll through the other patch or loop files contained in the same folder. The button on the right (the disk icon) is the Save button that allows you to save patches and instruments. You can use this function to organize the included patches in new folders that you create or to save patches and instruments you alter or generate from scratch.

PATCHES

Patches are files that contain settings for individual Reason instruments. Patches for instruments like the SubTractor and Malström synthesizers are purely data and contain only the settings needed to create sounds from the instruments. Patches for the samplers and Redrum drum machine contain the settings and also point the instrument toward the actual audio file that is used to create the sound.

PITCH BEND AND MOD WHEEL

All of Reason's instruments also contain MIDI pitch bend and mod wheel functionality, as shown in Figure 2.9. If your MIDI controller has a pitch bend wheel and mod wheel, you can use it to control these functions on your Reason instruments. You can also use your mouse to control the pitch bend and modulation wheels.

FIGURE 2.9
Pitch bend and
mod wheels

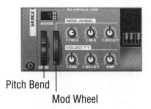

Pitch Bend

Mod Wheel

THE REASON BROWSER

As previously mentioned, all of Reason's instruments have a Browser button that opens the Reason Browser window (see Figure 2.10). Click the Browse button on any of the instruments to open the Browser window.

FIGURE 2.10

The Reason Browser

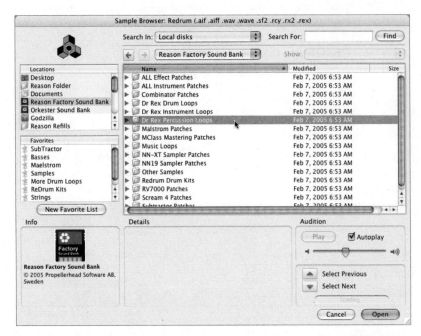

The Browser window can be modified a bit to make it more user friendly. Make sure that Autoplay (in the lower right corner) is turned on by selecting the check box. Autoplay allows you to preview loops and individual sound files as you browse.

You can keep frequently accessed ReFills, folders, and files in the Locations list at the top left of the Browser window. Add individual folders, complete ReFills, and single files or folders from within ReFills to the Locations list on the left by selecting and dragging them from the main window. Select an item in the Locations window to access its contents. You can remove any folder, file, or ReFill that you added to the Locations list by holding down the control, selecting it, and choosing Remove from the pop-up menu. (You can't remove the default locations: Desktop, Reason Folder Documents, and the Reason Banks.)

Below the Locations list is the Favorites list, which is a list of lists. You can add individual patches and loops to your Favorites lists by selecting and dragging as well. Create a new Favorites list by clicking the New Favorite List button. You may want to create a different list for different types of favorites. For example, I have a list of favorite patches for each Reason instrument, for different types of samples such as bass or keyboards, and for different types of Dr. Rex loops—drums, synthesizers, percussion, and so on. Click any Favorites list in the Favorites field to view its contents in the main Browser window. Select the file to load it into your Reason instrument.

You can remove or rename Favorites lists by holding down the Control key, clicking a list, and selecting the desired action from the pop-up menu.

The Reason Instruments

Reason's instruments are the heart of the program. You can use them individually to create a single melody line, drum track, or instrument performance, or you can put multiple instruments together to create an entire song. Each instrument contains its own unique abilities and possibilities. Once you've learned the basics of operating each Reason's instruments you can decide which ones will best suit your particular music and creative processes.

Creating a New Session

Open Reason's preferences by selecting Reason ➤ Preferences and then select the General tab from the drop-down menu at the top. Under Default Song, select Empty Rack, as shown in Figure 2.11.

FIGURE 2.11
Choose Empty Rack.

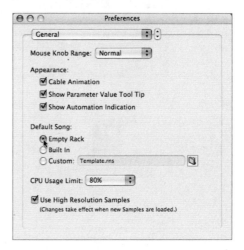

Reason's preferences give you multiple options for creating new sessions. Later on in this chapter, in the section "Creating a Template Session," I'll show you how to create a template session to take advantage of the instruments and effects you use most often, but for now you'll create your sessions from scratch.

Close the Preferences window. Choose File ➤ New.

The Reason Mixer 14:2

From the Create menu, choose Mixer 14:2. This creates what will be the main mixing console in any Reason session, as shown in Figure 2.12.

The Mixer is where you can raise and lower the volume of the individual tracks, as well as take advantage of functions like panning, simple equalization (EQ), and adding effects.

MULTIPLE MIXERS

In any Reason session you can add as many instances of the Mixer 14:2 as you like, routing the output of one into another. This allows you to create as many instruments as your processor power will allow.

FIGURE 2.12
The Reason Mixer 14:2

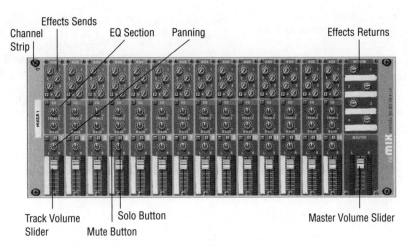

Channel Strip · Effects Sends · EQ Section · Panning · Effects Returns

Track Volume Slider · Solo Button · Mute Button · Master Volume Slider

Figure 2.13 shows a single channel strip from the Mixer console.

FIGURE 2.13
A single channel strip

Each channel strip is made up of three sections. The bottom section contains the Volume slider, which controls the volume for the assigned instrument. Above the Volume slider is the Pan knob, which sends the audio from your track to the left or the right speaker. Above the Pan knob are the Solo and Mute buttons for each track.

The middle section is a simple EQ for raising and lowering treble and bass frequencies on each track. You can turn the EQ on by clicking the EQ button in the top right corner of the EQ section.

In the top section are the Aux sends, which you'll use to apply effects to your tracks. I'll cover Aux sends later in this chapter in the "Effects" section.

Select the Mixer by clicking anywhere on the console so that it is highlighted with a light-colored outline. From the Create menu, choose Dr. Rex Loop Player.

Dr. Rex Loop Player

The Dr. Rex Loop Player, shown in Figure 2.14, is the most straightforward of the Reason instruments. As its name implies, the Dr. Rex Loop Player plays loop files and is a perfect tool for quickly creating backing rhythm and percussion tracks.

Along with its obvious drum and percussion related uses, the Dr. Rex can also play loops of any type of instrument, and its unique editing capabilities can be used to alter loops in both musical and nonmusical ways.

FIGURE 2.14
The Dr. Rex Loop Player

FIGURE 2.14
The Dr. Rex Loop Player

The Dr. Rex Loop Player plays .rx2 or REX files, which are loops that have been cut into sections called *slices*. The most common REX files are drum loops, but any instrument performance can be looped and made into a REX file using Propellerhead's Recycle software (sold separately). The Reason Factory Sound Bank comes with a number of REX drum loops and other instrument loops to get you started.

PLAYING LOOPS

To get started playing loops, follow these steps:

1. Click the Browse Loop button (with the folder icon) in the upper left corner of the Dr. Rex interface. The Reason Browser window will appear.

2. Under Locations choose Reason Factory Sound Bank.

3. Find the folder Dr. Rex Drum Loops, as shown in Figure 2.15.

4. Double-click the folder to open it and view the different categories of drum loops that are contained in the Reason Factory Sound Bank.

5. Open the folder Abstract HipHop. Select the file at the top of the list named Trh01_ SoleSide080_eLAB.rx2.

FIGURE 2.15
Select an RX2 file.

6. Click OK to load the file into the Dr. Rex Loop Player.

7. Preview the loop by clicking the Preview Loop button at the top of the Dr. Rex interface.

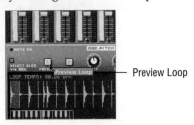 ——— Preview Loop

8. With the first loop still playing, use the Create menu to open a second Dr. Rex Loop Player.

9. Click the Browse Loop button and, in the Reason Factory Sound Bank, locate the folder `Dr. Rex Instrument Loops/Various Hip Hop Loops`.

10. Select the file `Hhp_Bassstar_093_Chronic.rx2` and click the OK button. Click the Preview loop button to hear the two loops playing together.

11. Use the Select Next Loop button on either of the Dr. Rex instruments to try out different combinations of loops.

12. Use the Select Previous loop button to return to the Hhp_Bassstar_093 loop.

13. Select File ➢ Save As to save the session as BassAndDrum1.rns.

You can add as many Dr. Rex Loop Players to your Reason song as your computer's processor can handle.

NAMING YOUR INSTRUMENTS

Each Reason instrument and effect you add to a session will give itself a name by default based on whatever type of instrument it is, such as DRREX 1 or MALSTROM 1. Once you have decided on a loop or patch for a particular instrument, it's a good idea to get in the habit of renaming your instrument right away. In a large session with multiple instances of the same instrument, things can get confusing.

To rename an instrument, click the name strip on the left side of the device and type whatever name you'd like in the field that appears. The name you choose will also appear alongside the instrument's volume slider in the Mixer 14:2.

ALTERING A LOOP

The Dr. Rex also gives you many options for editing and altering loops.

Load a loop into the Dr. Rex and listen to it by clicking the Preview Loop button.

Clicking the keyboard in the Loop window, as shown in Figure 2.16, will raise or lower the pitch of the loop, depending on where you click. Adjust the Oct knob above the Loop window to raise or lower the pitch an entire octave at a time.

FIGURE 2.16

The Keyboard window

EDITING SLICES

As mentioned previously, Rex loop files are drum and instrument loops that have been broken up into individual sections called slices. In the Dr. Rex environment you can edit these individual slices to create new rhythms and melodies from your existing loops. You can't save any changes you make to the actual REX file, but you can save the entire session and recall it.

Reopen the BassandDrum1.rns file you created in the "Playing Loops" section. Choose the Dr. Rex Loop Player playing the bass loop and highlight an individual slice by clicking in the window at the center of the Dr. Rex Loop Player, as shown in Figure 2.17

FIGURE 2.17

Select an individual slice from the bass loop.

Once a slice is selected and highlighted you can edit it by using the individual knobs underneath the Loop window:

♦ The Slice knob scrolls through the various slices that make up the REX file.

♦ The Pitch knob raises and lowers the pitch of the individual slice.

♦ The Pan knob sends the individual slice to the left or right speaker.

♦ The Level knob raises or lowers the volume of the slice.

♦ The Decay knob will shorten the length of the note. This is especially useful for editing REX files that are made up of a few longer slices if you want to eliminate unwanted notes at the end of a slice.

MORE EDITING OPTIONS

The Filter, LFO, and Amp Envelope sections on the right side of the Dr. Rex interface are all useful for making small or large changes to the sound of any loop you load into the Dr. Rex. These parameters are standard in any sampler or synth instrument and are covered in detail in Chapter 9, "Virtual Instruments."

NN-XT and NN19 Samplers

The NN-XT and NN19 are both samplers. The original version of Reason came with only the NN19. When the NN-XT was added in version 2, the NN19 was kept on, partly for the users who were familiar and comfortable with its interface and also because it's somewhat easier to use than the NN-XT. The NN19 is particularly useful if you are new to the concept of sampling and are still learning the basics or if you are planning on doing relatively simple sampling-related tasks. If you have a lot of experience with sampling or want to get into more complex functions, the NN-XT is the way to go.

USING THE NN19 SAMPLER

Create a new Reason session by selecting File ➤ New ➤ Create ➤ NN19 Digital Sampler. Figure 2.18 shows the NN19 Digital Sampler interface. As with any other instrument you create, this NN19 will be automatically routed through the Mixer 14:2 you created at the beginning of this session. Look for the NN19 channel strip on the Mixer 14:2 where you can now adjust the panning and overall volume for this sampler.

FIGURE 2.18
The NN19 Digital
Sampler

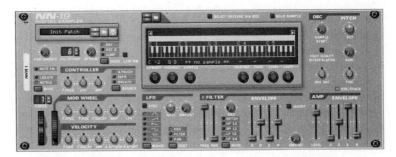

The simplest way to use the NN19 is to load a patch from the Reason Factory Sound Bank and then use your MIDI keyboard to trigger the sounds. To do this:

1. Click the Browse Patch button on the NN19 to open the Reason Browser.

2. Select the Reason Factory Sound Bank from the Locations list and locate the NN19 Sampler Patches folder. Within the folder you'll see more folders containing different instrument categories.

3. Open the Mallet and Ethnic folder. Select the patch VIBRAPHONE.smp and click OK.

4. Use your MIDI keyboard or use the Matrix Pattern Sequencer (see the "Matrix Pattern Sequencer" section later on in this chapter) to play the sample in the NN19.

PLAYING REX SLICES IN THE NN19

One interesting way to use the NN19 is to play slices of REX files. To load a REX file into the NN19:

1. Click the Browse Patch button on the NN19 to open Reason's Browser window.

2. In the Reason Factory Sound Bank, locate the folder Dr. Rex Drum Loops/Chemical Beats.

3. Load the file Chm02_Wildchild_125_eLab.rx2.

You can now use your MIDI keyboard to play the individual REX slices as a drum kit. You can trigger the samples by playing your MIDI keyboard in the C1 range, two octaves below middle C.

USING THE NN-XT ADVANCED SAMPLER

Some of the advantages that the NN-XT has over the NN19 include more outputs, more control over the individual samples that make up a patch, and the ability to import and use sample formats that the NN19 can't.

Finally, the NN-XT allows you to play and to create patches with multiple samples assigned to the same note, each one triggered by different velocity. This is called multilayered sampling and is especially useful for mimicking acoustic instruments, like piano. With a multilayered sample, you can press a key on your MIDI keyboard with more force and a louder, harsher sample will be triggered. When you play the same key gently the NN-XT will trigger a lighter, more delicate-sounding sample.

You'll look at a multilayered piano sample to get started using the NN-XT. Create a new Reason session and, from the Create menu, choose Mixer 14:2 and create an NN-XT Advanced Sampler. Figure 2.19 shows the NN-XT Advanced Sampler interface.

FIGURE 2.19
The NN-XT Advanced
Sampler

Click the Browse Patch button and in the Reason Factory Sound Bank locate the folder NN-XT Sampler Patches/Piano. Load the file A Grand Piano.sxt. Use your MIDI keyboard or the Matrix Pattern Sequencer to play the patch.

The Remote Editor

Click the small triangle on the bottom left to view the Remote Editor. This is where the NN-XT's sample editing functions take place. Using your mouse to scroll through the sampler editor window as shown in Figure 2.21, you can see how multiple samples are assigned to the same notes, creating a multilayered sample patch.

FIGURE 2.20
Inside view of a multi-
layered sample

The NN-XT's multilayering abilities allow you to create more complex, realistic sounding patches. In this case, different piano samples are assigned to different velocities, so different samples will be triggered depending on how hard you press the keys on your MIDI keyboard. Playing your MIDI keyboard softly will trigger a quiet sample, playing it hard will trigger a louder one.

The Remote Editor contains much of the functionality commonly found in hardware and software samplers. You can find more information on these parameters in the "Virtual Samplers" section of Chapter 9.

Importing Different File Formats

One of the advantages of the NN-XT is its ability to load other sample formats and then edit them in the sample editor. Here's how to take sections of a Rex loop and turn them into a new multilayered patch:

1. In the NN-XT you've already created, click the Browse Patch button and in the Reason Factory Sound Bank locate the folder Dr. Rex Instrument Loops/Various Hip Hop Loops.

2. Select the file Hhp_EPhit_095_Chronic.rx2 and click OK.

   Looking at the sample editor window, you can see that the NN-XT has loaded the REX file as two separate files made up of slices. Each slice is usually an individual note or *hit*. When you load a REX file in to the NN-XT, it automatically assigns each slice to a single key.

   This REX file is made up of only two notes. Just as in the NN19, the samples are triggered in the C1 range, two octaves below middle C.

3. Use your MIDI keyboard or the Matrix Pattern Sequencer to play the two notes.

4. In the Remote Editor window, use your mouse to select the first note of the top slice, and notice how the note becomes highlighted.

5. Increase the range of keys that will trigger the sample by moving your cursor to the left side of the highlighted sample, clicking your mouse, and dragging to the right.

   You can now use your MIDI keyboard to play the original sample across a wider range of notes. You can also use your mouse to drag the sample in the opposite direction to create a lower range.

6. Select the other sample and delete it by selecting Edit ➢ Delete Zones.

7. Now you'll load a sample from another REX file. This time, instead of loading the entire file, you'll load only one slice. Instead of the Browse Patch button, this time click the Load Sample button at the top of the Sample Editor window, shown in Figure 2.21.

FIGURE 2.21
The Load Sample button

8. Use the Browser to find `Dr. Rex Instrument Loops/Various Hip Hop Loops/ Hhp_BigOrch_092_Chronic.rx2`.

9. Double-click the file to open it and view the individual slices.

10. Select the `Hhp_BigOrch_092_Chronic.rx2 [1]` slice and click OK.

Use your MIDI keyboard to trigger the new multilayered sample patch. You can add as many samples as you want to the patch to create any number of different sounds. You can also assign different samples to different key ranges within the same patch.

If you'd like to reuse your patch later, click the Save Patch button, give your patch a name, and save it to your hard drive.

The SubTractor Analog Synthesizer

The SubTractor Analog Synthesizer isn't really an analog synthesizer. Like everything else on your computer, it uses digital information and processes it digitally; it merely mimics the functions of analog synthesizers.

The SubTractor is useful for creating hip-hop bass lines as well as techno melodies, synthesizer strings, percussion instruments, and various sound effects.

To begin the tour, choose File ≻ New to open a new Reason song. Use the Create menu to add a Mixer 14:2 and a SubTractor Analog Synthesizer to the session. Figure 2.22 shows the SubTractor interface.

FIGURE 2.22
The SubTractor
Analog Synthesizer

As with the other Reason instruments, you can load preexisting patches to get started. Click the Browse Patch button and, in the Reason Factory Sound Bank, locate `SubTractor Patches/PolySynths/Accorditor.zyp`. Use your MIDI keyboard or the Matrix Pattern Sequencer to preview the sound of the patch.

Using the Select Next Patch arrow, scroll through the patches in this folder to get an idea of the range of sounds that it's possible to create with the SubTractor.

You can also create your own SubTractor patches from scratch. Select Edit ≻ Initialize Patch. This returns the SubTractor to its original "clean slate" state. The Patch Name field next to the Browse and Save Patch buttons should read Init Patch.

Using the Matrix Pattern Sequencer or your MIDI keyboard to preview the sound, scroll through the 32 available waveforms in the Osc 1 (Oscillator One) section shown in Figure 2.23.

FIGURE 2.23
Oscillator One

USE THE MATRIX

While you are working on creating a new patch, or altering an existing one, you can keep a constant sound emanating from the device by hooking up a Matrix Pattern Sequencer. If you'd like to do this, skip ahead and read the instructions in the Matrix Pattern Sequencer section of this tutorial. The Matrix Pattern Sequencer works especially well for creating bass and melody lines with the SubTractor. When working with the SubTractor, try setting the resolution of the Matrix to ⅛. This plays slower notes with a longer interval between them so you can hear the output more clearly as you edit the patch.

These waveforms are the basic starting point for your patches, and each one has its best possible uses. For example, Waveform 29 is a good starting point for bell-like tones, Waveform 11 is good for organ sounds.

Here's how to use the SubTractor to create a hip-hop bass tone:

1. In the Osc 1 choose Waveform 17 by clicking the up arrow next to the Waveform display window. The next three parameters, Oct, Semi, and Cent, all affect the pitch of the waveform.

2. Click the down arrow next to the Oct display window to lower the pitch by one octave.

3. Add a second waveform to the patch by clicking the Osc 2 On/Off button below Oscillator 1.

4. In Osc 2, leave the waveform as the default Wave 0.

5. In the SubTractor's Filter 1 controls, try raising the Frequency (Freq) for harsher sounds or lowering it for more subdued sounds. Raise the Resolution (Res) fader for a more "techno" sound.

To save your patch, click the Save Patch icon, create a folder named SubTractor Patches and save the patch to your hard drive.

The Malström Graintable Synthesizer

The Malström is a combination of different types of synthesizers, making it an incredibly versatile instrument. Like the other Reason instruments, its basic operation is simple: you can browse and load the included patches (or patches from third-party ReFills), then use your MIDI keyboard or the Matrix Pattern Sequencer to trigger the sound. You can also create your own patches from scratch or edit and save existing patches that you have altered as new patches. Also like all of the Reason instruments, Malström has many editable parameters that allow you to create an amazing array of new sounds and patches.

Create a new Reason song and add a Mixer 14:2 and Malström Graintable Synthesizer to the session. Figure 2.24 shows the Malström interface.

FIGURE 2.24

The Malström Graintable Synthesizer

1. Click the Browse Patches button to open the Reason Browser window.

2. In the Reason Factory Sound Bank, locate `Malstrom Patches/ PolySynths`.

3. Select the patch `Air Pizz.xwv` and use your MIDI keyboard or the Matrix Pattern Sequencer to play the patch.

4. Use the Select Next Patch arrow to browse through the PolySynth patches to get an idea of the range of sounds available with the Malström synthesizer.

SETTING UP A NEW PATCH WITH THE MALSTRÖM

As with all of Reason's instruments, a lot of the fun and creativity is in creating your own original sounds from scratch. To create your own patches:

1. Choose Edit ➢ Initialize Patch.

   The Malström has two oscillators, located in the center of the device. These are your starting point for creating new patches. Oscillator A will be automatically turned "on" in the initialized patch.

2. Select a new graintable by clicking the up and down arrows next to the Osc A display window. (You can also view a list of all available graintables by clicking directly on the display window.)

3. Use your MIDI keyboard to preview some of the available graintables to get familiar with them.

ALTERING A GRAINTABLE

With the Malström, you can use the included graintables as starting points to create all kinds of different sounds. Start by using the mouse to adjust some of the parameters on both oscillators:

1. In the Oscillator A section, choose Sawtooth*16 from the graintable list by clicking the up arrow next to the display window.

2. Try raising and lowering the Shift and Motion parameters. The Octave, Semi, and Cent knobs all control the pitch, allowing you to raise and lower it incrementally or drastically.

3. To add a second graintable to the patch, turn on Osc B by clicking the On/Off button.

4. Click the Osc B Graintable display window and select square*4 from the list of available graintables.

5. Raising the Spread knob on the lower right above the Volume knob will send the sound generated by Oscillator A to your left speaker and the Oscillator B to your right speaker.

USING THE MODULATORS

Just above Oscillator A is Modulator A. The modulators can also have a drastic effect on the sound of your patch.

Raise the Pitch, Index, and Shift knobs first, then raise and lower the Rate knob to get an idea of how Mod A works.

Use the up and down arrows next to the Modulator Curve display to choose which waveform the modulator will follow.

Use the Modulator A Target button to determine if the modulator will be used on Osc A (up position), Osc B (down position), or both (middle position).

As you can probably guess, I'm only scratching the surface of what's available in the Malström. For more information on the Malström, check out Reason's included manual or the Propellerhead website.

USING RHYTHMIC PATCHES

The Reason Factory Sound Bank comes with seven folders containing different types of patches for the Malström. For example, the bass folder contains a few dozen synthesizer bass tones to get you started creating low-end tracks, and the FX folder contains odd sounds that are useful in creating ambient noise. These patches really show off the range of sound sculpting possibilities that the Malström holds.

The last folder in the list is the Rhythmic folder. As you scroll through these presets you may notice that they all have one thing in common: the Sync button in the Mod A section is turned on. These presets take advantage of the Malström's ability to sync perfectly with the Reason session's tempo, which gives you the ability to easily create synthesizer lines and patterns that are in time with the current session.

Follow these steps to load and play one of the Malström's rhythmic patches:

1. Create a new session and add a Mixer 14:2 and a Dr. Rex Loop Player and a Malström synthesizer.

2. From the Reason Factory Sound Bank load `Dr. Rex Drum Loops/Acoustic/Hip Hop/ Ahp_02_Live_078_Chronic.rx2` into the Dr. Rex.

3. Use the Browse Patch button on the Malström to locate and load the patch `Malstrom Patches/Rhythmic/FooledAgain.xwv`.

4. Click the Preview Loop button on the Dr. Rex to start the drum loop.

5. Wait for the first beat of the drum loop to come back around and hold down any single key on your MIDI keyboard.

You can hear how the rhythm of the Malström patch lines up perfectly with the rhythm of the drum loop. (If this synthesizer arpeggio sounds familiar, it's because it's based on the same arpeggio that you may have heard in the Who's classic rock song "Won't Get Fooled Again," also known as the theme song for the television show *CSI*.)

Redrum

Redrum is Reason's drum machine and much more. It can be used with the included Redrum kits as well as the kits that are available in many Reason ReFills, and you can build your own drum kits by loading WAV and AIFF files. In addition, as with the NN-XT Advanced Sampler, you can load the slices that make up REX files. For songwriting purposes, you can program up to 24 different beats in Redrum and then use the Reason Sequencer to arrange them in any order.

Create a new Reason song and add a Mixer 14:2 and Redrum drum machine to the session. Figure 2.25 shows the Redrum interface.

FIGURE 2.25
The Redrum drum machine

PROGRAMMING A BEAT

You'll start by loading a Reason drum kit and programming a simple beat.

1. Click the Browse Patch button to open the Reason browser.

2. Locate `Redrum Drum Kits/Hip Hop Kits/Hip Hop Kit 01` and click OK at the bottom right of the Browser window.

3. Click the Run button to start Redrum.

With Redrum running you'll be able to preview the beat you're creating as you work on it.

4. Click the Select button on channel strip 1, as shown in Figure 2.26.

Highlighting the select button on a channel allows you to program that channel's sample in the Reason Pattern Sequencer.

FIGURE 2.26
Select a channel for
programming.

5. Program a kick drum beat. Clicking with your mouse, highlight steps 1, 7, 11, and 14.

6. Select channel 3 and use your mouse to add snare hits on steps 5 and 13.

7. Select channel 6 and add hi-hat to steps 1, 5, 9, and 13. Now you've created a simple beat on Pattern A1.

8. Choose Edit ➢ Copy Pattern and select pattern A2.

9. Choose Edit ➢ Paste Pattern.

10. With pattern A2 and channel 6 still selected, add hi-hat on 3, 7, 11, and 15.

As you can hear, by using this copying and pasting method you can easily create multiple variations on a single beat. Use your mouse to switch between patterns A1 and A2 to hear how you might arrange a typical rhythm track.

To come up with some unexpected drum loops, try creating a pattern with one kit and then using the Select Next Patch button or the Reason Browser to change kits.

Choose File ➢ Save and save this Reason song as "Redrum One." You'll reopen this file later in the "Effects" and "Real-Time Automation" sections of this chapter.

TRIGGERING A SAMPLE WITH REDRUM

Redrum can also be used as a simple sampler device to preview WAV and AIFF files for use in a session.

1. Open the Reason session `BassAndDrum1.rns` that you created in the Dr. Rex tutorial.

2. Create a Redrum drum computer

3. Click the Browse Sample button for channel strip 1 in the Redrum.

4. Use the Browser window to open the folder `NN-XT Sampler Patches/Sound FX/Sound FX Samples`.

LOADING PATCHES

You may have noticed when you opened the NN-XT folder this time that there were no NN-XT patches visible. That's because when you are using a specific instrument's Browse function you will only see the patches and files that instrument can read and load. In this case, the Redrum can't be used to load NN-XT patches, but it can read the sample files that make up those patches.

---

1. Select the first sample, `Airaid.aif` and click OK to load it.

2. Make sure the Select button on channel strip 1 is on, and click the Step 1 button on the Redrum drum machine.

3. Start the REX files by clicking their Preview buttons above the waveform display.

4. Click the Run button on the Redrum.

5. Because this is a long sample, it starts over again before it finishes. Use the Length knob on the channel strip, shown in Figure 2.27, to shorten the length of the sample.

FIGURE 2.27
Shorten the sample by
reducing its length.

Use the Select Next Sample button in channel 1 to scroll through the various WAV files located in this folder.

Effects

Reason includes an amazing selection of effects, including reverbs, delays, distortion, compression, and modulation effects. These effects can be added to an entire session, individual instruments, or multiple instruments at once.

Return to Sender

Each Mixer 14:2 includes four effects sends, a common feature of most hardware mixing boards.

The way the sends work is that each track is internally wired to send its sound to an auxiliary (aux) track that contains an effect. The track that contains the effect then returns the effected signal to the original track. How much of a track's signal is sent to the effect is controlled by the Aux Send knobs at the top of each channel strip.

How much of the effected signal is returned to the original track is controlled by the Return knobs shown in Figure 2.28.

FIGURE 2.28
The Return section of the Mixer 14:2

Using the send/return functionality is a great way to apply a single effect to multiple instruments, which can simplify the mixing process and save processor resources.

To add effects to your Reason session, select and highlight the Mixer 14:2 then choose any effect from the Create menu. Reason will automatically route the new effect through the Mixer's Send and Return functions.

RV7000 Advanced Reverb

The RV7000 is the better sounding (and more complicated) of Reason's two included reverb effects. To try out the RV7000:

1. Create a new Reason song and save it as "Reverb Test."

2. Choose Create ➢ Mixer 14:2.

3. With the Mixer selected and highlighted, go back to the Create menu and choose RV7000 Advanced Reverb. Figure 2.29 shows the RV7000 interface.

FIGURE 2.29
The RV7000 Advanced Reverb

As mentioned earlier, by creating the RV7000 with the Mixer selected and highlighted, the RV7000 is automatically routed through the Mixer's Send and Return functions. Note that RV7000 has been added to the Return section at the top right of the Mixer.

4. Add the RV7000 effect to any track by raising the Aux 1 knob at the top of the Mixer's channel strip.

5. Click your mouse in the black space below the RV7000 so that any new instruments you create will be routed correctly.

6. Create a new Dr. Rex Loop Player and, using the Browse Loop function, locate `Dr. Rex Drum Loops/Acoustic/Hip Hop/Ahp01_Live_078_Chronic.rx2`.

7. Click the Preview button on the Dr. Rex to hear the loop.

8. Use your mouse to increase the Aux 1. This adds the reverb effect to the drum loop.

9. The Reason Factory Sound bank contains a folder of preset patches for the RV7000. Click the Browse Patches button on the RV7000 and, in the Reason Factory Sound Bank, locate the folder RV7000 `patches`.

10. Select the first patch and click OK.

11. With the loop playing, use the Select Next Patch button to scroll through the presets.

Scream 4 Distortion

One other Reason effect also has the ability to load and save patches: the Scream 4 Distortion.

The Scream 4 Distortion effect (see Figure 2.30) is every distortion pedal/box you can think of in one unit. Its uses range from adding subtle warmth to a track to all-out sonic destruction.

FIGURE 2.30
The Scream 4
Distortion

1. From the MMA `Audio/Reason` folder, open the Reason song `ScreamDemo.rns`.

2. Each Dr. Rex Loop Player in this session has been assigned a different Scream 4 patch illustrating the versatility of this effect.

3. Try soloing each of the Dr. Rex loops by clicking the Solo button on its channel strip in the Mixer 14:2.

4. Once a track is soloed, use your mouse to click the Bypass switch in the upper left corner of each Scream 4 and hear the original unprocessed loop.

5. Turn the Scream 4 back on, then use the Browse Patches button on each Scream 4 to try out different patches from the Reason Factory Sound Bank.

ADDING AN EFFECT TO A SINGLE INSTRUMENT

As the `ScreamDemo.rns` session illustrates, with Reason you can also add effects to one instrument at a time. Just select the instrument in the Reason window and create the desired effect from the Create menu, and the effect will be automatically connected to the selected instrument's output. The effect's output will then be routed directly to the Mixer 14:2.

DDL-1 Digital Delay Line

The DDL-1 Digital Delay (see Figure 2.31) is an all-purpose digital delay effect. It can be used to add an echo effect in large or small doses to any track or combination of tracks.

FIGURE 2.31
The DDL-1 Digital Delay

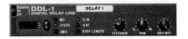

Take a look at the DDL-1 by using it in conjunction with the Dr. Rex Loop Player:

1. Create a new session and add a Mixer 14:2 and a Dr. Rex Loop Player. Load any drum loop or instrument REX loop from the Reason Factory Sound Bank into the Dr. Rex.
2. Use your mouse to select and highlight the Dr. Rex Loop Player in the Reason window and select Create ➤ DDL-1 Digital Delay Line.
3. Click the Preview button to hear the instrument through the delay effect.

   On the far right of the DDL interface you'll see the Dry/Wet knob. When the DDL-1 is created it defaults to completely wet. This means that when you add it to an individual instrument you will hear only the delay effect and not the original performance. Adjusting the knob completely to the left (to the Dry position) will have the opposite effect, totally removing the delay effect. You will probably want to use a setting somewhere in the middle so you can hear both the original performance and the delay effect.
4. Click the Unit button on the bottom left of the DDL to switch between milliseconds (ms) and steps as the increment of choice for your delay effect.
5. The steps setting will sync the delay with the session's current tempo. Use the scrolling arrows next to the LED display to change the delay time. Use the Step Length button to switch between sixteenth-note delay increments and eighth-note triplets. The milliseconds setting will allow you to set your own delay times.
6. Adjust the feedback knob for a more or less intense delay effect.

ECF-42 Envelope Controlled Filter

The ECF-42 Envelope Controlled Filter (see Figure 2.32) is perfect for creating sweeping effects like those heard in techno, house, and other dance music genres.

1. Create a new Reason song and add a Mixer 14:2 and a SubTractor Analog Synthesizer to the session.
2. Add a Matrix Pattern Sequencer to the SubTractor. (If you need a tutorial on this, skip ahead to the "Matrix Pattern Sequencer" section later in this chapter.)

FIGURE 2.32

The ECF-42 Envelope
Controlled Filter

3. Use the SubTractor's Browse Patch button to locate and load the patch SubTractor Patches/ MonoSynths/80's Dance Ld.zyp.

4. Click the Run button on the Matrix.

5. With the SubTractor selected, choose Create ➢ ECF-42 Envelope Controlled Filter.

6. Slowly raise the Frequency knob on the far left of the ECF to create a sweeping effect.

This sweeping effect can be automated using the techniques covered in the "Automating the Mixer or an Effect" tutorial later on in this chapter.

The ECF-42 also contains multiple choices for Low Pass and Band Pass filters as well as an ADSR envelope, For more details about Low Pass and Band Pass filters see the "Filters" section of Chapter 8, "Plug-in Effects." For more information on ADSR envelopes see the "Virtual Synthesizers" section of Chapter 9.

PH-90 Phaser

The PH-90 Phaser (see Figure 2.33) effect can be added to any instrument to help it stand out in a mix or to create new and interesting sounds. The Phaser is especially useful on synthesizers and on samples or loops of stringed instruments or voices.

FIGURE 2.33

The PH-90 Phaser

1. To try out the Phaser:

2. Create a new session with a Mixer 14:2 and a Dr. Rex Loop Player and a SubTractor Analog Synthesizer.

3. Select and highlight the Mixer, then choose Create ➢ PH-90 Phaser. Your new Phaser effect should be routed through Send and Return 1.

4. Set the tempo of the session to 85.

5. Use the Dr. Rex Browse Loop button to locate and load the loop Dr. Rex Instrument Loops/Guitar Loops/AcGT_Pop_C_085.rx2.

6. Click the Preview button to play the loop.

7. Add the Phaser effect by raising the Aux Send 1 knob on channel one of the Reason Mixer.

   You can drastically alter the Phaser effect by raising and lowering the Rate and Feedback knobs. For a longer, sweeping effect try lowering the rate. For a quicker, warbling sound, try increasing the rate.

8. Use the SubTractor's Browse Patch button to locate and load the patch SubTractor Patches/PolySynths/Analog Replicant from the Reason Factory Sound Bank.

9. Use your MIDI keyboard to play the patch. Add the Phaser effect with the Aux Send 1 knob. Try adjusting the Feedback and Rate parameters while triggering notes with your MIDI keyboard.

The Combinator

The Combinator device is new to Reason 3. The Combinator allows you to create new instruments from combinations of Reason instruments and effects. To get an idea of some of the possibilities, open a Combinator patch and look inside:

1. Create a new Reason song and add a Mixer 14:2. Choose Create ➤ Combinator. Figure 2.34 shows an empty Combinator device.

FIGURE 2.34
An empty Combinator device

2. Click the Browse Patch button to open the Reason Browser window.

3. In the Reason Factory Sound Bank, locate `Combinator Patches/Strings`.

4. Select the patch `The Alan Smith One Note Orchestra xt.cmb` and click OK.

5. Use your MIDI keyboard to hear what this Combinator patch sounds like.

Looking at the Combinator interface, you can see that this patch is made up of multiple instruments and effects. This patch includes a SubTractor synthesizer, two Malström synthesizers, and an RV7000 Reverb (as an aux send), all going into a Line Mixer 6:2 (a compact version of the Mixer 14:2) and, finally, the combined signal is processed by an MClass EQ.

Press the Tab key to view the routing and "wiring" of this Combinator patch, as shown in Figure 2.35.

FIGURE 2.35
The "wiring" of a Combinator patch

Create Your Own Combinator Patches

Using the Combinator you can create your own simple or complex instruments and patches. If you have a particular instrument/effect configuration that you use often, creating a Combinator version can be a great timesaver.

1. Chooser Create ➤ Combinator

2. Click your mouse in the Combinator creation area, and a red line will appear. This is where the instruments and effects that make up the Combinator patch will be created.

3. Add a Line Mixer 6:2 from the Create menu. This is a compact version of the Mixer 14:2.

4. With the Line Mixer 6:2 selected, create a DDL-1 Digital Delay Line effect device.

5. Click in the blank area again, then create an NN19 Digital Sampler and, in the Reason Factory Sound Bank, locate and load `NN19 Sampler Patches/Guitar/ACGUITAR.smp`.

6. Create a Malström Synthesizer and load the PolySynth patch `Airalogue.xwv`.

   Figure 2.36 shows your Combinator patch so far.

FIGURE 2.36
A new Combinator patch

7. On the Line Mixer device, locate the Aux button on the right side of channel 1.

8. Use your mouse to turn the knob to the right, adding the delay effect to the NN19 device.

9. Use your MIDI keyboard or the Matrix Pattern Sequencer to play the Combinator instrument you've created.

10. To save your new Combinator patch, click the Save Patch button on the upper right of the Combinator.

The Matrix Pattern Sequencer

The Matrix Pattern Sequencer is Reason's built-in MIDI controller that can be used to create bass lines, melody lines, and arpeggios with Reason's sampler and synthesizer instruments. It's especially useful if you are working on a laptop away from your home or studio or don't have a MIDI keyboard handy.

Basic Operation

The Matrix Pattern Sequencer (see Figure 2.37) is a great tool for creating bass tracks and melody lines, especially for users who don't have a MIDI keyboard in place. The Matrix can be hooked up to any instrument, though many users find it especially useful with the SubTractor and Malström Graintable Synthesizer .

We'll use the SubTractor to get a look at creating patterns with the Matrix Pattern Sequencer:

1. Create a new Reason song and add Mixer 14:2 to the session.

2. Create a new SubTractor synthesizer. Make sure the SubTractor is selected and highlighted in the Reason Instrument window.

3. With the SubTractor selected, choose Create ➤ Matrix Pattern Sequencer.

   Selecting the instrument before creating the new Matrix Pattern Sequencer will automatically attach the Matrix MIDI output to the SubTractor's MIDI input.

FIGURE 2.37
The Matrix Pattern
Sequencer

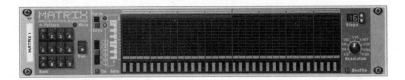

4. Click the Run button on the Matrix Pattern Sequencer. The Matrix will default to a pattern of single sixteenth notes.

5. Increase or decrease the pattern by using your mouse to adjust the Resolution knob.

6. Create patterns and melody lines in Matrix Pattern Sequencer by using your mouse to select and move notes.

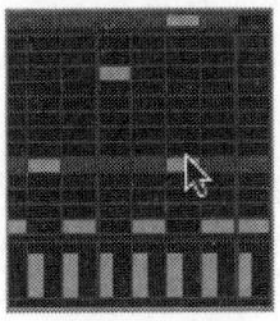

RANDOMIZE IT!

To use the Matrix to create a random pattern, select and highlight the Matrix in the Reason Instrument window then choose Edit ➤ Randomize Pattern. Creating random patterns is a good way to get an idea of what an instrument or patch will sound like in the context of a performance and get your creative ideas flowing. You can also edit a random pattern, keeping the notes that you think sound good and discarding or changing others.

Multiple Patterns

Like the Redrum drum machine, the Matrix Pattern Sequencer has 4 banks of 8 patterns, which you can use to create up to 32 different melody lines. See the "Automating the Matrix Pattern Sequencer" section later in this chapter for more instructions on how to use this function.

The Reason Sequencer

The Reason Sequencer is where you'll be doing all of your arranging, editing, and, of course, sequencing. As with all of Reason's instruments and plug-ins, you can start using the sequencer pretty quickly by getting a handle on some of the basic principles. If you want to go "deeper" with it (and there's a lot to learn, if you're interested) check out the Operation manual PDF in the documentation folder located in the same directory as the Reason program.

Edit Mode

To get a look at the Sequencer, create a new Reason song, add a Mixer 14:2 and an NN-XT, then, from Reason's Window menu, select Detach Sequencer Window.

In the upper left corner of the Sequencer you'll see the seven Edit Mode buttons shown in Figure 2.38.

FIGURE 2.38
The Edit Mode
buttons

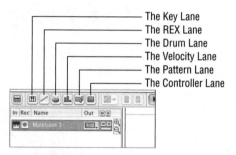

- The Key Lane
- The REX Lane
- The Drum Lane
- The Velocity Lane
- The Pattern Lane
- The Controller Lane

The first of these is the Edit/Arrange Mode button, which lets you toggle between the sequencer's two modes. The Arrange window, which we'll look at later, is where you will select and move sections or groups of MIDI information to arrange your tracks and complete songs. In the Edit Mode, shown in Figure 2.39, you can sequence notes, automate different parameters, and edit MIDI notes and information. Use the Edit/Arrange mode button to select Edit mode.

The next six buttons are relevant only in Edit Mode. These are the "Lane" buttons. Each one gives you access to different kinds of editing interfaces also known as *lanes*, where you can create and edit performances with Reason's instruments and effects. Let's add some instruments to get familiar with some of their functions. Load one of the piano patches into the NN-XT you created earlier. Make sure the NN-XT is selected in the Sequencer window.

THE KEY LANE

Click the Show Key Lane button. If any of the other lanes are showing, click their buttons to close them.

FIGURE 2.39
The Edit Mode
window

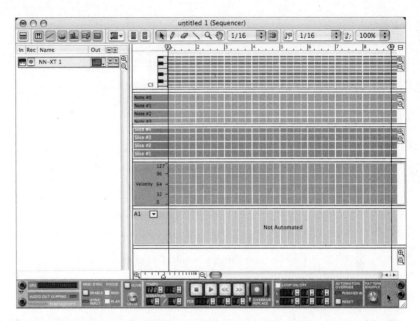

You will use the Key lane to add and edit MIDI notes. The keyboard on the left side of the Key lane can be used to preview the sounds of the instrument it's connected to. As you move your cursor over the keyboard you'll notice that it changes to a speaker icon with a plus sign. Click your mouse on any of the keyboard notes to preview the sound of the current NN-XT patch.

The Key lane can be used to create performances from scratch with just your mouse. To do this, select the Pencil tool.

With the Pencil tool selected, use your mouse to draw MIDI notes in the Key Lane window.

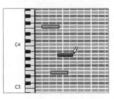

To play the notes, press the spacebar or click the Play button on the Transport bar at the bottom of the Sequencer window. Press Return to return the playhead to the beginning of the song.

To edit the notes you just created, choose the Selection tool.

You can use the Selection tool to grab and move notes around.

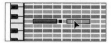

You can also use the Selection tool to lengthen or shorten notes by moving the cursor to the end of the MIDI event until the cursor changes to a two-sided arrow and then dragging.

THE REX LANE

Deselect the Key Lane button, then click the button to its right to view the Rex lane. You can use the Rex lane to rearrange Rex slices and create new drum patterns and melodies.

1. Choose ➤ Create Dr. Rex Loop Player.

2. In the Reason Factory Sound Bank, locate the folder `Dr. Rex Drum loops/Hip Hop`.

3. Select the file `Hhp_01_Classic_091_Chrnc.rx2` and click OK. Here you have to take a quick detour to the Loop section of the Transport bar.

4. Using your mouse, change the loop endpoint (the field to the right of the "R" label) to 5. This creates a four-measure loop.

5. Make sure the Loop On/Off button is lit. This means that, for now, when you press the Play button you'll hear a continuous loop of the first four measures of the song.

6. Once you have established the loop parameters, make sure that the Dr. Rex is selected in the Sequencer window, then go back to the Dr. Rex Loop Player interface and click the To Track button, shown in Figure 2.40.

FIGURE 2.40
Send the MIDI sequence to the sequencer track.

This sends all of the Rex slices to the Rex lane as individual MIDI events.

7. Use your mouse and the Selection tool to rearrange the Rex slices in the Rex lane to create new beats.

You can also use the Pencil tool to add new slices in the Rex lane.

THE REMAINING LANES

Each of the remaining lanes (see Figure 2.38) has its own functionality. As you get deeper into the Reason program you'll find your own uses for each lane.

Drum Lane   In the Drum lane you can use your mouse and the Pencil tool (just as you would in the Key lane) to arrange drum patterns with Redrum.

Velocity Lane   In the Velocity lane you can use the Pencil tool to make changes to the velocity of each MIDI note, determining how loud the note will play or which sample in a multilayered sample will be triggered.

Pattern Lane   The Pattern lane is where you will view the automation of the Matrix Pattern Sequencer and the Redrum drum machine. See the "Real-time Automation" section of this chapter.

Controller Lane   The Controller lane automates and edits MIDI controller functions, such as pitch bending, sustain, and volume parameters.

The Transport Bar

The Transport bar (see Figure 2.41) at the bottom of the Reason Sequencer is where you will find the controls for many of Reason's features. Aside from the obvious Play, Record, Fast Forward, and Rewind buttons, the Transport bar is also where you will control Reason's looping functions and click track.

FIGURE 2.41
The Transport bar

Arrange Mode

Once you've created events in the Edit window you can use the Arrange window in Arrange mode to move these events around, create groups of notes, and sequence your song. You'll use the Dr. Rex again to see how this is done.

1. Create a new Reason session.

2. In the Transport bar, create a four-measure loop as you did in the "Rex Lane" section.

3. Choose Create ➤ Mixer 14:2 ➤ Dr. Rex Loop Player.

4. In the Reason Factory Sound Bank, locate the folder `Dr. Rex Drum Loop/Abstract HipHop`. Select the file `Trh01_Soleside_080_eLab.rx2` and click OK.

5. Make sure Dr. Rex 1 is selected in the Sequencer window, then click the To Track button on the Dr. Rex to send the MIDI information to the sequencer track.

6. Toggle the Edit/Arrange Mode button to make sure you are in Arrange Mode.

   The new Dr. Rex groups appear in the Arrange window.

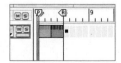

7. Click the Play button on the Transport bar to hear the loop.

8. In the Reason instrument window, click your mouse in the blank area below the Dr. Rex Loop Player. Use the Create menu to add another Dr. Rex Loop Player to your session.

9. In the Reason Factory Sound Bank, locate the folder `Dr. Rex instrument Loops/Various Hip Hop Loops` and load the file `Hhp_Brandywah_093-Chronic.rx2`.

10. Select Dr. Rex 2 in the Sequencer window and click the To Track button on the corresponding Dr. Rex device.

You now have two separate MIDI events to work with. One of the ways you can work within the Arrange window is to use the Selection tool shown in Figure 2.42 to highlight and move the events around the Sequencer window. Once you've highlighted a section with the Selection tool, you can use keyboard shortcuts to copy (⌘+C) and paste (⌘+V) events.

FIGURE 2.42
Use the Selection tool to rearrange groups.

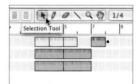

Recording and Grouping a Performance

Groups are sections or chunks of MIDI information that you combine to make copying, pasting, and sequencing easier to accomplish. This following steps show you how to record a simple performance and then use the Pencil tool to create and edit groups from the recorded MIDI events:

1. Create a new session and add a Mixer 14:2 and an NN-XT Advanced Sampler.

2. Load any one of the piano samples from the Reason Factory Sound Bank.

3. Make sure the NN-XT instrument is selected in the Sequencer window.

4. Press the Return key to move the playhead to the beginning of the song.

5. Make sure that the Reason Sequencer is in Arrange view. Get Reason ready for recording by clicking the red Record button on the Transport bar.

6. Start recording by clicking the Play button. Use your MIDI keyboard to play and record a performance.

NO MIDI KEYBOARD?

If you don't have a MIDI keyboard, you can use the methods covered in the "Matrix Pattern Sequencer" section to create your performance.

In the Arrange window you can watch the MIDI information being recorded as you play.

1. To create groups from your performance, set the Snap value by choosing from the Snap Value pop-up menu to the right of the Tools bar at the top of the Sequencer window.

2. Click the Snap to Grid button.

3. Use the Pencil tool to "draw" a group.

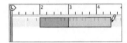

You can arrange groups by using the Selection tool to drag them from one section of a track to another or by copying and pasting them as you did with the Rex groups in the previous section.

You can also create new instruments and move groups between tracks. Figure 2.43 shows the previously recorded groups now triggering a Malström synthesizer.

FIGURE 2.43
Moving groups
between tracks

Tutorials

The following sections are tutorials designed to familiarize you with more of Reason's functionality and get you started on the process of creating and exporting complete songs and tracks. You'll start off looking at some of Reason's Automation functions.

Automating the Matrix Pattern Sequencer

Here's a quick way to familiarize yourself with automating playback of the Matrix Pattern Sequencer. The same techniques can be used to automate the Redrum drum machine.

1. Create a new Reason song and add a Mixer 14:2 and a SubTractor.

2. Attach a Matrix Pattern Sequencer to the SubTractor.

3. Use your mouse to click and select bank A and pattern 3, as shown in Figure 2.44, then choose Randomize Pattern from the Edit menu.

FIGURE 2.44
Select pattern A3.

4. Create random patterns on bank A/pattern 2 and bank A/pattern 1.

   For instructions, see the sidebar "Randomize It!" earlier in this chapter.

5. Return the playhead to Start by pressing Return. The Pos readout in the Transport bar should show 1/1/1.

6. Make sure you are in Edit mode in the Reason Sequencer window.

7. Click the Show Pattern Lane button.

8. Click the Record button first, then the Play button.

9. As the session plays, switch between patterns A1, A2, and A3. You will see the Automation recorded onto the Pattern lane, as shown in Figure 2.45.

FIGURE 2.45
The Pattern lane

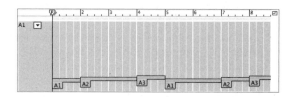

Real-time Automation

Open the file MMA_dub.rns in your MMA Audio/Reason folder. Press the spacebar or click the Play button in the Transport bar to start playback. Listen to the session once while keeping an eye on the Redrum drum machine. Notice the knobs that are highlighted on channel strip 8 and how they move throughout the session, changing the pitch of the hi-hat track and increasing and reducing the reverb effect. This is Reason's automation function in action. What you see in the Redrum is just the beginning. Reason allows you to automate an amazing range of functions on every device, including effects.

CREATING AUTOMATION

Creating automation on an instrument such as the Redrum or an NN-XT Sampler is straightforward. For this example, use the Redrum One file you created in the "Programming a Beat" subsection of the "Redrum" section.

1. Make sure the Redrum is selected in the Sequencer window and the track is armed to receive MIDI information.

   You can tell that a track is armed when the keyboard and red recording light on the far left are visible, as shown in Figure 2.46.

FIGURE 2.46
Arm the track to receive MIDI information.

2. Click the Record button on the Transport bar.

3. Click the Play button to begin recording.

4. Try changing the Pitch, Level, and Panning knobs on the snare (channel strip 2) or the rim shot (channel strip 3) while the song is playing back.

5. Once you've created some automation, press the spacebar to stop recording.

   The knobs you have adjusted should now have a green outline indicating that they have been automated.

6. Press Return to return to the beginning of the song.

7. Click the Play button to hear (and see) your newly created automation.

CLEARING AUTOMATION

If you are not happy with the automation you have created, follow these steps to clear it:

1. Use your mouse to move your cursor over the knob or button you have automated.

2. Control-click and select Clear Automation from the pop-up menu.

You can now start the process over again and create new automation from scratch.

AUTOMATING THE MIXER OR AN EFFECT

To automate the Mixer 14:2 or add automation to one of Reason's effects, you must create a Sequencer Track to record the automation.

1. Working with the Reason song from the previous section, choose Create ➤ Sequencer Track. A new sequencer track will appear in the Sequencer window.

2. In this case you want to create automation in the Mixer, so select Mixer 1 by clicking the device selector button on the right of the sequencer track, as shown in Figure 2.47. Rename the Sequencer Track Mix Automation.

FIGURE 2.47
Select the device you
want to automate.

3. Make sure the new sequencer track is selected in the Sequencer window and that it's armed to receive MIDI information.

4. Press Return to make sure you are at the beginning of the song, then click the Record button in the Transport bar.

5. Try adjusting Aux Send 2 (the delay effect) on the Redrum Groove track while the song is playing.

6. After you've recorded some automation, stop the song and return to the beginning of the session. Notice how the Aux 2 knob on the Redrum track has that familiar automation outline.

7. Try recording automation on other parts of the Mixer 14:2.

Every knob, slider, and button on the Mixer (and most instruments and effects) can be automated this way.

CREATING AND EXPORTING A COMPLETE SONG

The elements that make up a complete song are of course, up to you. You may want to use the sequencing functions from the previous section, the Dr. Rex loops, or the recording, grouping, rearranging, copying, and pasting techniques covered in other parts of this chapter. The following is one example of a Reason song created from scratch and some common methods for basic arrangements:

CREATING A SONG

To create a song, follow these steps:

1. Create a new Reason song.

2. Add a Mixer 14:2 and a Dr. Rex Loop Player.

3. Click the Preview button on the Dr. Rex.

By clicking the Preview button *before* you browse loops, they will play at the current session tempo as you scroll through the selection.

4. Click the Browse Loop button and select a loop to load into the Dr. Rex. Click the To Track button to send the drum sequence to the Sequencer window.

5. Add two NN-XT Advanced Samplers.

6. Use the Browse Patch button to load a bass sample into the first NN-XT from the Reason Factory Sound Bank/NN-XT Sampler Patches/Bass folder.

7. Use your MIDI keyboard or the Key Lane Editor to create a bass performance.

8. Use the Browse Patch button to load a piano sample into the second NN-XT from the Reason Factory Sound Bank/NN-XT Sampler Patches/Piano folder.

9. Use your MIDI keyboard or the Key Lane Editor to create a piano performance.

10. Add other instrument performances or Dr. Rex loops if you'd like to.

11. Use the grouping, copying, and editing functions to create a basic arrangement.

EXPORTING A SONG

When you are ready to export your song, use the following method:

1. Press Enter to return the playhead to the beginning of the song.

2. Scroll to the end of the song and locate the song end marker, shown here.

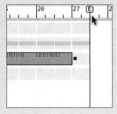

3. Drag the song end marker to one measure past the last measure of the song, also shown in the graphic. This will allow any last ringing notes to fade out.

4. Select File ➤ Export Song As Audio File, then choose between the AIFF and WAV formats and click Save.

5. Leave the default settings in the Export Audio Settings window as they are.

6. Click Export.

Creating a Template Session

Now that you are familiar with many of Reason's instruments and effects, here's how to create a template that contains the instruments, effects, and routing setups that you might use on a regular basis. This isn't written in stone—feel free to alter it in any way. You may have different effects that you prefer to use, or you may want multiple versions of some instruments and no versions of others.

1. Open a new Reason song and create a Mixer 14:2.

2. Make sure the Mixer is selected and create an RV7000.

3. With the RV7000 selected, create a Scream 4 Distortion.

4. With the Scream 4 selected, create a DDL-1 Digital Delay Line.

5. With the DDL-1 selected, create a PH-90 Phaser.

   The Effects Return strip on your mixer shown in Figure 2.48 should reflect the effects routing you've just set up.

FIGURE 2.48
The Effects
Return strip

MINIMIZING

To minimize all of the instruments effects and mixers simultaneously, hold down the Option key and click the minimize triangle in the upper left corner of any module.

---

1. Now add one each of Reason's instruments.

2. Minimize the instruments.

Figure 2.49 shows the complete session with all of the instruments and effects minimized.

FIGURE 2.49
The complete session

1. Choose File ➢ Save As and name the file `Template One.rns`.

2. Save the file in the Reason folder, which also contains the `Tutorial Song.rns` and the Reason Factory Sound Bank.

3. Now open Reason ➢ Preferences. Under the General tab in the Default Song section, select Custom, as shown in Figure 2.50.

FIGURE 2.50
Select Custom as the
default song.

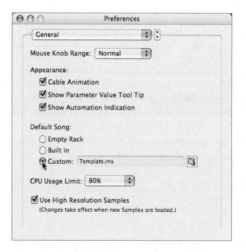

4. Click the folder icon to open the Reason Browser.

5. Locate the Reason folder and select the `Template One.rns` file, as shown in Figure 2.51.

FIGURE 2.51
Select the
template file.

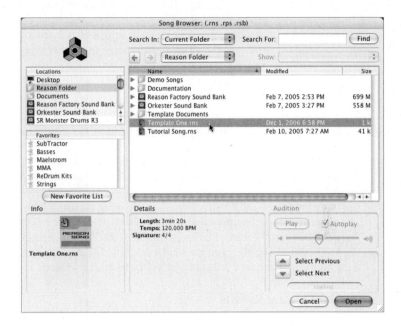

6. Click the Open button on the lower right.

ReWire

ReWire is a software protocol invented by Propellerhead that allows you to connect Reason with other music production programs. ReWire is now the standard communication protocol for music software. Propellerhead licenses ReWire for free to any company that wishes to use it. Each program that uses ReWire functions a bit differently. For example, when using Reason in a Pro Tools session you must do all of your tempo adjustments in the Pro Tools interface, but when you use Reason in conjunction with Ableton Live you can adjust the tempo in either program. These differences, however, are usually minor.

By using ReWire you can take advantage of all of the features that other music programs have that may be lacking in Reason, such as the ability to record live tracks and use various plug-ins. With ReWire you can take an entire, complex Reason session and route each individual track to individual tracks in the master program, allowing you to use plug-ins, effects, and automation for remixes, final mixes, and mastering.

At the opposite end of the spectrum, you can run your entire Reason session onto one stereo track in Pro Tools, Logic, Ableton Live or GarageBand, using one or more Reason instruments as a backing track or maybe working with a specific Reason synthesizer or sampler.

Reason and OS X

Reason has been a Mac-compatible program since the release of version 1 in 2000. As a result, Reason takes full advantage of OS X's architecture and it shows in its economical use of processor power and resources. While it's certainly possible to push your Mac to the limit with Reason, it takes some doing. Following as many of the OS X optimizing suggestions in Chapter 1, "Optimizing Your System," as is possible for your system will greatly improve your ability to create Reason songs with lots of instruments, effects, and automation.

More Power?

The current minimum system requirements for Reason 3.0.5 are Mac OS X 10.3.9 or later (10.4.4 or later required for use with Intel Macs), a G4 or G5 or Intel processor, 256MB RAM, and 2GB free hard disk space.

While it's possible to run Reason with the bare minimum, you'll want to have at least 512MB RAM and, if possible, up to 6GB of free space on your hard drive *after* the program is installed for virtual memory. As with any audio and music production program, the more RAM you have, the more you will be able to do. If you are planning on using Reason as a stand-alone program on an iBook or MacBook, you will definitely want to install more RAM than the minimum amount those models currently ship with. If you intend to use Reason in conjunction with ReWire, Ableton Live, Logic, or Pro Tools, I recommend at least 1GB of RAM. You can also get more out of Reason by quitting any unnecessary programs before launching a session.

Organizing ReFills

A large collection of ReFills can take up a lot of space. If you are utilizing the various free refills and demos that are available, it's a good idea to use a cleanup program like TidyUp! (also mentioned in Chapter 1) to make sure you are not taking up space with two versions of the same ReFill. Copies of the same ReFill can have different names, but Reason can only read one copy of a duplicate ReFill at a time. This can cause some confusion when browsing for patches and other files in the Reason Browser.

Also, for quick access to ReFills, keep them on the same drive and in one folder. You can utilize the Browser window to organize them by style, genre, or content and create Favorites menus based on your own needs.

Maximizing Processor Resources

Reason has a built-in CPU meter to let you know how much power you are using and how much you have left. The CPU meter is located at the bottom left of the Reason Transport bar, as shown in Figure 2.52.

FIGURE 2.52
The CPU meter

You can reduce the load on your CPU by eliminating processor-intensive effects and instruments. Reverb effects in particular use up a lot of resources. If you have more than one RV7000 in your session, try eliminating one or more and utilizing the Send and Return function of the Mixer 14:2 with a single reverb, as I covered in the "Effects" section earlier. Do this whenever you have multiple instances of any effects you may be working with.

Combinator devices can also take up a lot of power. If possible, use a single instrument in place of a Combinator device if you need more CPU. For example, you may be able to substitute an NN19 or NN-XT piano sample for a Combinator piano patch.

 Real World Scenario

CREATING BACKING TRACKS IN REASON

More musicians are finding that Reason can function as the primary DAW in their recording studio. For hip-hop artists in particular, a Reason session can contain all of the instruments, samplers, and arrangement options needed to create complete songs. I talked with Alexander of the San Francisco Bay Area hip-hop group Instant Messengers to get a look at some of his methods for creating a backing track from start to finish using Reason.

SETTING UP

Alexander's default session contains, in this order:

◆ The Mastering Suite

◆ A Main Mixer (14:2)

◆ Four effects: an RV-7 reverb, a DDL-delay, a chorus, and a compressor.

◆ Two NN19 samplers for melody lines and samples

◆ A SubTractor or Malström for bass

◆ A Redrum drum computer for the beat

GETTING STARTED

Alexander: "To start off, my weapon of choice is the NN19 Digital Sampler. I have all of the WAV samples that I've taken off different records and saved into separate folders that I can easily browse [with the Reason Browser] and use them as a starting point for a track. I also use the NN19 sounds from the Factory Sound Bank, like the pianos or a Rhodes patch.

"I don't use a MIDI keyboard. I'll create a loop [using the Loop On/Off button in the Transport bar], then open up the Piano Roll and work with that to create a melody—that's usually the starting point. Sometimes I'll use more than one melody or sample so I'll need more than one NN19."

BASS LINES

"For bass lines I use the SubTractor or the Malström. The [included] digital samplers have bass sounds, but a lot of them are kind of cheesy, trying to emulate bass guitars. I usually end up using synth-sounding basses from the SubTractor, sometimes the Malström. For EQ I use the two-band EQ on the mixing board [the Mixer 14:2], turning the highs down and turning up the lows.

"For the SubTractor I use the Factory sounds a lot—in the bass category [Reason Factory Sound Bank/ SubTractor Patches/Bass], there's a patch called Hyper Bottom that's the most generic sounding bass you can get, but it works really well.

"Once the melody and bass line are created, I group them, not a complete arrangement, just enough so I can loop them [in the sequencer window]."

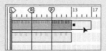

DRUM PROGRAMMING

"Once the bass line and melody or melodies are in place, from there I'll work on the drums. Sometimes I'll use samples, mostly from records. I'll record from my turntable into a four-channel mixer, then into the computer and then edit from there. I save the samples as WAV files and then open them in the Redrum.

"Along with my own samples I'll use drum sounds from different [Reason Factory Sound Bank] kits and mix and match the sounds.

"Usually what I'll do is use the Redrum Step Sequencer for the kick and snare to get at least one bar of how I want the drums to sound. I try not to use the Step Sequencer for hi-hat or cymbals, though. For cymbals I'll use the Copy Pattern To Track function and work in the Drum Lane."

To use the drum lane for greater control over the Redrum:

1. Select the Redrum track in the sequencer window.

2. Select and highlight the Redrum in the Reason window.

3. Use the Loop On/Off button in the transport bar to create a one or two-measure loop.

4. Deselect the Pattern Enable button in the Redrum.

5. Select Edit ➢ Copy Pattern to Track. This sends the Redrum pattern to the Sequencer as a group, or multiple groups if your loop is longer than one measure long.

6. Use the Edit/Arrange Mode button to switch to Arrange Mode.

7. Select the Show Drum Lane Button to view the Drum Lane sequencer.

The Drum Lane is exactly like the Piano Lane for the Redrum Drum Computer. You can trigger the Redrum by using the Pencil tool to draw notes directly in the Drum Lane.

By using the Drum Lane instead of the Redrum's step sequencer you'll have much better control over the hi-hat and cymbals. You can use the Snap To drop-down menu to divide the Drum Lane grid into much smaller increments, up to 1/64-notes.

To create a triplet feel with your hi-hat or cymbal tracks:

1. Use the Snap To drop-down menu to create an 1/8-note grid.

2. Select a hi-hat or cymbal track and use the Pencil tool to draw notes on each 1/8- note.

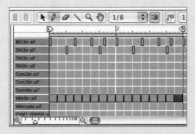

3. Select 1/8 T from the Snap To drop-down menu. The grid will change from 1/8-note divisions to 1/8-note triplet divisions.

4. Use the Pencil tool to create notes on some of the 1/8 T notes on the grid.

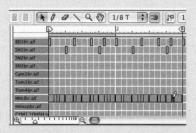

At this point, experimentation and chance can play a big role in creating a drum performance. You'll find that some notes sound rhythmically good and fit with your session while others just sound messy. Try experimenting with different patterns and using the Undo function when your ideas don't work out. Try viewing and adding smaller increments (1/16 notes and 1/16-note triplets, 1/32 notes, and so on) to your rhythmic variations. After you've worked with this method for a while, you'll begin to recognize patterns that work for you and you'll be able to program your beats with more precision.

ARRANGEMENTS

Once you've created a drum loop in the Drum Lane, return to the Arrange view and copy and paste the loop throughout the arrangement. You can then return to the Drum Lane and edit each instance of the loop by adding or deleting drum hits or rearranging the loop in any number of ways.

Alexander: "I'll usually create a few different variations on the beat, then move them around once I have the basic arrangement of the song, whether it's verse, chorus, whatever. I'll go through it and kind of tweak the transitions of the song, whether there's a crescendoing bass line before a new instrument comes in or maybe putting a crash (cymbal) on the first hit of a measure or a snare drop or beat dropping out on the fourth bar before something new comes in."

"Once the final arrangement is done I'll export the whole track as an AIFF file [File ➤ Export Song as Audio File]. Once that's done we can just bring it into Pro Tools to record vocals or burn a CD for a live backing track. One cool thing about Reason is that if I need to make any changes I can just go back and open the Reason file, make my changes and export a new track."

Instant Messengers' debut CD will be released in early 2007 on Simple Man Records. You can hear some of Alexander's Reason tracks at:

www.myspace.com/instantmessengers

www.myspace.com/alexanderspit

The Bottom Line

Create a new Reason song with a mixer, instruments, and effects   Reason songs can be made up of any configuration of instruments and effects. What instruments make up a particular session and in what order they appear will depend on how you prefer to work and the type of music you are creating, among other factors. The following is one possible template for working in Reason. Using the Tab key to toggle between front and back view of the Reason interface is a good way to begin creating your own routing configurations.

Master It   Create a new Reason song with a Mixer 14:2 and one each of Reason's instruments. Also include an RV7000 Advanced Reverb and a Scream 4 Distortion Unit as Send effects. Minimize the mixer and all of the instruments and effects.

Edit loops in the Dr. Rex Loop Player   Reason's Dr. Rex Loop Player can load and play back any file in the REX format. The most commonly used file in the Dr. Rex is the drum loop, though any instrument loop file can be converted to the RX2 format using Propellerhead's ReCycle program.

Master It   Open a drum loop in the Dr. Rex Loop Player and raise its overall pitch by one octave except for the first slice: lower that to one octave below the original pitch and pan it hard left.

Add effects as inserts and sends   Reason's included effects can be used to enhance an instrument track, to help out in a mix, or to create completely new sounds from instrument performances.

Master It   Create a Reason song with two Dr. Rex drum loops. Add reverb to both Dr. Rex Loop Players as a Send effect. Add a delay to the second Dr, Rex only as an Insert effect.

Create and save your own patches with the Malström Synthesizer   The Malström Graintable Synthesizer, like all the Reason instruments, comes with a large collection of included presets. More presets are available from many commercially available ReFills as well. The real fun with Malström, though, is investigating all of the possibilities it contains for creating your own sounds and saving them as original, recallable patches.

Master It   Use both of Malström's Oscillators and the Mod A LFO to create and save an original patch.

Create Automation on a Reason Mixer 14:2   Reason's Automation features can be used to introduce effects, adjust various parameters, silence a specific part or instrument, and much more. On the Reason Mixer, automation is especially useful for final mixes, raising and lowering tracks, and adding and reducing effects.

Master It   Create volume automation on channel 1 of a Mixer 14:2.

Chapter 3

Ableton Live

Even more than most other DAW software, Ableton Live is many programs in one. Live is an audio recording program, a looping sequencer, a MIDI sequencer, and of course, its original use: a live performance instrument.

Live continues to grow and add new functionality along the way. Along with the included audio and MIDI plug-in effects, Live now comes with a built-in sampler called Simpler and the Impulse drum machine. Live also includes the option to access more complex features, such as the Operator synthesizer and the cleverly named "Sampler" sampler. These two instruments are built in to the Live program and can be "unlocked" by purchasing an optional upgrade code.

Finally as one of the few programs that can work both as a ReWire slave *and* master, Live also makes an excellent companion to other programs such as Reason, GarageBand, Logic, and Pro Tools.

In this chapter, you will learn to

◆ Create MIDI performances in Live

◆ Use Live's included instruments and effects to create clips

◆ Edit audio loops in Live's audio Clip View

◆ Edit MIDI clips in Live's MIDI Clip View

◆ Use Live and Reason together in a ReWire session.

Live Basics

Ableton Live is available in two versions from www.ableton.com, a downloadable version and a boxed version. The boxed version contains some extra features, like the optional Essential Instruments collection. Some of the other extra files included in the boxed version can be purchased and downloaded from the Live website (see the section "Expanding Live" later in this chapter).

When you start Live for the first time, you'll see the Lessons View window containing information about Live's features and tutorials. (You can also access this window by choosing View ➤ Lessons.)

It's a good idea to go through as many of these as you can (especially the "Tour through Live") to familiarize yourself with Live's basic functions and features. I will also be covering many of these features in this chapter's tutorials.

Live's Major Features

One of Live's biggest selling points remains its ability to time-stretch and pitch shift loop files, allowing you seamlessly incorporate files of different tempos and pitches into cohesive songs. Originally available only to PC-based users of Sonic Foundry's (now Sony's) Acid program, this kind of looping technology has had a huge impact on the world of digital music. While Live was not the first Mac program to incorporate this feature, it was certainly the first to do it well. Other programs now include similar functions, but Live still remains ahead of the pack. One feature that sets Live apart is its selection of multiple algorithms, which you can apply to different types of loop files. The ability to apply one kind of algorithm to a drum loop and another to a piano or guitar loop and still another to an MP3 song file allows Live users to achieve much better-sounding results across the board than any other loop-based program.

Looping, as important as it is to working in Live, is only part of the story. Live's basic MIDI functionality is straightforward. Live's MIDI basics are easy to grasp and implement and, should you choose to explore them, the more complex features can keep you occupied endlessly as well.

You can also record directly into Live creating your own original tracks and loops, making it work as a standalone audio recording program.

The Mastering Demo Files

Included in the companion DVD is a folder named MMA Audio/Ableton Live. This folder contains some Live sessions and other related audio files that you'll be using in this chapter. If you haven't done so already, copy the entire MMA Audio folder to your desktop where you will have easy access to its contents.

Setting up a Live Template

Included in your MMA Audio/Ableton Live folder are two Template sessions, one each for Live 5 and 6. Since Live is a highly customizable program, these sessions have been included to make sure we're all viewing the same interface as we go through this chapter.

To install the Live Template:

1. Start Live.

2. Choose File ➢ Open Live Set.

3. Open the MMA Audio/Ableton Live/Live (5 or 6) Template folder.

4. Choose Live ➢ Preferences from the menu bar.

5. Select the File/Folder tab.

6. Click the Save button next to Save Current Set as Template.

7. Close Live's Preferences.

8. Choose File ➢ New Live Set.

You can use Live's Preferences to create a new Template session at any time. As you become more familiar with the program, you may want to create a more complex Template. Templates can include instruments, effects, and even audio files.

Session and Arrange View

Live offers two different basic modes of operation, the Session View and the Arrange View. Each view has it advantages depending on the type of project you are working on and your own preferred methods of creating music.

If you are composing and arranging primarily in Live as a stand-alone program you may find yourself starting projects in the Session window and finishing them in the Arrange window. Because it's much easier to access and learn many of Live's functions in the Session window, this is the method you'll be using for this chapter.

Whichever view you decide to work in, it's a good idea to become familiar with both modes of operation, as they each have their distinct advantages. Ultimately the best thing about Live is that it contains so many possibilities that you can use the method that works best for you.

SESSION VIEW

The Session View, shown in Figure 3.1, is Live's default window and will be visible when you first start the program. If you are seeing a different window (the Arrange View) click the Session View button (the three horizontal bars) in the top right corner of the Live interface.

FIGURE 3.1

Live's Session View

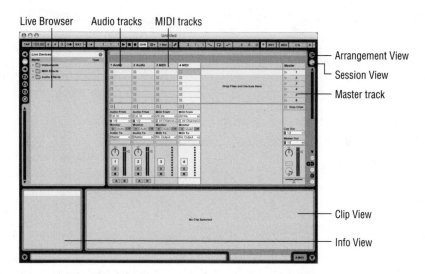

Some common uses for Session view include:

Live performance   If you are using Live in an improvised performance, you will probably work primarily in the Session view window, where you have immediate access to multiple clips that you can launch individually or simultaneously.

Composition   If you are composing music by mixing and matching loops, the Session view offers a straightforward way to organize your composition.

In this chapter, you will primarily be working in the Session View.

ARRANGE VIEW

Live's other mode of operation is the Arrange View. To access the Arrange View, click the Arrange View button below the Session View button.

Some common uses for the Arrange View include:

Working in ReWire mode   If you are using Live as a ReWire slave as an adjunct to a session in Pro Tools or Logic, you may end up working a lot in the Arrange window, which will give you a linear layout similar to the interface of those programs.

Composition   If you are used to working with other loop-based programs such as Sony's Acid (for PC) or GarageBand, you may be more comfortable working in the Arrange View where the setup and layout will be familiar to you.

The Live Interface

Let's take a look at some of the views and features that make up the Live interface.

THE LIVE BROWSER

Located on the upper left corner of the Live interface is the Live Browser. This is where you will access the files, instruments, and effects that will make up your Live sessions. Figure 3. 2 shows the Live Browser.

FIGURE 3.2

The Live Browser

Show/Hide Browser —
Device Browser —
Plug-in Device Browser —

File Browsers —

Hot-Swap —

Along the left side of the Live Browser are six buttons, from top to bottom:

The Show/Hide Browser button   This hides the Live Browser to make more room for the Session and Arrange windows, which I'll cover later.

The Live Device Browser   This button opens the Browser window containing all of your Live instruments and effects. Click the arrow next to each folder to open it and view its contents.

Plug-in Device Browser   Here you'll find all of your Audio Unit and VST plug-ins. These are third-party plug-ins that you may have on your system that will also work in your Live sessions. In order to use Audio units and VST plug-ins in Live, you must activate them in the File/Folder tab of Live's Preferences. For more information on using Audio Units and VST plug-ins in Live, see Chapter 8, "Plug-in Effects."

File Browsers   The next three buttons are your File Browser buttons. With these you can set up quick access to any audio files, such as loops and samples that you intend to use with Live.

The Hot-Swap Browser   This button is activated when you want to try out different samples in Live's sampler devices.

Adding loops, clips, instruments, or effects with the Live Browser is as easy as dragging them from the window on to the appropriate track. New tracks can also be created by double-clicking the loop, clip, instrument, or effect in the browser window. Some shortcuts that can help you navigate the Live Browser:

◆   If you've opened too many folders in any of the Browser views you can close all folders at once by double-clicking the Browser's button.

◆ You can "level up" by clicking the Parent Folder icon at the top of the Browser window.

◆ Click the Search icon in the top right corner of the Browser window to search for files, clips, presets, and plug-ins by name.

FIND YOUR GARAGEBAND LOOPS WITH THE FILE BROWSER

One of the main uses for the File Browser is to locate any loop files you would like to use in your Live projects. If you've installed GarageBand on your computer, you already have a library full of Apple Loops that can be used in Live. To use the File Browser to locate your GarageBand Apple Loops:

1. Select File Browser button 2 or 3.

2. Click the Parent Folder icon at the top of the file browser until you see your username or Home folder.

3. Your Apple Loops should be located in the following folder:

   ```
   Library/Audio/Apple Loops/User Loops/Apple Loops for GarageBand
   ```

If your Apple Loops are not located in this directory, you can use OS X's search function to locate them and then follow the correct file path with Live's File Browser.

INFO VIEW

If you are just starting to use the program, one of Live's most useful features is the Info View window located on the bottom left of the Live interface. With the Info View showing (select View ➤ Info if it's not currently visible), you can place your mouse over many of Live's buttons or fields and the Info View window will give you a detailed description of its function. Figure 3.3 shows a close-up of the Info View describing itself.

FIGURE 3.3
The Info View

SHOW/HIDE BUTTONS

The Live window features three triangular buttons, one each in the upper left, lower left and lower right corners. These are the Show/Hide buttons. You can use these to view or hide different fields in the Live window; they are handy if you find you need more room to work with tracks in the main window.

THE TRACK WINDOW

Taking up most of the center of the Live interface is the Track Window. This is the section in which you will do much of the work in Live, such as creating and deleting tracks, arranging clips, setting volume levels, and routing Live input and output when working in ReWire mode.

In the empty space in the center of the Track window is the Clip/Device Drop Area. You can create new Audio or MIDI tracks by dragging and dropping Live Clips, loops, instruments, or effects from the Live Browser on to the Clip/Device Drop Area.

Live has four different types of tracks that you will be working with:

◆ Audio tracks

◆ MIDI tracks

◆ Return tracks

◆ Master tracks

Audio Tracks

Figure 3.4 shows an audio track in the Session View window.

FIGURE 3.4
An audio track

To create a New audio track:

◆ Select Insert ➢ Insert Audio Track from the File menu.

◆ Use the keyboard shortcut Command+T.

◆ Drag an audio file (WAV, AIFF, or MP3) from the Live Browser or any location on your hard drive directly onto the Clip/Device Drop Area.

The top section of the audio track contains clip slots. These are used to load and play back audio files. Each audio track can hold many clips, but only one clip per audio track can be played back at a time.

Use the File Browser to open the folder MMA Audio/Ableton Live/All Loops and drag the file AcousGtr1.wav onto Audio Track 1's top clip slot. Figure 3.5 shows the clip in the clip slot.

FIGURE 3.5
An audio file in an
audio track clip slot

Use the triangular Clip Launch button located on the left side of the clip slot to play the clip.

Below the visible clip slots, above the I/O section, is the Clip Stop button. Click this button to stop playback of the clip.

The Input fields (labeled Audio From) in the I/O (in/out) section of the audio track can be used to route audio from ReWire devices like Propellerhead's Reason or to assign recording inputs from your hardware audio interface. Clicking either of these fields reveals a drop-down menu from which you can choose from your available audio routing options.

The Output section (labeled Audio To) can be used to route audio to outputs on your hardware audio interface or to other programs when using Live as a ReWire slave.

The Mixer section of each audio track (see Figure 3.6) contains the following parameters:

FIGURE 3.6
The Mixer section of
an audio track

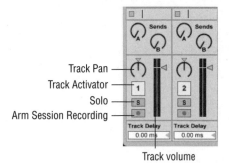

Track Pan Use the Track Pan knob to adjust panning for the selected track.

Track Activator Turns the track on and off. Can be used as a Mute button. Mute multiple track Command+clicking Track Activator buttons.

Solo button The Solo button mutes all but the selected track. Solo multiple tracks by Command+clicking Solo buttons.

Arm Session Recording Select the Arm Session Recording button to prepare a track for recording and to monitor its input. Arm multiple tracks by holding down the Command key and selecting multiple Arm Session Recording buttons.

Track Volume Use the Track Volume slider to raise and lower the track's volume.

MIDI Tracks

Figure 3.7 shows a MIDI track in the Session View window.

MIDI tracks in Live are used to create performances with virtual instruments. This includes Live's instruments such as the Operator, Sampler, Impulse, and Simpler, as well as third-party virtual instruments such as those covered in Chapter 9, "Virtual Instruments."

FIGURE 3.7
A MIDI track

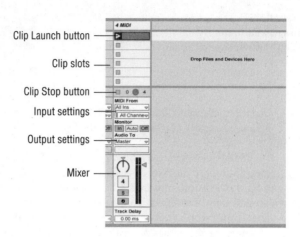

MIDI tracks and audio tracks have many similarities and a few key differences:

◆ Like the audio track, the MIDI track has clip slots for loading and playing back files. The difference is that MIDI clips contain more than just MIDI information. Loading a MIDI clip from the Live Browser will also load the virtual instrument and any effects it was created with.

◆ The Clip Launch and Clip Stop functions for MIDI tracks are the same as audio tracks.

◆ In the input (MIDI From) section of the MIDI track you can choose from your available MIDI inputs.

◆ The output (MIDI To) section works the same way as the audio tracks and can be used to route audio to outputs on your hardware audio interface or to other programs when using Live as a ReWire slave.

◆ In its default state, the Mixer section of the MIDI track looks different from the Mixer section of an audio track. Once you add one of Live's instruments, the Audio and MIDI track's mixer sections look identical.

Return Tracks

Figure 3.8 shows a return track in the Session View window.

FIGURE 3.8
A return track

Return Tracks in Live are the same as return tracks in any program. You can use return tracks to add a single effect or multiple effects like delay and reverb to multiple tracks, thereby reserving CPU power for other tasks.

To add an effect with a return track:

1. Use the Live Browser to add an audio file to Audio Track 1.

2. Click the Live Device Browser button to view the Device Browser.

3. Open the `Audio Effects` folder and choose an effect.

4. Drag the selected effect from the Browser window directly onto Return Track A.

5. Select View ➤ Sends from the File menu.

6. Raise the Send A knob on Audio Track 1.

Master Track

Figure 3.9 shows the master track in the Session View window.

FIGURE 3.9

The master track

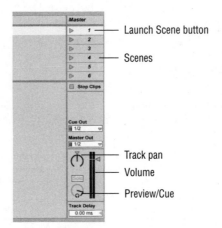

The top rows of the master track (where the clip slots are on MIDI and audio tracks) contain the Live session's scenes. A scene is comprised of all the clips lined up vertically across all of the tracks in the Track window.

Just as you can launch individual clips with the Clip Launch button, you can use the Scene button to launch entire scenes. To play a basic Live song arrangement in the Session view:

1. Open the file `MasterOne.als` from the `MMA Audio/Ableton Live/Live 6` folder.

2. Click a Launch Scene button to launch a scene.

3. While a scene is playing, click a different Launch Scene button to start a different scene. Live will automatically begin playing the next scene on the next measure's first beat.

4. Click the Stop Clips button to stop playback.

To create and arrange scenes:

◆ Select clips from the File Browser or other clip slots and drag them to any available clip slot.

◆ Copy clips by Option+dragging to open clip slots.

◆ Add new audio and MIDI files to the arrangement by dragging files from the Browser directly onto the Track window.

The Mixer section of the master track has a Track Pan knob and Volume fader that control the panning and master volume for the session, as well as a blue knob called the Preview/Cue volume knob.

PREVIEWING CLIPS

At the top left corner of the Live File Browser window is a button that looks like a pair of headphones. This button is only visible in any of the three File Browser views, not in the Device or Plug-in Device views. Turn this button on to activate the Browser Preview function. When Browser Preview is enabled, any clip you select in the Browser window will automatically play at the current session tempo, allowing you to get an idea of how the file will fit into your session. At the bottom of the master track is the Preview/Cue knob, which can be used to adjust the Browser Preview volume.

You can also add effects to the master track using the same drag-and-drop methods as audio, MIDI, or return tracks. Often a compressor or other mastering-related effects will be used in the final mixing process to establish a consistent output from the master track.

THE LIVE TOOLBARS

Along the top of the Live window you will see four toolbars. These contain all of Live's various tools. I'll describe some of the tools you'll be using in detail.

The first section, shown in Figure 3.10, contains Live's time-related functions.

FIGURE 3.10
Live's Time tools

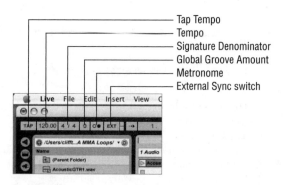

Tap Tempo Click your mouse rhythmically on the Tap Tempo button to set the tempo for the current session.

Tempo Displays the session's tempo. Click your mouse on the current tempo field and drag up or down to raise or lower the tempo.

Signature Denominator Displays the session time signature.

Global Groove Amount This field adjusts how much "groove" or "swing" is applied to a session's tracks. This is a way of adding a humanized feel to drum tracks and other performances.

Metronome This button turns Live's built-in metronome on and off.

External Sync Switch Can be used to sync Live with an external MIDI controller, which I'll cover in detail in Chapter 11, "MIDI."

In the center of the next toolbar, shown in Figure 3.11, are the Transport buttons, Start, Stop and Record, which are essentially the same as the similar functions in other programs.

FIGURE 3.11
The Transport buttons

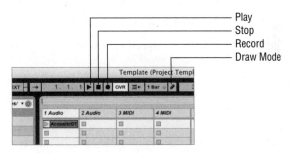

Play
Stop
Record
Draw Mode

Live's toolbars contain a number of other advanced functions that I won't be covering in this book. For more explicit instructions on using Live's toolbars, see the Live Lessons tutorials (select Help ➢ Lessons Table of Contents) or the Live Manual.

The other tool I'll cover is the Draw Mode switch (the Pencil icon at the far right, also shown in Figure 3.11). This switch is used to activate the Pencil tool in order to create and edit MIDI information in Live.

The third toolbar contains recording and looping functions I won't be covering in this book.

The toolbar on the far right contains the computer MIDI keyboard switch. When this switch is activated, you can use your computer's keyboard as a MIDI controller to play and record MIDI notes with Live's built-in instruments.

The other two buttons in this toolbar are the Key Mapping and MIDI mapping buttons, which I'll cover in Chapter 11.

Included Instruments

Live comes with built-in virtual instruments that you can use to create clips and tracks with by recording or manually creating MIDI performances:

Impulse A drum machine/percussion sequencer that comes with many preset drum kits. You can also drag and drop samples directly onto a blank Impulse instrument to create your own kits.

Simpler A basic sampler that come with some built-in instruments. You can create new simpler instruments by dragging and dropping WAV, AIFF and MP3 files directly onto the Simpler interface.

Sampler An advanced version of Simpler, new in Live 6. With Sampler you can create multi-layered sampler instruments and edit samples with complex built-in editing functions.

Operator Live's built-in synthesizer that contains many editable parameters for creating your own sounds and presets.

Impulse and Simpler are both automatically activated when you authorize the Live program. Sampler and Operator come with the downloaded or the boxed version of Live but have to be paid for and authorized separately. You can purchase authorization codes for Sampler and Operator from the Ableton website.

You can also try out Sampler and Operator in demo mode. In demo mode, you can use all the features, but you can't save or export your work. To try out Sampler or Operator:

1. Open Live's preferences by selecting Live ➤ Preferences.

2. Click the Products tab.

3. Choose Operator or Sampler from the Products list.

4. Click the Demo button at the bottom of the Preferences window.

To exit demo mode, select the instrument in the Preferences window Products list and click the Hide button at the bottom of the Preferences window. Live will exit demo mode when you create a new Live set.

Using Impulse

Creating drum performances with Impulse is easy, and Live incorporates some basic MIDI functionality to give your performances a more human feel. To create drum performance with Impulse:

1. Create a new Live session and click the Live Device Browser button.

2. Open the instruments category folder and open the Impulse folder.

   Contained in the Impulse folder are two preset subfolders: Acoustic, which contains (somewhat) natural-sounding drum kits, and Electronic, which contains synthetic drum kits. Many of these presets are a combination of the Impulse drum module and Live's included effects.

3. From the Acoustic folder, select the Big Rocker kit and drag it onto any MIDI track. You can also drag an Impulse kit directly onto the Clip/Device Drop Area to create a new track.

   At first glance you will not notice any change in your existing track in the Session View window; however, in the Track/Clip View field you will now see the Impulse drum machine and any effects contained in your Impulse kit. Figure 3.12 shows the Big Rocker Impulse kit.

FIGURE 3.12
The Big Rocker
Impulse drum kit

4. Select your Impulse track in the Session View window and double-click the first clip slot underneath the Track title bar to create a clip and to make the Clip View visible.

Here is where you will create your drumbeat or basic percussion rhythm.

5. The current Clip View value should be set to 1/16. To make sure this is the case, Control+click anywhere inside the MIDI Note Editor and select Fixed Grid: 1/16 from the pop-up menu (Figure 3.13).

FIGURE 3.13
The MIDI Note Editor
and pop-up menu

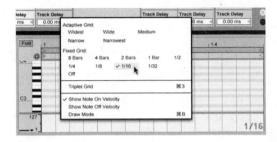

6. Double-click in any empty slot to create a MIDI note.

7. Once you've created a note, double-click it again to delete it.

8. Move notes around by clicking in the center of the note and dragging the note to a new location.

Figure 3.14 shows a drum performance in the MIDI Clip View window. If you are not familiar with basic drum programming, you can set up your own performance using Figure 3.14 as a guide, drawing notes on the kick drum track at beats 1, 3, 9, and 11 then on the snare track at beats 5 and 13.

FIGURE 3.14
A drum performance
in the MIDI Clip View

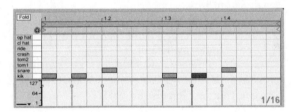

You can also use your MIDI keyboard to trigger Impulse's sounds and create a performance. The first drum (usually the kick drum) in any Impulse kit will correspond to the note C3 on your MIDI keyboard. For more on this, see the "MIDI Recording" section later in this chapter.

DRAW MODE

You can also create performances in Draw Mode. Activate the Draw Mode by clicking the Draw Mode button (Pencil icon) at the top of the screen or by using the keyboard shortcut Command+B. In Draw Mode, click an empty slot once to create a MIDI note. Click the note a second time to erase it.

You can also select an empty note, hold down your mouse, and drag to the left or right to create or erase a series of notes.

CREATING AND SAVING A NEW KIT

If none of the included Impulse kits are exactly what you're looking for, follow these steps to create your own basic kit from any drum (or other instrument) samples:

1. Select the Impulse folder in the Live Device Browser and drag it to an empty MIDI track or blank spot on Clip/Device Drop Area.

2. Using Live's File Browser window, open the folder MMA Audio/Ableton Live/Impulse. Select the file KickOne.aif and drag it from the Browser window onto the first open slot on the Impulse interface (above the Start knob). You can also drag and drop any WAV, AIFF or MP3 files from anywhere on your hard drive directly onto any sample slot in Impulse window.

3. Add the SnareOne.aif and the HiHat.aif files (in the same folder) to the kit.

4. Select and highlight the kick drum sample in the Impulse window as shown in Figure 3.15.

FIGURE 3.15
Select and highlight
the kick drum sample.

Selecting and highlighting a sample allows you access to Impulse's individual sample editing functions. Impulse's edit functions are located in the middle row of the interface and include transposing, panning, and volume parameters. Once you adjust any settings for an individual sample, you can preview the changes by clicking the Play button (triangle icon) in the sample's slot, also seen in Figure 3.15.

To save your new kit, click the Save Preset button (disk icon) in the top right corner of the Impulse interface. Type a name for your new kit and press Return. The new kit will be added to the Impulse folder by default.

You can also create a new folder for your original kits. To create a new folder, Control+click your new kit in the Live Device Browser and choose Create Folder from the pop-up menu. Name your folder, then drag your new Impulse kit into it.

SAVING CLIPS

Saving a Live clip means saving your actual performance along with any information Live needs to recall the performance. This includes any Impulse kit or other Live instrument and any effects that may have been used to create the clip (I'll cover Live's effects in the "Audio Effects" section later in this chapter).

To save your drum performance as a recallable Live Clip:

1. Select File Browser 1, 2, or 3 in the Browser window.

2. Select a location for your new folder, such as the desktop or the MMA Audio/Ableton Live folder.

3. Control+click anywhere in the Browser window and select Create Folder from the pop-up menu.

4. Name the new folder.

5. Select the clip you want to save in the clip slot.

6. Drag the clip directly onto your new folder in the Browser window.

7. Name the new clip.

DRUM ARRANGEMENTS

After you create the basic rhythm for your song, you can create multiple parts on the same MIDI track for different sections of the song. Double-click any blank clip slot to open the MIDI Note Editor and create a new clip or loop.

You can also create a copy of a drum clip by Option+dragging the clip to a blank clip slot. Use the MIDI Note Editor to create a variation of the loop using the clip copy.

Using Simpler

As the name implies, Simpler is sampling at its most basic. To get started with Simpler, try out one of the included Simpler instruments:

1. Open the Live Device Browser window.

2. Open Instruments/Simpler/Keys.

3. From the Keys folder, drag and drop the Korgan preset onto any empty MIDI track or directly onto the Clip/Device Drop Area.

4. The new Simpler instrument will appear in the Device View at the bottom of the Live Interface. Figure 3.16 shows the new Simpler instrument.

FIGURE 3.16

The Korgan Simpler instrument

Sample display

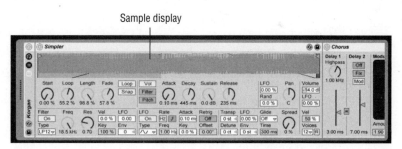

Creating a performance is essentially the same in Simpler as it is with Impulse. First, select your Impulse track in the Session View window and double-click the first clip slot underneath the Track title bar to create a clip and to make the Clip View visible in the Track/Clip view. Then create a performance in the MIDI Clip View (see the earlier "Using Impulse" section for instructions).

One major difference between the two instruments is that with Simpler you will want a much wider range of notes to choose from.

To access the lower or higher registers of the Simpler instrument, move your mouse to the left side of the MIDI Note Editor window just past the piano keys. The cursor changes to the Resize tool, which is a hand icon holding a magnifying glass, shown in Figure 3.17.

FIGURE 3.17
The Resize tool

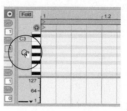

Drag up or down to access a different section of the keyboard range. Drag left to right to view larger notes, or drag right to left to view smaller notes.

CREATING A SIMPLER INSTRUMENT

You can create your own Simpler instruments by dragging and dropping samples from the Browser window or the OS X Finder onto an empty Simpler:

1. Choose File ➤ Open Live Set to create a Live set.

2. From the Live Device Browser, drag the Simpler (the device, not a preset) onto an empty MIDI track. You'll see an empty Simpler Device in the Clip/Device view at the bottom of the Live interface.

3. Use the File Browser to open the folder `MMA Audio/Ableton Live/Simpler`.

4. Drag the `PianoC3.wav` file onto the Sample Display area of the Simpler instrument.

5. Create a new clip using the methods covered earlier, or see the "MIDI Recording" section later in this chapter for more advanced techniques.

6. Save the new instrument by clicking the Save Preset button on the top right corner of the Simpler interface.

7. Name the new instrument and drag it into any folder, or create a new folder by Control+clicking the Simpler Device in the Browser window and selecting Create Folder from the pop-up menu.

EDITING SAMPLES

Simpler contains many functions that will be familiar to users of hardware and software samplers. The first section below the Sample Display window contains the Start, Loop, Length, and Fade controls. You can use these controls to adjust these parameters, which will noticeably affect your sample.

The next section contains a choice of three ADSR (Attack, Decay, Sustain, Release) envelopes, one each for the volume, filter, and pitch parameters of the sample. At the bottom of the Simpler interface are the filter and LFO (Low Frequency Oscillator) parameters. For more information on ADSR envelopes, filters, LFOs, and virtual samplers, see the sections "Virtual Samplers" and "Virtual Synthesizers" in Chapter 9.

Using Sampler

New in Live 6 is the included Sampler device. Sampler is a multisampling device (which means you can add more than one sample to the instrument you create) that contains all of the features commonly found in virtual samplers.

Activate Sampler by opening Live's Preferences and selecting the Products tab. Select Sampler from the Products list and click Unlock if you have purchased a serial number for Sampler. If you haven't purchased a serial number, click the Demo button to work with Sampler in demo mode. This means you'll have complete access to all of Sampler's features but won't be able to save your Live sets or export loops, tracks, or finished songs.

To get started using Sampler, open Sampler in the Live Device Browser window, then drag the Sampler Device onto any empty MIDI track. Use the Live File Browser to open MMA Audio/Ableton Live/Sampler, and drag the file PianoC3.wav directly onto the Sampler Sample window. Figure 3.18 shows the Sampler's main window with a single file loaded.

FIGURE 3.18
The Sampler interface

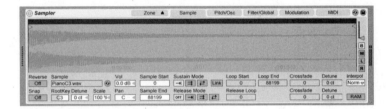

You can now begin to create a multisample:

1. At the top of the Sampler window click the Zone tab to view the Zone Editor (Figure 3.19).

   As you can see, the PianoC3.wav sample has been mapped across the entire keyboard. This is the sample's "zone." Mapping a single sample across an entire keyboard is what the Simpler instrument does by default. By contrast, with Sampler you can adjust the default mapping and add more samples to the instrument.

FIGURE 3.19
Sampler's Zone Editor

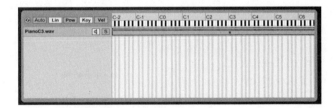

2. Place your mouse at either end of the Zone, then drag inward to shorten the zone. For this sample, create a one-octave range, as shown in Figure 3.20.

FIGURE 3.20
A one-octave range in the Sampler

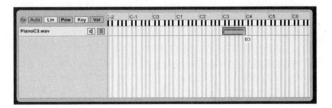

3. Add the other four piano samples to the instrument by dragging them from the MMA Audio/Ableton Live/Sampler folder directly onto the sample layer list on the left side of the Zone Editor.

4. Resize each of the sample zones to be one octave in length.

5. Drag each one-octave zone to the appropriate location in the Zone Editor window according to the sample's name. For example, place PianoC1.wav in the C1 octave range, PianoC2.wav in the C2 octave range, and so on.

   Figure 3.21 shows the how the samples should be mapped in the Zone Editor.

FIGURE 3.21
A mapped out
multisample

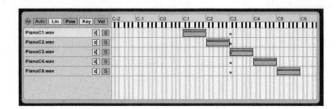

By default, Sampler will make C3 the root note of each sample you add to the instrument. This means the multisample's low notes are currently too low and its high notes are too high. You can see the default Root Key in the Zone Editor—it's the tiny "R" located on each sample layer at C3.

6. For this instrument, the Root Key should be set as the first note of each octave. Adjust the Root Key by Option+clicking the first note of any zone in the Zone Editor or by Option+dragging the small "R" from its current setting to the new location.

   You can also adjust the Root Key by selecting a sample in the Sample Layer List, clicking in the Root Key box at the bottom left of the Sampler interface, and dragging up or down.

7. Save your new multisample by clicking the Save Preset button on the top right of the Sampler Interface.

Use your MIDI keyboard or create a MIDI clip to try out the new instrument. As you can tell, this is far from a perfect sampled piano instrument. However, if you invest the time into creating them, Sampler can provide many more intricately mapped out samples. Sampler also makes a great alternative to the Impulse instrument if you want to create drum or percussion kits with more than Impulse's eight available sample slots.

Sampler contains many other features you'd expect to find in a virtual sampler such as velocity mapping, filters, oscillators, and MIDI mapping. For more information on Sampler's features, see the Live manual and the Sampler tutorial in the "What's New in Live 6" lessons, which you can access by selecting Help ➢ Lessons ➢ Table of Contents from the menu bar.

Included Effects

Ableton Live comes with a big collection of included plug-in effects. Open Live's Device Browser to see separate folders for two different types of effects: MIDI Effects and Audio Effects.

MIDI Effects

MIDI effects can be used on any MIDI track or MIDI instrument clip. Live's MIDI Effects are as follows:

Arpeggiator   Creates arpeggios. Includes many editable parameters to control speed, octave range, and note selection.

Chord   Turns any single note into a chord. Create your own chord forms or use any of the included presets.

Pitch   Inserts the pitch effect on any track; use the Pitch Transposition knob to raise or lower the pitch of any MIDI performance.

Note Length   Automatically assigns all of your MIDI notes the same length. This plug-in can be useful for quickly creating a consistent performance.

Random   Creates a random performance from your MIDI notes. Different presets will create different kinds of randomness, or create you own settings and save them.

Scale   Can assign any MIDI notes in a performance to fit a predetermined scale.

Velocity   Assigns a velocity range to a MIDI performance. This means that no matter how hard you press the keys on your MIDI keyboard, the notes will fall within a certain velocity range. This plug-in can be used to create a uniform performance (the compression presets) or to add dynamics.

To add a MIDI effect to a track:

1. Click the Live Device Browser button and open the MIDI Effects folder.

2. Select an effect and drag it from the Browser window directly onto a MIDI track or into the MIDI Track View window.

3. Each MIDI effect also contains a list of presets. Click the triangle next to the effect name in the Browser window to view the included presets. To add a MIDI effect preset to a track, select and drag the preset directly onto a MIDI track or into the MIDI Track View window.

MIDI effects will automatically be placed before the virtual instrument in the Track View window. You can add multiple MIDI effects to a track and arrange them in any order. Figure 3.22 shows the Arpeggiator and Velocity effects in the Track View window.

FIGURE 3.22
MIDI effects in the
Track View

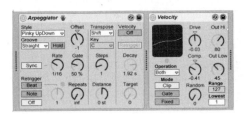

Audio Effects

Below the `MIDI Effects` folder in the Live Browser window is a folder containing Live's 24 built-in audio effects, including filters, delays, modulation effects, distortion, EQs, reverbs, and compressors. Live also contains some interesting effects that don't necessarily fall into a specific category such as Beat Repeat, Erosion, and Vinyl Distortion.

Live's audio effects can be added to either audio or MIDI tracks. To add an audio effect:

1. Select the effect by name or select a preset from inside the effect's folder and drag it directly onto an audio or MIDI track.

2. The effect will appear in the Track View at the bottom of the Live interface. You can also add effects by dragging from the Live Device Browser directly onto the Track View. Figure 3.23 shows the Filter Delay effect in the Track View.

FIGURE 3.23
The Filter Delay effect

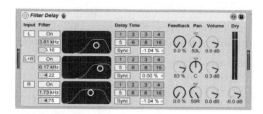

3. Add more effects to a chain by dragging them from the Live Device Browser to a track.

4. Rearrange the effects order in the Track View by clicking the effects title bar and dragging.

Expanding Live

Another strong feature of Live is the ability to expand on its included functionality. Using third-party instruments and effects or the free expansion content provided by Ableton can open up many creative possibilities.

LIVE PACKS

Live users who have installed the downloadable version can access additional files for Operator, Simpler, and Impulse as well as the files that were included in Live 4 from www.ableton.com/livepacks. After you download the files to your hard drive, double-click them to install the included files in your Live Library. When you restart Live, you'll be able to access new instruments in the Operator, Impulse, and Simpler devices or by looking in your Live Clips folder. You can see which Live Packs are already installed by opening Live's preferences and clicking the Live Packs tab.

LIVEFILLS

TrackTeam Audio has created a series of patches, kits, and clips called *LiveFills* (the concept is based on Reason's ReFills expansion packages). TrackTeam's LiveFills range in price from $39 to $59 and are available in bundles if you want to save a few dollars. Demo versions of each LiveFill are also available. Go to www.trackteamaudio.com for demo downloads and more information.

THIRD-PARTY EFFECTS AND INSTRUMENTS

Live supports the Audio Unit and VST plug-in formats for both plug-in instruments and plug-in effects. Activate Audio Units and VSTs by opening Live's Preferences, selecting the Plug-in tab, and turning Use Audio Units and Use VST Plug-in System Folders on.

Using Audio Unit and VST effects and instruments in Live and other DAW programs is covered in detail in Chapters 8 and 9.

Live Clips

A Live clip can be as simple as an audio file, such as an Apple Loop or WAV format loop, or a MIDI performance and instrument. Live clips can also be as complex as an audio file that has been transposed and adjusted in the Clip View with added effects or a MIDI clip with added effects and envelopes.

Audio Clips

Select any clip in any audio track clip slot to view its properties in the Clip View at the bottom of the Live Interface. Figure 3.24 shows an audio clip in the Clip View with all of the available boxes that can be used to adjust an audio clip (they won't all necessarily be showing, however). From left to right, the Clip View includes the Clip Box, the Launch Box, the Sample Box, and the Envelopes Box.

FIGURE 3.24

The Audio Clip View

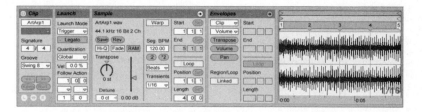

The Clip Box   In the Clip Box you can set some of the clip's basic properties such as the name of the clip, the color it will be represented by in the Live interface, and its time signature. This is the only box that will always be showing.

CLIP VIEWS

At the bottom of the Clip Box are three buttons. These are the Clip View Show/Hide buttons that can be used to hide sections of the Clip View that aren't being used in order to make more room for the Note Editor. By clicking any of these three buttons you can show or hide (from left to right) the Launch Box, Sample Box, or the Envelopes Box.

The Launch Box   In the Launch Box you can set a number of parameters that control how and in what order Live plays your clips in the Session window.

The Sample Box   The Sample Box contains many of the most important functions you'll use when working with audio clips and loops. As you'll see in the next section, this is where you will do much of the pitch-shifting and time-stretching, as well as volume adjustments.

The Envelopes Box   The Envelopes Box can be used to create pitch transposition, panning, or volume automation for any audio clip. This box can also be used to automate panning and volume of the mixer and Send/Return effects.

MIDI Clips

MIDI clips are similar to audio clips but with some important differences. Figure 3.25 shows the Clip View for a MIDI clip with all of the available parameter boxes showing.

FIGURE 3.25
The MIDI Clip View

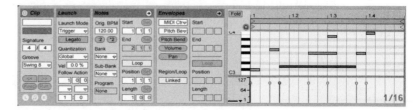

You can see that the Clip and Launch boxes are exactly the same for MIDI and audio clips. The Audio Clip Sample Box, however, is replaced by a Notes Box in the MIDI Clip View. The Notes Box has fewer features than the Sample Box. Many of the adjustments such as pitch shifting and volume changes that are available in the Audio Clip View can also be made to MIDI clips, but they take place elsewhere in the Live interface.

The MIDI Clip View's Envelope Box is similar to the audio Clip View's but with some added features particular to MIDI tracks, such as modulation and expression automation.

Live Tutorials

The tutorials in the following sections will get you started with some of Live's most important functions, including working with audio loops and introductions to both audio and MIDI recording. When it comes to looping and recording, Live offers some different and original options not available in other DAW software and these differences open up some interesting creative possibilities.

Working with Audio Loops

Loop files in AIFF or WAV format are one of the building blocks of Live sessions. Live treats these files (and their cousins the Apple Loop and the Acid file) in the same way. In MMA `Audio/Ableton Live/All Loops`, drag and drop the file `SynBassArp2.wav` onto any available audio track clip slot.

Select the clip in the clip slot to view the clip's properties in the Clip View window at the bottom of the Live interface.

On the bottom left of the Clip View window are the three Show/Hide buttons. Click the Show/Hide Sample Box button so that the Sample Box is showing.

In the Sample Box you can make a number of basic adjustments to the loop. Two of the most often used features of the Sample Box are the Transpose knob and the Clip Gain slider, both located on the bottom left of the Sample Box, as shown in Figure 3.26. To hear the effects of these features, follow these steps:

1. Use the Clip Launch button in the audio track to play back the selected clip.

2. With the clip playing, adjust the Transpose knob, raising and lowering the pitch of the clip.

3. Adjust the Clip Gain slider, raising and lowering the clip's volume.

FIGURE 3.26

The Sample Box

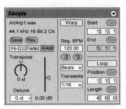

The middle of the Sample Box contains the Warp settings. Turning off the Warp button will cause the selected clip to play at its own unaltered tempo. The Seg. BPM field shows Live's guess at the selected loop's tempo. Play the loop back at double speed by clicking the :2 (halve tempo) button. Slow the loop down by clicking the *2 (double tempo) button.

Below the tempo settings is the Warp Mode selector, which is set to Beats, the default Warp Mode, in Figure 3.26. Choose from five different modes depending on the audio instrument content of the selected loop. Place your cursor over the Warp Mode box to view a list of suggestions for audio files and modes in the Info View.

On the right side of the Sample window are settings for setting the beginning and end point for the selected loop and the length and position for the loop markers in the Note Editor field.

CREATING AND SAVING AN AUDIO CLIP

In this section you'll create and save a new, recallable audio clip:

1. Create a new Live Set.

2. Select File ➢ Save Live Set As.

3. Name the new set Clip Project and save it to the desktop. A new folder with your Live set's name will be created on the desktop.

4. Select any audio file from the MMA Audio/All Loops folder and drag it to an open clip slot in any audio track.

5. Double-click the clip to open the Sample Display window at the bottom of the Live interface.

6. Use the Transpose knob to adjust the clip's pitch.

7. Use the Volume slider to adjust the clip's volume.

8. Use the Live Device Browser to open the Audio Effects folder.

9. Add the effect to the clip by selecting any effect preset and dragging it onto the audio track.

10. Use the File Browser to view the desktop.

11. Select the clip in the clip slot and drag it directly onto the Live Set's folder in the File Browser window.

12. Name the clip.

13. Delete the original clip and select the new one in the Browser window.

14. Drag the new clip onto any available audio track.

The new clip will contain all of the changes you made to the original file as well as any added effects. All of this information is stored within the clip file.

CREATING AND SAVING A MIDI CLIP

You can use the techniques covered in the previous section to create MIDI clips as well. To create a MIDI clip:

1. Create a new Live Set and save it to the desktop.

2. Create an Impulse beat or Simpler performance.

3. Add any effects to the MIDI clip.

4. Select it in the clip slot and drag it to the project folder.

COLLECTING AND SAVING

Once you've added any clips to a project folder, the final step should always be to select File ➢ Collect All and Save.

When you save a clip, the file that is created doesn't contain the audio. It "points" to the information that makes up the clip, telling Live to look for and load the audio file and any effects and then to automatically make the appropriate settings. The Collect All and Save command instructs Live to make copies of all of your audio files and place them in the project folder.

This means that if the original samples that were used to create a clip end up missing or moved, it won't make any difference because Live will be drawing from the copies saved in the project folder. This also means you can share projects across different computers.

It is especially important to use Collect All and Save if you are using Simpler, Sampler, or Impulse devices to make MIDI clips. The command will save every individual sound that makes up a particular virtual drum kit or instrument in a subfolder within the project folder.

Envelopes

Live clips and tracks include an Envelope Editor, which contains similar features for audio and MIDI loops and tracks. Make sure the Envelope Editor is showing in the Clip View by clicking the Show/Hide Envelopes Box button on the bottom left of the Clip View area. You may also want to hide the Launch Box and the Envelopes Box since you won't be using them in this section. Figure 3.27 shows a close-up of the audio clip Envelopes Box.

FIGURE 3.27
The Envelopes Box

USING AUDIO ENVELOPES

Using the Envelopes Box on audio loops is a great way to make micro-edits such as changing a single bad note or adjusting the volume of one section of a loop.

1. Use the File Browser to open the folder `MMA Audio/Ableton Live/All Loops`.

2. Select the file `LoudNote.wav` and drag it to any available audio track clip slot.

3. Click the Clip Launch button to play the loop.

   As you can hear, the loop contains one note that is significantly louder than the rest.

4. There are two drop-down menus at the top left of the Envelopes Box, the Device Chooser and the Control Chooser. Below the Control Chooser menu is the Clip Envelope Quick Chooser. Use the Control Chooser drop-down menu or the Quick Chooser to select the Volume parameter.

5. In the Note Editor, locate the one note that is louder than the rest (it shouldn't be too hard).

6. The red line at the top of the Note Editor is called the Breakpoint Envelope. Double-click the Breakpoint Envelope to create breakpoints. Double-click any breakpoint again to delete it.

   Working with breakpoints in Live can take a little getting used to. You might want to take some time here to create and move around some breakpoints to get an idea of how they can be used to create sudden or gradual shifts in volume.

7. Create four breakpoints on the Breakpoint Envelope around the louder note.

8. Use the two outside breakpoints to zoom in on the beginning and end of the loud note.

9. Use the two center breakpoints to adjust the volume of the note. Figure 3.28 shows the edited clip.

FIGURE 3.28
An audio clip
edited with volume
breakpoints

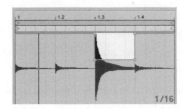

Audio Recording

Audio recording with Live is somewhat different from recording with most audio recording programs. Since much of Live's focus is on working with loops and clips, getting used to Live as a recording program can be a little strange at first.

MIDI ENVELOPES BOX

The MIDI Envelopes Box is similar to the audio Envelopes Box, but the Transpose button is replaced with the MIDI equivalent, a Pitch Bend button. In the MIDI Envelopes Box you can perform many of the same kinds of editing and modulation tasks for MIDI clips and tracks as you can for audio clips and tracks with the Audio Envelopes Box.

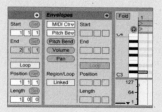

SETTING UP AUDIO RECORDING

To set up Live's Audio recording preferences, follow these steps:

1. Choose Live ➤ Preferences.

2. Click the Audio tab.

3. Select your Audio Input Device from the drop-down menu.

4. Select your Audio Output Device from the drop-down menu.

5. Click the Input Config button to set up the hardware interface inputs you'd like to activate to use with Live.

6. Click OK.

7. Close Live's Preferences.

RECORDING IN SESSION VIEW

Live is now set up for audio recording. To record onto an audio track:

1. If necessary, activate Live's click track by clicking the Metronome button in the top left toolbar.

2. Make sure your audio interface is powered up and ready and your instrument is connected to one of its inputs.

3. Make sure the track's I/O section is showing by selecting View ➤ In/Out. All of the necessary routing will take place in this section.

4. Make sure the Input Type field (under Audio From) reads "Ext. In" in order to receive audio signal from your audio input device.

5. Select an input channel from the Input Channel drop-down menu.

6. Click the Arm Session Recording button.

   You should now be able to hear the instrument you are preparing to record. When you arm a track for recording, the clip slot buttons all become round Record buttons, as shown in Figure 3.29.

7. Click any of the round clip slot buttons to begin recording in the selected clip slot.

FIGURE 3.29

Click a clip slot Record button to begin recording.

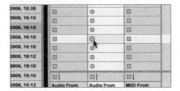

8. Click the Stop button in the Transport bar to stop recording.

RECORDING IN ARRANGE VIEW

If you are working in Arrange View, you may prefer to record your audio there. Steps 1 through 5 of "Recording in Session View" also apply to recording in Arrange View.

When recording in Arrange View, however, you will use the Transport bar at the top of Live interface to begin recording.

1. Double-click the Stop button to return the playhead to the beginning of the session.

2. Click the Global Record button.

3. Click the Play button to begin recording.

AUDIO EDITING

Once you've created a recording on an audio track, you may want to edit it or create a loop from a section of the recorded audio. You can use the Note Editor (shown in Figure 3.30) to edit your performance.

FIGURE 3.30

An audio recording in the Note Editor

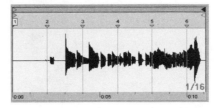

Move your pointer to the top of the Note Editor and select either end of the gray bar at the top, called the Loop Brace, to lengthen or shorten an audio or MIDI loop. Figure 3.31 shows the Loop Brace being resized to create a shorter loop.

FIGURE 3.31

Resizing the Loop Brace

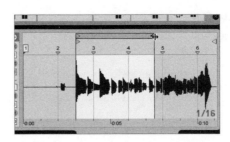

MIDI Recording

Live's MIDI recording functions are easy to start using. The included instruments are a good way to get familiar with creating virtual instrument performances. Used in conjunction with third-party virtual instruments (which I'll cover extensively in Chapter 9), you can use these techniques to take full advantage of Live's music-making possibilities.

ACTIVATING MIDI DEVICES IN LIVE

In order to use any MIDI device in Live you have to activate it in Live's preferences:

1. Make sure your MIDI keyboard and/or interface are properly connected and powered up.

2. Select Live ➤ Preferences and click the MIDI/Sync tab. The bottom half of the MIDI/Sync window contains a list of your available MIDI inputs.

3. In the Track column, click buttons to turn your desired MIDI inputs on.

   Figure 3.32 shows the MIDI/Sync Preferences tab.

FIGURE 3.32
The MIDI/Sync
Preferences tab

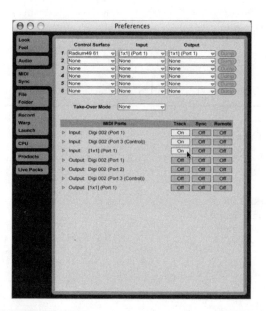

You'll use Live's built-in Simpler sampler for the following examples. MIDI performances can be created using these methods with any virtual instrument including third-party Audio Unit and VST instruments (covered in Chapter 9).

SIMPLE CLIPS

Simple clips can be created using your MIDI keyboard and Live's loop recording function; just follow these steps:

1. Using the Live Device Browser, select Instruments ➤ Simpler ➤ Keys ➤ FM Piano.

2. Drag the FM Piano onto an empty MIDI track.

3. Click the track's Arm Session Recording button.

4. Activate the Metronome, located on in the toolbar on the top left side of the Live interface.

5. Create an empty clip by double-clicking anywhere in an empty clip slot *except* the Record button.

6. Click the Clip Launch button to begin recording, and play your MIDI instrument. Live will record the notes you play. The clip will play on a continuous loop, allowing you to add more notes on each pass.

7. Click the Clip Stop button to stop recording.

LONGER PERFORMANCES

You can also create longer MIDI performances in Live. One of my favorite methods of working with MIDI tracks in Live is to create longer performances and edit them in the MIDI Note Editor, either fixing mistakes or taking sections of a performance and creating loops. You can use this recording technique to add complete tracks to a session or to improvise a solo part.

1. Follow steps 1–4 in the preceding "Simple Clips" section.

2. Click the clip slot Record button to begin recording.

3. You can view the recording as it's happening by double-clicking the clip in the clip slot.

As noted, this process is similar to creating a clip. Unlike that process, however, with MIDI you can create an ongoing performance instead of working within the confines of one or two repeating measures.

Once you've created a performance, if it's not currently showing in the MIDI Note Editor, you can view your performance by double-clicking the clip in the clip slot. Adjust the Loop Brace to select a section of the MIDI recording to create a loop, then fix, create, or delete notes in the Note Editor.

Ableton Live with Reason and ReWire

Ableton Live can act as both ReWire master and ReWire slave. This means that when working with a ReWire master (such as Logic or Pro Tools) Ableton Live, acting as a slave program, will follow commands and protocols from those programs. I'll cover Live as a ReWire slave in Chapter 4 "Pro Tools," Chapter 5 "Logic," and Chapter 6 "GarageBand."

When working with Reason, the opposite will be true: Live will be the master program and Reason will follow its direction. You can also use Live and Reason side-by-side as slave programs to your DAW master or host program.

Reason and Live make an excellent combination. Each program's features nicely complement the other's. Reason's collection of synths, samplers, and instruments combined with Live's looping functions and audio recording capabilities make a great team. In this section, I'll show you how to set up two kinds of ReWire session with Live and Reason.

Make sure the most current version of Reason is installed. You can also try out the following tutorials by using the Reason Demo downloadable from www.propellerheads.se.

When using any two programs together via ReWire, you will always start your master program first—in this case, Live. When you start Reason with Live already running, Reason will automatically "ReWire" itself to Live.

Once both programs are up and running, you'll set up Live's input tracks for Reason's output. There are multiple options in Live for routing Reason's audio output:

♦ You can send Reason to a single stereo track.

♦ You can route the audio to two panned mono tracks.

♦ You can route individual instruments and Reason outputs to individual Live tracks, giving you much more control over the mixing process.

Stereo Routing

To configure a single stereo track routing for Live and Reason:

1. Start Live and create a new Live set in Session View.

2. Start Reason and create a new Reason song or open ReasonLive1.rns from the MMA Audio/ Live Reason folder.

3. Make sure the I/O section, shown in Figure 3.33, is showing in the Session View.

FIGURE 3.33

The I/O section in Session View

If the I/O section is not currently showing, you can make it visible in the following ways:

♦ Select In/Out from the View menu.

♦ Use the keyboard shortcut Command+Option+I.

♦ Click the Show/Hide In/Out button on the right side of the Session View window.

4. In the Live interface, select the first unused audio track.

5. Under Audio From at the top of the I/O section, choose Reason.

6. In the Input Channel menu below Audio From, choose 1/2: Mix L,Mix R.

7. Under Monitor, click the In button to enable monitoring.

Figure 3.34 shows a Live track I/O configured for Reason and ReWire.

This is a standard stereo ReWire routing. You can use this configuration for a quick and easy way to add Reason and other ReWire instrument tracks to any Live session.

FIGURE 3.34
Audio track's I/O
configured for Reason

Complex Routing

As you may have noticed from clicking the Input Channel drop-down menu, Live gives you the option to route ReWire instruments into Live in up to 32 stereo or 64 individual mono tracks. This will require some rerouting in both programs. To create the necessary routing in Reason and Live:

1. Create a new Live set with three audio tracks.

2. Start the Reason program and load the file `LiveReason2.rns`.

3. In Reason, press Tab to view the "backside" of the instrument rack. At the top of the virtual rack is the Reason Hardware Interface. This is where the audio is routed out of Reason. When you create a Mixer 14:2 device, Reason automatically routes everything into the mixer and then in stereo to tracks 1 (left) and 2 (right) in the Reason Hardware Interface.

    Since this session was created without a Mixer 14:2, only the first instrument was routed automatically; the rest had to be set up manually, as will any new Reason instruments you add to the session. Figure 3.35 shows the backside of the Reason Hardware Interface.

FIGURE 3.35
The back of the Reason
Hardware Interface

4. Create a new Malström Synthesizer and route its audio to the Reason Hardware Interface by selecting Left: Filter: A and dragging it to Input 5 on the Hardware Interface.

5. Select Right: Filter B and route its audio to Input 6.

6. Back in the Live Program, open the input drop-down menus for the first three audio tracks and select Reason from the Audio From drop-down menus.

7. For the first track's input channel, select 1/2 Mix L, Mix R.

8. For the second track's input channel, select 3/4 Channel 3, Channel 4.

9. For the third track's input channel, select 5/6 Channel 5, Channel 6.

You can also route instruments from Reason to Live mono tracks.

CREATING A SESSION FROM SCRATCH

Now that I've covered many of the elements that make up a Live session, let's put them all together. You'll create and export a (relatively) simple complete arrangement.

When you're working on the following examples, don't get too caught up in creating the perfect musical piece. Once you understand the process of creating arrangements in Live, your ability to incorporate Live's instruments and functions into more cohesive musical work will improve.

Start by creating a single scene from multiple sources:

1. Select File ➤ New Live Set.

2. Save the new set to any location on your hard drive.

Next, create a simple drum loop with an Impulse kit:

1. Use the Live Device Browser to open the Impulse folder.

2. Select one of the acoustic or electronic kits and drag it to an empty MIDI track.

3. Select the MIDI track and double-click one of the clip slots to create a new blank clip.

4. Program a simple drum pattern.

Now that you have a rhythmic foundation, you can move on to adding some melodic and loops:

1. Use one of the File Browser buttons to open MMA Audio/All Loops (or any other folder containing AIFF or WAV loops).

2. Click any loop to preview it and see if the loop will work alongside the beat you created.

3. When you have chosen an audio loop file, drag it directly to any open audio track.

4. Press the Clip Launch button to play the loop along with the drum track.

5. Use this method to add at least two or three loops to your session from any sources.

You can also add clips from Live's library.

Next, you'll create a MIDI clip with a Simpler instrument:

1. Use the Live Device Browser to choose one of the preset Simpler instruments and add it to your session.

2. Create a MIDI performance using your mouse or one of the MIDI recording techniques we've covered.

You should now have a scene made up of multiple audio and MIDI tracks, similar to the one shown here.

Now create two more scenes:

1. To stop playback of all the current clips, click the Stop Clips button on the master track.

2. Select and highlight the Scene slot in the master track.

3. Use the keyboard shortcut Command+D to duplicate the scene twice.

4. Remove two clips, either audio or MIDI, from the first scene.

5. Remove one clip, either audio or MIDI, from the second scene.

Finally, you'll create and record an arrangement of the three scenes:

1. Double-click the Stop button in the Transport bar to return the song position to 1.1.1.

2. Click the Record button in the Transport bar to prepare Live for recording.

3. Launch the first scene in your arrangement to begin recording.

4. Use the other Launch Scene buttons to launch scenes in any order.

5. Click the Stop button in the Transport bar to stop recording.

6. Click the Arrange View button to view the arrangement you created.

To export your arrangement as an AIFF or WAV file:

1. Choose File ➤ Render to Disc.

2. Select the correct settings for your song file and click the OK button.

3. Choose a location or create a new folder for your exported song and click the Save button.

Live and OS X

Ableton Live was the first time-stretching and pitch-shifting looping program to catch on with Mac users. From OS 9 through every version of OS X and now with Universal Binary compatibility, Ableton Live has been consistently updated and adapted to every new development in the Mac world.

Keep up to Date

The minimum system requirements for the current version of Live 6 are a G3 or faster, 512MB RAM and OS X 10.2.8 or later. The more up to date your computer and operating system are and the more installed RAM you have, the better your results will be with Live.

As of version 5.2, Live is optimized to run natively on Macs with Intel processors. If you are using Live 5 make sure you are running the latest available version. Running a version of Live 5 that is not Universal Binary compatible on your Intel Mac can result in a significant loss of power.

Freezing Tracks

Since Live is a resource-intensive program, you may find yourself running out of processor power. Live has a cool built-in feature called Freezing to help get around this. Freezing a track renders the track or clip in its current state—including all effects, edits, and adjustments to pitch and volume—and saves it to your hard drive, freeing up all of the resources that were being used to alter the file.

To freeze a track, select the track or any clip and choose Edit ➢ Freeze Track. Freezing a track will highlight all of the track's "frozen" parameters.

Figure 3.36 shows a frozen track in the Track View.

FIGURE 3.36
A frozen track in Live

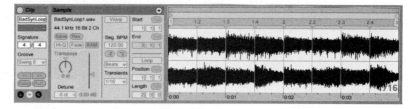

Freezing has another use: Ableton uses Audio Unit and VST plug-ins and virtual instruments. When using Live as a ReWire slave, however, your Audio Units and VST plug-ins won't work. This can be a problem if you create a session in Live and then want to open it as a ReWire session. By freezing tracks, you can open them as part of a ReWire session with all of your third-party instruments and effects in place. This method will work in all DAW programs that use Live as a ReWire slave; it's covered in detail in the "Pro Tools and Ableton Live" section of Chapter 4, "Pro Tools."

CPU Meter

You can keep an eye on how much processor power you are currently using by checking Live's built-in CPU meter, located at the top right of the Live interface. Some suggestions for reducing the CPU load when working in Live:

◆ Quit all unnecessary programs. Any programs running in the background can cause an unneeded drain on Live's resources.

- ◆ Use return tracks to add effects. If you have multiple similar effects you can consolidate them by placing a single instance on a return track and routing your tracks signal to the effect using the Send knob.

- ◆ Use the Collect All and Save function from the File menu. This is especially important if you are using loops and clips from multiple drives.

NEW SESSIONS, ORGANIZATION, AND CPU

When I'm working on a new session for the first time I usually keep it on the desktop. This way I have quick access to it in the File Browser 2. When it's time to save, I use the Collect All and Save function, then move the session to a new location on an external hard drive.

Running a self-contained Live session from a fast external hard drive can sometimes free up to 5 to 10 percent of your available CPU, depending on the number of tracks, effects, and samples in your Live session.

Locations

One of the biggest hassles when using lots of loops and clips with Live is keeping them all organized. In order to quickly access my audio files, I have the File Browser set up in the following way:

File Browser 1   This one is set by default to the Ableton Library. Your Ableton Library should be located in `Applications/Ableton Live 6/`.

File Browser 2   Since much copying of files and downloading ends up on the desktop, it makes sense to have one of the File Browsers dedicated to this location.

File Browser 3   This one is set to the drive that holds most of my loops and sample files.

 Real World Scenario

COMPOSING FOR VIDEO WITH LIVE

With its combination of looping features and MIDI-controlled virtual instrument functionality, Ableton Live seemed like almost the perfect tool for soundtrack composition. However, prior to version 6, I avoided using Live for this purpose because it didn't contain built-in support for video. It would have been possible to use ReWire to route Live to a DAW program such as Logic that had built-in video support, but because importing and working with video files is usually very processor-intensive it seemed like the combination of two DAW programs and a large video file might slow things down too much to work effectively.

One of the things that makes Live such a great program is that its programmers continue to pay close attention to the needs and wants of the program's users. As a result of many Ableton Live users requesting the addition of video support, Ableton has included this functionality in Live 6.

When the Internet video station D7TV (www.d7tv.com) asked me to provide the theme music for a new show called *Rock Court*, it seemed like a perfect chance to check out Live's new video support for AVI and QuickTime movies.

You'll need to work in Arrangement View since the video import function doesn't work in Session view.

I was provided with a video montage that would make up the opening sequence of each episode. Getting this file into Live was as easy as dragging and dropping. I should mention here that Live does not support MPEG video; your video needs to be in AVI or QuickTime (MOV) format. If the video you want to work with is not in a Live-supported format, you can use Apple's QuickTime Pro (a very inexpensive upgrade from the QuickTime program included with OS X) to convert just about any video file to AVI or MOV format. To upgrade to QuickTime Pro, start QuickTime from your Applications folder and select QuickTime Player ▷ Buy QuickTime Pro.

To use Live to compose for video in real time:

1. Create a folder to hold your video clip or clips.

2. Start Live and save your Live session to the folder containing your video clips.

   You'll want to keep the video and the Live session together. If you move the video file to a new location after importing it, the video won't be visible in Live anymore. Another option is to choose File ▷ Save Set Self-Contained after importing your video file.

3. If Live's Video Window isn't showing, choose View ▷ Video Window to make it visible.

   Live's video window can be resized by clicking and dragging at the bottom right of the window.

4. Drag and drop loops from the loop browser or use Live's built-in instruments or third-party MIDI virtual instruments to compose your soundtrack music.

   One of the things I especially like about working in Live for this kind of project is the ability to quickly set up a drum loop, then play a virtual MIDI instrument over the drum loop in real-time.

5. If you want to loop a section of video, set the Loop Region using the Loop/Punch-Recording Region bar just above the individual tracks in the Arrangement View window.

6. If you want to place a sound effect or musical event at a specific location to match an event taking place in the video, use the keyboard shortcut Command+4 to turn Live's Snap to Grid functionality off. Use the same keyboard shortcut to turn Snap to Grid back on after you have placed your file.

For video files that contain audio, Live automatically imports the sound. This can be very helpful if you are trying to compose music around dialogue. If you prefer to work without the included sound:

1. Select the video track in the Arrange window to view the Clip view.

2. Use the Clip Gain fader in the Clip View window to lower the volume

There are still two drawbacks to creating your soundtrack pieces in Live: Live doesn't export video (yet), and Live doesn't have the more accurate MIDI time-code functionality that you can find in Logic and Pro Tools. However, the ability to import QuickTime and AVI movies is a huge step in the right direction.

The Bottom Line

Create MIDI performances in Live   Live's built-in instruments, the Impulse Drum kit and Simpler virtual sampler, can be used to create loops or entire tracks by using your MIDI keyboard or manually creating a performance in the Note Editor.

   Master It   Create a basic MIDI loop using one of Live's Simpler virtual sampler presets.

Use Live's included instruments and effects to create clips   Live's audio and/or MIDI playback and editing functions can be combined with the program's built-in effects to create recallable clips.

   Master It   Create and save a reusable MIDI clip with an Impulse drum sequencer kit and a ping-pong delay effect preset.

Edit Audio loops in Live's audio Clip View   Live's ability to time-stretch, adjust, and edit audio loop files is one of its most useful features. Most of this editing takes place in Live's Clip View at the bottom of the Live interface.

   Master It   Add an audio loop file to a Live set; adjust its pitch, volume, and panning; and save it as a clip.

Edit MIDI clips in Live's MIDI Clip View   The MIDI Clip View is similar to the Audio Clip View, with a few significant differences having to do with functions that are specific to each format.

   Master It   Create a MIDI loop with Simpler, then pitch shift the second half of the loop using the Note Editor and Envelopes Box.

Use Live and Reason together in a ReWire session   With Propellerhead's ReWire protocol, you can use Reason and Live together. Combining the two programs allows you to take advantage of Live's audio recording and looping functions and Reason's samplers, synthesizers, and effects in a single session.

   Master It   Create a new Live set and Reason song with a Mixer 14:2 and a Dr. Rex Loop Player. Route Reason's output to a single stereo track in Live. Add some Live clips, then save the project in a single folder.

Chapter 4

Pro Tools

Considered by many people to be the industry standard audio recording software, there is certainly no doubt that Pro Tools is used in many professional recording, film, and post-production studios. Much of what you hear today in movies, on television, and certainly on the radio has in some way involved the use of Pro Tools.

In this chapter, you'll learn to

◆ Create and save a new Pro Tools session

◆ Add plug-in effects to Pro Tools tracks

◆ Process audio with AudioSuite plug-ins

◆ Create automation on Pro Tools tracks

◆ Use Pro Tools as a ReWire master with Reason

Pro Tools Basics

Pro Tools is now available in multiple formats for the user's needs and budget. The lessons and tutorials in this chapter will primarily take place in the Pro Tools LE environment but, except where noted, will pertain to all currently available versions of Pro Tools. The following are the currently available Pro Tools formats:

Pro Tools HD   The current high-end version of Pro Tools is the HD system, which is available in three configurations: HD1, HD2, and HD3. HD systems come with their own HD Core cards that are installed in available PCI slots in your CPU. HD systems also require Pro Tools hardware interfaces. HD systems start around $8,000, not including the required Pro Tools hardware interface. Pro Tools HD offers unlimited tracks and the power to run many plug-ins at once, and it comes with lots of cool plug-ins and software.

Pro Tools LE   For the smaller recording studios and home studios, there is the Pro Tools LE system. Pro Tools LE and the included Digi 001 hardware interface were introduced in 1999 as a way of making Pro Tools available to the entry level or nonprofessional recording enthusiast. The current generation of Pro Tools LE hardware includes the Mbox 2 Pro, the Digi 002, and Digi 002 Rack.

> **Mbox 2 Pro**   The Mbox 2 Pro is a simple FireWire-powered interface with two audio inputs as well as a MIDI in and MIDI out. The Mbox comes with Pro Tools LE software as well as a number of bundled plug-ins and third-party software.

The Digi 002   The Digi 002 is a FireWire audio and MIDI interface as well as a hardware mixing board. Aside from its main use as a Pro Tools interface and controller, the Digi 002 can be also used as a stand-alone mixer.

Digi 002 Rack   The Digi 002 Rack is a FireWire-based, rack-mountable hardware interface with eight analog inputs and outputs as well as MIDI I/O and digital and optical input and outputs.

Pro Tools M-Powered   Pro Tools M-Powered, the most recently introduced version of Pro Tools, can be run on any system using any of the M-Audio hardware interfaces, bringing Pro Tools to an even wider range of recording studios. Pro Tools M-Powered costs $299 and is sold separately from your audio interface. M-Audio interfaces range from the simple $99 USB-powered transit with a single ⅛-inch stereo input to the midpriced FireWire Audiophile (with MIDI I/O) to the Octane eight-channel pre-amp, which sells for around $700. Pro Tools M-Powered comes with 35 included RTAS and AudioSuite plug-ins and supports all of the ReWire programs and third-party plug-ins that Pro Tools LE does.

Today, with Pro Tools' increased functionality, higher sample and bit rates, more included plug-ins, and the ability to use it in conjunction with other programs, it is quite possible to make high-quality audio recordings for compact discs, demos, or soundtracks for movies and television in your home or professional studio with any version of Pro Tools.

More information on Pro Tools HD, LE, and M-Powered software and hardware can be found at http://www.digidesign.com and http://www.m-audio.com.

Tech Support

Digidesign offers a number of tech support options, including a searchable database that you can use to resolve any issues you might be having regarding the setup and operation of Pro Tools systems. You can access this by going to http://www.digidesign.com and clicking the Support tab at the top of the page. To access the Digidesign support database, click Support Search and select Answerbase from the drop-down menu.

Type your question or any error messages into the search field. The Answerbase contains an archive of many of the problems and their solutions discovered over the years by Pro Tools users.

If you can't find the answers you need on their website, you can also contact Digidesign's tech support via phone or e-mail. When you buy a Pro Tools system you are entitled to free phone support for a limited period of time, depending on the system you bought. Once that time period has expired, you can purchase phone support by using the Digidesign ProAxess telephone line.

User Forum

One of the best resources for Pro Tools support is the Digidesign Users Conference (DUC) forum (http://duc.digidesign.com). In these forums you can communicate directly with other Pro Tools users and get suggestions and tips to help you solve any technical problems and enhance your Pro Tools experience. If you are having problems with your Pro Tools setup, it can be especially helpful to correspond with other users running the same brand and model of computer or utilizing the same third-party applications and hardware. The DUC is also a great resource when deciding what kind of Pro Tools system, interface, and operating system is best for your needs.

The DUC forum is divided into sections reflecting each Digidesign product and system. There's even a section for discontinued products. You can also search within topics for the answers to specific questions or solutions to any problems you may be experiencing.

Setting Up Pro Tools

Pro Tools systems and their included interface(s) come with software installation discs. However, these discs may not contain the most recent version of the software, as Pro Tools is updated fairly regularly. Even if you bought Pro Tools recently, it's worth checking for updates, because Digidesign frequently offers minor updates with bug fixes and increased functionality, as well as plug-in updates. You can keep up to date on these by visiting `http://duc.digidesign.com` and clicking the Digidesign Announcements link near the top of the page.

Every Pro Tools system will require a different cabling, routing, and hardware setup depending on the kind of Pro Tools system you've purchased and the hardware (mixers, analog/digital (A/D) converters and studio monitors) that makes up your recording environment. For information on your specific equipment, consult Digidesign's included Quick Start guide and other documentation.

Creating Your First Session

Start up Pro Tools and what do you see? Nothing.

When you open Pro Tools, a session is not automatically created. To view the Pro Tools interface, you have to create a new session by selecting File ⊳ New Session. You'll see a dialog box, shown in Figure 4.1, which gives you the chance to make some general settings for the session.

For the purposes of this chapter, choose settings that are compatible with all of the existing versions of Pro Tools:

Audio File Type	BWF (.WAV)
Sample Rate	44.1 KHz
Bit Depth	16 Bit

FIGURE 4.1
The New Session
dialog box

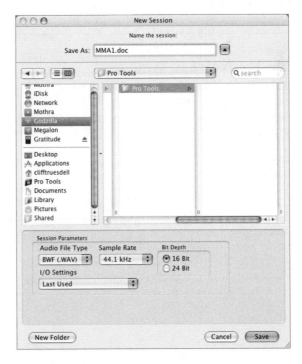

Finally, name the session.

You'll also want to make a decision here about where you are going to save your files. As I covered in Chapter 1, "Optimizing Your System," whenever possible it's a good idea to save your sessions to an external hard drive. Saving your sessions and audio files on a FireWire-connected drive will give you a faster response time and increase the number of plug-ins and effects you can use in a single session. It's also a good idea to create a catch-all Pro Tools session folder to keep all of your session files in one place. Once you've made these decisions, click the Save button.

When you create and name a Pro Tools session, a folder is automatically created that will contain your PTF file (the Pro Tools session file). Inside that folder will be a folder for your session's audio files (cleverly named Audio Files) and separate folders for other information that a Pro Tools session may generate, including one folder that contains the information used to make up fades and cross fades and another that keeps backup copies of your current session.

AUTOMATIC FILE BACKUP

Pro Tools will automatically create backup versions of your current sessions. This is a useful function that can save your work after a crash or to reference an earlier version of a session you are working on. You can choose how often you'd like Pro Tools to back up your files and how long you'd like to keep them for. Pro Tools will automatically create a folder for these files named Session File Backups and place it in your session folder. If you need to access a backup file, just open the folder and double-click the file to open it as you would any Pro Tools session file.

To set your backup options, select Pro Tool ➤ Preferences and click the Operation tab at the top of the Preferences window. On the right side in the Auto Save field, choose the number of recent backups to keep and the frequency (in minutes) with which Pro Tools creates new backup files. I recommend saving a backup every five minutes, although your settings are a matter of personal preference. The process doesn't really interfere with your systems performance, so if you feel the need for more frequent backups that's your call.

The Pro Tools Edit Window

As soon as you save your file, the Pro Tools Edit window (Figure 4.2) and Mix window appear. These are the two windows that you will be doing most of the work in. For now, close the Mix window and leave the Edit window open. Both windows contain many of the same functions placed in different locations and with a different focus. We'll look at the Mix window in more detail later on.

FIGURE 4.2
The Edit window

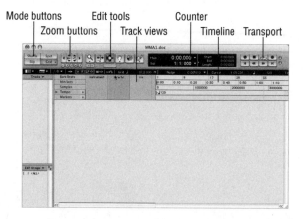

Creating Tracks

There are five different types of tracks that make up a Pro Tools session. To create tracks, choose Track ➢ New and the New Tracks dialog box will appear. You can use the New Tracks dialog to create a single track or multiple tracks at once. New in Pro Tools 7 is the ability to create different *kinds* of tracks at once: by clicking the + button on the right side of the New Tracks dialog box you can create as many different types of tracks as you want, all at the same time.

To get started exploring the different types of tracks, create one each of the following, as shown in Figure 4.3.

FIGURE 4.3

Create multiple tracks.

- ◆ Mono Audio Track

- ◆ Stereo Audio Track

- ◆ Stereo Aux Input

- ◆ MIDI Track

- ◆ Instrument Track

- ◆ Stereo Master Fader

VERSIONS OF PRO TOOLS

There are some minor variations in the interface for the HD, LE, and M-Powered versions of the Pro Tools program. For the purposes of this chapter, we'll be using screenshots from the Pro Tools HD and LE versions. With a few noted exceptions, the functions described in this chapter will work for every current version of Pro Tools.

MONO AUDIO TRACK

Figure 4.4 shows the most commonly used track, the mono audio track. This is the kind of track that gets used to record guitar, vocals, individual drum tracks, and so on. Any instrument or sound from an external source can be recorded onto a Mono audio track.

FIGURE 4.4
A mono audio track

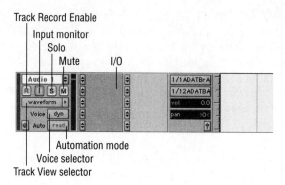

Located just below the Track Name field (in this case Audio 1) are the following elements:

Track Record Enable   This button, labeled "R," must be turned on before you can record onto the track. When a track is Record-enabled, this button will become a flashing red light. When you are actually recording onto the track, it will remain solidly red.

Input monitor   This allows you to hear the instrument without actually recording. This feature is only available on Pro Tools HD.

Solo   This button, labeled "S," plays the selected track while muting all other tracks.

Mute   This button, labeled "M," silences the selected track.

Track View selector   Just below the Record, Solo, and Mute buttons is the Track View selector. The default view is the Waveform view, showing the peaks and valleys of the audio that is recorded onto the track. You can also choose to view and edit other parameters, such as Track Panning and Track Volume. Figure 4.5 shows the Track View Selector pop-up menu.

FIGURE 4.5
The Track View
selector

Voice selector   Just below the Track View selector is the Voice selector. Select Off in the Voice selector pop-up menu if you want to turn off (silence) the track. Unlike a muted track, a track with its voice turned "off" cannot be accidentally reactivated.

Automation mode   The Automation Mode selector gives you choices about how you'd like to use Pro Tools track automation features. We'll look at Pro Tools Volume, Panning, and Plug-in Automation features later in this chapter.

The I/O Section

The I/O (input/output) section, shown in Figure 4.6, controls where the audio signal comes from and where it's going.

FIGURE 4.6
The I/O section

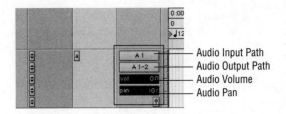

Audio Input Path
Audio Output Path
Audio Volume
Audio Pan

From top to bottom:

Audio Input Path selector Currently set to its default of A1, this where the audio signal coming in to Pro Tools is routed to the track. If your instrument or microphone is plugged into the first input of your Digidesign hardware interface, the input path for the track is A1. The second input of your hardware interface is routed to A2, and so on.

Audio Output Path selector This shows where your audio is being routed for monitoring. In general, and for the purposes of this chapter, this should remain at its default setting of A1–2.

Audio Volume indicator/pop-up slider This controls the track volume. Click the volume indicator to view the pop-up slider and drag to raise and lower the volume.

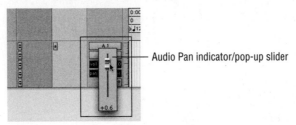

Audio Pan indicator/pop-up slider

Audio Pan indicator/pop-up slider Drag the slider to choose the panning for the track, placing its audio output in the right or left speaker, or leave it at zero, directly in the middle.

STEREO AUDIO TRACK

Stereo audio tracks are useful for recording live performances, such as a drum kit or group of musicians, captured with a stereo microphone. Stereo audio tracks are essentially the same as mono tracks with the added feature of the left and right channel panning options.

AUX INPUT TRACK

Aux is short for "auxiliary." Aux input tracks are tracks you can hear but that do not create digital/audio waveforms. Aux input tracks do not have a Record button. If you want to record the output of an aux input, you can do so by routing its output signal to an audio track. Some uses for aux input tracks include click tracks, adding effects, and ReWire programs, all of which I'll cover later in this chapter. Figure 4.7 shows an aux input track.

FIGURE 4.7

An aux input track

When you create an aux input track the sound is turned off by default. To make an aux input audible you can drag the track's Audio Volume slider, or you can Option+click the Audio Volume, indicator to instantly raise the track volume to an audible level.

MIDI TRACK

MIDI tracks record and edit MIDI information. By themselves they do not play any audio; they must be routed to instrument that is placed on an aux or audio track. The Track View selector of a MIDI track gives the option to view the different editable MIDI parameters, such as velocity and pitch bend. In the I/O section of a MIDI track, you will choose which MIDI controller input to use and which MIDI device should receive it (output). MIDI volume is measured numerically from 0 (silent) to 127 (loudest). Figure 4.8 shows a MIDI track.

FIGURE 4.8

A MIDI track

INSTRUMENT TRACK

Instrument tracks are a new feature in Pro Tools 7 that allow you to combine MIDI tracks with instruments that are triggered by MIDI.

For sessions that use instrument tracks, be sure to choose View ➤ Edit ➤ Instruments and View ➤ Edit Inserts in order to make sure the Instruments view and Inserts view are showing. Figure 4.9 shows an instrument track.

FIGURE 4.9

An instrument track

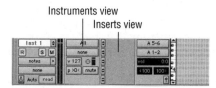

Instruments view

Inserts view

STEREO MASTER FADER

Every session should have a stereo master fader. The stereo master fader is where all of your tracks come together to create a stereo mix. Use the stereo master fader to control the overall volume of your mix. Figure 4.10 shows a stereo master fader.

FIGURE 4.10

A stereo master fader

NAMING TRACKS

To rename a track:

1. Double-click the current track name, for example, Audio 1.

2. Rename the track in the dialog box that appears.

3. Click the Previous or Next button to rename other tracks.

PRO TOOLS FILE NAMING

Pro Tools names the audio files it creates based on what you have named a track, so when you create new tracks be sure to name them *before* you record anything onto them. Naming tracks right away will help keep your session organized. It's a good habit to develop, because somewhere down the road you may have to locate a stray audio file. I can tell you from experience that searching through 400 SDII files, all named Audio 1 is no fun at all.

There's not a lot of room on the track header, but try and be as precise as possible. For example, if you're recording two different guitar players in the same session, name the individual audio tracks with the musician's initials followed by "GTR." If you're recording one guitar amp with two different microphones simultaneously, you may want to include a microphone model number as well. A typical track name might look like this: "CB GTR U87." If you run out of space, try using lowercase letters. It may be harder to read, but you can fit a bit more information.

You can also add information about a track in the Comments sections by selecting View ➤ Edit Window ➤ Comments. This is especially useful if there's another engineer on the session who may need to know some information about a track.

MODE BUTTONS

In the upper left corner of the Edit window, you'll see the four Mode buttons shown in Figure 4.11.

FIGURE 4.11
The Mode buttons

Each mode is appropriate for different operations or types of work you may be doing. The four modes are as follows.

Shuffle   Automatically moves audio regions into place to replace deleted regions; Shuffle mode is used for advanced editing techniques.

Spot   Opens a dialog box that allows you to move each audio file to a location. Spot mode is often used for syncing audio and video by selecting exact locations based on MIDI information.

Slip   Edits and moves audio and MIDI notes and regions freely around your session.

Grid   Lets you create and edit all of your audio and files in precise increments. This is especially useful when working with loops and MIDI instruments and when using virtual instruments through ReWire.

THE ZOOM BUTTONS

Next to the Mode buttons are the Zoom buttons, shown in Figure 4.12.

FIGURE 4.12
The Zoom buttons

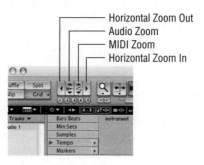

From left to right these are as follows.

Horizontal Zoom Out Allows you to access a wider view of the current session or track.

Audio Zoom Allows you to increase and decrease the size of recorded waveforms for more precise editing. Use this button to make smaller, "quiet" audio waveforms large enough to edit properly.

MIDI Zoom Zooms in on MIDI tracks, allowing you a closer look at the MIDI notes and other editable parameters.

Horizontal Zoom In Gives a closer view of the track or region that you are working on.

Zoom Presets The five buttons at the bottom are the zoom presets. They range from the default 1 preset, which zooms out for an overview of the session, to the 5 preset, which zooms in on the cursor's current location.

THE TOOL BUTTONS

To the right of the Zoom buttons are the Tool buttons, shown in Figure 4.13. You'll be using most if not all of them on a regular basis, so it's a good idea to get as familiar with these as possible.

FIGURE 4.13
The Tool buttons

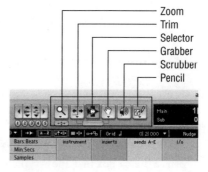

The Tool buttons from left to right are as follows:

Zoom Magnifies a section of a track or session.

Trim Deletes unwanted audio form the beginning or end of a track. Can also be used to remove MIDI notes and sequences.

Selector   Selects a playback starting point or highlights a section of audio or MIDI data for looping, editing, copying, or deleting.

Grabber   Moves sections of audio or MIDI data around a track or onto a new track in a session.

Scrubber   Plays parts of an audio file at slower speeds to locate an edit point.

Pencil   Draws and edits MIDI notes and edits audio waveforms by hand.

I'll cover uses for some of these tools once we've created some audio files to work with.

The Counter Window

The Main Counter and Sub Counter let you know where the playhead is in your Pro Tools session. For this chapter, the Main Counter should be set to minutes and seconds. To set the Main Counter, click the Main Counter Selector (the triangle just to the right of the displayed numbers), as shown in Figure 4.14, and choose Min:Secs (minutes and seconds).

FIGURE 4.14
Set the Main Counter.

Pro Tools will automatically set the Sub Counter to Bars:Beats.

The Transport Bar

The Transport bar, shown in Figure 4.15, controls all of Pro Tools' playback and recording functions.

FIGURE 4.15
The Transport bar

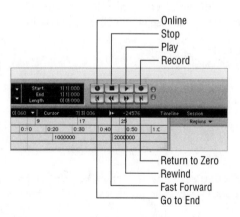

Selecting the Online button causes Pro Tools to wait for an outside MIDI source (such as a note played on a MIDI keyboard) to let it know when to start recording. Return to Zero moves to the beginning of the session.

Just below the Counter window is the Grid Value selector.

This where you will set the units of measure for all of the session's tracks when working in Grid mode.

For the sessions in this chapter, make sure there is a check mark next to Bars:Beats and set the value to ¼ Note, as shown in Figure 4.16.

FIGURE 4.16

Set the Grid value.

Changing Edit Window Views

Pro Tools gives you some control over which parts of the interface you want to have showing. Just below the Mode buttons is the Edit Window View selector.

Clicking the Edit Window View selector opens the pop-up window shown in Figure 4.17, which allows you to choose which fields you would like to have visible in the Edit window.

FIGURE 4.17

The Edit Window
View Selector pop-up

For the rest of this chapter, make sure that the Instruments, Inserts, and I/O Views are showing. Your basic tracks should always look like the track shown in Figure 4.18.

FIGURE 4.18

The Track view for
this chapter

Saving Sessions

Once you have had a look at all of Pro Tools basic features, take a look at the Save options in the File menu. Pro Tools gives you three options for saving your sessions: Save, Save As, and Save Copy In.

Save Saves your current file in its current state.

Save As Saves a new PTF file in any location you select.

Save Copy In Creates a copy of your Pro Tools session in any location you choose and gives you numerous options for copying associated files (like audio files and plug-in settings). You can also use the Save Copy In function to export your session's audio files in different formats (WAV, AIFF, or SDII), sample and bit rates or to save your sessions in older Pro Tools file formats in order to open them on older systems. Figure 4.19 shows the Save Copy In window.

FIGURE 4.19
The Save Copy In window

For now, select File ➢ Save to save your session. This will also lock the changes you've made to the track views and mode selection so they will become a part of your next sessions.

Creating an Audio Only Session

The most basic kind of Pro Tools session is purely audio based. This session will involve no MIDI instrumentation, imported loop files, or ReWire programs. If you are recording a singer/songwriter, a quick acoustic demo, or a rock band with basic guitar/bass/drums instrumentation, you can keep your sessions simple by using only Pro Tools' audio recording capabilities.

Since this is a good way to get familiar with the basic functions of Pro Tools, we'll start things off with an audio-only session.

1. If you still have a Pro Tools session open, select File ➢ Close Session.

2. To create a new session select File ➢ New Session.

3. Name the new session Audio 1. Keep the same file type, sample rate, bit rate, and I/O settings you used on our first example session and click the Save button.

4. Select Track ➢ New and create the following tracks:

   ◆ Three mono audio tracks

   ◆ One mono aux input

   ◆ One stereo master fader

CREATING A CLICK TRACK

Pro Tools comes with a built-in click track that you can add to your sessions to help keep your musicians in time. The click track is also useful if you plan to do any looping of sections from a recorded performance.

To set up a click track in Pro Tools:

1. Click the Grid Mode button and make sure that Pro Tools is in Absolute Grid Mode. In Absolute Grid Mode all of your audio files will snap to the selected grid amount, always. (In Relative Grid Mode it's possible for files to be moved away from the Grid.)

2. Make sure that you followed the instructions for setting the Grid value in the previous section of this chapter.

3. Click the Aux Input Track Name field and name the track Click.

4. Option+click the Audio Volume indicator or use the Audio Volume pop-up fader to raise the track volume to zero.

5. In the Inserts view, choose Plug-in ➤ Instrument ➤ Click (Mono). Figure 4.20 shows the Click instrument.

FIGURE 4.20
The Click Track
window

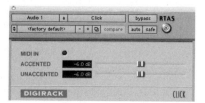

SILENT AUXES?

When an aux input track is created its audio output is turned off by default. In order to hear the audio output of an aux input track, you'll need to Option+click the Audio Volume indicator or use the Audio Volume pop-up fader to raise the track volume to zero.

You can change the sound of your click track by clicking on the Librarian menu (the field that reads <factory default> in Figure 4.20) and selecting from the list of sounds. Turn off the click track at any time by clicking the track's Mute button.

RECORDING A SIGNAL

Now we get to "fun" part: actually recording audio tracks with Pro Tools. However, the following steps are only part of the process of creating good tracks. Once you have the following steps mastered, you'll also want to spend some time figuring out the best ways to get strong, consistent audio signals from your instruments, microphones, and audio interface.

ROUTING AUDIO

Every studio is set up differently and contains different devices, instruments, and monitoring and playback functionality. Because of the complexity and the vast number of possibilities for different studio configurations, I am going to assume here that your hardware and playback are set up and functioning properly.

If, after following the instructions in the next section, you are having difficulty recording or playing back your audio, consult your software and hardware documentation, contact Digidesign tech support, or seek help in the Digidesign Users Conference forums.

To begin recording audio with Pro Tools:

1. Name the track according to the instrument you plan to record.

2. Plug your instrument or microphone into Input 1 on your Pro Tools interface, or route the signal to Input 1 through your pre-amp or mixing board.

3. Click the Audio Input Path selector and select A1 as your interface input, as shown in Figure 4.21.

FIGURE 4.21
Select input A1.

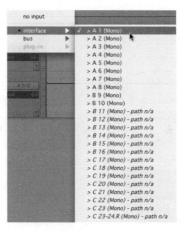

4. Arm the track for recording by clicking the Track Record Enable button, shown in Figure 4.22.

FIGURE 4.22
Click the Track Record
Enable button.

5. To begin recording you can either:

   ◆ Click the Record button in the Transport bar, then the Play button *or*

   ◆ Press Command+spacebar.

6. To stop recording, press the spacebar or click the Stop button in the Transport bar.

Take at look at the waveform of the recorded file. You want to have a clearly visible waveform, but at the same time it's important make sure that the track is not peaking. Any clipping or digital distortion needs to be addressed by lowering the volume of your pre-amp or the instrument or amplifier you are recording. Adjusting the Audio Volume indicator in Pro Tools only affects what you are hearing, not what is being recorded.

TEMPO CHANGES

As you are recording you will hear the click track you created playing at its default tempo of 120BPM (beats per minute). To silence the click track, click the Mute button (marked "M") on the Aux Input Track header.

To change the session tempo:

1. Press the Return key to return the playhead to the beginning of the session. The Main Counter should read 0:00.000.

2. Click the Add Tempo Change button, shown in Figure 4.23.

FIGURE 4.23
The Add Tempo
Change button

3. In the Tempo Change dialog box, shown in Figure 4.24, change the BPM to the tempo you want for the session.

FIGURE 4.24
Change the BPM.

DUDE, WHERE'S MY AUDIO?

Occasionally something will happen that will throw your Pro Tools audio routing out of whack. It could be importing a session from another Pro Tools system or the temporary addition of a new hardware interface for more audio inputs, or possibly another engineer chose to route their session differently and then forgot to return your settings to their original configuration. A quick way to fix this is to open an older session that contains your original settings, then close the session and create a new one. Be sure to choose Last Used for the I/O settings in the session parameters window.

It's also a good idea to keep a backup copy of your basic I/O setup. You can do this by choosing Setup ➢ I/O and clicking the Export Settings button at the bottom of the window. Name the exported settings Basic or something similar. When your I/O setup gets thrown out of whack, just click the Import Settings button and bring your old settings back into place.

Adding an Insert

The simplest way to add an effect to a track is as an insert, which means exactly what it sounds like: you insert the effect onto your track.

To add a delay effect as an insert on the track you've just recorded, follow these steps:

1. If the Inserts view isn't showing in the Edit window, choose View ➢ Edit window and make sure Inserts has a check mark next to it.

2. Click Insert Selector A, shown in Figure 4.25.

FIGURE 4.25

Choose Insert Selector A.

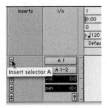

3. Navigate the Pro Tools plug-in selection as follows: Plug-in ➢ Delay ➢ Medium Delay II (Mono), as shown in Figure 4.26. When adding an insert to a stereo track, choose the stereo version of the plug-in.

FIGURE 4.26

Add the Medium Delay II plug-in.

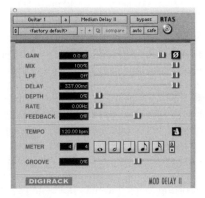

You can apply plug-ins before or after recording a track. Pro Tools records the audio file before the inserted effects. As a result, the actual audio file that Pro Tools creates is not affected by the plug-in. You can change, remove, or add multiple effects to a track at any point in the recording and mixing process. You can insert up to five effects on a single track.

For more information on inserts, see the "Plug-in Effects" and "Included Software" sections later in this chapter.

WATCHING THE MASTER FADER TRACK

As previously mentioned, the master fader track is the sum of all the other tracks. It's important, especially when mixing down, to keep an eye on the LED in the track header and make sure it doesn't go into the red zone. If you are pushing the overall volume to the limit, you can lower the volume for each track individually.

Another way to lower the volume of your session is to select <All> from the Edit Groups section in the lower left corner; lowering the volume on any one track will then lower the volume for all the tracks in your session simultaneously.

Make sure you deselect the <All> group when you're done, or you could end up making other changes to all of your tracks that might be hard to undo.

RECORDING MORE TRACKS

If you are going to use the same instrument and input to record your next track, you can change the new track's Audio Input Path selector field to A1.

If you are using the second input on your Digidesign hardware interface, leave the new track at its default input, A2.

If you are using an interface with more than two inputs, the audio input you are using on your hardware interface should correspond with the Input Path selector on the track you plan to record on.

It's also important to make sure the track that you are recording to is the only one that is armed for recording; otherwise you could end up recording over a perfect take by mistake.

BASIC EDITING

Once you have the basics of recording audio performances down, you will want to start taking advantage of Pro Tools' powerful editing tools. You should also be aware while you are learning these techniques that many of these edit functions have similar applications with MIDI tracks.

For the following examples, you can either record your own audio or drag and drop one of the WAV or AIFF files from the MMA AUDIO FILES folder from the included DVD-ROM directly onto any blank area in the Edit window workspace.

Let's start with the Trim tool. The Trim tool has two modes, standard and TCE (Time Compression and Expansion). The TCE mode works something like the time-stretching functions in Garage-Band and Live, altering the tempo of a track or loop without changing its pitch. TCE mode is useful when importing loops that may not be in the same tempo as the current session.

The Trim tool performs *nondestructive* editing, which means that the actual recorded audio file is not affected by any editing you do.

For this session, make sure you have selected the Trim tool's Standard mode.

1. Click the Trim tool button and move your cursor to any spot near the end of a recorded region, as shown in Figure 4.27.

FIGURE 4.27
Select a section
to edit.

2. Click the waveform and drag the cursor to the left. The Trim tool will erase a section of the recorded audio. Figure 4.28 shows the waveform in the process of being trimmed.

FIGURE 4.28
Trim a section
of audio.

3. Place the cursor near the end of the waveform again. This time, click and drag to the right. Now you'll see your track restored to its original state.

When you use the Trim tool in Grid mode, your edits will automatically conform to the grid; this is handy for creating loops but otherwise limits your editing capabilities. If you need to do more precise editing, use Slip mode. Change to Slip mode by clicking the Slip mode button in the upper left corner.

UNDO AND REDO

As with most Mac programs, the Undo command in Pro Tools is Command+Z. Redo is Command+Shift+Z. Most editing functions can be undone and redone, but certain functions are not affected by Undo and Redo, such as creating and deleting tracks and volume and pan changes made in the I/O section of a track.

Using the Selector Tool

The Selector is probably the most used tool in Pro Tools. Among other tasks, the Selector can find locations to stop and start playback or highlight parts of an audio or MIDI track for editing or looping. Another common use of the Selector is to split tracks into new regions:

1. Click the Selector tool, then choose an edit point by clicking anywhere on one of your audio waveforms, as shown in Figure 4.29.

FIGURE 4.29
Choose an edit point.

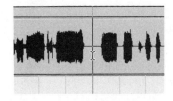

2. Press Command+E to split a track wherever you place the cursor.

You can use the same keyboard shortcut to separate an entire region by first clicking and dragging over a section of the track with the Selector tool, then applying the shortcut. Figure 4.30 shows two newly separated regions.

FIGURE 4.30
Create a new
edit region.

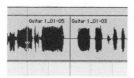

Using the Grabber Tool

Once you split a track or create a new, separate region, you can use the Grabber tool to move the region or track around in your session. You can either place the region in a different location on the same track or move it to a different track. This is especially useful for editing performances and when working with loops to create arrangements. Figure 4.31 shows the Grabber tool moving one of the new regions to another track.

FIGURE 4.31
Place the region on
another track.

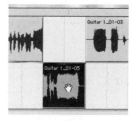

Duplicating and Copying

To duplicate a track or region, use the Selector tool, select an entire track or region by double-clicking inside it, then press Command+D. The Duplicate command will place the copy directly after the original track or region. Figure 4.32 shows a region that's been duplicated twice.

FIGURE 4.32
Duplicate the
new region.

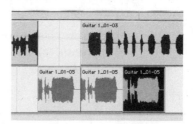

To copy a track or region to another track or section of a track, press Command+C on the selected track or region. To paste the track or region, use the Selector tool to choose a location within the session to place the copy, then press Command+V to paste it.

VOLUME AUTOMATION

Pro Tools' volume automation options can come in handy when working with an uneven instrument or vocal performance or if you want to make one section of a performance, such as a guitar solo, stand out in a mix. Used on the master track, volume automation can also create a fade-out at the end of a song. As with many of the functions in Pro Tools, there are multiple ways to achieve the same results. Here's how to manually create volume automation in a Pro Tools session:

Use the Track View selector to choose Volume view, as shown in Figure 4.33.

FIGURE 4.33
Choose the
Volume view.

The edit points that you will use to automate the track are *breakpoints*. To create a new breakpoint, use the Grabber tool to click the graph line. Create a second breakpoint and use the Grabber to drag it downward to lower the track volume, as shown in Figure 4.34.

FIGURE 4.34
Create breakpoints.

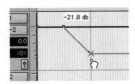

You can have as many breakpoints as you want on a track, creating complex volume adjustments. To delete breakpoints, use the Selector tool to highlight them, as shown in Figure 4.35, then press Delete.

FIGURE 4.35
Highlighted
breakpoints

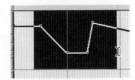

Once you add volume automation to a track, you won't be able to adjust the volume using the Volume indicator/pop-up fader—you'll have to make all future volume adjustments using the breakpoints in the Volume Track view. You can, however, use the Automation Mode selector to turn the track's automation off, as shown in Figure 4.36.

FIGURE 4.36
Turn off automation.

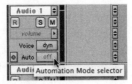

With automation turned off, you are again able to adjust the Volume indicator with your mouse.

PANNING AUTOMATION

The same techniques used to create volume automation can be used to create panning automation. Use the Track View selector to choose Pan view. Using the mouse and the Grabber tool, use the methods you just used to create volume automation to create panning automation on your track. Figure 4.37 shows different ways to draw panning automation on the same track.

FIGURE 4.37
Different ways to draw panning automation

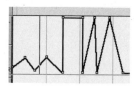

THE MIX WINDOW

To get a look at Pro Tools' mixing functions, create a new session and name it Mix One. Add the following tracks to the session:

◆ Two mono audio tracks

◆ One stereo aux input

◆ One stereo instrument track

◆ One stereo master fader

Choose Window ➢ Mix to view the Mix window. Make sure View ➢ Narrow Mix is deselected (with no check mark next to it) so that you have the best possible view of your tracks.
Figure 4.38 shows the Pro Tools Mix window.

FIGURE 4.38
The Mix window

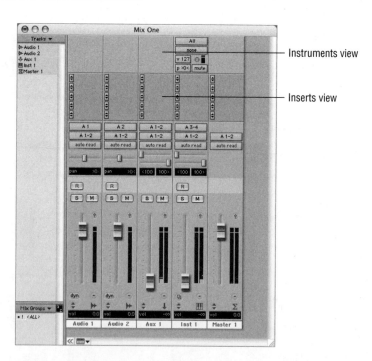

Instruments view

Inserts view

As you can see, the Mix window contains all of the same information that the Edit window has, but without the Waveform view.

At the top of each channel strip you have the same Instrument, Inserts, and Send views available, depending on which you want to have visible. Choose View ➤ Mix Window ➤ to make these sections visible or hidden.

Figure 4.39 shows the bottom half of an audio track channel strip containing the I/O (input and output) information for each track. Below the I/O section you will find the Panning slider and, just below that, the Arm For Record, Solo, and Mute buttons.

FIGURE 4.39

A single channel strip

While the main advantage of the Mix window is a clearer view of the Volume and Panning functions, many Pro Tools users choose to do both their recording and their mixing in the Edit window. It's a good idea to try working in both and see which is a better fit for your methods and needs.

Plug-in Effects

Every Pro Tools system comes with an extensive set of plug-in effects. These include the DigiRack effects, the Bomb Factory bundle, and any other plug-ins that may be included as part of Pro Tools Ignition Pack, HD pack, and other promotions.

Digidesign also frequently releases new plug-ins that owners of Pro Tools systems can download and add to their existing collections.

Along with the included plug-ins, Digidesign and other companies have also created a huge array of other effects that can be used with Pro Tools. Many of these third-party plug-in effects are covered in Chapter 8 "Plug-ins."

AudioSuite, Real Time AudioSuite, and TDM

AudioSuite, Real Time AudioSuite, and TDM (Time Division Multiplexing) are Digidesign's names for their plug-in formats used within the Pro Tools environment. Other plug-in types such as Audio Units and VST will not work within Pro Tools (though you can get VST plug-ins to work with a plug-in wrapper program such FXpansion's VST to RTAS program; see Chapter 8). AudioSuite, Real Time AudioSuite, and TDM plug-ins will only work within the Pro Tools environment.

TDM   TDM plug-ins work with Pro Tools HD systems. They use power from HD system's Core and Accel cards. TDM plug-ins are added to your tracks as *inserts*. This means that Pro

Tools plays back your audio track, runs it through the inserted effect, then runs it out through your speakers or headphones. The actual recorded audio is not affected in any way.

HTDM   HTDM (Host TDM) plug-ins are similar to TDM plug-ins. They work with HD systems but, unlike TDM plug-ins, they draw their power from the host system's processor.

Real Time AudioSuite   The Real Time AudioSuite (RTAS) format will work with every Pro Tools system. Like TDM plug-ins, these are added to your tracks as inserts and do not affect the recorded signal, only the output. RTAS plug-ins draw their power from your computer's CPU and virtual memory.

AudioSuite   These are accessed from the AudioSuite menu and are used to process audio regions that you have selected in the Pro Tools Edit window. This applies the effect to the actual sound file and in some cases you can overwrite the original file.

You'll find that some effects are available both as AudioSuite and also as TDM/RTAS plug-ins, while some are available as one or the other. The following sections divide the plug-ins into different categories and cover some of the key elements and commonly used techniques relevant to each type of effect.

DigiRack Plug-ins

The most formidable list of included plug-ins are the DigiRack effects. This includes many basic and frequently used plug-ins including:

◆ Delays

◆ Compressors

◆ EQs

◆ Reverbs

DELAYS

Digidesign has included multiple delays for multiple uses. Whether you are looking for a quick slapback echo for a vocal track, a long ringing delay to create a chiming guitar tone, or spaced-out dub effects, there's a DigiRack delay that can get the job done. They include:

◆ Extra-Long Delay

◆ Long Delay

◆ Medium Delay

◆ Mod Delay II

◆ Multi-Tap Delay

◆ Ping-Pong Delay

◆ Short Delay

◆ Slap Delay

Delay plug-ins such as the Short, Long, and Medium Delay plug-ins are easy to use. You'll add them to your tracks as inserts and adjust the settings to achieve the sounds you want. You can switch between delay effects, try out other plug-ins, or remove all effects from your track at any time.

To try out delay effects:

1. Create a Pro Tools session named Delay Tests.

2. Make sure the Inserts view is visible.

3. Create a mono audio track and add the Medium Delay as an insert.

4. Record a quick vocal or instrumental performance (or use one of the audio files from the MMA Audio folder).

Figure 4.40 shows the Medium Delay plug-in.

FIGURE 4.40

The Medium
Delay plug-in

On all of the Pro Tools RTAS and TDM delay effects the Mix slider's default setting is 100%, which means that when you add a delay effect all you hear is the effect and not the original recording. To hear both the original track and the delay effect, adjust the mix slider, for example, from 100 % to 50%.

If you've made adjustments to your plug-in and want to save the preset for later, choose Save Settings As from the Preset menu.

TEMPO SYNC

The delay effects all have built-in tempo syncing abilities, allowing you to automatically sync the speed of the delay effect with the current tempo of your Pro Tools session. When the Tempo Sync button is activated, it will turn orange and the Adjust Tempo slider will disappear.

Adjustments to the session's tempo will be automatically reflected in the plug-in window.

USING AUDIOSUITE DELAYS

Aside from the included TDM/RTAS insert delays, you'll also have a few delays available from the AudioSuite menu. To apply an AudioSuite delay:

1. Select an audio region or multiple audio regions in the Pro Tools Edit window using either the Selector tool or the Grabber tool.

2. From the AudioSuite menu, choose the delay effect you wish to use. Figure 4.41 shows the Multi-Tap Delay.

FIGURE 4.41
The AudioSuite
Multi-Tap Delay

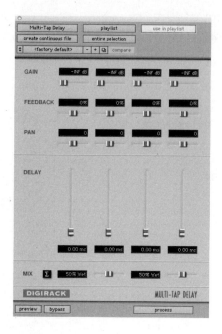

3. Set the effect either by using one the preset menu or manually adjusting the effects parameters.

4. Preview the effect by clicking the Preview button on the lower left.

5. If you are satisfied with the effect, click the Process button.

6. If you are not satisfied with the result after you've applied the AudioSuite effect, you can undo the effect by pressing Command+Z.

Dynamics III

While keeping the previously included Dynamics II plug-ins, Digidesign recently introduced a free upgrade, the Dynamics III plug-ins:

◆ Compressor/Limiter

◆ Expander/Gate

◆ De-Esser

The Dynamics III plug-ins are free and are compatible with any system running Pro Tools 6.7 or higher.

Let's take a look at the versatile Compressor/Limiter plug-in (Figure 4.42):

1. Create a new session and add a mono audio track.

2. In the Inserts view, add the plug-in Dynamics ➤ Compressor/Limiter Dyn 3 (mono).

3. Record an instrument or vocal performance (vocals work best), or drag and drop the file DRUMWAV1 from the MMA Audio folder.

4. Try out the Brickwall, Pump, and Vocal Levelor presets to get an idea of the both subtle and dramatic effects that are possible with the Compressor/Limiter. Figure 4.42 shows the plug-in with the Vocal Levelor preset.

FIGURE 4.42

Pro Tools Compressor/
Limiter plug-in

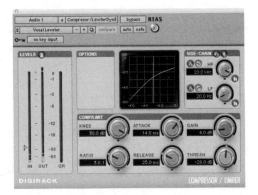

PLUG-IN TIPS

Take note of these tips to work with plug-ins more efficiently:

Keyboard Shortcuts   Many Pro Tools plug-ins respond to keyboard shortcuts. For example, on the Compressor/Limiter try Option+clicking any knob to return it to its default state. You can also Command+click any knob to make small adjustments.

Presets   Many of Pro Tools included plug-ins (and third-party plug-ins) come with existing presets. Click the Librarian menu field (labeled <factory default> when you first open the plug-in) to access these presets (and select from the list that appears.

If you've adjusted a plug-in and wish to save the changes for use on another track, you can save your own presets by clicking the arrows next to the Librarian menu and selecting Save Settings As from the pop-up menu.

Reverb Plug-ins

All Pro Tools systems include the D-Verb reverb plug-in. This is a simple but effective reverb effect that can be used on everything from vocals to drum kits. Let's take a look at this effect:

1. Create a new session and add a stereo audio track.

2. Drag MMA Audio /DRUMWAV1 onto the audio track.

3. In the Inserts view add the plug-in Multi-Channel Plug-in ➤ Reverb ➤ D-verb (stereo) on Insert A.

4. Listen to the default setting of the D-verb plug-in. Figure 4.43 shows the D-Verb plug-in.

FIGURE 4.43
The D-Verb reverb plug-in

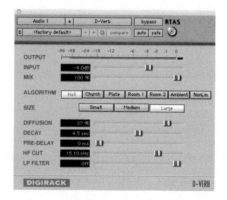

Just like the delay plug-ins, the D-Verb's mix slider defaults to a setting of 100%, meaning you hear only the effect and not the original file. The D-Verb has numerous basic settings to choose from. Try out different combinations like Small/Church and Medium/Room 2 to get an idea of the range of available sounds.

EQ Plug-ins

Along with the Dynamics plug-ins, Digidesign recently upgraded the included EQ plug-ins: they still have their standard 1- and 4-band EQs but also added the EQ III plug-ins. If you have an older Pro Tools system, you can download and install these new plug-ins for free.

In the Filter section, the 1-band EQ contains a single knob that demonstrates how all of the EQ III plug-ins work.

Figure 4.44 shows the 1-band EQ III.

♦ Select the Q knob in the Filter section to adjust the width (labeled "Q") of the selected frequency range.

♦ Select the Freq knob to choose the actual frequency.

♦ Adjust the Gain knob to increase or reduce the selected frequency.

You can also use the 1-band EQ to quickly add a Low Pass or High Pass filter to a track using the Type buttons in the lower left corner.

FIGURE 4.44
The 1-Band EQ plug-in

Bomb Factory Plug-ins

In 2004, Digidesign bought the rights to many Bomb Factory plug-ins. Since then Digidesign has included a number of these plug-ins with every Pro Tools system:

BF76   Based on the world-famous 1176 compressor. A great alternative to the Compressor/ Limiter and cool on drums and vocals. Works as TDM, RTAS, and AudioSuite.

BF Essentials Clip Remover   Repairs clipping or peaking tracks. AudioSuite only.

BF Essentials Correlation Meter   Finds and fixes phase problems on tracks and submixes. RTAS only.

BF Essentials Meter Bridge (HTDM, RTAS)   Works like any VU meter on single tracks, submixes, or your master track. TDM and RTAS.

BF Essentials Noise Meter   This mono or stereo three-in-one plug-in works as an A-weighted noise meter, a Robinson-Dadson equal-loudness meter, and a VU meter with 100dB of visual range. RTAS only.

BF Essentials Tuner   Works as a straightforward tuner for guitar, bass, or other stringed instruments. RTAS only.

Funk Logic Mastererizer   Works as a lo-fi sound destruction effect. Comes with tons of presets for adding noise and distortion to your tracks. RTAS and AudioSuite.

Add the Bomb Factory plug-ins to your sessions as inserts or use them to process audio, just as you would any other plug-in effects. For more information on the Bomb Factory plug-ins, how they work, and what they do, see your included documentation.

Plug-in Automation

You can automate just about any parameter of your Pro Tools TDM and RTAS plug-ins. Here's how to do some simple manual automation with a delay plug-in:

1. Create a new session and add a stereo audio track.

2. Set the session tempo to 140BPM

3. Drag and drop the file DRUMWAV1 from the MMA Audio files folder to the stereo track and use the Grabber tools to place it at the beginning of the track.

4. Select the loop and press Command+D to duplicate the loop over eight bars.

5. Add the Medium Delay plug-in.

6. In the Medium Delay plug-in window, click the Plug-in Automation Enable button.

This opens the Plug-in Automation dialog, where you'll decide which parameters you want to automate.

7. Select the Mix Left parameter from the list and click the Add button to add it to the list of parameters that will be automated. The result is shown in Figure 4.45.

FIGURE 4.45

The Plug-in Automation dialog box

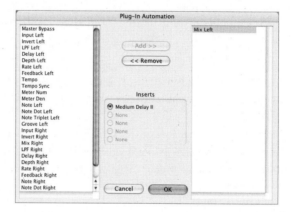

8. Command+click or Shift+click to select multiple parameters. Click the Add button to add selected parameters to the list.

9. Click the OK button. The parameters available for automation are now highlighted in red.

10. Click the Automation Mode selector on the track header, shown in Figure 4.46, and select Write from the pop-up menu.

FIGURE 4.46

The Automation Mode selector

Your plug-in is now ready to be automated.

11. Press the spacebar to start the session. As the song plays, adjust the mix left settings on the Medium Delay plug-in.

12. Press the spacebar to stop the session and change the Automation Mode selector to Read.

13. Play the session again to hear your automation. Watch the sliders move on the Medium Delay plug-in.

Plug-in automation can also be created with breakpoints just as volume automation can. To view the automation you've created, click the Track View selector and choose (fx a) Medium Delay II ➢ Mix Left, as shown in Figure 4.47.

FIGURE 4.47
View the plug-in automation.

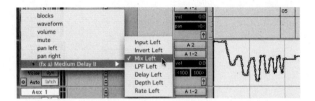

Just like volume or panning automation, you can use the Grabber tool to adjust the automation parameters. And, as with any Pro Tools automation, you'll find it's significantly easier to manipulate the breakpoints by switching from Grid mode to Slip mode.

Sends and Busses

One common mixing technique is applying plug-in effects to multiple instruments and performances by sending them to a single aux track. This is achieved by using Pro Tools *sends* to route an audio signal from its original audio track to another track containing the effect(s).

THE SENDS VIEW

Make sure View ➢ Edit Window ➢ Sends A–E has a check mark next to it.

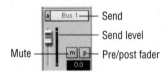

These are the elements that make up a send, from top to bottom:

Send   Clicking the Send selector will allow you to choose where you want to send your audio. Command+click the Send selector to choose from a list of available sends, in this case A–E.

Send Level   The Send Level fader determines the amount of signal being sent. This fader is silent by default. Option+click the fader to make the send audible.

Send Panning   On mono sends there will be a single slider (Pro Tools HD only; on mono sends in Pro Tools LE and M-Powered there is no panning function). On stereo sends (on all systems) there will be two sliders that you can use to determine the location of your send in the overall mix.

Mute   Marked "M." The mute button silences the send.

Pre-/Post-Fader   Marked "P." When the Pre-/Post-Fader button is turned on, any adjustments you make to a track's main volume slider will have no effect on the send.

Creating a send assignment also automatically opens up the Send window, shown in Figure 4.48.

FIGURE 4.48

A mono Send fader

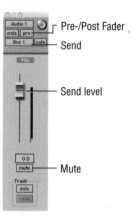

Send faders contain the same features as sends but in a larger and easier to access configuration. You can use whichever you are more comfortable with to control your sends.

SETTING UP A SEND

For this example, use the D-Verb (but this method can be used just as easily with a delay or dynamic effect).

1. Create a new Pro Tools Session.

2. Add two stereo audio tracks and one stereo aux input.

3. From the MMA Audio folder drag and drop the files DRUMWAV1 and PIANOWAV1 directly onto their own audio track.

4. Make sure there is a check mark next to Options ➢ Loop Playback.

5. Enable the Sends View by choosing View ➢ Edit Window ➢ Sends A–E.

6. On each of the audio tracks, use Send Selector A to select Bus 1-2 (Stereo).

7. Option+click the faders on each send to make them audible.

8. Change the aux track's audio input to Bus 1-2.

9. Option+click the aux track's volume indicator to raise the track volume.

10. On the aux input track, add the stereo D-Verb plug-in as an insert.

    Figure 4.49 shows the I/O routing for this session.

11. Use the Grabber tool or the Selector tool to highlight one of the loops and start playback of the session.

12. With the tracks playing, adjust the Send faders, aux track volume and D-Verb parameters.

You can add multiple effects to a single aux track or create multiple auxes with different effects. The routing is up to you. For Pro Tools LE and M-Powered users, sends and busses can be an excellent way to conserve processor power.

FIGURE 4.49
The I/O routing

> **OUT OF PHASE**
>
> Adding multiple effects as inserts or sends can cause subtle phase problems on M-Powered and LE Pro Tools systems. This happens when your tracks are delayed slightly as plug-ins process the audio signal. Slightly delayed tracks won't line up perfectly with the rest of the tracks in your session. This small amount of delay can lead to thinner or washier sounding mixes. To fix this problem, Pro Tools includes a plug-in called the Time Adjuster, which is accessed from your Plug-in ➤ Delay menu. Use the Time Adjuster presets to compensate for up to five plug-in effects on each track or send.
>
>

Included Software

Pro Tools HD and LE systems all come with assorted included software, including plug-ins and LE (*Light Edition*) versions of popular software. These programs are generally significantly limited in their functionality when compared to the full versions. Still they offer a great chance to become familiar with the basic functions of some great programs. Also, if you find them useful you can, in most cases, upgrade to the full versions of these programs for a substantial discount.

Some of the software that is currently included with every Pro Tool system:

- Ableton Live Lite 5
- Propellerhead's Software Reason Adapted 3
- FXpansion BFD Lite drum module
- IK Multimedia SampleTank 2 SE
- IK Multimedia AmpliTube LE
- IK Multimedia T-RackS EQ

The following sections cover the basic operation of each of these programs in conjunction with Pro Tools HD, LE, and M-Powered.

Ableton Live Lite 5 Digidesign Edition

Ableton Live's Digidesign Edition is a limited-feature version of the Live program covered in Chapter 3, "Ableton Live." If your version of Pro Tools shipped with an earlier version of Live Lite for Digidesign, you are eligible for a free upgrade to Version 5. To upgrade your software go to

`http://www.ableton.com/free-digidesign-upgrade`
and enter your Live for Digidesign serial number.

LIVE LITE FEATURES

Live Lite allows you to create the following:

◆ Up to four audio tracks

◆ Up to four MIDI tracks

◆ Up to four scenes

◆ Limited number of effects per track

Live Lite Digidesign Edition works both as a ReWire plug-in and as a stand-alone program. Although you can't add as many tracks or effects, Live Lite otherwise functions in essentially the same ways as the full version.

ADDING LIVE LITE TO A PRO TOOLS SESSION

To add Live Lite to a Pro Tools session:

1. Create a new Pro Tools session or open an existing one.

2. Choose Track ➤ New and create a stereo aux input track.

3. Option+click the Audio volume indicator to raise the track volume to 0.

4. Make sure that the Inserts View is showing (View ➤ Edit Window ➤ Inserts).

5. In the Inserts View, click Insert Selector A and choose Multi-Channel Plug-in ➤ Instrument ➤ Ableton Live.

6. In the DigiRack ReWire window that appears, make sure that Live Lite's output is routed to Mix L – Mix R as shown in Figure 4.50.

FIGURE 4.50
Check Live's output
routing.

7. Add loops and clips in Live.

8. Use Pro Tools to stop, start, and adjust the tempo of the session.

For more instruction on using Ableton Live and Pro Tools together, see the "Pro Tools and Ableton Live" section later in this chapter.

Ableton offers a special upgrade price for Live Lite users who want to move up to the full version of Live. For information on this, visit `http://www.ableton.com`.

Reason Adapted 3

Reason Adapted is the Light Edition of Propellerhead's Reason 3 software. Created specifically for use with Pro Tools systems, Reason Adapted 3 contains all of the Reason instruments in a locked configuration. While you cannot add or delete instruments, you can work with the included ones in much the same way that you work with instruments in the full version of Reason, adjusting various parameters and loading samples and sounds from the included sound bank. Reason Adapted is an excellent way to learn the basics of Reason and familiarize yourself with some of the possible uses for Reason in creating your music.

Figure 4.51 shows the Reason Adapted for Digidesign window.

FIGURE 4.51

Reason Adapted for Digidesign

FEATURES OF REASON ADAPTED 3

Reason Adapted contains the following devices:

◆ A Redrum drum machine device

◆ A Dr. Rex Loop Player device

- Two SubTractor Analog Synthesizer devices

- An NN19 Sampler device

- An RV7000 advanced reverb device

- A DDL-1 digital delay device

- A Comp-01 compressor device

- A Mixer 14:2 device

If you have an earlier version of Reason Adapted (2.5), there is at this time no upgrade option.

ADDING REASON ADAPTED 3 TO A PRO TOOLS SESSION

Adding Reason adapted to a Pro Tools session is essentially the same as using the full version, but with limitations:

1. Create a new Pro Tools session or open an existing one.

2. Choose Track ➤ New and create a Stereo instrument track.

3. Option+click the Audio volume indicator to raise the track volume to 0.

4. Make sure that Inserts View is showing (View ➤ Edit Window ➤ Inserts).

5. In the Inserts View, click Insert Selector A and choose Multi-Channel Plug-in ➤ Instrument ➤ Reason Adapted.

Even with its limitations you can use the Reason Adapted program in many of the same ways you would use the full version. See Chapter 2, "Reason," for descriptions of the individual Reason Instruments and how to use them in conjunction with the Reason Mixer and Sequencer. For more instruction on routing the Reason program, see the "Pro Tools and Reason" section later in this chapter.

IK Multimedia SampleTank 2 SE

Users who own SampleTank SE can download and install a free update. If you have tried to use SampleTank SE and been frustrated by its nonintuitive interface, you will be pleasantly surprised by SampleTank 2 SE. It's much easier to use and includes some nice sounds.

ADDING SAMPLETANK 2 SE TO A PRO TOOLS SESSION

To add SampleTank 2 SE to a session:

1. Create a stereo instrument track and choose Multi-Channel Plug-in ➤ Instrument ➤ SampleTank 2 SE.

2. In the MIDI Output selector in the Instrument view, choose SampleTank 2 SE ➤ Channel 1. Figure 4.52 shows the SampleTank 2 SE interface.

3. Option+click the Audio Volume indicator to raise the volume to make the track audible.

FIGURE 4.52

SampleTank 2 SE

4. Make sure that the MIDI Input selector is set to All or to the appropriate predefined MIDI input.

5. In the SampleTank window Channel 1 will be automatically selected.

6. Load the Church Organ patch from SampleTank's Browser column by double-clicking it. Figure 4.53 shows the Church Organ patch.

FIGURE 4.53

Select the Church
Organ patch.

7. Use a MIDI keyboard to trigger notes or use the Pencil tool to draw notes directly on the instrument track in Pro Tools.

USING SAMPLETANK 2 SE EFFECTS

SampleTank 2 SE comes with dozens of included instruments, including drum kits, sampled instruments, and synthesizers, as well as many built-in effects. Multiple effects can be applied to each instrument. These effects include saturation/distortion, equalization, reverb, and flanger/chorus/phaser effects.

Select the Reverb effect in the Effects field as shown in Figure 4.54.

FIGURE 4.54
Select the Reverb
effect.

Using the Effect Parameter knobs, adjust the time, color, density, size, and level of the reverb effect. From the menu beneath the Reverb effect that currently reads No Eff, choose any of the 31 other effects and add it to the current sample.

If you have added an effect or adjusted any of the other settings and wish to save the sound for future use, click the Save As button at the top of the SampleTank window.

More on SampleTank 2

SampleTank 2 Free is IK Multimedia's free/demo version of SampleTank 2 and can be used in any DAW program. SampleTank SE 2 and SampleTank Free are similar in their features and functionality. For a more in-depth look at SampleTank's features, see Chapter 9, "Virtual Instruments."

IK Multimedia AmpliTube LE

AmpliTube LE is the "light" version of the AmpliTube virtual amplifier program. For the home recording enthusiast, this is one of the most useful plug-ins included with Pro Tools. AmpliTube LE mimics the sounds of many different guitar amplifiers and cabinets, putting a large array of electric guitar and bass sounds at your disposal. Just plug your guitar or bass directly into your Pro Tools hardware interface, add AmpliTube LE to a track, and begin recording.

The full version of AmpliTube is available from `http://www.AmpliTube.com`. If you have a Syncrosoft USB key, you can download and try out the demo version of AmpliTube 2. AmpliTube 2 is covered in detail in the "Virtual Amplifiers" section of Chapter 9.

AmpliTube also offers AmpliTube Live, which works as a stand-alone program, and AmpliTube UNO Free, a simple, fun stand-alone amplifier.

To try out this plug-in, create a new session named AmpliTube LE Test. Select Track ≻ New and create a single mono audio track. Then, in the Inserts view, choose Insert Selector A and navigate to `plug-in/Other/AmpliTube LE`. Note that it's possible that AmpliTube LE will be in a different folder; if it's not under `Other`, try the `Instruments` or `Dynamics` folders.

Figure 4.55 shows the AmpliTube LE plug-in interface.

FIGURE 4.55
The AmpliTube
LE plug-in

As with many of the other Pro Tools plug-ins, you can choose from a list of presets from the Librarian menu, which reads <factory default> in Figure 4.55. You can also adjust AmpliTube LE's knobs and built-in effects to create and save your own presets. To use AmpliTube LE on a guitar or bass track:

1. Plug your electric guitar or bass directly into your hardware interface or mixing board.

2. Choose a track to record onto. Name the track and arm it for recording.

3. Add the AmpliTube plug-in and try out some of the presets.

4. Locate a preset you like and use its current settings to record your guitar or bass track.

   If you find that a particular preset is close to what you want but not exactly right, you can change any of the AmpliTube LE settings to achieve the sound you are looking for. AmpliTube LE has a pretty extensive range of editable features, including reverb and delay effects and different amplifier choices.

5. If you'd like to keep your settings for future use, select Save Settings As from the Settings menu to create your own reusable preset.

6. Record a guitar or bass performance.

Even you have recorded a track, if you decide to you are not happy with the current AmpliTube LE sound you can change the settings, try out different preset, and work with the plug-in to shape the sound you want.

Xpand!

Xpand! Is Digidesign's new sample playback/synthesizer plug-in. It comes with every new Pro Tools system. If you bought your Pro Tools system before Xpand! was released, you can get a free copy (well, almost free—you pay for shipping costs) at http://www.digidesign.com.

XPand! has 28 categories of presets to choose from including synthesizers, percussion, and sampled instruments like piano and strings.

Figure 4.56 shows the Xpand! Instrument plug-in.

FIGURE 4.56

The Xpand! sampler/
synthesizer

ADDING XPAND! TO A PRO TOOLS SESSION

You can add Xpand! to any Pro Tools session as a plug-in on an instrument track:

1. Create a new session or open an existing one.

2. Choose Track ➢ New and create a new instrument track.

3. Make sure that Instrument view and Inserts view are showing in the Pro Tools Edit window.

4. Choose Plug-in ➢ Instrument ➢ Xpand! from the Inserts menu.

5. Choose one of the over one thousand included presets from the Librarian menu to try out XPand!

6. Use your MIDI keyboard to play Xpand! or use the Pencil tool to draw notes directly onto the instrument track.

CREATING PATCHES

You can also create your own original patches with XPand! using some of the more than 500 included sounds. You can use single sounds or combine and edit multiple sounds to create an unlimited number of ideas:

1. In the Librarian menu, scroll to the bottom and choose Init to initialize XPand!.

2. Click the blank space in Section A to choose a sound or sample. Figure 4.57 shows XPand! with one sample added.

   You can add up to four different samples in a single patch.

FIGURE 4.57
Choose a sound or
sample for your patch.

Just above Section A you'll see the Mix, Mod, Arp, and FX tabs. Mix is the current view. This is where you'll adjust the volume and panning for each sample.

3. Click the Arp tab to open the arpeggiator. To activate the arpeggiator for an individual sample, click the On button. Try adjusting the mode and the rate for different variations on the arpeggio.

4. Click the FX tab to view the available effects for Xpand!. FX 1 and FX contain delays and echo effects as well as flanger/phaser effects that you can add to each individual sample.

To save a patch, click Xpand!'s Settings menu and select Save Settings As. You can save your new patch to one of the existing folders or create a new folder for your original patches.

Creating Templates

One way to save a lot time when you're working with Pro Tools is to create template sessions containing the types of tracks you commonly use. You can also add volume adjustments, panning, plug-ins, plug-in settings, ReWire instruments, and MIDI routing to the included tracks in your template session.

You can use this method to create any kind of template you want. The following template is one that can be used for a basic audio session:

1. Create a Pro Tools session and name it Demo Template.

2. Select Track ➤ New and create the following tracks in this order:

    ◆ Four mono audio tracks

    ◆ One mono aux input

    ◆ One stereo instrument track

    ◆ One stereo master fader

3. Name the tracks as follows:

    ◆ Vocals

    ◆ GTR L

    ◆ GTR R

    ◆ Bass

    ◆ Click

    ◆ Reason

4. Using the methods I covered in earlier sections of this chapter, add the following plug-ins and instruments:

Vocals	Digi Compressor w/ Vocal Levelor preset
GTR L	AmpliTube LE w/ amp setting of your choice
GTR R	AmpliTube LE w/ amp setting of your choice
Bass	Digi Compressor w/ Basic Bass preset
Click	Pro Tools Click Instrument
Reason	Reason Adapted ReWire Instrument

5. Option+click the Audio Volume indicator on the two aux inputs to make the tracks audible.

6. Pan GTR L all the way to the left and GTR R all the way to the right.

7. Close the session and select the Demo Template.ptf file from your hard drive.

8. Press Command+I to open the file's Info window.

9. Put a check mark next to Stationery Pad, as shown in Figure 4.58.

10. Drag the Demo Template file to the dock.

Now, when you click the icon in the dock, a new copy of the session will be created containing all of your plug-ins and track settings.

FIGURE 4.58
Select Stationery Pad.

DON'T RECORD AUDIO WHILE CREATING A TEMPLATE

While you're creating the original template file, don't record any audio. Doing so will make the audio file a part of the template. Pro Tools will then try and locate the files every time you create a new session from the template.

Pro Tools and Reason

The combination of Pro Tools and Reason is powerful. Where one program lacks, the other's strengths come in to play. Pro Tools has great digital audio recording and editing abilities for working with original tracks. Reason brings sampling, looping, and of course its excellent synthesizers to the table. As I touched on in the "Reason Adapted 3" section earlier in this chapter, you can route your Reason Instruments into Pro Tools as a single stereo track or as individual outputs for each Reason instrument or effect. In this section I'll cover multiple aspects of using Reason and Pro Tools together along with Reason's included ReFills—the Reason Factory Sound Bank and the Orkester ReFill.

For this section it's recommended that under Reason's preferences you select Empty Rack as the default song.

In Pro Tools these sessions should take place in Absolute Grid mode with the grid value set to Bars:Beats and ½ note.

A Basic Session

First I'll cover one of the simplest possible uses of Reason in Pro Tools: creating a click track. Often musicians are more comfortable with a customized click track sound over Pro Tools' included (and limited) choices. You can use Reason to create a distinctive and/or more pleasing sound to keep your musicians in time with the session:

1. Create a new Pro Tools session.

2. Make sure the basic settings follow the guidelines covered at the beginning of this section.

3. Create a stereo aux input.

4. Option+click the Volume indicator to make the track audible.

5. Select the Insert Selector A and choose Multi-Channel Plug-In ➤ Instrument ➤ Reason (Stereo).

6. Reason should load automatically and open your default Reason session. As I mentioned in the previous section, your default Reason session should be Empty Rack, which you can select in Reason's General Preferences window.

7. Create a Mixer 14:2 and add a Redrum drum machine and Dr. Rex Loop Player.

Now you have a couple of options for creating a click track. To use the Redrum drum machine:

1. Click the browse Sample button on Redrum's channel strip one. You have thousands of samples in multiple locations to choose from for your click track.

2. Browse through the folder `Redrum drum kits/x-clusive drums-sorted` to find a good sample for your click track. You'll find many of the samples that make up the included Redrum drum kits; the `Rimshots` and `Percussion` folders have especially good samples.

3. Select a sample.

4. Add notes in the Redrum step sequencer. For a standard 4/4 click track try adding notes at 1, 5, 9, and 13 (see Figure 4.59).

FIGURE 4.59
Program the Redrum.

5. Adjust the Resolution knob (just above the Step sequencer) to speed up or slow down the click track.

To create a click track using the Dr. Rex Loop Player, create a Dr. Rex Loop Player, click the Browser Loop button, and locate the folder `Reason Factory Sound Bank/Dr. Rex Percussion Loops`. Try the Tambourine or Shaker loops as click/tempo tracks.

Some of the other percussion loops may also work, depending on the session. If you have other ReFills, they may contain more appropriate loops for click and tempo.

Controlling Multiple Instruments

With Reason and ReWire you can use multiple instrument tracks to control different Reason instruments.

1. Create a new Pro Tools session.

2. Create a stereo instrument track and add Reason as an insert.

3. Option+click the Volume indicator to make the track audible.

4. In Reason, create a Mixer 14:2, a Malström Graintable Synthesizer, and a SubTractor Synthesizer.

5. On the instrument track's MIDI output selector, choose the Malström synth, as shown in Figure 4.60.

FIGURE 4.60

Choose the Malström synth from the MIDI output selector.

6. Use your MIDI keyboard to record a performance, or use the Pencil tool to draw MIDI notes on the instrument track.

7. Create another stereo instrument track.

8. Choose the SubTractor from the new track's MIDI output selector.

9. Create a performance on the new instrument track.

When you play the performance back you'll hear both instruments. Set the volume and panning levels in Reason.

You can create as many Reason instruments as you want, as well as new instrument tracks to control them. You're limited only by your computer's processor power.

Routing Multiple Outputs

With ReWire you can also send the output of multiple instruments to multiple tracks in Pro Tools. This can be useful if you want to apply a Pro Tools plug-in to a Reason track or if you want to use Pro Tools as the mix environment for a Reason song. To route individual instruments:

1. Create a new Pro Tools session with three stereo aux tracks.

2. Option+click each track to make it audible.

3. Add Reason as an insert on each track. For the stereo tracks choose Multi-Channel Plug-in ➤ Instrument ➤ Reason.

4. In the ReWire window, change the Reason output on the second stereo track to Channel 3– Channel 4, as shown in Figure 4.61.

FIGURE 4.61

Change the Reason output in Pro Tools.

5. Change the third track's ReWire output to Channel 5–Channel 6.

6. Change the two mono tracks to Channel 7 and Channel 8, respectively.

7. Now switch to the Reason interface, and create a new empty Reason song. Do *not* create a Mixer 14:2. Creating a Mixer will automatically route your new Reason instruments through its output, which you don't want in this case.

8. Add two Dr. Rex Loop Players to the Reason song. Use the Reason Browser to load a different drum loop into each instrument.

9. Click the Preview Loop button on the Dr. Rex Loop Players.

10. Press Tab on your Apple keyboard to view the routing of the Reason song. The output of the first Dr. Rex Loop Player is already routed to Inputs 1 and 2 in the Reason hardware interface.

11. Route the outputs of the second instrument to Inputs 3 and 4, as shown in Figure 4.62.

FIGURE 4.62

The output routing in the Reason hardware interface

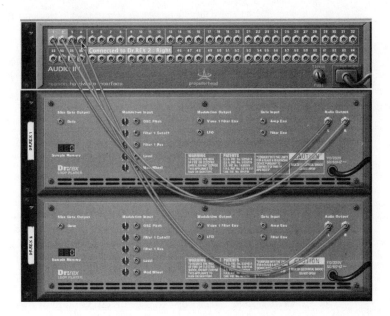

You can now use the Pro Tool instrument tracks to control the volume and panning of each Reason instrument. Using this method you can route as many instruments as you wish in either mono or stereo configurations. On any track you can use either the Reason Sequencer window or the Pro Tools instrument track to draw, record, and edit MIDI data.

RECORDING THE OUTPUT OF AN AUX OR INSTRUMENT TRACK

When you finish a Pro Tools session and bounce your song down in a final mix, the output of any ReWire Instrument that you have added to an aux input or instrument track will be included in the mix.

However, if you want to take advantage of Pro Tools' audio editing tools and functions, you'll have to create an audio file from the output of your Reason song or other ReWire instrument.

The problem here, as you may have noticed, is that there's no Record button on an aux input, and the Record function on an instrument track only captures MIDI data. You might think that the solution would be to insert your ReWire track onto a stereo audio track and click Record. Unfortunately, that doesn't work either. In order to send the output of your Reason track into an editable audio track you have to do as follows:

1. Create a stereo aux input or instrument track for the Reason session or for the individual Reason instrument you'd like to record.

2. Create a stereo audio track.

3. Change the output of the Reason aux input track to Bus 1-2.

4. Change the input of the new audio track to Bus 1-2.

5. Click the Track Record Enable button to arm the audio track for recording.

6. Do a test run to check the levels of the new recording.

7. Make any necessary volume adjustments on the aux track.

8. Click Record in the Transport bar, then click Play to begin recording.

9. Mute the original aux input or instrument track.

10. Deselect the Track Record Enable button.

11. Use any of Pro Tools editing functions to work with your new audio file.

Pro Tools and Ableton Live

Combining Ableton Live's looping functions and Pro Tools audio recording abilities makes for a formidable duo. While Pro Tools now contains some pretty advanced looping functions (especially with regard to WAV files and REX loops), your sessions and songs can still benefit greatly from Live's advanced looping abilities and easy to use included instruments.

I've touched on a couple of the basics in the "Ableton Live Lite 5 Digidesign Edition" section earlier in this chapter, but there are many more possibilities available with the full version. If you don't own Live, a trial copy of the current version of the program is always available from http://www.ableton.com.

A Basic Session

Live will be running as a slave to Pro Tools. However, even with Live in ReWire slave mode you can still create your Live songs using the same methods you would if you were using Live as a stand-alone program. You can stop and start the session in either the Live or Pro Tools window. You can turn looping on and off and set the area of the session you wish to loop in either program. Tempo settings must be made in Pro Tools, though.

Let's start by covering the most basic session you'll create: a stereo session where you'll add Live as a stereo insert on an aux input track.

1. Create a new Pro Tools session and create a stereo aux input track.

2. Using Insert Selector A, add Live as a ReWire instrument by choosing Multi-Channel Plug-in ➢ Instrument ➢ Ableton Live.

Don't Stop Here!

Do not start the Live program until after you have created an aux input and added Live as an insert. Live will not run as a ReWire slave until you have completed these steps.

---

1. Make sure that the output in the ReWire window is set to Mix L – Mix R as shown in Figure 4.63.

FIGURE 4.63
The ReWire output settings

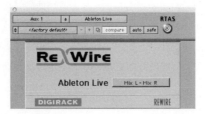

2. Option+click the Audio Volume indicator to make the track audible.

3. Open the Live program (unlike Reason, Live will not start up automatically when added to a track).

4. Add loops or clips to the Live session or create performances with the Impulse, Simpler, or Operator. You can work in either Arrange view or Session view.

You can use Live's built-in instruments just as you would in typical Live session. Unlike Reason, however, Live's MIDI controlled instruments will not appear as options for MIDI output in Pro Tools MIDI tracks or instrument tracks. All of your MIDI recording and editing will have to take place within the Live environment.

One important thing to note here: all of your VST and Audio Unit plug-ins and instruments will be disabled when Live is running in ReWire mode. However, there is a way to open previously created Live sessions that contain plug-ins and effects that I'll cover later on in the "Live, Plug-ins and ReWire" section of this chapter.

Multiple Output Session

Using ReWire, you can also route your individual Live tracks to individual Pro Tool tracks. This gives you greater control over your mixing, allows you to use Pro Tools RTAS and TDM plug-ins on Live tracks, and can be used to mix any of your live sessions in Pro Tools.

Here's a possible configuration that covers the basic principles behind routing multiple inputs and outputs between Live and Pro Tools:

1. Create a new Pro Tools session and add two stereo aux input tracks and two mono aux inputs.

2. Add Live as an insert to each aux track.

3. Open the ReWire plug-in window for the first aux input and change the Ableton Live output to Bus 03–04 as shown in Figure 4.64.

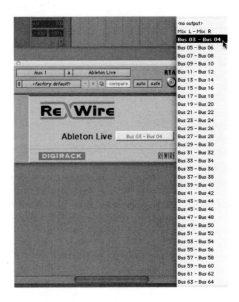

FIGURE 4.64
Routing in the ReWire window

4. Change the second aux input to Bus 05–06.

5. Change the third and fourth mono aux inputs to Bus 07 and Bus 08.

6. Start Live and create a new Live set with two audio tracks and 2 MIDI tracks.

7. In Live's Session view, make sure that I/O is showing.

8. In the first audio track under Audio To, change the top field to ReWire Out as shown in Figure 4.65.

FIGURE 4.65
Routing in the Live window

9. In the bottom field, choose Bus 3/4.

10. Route Track 2 to Bus 5/6.

11. Route the next two tracks as individual mono outputs by scrolling down to the bottom half of the output list. Choose any routing configuration you like. Generally, drum tracks are routed in stereo, while single instruments like a guitar loop or vocal track are routed in mono.

Live, Plug-ins, and ReWire

Audio Units and VST plug-ins are disabled when running Live as a ReWire slave. If you've created a session in Live that contains Audio Unit and/or VST plug-ins effects or instruments and you want to mix in Pro Tools, there is a way to work around this by taking advantage of Live's Freeze Track function:

1. Open your Live session in stand-alone (not ReWire) mode.

2. Select each track that contains an Audio Unit or VST plug-in effect or virtual instrument. Select Edit ➢ Freeze Track. This renders each track to your hard drive, including all effects. On tracks that are created using a VST or Audio Unit synthesizer or sampler the output is turned into a complete audio file.

3. Save the Live session as a self-contained set by choosing File ➢ Save Set Self-Contained.

4. Close Live, then start Pro Tools.

5. Create your stereo aux input or multiple inputs in Pro Tools.

6. Start Live and choose File ➢ Open Recent Set ➢ *your file*.als.

You can now set up all of your track routing as you would in any other ReWire session. You will not be able to edit any of the frozen tracks in Live. If you unfreeze them they may become silent or lose any added effects permanently. If you need to rearrange or edit your frozen tracks, try recording their output by routing the signal from an aux input track to an audio track as I covered previously in the "Recording the Output of an Aux or Instrument Track" sidebar.

Using the Workspace

Live's Browser window allows you to set three locations to browse for loops and clips to include in your Live sessions. If you are more comfortable working with Pro Tools' workspace browser or already have multiple locations defined with the workspace you can use this in conjunction with Live. You'll find this comes in handy especially with some files that don't loop well in Pro Tools but respond better in Live.

1. Open the workspace by selecting Window ➢ Workspace or pressing Option+; (semicolon).

2. Use the workspace to browse to any location where your loops are stored. Figure 4.66 shows the Pro Tools workspace.

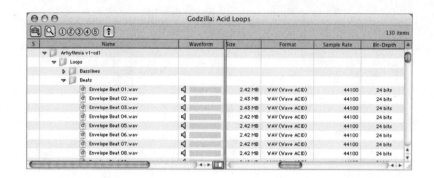

3. Preview loops in the workspace by clicking the speaker icon next to the loop.

4. When you locate a loop you want to add to your session, select it in the workspace then choose Reveal in Finder from the toolbox drop-down menu in the upper left corner of the workspace.

5. Drag the loop from the Finder directly onto any open Live audio track.

Pro Tools and OS X

Pro Tools and Apple computers go way, way back. In fact, in the beginning Pro Tools was a Mac-only program. Pro Tools is often one of the first programs to take advantage of advances in Apple technology. In most cases when a new operating system is released, or even when a radical change like Apple's switch to Intel Processors occurs, it doesn't take long for Digidesign to prepare a compatible version of Pro Tools. Still, when buying a new Apple computer or operating system for a Pro Tools system, it's a good idea to wait a bit and avoid being on the cutting edge. Occasionally there will be some major bugs or problems related to a new operating system or new model of computer that need to be worked out. You're much better off letting someone else be the guinea pig for a while before you make the plunge.

It's also good idea to research as extensively as possible how your Mac and external hardware will interact with Pro Tools before you buy a system. There may be known incompatibilities or difficulties that some users have had in the past that a quick check of the Answerbase or a search of posts in the Digidesign Users Conference could turn up. A couple years ago I helped a friend set up a Pro Tools–based studio that wouldn't run for more than two minutes without crashing. After many hours of troubleshooting with no success we did a search on the DUC forums, including his model number and peripherals in the search criteria. We found out that using his model of G4 in conjunction with a FireWire 800 drive was causing Pro Tools to crash. In the end it turned out that we could have saved a lot of time and headaches by researching the equipment beforehand.

Buffer Settings

Using multiple plug-ins and virtual instruments and/or recording multiple tracks at once can sometimes overwhelm your system, causing it to freeze, crash, or display various error messages.

Some of the most common error messages will tell you that you need to adjust your Buffer settings. This is done in Pro Tools by choosing Setup ➤ Playback Engine and selecting from the H/W Buffer Size menu shown in Figure 4.67.

FIGURE 4.67
The H/W Buffer
Size menu

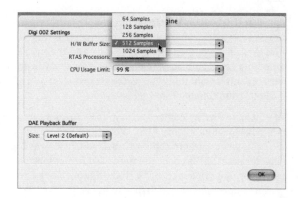

If your buffer is set too high you will experience some latency in your monitoring. Set the buffer too low and your sessions will stop. The solution is to try and find the middle ground—try 512 samples for starters. If you continue to get error messages, try removing plug-ins and using AudioSuite to apply any necessary effects to tracks.

Keeping an Eye on the Disk Usage

Pro Tools includes two handy little functions that let you keep an eye on how much CPU power you are currently using and how much disk space you have left. Select Window ➤ System Usage to view the System Usage meter shown in Figure 4.68.

FIGURE 4.68
The System
Usage meter

The CPU bar is the most important, letting you know how much power you're using and how much is left. Remember that certain plug-in effects take-up much more power than others. If you are working on an M-Powered or LE system, using lots of virtual amplifiers like AmpliTube and reverb effects like D-Verb can take up enough power to stop your sessions cold.

The other meter is the Disk Space meter shown in Figure 4.69.

FIGURE 4.69
The Disk Space meter

Access the Disk Space meter by selecting Window ➤ Disk Space from the Pro Tools menu. This meter shows how much room is left on each of your drives, as well as how many minutes of recording you have left at the current session's sample and bit rates.

 **Real World Scenario**

SIDE-CHAINING

Side-chaining is using the signal from one track to trigger or adjust an effect (usually volume or compression related) on another track. This process is sometimes known as "ducking," and you often hear it on the radio when a DJ begins talking and the music playing is automatically lowered. Another noticeable use of side-chaining in a mix is an acoustic guitar that gets much quieter whenever vocals come in. This is something you can hear quite clearly in many older recordings, especially folk records like Bob Dylan's *Another Side of Bob Dylan*.

Side-chaining also has subtler uses in your audio mixes. In one case I recorded a CD for the punk-influenced hard rock band Motorhome. Most of the songs had lead guitar fills throughout their entire arrangements. Generally, when you are recording electric guitars it's very important to make sure that the lead and rhythm guitar tones are distinct enough from each other to stand out. In this case we didn't notice until everything was packed up and taken out of the studio that our lead guitar fills were consistently getting lost because they were in sonic competition with the rhythm guitar. We tried automation, but this turned out to be difficult because certain tracks had so many lead fills that automating each one precisely would have taken up most of the time we had allotted to mix the CD.

We solved the problem by adding a compressor plug-in on one of the rhythm guitar tracks, then adding a side-chain so that the sound of the lead guitar automatically lowered the signal of the rhythm guitar track. This kind of side-chaining can help control any competing instruments in your mixes.

Here's a quick way to set up a side-chain in Pro Tools to familiarize yourself with the process:

1. Record an instrument performance. Acoustic rhythm guitar in particular will suit itself to this experiment. Whatever instrument you record, make it a consistent performance with no stops or noticeable dynamics.

2. Record a second track that consists of a "stop and start" performance.

Any instrument or vocal will work (in fact, using a side-chain with a vocal/acoustic guitar recording is often a very good idea). Guitar fills or keyboard flourishes will also work well.

3. Add a Pro Tools Compressor to the first track you recorded.

4. Make sure Pro Tools' Sends view is showing (View ➤ Edit Window ➤ Sends A-E).

5. Select the second track and route Send A to Bus 1.

6. Raise the Sends volume in the Sends view.

7. Click the Key Input at the top left of the Compressor's interface and choose Bus 1.

8. Click the Side-Chain key button on the right side of the interface to turn side-chaining on.

Here are some possible settings to start off with:

- 2:1 Ratio
- Fast Attack 10–30ms
- Longer release (around 750ms)
- Knee in the Middle (around 100)
- Raise and lower the threshold depending on the track

9. Try raising and lowering the Ratio setting to create a subtler or a more dramatic effect.

Your settings will vary greatly from session to session, depending on the instruments involved and how much of an effect you want to produce.

Round Robin Allocation

You can alleviate a lot of the strain on your system by choosing to use Pro Tools' Round Robin allocation to distribute newly recorded files onto folders on multiple hard drives. To set up Round Robin allocation:

1. Create a new Pro Tools session.

2. Before you add any tracks, choose Setup ➤ Disk Allocation.

3. In the Disk Allocation window, select all three boxes: Custom Allocation Options; Create Subfolders for Audio, Video, and Fade Files; and Use Round Robin Allocation for New Tracks.

4. Click OK.

5. Create four new mono audio tracks.

6. Open the Disk Allocation window again.

7. Click the Root Media Folder selector for Track 1 as shown in Figure 4.70.

FIGURE 4.70
The Root Media Folder selector

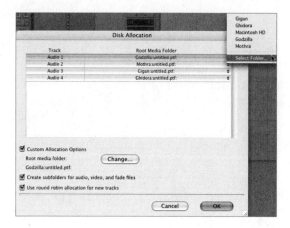

8. Choose Select Folder.

9. Create a new folder for the audio and data files Pro Tools will create for this track.

10. Repeat the procedure for the other tracks.

If you have two external hard drives, you may want to assign every other track to a specific folder. It's a good idea to do all of your allocations at the beginning of a session. If you have three (or more) drives, you can assign every third track to a different drive, and so on.

Remember that when you create any new tracks they will not automatically be routed to the folders you created. You have to open the Disk Allocation every time you create a new track or tracks.

TAKE IT WITH YOU

Any session created in Pro Tools 7 can be opened on any other Pro Tools system, including older systems running previous versions of Pro Tools. Pro Tools sessions are also portable between Mac and PC. Just burn your session folder to a CD-R or DVD-R. This is especially useful if you want to use Pro Tools in your home studio or to record a mobile session and then do final mixes or overdubs in another location. However, keep in mind if you are going to be moving your session from a system that uses TDM plug-ins to an M-Powered or LE system you should remember to switch out any TDM plug-in effects with RTAS plug-ins, which are compatible with all versions of Pro Tools.

The Bottom Line

Create and save a new Pro Tools session   Every time you start a new Pro Tools session, decisions will have to be made about location, file format, and settings and the types of track to be included. These decisions will impact the rest of the session in various ways and will also play a part in determining compatibility with other Pro Tools systems, should you end up working on a session in multiple studios.

Master It   Create a new Pro Tools session with the WAV file format, containing a mono audio track, a stereo instrument track, one mono *and* one stereo aux input, and a Stereo Master Fader track.

Add plug-in effects to Pro Tools tracks   Pro Tools includes a wide range of plug-in effects, which will be used in some capacity in almost every recording session.

Master It   Add Pro Tools' RTAS Medium Delay and D-Verb plug-ins to a mono audio track.

Process audio with AudioSuite plug-ins   Pro Tools AudioSuite plug-ins can make permanent changes to your audio tracks.

Master It   Process an audio track with Pro Tools' Multi-tap delay AudioSuite effect.

Create volume automation on a Pro Tools track   Pro Tools has a number of automation features built in to the program. Automation can adjust volume levels, panning, many of the parameters of any plug-in effects or virtual instruments, and more.

Master It   Use the Pencil tool and the Grabber tool to create and adjust volume automation on a Pro Tools audio track with breakpoints.

Use Pro Tools as a ReWire master with Reason   Using Propellerhead's ReWire protocol allows you to sync two DAW programs together, taking advantage of the strengths and features of each program. Host programs like Pro Tools can control all the output and functionality of slave programs like Propellerhead's Reason. Since all versions of Pro Tools come with Reason Adapted for Digidesign, every Pro Tools user can take advantage of this excellent feature.

Master It   Add Reason or Reason Adapted for Digidesign to a Pro Tools session as a ReWire slave.

Chapter 5

Logic

Logic is an amazing and very complex program. Originally created by the German company Emagic to run on both Windows and Mac operating systems, Emagic was bought by Apple in 2002 and the Windows versions of the program were discontinued. Now that Logic is owned by Apple, the program has incorporated and informed some aspects of GarageBand. Both programs now share many features, such as Apple Loop support and similar loop browsing functions. Logic also contains all of GarageBand's virtual instruments. In fact, as I'll cover in Chapter 6, "GarageBand," you can create sessions in GarageBand and open and edit them seamlessly in Logic.

Of all the programs covered in this book, Logic is possibly the most in-depth, complex, and full-featured music-making program. Because it has so many included features, instruments, plug-ins, audio and MIDI editors, and routing possibilities, Logic can be somewhat intimidating at first. Much of what I am going to do in this chapter is set out to demystify Logic and show you simple, direct ways to access some of its best functions. As with any program, once you understand the basic concepts of Logic, the more complicated ones will quickly begin to make sense.

In this chapter, you will learn to

◆ Create an Autoload session

◆ Use Logic's Loop Browser

◆ Use Logic's editing tools

◆ Create MIDI performances with Logic's virtual instruments

◆ ReWire Logic with Reason and Ableton Live

Logic Basics: Logic Pro and Logic Express

Logic is available in two versions. The complete program is called Logic Pro and the "light" version of the program is Logic Express. Both versions have essentially the same interface and many of the same features. The major differences between the two programs:

Support for Surround Sound   Logic Pro contains support for surround mixing.

TDM Support   Logic Pro can be used in conjunction with Digidesign's Pro Tools TDM hardware and DSP (Digital Signal Processing) cards (both versions can be used with Pro Tools LE and M-Powered interfaces).

More Instruments and Effects   Both versions contain lots of great virtual instruments and plug-in effects, but Logic Pro includes some instruments and effects like the Ultrabeat drum module and the Space Designer reverb effect not available in Logic Express.

The two programs also contain many minor differences in functionality and available options. Much of what I'll cover in this chapter applies to both versions of the program. Features that are only available in the Pro version will be noted as such.

As I will point out continuously in this chapter, Logic is a highly customizable program with many, many features. Quite often there are multiple ways to perform tasks, such as recording and editing functions. Many of the tutorials in this chapter show one or two ways to perform tasks that could possibly be accomplished using other methods as well. The more you work with Logic the more you will find methods of operations that work best for you. Exploring Logic's many file menu options and experimentation in general is definitely encouraged.

Setting Up Logic

The first time you run Logic you will be prompted to set certain parameters and functions with the Setup Assistant. If you've already done this you'll need to run the Setup Assistant again to prepare for the tutorials in this chapter. You can run the Setup Assistant again by opening the Logic menu (which is called Logic Pro or Logic Express, depending on your version) and then selecting Preferences ➤ Start Logic Setup Assistant.

STARTING OVER FROM SCRATCH

For the tutorials and exercises in this chapter you'll be working with the Logic's default settings. If you have already been working in Logic or have changed any parameters you can return Logic to its default state by selecting Logic ➤ Preferences ➤ Initialize All Except Key Commands.

---

1. The first window of the Setup Assistant (Figure 5.1) scans your system for MIDI and audio devices. Make sure any hardware audio interfaces, MIDI controller(s), and any other MIDI devices are connected, then click the Next button.

FIGURE 5.1
The Setup Assistant

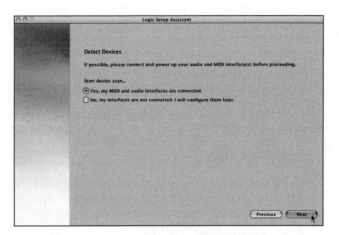

2. The second window asks you to choose which device will be your default audio interface. Choose your preferred device from the list. If you do not have an audio interface connected, you can use your Mac's built-in audio. If you are using Logic Pro and have Digidesign Pro Tools TDM hardware, select the TDM support with Logic box at the bottom of the window.

3. The third window is the Core Audio Mixer Setup. This window allows you to set the number of audio tracks, busses, virtual instrument tracks, and outputs your default sessions will have. Create the following custom setup:

Choose Custom from the Mixer Presets drop-down menu, then use the sliders to set the following parameters:

Audio Tracks	4
Audio Bus Channels	4
Audio Instruments	4
Audio Inputs	At least 2, but you can select a higher number if you want to use multiple inputs and your audio interface has them available.
Audio Outputs	2

CHANGE IT LATER

These settings in the Core Audio Mixer Setup window apply only to the tutorials and exercises in this chapter. All of these settings can be changed later for more complicated routing options. When you return to Logic's Setup Assistant you will almost certainly want to increase the number of audio tracks and audio instruments as well as changing the Audio Input and Output settings to match your devices and needs.

1. The fourth window lets you choose your preferred audio input setup. This is a personal preference. As the hint at the bottom of the screen says, whichever choice you make here, you can always route individual tracks manually later on.

2. In the fifth window, choose your default key commands. If you are working on a laptop, choose Logic v7 for PowerBook. If you are working on a desktop, choose Logic v7 for Pro Keyboard. Logic also gives you the option to customize your key commands, which I'll cover later in this chapter.

3. In the sixth window, check the box next to Activate Dock Autohide. If you have more than one monitor, click the Identify Monitors button to set up multiple monitors with Logic.

4. The seventh window displays all of your MIDI devices. If there are any devices in this window that you don't want to use with Logic, select them and click the Remove button. If there are any devices you wish to use that are not on the list, click the Add button and fill in the relevant information in the New External MIDI Device dialog box, then click Add.

5. Click the Finish button. Logic will restart automatically.

The Arrange Window

Much of the work you do in Logic will be done in the first window you'll see when Logic starts up. This is the Arrange window, shown in Figure 5.2.

The largest section of the Arrange window is the Timeline. This is where all of your audio and MIDI files will exist, including loops and "live" recordings.

To the left of the Timeline is a column of tracks that make up a Logic session. Select any audio track, then take a look at the far left side of the Arrange window. You'll see four separate fields, shown close up in Figures 5.3 and 5.4.

FIGURE 5.2

The Arrange window

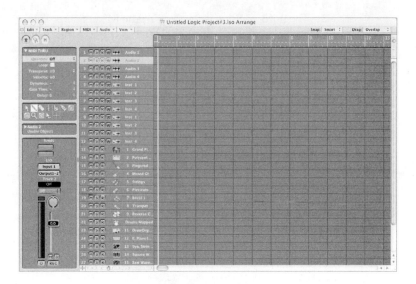

FIGURE 5.3

The MIDI Thru, Tools, and Object Parameters boxes

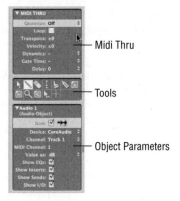

— Midi Thru

— Tools

— Object Parameters

These are, from top to bottom:

MIDI Thru/Region Info box   Here you can set MIDI parameters for any selected MIDI track. This box also automatically displays information about any audio or MIDI region you have selected in the Timeline.

Tools box   These are Logic's editing tools. I'll cover these in detail later in this chapter.

Object Parameters box   In this box you can set up the input and output for your tracks and choose which elements, such as inserts and sends, will be visible. The settings in this box change depending on the type of track you have selected. Audio tracks, instrument (MIDI) tracks, and GM (General MIDI) tracks all contain different parameters.

Channel Strip   In the channel strip (Figure 5.4) you can set audio parameters like volume and pan settings for any selected audio or MIDI track. You can also add effects and route the track's input and output. Get a better look at the channel strip by minimizing the Object Parameters and/or MIDI Thru box. Like the Object Parameters box, the channel strip changes depending on the type of track you have selected.

FIGURE 5.4
The Channel Strip

Creating an Autoload Song

Now I am going to cover the basic operation of Logic's audio recording and MIDI-controlled virtual instruments. As you work with Logic you'll find that one of its great assets is flexibility. You can customize the work environment to suit your needs. In order to simplify our workflow you're going to eliminate some of the unnecessary tracks and options from Logic's Arrange window and make some other, more useful functions available.

You're going to set up a basic template, also known as the Autoload song. Templates in Logic can contain complex routing, preloaded instruments and track configurations, and more. To get familiar with some Logic basics, you're going to create a very simple Autoload song.

When Logic starts up after you've completed the Setup Assistant, there will be three sets of tracks in the Arrange window:

Audio tracks   Used to record and edit live instrumentation, play back Real Instrument Apple Loops, and import audio files in any format that Logic can read (WAV, RX2, AIFF, and so on).

Instrument tracks   Used for virtual instruments like synthesizers, samplers, and drum machines, triggered by MIDI information. There are multiple ways to record and edit MIDI information in Logic, which we'll cover in detail.

General MIDI Device tracks   Used to control external MIDI devices.

We won't be working with General MIDI Device tracks, so you can simplify things by eliminating them from your Autoload song:

1. Select the Grand Piano track in the Arrange window (track 9). Press the Delete key on your Apple keyboard.

2. Use this method to delete all of the remaining General MIDI Device tracks. You should now have a total of eight tracks: four Audio tracks and four Instrument tracks.

3. Select Audio Track 1.

4. Minimize the MIDI Thru box and Object Parameters box so that you have a clear view of the Arrange window's channel strip.

5. In the Arrange window's menu, select View ➤ Track Solo Buttons.

MULTIPLE MENUS

When you are working in Logic there are often two separate groups of menus. There are the standard menus at the top of your screen, just as in any Mac program, but in many of Logic's windows, there is also a second group of menus within the window you are working in. For example, at the top left of the Arrange window you'll see Edit, Track, Region, MIDI, Audio, and View menus.

This can sometimes be very confusing when trying to follow instructions pertaining to Logic's features. To clarify things in this chapter I'll refer either to the menu "in the menu bar" or the menu in a specific window. For example, "the Edit menu in the Arrange window."

Now all of your Audio and Instrument tracks should have visible Mute (M), Solo (S), and Record (R) buttons.

The Arrange window's View menu contains many different view options and can be used at any time to customize your sessions or templates.

Figure 5.5 shows how the tracks and parameter boxes should look in your Autoload session when you have an empty Audio track selected in the Arrange window.

FIGURE 5.5

Eight tracks in the track column

Now that you've got your Autoload song set up, you need to save it as a template. From the menu bar, choose File ➤ Save as Template. Name the session Autoload in the Save Document As dialog, then in the menu bar choose File ➤ Close to close the session.

Creating a New Session

Now that you've created and saved an Autoload song, Logic will use it as the default template every time you create a new session. To create a new session using your Autoload song:

1. From the menu bar, choose File ➤ New.

   Figure 5.6 shows the New Song dialog box.

2. Leave the Use Song Template box unchecked *or* put a check mark in the box and choose User ➤ Autoload from the Template drop-down menu. Either way the Autoload song will be used as the default template for your sessions.

3. Name the project in the Name field.

4. Use the Set button to choose a location for the new project. This will automatically become the default location for all of your Logic sessions. However, you can change it anytime you create a new session.

5. Click OK.

FIGURE 5.6
The New Song
dialog box

OTHER TEMPLATES

Logic also comes with other template files. These templates can be used for different types of sessions; they also make a good introduction to some of the more complex routing possibilities available in Logic. To open any of the included templates:

1. From the menu bar, choose File ➤ New.

2. Put a check mark in the Use Song Template box and choose any template from the Template drop-down menu.

The Mixer Window

Logic's Mixer window controls the volume and panning for all of the tracks in our sessions, and you'll also be using the Mixer window to do your audio routing and assigning virtual instruments and effects to tracks.

To open the Mixer window you can do any of the following:

◆ Double-click one of the Audio Tracks.

◆ Use the keyboard shortcut ⌘+2.

◆ Figure 5.7 shows the Mixer window.

CHOOSE YOUR WEAPON

There are frequently many ways to accomplish the same objectives in Logic. Anything you do with a channel strip in the Mixer window can also be done by selecting a track in the Arrange window and using the Arrange window's single channel strip. In order to keep things simple in this tutorial, we will do much of our work in the Mixer window. If you are more comfortable working in the Arrange window, the following actions can be done in either place:

◆ Routing audio from your hardware interface to an audio track

◆ Adding effects

◆ Adding virtual amplification to an instrument

◆ Adding MIDI instruments to a session

◆ Automation

FIGURE 5.7
Logic's Track Mixer
window

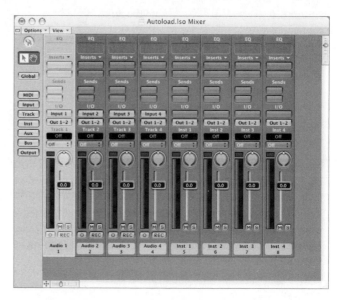

In this section we'll be dealing primarily with two distinct kinds of channel strips that appear in the Mixer window: the Audio channel strip and the Instrument Track channel strip.

AUDIO CHANNEL STRIPS

Audio channel strips are where you will do much of the work pertaining to audio tracks in Logic. Audio tracks can be original recorded performances or Apple Loops from GarageBand or any other loop library. Figure 5.8 shows an Audio channel strip.

The elements that make up the channel strip are, from top to bottom:

Channel EQ Click here to open an EQ plug-in for each individual track. This will automatically insert an EQ plug-in into the Inserts field just below.

Inserts You can add multiple effects on each track here.

FIGURE 5.8
An Audio
channel strip

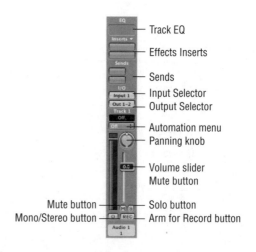

Sends Allows you to route the audio from each track to a separate bus track for creating sub-mixes or adding effects to multiple tracks.

I/O Selectors Allows you to choose where your audio will be coming from, specifically which input on your hardware interface. The output field (labeled Out 1–2 on Figure 5.8) determines where your track's audio is routed. For our sessions this will be kept at its default setting, which sends all of your track's outputs to Out 1–2.

Automation menu Allows you to choose how Logic responds to your automation commands for each track. I'll cover automation in a later section.

Panning knob Adjusts the panning for each track, sending it to the right or left speaker.

Volume slider Adjusts the track's volume.

Mute and Solo buttons Clicking the Mute button, marked "M," silences the track. The Solo button, marked "S," plays the track and silences the rest of the tracks in the session.

Mono/Stereo button Turns a mono track into a stereo track and vice versa.

Arm for Record button Prepares the track for recording. Clicking this button for the first time in each session will open up a dialog box asking you where you would like your recorded files to be placed.

INSTRUMENT TRACK CHANNEL STRIPS

Figure 5.9 shows an Instrument Track channel strip.

FIGURE 5.9
An Instrument Track
channel strip

Instrument Track channel strips are essentially the same as audio track channel strips with a few very important differences:

- The Input section of the I/O section is used to select a virtual instrument.

- There's no Mono/Stereo button. Whether an instrument track is mono or stereo is determined by the instrument or any effects you are using.

- There's no Arm for Recording button. Recording is automatically enabled by selecting the track in the Arrange or Track Mixer window.

The Transport Bar

The Transport bar at the bottom of the screen is shown in Figure 5.10.

FIGURE 5.10
The Transport bar

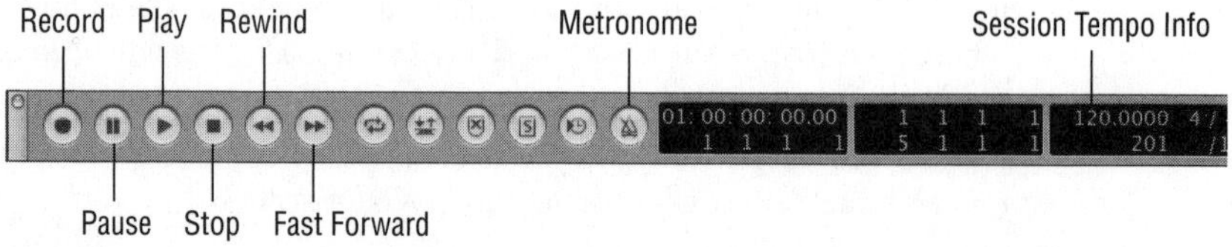

Record   Play   Rewind   Metronome   Session Tempo Info

Pause   Stop   Fast Forward

The Transport bar controls and displays information relevant to Logic's recording and playback functions. The first six buttons are the standard Record, Pause, Play, Stop, Rewind, and Fast Forward. The button farthest to the right turns Logic's metronome on and off.

Session tempo information is displayed in the second pane from the right. Logic's default session tempo is 120BPM. Tempo can be adjusted by using your mouse to click the tempo field and raise and lower the tempo, or by double-clicking the Tempo field and using your keyboard to type a new tempo. Press the Return key to set the new tempo.

Key Commands

Some of Logic's default keyboard shortcuts include:

Key	Action
Spacebar	Stop and start play
0	Stop play and return to the beginning of the session
]	Fast forward
[	Rewind
⌘+1	Open the Arrange window
⌘+2	Open the Track Mixer

One of Logic's many customizable features is the ability to assign your own keyboard shortcuts. This can be very useful if you are used to working with specific commands in another program or you wish to assign or reassign a keyboard shortcut to a frequently used function.

Here we'll assign a new keyboard shortcut for the recording function:

1. From the menu bar, select Logic ➤ Preferences ➤ Key Commands.

2. Click the triangle to the left of Global Commands to view the list. Figure 5.11 shows the Key Commands dialog box.

3. Select the Learn by Key Label button.

4. Press the ⌘ (Command), Ctrl (Control), and equal (=) keys on your Apple keyboard.

You have now assigned the keyboard shortcut ⌘+Control+= to the Logic's record function.

Scroll through the various categories and lists in the Command column. As you can see, Logic contains hundreds of potentially assignable keyboard shortcuts. If you attempt to assign a key command that already belongs to another function, a pop-up window will appear asking if you want to replace the existing keyboard shortcut.

FIGURE 5.11
The Key Commands
dialog box

Assigning a new key command is a permanent change to all of your Logic projects. To return to the default key commands select Preferences ➤ Start Logic Setup Assistant and choose one of the Logic default sets when you get to the Key Commands window.

Recording into Logic

To make sure that you are ready to record:

1. From the menu bar, select Logic ➤ Preferences ➤ Audio.

2. Select the Drivers tab.

3. Select the Core Audio tab.

4. Make sure the Enabled box is checked.

5. Select your recording interface from the Driver menu, shown in Figure 5.12.

6. Close the Audio Preferences window and return to the Logic interface.

FIGURE 5.12
Select your audio
interface.

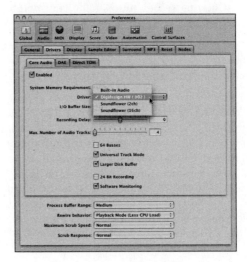

There are multiple ways to proceed from here with the routing and recording process; the following method is one of the simplest:

1. In the Arrange window, double-click Audio Track 1 to open up the Mixer window.

   When the Mixer window opens, Track 1 will be selected.

2. Click the Input field in the I/O section and choose your audio input from the drop-down menu shown in Figure 5.13.

FIGURE 5.13
Select an input.

3. Click the Record button at the bottom of the channel strip. You will be prompted to select a location where your recorded audio files will reside. If possible, choose a location on an external drive.

4. Press the 0 key on your numeric keypad or Mac keyboard to return the playhead to the beginning of the session.

5. Click the Record button in the Transport bar. Logic will begin recording after a four-beat count off.

You can add any of Logic's included effects or third-party plug-in effects before or after the recording process. For information on how to use plug-in effects with Logic see the section "Included Effects" later in this chapter.

Creating a MIDI Performance

Logic's MIDI capabilities are one of its biggest selling points. Combine the included virtual instruments with Logic's ability to create and edit complex MIDI performances and you have a program that is pretty much everything you need to create music in one package.

This is also where things can get extremely complicated for the users who are not familiar with (or not interested in) advanced MIDI recording and editing techniques. In this section we'll take a look at some quick and painless ways to create MIDI performances. We'll also take a look at Logic's easiest-to-use MIDI editor, the Matrix Editor. For more advanced MIDI implementation in Logic see the "MIDI and Logic" section in Chapter's 10, "Apple Loops."

INSERT A MIDI INSTRUMENT

1. Create a new Logic session and save it in your Logic Sessions folder.

2. In the Arrange window, double-click the first instrument track to open the Mixer window. The instrument track will be automatically selected in the Mixer window.

3. The input field in the I/O section of the instrument track channel strip will be blank. Click your mouse here to add a virtual instrument to the track. For this example we'll use Logic's ES-1 Synthesizer. Add the ES-1 to the track from the pop-up menu by following the path Stereo ➢ Logic ➢ ES-1.

Use one of the methods in the following sections to create a MIDI performance.

Create a Performance with a MIDI Keyboard

The easiest way to create a MIDI performance is with a MIDI keyboard. If you have a MIDI keyboard and/or other MIDI interface, they were set up to work automatically with Logic when you used Logic's Setup Assistant.

Once your MIDI connections are in place and working properly, your MIDI keyboard will trigger any instrument track that is selected in either the Arrange or Mixer window.

1. Close or hide the Mixer window by clicking the Close or minimize button at the top left of the window.

2. In the Arrange window select the instrument track containing the ES-1 synth.

3. Click the Record button on the Transport bar.

4. After a four-beat count-off, Logic will begin recording your MIDI performance.

Figure 5.14 shows a MIDI recording in the Arrange window.

FIGURE 5.14
A MIDI recording in
the Arrange window

Create a Performance without a MIDI Keyboard

Even without a MIDI keyboard you can still create MIDI performances in Logic. The easiest way to do this is with the included Caps Lock onscreen keyboard, which you can access by pressing the Caps Lock on your Apple keyboard. Figure 5.15 shows the Caps Lock keyboard.

1. In the Arrange or Mixer window, select any instrument track containing a virtual instrument.

2. Type on your Apple keyboard to "play" the Caps Lock keyboard.

3. Once you are familiar with the Caps Lock keyboard, use the zero (0) keyboard shortcut to return to the beginning of the session.

FIGURE 5.15
The Caps Lock
keyboard

4. Click the Record button in the Transport bar to begin recording a performance.

5. Click the Stop button to finish recording.

6. Listen to your recording.

7. Use the Undo keyboard shortcut (⌘+Z) to delete your performance and rerecord it, or use the editing features covered in this chapter to adjust your performance.

CREATE A PERFORMANCE IN THE MATRIX EDITOR

Of all of Logic's MIDI editors, the easiest to use and understand is the Matrix Editor. While the Matrix Editor also has many interesting and complex functions, its basic operation is pretty straightforward.

You can open the Matrix Editor by doing any of the following:

◆ Clicking any MIDI region in the Arrange window.

◆ Selecting Windows ➢ Matrix Edit from the menu bar.

◆ Using the keyboard shortcut Command+6

◆ Figure 5.16 shows the Matrix Editor.

Here you'll use the Matrix Editor to create a simple MIDI performance:

1. Select any instrument track that contains a virtual instrument in the Arrange or Mixer window.

FIGURE 5.16
The Matrix Editor

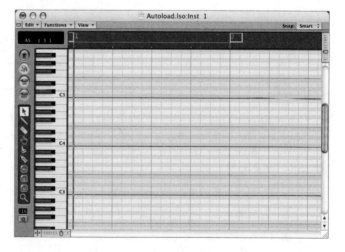

2. In order to use the Matrix Editor, you'll need an audio region to edit. Create a region by selecting the Pencil tool (the second tool in the top row of the Toolbox in the Arrange window) then clicking in the Timeline.

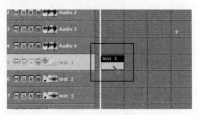

3. Any region you create will automatically be one measure long. You can lengthen or shorten the region by moving the Pencil tool to the end of the region, then clicking and dragging to resize it.

4. Double-click the region to open the Matrix Editor.

5. Select the Pencil tool (second from the top) from the Toolbox on the left side of the Matrix Editor.

6. Use the Pencil tool to create notes by clicking in the Timeline of the Matrix Editor.

7. Lengthen and shorten MIDI notes by moving the mouse to the beginning or end of a note and clicking and dragging.

8. Move notes around in the Matrix Editor by selecting and dragging with either the Arrow or Pencil tool.

Figure 5.17 shows a note being moved in the Matrix Edit window.

FIGURE 5.17
Moving notes around
the Matrix Edit
window

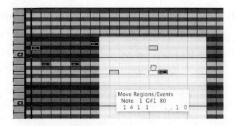

More editing techniques in the Matrix Editor are covered the "Basic Editing" section of this chapter.

The Loop Browser

If you've ever used GarageBand's Loop Browser, then Logic's Apple Loop Browser will be very familiar to you. To start working with Logic's Apple Loop Browser:

1. Create a new Logic session.

2. From the menu bar, select Audio ➤ Loop Browser. Figure 5.18 shows the Loop Browser.

3. The three buttons in the top left corner of the Loop Browser are used to choose the Loop Browser view. Choose the center button to view instrument, genre, and mood categories.

FIGURE 5.18
Logic's Apple Loop
Browser

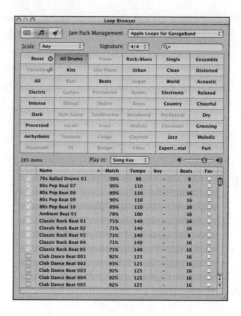

4. Click the All Drums category at the top of the window to display all of your Apple Loop drum loops in the window at the bottom of the Loop Browser.

   Files with a blue icon are Real Instrument loops—that is, "live" audio performances. Files with a green icon are Software Instrument loops, created with virtual instruments and MIDI data.

5. Click any file in the display pane to preview the loop at the current session tempo.

6. Add a loop to your session. To add a Real Instrument loop to your session, drag the file directly from the Loop Browser to any available audio track. To add a Software Instrument loop, drag it from the Loop Browser directly onto any available Instrument or audio track.

When you place a Software Instrument loop on an instrument track, Logic will automatically assign the appropriate virtual instruments and effects to the track's input and inserts. The MIDI data that triggers the virtual instrument can be manipulated and edited in the Arrange window or Logic's MIDI editors.

Adding a Software Instrument loop to an Audio Track will automatically convert the loop to a Real Instrument loop. This can be very useful if you prefer to work with Real Instrument loops or want to use Logic's audio editing functions instead of MIDI editing.

Cycle Regions

A cycle region is a section of your Logic session that is selected and played back as a continuous loop. Cycle regions can be used as tools for creating songs or finding and identifying any problems in a specific region or a specific section of session. You can also edit audio and MIDI tracks while they are being played back as part of a cycle region.

Create a cycle region by clicking and dragging at the very top of the Timeline in the Arrange window. Figure 5.19 shows a Real Instrument loop and a four-measure cycle region.

FIGURE 5.19

A four-measure
cycle region

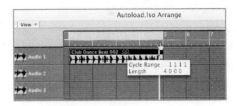

Basic Editing

Logic has multiple editing features and windows, some of which take some getting used to. However, once you get the basic concepts down, the process speeds up significantly.

Basic arrangement editing as well as cutting and pasting can be accomplished in the Arrange window. We'll start by looking at the editing tools available and move on to trying out editing in the Arrange window and Matrix Editor.

ARRANGE WINDOW EDITING TOOLS

Each of Logic's windows has it own set of tools. The Arrange window contains the most comprehensive set, many of which will be replicated in other windows. To get an idea of how each tool works, drag and drop a Real Instrument loop from the Loop Browser or any WAV or AIFF file directly onto any audio track in the Arrange window.

The tools available in the Arrange window, as shown in Figure 5.20, are as follows.

FIGURE 5.20

Logic's Arrange
window Toolbox

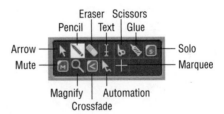

Arrow   Selects single or multiple regions. The Arrow tool can be used to lengthen, shorten, or loop a region or to move it to a new location in the Arrange window.

Pencil   Creates and selects regions. Click the Pencil tool on any blank area of the Timeline to create a new region. Like the Arrow tool, the Pencil tool can also be used to lengthen, shorten, or loop a region or to move it to a new location in the Arrange window.

Eraser   Deletes regions.

Text   Names or renames track and regions.

Scissors   Splits regions. Click anywhere on a region to split it into multiple regions.

Glue   Combines multiple regions into a single audio or MIDI region. With the Glue tool selected, hold down the Shift key while selecting adjacent regions to combine them.

Solo   Solos and plays back any selected region.

Mute   Mutes any region; click it a second time to unmute it.

Magnify   Zooms in on any track or region. A single click without dragging returns the Arrange window to its original view.

Crossfade   Creates crossfades between two adjacent regions. This is especially useful for eliminating pops and clicks from adjacent regions that start or end abruptly.

Automation   Accesses Logic's automation features, which are covered later in this chapter.

Marquee   Selects specific sections of a region for editing.

Many of the editing tools available in the Arrange window are used in Logic's other windows as well, usually performing similar functions.

EDITING IN THE ARRANGE WINDOW

The following example uses a MIDI performance, but the techniques covered also apply to audio recordings, Software Instrument loops, and Real Instrument loops.

1. Create a new Logic project.

2. Double-click the first instrument track in the Arrange window to open the Track Mixer.

3. In the Track's I/O section, choose Stereo ➢ Logic ➢ ES-1 to add an ES-1 Synth virtual instrument to the track.

4. Use your MIDI keyboard or the Caps Lock keyboard to play the ES-1.

5. Return to the Arrange window and record at least a four-measure performance.

6. Use the Magnify tool or the sliders at the top right and bottom left of the Timeline to increase the viewing size of your new performance.

7. Select the Scissors tool and use it to divide your MIDI performance into separate regions as shown in Figure 5.21.

FIGURE 5.21
Divide the performance into separate regions.

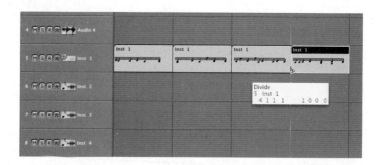

SPLIT, SHORTEN, OR KEEP?

Sometimes when splitting a MIDI performance into multiple regions you'll encounter a pop-up message that says "Overlapping Notes Found!" and asks what you'd like to do with the offending notes. Select Split to divide them between the two regions, select Shorten to cut the notes off at split point, or select Keep to leave them as they are.

Each region can now be edited or adjusted individually. Try these different options on individual regions:

◆ Use the Mute tool to mute any region.

◆ Select the Solo tool and click at the beginning of a region to play it back.

◆ Double-click any region to open it in the Matrix Editor.

◆ Use the Erase tool to erase any unwanted regions.

◆ Use the Arrow tool to lengthen, shorten, or loop any selected region.

 Real World Scenario

FIXING A FLAWED PERFORMANCE

One of the biggest effects that digital audio recording has had on the process of creating music is the ability to fix or correct imperfect performances. Whether this is a good thing or not is the subject of much debate. While I certainly agree that there's no substitute for a talented musician performing their part well, in many cases the "magic" of digital editing can save you a lot of time and headaches. It's also very nice to be able to fix problems you might not have noticed the first time around without having to set up all of your equipment, microphones, and so on all over again.

Another thing I really like about digital editing is that today's digital editing gives nonmusicians the ability to put together a cohesive performance from bits and pieces of otherwise imperfect takes. This means, for example, that someone (not unlike myself) who may not be the best piano player in the world can still realize musical ideas without needing years of piano lessons.

I'm going to use a couple of imperfect audio files to demonstrate how you might use Logic's Arrange window editing tools to fix bad performances.

1. Create a new Logic Project from your Autoload song.

2. Locate the MMA Audio\Logic\Loops folder and drag the files SweetRoll.aif and BoffGuit.aiff onto two audio tracks.

3. Line both tracks up at the beginning of the Timeline and create a four-measure cycle region.

4. Listen to the cycle region.

5. In order to get a better look at the two regions, use the sliders at the top right and bottom left of the Arrange window to increase the size of your track views.

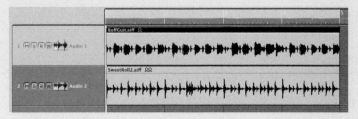

Listening to these two performances, you can hear the obvious mistakes. The third measure of the guitar performance contains nothing but wrong chords. The second measure of the drum performance sounds like someone falling down a flight of stairs. Now let's fix them.

1. Select the Scissors tool.

2. On the guitar track, make cuts at the beginning and end of the third measure.

3. Use the Eraser tool to delete the now separate third measure.

4. Choose one of the following options for fixing the track. You can either:

   ◆ Select the Arrow tool and Option+Drag a copy of the fourth measure to the third measure.

   ◆ Delete the fourth measure, select the Arrow tool, and use Logic's looping functions to loop the first two measures.

5. Select the Scissors tool again and use it to separate the second measure of the drum track.

6. Select the Eraser tool and delete the second measure of the drum track.

7. Use the Arrow tool to loop the first measure of the drum track.

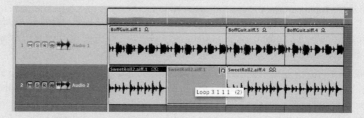

Many mistakes won't always be this clear cut and happen conveniently at specific locations within a performance, so using an entire good measure (or two) to replace a bad section is often your best bet.

MIDI EDITING WITH THE MATRIX EDITOR

Double-clicking any MIDI region in the Arrange window's Timeline will open the Matrix Editor. As you've seen, the Matrix Editor can create and arrange MIDI performances. The Matrix Editor can also work with Software Instrument loops and edit different aspects of any MIDI track.

CHANGING YOUR DEFAULT MIDI EDITOR

By default, double-clicking a MIDI region in the Arrange window Timeline will open the Matrix Editor. If you decide that you would rather use a different MIDI editor you can change this by using the menu bar to select Logic ➤ Preferences ➤ Global then choosing the Editing tab. From the Double-clicking a MIDI Region Opens drop-down menu you can select any of Logic's MIDI editors.

To get familiar with some of the Matrix Editor's functions, you'll work with an Apple Loop. In a new Logic session, open the Loop Browser and drag any Software Instrument loop onto any instrument track. Then double-click the loop in the Arrange window Timeline to open the Matrix Edit window.

On the left side of the Matrix Edit window are the Matrix Edit tools. These are basically the same as the Arrange window tools with some additions and differences. To familiarize yourself with the Matrix Editor, try adding Software Instrument Loops from the Loop Browser and then editing them in the Matrix Edit window. The main difference between the Arrange window tools and the Matrix Edit window tools are the Matrix Edit window's Quantize and Velocity tools, as well as the different functionality of the Arrow and Pencil tools.

Quantize tool   Third from the bottom, the Quantize tool is one of multiple ways to quantize your performances in Logic. With the Quantize tool selected, click and hold your mouse on any single note. Select a quantization amount from the pop-up menu. You can also use the Quantize tool to "lasso" and quantize multiple note.

Velocity tool   Second from the bottom, the Velocity tool raises and lowers the velocity (volume) of selected notes. With the Velocity tool selected, click and hold your mouse on any single note. Then drag up or down to change the volume of the selected note. You can also use the Velocity tool to lasso and raise or lower the velocity of multiple notes.

The Arrow or Pencil tool   Both the Arrow tool and the Pencil tool can be used to lengthen or shorten notes. Select a note with either tool and move your cursor to the end of the note. Click and drag to resize the note. Figure 5.22 shows a MIDI note being resized.

Figure 5.22
Resizing a note in the
Matrix Editor

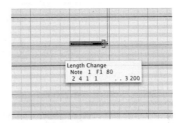

New Loops from Old Loops

One of my favorite tricks is editing a Software Instrument loop in the Matrix Edit window then saving it as a new loop. Once you've rearranged a loop by adding or removing notes in the Matrix Edit window, add the "new" loop to the Loop Browser:

1. Use the Arrow tool to select the region in the Arrange window.

2. From the Arrange window menu, choose Region ➢ Add to Apple Loops Library.

3. Name the loop and fill in the appropriate metadata.

You can even take things a step further by dragging the newly saved loop from the Loop Browser to an audio track to convert it to a Real Instrument loop and *then* saving the Real Instrument loop to the Loop Browser as well.

Logic Instruments

Logic's included instruments are another one of its strongest features. Realistic keyboards, complex virtual synthesizers, and an excellent sampler that can import multiple file types are all built in to the Logic program. Combined with Logic's effects and MIDI editors, these virtual instruments can create music in just about any style imaginable.

The Keyboards

Logic includes three virtual keyboards based on popular instruments that can be used across the musical spectrum. Logic's virtual organ, clavinet, and electric piano each contain various instrument models, presets, and built-in effects for creating an incredible range of keyboard sounds suitable for use in any genre.

EVB3 TONEWHEEL ORGAN

Based on the Hammond B3 the EVB3 Tonewheel organ is a very realistic-sounding virtual organ instrument. Its preset categories include Pop, Rock, Jazz, Theatre, and Vintage Organ Emulations. The EVB3 allows you to adjust the settings just as you can with a "real" organ, including adding and removing click sounds to each note, a variety of vibrato settings, and various drawbar configurations for creating wildly different sounds. In the bottom right corner of the plug-in interface you can choose from a list of virtual cabinet types.

Add the EVB3 to any session by clicking the input field of any instrument track and selecting Stereo ➤ Logic ➤ EVB3 (Tonewheel Organ). Figure 5.23 shows the EVB3 Tonewheel organ.

FIGURE 5.23

The EVB3 Tonewheel organ

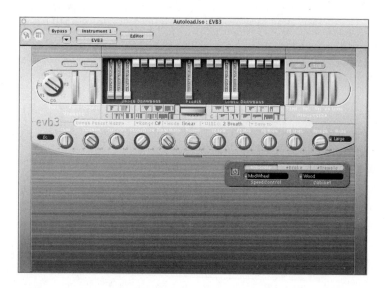

EVD6 ELECTRIC CLAV

The EVD6 Electric Clav is based on the Hohner Clavinet D and contains some fantastic Clavinet sounds like those featured prominently in Stevie Wonder's "Superstition" or Led Zeppelin's "Houses of the Holy." It also has presets for other stringed instruments and sounds including guitars and harps and organs. The Effect Sounds and Other Instruments categories contain some unexpected bonuses as well.

Add the EVD6 to any session by clicking the input field of any instrument track and selecting Stereo ➤ Logic ➤ EVD68 (Electric Clav). Figure 5.24 shows the EVD6 Electric Clav.

◆ On the left side of the interface are the string parameters. Use these sliders to adjust the setting for the basic tone settings and instrument sound.

◆ In the middle of the interface are the pickup settings. Click in the Pickup Mode field to choose the pickup emulation.

FIGURE 5.24
The EVD6
Electric Clav

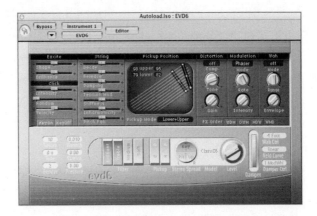

FIGURE 5.24
The EVD6
Electric Clav

◆ On the right side of the interface are the effects: distortion, modulation, and wah. Click in the field just above the parameter knobs to adjust the distortion level or to choose the type of modulation effect or type of wah effect. Use the parameter knobs to adjust the levels and intensity of the various effects.

EVP88 ELECTRIC PIANO

The EVP88 is a warm-sounding and very realistic electric piano. The included presets demonstrate the different genres most commonly associated with electric piano: funk, jazz, and rock. The EVP88 is also capable of creating some very nice ambient tones, especially when combined with a delay or reverb plug-in effect. Most of the EVP88's instruments and presets are very responsive to MIDI velocity. Playing your MIDI keyboard "hard" or creating MIDI notes at a high velocity will create a very different tone than a more delicate or lower velocity performance.

Add the EVP88 to any session by clicking the input field of any instrument track and selecting Stereo ➤ Logic ➤ EVP88 (Electric Piano). Figure 5.25 shows the EVP88 electric piano.

FIGURE 5.25
The EVP88 electric
piano

The EVP88 has a lot of great sounds and is very easy to adjust:

◆ Use the Selector knob at the top of the interface to choose one of the 15 different models.

◆ Use the Voices knob to choose up 88 notes of polyphony.

◆ Use the tuning knob to adjust the instruments tuning incrementally.

◆ On the bottom right side of the interface are three separate fields containing modulation effects: phaser, tremolo, and chorus.

Logic's Synths

Logic has multiple included synthesizers, any one of which can keep you occupied for days at a time. Each one has its own set of practical applications and is conducive to a wide range of sounds or styles. We'll take a quick look here at some of Logic's synthesizers, describing their basic functions and suggesting some possible applications.

For in-depth descriptions of common synthesizer parameters see Chapter 9, "Virtual Instruments."

THE BASIC SYNTHS

Logic's simplest synthesizers are very easy to use. They all contain easily adjustable parameter knobs and sliders and a set of simple presets to give you an idea of the available sounds and possibilities in each instrument.

The ES M (ES Mono)

Add the ES M (ES Mono) synthesizer by selecting Mono ➤ Logic ➤ ES M from any instrument track I/O. The ES M is a mono (single voice) synthesizer most often used to create bass tracks. Its presets are for the most part techno/electronic bass-oriented. To try out the ES M synth:

1. Choose any of the included presets.

2. Use the 8, 16, and 32 buttons to set the octave of the synth.

3. Use the Mix knob to choose the mix of the two waveforms.

4. Adjust the Glide knob to control how the one note slides upward or downward into the next.

The ES E (Ensemble Synth)

The ES E contains a list of presets to get you started. Try out the Ice Synth, Pulse Sweeps, and Vintage Classic Pad presets to get an idea of the kinds of sounds you would use ES E for. This synthesizer is especially useful for ambient sounds, swells, and long sustained notes.

The ES P (E Poly)

The ES P synth is an extremely versatile instrument and is somewhere in the middle of the spectrum as far as ease of use goes.

Add it to any session by clicking the input field of any instrument track and selecting Stereo ➤ Logic ➤ ES P (Polyphonic Synth).

1. Figure 5.26 shows the ES P synthesizer.

Use your MIDI keyboard or the Caps Lock keyboard to try out the presets like Effect Take Off, Game Boy, and Juno Pad to get an idea of the range of available sounds.

FIGURE 5.26
The ES P synth

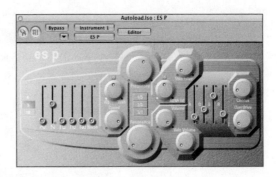

Here's a brief tutorial to get you started:

1. Select the preset Lead Pad from the preset menu (the upside down triangle at the top left of the instrument interface).

2. Click the 4, 8, or 16 button to change the octave range of the ES P.

3. The output of the ES P is made up from the six faders on the left side of the synth. The first five faders control various waveforms, and the sixth adds noise. Try raising and lowering the faders to create new sounds.

4. On the right side of the synthesizer interface are the ADSR sliders, controlling the standard Attack, Decay, Sustain, and Release functions found on many synthesizers. Use your mouse to change these settings.

For more information on these parameters, see Chapter 9.

INTRODUCING THE "DEEPER" SYNTHS

The next level of Logic synths are even more complex. These synths feature complex sound-generating and routing features as well as lots of included presets. These synths include the ES1, ES2, and Sculpture synthesizers. The ES2 is a virtual-analog synth with a great collection of presets and the ability to generate an incredible range of sounds.

When it comes to Logic's more involved synthesizer instruments, however, one in particular stands out, the Sculpture synthesizer. Sculpture is an entirely new type of synthesizer based on new types of synthesis. Sculptures starts with a virtual "string" and the actual sounds are created by up to three virtual "objects" which can vibrate the string in different ways. From there the signal passes through virtual "pickups" similar to those on an electric guitar or other amplified instrument. From the pickups the signal is then routed through various envelopes, shapers, filters, and effects, each one capable of drastically altering the sound produced by the Sculpture. Figure 5.27 shows the Sculpture Synth.

Add Sculpture to a track by clicking the Input field and selecting Stereo ➤ Logic ➤ Sculpture (Modeling Synth).

FIGURE 5.27

The Sculpture Synth

FIGURE 5.27

The Sculpture Synth

Sculpture comes with a few hundred presets that cover some of the range of possibilities available. Try out some of Sculpture's included presets from the Settings menu.

To begin getting familiar with Sculpture, you'll go through the steps of creating a new preset:

1. From the Settings menu, choose #default or Factory ➢ #default.

2. Use your MIDI keyboard to play the default sound. It sounds very much like a nylon-stringed guitar.

3. In the very center of the Sculpture window is a square with the word "Material" in the middle. In each of the four corners are different sound types. Use your mouse to navigate the Material box and select one of the four corners or any other location.

4. On the left side of the Sculpture interface are the three objects that create sounds. The default preset is the sound of the string being vibrated by Object 1. Try turning off Object 1 and listening to the sound of Objects 2 and 3.

   The active objects are highlighted in blue. At least one object must be active to create a sound with Sculpture. You can use any single object or a combination of multiple objects to create sounds.

5. Now deselect Objects 2 and 3 and turn Object 1 back on.

6. Each object has a Type field that you can use to select a different type of interaction between the object and the string. Object 1's Type field currently reads "Impulse." Click the word "Impulse" to view the other choices in the type menu.

7. From the object the sound travels to the pickups in the left center of the interface. Adjust the pickups by moving the controls marked A and B and 1, 2, and 3.

8. Next, the sound travels to the Amplitude envelope. Located to the right of the Material box, the Amplitude envelope contains a standard ADSR (Attack, Decay, Sustain, and Release) envelope and a Level knob, which you can use to raise or lower the overall volume of the preset. Adjust any of the ADSR settings and use the Level knob to raise the overall volume of the preset.

9. Next in the signal chain is the filter, located underneath the Material box. Turn on the Filter by clicking the word Filter. Click one of five EQ filters underneath the filter knobs: HiPass, LoPass, Peak, BndPass, or Notch.

10. To the right of the Filter are the Body EQ controls. Turn them on by clicking the Body EQ button on the left side of the field.

11. At the top right of the Sculpture are the Stereo Delay controls, which can be used to add long, short, simple, or extremely complicated delay effects to your preset. Click the Stereo Delay button to turn the delay effect on.

12. Save your preset by selecting Save Settings As from the presets drop-down menu. Use the dialog box to create a new folder to save your original presets in.

Once you've created a new preset with a single object, try activating the other objects. Changing an object's type or any other parameter can have a drastic effect on the overall sound of a preset.

ULTRABEAT DRUM SYNTH (LOGIC PRO ONLY)

Logic's Ultrabeat drum machine is one of its coolest included instruments. Following the same pattern as many of Logic's features, Ultrabeat can be operated using very basic programming methods, but if you choose to go deeper with it you can access some very intensive sound-shaping and editing features.

Using Ultrabeat

To get started with the Ultrabeat:

1. Create a new Logic session with your Autoload song.

2. Double-click the first instrument track and open the Mixer window.

3. Select the input field in the I/O section and choose Stereo ➤ Logic ➤ Ultrabeat (Drum Synth). Figure 5.28 shows the Ultrabeat Drum Synth.

The Ultrabeat is divided into three main sections:

Drum Mixer   On the left side of the Ultrabeat is the Drum Mixer, where you will see a list of all of the currently available sounds. Each sound has its own Mute and Solo buttons and Panning knob. Click your mouse on the vertical keyboard at the far left of the window to preview any sound. You can also use your MIDI keyboard to play the Ultrabeat and preview sounds. Ultrabeat's sounds are mapped to the note range C1–C3 on your MIDI keyboard.

Synthesizer   Taking up most of the instrument's real estate in the middle/right section of the Ultrabeat is the synthesizer. This is one of the most complex drum sample editors you'll find anywhere. The synthesizer contains two separate oscillators, one at the top and one at the bottom. There's also a noise generator, multiple filters, distortion effects, and more.

FIGURE 5.28

The Ultrabeat
Drum Synth

Sequencer   The bottom section of the Ultrabeat contains the sequencer. This is where you can create drum patterns and sequences with the Ultrabeat. The step sequencer is very easy to operate and control and is programmed by mouse clicks and dragging.

Aside from the ability to create and extensively edit and shape the sounds of your own drum kits, Ultrabeat also comes with many kits already installed. You can access these from the Settings/ Presets menu (the upside-down triangle) at the top of the plug-in window. Let's use one of these kits to take a look at using Ultrabeat's sequencer:

1. Use the Settings button to view the available drum banks and drums kits.

2. Select and load the kit Drum Sets ➢ Analog Electro kit.

3. Turn the Ultrabeat sequencer on by clicking the Power button near the bottom left.

4. Click the Play button to right of the Power button to play the sequence.

5. Take a look at the sequencer while the pattern is playing: By default, when you loaded the Analog Electro kit the kick drum was selected in the Drum Mixer. Click the kick drum's Solo button to hear it alone. You can see the notes that are triggering the kick drum in the sequencer.

To add more notes to the kick drum sequence:

1. Click your mouse on an empty note in the sequencer.

2. Drag your mouse up or down to set the velocity of the note.

3. Drag your mouse to the left or right for a longer note.

4. Delete notes in the sequencer by clicking the highlighted note number at the top of the sequencer to "turn off" a note.

5. Unsolo the kick drum to hear the entire sequence again.

As the sequence plays you can see certain parameters from the sequencer reflected in the Drum Mixer. When a note is triggered in the sequencer, the corresponding keyboard note in the drum mixer turns blue momentarily. Additionally, any drum sound that is used in the current sequence will have the letters "sq" in white next to its name in the Drum Mixer.

Adding a Sequence to Your Session

There are many ways to incorporate Ultrabeat into your sessions. For example, it's possible to create multiple sequences with Ultrabeat and use MIDI information to trigger them externally in any order. Or you can play the Ultrabeat in real time with your MIDI keyboard or the Caps Lock keyboard and record the performance just like any virtual instrument. The following tutorial shows you a quick way to create multiple sequences in Ultrabeat and add them to your sessions:

1. Use the settings menu to load the kit Tutorial Settings ➢ Tutorial Kit.

2. Turn the sequencer on and create a simple beat using the kick drum snare drum and hi-hat. If you are not familiar with drum programming, use the following to program a beat:

   ◆ Kick drum 1, 5, 13, 15, 21, 23, 27

   ◆ Snare drum 9, 25

   ◆ Hi-hat 1, 5, 9, 13, 17, 21, 25, 29

3. Once you have created a beat, select the Pattern button on the bottom left of the Ultrabeat window.

4. Drag the Pattern button directly onto the track in the Arrange window containing the Ultrabeat instrument. This will create a new MIDI region containing the drum sequence.

5. Place the region at the beginning of the Logic song in the Timeline.

6. Turn off the Ultrabeat sequencer and play back the sequence.

   The MIDI region you've created works exactly like any other MIDI region in Logic. You can edit or loop the region in the Arrange window or double-click the region to open the Matrix Editor.

7. Return to the Ultrabeat window and create a variation on the drum pattern.

8. Click and drag the Pattern button to the same track in the Arrange window to add the new sequence.

9. Arrange the sequences in any order in the Arrange window.

Using this method, create and add multiple patterns to your sessions with Ultrabeat.

THE EXS24 MKII SAMPLER

The EXS24 mkII comes with Logic Pro only. Logic Express comes with a sampler called the EXSP24 Sample Player. The Logic Express version is not able to load or import samples from other libraries, but it does come with many of the same included instruments, access to GarageBand instruments, and sample editing functions.

Logic Pro's ESX24 Sampler (Figure 5.29) is an extremely powerful sampling instrument that comes with a huge collection of already installed instruments. This includes all of GarageBand's instruments and presets, as well as a collection of pianos, stringed instruments, ethnic instruments, drum kits, and much more. You can create your own EXS24 instruments from AIFF or WAV samples REX files or any other audio source.

FIGURE 5.29

The EXS24 interface

Aside from the included sample library, the ESX24 is also capable of loading sampled instruments from many different file formats including WAV, AIFF, AKAI, SampleCell, and RX2.

To use the ESX24 in a session:

1. Create a new session and double-click any available instrument track to open the Mixer window.

2. Add the ESX24 to the I/O section of the instrument track by selecting Stereo ➤ Logic ➤ ESX24 (Sampler).

3. Load any of the included sampler instruments by clicking the black field at the top of the silver panel on the right side of the EXS24 interface. Select from any of the available categories to load an instrument. Figure 5.30 shows an instrument loaded in the silver panel area.

4. Use your MIDI controller or the Caps Lock keyboard to play the instrument or use the Matrix Editor to create a MIDI performance.

FIGURE 5.30

An instrument loaded
in the EXS24 mkII

Here you'll create a simple multisampled piano instrument:

1. Create a new session and double-click any available instrument track to open the Mixer window.

2. Add the ESX24 to the I/O section of the instrument track by selecting Stereo ➤ Logic ➤ ESX24 (Sampler).

3. Instead of selecting an instrument from the Instrument menu, click the Edit button near the top right corner of the ESX24 interface. This will open the EXS24 Instrument Editor. You may have to move the EXS24 interface out of the way to access the Instrument Editor window.

4. Select Instrument ➤ New from the Instrument Editor's menu.

5. Select Instrument ➤ Save As from the Instrument Editor's menu.

6. Name the Instrument New Piano and save it in the `Sampler Instruments` folder.

7. Choose Zone ➤ Load Multiple Samples from the Instrument Editor's menu.

8. Use the Load Multiple Samples dialog box to locate the folder `MMA Audio\Logic\EXS24`.

9. Click the Add All button to add all of the folder's piano samples.

10. Click Done.

11. In the Load Multiple Samples pop-up window that appears next, select "Auto Map" by Reading the Root Key from the Audio File.

12. Click OK.

13. Figure 5.31 shows the new EXS24 Instrument's Editor window.

FIGURE 5.31
The EXS24's Instrument Editor window

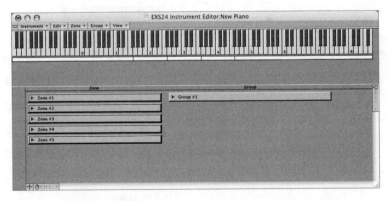

To load and play your new EXS24 instrument:

1. Select Instrument ➤ Save in the Instrument Editor window and then use the Close Window button on the top left to close the Instrument Editor window.

2. Click the Load Instrument field at the top of the silver panel in the EXS24 interface and select Refresh Menu.

3. Click the same field again and select Sampler Instruments ➤ New Piano.

4. Use your MIDI controller or the Caps Lock keyboard to play the instrument, or use the Matrix Editor to create a MIDI performance.

The EXS24 has many more features, including all of the editable parameters typically found on any sampler device, which are discussed in Chapter 9.

Included Effects

Another one of Logic's biggest strengths is the included plug-in effects. Both Logic Express and Logic Pro come with a wealth of effects, including multiple reverbs, delays, compressors, modulation effects, EQs, and more. In addition, each of the included plug-ins comes with a number of presets to highlight its abilities and to get you started applying the effect to your MIDI and audio tracks.

PRE-FADER RECORDING

All recording in Logic takes place "pre-fader." This means that you can add effects as you are recording, but the actual effect is not recorded onto the track. This can work either in your favor or against you depending on how you proceed. For example, recording a vocal track with lots of reverb and chorus may sound better as it's being recorded, but when you go to mix the track and want to remove some of the effect you may find a weak vocal performance that was masked by the effects. On the other hand a vocalist's confidence can often be boosted by adding a slight effect (like compression or delay), which can then result in a better performance.

Logic's effects are accessed by adding them as "inserts"—inserting them into the signal path on a selected track. You can add effects to a track by using the channel strip in the Arrange window or selecting a channel strip in the Mixer window.

To add an effect, click any open (empty) insert field, and then:

◆ For a mono track, select Mono ➤ Logic and then choose the effect category and effect.

◆ For stereo tracks, choose Stereo ➤ Logic then the effect category and effect.

Once you have added an effect, its interface will appear. Most Logic effects have presets to get you started with the effect or to access commonly used parameters. Open the effect's presets menu by clicking the upside-down triangle near the upper left corner of the plug-in window. Figure 5.32 shows the preset menu of Logic's Tape Delay effect.

Delays

Logic comes with three included delay effects, useful for different situations and musical styles.

Sample Delay   Sample Delay is the simplest, allowing you to delay the signal by tiny increments (samples) in order to correct minor phase problems and other issues associated with multichannel microphones.

Stereo Delay   Logic's most standard delay effect is the Stereo Delay. Added to any stereo track you can control the left and right delays separately or together. You can also control the feedback for each channel and mix the two signals through the "crossfeed" parameters.

FIGURE 5.32

FIGURE 5.32
The Tape Delay Effect
preset menu

Tape Delay   The Tape Delay simulates vintage tape-based effects units like the Echoplex and Roland Space Echo. The Tape Delay is useful for all kinds of music, especially reggae/dub styles and psychedelic rock.

Try out the Tape Delay plug-in effect with the following exercise:

1. Open the Loop Browser and in the Organ category locate one of the Island Reggae organ loops.

2. Drag the loop from the Loop Browser onto any audio track in the Arrange window.

3. Create a cycle region the length of the loop.

4. Add the Tape Delay as an insert on the organ track and begin playback.

5. Select the preset Space Dub Delay.

6. During playback, raise and lower the Feedback slider on the left side of the Tape Delay interface. Figure 5.33 shows the Tape Delay with the Space Dub Preset.

FIGURE 5.33
The Tape Delay
interface

Distortion

Logic comes with eight distortion-related plug-ins. Many of these serve similar functions. You can use the Clip Distortion, Distortion, Distortion II, and Phase distortion plug-ins to overdrive and distort your tracks. Each distortion plug-in has a series of presets to try out. Try applying a small amount of a distortion effect to make a track stand out in a mix. Apply a larger amount to create lo-fi tracks, like extremely overdriven drum loops.

Let's take a look at Logic's most in-depth distortion effect for guitar and bass players, the virtual amplifier plug-in Guitar Amp Pro. (Logic Express contains a light version called Guitar Amp that is very similar but doesn't have the ability to save changes to presets.)

Figure 5.34 shows the Guitar Amp Pro plug-in.

FIGURE 5.34

The Guitar Amp Pro plug-in

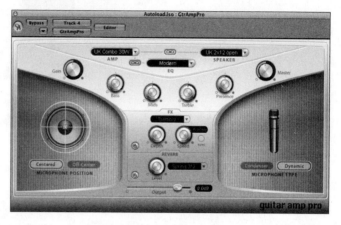

To use Guitar Amp Pro:

1. Plug your guitar or bass into your audio interface. Make sure the input you are using on your audio interface corresponds to the input field on the I/O section of the selected channel strip.

2. To make sure the signal is routed correctly, arm the track for recording by clicking the Record button at the bottom of the channel strip. If your setup is working correctly you should now hear your guitar through your speakers or headphones.

3. To add Guitar Amp Pro to the selected channel strip as an insert, choose Stereo ➤ Logic ➤ Distortion ➤ Guitar Amp Pro.

4. Select a preset from the Amp menu at the top of the interface. You can also create your own presets by adjusting the parameters of the virtual amplifier.

At the top of the Guitar Amp Pro window you'll see the drop-down menus where you can create your own presets by choosing any combination of the 11 different kinds of amps, 4 basic EQ settings, and 15 cabinet (speaker) types.

In the middle section you'll see the standard parameters for any guitar amplifier: Gain, Bass, Mids, Treble, Presence, and Master volume. In the center of the window you can add a tremolo or vibrato effect and/or a reverb effect. These effects are turned on and off by clicking the power buttons on the left side of each effect's field.

On the left and right side are the microphone position and microphone type settings. Choosing the Off-Center and Condenser settings will give you a roomier sound. Choose the Centered and Dynamic settings for a closer, tighter sound.

Dynamics

Logic's dynamics plug-ins include two limiters, two gates, and three compressors. At opposite ends of the spectrum are the very basic Silver Compressor and the more complicated Multipressor. Let's take a look at the middle ground, the Compressor shown in Figure 5.35.

FIGURE 5.35

The Compressor plug-in

1. Create a new Logic project.

2. Open the Loop Browser and select the All Drums Category.

3. Select the Software Instrument Loop Classic Rock Beat 02 and drag it to a audio track (this converts it to a Real Instrument loop).

4. Add the Compressor to the drum track as an insert by selecting Mono or Stereo ➤ Logic ➤ Dynamics ➤ Compressor.

5. Create a cycle region the length of the loop and press the spacebar to begin playback.

   The Compressor plug-in comes with a very impressive list of presets covering everything from final mix compression to drum kits, vocals, and stringed instruments. You can use these presets as they are or as a starting point for creating your own presets. These presets also make an excellent introduction to the use of digital compression effects.

6. Click the preset menu button (the upside-down triangle at the top left of the plug-in interface) and from the Compressor Tools preset category try out the FX Pump It Up preset.

7. Click the Bypass button at the top left of the plug-in interface to compare the dry and effected track.

With this preset you can hear how adding the compressor to the track brings out certain overtones in the snare drum and adds a more "live" feeling to the drum track.

For more information on digital compression, see Chapter 8, "Plug-ins."

EQ

Logic comes with multiple EQ plug-ins for different applications. The DJ EQ, High Shelving EQ, and Low Shelving EQ are used for quick adjustment of specific frequencies. The Fat EQ is a five-band parametric EQ with no included presets.

The Channel EQ can be accessed by clicking the Channel EQ field at the top of every channel strip or by choosing Mono or Stereo ➤ Logic ➤ EQ ➤ Channel EQ. This is the most comprehensive of the included EQ plug-ins. It also comes with a very large collection of presets for vocals, drums, a wide range of instruments, and final mixes and mastering. Figure 5.36 shows the Channel EQ plug-in.

One of the coolest things about the Channel EQ presets is that there are multiple presets for similar things. For example, when equalizing a bass track you might try the Bass Boost or Modern Jazz Bass presets. If those don't work for your track, you can also try one of the Bass Improve presets from the Miscellaneous EQ Tools category.

FIGURE 5.36

The Channel
EQ plug-in

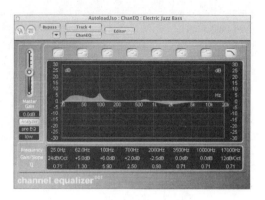

Modulation Effects

Logic includes the entire range of modulation-based effects, including Chorus, Phaser, Flanger, Tremolo, and Vibrato. Each of these effects has its own set of presets and can be added to audio or instrument tracks. The Modulation Delay effect combines multiple effects in one unit with adjustable presets for chorus, flanging, and tremolo effects. One of my favorite Logic effects is the Ringshifter Ring Modulator shown in Figure 5.37.

FIGURE 5.37

Ringshifter Ring
Modulator

Ring modulators are sometimes used on guitars for techno, machine-like effects. The Ringshifter can also be to achieve interesting robot-like vocals or strange vocal sounds like those on the Nine Inch Nails song "Gave Up." Ring modulators are often associated with adding nontraditional and sometimes nonmusical elements into a mix. The Ringshifter is much more than just a ring modulator, though. It also contains some great-sounding more traditional possibilities.

1. Use the Loop Browser to locate the loop `Acoustic Noodling 03` in the Guitar category.

2. Drag and drop the loop onto the Arrange window and create a two-measure cycle region.

3. Add the Ringshifter as an insert effect.

4. Select the preset Yaiih from the bottom of the preset list. This is one of the more standard-sounding presets.

5. Adjust the giant frequency knob in the center of the Ringshifter interface for traditional phaser-like modulation effects.

6. Try out some of the other presets. Most of them are pretty dramatic and contain interesting overtones or added rhythmic artifacts.

7. To create less dramatic presets:

8. Select an instrument track and add a virtual instrument. Use something that contains very simple legato notes, like a cello sample in the EXS24 or a basic synth tone.

9. Add the Ringshifter as a plug-in effect.

10. Use your MIDI keyboard or the Caps Lock keyboard to play the instrument and effect while you make the following adjustments:

    A. Select the #default preset.

    B. Click the Dual button in the top left corner of the Ringshifter interface.

    C. Select the Frequency knob in the center and make minor adjustments to the left or right.

    D. Click the Power button in the LFO field.

    E. Select the LFO slider to the right of the frequency knob and raise it slightly (try around the 0.400 range).

11. Save a preset by selecting Save Settings As from the preset drop-down menu.

Try making minor adjustments to the other parameters to create subtler effects with the Ringshifter.

Reverb

The included reverb plug-ins range from simple (AVerb) to the somewhat complicated (Platinum Verb) to the really incredible (the Space Designer). The EnVerb is fairly straightforward but also contains some very impressive and dramatic presets, including a number of reverse reverb effects. The Space Designer (Logic Pro only) is shown in Figure 5.38.

FIGURE 5.38

The Space Designer

The Space Designer is an exceptionally complex plug-in and comes with 36 *categories* of presets. Some categories even contain subcategories (check out Misc. Rooms and Misc. Reverbs in particular). Some preset categories contain more than 30 individual presets.

Aside from the drum, instrument, and vocal presets the Space Designer contains some pretty amazing, very different reverb-based effects. Many of these are located in the Misc. Delays and Effects Delays categories.

To adjust the results of the Space Designer, use the two sliders on the right side of the interface. The Direct slider adjusts how much of the original (dry) signal is output. Raising the Reverb slider adds more of the selected preset to the track.

Special

The Special category contains plug-ins that may not fall into any specific category. This category includes:

- ◆ Denoiser
- ◆ Exciter
- ◆ Grooveshifter
- ◆ Pitch correction
- ◆ Pitch Shifter II
- ◆ Spectral Gate
- ◆ Stereo enhancer
- ◆ Subbass
- ◆ Stereo spread
- ◆ Vocal enhancer

Automating Effects

Creating automation on Logic effects is very simple. I'll use the Stereo Delay as an example:

1. Use the Loop Browser to add any drum loop to an audio or instrument track.

2. Add the Stereo Delay as an insert effect.

3. Located on the channel strip just above the Level meter and Pan knob is the Automation field. Click the Automation drop-down menu and choose Write.

4. Press the zero (0) key on your Apple keyboard to start the session from the beginning.

5. Press the spacebar to begin playback.

6. Adjust any parameters on the Stereo Delay.

7. Click the Automation drop-down menu and choose Read.

8. Start playback from the beginning of the session to hear your automation.

Adding Effects on Bus Tracks

One common way to utilize effects in any DAW program is to put the effect on an auxiliary (or aux) or bus track then route ("send") a signal from the audio or instrument track to the effected bus or aux track. This allows you to leave your original track unchanged and also lets you use a single effect on multiple tracks. Each DAW handles this kind of effects processing differently, often with different names for the same kinds of functionality. For example, I've covered similar territory in other chapters, such as Reason's Send and Return channels on its included mixer and Pro Tools sends and aux tracks.

In Logic this is accomplished by using sends and bus tracks, as I'll cover in the next section.

VIEWING THE BUSSES

In order to use the bus tracks, you have to make them visible in our Logic session. To do this:

1. Create a new Logic session.

2. Locate the file DrumLogic1.aif in the MMA\Logic\Loops folder.

3. Drag and drop the DrumLogic1.aif file onto any audio track.

4. Double-click the track header to open the Track Mixer.

5. Click the Global button on the left side of the Track Mixer. This allows you to see all of the available tracks in this session, including the aux tracks, bus tracks, and Master fader.

6. Scroll to the right to view the bus tracks and Master fader.

7. Double-click the tracks Bus 1 and Bus 2 to make them visible in the Arrange and Track Mixer windows.

8. Deselect the Global button. Figure 5.39 shows the Bus 1 and Bus 2 tracks in the Track Mixer window.

MIX AND MATCH

Here's another example of there being multiple ways to work in Logic. I prefer to do most of my routing and mixing in the Track Mixer, but you can also do the same kinds of work in the Environment window, which has all of the available tracks visible. To access the Environment window, go to the menu bar and choose Windows ➤ Environment or Audio ➤ Audio Mixer.

FIGURE 5.39
Bus 1 and 2 in the
Track Mixer

ROUTING EFFECTS

Now that your bus tracks are visible, you can use them to add a reverb effect to two different tracks:

1. Use the Loop Browser to add any two loops to Audio Tracks 1 and 2.

2. Add the EnVerb as an insert on the Bus 1 track (Stereo ➤ Logic ➤ Reverb ➤ EnVerb).

3. Select the Reverse Reverb Long preset.

4. Select the first audio track, click in the top Sends field and choose Bus 1. A knob will appear to the right of the Sends field.

5. Use the knob to raise the amount of signal being sent to the Bus 1 track.

   Figure 5.40 shows the Sends section of audio track one's channel strip.

FIGURE 5.40
The Sends field on
Audio Track 1

6. Create a send to Bus 1 on Audio Track 2 and raise the Send knob.

7. Add a plug-in effect on Bus 2 and create a second Send on Audio Track 1.

A ReWire Session with Logic and Reason

While previous versions of Logic made the ReWire process a bit more complicated than it needed to be, the general consensus is that in Logic 7.2 Apple finally has the ReWire implementation worked out. Logic even incorporates stereo ReWire tracks to make the process easier.

One of the great ways to take advantage of ReWire is to create a song in Reason and then use another program (such as Logic) to do your final mixes. This allows you to take advantage of the compressors, EQs, and other plug-in effects contained in Logic that aren't available in Reason. It also gives you a chance to utilize Logic's virtual instruments or add your own live performance audio tracks.

For these sessions in Reason's Preferences the default song should be "Empty Rack." If you don't own Reason but would like to try the following tutorials, you can use the Reason Demo available at `http://www.propellerheads.se`.

With any ReWire session, you'll open the master program first, in this case Logic. To get started with Logic and Reason:

1. Create a new Logic project or open an existing project.

2. Start Reason and create a Mixer 14:2 and a Dr. Rex Loop Player.

3. Select an empty instrument track in Logic's Arrange window.

4. The Object Parameters box is located just below the Tools box in Logic's Arrange window. If the Objects Parameters box is minimized, click the triangle on the left side of the box to open it.

5. Use the Text Tool to rename the track "Reason" in the Object Parameters box.

6. In the Object Parameters box, select Channel ➤ ReWire Stereo ➤ Reason ➤ RW: Mix L/R.

   Figure 5.41 shows the track settings in the Object Parameters box.

7. In Reason, use the Browse Loop button on the Dr. Rex Loop Player to Load any REX loop from the Reason Factory Sound Bank and click the Preview button on the Dr. Rex.

FIGURE 5.41
The Object
Parameters box

You will have audio from Reason routed to a single stereo track in Logic. Double-click the "Reason" track in Logic's Arrange window to open the Track Mixer. Here you can adjust the pan and volume settings and add effects as you would with any other track.

Using this simple configuration you can create arrangements in both Logic and Reason simultaneously. You can also use this configuration to open an existing Reason song and add it to a Logic session. If you are using Reason to create simple backing tracks or taking advantage of a single instrument, this simple setup will be all you need to use the two programs together.

Complex Routing

In order to take full advantage of Logic's plug-in and/or mixing capabilities, you will want to create more complex routing, sending individual tracks from Reason to individual tracks in Logic. To do this:

1. Create a new Logic session.

2. Select the first instrument track in Logic and, in the Object Parameters box, name it Dr. Rex One.

3. With the track selected, in the Object Parameters box select Channel ➤ ReWire Stereo ➤ Reason ➤ RW: Mix L/R.

   Even though it reads "Mix L/R," another name for this setting could be ReWire 1/2 since you are actually routing the signal through Reason's output 1 and output 2.

4. Select the second instrument track and rename it SubTractor One.

5. In Logic's Object Parameters box, select Channel ➤ ReWire ➤ Reason ➤ RW: Channel 3.

6. Create a four-measure cycle region in Logic.

7. Start Reason and select File ➤ Open.

8. Use the Open File dialog box to locate the file `LogicReason2.rns` in the `MMA\Logic\ReWire` folder.

9. Press the Tab key on your Apple keyboard to view Reason's output routing.

   In most Reason sessions all of your instruments will be routed through a Mixer 14:2 and the output of the Reason Hardware Interface will be routed through Outputs 1 and 2. However, this session has no Mixer 14:2, and in sessions with no Mixer 14:2 the first instrument you create (in this case the Dr. Rex Loop Player) will automatically be routed to Outputs 1 and 2 on the Reason hardware interface. Every instrument you create after that will have to be routed manually.

10. Click the Audio Output of the SubTractor to create a virtual cable.

11. Drag the virtual cable to Input 3 on the Reason hardware interface. The output of the SubTractor is now routed to the SubTractor One track in Logic.

12. Use the Browse Loop button to load a loop into the Dr. Rex Loop Player, then click the To Track button to send the Dr. Rex Loop to the Sequencer track.

13. Create a performance with the SubTractor using your MIDI keyboard or the Key Lane.

14. Start playback in either Reason or Logic.

Since the Dr. Rex and the SubTractor are on different tracks in Logic, you can apply different effects to each track or adjust the volume and panning levels separately.

From here you can create more ReWire inputs in Logic, then create more Reason instruments and route them to individual tracks in Logic. Use this setup to take existing Reason songs and mix them in Logic or create entire new song by routing instruments.

Controlling Reason Instruments in Logic

If you are comfortable with Logic's MIDI editing functions you may decide to do all of your MIDI editing for a ReWire sessions within Logic.

To use Logic to control individual Reason instruments, you need to create ReWire Objects in the Environment window and route them to individual instrument tracks. The ReWire Object you create will send the MIDI data from Logic directly to the Reason instrument.

Once you have a configuration you'd like to work with, you may want to save both the Logic project and Reason song as recallable templates. You'll be working with mono tracks only in this section.

1. Create a new Logic project.

2. Select the first instrument track and, in the Object Parameters box choose Channel ➤ ReWire ➤ Reason ➤ RW:Mix L.

OBJECTS AND ENVIRONMENTS

Logic Environments are considered the "brain" of the program. Customizing Logic Environments is one of the ways that advanced users can take advantage of even more features and functionality in Logic. Objects are the "pieces" that make up a Logic Environment. Without getting too deeply into what is one of the most complicated and confusing aspects of the program, you'll be using an Environment window to create a ReWire Object for routing MIDI information to Reason.

---

3. Select the second instrument track and, in the Object Parameters box, choose Channel ➢ ReWire ➢ Reason ➢ RW:Mix R.

4. In the Object Parameters box, rename the first track Synth 1 L and the second track Synth 1 R.

5. Double-click the track Synth Track 1 L to open the Track Mixer window.

6. Start Reason and create a Malström Synth. The synth will automatically be routed to Reason's first two outputs. If you have a MIDI keyboard or other controller connected, make sure to *deselect* the Malström in the Reason Sequencer so that your MIDI keyboard is not triggering the device.

7. In Logic's Track Mixer, select and highlight Synth Track 1 L, then choose Windows ➢ Environment to open the Environment window.

8. From the Environment window's menu, choose New ➢ Internal ➢ ReWire to create a new ReWire object.

9. Select the ReWire object in the Environment window and, in the ReWire Object Parameters box, choose the following settings:

Device	Reason
Bus	6
Channel	Malström 1

10. Click your mouse near the top of Synth 1 L track in the Environment window to select and highlight the track.

11. Connect the track to the ReWire object by clicking and dragging from the top right corner of the channel strip, creating a virtual "wire" to the ReWire object.

Figure 5.42 shows the cabling in the Environment window.

FIGURE 5.42
The ReWire Object connected to the Synth 1 L track in the Environment window

12. Close the Environment window and the Track Mixer window.

13. Use your new ReWire object to record a performance from your MIDI controller or use the Pencil tool and the Matrix Editor to create a performance.

Adding More Reason Instruments to a Logic Session

You can use the method outlined in this tutorial to add as many Reason instruments as you want to your sessions:

1. Create a SubTractor synth in Reason. Route its output to Channel 3 on Reason's hardware interface.

2. In Logic, choose the third instrument track in the Arrange window.

3. In the Object Parameters box, choose Channel ➤ ReWire ➤ Reason ➤ RW: Channel 3.

4. Rename the track SubTractor 1 in the Object Parameters box.

5. Make sure the track is selected in the Arrange window and choose Windows ➤ Environment.

6. In the Environment window, choose New ➤ Internal ➤ ReWire.

7. In the ReWire Object Parameters box choose the following settings:

Device	Reason
Bus	6
Channel	SubTractor 1

8. Click the top of the SubTractor 1 channel strip to select and highlight it.

9. Use the virtual connector that appears in the top right corner of the channel strip to "wire" the track to the new ReWire object.

10. Close the Environment window.

Whichever track is selected and highlighted in the Environment window, Track Mixer, or Arrange window, your MIDI controller will trigger the audio from the track's assigned Reason instrument.

A ReWire Session with Logic and Live

Many of Logic's built-in features, including its use of Apple Loops, are great, but Live has specific looping capabilities that set it apart. Logic certainly does a lot of things well, but Live does looping better. There are lots of possibilities and reasons for combining the two programs. A typical Logic/Live session might consist of an arrangement created in Live with some extra virtual instrumentation or live audio recording added in Logic.

Whatever the reason, combining the two programs in a single session makes for a very powerful music tool. We'll start with a basic stereo routing and then explore more complex routing.

Basic Stereo Routing

To set up basic stereo routing between Logic and Live:

1. Start Logic and create and save a new session.

2. Select an empty instrument track in the Arrange window.

3. The Object Parameters box is located just below the Toolbox in Logic's Arrange window. If the Objects Parameters box is minimized, click the triangle on the left side of the box to open it.

4. Use the Text tool to rename the track Live One in the Object Parameters box.

5. In the Object Parameters box, select Channel ➢ ReWire Stereo ➢ Ableton Live ➢ RW: Mix L/R.

6. Start Live.

7. Add a MIDI or audio clip to any of the Live tracks and launch the clip. Launching the clip will simultaneously begin playback of the Logic session.

8. Double-click the Live One track in Logic's Arrange window to open the Track Mixer.

9. Use the Live One track's channel strip to adjust the panning and volume of Live's output.

10. Create an arrangement in Live's Session view or Arrange view and/or in the Logic Timeline.

Complex Routing

An excellent way to take advantage of Logic's EQs and other features is to mix your Live sessions in Logic. To set up more complex routing in Live:

1. Create a new Logic project.

2. Select an empty instrument track in the Arrange window.

3. If the Objects Parameters box is minimized, click the triangle on the left side of the box to open it.

4. In the Object Parameters box, select Channel ➢ ReWire Stereo ➢ Ableton Live ➢ RW: Mix L/R. This sets up the ReWire input for Bus 1 and 2 from Live as well as the master volume output.

5. Select the next available instrument track and, in the Object Parameters box, select Channel ➢ ReWire Stereo ➢ Ableton Live ➢ RW: Bus 03/04.

6. Start Live and add an audio or MIDI clip to any two tracks.

7. Select the first track that you have created or added a clip to and, in the Audio To section (Figure 5.43), select ReWire Out.

8. In the Output Channel drop-down menu (also Figure 5.43), select Mix L/R.

FIGURE 5.43
Live's ReWire output
configuration

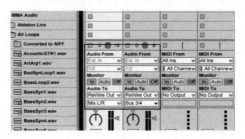

9. Select the next track and choose the ReWire Out and Bus 3/4 from the output drop-down menus.

You can use this routing configuration to create as many input/output configurations as your Live session needs.

Logic and OS X

Because Logic is now owned and updated by Apple, it has been and will continue to be one of the first programs to take advantage of any changes to Apple hardware and operating systems. Logic 7.2, the most recent version as of this writing, was released in 2006 and will run natively on Macs containing both Power PC and Intel processors.

Automatic Updating

One advantage to using Logic is that, since it is an Apple program, you can use OS X's built-in Software Update feature to automatically download and install any updates to the current release of Logic.

To install an update of the Logic program, choose Software Update from the Apple menu and OS X will automatically locate any available updates.

Freeze Tracks

Logic's instruments and plug-ins are extremely processor intensive. Even the most up-to-date Macs with lots of RAM can benefit from Logic's Freeze Track function. Freezing tracks renders all of the MIDI performances, audio performances, and any editing and/or plug-in effects on a track to a noneditable file. You cannot edit, change, or loop a frozen file in any way without first unfreezing the track.

To freeze and unfreeze any Audio or MIDI track:

1. Stop playback of the current Logic session.

2. Click the Freeze Track button shown in Figure 5.44.

FIGURE 5.44
The Freeze Track
button

3. Start playback. Logic will render the frozen track before playback begins.

4. Click the Freeze Track button a second time to unfreeze any track.

The Bottom Line

Create an Autoload session   Creating an Autoload session saves time, simplifies your Logic experience and can be used to automatically create your own customized Logic session by default whenever you start the program.

> **Master It**   Use the Logic Setup Assistant to set up Logic, then create your own Autoload template.

Use Logic's Loop Browser   Logic's built-in Loop Browser gives you quick access to all of your Real Instrument and Software Instrument Apple Loops.

> **Master It**   Use the Loop Browser to add a Real Instrument and Software Instrument loop to a Logic session, then convert a Software Instrument to a Real Instrument.

Use Logic's Arrange window editing tools   Logic's Arrange window contains a palette of editing tools that you can use to edit audio and MIDI tracks. The edit tools can fix major or minor problems in your audio or MIDI recordings or create entirely new performances out of existing tracks and loops.

> **Master It**   Use the Arrange window edit tools to cut an Apple Loop, audio, or audio performance into three separate regions. Mute one of the regions. Drag one of the regions to a new track and loop it.

Create MIDI performances with Logic's virtual instruments   Logic's collection of virtual instruments includes keyboards, drum modules, synthesizers, and the all-purpose EXS24 sampler. Using these instruments, you can create single tracks, multiple tracks, or complete performances.

> **Master It**   Add an ES1 synthesizer to your Logic song and use the Caps Lock keyboard to create and record a simple MIDI performance.

"ReWire" Logic with Reason and Ableton Live   Using Propellerhead's ReWire to connect Ableton Live and/or Reason to Logic has gotten easier with each successive Logic update.

> **Master It**   Create a new Logic session using a Dr. Rex Loop Player in Reason as a drum track.

Chapter 6

GarageBand

GarageBand is one of the five programs in Apple's iLife suite, which also includes iPhoto for organizing and editing digital pictures; iWeb for creating simple websites; the entry-level DVD authoring program iDVD; and iMovie, a digital video editing program. Apple updates the iLife suite every year. The current version comes with every new Apple computer and is also available at your local computer store and at `http://www.apple.com`.

Considering its cost and available functions, GarageBand is an incredible value, possibly the best bang for your buck in the music software market today. While GarageBand does have its limitations, it can be very useful in a number of situations, and it's a safe bet that Apple will keep adding new functionality, effects, and instruments with each future release.

GarageBand combines audio recording, looping, built-in MIDI instruments, and sequencing in one easy-to-use package. The current version, GarageBand 3, also has added functionality that lets you create your own podcasts and add soundtracks to projects created with Apple's iMovie and iDVD programs. For Mac owners just starting out in the digital recording world, GarageBand represents an excellent opportunity to learn the basics of digital music making without breaking the bank. For more experienced users, GarageBand may not be the DAW of choice, but I find it to be very useful for a number of things, including recording band rehearsals, making quick demos, creating Apple Loops and podcasts, and using it as a kind of sonic sketchpad for quickly getting ideas down.

GarageBand also shares many features with Apple's Logic Express and Logic Pro, which makes for a great segue into learning those programs. GarageBand, like all of the DAW programs I'm covering in this book, can also be used as a ReWire host with Reason, Ableton Live, and any other ReWire-compatible programs. In short, GarageBand is definitely worth a close look for anyone who is creating music on a Mac.

In this chapter, you'll learn to

◆ Use GarageBand's Musical Typing keyboard

◆ Locate specific kinds of loops and add them to a session

◆ Create a drum track using GarageBand's Software Instruments

◆ Add effects to a GarageBand track

◆ Export a GarageBand song to iTunes

GarageBand Basics

Since GarageBand is a relatively simple program, the process of installing, setting up, and starting to use the program is pretty easy. However, there are a few things you can do to help get things running smoothly, and I'll cover them in this next section.

Installing GarageBand

GarageBand and all of its included loops, effects, and instruments will be automatically installed when you install iLife. You can also choose the option of performing a custom installation from your iLife DVD, installing only the GarageBand program and its sound files.

To perform a custom installation:

1. Insert the iLife DVD into your DVD drive.

2. Click the Install icon and proceed as you normally would.

3. Once you choose which drive to install GarageBand onto, click the Custom Install button.

4. Deselect the programs you don't wish to install.

Your First Session

The first thing you'll see when you open GarageBand is the menu asking what kind of project you'd like to create. GarageBand has three different templates to choose from: Music Project, Podcast Episode, and Movie Score. Click the button next to New Music Project. This is the template you will be primarily working with in this chapter.

In the dialog box that appears, type a name for your project and choose a location where you'd like to save your new session. If possible create a folder on an external drive to record and save your GarageBand sessions in.

Setting Preferences

GarageBand's preferences are also straightforward, especially compared to other DAW programs. Let's take a look here at a few settings you might want to change depending on how you'd like to work with GarageBand.

GENERAL PREFERENCES

Open GarageBand's preferences window by selecting GarageBand ➢ Preferences. The first tab is the General Preferences. Here you will want to fill in a name for your GarageBand iTunes Playlist. Also fill in the Composer Name (that's you) and Album Name fields, as shown in Figure 6.1.

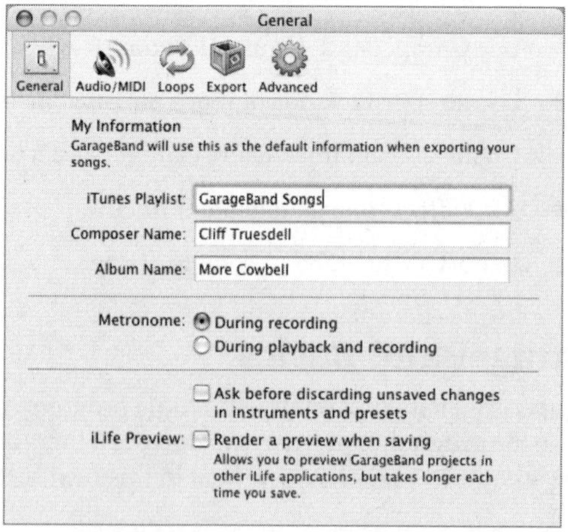

FIGURE 6.1
GarageBand's General
Preferences

These settings determine how your files will be organized when you mix down your songs and export them to iTunes.

MIXING DOWN

Unlike other DAW programs GarageBand does not offer you much control over file formats when you mix a song down. Basically, you have two choices: you can choose the Export to Disc option, which saves your song as an AAC file (see Chapter 13, "Post Production," for more on file types), or you can choose the Send Song to iTunes option, which will automatically mix your song to AIFF format and add it to your GarageBand iTunes Playlist.

Next you'll choose your metronome settings: whether you want to hear the metronome during recording and playback or just during recording. (During a session you can turn the metronome off altogether by using the keyboard shortcut Command+U or selecting Control ➤ Metronome.)

If there's a check mark in the field next to Ask Before Discarding Unsaved Changes in Instruments and Presets, remove it. This will prevent you from altering any of GarageBand's instruments and presets by mistake.

If you are planning on using your GarageBand projects in conjunction with iPhoto, iMovie, or iDVD put a check mark in the iLife Preview box. If you are not planning on doing this, leave it blank.

AUDIO/MIDI

If you own a USB or FireWire audio interface, you can use it to record directly into GarageBand and play back audio for monitoring purposes. If you don't have a hardware audio interface, every Mac will have a ⅛-inch (3.5mm) line-out jack that you can use to hook up speakers for audio output.

Most Macs will also have another ⅛-inch (3.5mm) line-in jack, which you can use to record instruments directly into your computer. GarageBand will choose this as your default audio input.

If you have an external hardware audio interface that you would like to use, click the Audio/MIDI tab in GarageBand's Preferences. Select the interface you'd like to use from the Audio Input and Audio Output fields.

GarageBand handles MIDI in a simple way: it works automatically with any MIDI device that you connect.

You can raise or lower the keyboard sensitivity to adjust the default velocity of GarageBand's built-in keyboard. This will not affect the velocity of notes played on your external MIDI keyboard in any way.

LOOPS

In the Loops preferences, I like to keep the Filter for More Relevant Results option unchecked. Choosing to filter the results will limit the loops you'll see in a search to those that are in or close to the key of the current song. Limiting these search results to a specific key doesn't leave room for the happy accidents that are an important part of the creative process.

If processor power is an issue, you may want to put a check mark in the Convert to Real Instrument box. This setting automatically converts your Software Instrument loops to Real Instruments, which may give you fewer editing options but saves a fair amount of your systems resources.

EXPORT

The Export settings are mostly for podcasts and iMovie scores. However, if you want to export your GarageBand songs directly to AAC format, you can choose the setting here.

The GarageBand Interface

Now that you've created your session, the GarageBand window will open up. At the top you'll see the Grand Piano track that every GarageBand session starts with, shown in Figure 6.2.

FIGURE 6.2
GarageBand's default
Grand Piano track

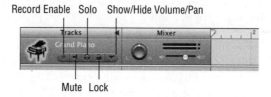

The section that contains the name of the track is called the *track header*. The five buttons in the track header, just below the track name are, left to right:

Record Enable   When this button is on (red), indicates the track is ready for recording.

Mute   Silences the track.

Solo   Plays the track by itself. You can also "solo" multiple tracks at once to hear how various combinations of your tracks will sound together.

Lock   Renders the track to your hard drive, preventing you from editing it in any way. This frees up processor power.

Show/Hide Track Volume/Pan   Reveals a "track within a track" which you can use to automate the volume and panning of each track with *control points* (see the sidebar "Control Points"). Click the field that currently reads Track Volume to choose between Track Volume view and Track Pan view. Figure 6.3 shows the Track Volume view with added control points.

FIGURE 6.3
Automate volume
with control points.

CONTROL POINTS

Control points are used to control the Volume and Panning automation functions on your Garageband tracks. You can create and adjust control points by clicking and dragging the straight line in the Volume or Pan track window, as shown in Figure 6.3.

THE MIXER

Next to the track header is GarageBand's Mixer section. Unlike most DAW programs, which split up mixing and editing into separate windows, GarageBand keeps these functions in one simplified interface. The Mixer contains a Panning knob for placing your tracks in the left or right speaker and a Volume slider for adjusting the level of your track.

To return the volume to zero and the panning to dead center, hold down the Option key then click the knob or the slider.

THE TIMELINE

The large gray area to the right of the track header and Mixer section is the GarageBand Timeline, which is where you will do all of your arranging and recording.

In the Timeline you'll see a thin red line with an upside-down triangle on top. This is the playhead, which lets you know where you are in a song as it's playing back. Keep an eye on the triangle at the top of the playhead during playback of your sessions. When you're pushing your Mac's memory and processor limits the playhead will first turn yellow, then orange, then red before it stops the session. If this happens, you'll have to either remove tracks or effects from your session, or use the Lock Track button to free up some of your computers resources.

CONTROL BAR

On the bottom right of the GarageBand window are three buttons, shown in Figure 6.4, which are, from left to right:

FIGURE 6.4
New Track, Loop Browser, and Track Editor buttons

New Track   Track Editor

Loop Browser

New Track   Click this to create a new Real Instrument or Software Instrument track. New tracks can also be created by choosing Track ➤ New Track or by using the keyboard shortcut Command+Option+N.

Loop Browser   This opens up the Loop Browser, where you can locate Apple Loops to add to your session. You can also open the Loop Browser by using the keyboard shortcut Command+L.

Track Editor   Opens GarageBand's Track Editor, where you can edit and adjust your loops and tracks. The Track Editor can also be opened with the keyboard shortcut Command+E.

Moving to the right you'll see the Transport bar, shown in Figure 6.5.

FIGURE 6.5
The Transport bar

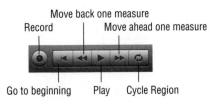

Record   Move back one measure   Move ahead one measure

Go to beginning   Play   Cycle Region

Here you'll find the Record, Move Back One Measure, Play, and Move Ahead One Measure buttons. The button on the far right of the Transport bar (with two curved arrows) is the Cycle Region button (see the sidebar "Cycle Regions").

CYCLE REGIONS

Creating a cycle region tells GarageBand to continuously loop one section of a session. You can do this by clicking the Cycle Region button in the Transport bar or by typing the letter "C" on your Apple keyboard. A yellow line will appear at the top of the GarageBand Timeline, which controls the length and area of your loop. Drag the cycle region to another part of your session and to lengthen or shorten the looped playback.

Cycle regions can be useful when working with Apple Loops, editing tracks, or rehearsing a section of a performance before recording it. A cycle region can be as long or as short as you want, but generally you will probably want to work with 4-, 8- or 16-measure cycle regions.

Figure 6.6 shows the time display to the right of the Transport bar, which tells you the position of the playhead and the tempo in beats per minute (BPM) of your session. GarageBand by default starts every session at 120BPM. Click Tempo in the time display and a slider will appear that you can use to speed or slow the tempo of your session.

FIGURE 6.6

The time display

Just to the right of the time display is the Master Volume slider.

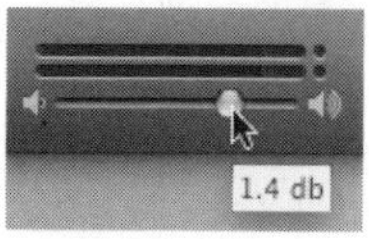

This is where you can control the overall volume for your session. Keep an eye on this section throughout the recording and arranging process; always make sure that the master level meters above the slider don't go too far into the red zone.

Finally, the two buttons on the lower right side of the window, shown in Figure 6.7, are the Track Info button and the Media Browser button.

FIGURE 6.7

The Track Info and
Media Browser
buttons

The Track Info button opens the Track Info window on the right side of the Timeline, which contains the virtual amp settings, effects, and routing information for any Real or Software Instrument track you may have selected. The Media Browser button opens the Media Browser, which you can use add images, iTunes songs, and iPhoto images to your podcast Episode projects, as well as iMovie files to your Movie Score projects.

REAL INSTRUMENT AND SOFTWARE INSTRUMENTS

There are two different types of loops and tracks in GarageBand: Real Instruments and Software Instruments.

Software Instruments are basically MIDI tracks that trigger sampled sounds. The main advantage of working with Software Instruments is the ease with which they can be created, edited, and altered. It's easy to time-stretch, change the pitch, and even substitute a different instrument.

Real Instruments are actual audio recordings of live performances, such as a live drum kit, guitar, keyboard, or external synthesizer. The main advantage to Real Instrument loops and tracks is that they tend sound more human and natural. You can still use GarageBand's editing, time-stretching, and pitch-shifting features on Real Instrument tracks and loops, though the quality of your tracks after editing may suffer a bit more than when the same techniques are applied to Software Instrument tracks and loops. Real Instrument loops also use less of your processor's resources, so on sessions where resources are an issue you may want to use Real Instrument loops whenever possible.

Working with Loops

The easiest way to get started with GarageBand is to use the Loop Browser to preview loops and then add them to your GarageBand projects. Click the Loop Browser button or choose Control ➤ Show Loop Browser to view the Loop Browser, shown in Figure 6.8

FIGURE 6.8

The Loop Browser

Click any one of the descriptor fields (Beats, Piano, Acoustic, and so on) to view the loops in that category. As you can see, some of the keyword buttons are instruments like Drums and Bass, while some are descriptions of sound or feel, such as Distorted and Relaxed. You can click multiple keyword buttons to find specific types of loops. For example, selecting the categories All Drums, Electronic, and Distorted will narrow down the results to just a few choices. You can also type keywords into the search field located at the bottom off the Loop Browser. For example, select the All Drums descriptor and type the word **Motown** in the Search field, then press Enter to locate all of your Motown-style drum loops.

Selecting a keyword button will bring up a list of possible loops on the right side of the Loop Browser. Once you locate a loop that you may want to use, preview it by clicking it in the list.

Customizing the Loop Browser

GarageBand's built-in Loop Browser automatically organizes and gives you instant access to all of your Apple Loops and any other loop files you may add to your collection as you continue to work with GarageBand. Here are some ways to customize the Loop Browser to better suit your needs.

View the Whole Browser   If you move your cursor to the dark gray area above the Loop Browser you'll see that in certain spots the cursor will turn into a hand. Use this to drag upward and view the entire Loop Browser.

Move Keywords   If you have certain categories that you work with often, you can click and drag them to a new location in the browser.

Add Keywords   If you added a loop or loops that don't fall into the categories you currently see in the Loop Browser, there are more keywords available. For example, if you just added a folder of oboe loops, you can add an Oboe Category to the Loop Browser. Control+click a keyword button, then choose Instruments ➤ Woodwind ➤ Oboe from the contextual menu (Figure 6.9).

FIGURE 6.9

Add a new keyword to
the Loop Browser.

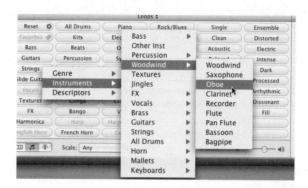

There are loops categories for each piece of the drum kit (kick, snare, cymbal), different types of vocals (male, female, choir), as well as many others.

View Loops by Folder   Apple's Jam Packs are collections of additional loops and Software Instruments for GarageBand. If you add any of Apple's GarageBand's Jam Pack loop libraries or third-party loop collections, you can browse them by clicking the Loops at the top of the Loop Browser. Figure 6.10 shows the different loop collections.

FIGURE 6.10

View different loop
collections.

Selecting GarageBand in the menu that appears will display only the loops that came with GarageBand. Selecting My Loops will show loops you've created and single loops you've added to the Loop Browser. In the Other category are Jam Packs and any complete folders you've added to the Loop Browser. If you can't find a loop you're looking for, make sure you have Show All selected in the Loops pop-up menu and that under Preferences ➤ General you've unchecked the Filter for More Relevant Results check box.

ADDING LOOPS TO A SESSION

To add a loop to your session, select a loop that you'd like to use then drag it from the Loop Browser directly onto the GarageBand Timeline. GarageBand will automatically create a new track for the loop. Figure 6.11 shows a Real Instrument loop (Cop Show Clav 01.1) and a Software Instrument loop (70s Ballad Piano 01) in the Timeline.

FIGURE 6.11

A Real Instrument and
a Software Instrument
in the Timeline

To repeat a loop, move your cursor to the end of loop in the Timeline, at the top of the loop. When the cursor changes to what looks like a curved arrow (as shown in Figure 6.11), click your mouse and drag to the right.

For more information on working with loops in GarageBand, see Chapter 10 "Apple Loops."

Included Instruments

GarageBand comes with a large collection of included instruments including:

◆ Drum kits

◆ Guitars

◆ Horns

◆ Pianos

◆ Organs

◆ Synthesizers

Each instrument has a variety of included settings that can be altered and saved as presets for use in other GarageBand projects. But you are not limited to the included instruments. You can expand your collection of GarageBand Instruments with Apple's Jam Packs (which also include Apple Loops) as well as packages from other third-party loop libraries like Drums on Demand and PowerFX.

Recording with Software Instruments

Every GarageBand music project starts with a default Grand Piano Software Instrument track. If you have a MIDI keyboard you can use it to play the Grand Piano instrument. Open GarageBand's preferences again and select the Audio/MIDI tab.

If you don't have a MIDI keyboard connected to your computer, you can use one of Garage-Band's two built-in keyboard functions:

◆ To use your mouse to play Software Instruments, select Window ➢ Keyboard (see Figure 6.12).

FIGURE 6.12
Use your mouse
to trigger notes on
GarageBand's built-in
keyboard.

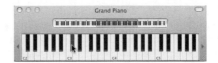

◆ To use your Apple keyboard to play Software Instruments, choose Window ➢ Musical Typing.

We'll cover the Musical Typing feature in more detail in the section "Musical Typing."

CREATE A DRUM TRACK

First create a new Software Instrument:

1. Select Track ➢ New Track.

2. Select Software Instrument in the dialog box and click Create.

The Track Info window, shown in Figure 6.13, will open on the right side of the GarageBand window. The new track will be created by default as a Grand Piano instrument, but you can change this easily.

FIGURE 6.13

The Track Info window

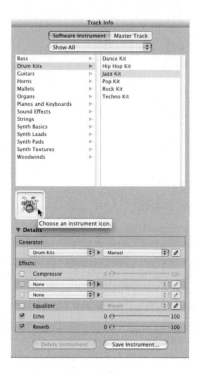

3. Select the Drum Kits category and choose one of the kits from the list of available instruments.

IT'S IN THE DETAILS

To see the Details view at the bottom of the Track Info window, click the sideways triangle next to Details. This section of the Track Info window is where you'll find all the settings and effects that make up whatever instrument or loop you are currently working with. I'll cover this in more detail further on, but for now it's good to get in the habit of always having the Details view visible.

When you are ready to record, make sure the Record Enable button in the track header is on (red) and click the Record button in the Transport bar at the bottom of the GarageBand Timeline.

Use your MIDI keyboard or one of the built-in keyboards to trigger the various sounds that make up the drum kit. Record your performance and then listen back. Don't worry about any imperfections (even if it's *all* imperfections). I'll cover editing tracks shortly.

CREATE A KEYBOARD TRACK

For right now, create another Software Instrument performance:

1. Create a new Software Instrument track and select the Organ Instrument category in the Track Info window.

2. Choose one of the Organ presets.

3. Make sure the track's Details view is showing. If not, click the Details triangle at the bottom of the Track Info window.

4. Use your MIDI keyboard or one of the built-in keyboards to preview the organ sound.

5. Click the Edit Preset button to view the organ instrument's changeable parameters

The parameters are shown in Figure 6.14.

FIGURE 6.14
The Tonewheel Organ
Edit Preset window

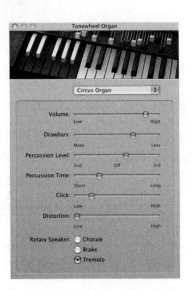

6. Try adjusting the various parameters to create a new sound.

7. If you would like to save the adjusted instrument, select Make Preset from the drop-down menu.

8. Arm your track for recording and record a performance of the selected piano instrument.

One cool feature of GarageBand is that once you have created a performance with a Software Instrument in GarageBand, you can change the track to any other instrument.

To preview what other instruments will sound like on your organ performance track:

1. Create a cycle region by pressing the C key.

2. Adjust the length of the cycle region.

3. Start the GarageBand song.

4. With the song playing, choose another category and instrument in the Track Info window.

FIX IT IN THE MIX

Once you've recorded a performance you can use the Track Editor to clean up any mistakes and use quantization to fix any timing issues.

1. Double-click the recorded track in the Timeline to open the Track Editor, shown in Figure 6.15.

FIGURE 6.15
GarageBand's
Track Editor

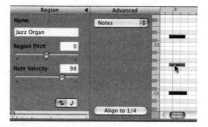

2. Select and move any wrong notes. To delete a note, select it with your mouse and press the Delete key.

3. To fix the overall timing of your performance, select a note then choose Edit ➢ Select All (or use the keyboard shortcut Command+A). You can also drag in the Track Editor to select a few notes at a time.

4. Click the Align button at the bottom of the Track Editor.

You can adjust the amount of quantization applied to your performance by moving the Zoom slider on the bottom left of the Track Editor window. As you move the Zoom slider to the right you'll see the quantization increments on the Align button become smaller.

Find the right amount of quantization for your performance by clicking the Align button and listening back.

If the performance changes too drastically, choose Edit ➢ Undo Fix Timing Region, then move the Zoom slider to the right and try a smaller amount of quantization.

THE GARAGEBAND SYNTHESIZERS

In my opinion GarageBand's coolest "secret weapons" are its included synthesizers. A wide range of different synthesizer types is represented here, with each one containing its own unique characteristics and great preset sounds. Each synthesizer includes lots of adjustable parameters for creating individual presets. The included synthesizer instrument categories are as follows:

- ◆ Synth Basics
- ◆ Synth Leads
- ◆ Synth Pads
- ◆ Synth Textures

Synth Preset Instruments

Within each category is a list of presets. Let's take a look at one of the presets to get an idea of how GarageBand's synthesizer instruments work. To use the Moonbeam preset, follow these steps.

1. Create a new GarageBand music project.

2. Double-click the track header to open the Track Info window.

3. From the Synth Leads category choose the Moonbeam preset.

4. If the Instrument's details are not showing, click the Details button at the bottom of the track info window.

5. Use your MIDI keyboard or GarageBand's Musical Typing to preview the sound of the Moonbeam preset.

6. Figure 6.16 shows the Details view for this preset.

FIGURE 6.16
The Details view of the
Moonbeam preset

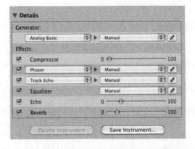

At the top of the Details view is the Software Instrument Generator drop-down menu. This menu shows which of GarageBand's instrument modules are being used to create the sound of the instrument; in this case it's the Analog Basic synthesizer.

Further down in the Details view you can see which effects have been added to the preset. In this case this preset includes various effects, including a Phaser and a Track Echo (delay) plug-in. Quite often the most striking synthesizer sounds are a combination of the instrument and various effects. There's more on GarageBand's included plug-in effects in the "included Effects" section of this chapter.

Click other Instrument categories and presets to preview their sounds and see which generators and effects are used to create the some of GarageBand's preset synthesizer sounds.

GARAGEBAND MODULES

You'll notice on the Generator menu of GarageBand modules that there are other instruments besides the various synthesizers. These are the GarageBand modules that are the building blocks for all of the GarageBand instruments. Just as you can use the Synth modules to create your own synths, you can also use the other instrument modules to create your own pianos or organs or horn sections.

At the bottom of the Generator menu you see Audio Unit Modules. These are third-party Audio Unit instruments that can be used in GarageBand as well as any program that supports the Audio Unit format. For more information see Chapter 9, "Virtual Instruments."

Creating Original Synths

The real fun here is in creating your own original synthesizer sounds. To do so, follow these steps:

1. Create a new Software Instrument track and double-click the track header to open the Track Info window.

2. Click the drop-down menu to view the list of available GarageBand modules.

   At the top of the list you'll see GarageBand's five Analog Synth modules. Further down the list are the three Digital Synth modules, and below them the two Hybrid Synth modules. This is a total of ten different synthesizers. Combined with GarageBand's plug-in effects, you can create a dazzling array of sonic possibilities.

3. Choose the Digital Basic GarageBand module.

4. To the right of the Generator menu is the Preset menu. Try the FM Bells C or FM Polysynth presets from this list.

5. Click the Edit Preset button (the Pencil icon to the right of the Preset menu) to view the Digital Basic module's Edit window.

6. Adjust some of the parameters to come up with a new and interesting sound.

MORE ABOUT VIRTUAL SYNTHESIZER PARAMETERS

For a better understanding of what some of the virtual synth parameters do and how virtual synthesizers work, see the section "Synthesizer Basics" in Chapter 9, "Virtual Instruments."

7. Add effects to your new synthesizer sound. Some good choices for synth effects include phaser, flanger, and delay. Try out different combinations of these and other effects.

To save your new synth instrument, select one of the four Synth Instrument categories in the Track Info window and click the Save Instrument button on the lower left. Name your instrument in the dialog box that appears.

You can now load your instrument whenever you like for use in other GarageBand sessions.

Recording with Real Instruments

Real Instrument tracks are the tracks you'll use to record your live instruments, such as electric guitar, bass, or a vocal track. You can also use a microphone to record other instruments such as horns, percussion, or piano.

To record onto a Real Instrument track, you'll either need a hardware audio interface or the right adapters to connect your guitar, microphone, or other instrument to your Mac's built-in ⅛-inch (3.5mm) line in.

Once you have your connections in place:

1. Create a new Real Instrument track by clicking the New Track button on the bottom left of the Timeline or selecting Track ➤ New Track.

2. Choose Real Instrument from the dialog box.

   Creating a new Real Instrument track will automatically open the Track Info window on the right side of the screen.

3. In the Track Info window, select the type of instrument you plan to record or select Basic Track ➤ No Effects to record "clean," without any added effects or virtual amplification.

4. Choose your input channel from the Input menu shown in Figure 6.17.

5. Turn monitoring on from the Monitor drop-down menu, also shown in Figure 6.17.

FIGURE 6.17
Choose an input and turn Monitor on.

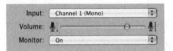

6. Drag the Volume slider to the right so you can hear your instrument.

7. Make sure the Record Enable button is lit on your new track.

8. Click the Record button in the Transport bar to begin recording. To turn GarageBand's click track on or off select Control ➤ Metronome.

9. Press the Spacebar to stop recording.

Figure 6.18 shows a newly recorded Real Instrument track.

FIGURE 6.18
A Real Instrument recording

After you record your track, you can use the Track Editor to edit your performance. To delete or separate part of a performance:

1. Double-click the track in the Timeline to open the Track Editor.

2. Move your cursor on the bottom of the waveform in the Track Editor until it changes to what looks like a plus (+) sign, shown in Figure 6.19.

FIGURE 6.19
Editing a Real
Instrument track

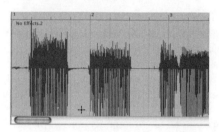

3. Click and drag your mouse over the section you'd like to remove or separate.

4. Release your mouse, then single-click in the selected area. You have now created a new audio region, as shown in Figure 6.20.

FIGURE 6.20
A new audio region

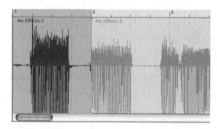

At this point you have a number of options for what you can do with your new region:

◆ To adjust the region's pitch, use the Track Editor's Pitch slider.

◆ To delete the region, select the newly created region in the Timeline and press the Delete key on your Apple keyboard.

◆ To move the region to a new track, click the New Track button and create a new Real Instrument track. Select the new region in the Timeline and drag it onto the new track.

◆ To loop the new region, loop it as you would any Real Instrument loop.

Included Effects

GarageBand comes with a number of built-in effects that you can add to your tracks to help them stand out in a mix or to create entirely new sounds. You can add effects to any GarageBand tracks, including Apple Loops and Software Instrument or Real Instrument tracks. Effects can be added before or after recording.

Adding Effects to a Track

To add an effect to a Software or Real Instrument track:

1. Add a Real or Software Instrument loop to the Timeline or record a Real or Software Instrument performance.

2. Choose the track you'd like to add an effect to and double-click the track header to open the Track Info window.

3. Click the Details triangle in the lower right corner of the Track Info window to open the Track Details view.

4. At this point you can do the following:

- ◆ Put a check mark in the box next to the Compressor, Equalizer, Echo, or Reverb to add basic versions of these effects. These effects all have a slider you can use to choose how much of an effect you'd like to apply.

- ◆ The Equalizer has a drop-down menu (which currently reads "Manual"). Choose from any of the included presets.

- ◆ Just above the Equalizer are drop-down menus that you can use to add two additional effects to the track.

The Effect drop-down menus list all of your built-in GarageBand effects.

AUDIO UNIT EFFECTS

At the bottom of each of the Effects drop-down menus, below the GarageBand Effects, is a list of Audio Unit plug-ins featuring a number of plug-ins that come with OS X and which will work with any audio program that supports the Audio Unit format. This includes GarageBand as well as Ableton Live, Logic Pro, and Logic Express. If you have installed other software such as Native Instruments Reaktor or another virtual synthesizer program, it may also appear on the list, as will any third-party Audio Unit plug-ins. You can expand your collection of Audio Units significantly by searching the Internet for new Audio Unit plug-ins. Many are available for free download through http://www.iCompositions.com and http://www.MacJams.com. Try using Google to search for "Audio Units" or "Free Audio Units."

Audio Unit plug-ins will be covered more extensively in Chapter 8.

Let's take a look at some of the included GarageBand effects and presets.

1. Create a new GarageBand Song and set the tempo to 100BPM.

2. Open the Loop Browser and add the drum loop Motown Drummer 14 to the Timeline.

3. Create a two-measure cycle region and click the Play button.

4. Double-click the track header to open the Track Info window.

5. With the loop still playing, use the first additional Effects menu, shown in Figure 6.21, to add the flanger effect from the list of GarageBand effects.

FIGURE 6.21
Add an additional effect.

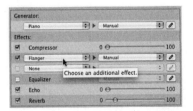

Using Effect Presets

Effect presets, as the name implies, are precreated settings for GarageBand effects. Using the GarageBand song you created in the previous section, let's look at using presets.

1. Try out some of the presets from the pop-up menu to the right of the flanger effect.

   Some of the presets, such as Dolphin Flange and Intergalactic Police will cause a drastic change in the sound of your loop; others will be subtler.

2. Open the Loop Browser again and add the piano loop Classic Rock Piano 01 and to the Timeline.

3. Double-click the track header to open the Track Info window.

4. Press the spacebar to start the song.

5. With the song playing, select the GarageBand effect Track Echo from one of the Effects drop-down menus.

6. Click the Edit Preset button to open the effect window.

7. Try out some of the different settings from the presets drop-down.

Creating Your Own Effect Presets

The Pencil icon to the right of the Preset menu for each effect is the Edit Preset button for the effect, which is similar to Edit Preset button for GarageBand's instruments. Click the Edit Preset button to view a plug-in's interface and manually change its settings.

Figure 6.22 shows the Equalizer plug-in window.

FIGURE 6.22
Settings for the
Equalizer plug-in

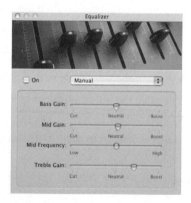

You can also use presets as a starting point and adjust the parameters to your taste to create your own sounds and presets.

To create your own presets for any effect:

1. Click the Edit Preset button (the Pencil icon) to open the effect window. In this case, open the effect window for the flanger that you added in the previous section. The window is shown in Figure 6.23.

FIGURE 6.23
Settings for the
Flanger's Dolphin
Flange preset

2. Make any adjustments you want to the effect.

3. Select Make Preset from the drop-down menu at the top of the effect window.

4. Name the preset and click Save.

You can now recall and use this preset any time you apply the flanger effect to a track.

GarageBand Tutorials

These tutorials are designed to further familiarize you with GarageBand's functions and features. There's also a section on working with loops in GarageBand in Chapter 10 and a section on MIDI and GarageBand in Chapter 11, "MIDI."

Using the Track Editor

GarageBand's built-in Track Editor can be used to make slight adjustments or drastic changes to your loops and tracks. Here are some basic tips and trick for making the most out of this powerful feature.

EDITING SOFTWARE INSTRUMENT PERFORMANCES

One use for the Track Editor is rearranging MIDI information to alter Software Instrument loops and tracks:

1. Create a new GarageBand Session named Track Editor.

2. Drag the drum loop 80s Pop Beat 09 onto the Timeline.

3. Create a four-measure cycle region and click the Play button to start the audio and listen to the loop.

4. Double-click the loop in the Timeline to open the Track Editor.

5. With the audio playing, use your mouse to select the MIDI notes that trigger the kick drum, as shown in Figure 6.24.

FIGURE 6.24
Select multiple notes
in the Track Editor.

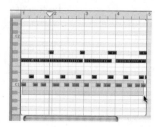

6. Experiment with some of the following:

- ◆ Try completely changing the loop by dragging the kick drum notes up or down so that they trigger another instrument.

- ◆ Use the same method to grab the notes that trigger the hi-hat or snare drum.

- ◆ Add notes to the loop by holding down the Command key and clicking in the Track Editor window.

- ◆ Remove notes by selecting them and pressing the Delete key on your Apple keyboard.

By adding, removing, and rearranging the existing notes, you can create a loop with a slightly different feel or an entirely unrecognizable performance.

EDITING REAL INSTRUMENT TRACKS

You can also use the Track Editor to edit your Real Instrument tracks and loops. The following example covers some of its more advanced features.

1. In the Loop Browser, drag the bass loop Edgy Rock Bass 07 onto the Timeline.

2. Double-click the track in the Timeline to view it in the Track Editor.

3. Move your mouse to the center of the waveform in the Track Editor until the cursor changes to the selection tool, which looks like crosshair or a plus (+) sign.

4. Click and hold your mouse to select only the last measure of the loop, as shown in Figure 6.25.

FIGURE 6.25
Select the last mea-
sure of the loop.

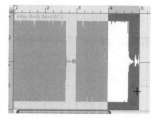

This takes a bit of practice to get right. Remember that you can undo any mistakes with the keyboard shortcut Command+Z.

5. Release the mouse, then click anywhere in the selected area to separate the region. This breaks your loop into two separate, distinct regions, which can now be edited individually. You'll also see in the Timeline that the loop has been separated into two sections.

6. Click your mouse near the top of the new region and drag it all the way to the left in the Track Editor.

7. Move your mouse to the upper right corner of the new region and, when you see the loop cursor, drag the loop so it covers the entire cycle region, as shown in Figure 6.26.

FIGURE 6.26

Loop the new region.

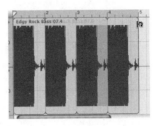

Musical Typing

Let's take a look at GarageBand's built-in Musical Typing feature. This is GarageBand's solution for users who don't have access to a MIDI keyboard. It's especially useful if you're working on a laptop.

CREATING A PERFORMANCE

One of the great things about the Musical Typing keyboard is that it offers you different ways of doing things depending on what you are most comfortable with. Use the following steps to start creating music with the Musical Typing keyboard:

1. Open a new GarageBand music project or an existing session and create a Software Instrument—the default Piano will work just fine.

2. Activate the click track or choose a simple drum beat loop to keep time.

3. From the menu, choose Window ➤ Musical Typing or use the keyboard shortcut Shift+Command+K to view the Musical Typing keyboard, shown in Figure 6.27.

FIGURE 6.27

The Musical Typing keyboard

4. Experiment with the keyboard.

The keys and their functions are clearly marked on the keyboard. You can use letters "a" through the single quote (') symbol to play musical notes, while various other keys perform a range of functions including pitch shifting, sustain, and modulation.

One of the first things you might notice is that you can only work in one octave at a time. That's not much room to maneuver, but with practice and some creative overdubbing and editing, you can achieve some pretty good results.

To switch between octaves, you can click and drag the highlighted blue section of the long keyboard at the top of the window, mouse-click the yellow plus (+) and minus (–) buttons on the lower left, or type the "Z" or "X" keys on your keyboard.

The modulation function is most appropriate for synthesizer sounds and won't have much of an effect on the piano. Click the track header and select the Instrument Category Synth Basics and the Instrument Modern Prophecy. Hold down the letter "A" on your keyboard and click between the purple Off (the number 3) and Max (the number 8) buttons too hear the effect of modulation on an instrument.

Use the Track Info window to choose the Grand Piano instrument again and check out the Musical Typing Sustain function. Using the Tab key to trigger the sustain will also work in conjunction with a MIDI keyboard, which is handy if you don't have a sustain pedal. Hold down the Tab key on your keyboard and select notes with your mouse, or type them on your Apple keyboard.

HUMANIZING YOUR PERFORMANCE

One of the biggest drawbacks to Musical Typing is that you have no control over the dynamics of your performance. GarageBand automatically gives each note the same velocity. This can make your tracks sound lifeless or flat. You can work around this by doing some after-recording work in the Track Editor:

1. Double-click the track header and select Grand Piano from the Piano Instrument Category.

2. Using Musical Typing and your keyboard, record some chords or notes. About eight bars should be enough.

3. Listen back to your performance. You'll notice that every chord or note has the same performance quality.

4. Close the Musical Typing window and double-click the track in the Timeline to open the Track Editor.

5. From the Track Editor's Advanced section (shown in Figure 6.28) select Expression.

6. Create control points by Command-clicking in the selected Track Editor field, also shown in Figure 6.28. You can create a new control point with each mouse click.

FIGURE 6.28
Varying the expression of a performance in the Track Editor's Advanced section

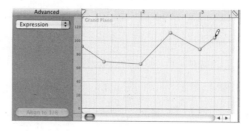

7. To delete a control point, select it and press Delete on your keyboard.

You can use these control points to create dynamics in your performance. Subtle variation works best, but you can also create a wide dynamic range by moving control points closer to the top or bottom of the Track Editor.

Pitch Shifting

GarageBand's different pitch-shifting features are a fun and easy way to work with loops and tracks and explore new ideas and possibilities.

PITCH SHIFTING WITH THE TRACK EDITOR

Using the GarageBand's Track Editor, you can pitch-shift individual loops and entire tracks.

1. Create a new GarageBand music project.

2. Open the Loop Browser, drag the loop 70s Ballad Piano 01 into the GarageBand Timeline, and create a four-measure cycle region.

3. Double-click the track in the Timeline to open the Track Editor.

4. Press the spacebar to play the cycle region.

5. With the cycle region playing, adjust the Region Pitch slider in the Track Editor window.

You can use the Region Pitch slider to raise or lower the loop by up to three octaves. You can also cut a loop or track into sections (regions) and adjust the pitch of each region:

1. Select the loop in the Timeline.

2. Move the playhead to the center of the loop.

3. Select Edit ➢ Split to separate the track into two regions.

4. Click in any blank area of the Timeline to deselect the piano loop.

5. Select either region in the Timeline *or* the Track Editor and adjust its pitch with the Region Pitch slider.

PITCH SHIFTING WITH THE MASTER TRACK

You can also use the master track to pitch-shift entire sections of a GarageBand session at once. To access pitch shifting on the master track:

1. Make the master track visible by selecting Track ➢ Show Master Track or use the keyboard shortcut Command+B.

2. Click the field in the master track header that reads Master Volume and change it to Master Pitch.

3. Add control points along the master track in the Timeline as shown in Figure 6.29.

FIGURE 6.29
Use control points on the master track to pitch-shift entire sections of a song.

Pitch shifting on the master track works seamlessly with Software Instrument tracks loops but can sometimes be problematic with Real Instruments. Listen carefully to your session to make sure your tracks are being shifted correctly before you mix down.

Drum and percussion loops and tracks will not be affected by pitch-shifting in GarageBand, whether you are using the Track Editor or the Master Pitch track.

Exporting to iTunes

After you create a complete song, the final step is to get it ready for exporting. The master track is where of all of your loop tracks and Real and Software Instrument tracks come together in a final mix. To view the master track choose Track ➤ View Master Track.

1. Double-click the master track header to view the Track Info window. Here GarageBand gives you different options for adding effects to the master track and your overall mix.

2. Select any preset and open the Details view to see what kinds of effects are added in each preset. Even the Basic ➤ Default preset has a small amount of echo and reverb added to it.

3. For a completely dry track without any effects, deselect the Echo and Reverb effects and click the Save Master button at the bottom of the Track Info window.

4. Play back your track and make sure the Volume meter above the Master Volume slider doesn't peak.

5. Make sure that the Cycle Region function is turned off. (If you have an active cycle region, only that section of your song will be exported.)

6. When your track is ready for exporting, choose Share ➤ Send Song to iTunes.

Your song will automatically be sent to an iTunes playlist with the name you chose when you set your GarageBand Preferences at the beginning of this chapter.

Podcasting with GarageBand

When Apple introduced GarageBand 3 in iLife '06, the upgraded program contained a number of new features designed to make GarageBand the program of choice for Apple users who want to create their own podcasts. These features include voiceover tracks already set up with EQ and effects for optimum spoken word recordings, a separate track for podcast images, and a Media Browser window to access those images as well as iTunes playlists.

RECORDING YOUR VOICE

You'll need a microphone (obviously) and either an audio interface or preamp. You can also record directly into your Mac's ⅛-inch (3.5mm) audio input.

Once you have your microphone and connections in place, you'll follow exactly the same steps you would for any Real Instrument recording:

1. Create a new GarageBand podcast episode session and name it "Podcast One." As you can see, when you create a new podcast episode the GarageBand interface changes dramatically. By default GarageBand will create four new tracks:

   Podcast Track You can add images to your podcast by dragging them directly from the Media Browser on the right side of the screen to the Artwork Track.

Male and Female Voice Tracks   These tracks are set up with preset effects to automatically enhance male or female voiceover tracks.

Jingles Track   In a podcast episode session, clicking the Loop Browser button will open it in Podcast Sounds View. Click the Jingles categories to see a list of 200 included jingles.

Radio Sound Track   Use the Loop Browser to add radio sound effects from the Stingers and Sound Effects menus.

2. Arm the Male or Female voice track for recording.

3. Double-click the track header to view the Track Info window.

4. In the Track Info window, turn monitoring on and raise the Volume slider.

5. Do a few recording tests to get comfortable with the microphone and to make sure the volume isn't too high or too low.

ADD SOUND EFFECTS AND LOOPS

One frequently used technique is to have a loop or song playing in the background during voiceovers; these are called *beds*. You can use any of the included jingles, stingers, or sound effects for your background music. GarageBand loops are also an excellent resource for podcast beds. Drag the sound files you want to use onto the Timeline and arrange them as you like. You can use control points and track volume automation to fade them in and out under your voiceover, or you can use the Ducking feature, which allows you to set which tracks will be prominent at any time in a podcast mix.

Figure 6.30 shows the Ducking buttons on the right side of the mixer.

FIGURE 6.30
The Ducking buttons

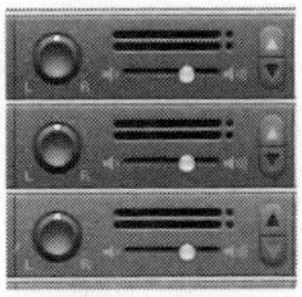

To make a track dominant, click the top (yellow) ducking arrow. To cause a specific track to "duck" (recede into the background), click the bottom (blue) ducking arrow.

Try using effects like reverb, delay and echo, and compression on your voice. You can use them lightly to add atmosphere and ambience or dramatically to create obvious sound effects.

THE MEDIA BROWSER

Aside from the default tracks, the other major difference between podcast episodes and music projects is the Media Browser. The Media Browser is where you can access songs and images to include in your podcast. It's also used in Movie Score Projects to choose movie files. Shown in Figure 6.31, the Media Browser should open automatically when you create a new podcast episode or movie score project.

If the Media Browser is not currently showing, open it by clicking the Media Browser button on the lower right side of the GarageBand window.

FIGURE 6.31

The Media Browser

USING THE MEDIA BROWSER

You can also open and use the Media Browser in a music session. In fact, if you want to, you can turn a music session into a movie score or podcast by dragging images, songs, or movies from the Media Browser onto the GarageBand Timeline.

ADDING SONGS TO A PODCAST

If you are doing a music show and want to add songs to your podcast, or if you want background music for your podcast other than GarageBand included sounds and loops, you can add complete songs to the GarageBand Timeline and use control points to vary the volume as needed:

1. Open iTunes and make a playlist of songs you want to use in your podcast.

2. Open the Media Browser in GarageBand and click the Audio tab.

3. Locate your playlist and drag any song you want to use directly onto the GarageBand Timeline.

   You can drag most AIFF, MP3, and AAC files directly onto the GarageBand Timeline from iTunes.

DO IT AGAIN

One of the advantages to podcasting, as compared to live radio, is that with a podcast, you don't have to always get it right the first time. If you make a mistake in your recording, choose Edit ➤ Undo and try again. If your recording is perfect, except for a section somewhere in the middle, you can always punch in and fix it. To do this:

1. Move the playhead to just before the spot you want to fix.

2. Record a new performance.

3. If your new recording starts too early or ends too late, you can drag the original file back into the right position. To do this, place your cursor on the bottom half of the track at the spot where your original recording ends, then click and drag forward.

EXPORT TO ITUNES

Once you have your podcast arranged to your liking, choose Share ➤ Send Song to iTunes. In iTunes, you'll want to convert the file from the default AIFF format to MP3 or AAC to reduce the file size. For a longer podcast, you might want to choose a lower-quality file size. These settings can be changed in GarageBand's preferences by clicking the Export tab.

PODCAST RESOURCES

For information on sharing your podcast through blogging and RSS feeds, check out these sites:

http://www.blogger.com

http://www.feedburner.com

http://www.apple.com/podcasting

http://www.apple.com/support/garageband/podcasts

 Real World Scenario

SOUND TRACKING

Because of the limitations of GarageBand's video export functions and its difficulty with handling large video files, GarageBand is not a program that you would use for a professional video project. It does, however, make a great easy-to-use and inexpensive tool for simple soundtrack composition, especially for your home movies and DVD projects.

If you're working on a large video project, it's a good idea to create three- to four-minute individual iMovie sessions, which you can then import into GarageBand without overtaxing your processor and hard drive resources. The following steps will show you how to add a soundtrack to any iMovie file:

1. Create a new GarageBand session and choose the New Movie Score template. GarageBand will automatically open up the Media Browser window on the right side of the GarageBand interface.

2. Click the Movies tab to view your iMovie projects.

3. Drag any iMovie project onto the video track. GarageBand will automatically create a video sound track containing your movie's original sound. You can delete or mute this track if you choose.

4. Create your soundtrack from loops, live instrumentation, or a combination of the two.

5. Double-click any of the track headers to open the Video Preview box in the Media Browser. This allows you to view your video while arranging or recording your tracks.

6. When you're ready to export the finished movie choose one of the following:

   ◆ Share ➤ Send Song to iTunes to send the video directly to your iTunes video collection.

   ◆ Share ➤ Send Movie to iDVD to add your movie to a DVD project.

   ◆ Share ➤ Export as QuickTime Movie to save your movie as a QuickTime MOV file.

GarageBand and ReWire

All ReWire-compatible programs will work with GarageBand, though there are some limitations. GarageBand does not function in exactly the way other ReWire host programs do in one important way: in GarageBand, audio is routed from the ReWire slave to an "invisible" track. You must control the volume levels entirely within the slave program. You are also not able to route multiple outputs from your ReWire slave programs into GarageBand.

A GarageBand/Reason Session

Using GarageBand and Reason together is a great way to take advantage of GarageBand's looping abilities in conjunction with Reason synthesizers—or the other way around. It all depends on your particular style of music making and how you like to work. Either way, the two programs complement each other nicely. To set up a ReWire session with GarageBand:

1. Since GarageBand is the master program, start GarageBand first. Either create a new GarageBand music project and add some loops and/or audio, or open an existing project.

2. Start Reason and create a new session or open an existing one.

3. Start playback in either GarageBand or Reason.

4. Add and record new tracks or instruments as you wish in either program.

Once you have resolved any troubleshooting issues (if necessary—see the sidebar "Troubleshooting Reason and GarageBand"), GarageBand and Reason work together very well. Many functions can be performed in either program, depending on how you prefer to work. You can adjust the cycle region, stop or start playback, and adjust the tempo in either program.

TROUBLESHOOTING REASON AND GARAGEBAND

If you have both Ableton Live and Reason installed on your computer, there is one common problem that occurs when using GarageBand and ReWire. If Reason is running in ReWire mode and is responding to stop and start commands but no sound is coming through, it may be that Ableton Live is causing the problem. This has been a known issue for a while and it's a bit perplexing why Apple hasn't addressed it yet. The following is a workaround for this problem:

1. Locate the folder User/Library/Application Support.

2. Remove any Ableton files or folders (move them to the Desktop or another location, not the Trash, as you will need to return them later).

3. Log off or restart your computer.

When you start up your session again, Reason's output should be correctly routed through GarageBand.

MIX-DOWN

After you create a complete song using elements from GarageBand and Reason, use the same mix-down methods covered in the "Exporting to iTunes" section earlier in this chapter.

Ableton Live and GarageBand

Ableton Live and GarageBand contain many similar features, such as looping and virtual instrumentation functionality, though they're implemented in noticeably different ways. Each program also has its advantages, for example, GarageBand's included instrument collection and Live's advanced loop editing features. By using Live (or one of the "light" versions of Live) in conjunction with GarageBand you can access the best features of both programs in a single session.

USING APPLE LOOPS IN ABLETON LIVE

Ableton Live contains all of the looping functions that GarageBand contains and more. In fact Ableton's looping abilities go far beyond what GarageBand is capable of. If you do choose to use the two programs together through ReWire, you should consider doing as much of your session's looping as you can within Live.

To access your GarageBand Apple Loops in Live:

1. Locate your Apple Loops For GarageBand folder. This may be under User/Library/Audio/Apple Loops or another location. If necessary, use Spotlight or search your hard drive for this folder.

2. Make a note of the path and use Live's Browser window to locate and open the folder.

3. Select the Arrange view.

4. Drag the Apple Loop file 70s Ballad Piano 01 to any track in the Arrange view window.

5. Use your spacebar to play back the file.

Depending on your settings, Ableton Live may read GarageBand's Apple Loops at a different tempo than GarageBand does when added to a session. For example, the loop 70s Piano Ballad 01, which is read as having a default tempo of 80BPM in GarageBand, shows up as having a default tempo of 160BPM in Live. You can easily correct this by taking advantage of Live's Warp function:

1. Double-click the file in Live's Arrange window to open the Sample Display at the bottom of the window.

2. In the Warp section shown in Figure 6.32, click the :2 button to cut the default tempo in half.

FIGURE 6.32
The Warp section of
Live's Sample Display

3. You may also notice warbly sonic artifacts in the loop. To smooth this out, select the Tones setting from the Warp Mode menu.

HALF-TIME OR DOUBLE-TIME?

By cutting the default tempo in half, you actually double the speed of the current loop's playback. This is covered in more detail in Chapter 10 "Apple Loops."

The different Warp Mode settings adjust how Live reads the Apple Loop and are covered in more detail in Chapter 3, "Ableton Live."

A LIVE/GARAGEBAND SESSION

To run Ableton Live and GarageBand together through ReWire, follow these simple steps:

1. Start GarageBand (the master program) and create a new music project or open an existing one.

2. Start Ableton Live and add clips or loops to the project to make sure the audio is being routed to GarageBand.

3. Add more loops and clips to the Live session and more Real and Software Instrument performances to GarageBand.

4. Use GarageBand to adjust the tempo and to start and stop the session.

5. Use the same mix-down and exporting techniques you would use in any GarageBand session.

GarageBand to Logic

Apple introduced GarageBand in 2004 when it launched the first version of its iLife suite of programs. In September 2004 when Logic 7 was released it incorporated many of GarageBand's features, including access to GarageBand instruments and support for Apple Loops. It also included the ability to open GarageBand projects, making the upgrade path from GarageBand to Logic very easy.

If you've worked with a GarageBand a lot or a little and you'd like to give Logic Express a try, you can download a 30-day trial version from:

```
http://www.apple.com/logicexpress/trial
```

All of your GarageBand projects will open seamlessly in Logic, allowing you to add more instruments or loop tracks and take advantage of Logic's editing functions, effects, and more.

For more information on using Logic Pro and Logic Express, see Chapter 5, "Logic."

GarageBand and OS X

Because GarageBand is an Apple program, the current version will be updated automatically when you run the Software Update. GarageBand also works seamlessly with other Apple programs, especially the other iLife programs, such as iDVD, iMovie, and iPhoto.

Installing GarageBand on an External Hard Disk

When you use Apple's installer, GarageBand and the rest of the iLife programs can only be installed on the same drive as your operating system. This prevents you from taking advantage of the benefits of running the audio application from a faster external drive. Luckily there's a nifty little program called GarageBand Anywhere that allows you to install GarageBand on any external drive. Unfortunately (as of this writing), GarageBand Anywhere does not support *installing* GarageBand 3 on an external hard disk. However, you can still use GarageBand Anywhere to *move* your existing copy of GarageBand 3 to an external drive.

You can download GarageBand Anywhere from `http://www.gb-anywhere.webhop.net` or by searching for it on `http://www.versiontracker.com`.

Click the GarageBand Anywhere icon to run the program. Select a drive from the Move To menu. Click the Move button as shown in Figure 6.33.

FIGURE 6.33
Move GarageBand to
an external drive.

GarageBand Anywhere will move GarageBand and all of its associated files to whatever drive you have selected. It will also create an Applications folder where the GarageBand application will reside and a Library folder for your Apple Loops, Software Instruments, and documentation.

Maximizing Processor Power

The color of the playhead is the best indicator of how much processor power is being used. If it's clear or white, you have plenty of room to maneuver. As you use more of your system's resources, the playhead turns yellow, then orange, and finally red before GarageBand tells you that there's not enough power.

LOCKING TRACKS

In GarageBand the first thing you can do to free up more power is to lock your tracks. Locking a track copies the track's audio to your hard drive, including any effects and edits, then reads it from there. Locking Software Instrument tracks, in particular those that are using a lot of effects, will free up your processor quite a bit. Locking is especially useful in the mixing process. To lock any GarageBand track, click the Lock Track button on the track header shown in Figure 6.34.

FIGURE 6.34

Lock tracks to save resources.

If you need to make any changes you can easily unlock the track by clicking the button again.

CONVERTING SOFTWARE LOOPS TO REAL INSTRUMENT LOOPS

Another strategy for saving system resources is converting Software Instrument loops to Real Instrument loops. Under GarageBand Preferences ➤ Advanced, check the Convert to Real Instrument check box.

If you already have sessions using Software Instrument loops with added effects, here's a quick tutorial describing how to convert them to Real Instrument loops:

1. Create a new GarageBand Session and, in the Loop Browser, find the loop Funky Pop Bass 01.

2. Make sure the Convert to Real Instrument check box is checked in the Advanced Preferences.

3. In the Effects menu, add phaser and boost the echo effect.

4. Close out the Track Info window and select the track in the Timeline.

5. Choose Edit ➤ Add to Loop Library and, in the dialog box, change the name of the file to Funky Pop Phase Echo.

6. Drag the file Funky Pop Phase Echo from the Loop Browser to the Timeline.

GarageBand will automatically convert your Software Instrument loop to a Real Instrument loop with all the effects applied.

PRINTING EFFECTS ON COMPLETE TRACKS

If you have a session with many Real or Software Instrument tracks that use virtual amps or a lot of plug-in effects, you may run out of power. One way to fix this problem is to "print" your settings by sending your track to iTunes and reimporting it back into GarageBand. This is similar to locking tracks but allows editing of the printed track on the fly.

1. Once you have the settings for your virtual amp or plug-ins worked out, solo the track and choose File ➤ Export to iTunes; iTunes will automatically give the track the same name as your session.

2. Rename the track and drag it directly from your iTunes playlist back into your GarageBand session.

3. Click the track header and rename the new track.

4. Mute or delete the original track.

GARAGEBAND RESOURCES

To learn more about GarageBand, check out the included help files and the tutorials available at `http://www.apple.com/support/garageband`. There are a few independently run sites that also contain lots of resources. One is `http://www.iCompositions.com`, which has user forums, free loops, and plug-ins for download, as well as excerpts from various GarageBand books and more. Another great site is `http://www.MacJams.com`, which also has forums, loops, tips, useful links, and other resources.

The Bottom Line

Use GarageBand's Musical Typing keyboard GarageBand's built-in keyboard and Musical Typing features make it possible to use your computer's keyboard to create music quickly without attaching a MIDI controller. The Musical Typing keyboard can be especially useful on a laptop if you are traveling or unable to hook up your MIDI devices for any reason.

> **Master It** Use the Musical Typing keyboard to create a performance with one of the GarageBand synthesizers.

Locate specific kinds of loops and add them to a session GarageBand's Loop Browser organizes loops by various attributes such as instrument type, genre, and other keywords. The Loop Browser also contains a section where you can view information about the selected loops such as key and original tempo.

> **Master It** Create a four-measure cycle region, then add a Real Instrument drum loop and a Software Instrument bass loop. Finally, locate a Real or Software Instrument guitar loop that fits musically with the other loops.

Create a drum track using GarageBand's Software Instruments GarageBand's Software Instruments include drum kits, basses, pianos and organs, and a large collection of different types of synthesizers. All of the included instruments can be used to create loops and complete tracks.

> **Master It** Create a drum loop using your MIDI keyboard and one of GarageBand's included virtual drum kits. Then use the Editor window to fix any mistakes or inconsistencies.

Add effects to a GarageBand track GarageBand's built-in effects, OS X's built-in Audio Unit effects, and any third-party Audio Unit plug-in effects are all accessible from the Track Info window and can be added to any Real or Software Instrument track.

> **Master It** Create a new track with any loop from the Loop Browser and add two plug-in effects.

Export a GarageBand song to iTunes GarageBand automatically mixes your songs down into the iTunes program. From there you can add metadata, burn CDs, or convert songs into other formats.

> **Master It** Create a song on GarageBand using loops or loops and your own audio recordings, then export it to iTunes.

Chapter 7

More Useful Software

In this chapter I'll cover some programs that can be useful to you no matter what your primary recording software is. The programs covered in this chapter represent some of the best of what's available for OS X. Each section is designed to give you an overview of the software and some tutorials to familiarize you with the program's interface and some of its basic functionality. All of the programs covered in this chapter have demo versions available, so you can try these programs out yourself and see which ones will suit your style and workflow.

Some of the programs I'll be covering perform similar functions, but each works in its own unique way. Some programs, like Celemony's Melodyne software, introduce new ways to perform familiar tasks, while others, like Audiofile's Wave Editor, add some interesting variations to familiar editing processes.

In this chapter, you will learn to

◆ Create and edit loops, samples, and other audio files with an audio editor

◆ Use Audio Units and VST plug-ins outside of a host program

◆ Batch convert audio files

◆ Create a loop or sample from a DVD

◆ Scan a hard drive or folder for all of its audio files

Get Ready

To get the most out this chapter, it will help to have at least one virtual instrument and some plug-in effects installed.

We'll be working with programs that use Audio Units and VST format instruments, so for a virtual instrument I recommend downloading and installing the freeware Crystal synthesizer, which is available in both formats. Crystal is available from `http://www.greenoak.com/crystal`.

For more information on using and expanding the Crystal synthesizer see the "Virtual Synthesizer" section of Chapter 9, "Virtual Instruments."

For a set of plug-ins, I suggest downloading the Pluggo Junior suite of free plug-ins. Pluggo Junior is a set of ten selected effects from Cycling '74's Pluggo suite, which contains over 100 effects and instruments. Pluggo Junior contains Audio Unit, VST- and RTAS-compatible plug-in effects and is available from `http://www.cycling74.com/pluggo`.

Pluggo and Pluggo Junior are covered in detail in Chapter 8 "Plug-ins."

Default Playback Devices

You'll be installing and using a wide range of software throughout this chapter and the rest of the book. As you work with different programs, you will be creating many audio files, whether by bouncing a final mix, playing a virtual instrument, or exporting a processed file from an audio editor.

As you install and work with different programs and plug-ins, you'll find that a new program will often make itself the default program for opening a certain file type. For example, for most Mac users the default program for opening any MP3 is iTunes. This means that every time you double-click an MP3 file, iTunes will automatically start up and play the file. Furthermore, every MP3 file on your computer will be represented by the iTunes icon.

Certain file types may become associated with programs that may not be the most convenient or appropriate default program. For example, Pro Tools likes to make itself the default program for opening AIFF files. This means that every time you create and export an AIFF file from any program and then double-click it to listen back, Pro Tools will start up and try to import the file.

I recommend setting up QuickTime as your default playback program for AIFF and WAV files. QuickTime makes a good choice for a number of reasons:

◆ It's installed on every Mac.

◆ It opens quickly, each file in a single window.

◆ It has a built-in feature that's great for previewing loop files (use the keyboard shortcut Command+L to loop playback in QuickTime).

To make QuickTime your default playback program for a specific file type:

1. Locate any file of the appropriate type—AIFF, WAV, and so on.

2. Select the file in the Finder and use the keyboard shortcut Command+I to open the Get Info window.

3. In the Open With field (Figure 7.1), use the drop-down menu to select the most recent version of QuickTime Player.

4. Click the Change All button.

5. Click Continue in the confirmation pop-up window.

FIGURE 7.1
The Get Info window

If you have a specific program you prefer to work with, or if you'd like to assign a specific file type to a specific program, use the Get Info window to do so.

Installing new programs or working in others can cause your settings to change, sometimes frequently. Keep an eye on default icons of any files you export to make sure the settings you've chosen are still in place. You can always go back and change the default playback program again at any time.

AudioFinder

AudioFinder is available from `http://www.icedaudio.com` for $69.95. The purchase price includes unlimited updates for life.

There is a demo version available, with access to much of AudioFinder's functionality. However, when using the demo version, audio processing functions will be disabled after starting the program in trial mode a number of times.

AudioFinder is many programs in one, but at its core it's an organizational tool. It gives you very straightforward ways to organize and access all of the loops, samples, and other audio files that reside on your computer or any attached hard drives.

As the program grows, more features are constantly being added, including an audio editor and a plug-in manager.

Some of the things you can do with AudioFinder:

◆ Convert between many file formats including RX2 to AIFF or WAV files

◆ Apply effects to loops and samples and save the results as a new file

◆ Select individual loops from various collections and send them to a new folder

◆ Browse your audio files by categories like BPM or instrument type

◆ Create sample instruments for Logic's EXS samplers

◆ Manage all your plug-in effects and instruments, regardless of format

AudioFinder is one of the best deals going for audio-related software. Also included with your license is unlimited updating: you get every new version for free for life, and you can request authorization codes for AudioFinder for every computer you own.

These tutorials were written using AudioFinder 4. AudioFinder is one of the most frequently updated programs I've come across. It's possible that some of the features covered in this section may have since been updated or moved around. If you find that this is the case, please refer to the Iced Audio website for information on any recent updates and added features.

Setting up AudioFinder

When you start AudioFinder for the first time, a dialog box will appear asking where your audio files are stored. Select your main hard drive to set it as the root folder for future searching, browsing, and scanning.

There are two basic ways to use AudioFinder to locate and work with your audio files:

◆ You can use AudioFinder's Browser to browse a specific location (folder or drive) on your computer.

◆ You can use the AudioFinder's Scanner to catalog all of the audio files on your hard drive or another more specific location such as a folder, directory, CD, or DVD-ROM.

Figure 7.2 shows AudioFinder's Browser window.

FIGURE 7.2
AudioFinder's
Browser window

WHAT'S IT DOING?

When I say that AudioFinder organizes all of your audio files, I mean that it catalogs them. AudioFinder doesn't actually move any files around (unless you tell it to).

AudioFinder creates a list of all the sound files it finds on your hard drive or in a specific folder and presents you with that list in such a way that you can preview and select the files. It's kind of like an audio-only version of Apple's Spotlight search feature.

Once AudioFinder catalogs your entire collection, you can search for specific types of files by name or by other criteria like file type.

AudioFinder *can* also copy and move your files around as well, but only if you tell it to.

Scanning

In order to utilize AudioFinder's organizational functionality you'll want to have the program scan your system for all of your available audio files.

EXCLUDE MP3 FILES

If you have a collection of MP3 files residing on any of the drives you intend to scan and you have it organized and cataloged in iTunes, you may want to exclude these from the AudioFinder results. To do this, choose Scanner ➤ Scan Item Type Setup and remove the check mark next to MP3, as shown in Figure 7.3.

DEFAULT SCAN

The first time you run AudioFinder you should have it scan your entire hard drive and external drives. If you are doing a lot of recording, this can turn up a vast amount of audio files, including every track you have recorded that is currently saved on any internal or external drives. You may be surprised to find a number of files you forgot about or didn't know existed.

FIGURE 7.3
Exclude MP3 files
from your scan.

Scanning your entire system can take a while, but having a complete catalog of every audio file in your system can come in handy any number of ways and is well worth the wait.

1. Start AudioFinder.

2. Click the Home button in the Browser window (the button with a house icon, second from the left at the top of the AudioFinder window).

3. Select the Volumes folder if you would like to scan your entire system, including external hard drives. Or, if you prefer, select a specific drive from within the Volumes folder to scan that drive only.

4. Click the Scanner tab. Figure 7.4 shows the Scanner window.

5. Select Live Scan From Browser.

6. Once the scan has completed, click the Save Default button at the bottom of the Scanner window.

FIGURE 7.4
AudioFinder's
Scanner window

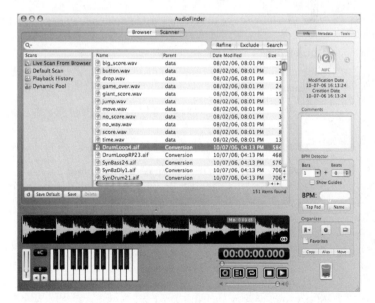

This complete cataloging of your system is now saved as the Default Scan. You can access this at any time by selecting Default Scan in the Scanner window. Scroll through the list to see all of the audio files currently residing on your hard drive.

You can now use the Search field at the top of the Scanner window to locate files by name or the name of the folder they are located in. Try searching for keywords like Apple Loops and Garage-Band. If you have installed GarageBand, Live, Logic, or any other audio program, scanning your system with AudioFinder will turn up any loops or samples associated with those programs.

You can also use the scanner for more refined searches. To scan a specific folder or drive:

1. Select the folder or drive in the Browser.

2. Click the Scanner tab at the top of the AudioFinder window.

3. Select Live Scan From Browser.

4. Once the scan is complete you can save it by clicking the Save button at the bottom of the Scanner window (to delete a saved scan, click Delete).

Browsing

The other way to locate files in AudioFinder is the Browser window. Select the Browser tab at the top of the AudioFinder window and click the Home button. This brings you to your hard drive's root folder. From here you can access any location on your computer:

◆ To browse your hard drive, secondary or external drives, or a CD or DVD, open the Volumes folder.

◆ To locate your Apple Loops For GarageBand folder, select `Volumes\Your Hard Drive\ Library\Audio\Apple Loops\Apple Loops for GarageBand`. (It's also possible that your GarageBand loops will be located under *yourusername*`\Library\Audio\Apple Loops`, especially if there's more than one user on your computer.)

◆ To browse the desktop, select `Users\`*yourusername*`\Desktop`.

Bookmarks

Bookmarking your most commonly used folders will give you quick access to their contents. To bookmark a folder:

1. If you haven't done so already, copy the `MMA Audio` folder to your desktop from this book's companion DVD.

2. Locate the `MMA Audio` folder with the Browser and select it to view its contents.

3. Click the Bookmark button on the top left of the AudioFinder window and choose Add Selection to Organizer Bookmarks from the drop-down menu.

Use the Browser to check out any other locations on your hard drive. When you want to return to the MMA Audio folder, click the Bookmark button and select MMA Audio from the drop-down menu.

Playing Files

Once you have scanned or browsed your way to an audio file, you can use AudioFinder to play back the file as a one-shot or as a loop. Select any file in the Scanner or Browser window and it will play automatically.

Located at the bottom of the AudioFinder interface is an area where you can see the selected file's waveform. Beneath the waveform display you can see the playback buttons shown in Figure 7.5.

FIGURE 7.5
The sample playback buttons

These buttons give you a number of different options for playing the audio file. They are from left to right:

Play a Random Sound   Plays a random loop or sample from the files within the selected folder.

Autopilot Play   Continuously plays random loops or samples from the selected folder.

Loop   Plays back the selected file as a continuous loop. Click the button again to stop play.

Stop   Stops playback.

Play   Plays the selected file.

Try out AudioFinder's playback features:

1. In the Browser window open the MMA Audio\AudioFinder folder and select the audio file DrumLoopAF.wav.

2. Click the Loop button to play back the selected file as continuous loop.

3. Click the Loop button again to stop the loop.

4. Select a different file in the Browser window and preview it using the Loop button.

Copying Files to a New Location

AudioFinder gives you multiple choices for copying loops to another location. This is especially useful if you are compiling loops or samples from various sources for a project or track.

The easiest way to copy a track is to drag it directly from the AudioFinder window to your desktop or another folder. With some programs, such as GarageBand and Live, you can drag and drop files directly from AudioFinder into the program interface. In others you may have to copy the loop or sample to the desktop first to make it work.

In the lower right corner of the AudioFinder interface is the Organizer, shown in Figure 7.6.

You can use the Organizer to create new folders to hold your personalized collections of audio files. To create a new library:

1. In the Organizer, click the Bookmark button (the one that looks like a ribbon) and select Other from the pop-up menu that appears.

2. Use the dialog box to create a new folder on your desktop named My Samples.

FIGURE 7.6
The Organizer

3. Click the Bookmark button again and make sure that My Samples is the selected folder.

4. Select any file in either the Browser or the Scanner window and click the Copy button in the Organizer.

AudioFinder will automatically create a copy of the file in your My Samples folder. You can also do the following with the Organizer:

♦ Click the Alias button to create a shortcut to your file in the selected folder.

♦ Click the Move button to move the file from its current location to the selected folder.

Converting Files

One of AudioFinder's useful features is its ability to quickly convert files to and from multiple formats. Conversion can be done in the Browser or Scanner window but for organizational reasons it's best to work in the Browser window.

BASIC CONVERSION

Locate and select any audio file in the Browser window or select multiple files at once by Shift+clicking or Command+clicking. Choose File ➢ Convert, then choose the format you want to convert to.

A new file will be created within the same folder with "–Converted" added to the file name.

CUSTOM CONVERSION USING ITUNES

To convert to MP3 or AAC format or to have more control over the Sample Rate and Bit Rate for your converted WAV and AIFF files, you can use AudioFinder's Convert Using iTunes command. However, settings for the converted files will be determined by settings you create beforehand in your iTunes Preferences, so you should do that first. To set your iTunes Preferences:

1. Open iTunes and select iTunes ➢ Preferences.

2. Click the Advanced tab.

3. On the Advanced tab, select the Importing tab.

4. From the Import Using drop-down menu, select a format.

5. Select Custom from the Settings menu and then make the changes you want in the dialog box that appears. Close iTunes.

6. Open AudioFinder and select the file or files you want to convert.

7. Select File ➢ Convert Using iTunes.

8. From the Select Conversion Format dialog box, choose your preferred format from the list of file format encoders—MP3, AAC, Apple Lossless, AIFF, WAV—then click the OK button.

Converted files will appear in iTunes in an automatically created playlist named AudioFinder Converted. You can drag these files directly from the iTunes window to copy them to a new location or select them in the iTunes window and use the keyboard shortcut Command+R to open the file in OS X's Finder window.

Adding Effects

With AudioFinder you can add a single AudioUnit effect to any audio file:

1. Locate the file DrumLoopAF.wav in the Browser window.

2. Choose AudioUnits ➢ Apple ➢ AUMatrixReverb.

3. Click the Loop button to play back the file and the added effect as a continuous loop.

4. Adjust the AUMatrixReverb or choose a preset from the Factory Preset drop-down menu at the top of the plug-in interface to create the effect you want.

5. Select AudioUnits ➢ Process to permanently add the effect to the loop.

AudioFinder will automatically create a new file with -AUProcessed added to the file name.

Editing Files

AudioFinder's included Meta Editor can perform a number of audio editing tasks, mostly associated with samples and loops.

Double-clicking any audio file in the Browser or Scanner window will open the Meta Editor.

To try out the Meta Editor, navigate the Browser to MMA Audio\AudioFinder and double-click the DrumLoopAF.wav file to open the Meta Editor.

Figure 7.7 shows the audio file DrumLoopAF.wav in the Meta Editor window.

FIGURE 7.7

The Meta Editor

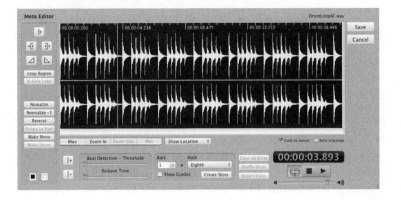

On the bottom right side of the Meta Editor is the Transport bar, which has only three buttons, Loop, Stop, and Start. Click the Start button to play the file; click the Loop button to turn looping on to play the file as a continuous loop.

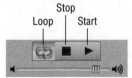

The Meta Editor has a selection of basic tools for editing your audio files. The Tools section is located on the left side of the Meta Editor.

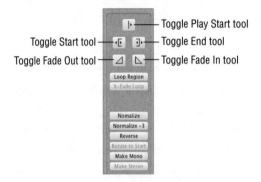

From top to bottom:

Toggle Play Start tool   Turns on the Play Start Cursor, which sets where playback of the audio file begins. With the Toggle Play Start tool selected, move the Play Start Cursor to any location within the audio file and double-click the Stop button on the lower right of the Meta Editor. Then click the Play button to begin playback of the audio file.

Toggle Start tool   Sets a new start point for the audio file. Click the Toggle Start tool and move the Start Cursor to the right. All audio to the left of the Start playhead will not be included in the loop.

Toggle End tool   Sets a new end point for the audio file. All audio to the right of the End Playhead will not be included in the loop. Use the Toggle Start and Toggle End tools to create "loops within loops."

Toggle Fade-In tool   Creates a fade-in from the start of the loop. Adjust the length of the fade by clicking and dragging the circle at the top of the Editor window.

Toggle Fade-Out tool   Creates a fade-out at the end of the loop. The fade tools are very useful for cleaning up clicks and pops at the beginning and end of sound files.

Loop Region button   Creates region markers within the audio file that some sampler applications can use to stop and start the file.

X-Fade Loop button   Opens the Crossfade dialog box, allowing you to create a crossfade within the Loop Region for better playback in the sampler applications that can access the Loop Region settings.

Normalize button   Makes the loop as loud as possible without clipping.

Normalize –3db button   Makes the selected file as loud as possible without clipping, then subtracts 3db.

Reverse button   Reverses the loop or selected region within the loop.

Rotate to Start button   Use this button in conjunction with the Toggle Play Start button. Click the Toggle Play Start button and move the Play Start cursor to any location within the file. Then click the Rotate to Start button to start the loop from the selected location.

Make Mono button   Converts stereo files to mono.

Make Stereo button   Converts mono files to stereo.

Plug-in Manager

AudioFinder also contains a plug-in managing function that you can use to enable and disable any plug-ins installed on your computer. This can be useful if you've got many plug-ins installed that you are not using but don't want to delete or if your DAW or other programs are crashing on startup, which can often mean a bad plug-in.

To disable a plug-in with AudioFinder's Plug-in Manager:

1. Select Window ➢ Plug-in Manager (Command+P).

2. Choose a plug-in format from the drop-down list at the top of the window.

3. Select the plug-in you wish to disable from the Enabled Plug-ins list.

4. Click the Disable button at the bottom of the list, then click OK.

You can also do the following:

◆ Reenable a plug-in by selecting it in the Disabled Plug-ins list and clicking the Enable button.

◆ Disable all of the plug-ins on the list at once by clicking the Swap Lists button at the bottom of the window.

And the Beat Goes On...

As you can tell by now, AudioFinder has a lot more to it than just the organizational components. As a program that adds new features to just about every update along the way there's really no telling what's in store for in AudioFinder's future updates.

Audio Hijack/Audio Hijack Pro

Audio Hijack, from Rogue Amoeba (`http://www.rogueamoeba.com`), is a recording program that can "grab" the audio output from any program on your Mac and create an audio file. Some of the things Audio Hijack can be used for include recording streaming audio off of the Internet or creating loops and samples from QuickTime movies, DVDs, or songs in your iTunes Library. Audio Hijack costs $16. The "Pro" version, with even more features and functionality, costs $32.

Demo versions will work for ten days and are fully functioning, except that any recordings over ten minutes long will have intermittent noise.

Looping and Sampling with Audio Hijack

Each Audio Hijack recording is considered a "session." Audio Hijack places all of the recorded files for each session on the desktop by default. For this session you'll create a new folder for the Audio Hijack recording:

1. Start the Audio Hijack program.

2. Select the program you want to hijack from the Sessions list.

3. Make sure the Inspector window is showing. If it's not, choose Control ➤ Show Inspector. Figure 7.8 shows the Audio Hijack's Main and Inspector windows.

FIGURE 7.8
Audio Hijack's interface

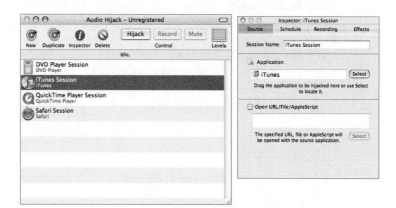

4. Click the Recording tab in the Inspector window.

5. Under Save Recorded Files To, click the Select button.

6. Use the dialog box to create a new folder on your desktop named Audio Hijack Files.

7. Click Choose.

For this example I used Audio Hijack to create a drum loop from a song in my iTunes library. I chose this particular drum break (from a band named after insects and an album named after the "road" they were recording on) because it contains a number of sections that could be edited and looped as well as a very nice isolated kick drum sound that could be extracted. Now you try it:

1. Start the Audio Hijack program.

2. Select iTunes Session in the Audio Hijack window.

3. Click the Hijack button at the top of the Audio Hijack window. The iTunes program will start automatically.

4. Locate the song you wish to use in iTunes.

5. Locate the section of the song you want to capture.

6. Click the Record button at the top of the Audio Hijack window.

7. Click the Play button in iTunes (Audio Hijack will wait for you to click the Play button in iTunes before it actually begins recording).

8. Stop playback in iTunes to end recording.

9. Click the Record and Hijack buttons again in Audio Hijack to finish the session.

10. Locate the file that Audio Hijack has created and open it with your default audio playback device.

You can now edit the file in your DAW program or audio editing program.

Audio Hijack Pro

Audio Hijack Pro contains all of the features of Audio Hijack but adds more functionality to the mix. Audio Hijack Pro's extra features include:

◆ The ability to add metadata to your files such as artist information and comments

◆ The Recording Bin, an iTunes-style playlist for quick access to your recordings

◆ CD burning

◆ The ability set up a default audio editor to edit your recordings

◆ Support for Audio Units and VST effects

SETTING UP

Before you start using Audio Hijack Pro, you will want to install the Instant Hijack function. This will allow you to begin recording from any source without having to restart the source program:

1. Start the Audio Hijack Pro program.

2. Select Audio Hijack Pro ➤ Install Extras.

3. Click the Instant Hijack tab.

4. Click the Install button.

5. Log off or restart your computer to finish the installation process.

SAMPLING WITH AUDIO HIJACK PRO

I'll use Audio Hijack Pro to create a spoken word sample from a DVD then add some effects:

1. Choose a DVD to sample. Insert the DVD into your DVD drive and locate the section you'd like to record.

2. Pause the DVD.

PUBLIC DOMAIN

Most commercial DVDs are copyright protected, meaning that you can't use their audio contents in a commercially available recording without "clearing" any samples with the copyright owner. There are many older movies available that fall into the category of public domain, which means their copyrights have expired and were not renewed. Finding out what's in the public domain and what's not can be tricky. Internet searches and websites like http://www.openflix.com can often be helpful in locating information and titles. Many public domain movies are also available for viewing and download from: http://www.archive.org/details/movies.

---

3. Choose Video ➤ Half Size to play the DVD in a smaller window.

4. Start Audio Hijack Pro.

5. Select DVD Player from the Component list on the left side of the screen. Figure 7.9 shows a DVD Player Audio Hijack session.

FIGURE 7.9
A DVD Player Audio
Hijack session

6. Click the Recording tab in the center of the Audio Hijack Pro window.

7. Set the recording format to For Burning to CD. This will create your audio files as 16-bit stereo AIFF files, which can be opened and read in every audio recording and editing program.

8. Click the Effects tab to view the Effects window. At this point you can add to the recording any Audio Unit, VST, or LADSPA effects that are installed on your system. Audio Hijack also has 20 of its own built-in effects. Effects like delays and intense reverbs can be used for drastic results. You can also use plug-ins such as a compressor or EQ to enhance or clean up the sound.

9. Add Audio Hijack Pro's built-in reverb effect by clicking your mouse in any empty effect slot and selecting 4FX Effect ➤ Reverb.

10. Click the Hijack button at the top of the screen to prepare for recording.

11. Start playback of the DVD player to hear what the effect will sound like.

    You can toggle between the effected and clean sound by selecting and deselecting the Hijack button. To remove the effect, select it in the Effects window and press the Delete key on your Apple keyboard.

12. Click the Record button to begin recording.

13. Click the Record button again to stop recording.

14. Click the Hijack button to end the recording session.

To play back the Audio Hijack Pro recording select Recording Bin at the top of the Components window. Figure 7.10 shows the Audio Hijack Recording Bin.

FIGURE 7.10
The Audio Hijack
Recording Bin

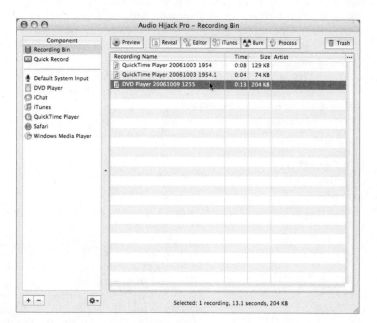

There are seven buttons across the top of the Recording Bin that you can use to determine what to do with your file. From left to right:

Preview   Plays back your file in a QuickTime-style playback window.

Reveal   Locates the sound file on your hard drive. Use this feature to drag and drop the file into another program such as an audio editor or DAW.

Editor   Opens your default audio editor. Assign a default audio editor by selecting Audio Hijack Pro ➤ Preferences and clicking the Set button next to the Audio Editor field. Use the dialog box to locate your preferred audio editor.

iTunes Opens the file in iTunes and add it to your iTunes library.

Burn Burns any selected files to an Audio CD.

Process Lets you chose from a number of iTunes-related scripts. Add the file to your iPod, convert file formats and more.

Trash Moves the selected file to the Trash.

Audio Hijack and Audio Hijack Pro are fun, inexpensive programs that make quick sampling and capturing audio from any OS X programs easy to accomplish.

Audacity

Audacity is an open source freeware audio recording program, available from `http://audacity .sourceforge.net`, which can be extremely useful for quick recording and editing tasks that might be more involved or complicated in your DAW program. For audio processing Audacity has its own built-in plug-ins and, by installing the separate VST enabler, you can also use many of your VST plug-ins. Audacity also has the ability to import and export many different file types including standard WAV and AIFF formats. MP3 exporting can be enabled by downloading and installing the LAME MP3 Encoder.

Because it's free, easy to use, and has multitracking capabilities and many included effects, Audacity is very popular with podcasters.

There are usually multiple versions of Audacity available, both the recommended download and the beta version of an upcoming release. It's a good idea to stick with the recommended download for maximum stability.

Installing Audacity is as simple as dragging the Audacity folder to your Applications folder. Double-click the Audacity icon to start the program. Figure 7.11 shows the Audacity interface.

FIGURE 7.11
The Audacity
interface

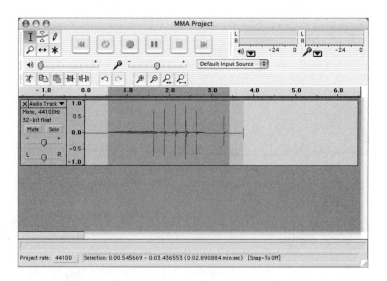

Basic Multitrack Recording

Audacity doesn't have many of the advanced features or options that many commercial recording and editing programs have. You can multitrack record but only by adding one track at a time. This makes Audacity a great program for creating a quick demo or capturing an off-the-cuff live performance, but it's not a good choice for more intricate recording. To record in Audacity:

1. Select Audacity ➤ Preferences ➤ Audio I/O and choose the playback and recording devices.

   If you are recording and/or monitoring through a hardware interface, select it from the drop-down menu or use your Mac's built-in audio for recording and playback.

2. Enable monitoring by selecting Hardware Playthrough (Play New Track While Recording It).

   If you find that you are unable to monitor your track while recording, return to the Audio I/O Preferences and select Software Playthrough.

3. If you want to hear previously recorded tracks while recording new tracks, select the Play Other Tracks While Recording New Ones check box.

4. Choose whether to record in mono or stereo. To record mono tracks leave the Channels setting at 1 (Mono). To record stereo tracks choose 2 (Stereo) from the drop-down menu.

5. Click OK to return to Audacity's main window.

6. Make sure your microphone or instrument is properly connected.

   Figure 7.12 shows Audacity's Transport bar.

FIGURE 7.12
Audacity's
Transport bar

7. Click the red Record button to begin recording and the yellow Stop button to stop recording.

8. Use the purple Rewind button on the left to return to the beginning of the recording. Use the green Play button to play back your recording.

9. To add a second track, click the Rewind button to return to the beginning of your session and then click the Record button. Audacity will automatically create a new track and begin recording.

Mixing

Mixing in Audacity is done right in the Recording window. Once you've created some tracks in Audacity you can use the track header section on the left side of each track to set the volume levels and panning. Figure 7.13 shows a track header in the main window.

FIGURE 7.13
A track header in
Audacity

At the top of the track header is a drop-down menu (labeled Audio Track in Figure 7.13) from which you can do the following:

◆ Rename the track.

◆ Move the track up or down in the window to better organize your mixing process.

◆ Change the track view from Waveform to Spectrum or Pitch.

◆ Set Mono or Stereo properties.

◆ Set Sample Rate or Bit Rate properties.

Editing

Audacity's six editing tools are located at the top left of the interface (Figure 7.14).

FIGURE 7.14
Audacity's
editing tools

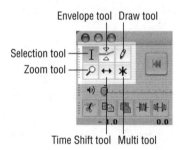

Selection tool Selects sections of audio for processing, copying, and deleting.

Envelope tool Creates volume envelopes, raising and lowering the volume of a track.

Draw tool Manually edits waveforms.

Zoom tool Gives you a close-up view of sections

Time Shift tool Moves audio forward and backward within the track.

Multi tool Lets you use different tools, depending on where you place the cursor on a track.

Saving and Exporting

Audacity gives you lots of options for saving and exporting your files. From the File menu you can choose from the default choices: Export as WAV, Export as MP3, or Export as Ogg Vorbis.

EXPORT AS MP3

For legal reasons Audacity is not able to include the ability to export MP3 when you download the program. In order to use the MP3 export option you have to download and install the separate LAME MP3 exporting encoder available at `http://spaghetticode.org/lame` or on the Audacity download page. Here's how to install the MP3 exporter:

1. Download and unstuff the `LameLib-Carbon.sit` file.
2. Place the LameLib file in your Audacity folder (in the Applications folder).
3. Open Audacity and create a quick recording.
4. Choose File ➢ Export as MP3.
5. Use the dialog box to locate the LameLib file.
6. Fill out the appropriate track data in the export dialog box.
7. Click OK.

You can now use the Export as MP3 function at any time. Audacity will automatically locate the LameLib from now on.

EXPORT AS AIFF

You can also change the Export as WAV function to Export as AIFF:

1. Select Audacity ➢ Preferences and click the File Formats tab.
2. In the Uncompressed Export Format field, choose AIFF (Apple/SGI 16 Bit PCM).
3. While you're there, you'll notice the Other option at the bottom of the list. Select this to get a look at the very impressive list of possible file formats you can export from Audacity.

You can also choose File ➢ Export Multiple to export all the tracks in a session as individual WAV or MP3 files.

Using Effects

Audacity includes a number of built-in effects as well as any Audio Unit effects you have installed. Effects in Audacity can be added to entire tracks or sections of tracks.

1. Use the Selection tool to select a section of audio, or use the keyboard shortcut Command+A to select the entire track.
2. Select an effect from the Effect menu. Figure 7.15 shows Audacity's Phaser plug-in effect.
3. If necessary, adjust the effect's parameters and use the Preview button to listen to the effect before processing the file.

FIGURE 7.15
Audacity's
Phaser effect

USING VSTs

You can also use many of your VST plug-in effects in Audacity by downloading and installing the VST Enabler:

1. Download the VST enabler from `http://www.audacityteam.org/vst`.

2. Unzip the VST Enabler folder.

3. Place the file `vst-bridge.so` in the folder `Applications\Audacity\Plug-ins`.

Some of your VST plug-ins will appear below Audacity's included plug-ins in the Effects menu. Not all of your VSTs will work in Audacity and some may function differently. Whenever possible I recommend using Audacity's included effects instead.

Resources

Since Audacity is freeware, much of the documentation that exists is created by users and also shared freely. You can find an online manual here:

> `http://audacity.sourceforge.net/onlinehelp-1.2`

More information and a users' forum can be found at here:

> `http://www.audacityteam.org`

A user-updated online encyclopedia is available here:

> `http://www.audacityteam.org/wiki`

Wave Editor

Audiofile Engineering's Wave Editor, available from `http://www.audiofile-engineering.com`, is an audio editing program that combines both standard and innovative editing techniques. Along with the usual features you would expect from an audio editor—volume adjustment, cross-fading, effects, and so on—Wave Editor has some interesting new ways to work with sound files, including the ability to work with multiple layers within a single file much like as you would in an image editor.

Wave Editor costs $250 and works with OS X 10.4 and higher. The demo version is fully functional for 15 days.

Wave Editor Basics

Wave Editor's main window is only visible once you opened an audio file. Locate and open an audio file by choosing File ➤ Open.

Figure 7.16 shows Wave Editor's main window with a looped WAV file.

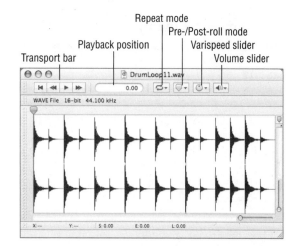

The top of the window contains Wave Editor's main controls, from left to right:

Transport bar Includes the Back (to the beginning of the file), Rewind, Play, and Forward buttons.

Playback position Displays in seconds the current position of the playhead.

Repeat mode Opens a menu for setting the looping function. Choose from Off (no looping), Selection (loops only the area selected with your mouse), Playback Loop (plays the loop once), and Entire File (loops the whole file continuously).

Pre/Post-roll Opens a menu allowing you to choose to add pre-roll or post-roll when playing back the sound file. The Options choice at the bottom of the menu opens a dialog box containing pre- and post-roll parameters. These settings work with Wave Editor's recording functionality. Pre- and post-roll are the amount of audio you will hear before and after creating a new recording on an existing audio file.

Varispeed slider Adjusts the playback tempo of the current file.

Volume slider Changes how loud the sound file plays.

Editing a Sound File

Wave Editor includes many of the usual sound file editing options. To use Wave Editor's basic functions:

1. Select File ➤ Open and locate the `MMA Audio\Wave Editor` folder on the book's companion DVD.

2. Select any WAV file. You can preview the folder's WAV files in Wave Editor's Open File dialog box by clicking the Play button.

3. Choose a file and click Open.

4. Select a section of the audio file.

5. Use the standard OS X keyboard shortcuts to edit the audio file: Command+X to cut, Command+C to copy, and Command+V to paste sections of the audio file.

6. Use Command+N to create a new audio file and copy and paste between the two files.

The Processor Window

Figurer 7.17 shows the Wave Editor's Processor window.

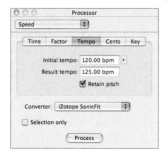

FIGURE 7.17

The Processor window

Open the Processor window by selecting Window ➢ Processor or using the keyboard shortcut Command+Shift+P. The commands available from the Processor window drop-down menu (labeled Speed in Figure 7.17) include the following:

Change Gain   Raises or lowers the volume of an audio file or selected region.

Normalize   Raises the volume of the highest peak in your audio file as high as possible without "clipping" or creating digital distortion.

Invert Phase   Corrects any phase problems encountered in the recording process.

Trim   Eliminates dead space at the beginning and end of audio files.

Speed   Changes the playback speed of an audio file. This is especially useful for adjusting the tempo of loop files.

Reverse Audio   Reverses an entire audio file or selected region of an audio file.

Remove DC Offset   Removes the clicks or pops at the beginning or end of an audio file caused by DC offset.

DC OFFSET

DC offset is a slight inaccuracy or variation in your audio files that can happen when your signal is converted from analog to digital by your audio interface. DC offset isn't usually a big problem in most digital recording situations, but it does show up from time to time. It's most noticeable in pops or clicks that may occur at the beginning or end of a file that contains DC offset.

Convert Sample Rate   Converts the sample rate of the file anywhere from 22,050Hz to 192,000Hz.

Thresholds   Create new labels at selected points throughout the selected audio file.

WORKING WITH LAYERS

To create a new layer in a Wave Editor file:

1. Choose File ➤ Open and locate any WAV, AIFF, or RX2 file.

2. Highlight a section of the audio file and use Command+C to copy the selection.

3. Choose Layer ➤ Add Layer. Adding a new layer will open the Layers panel on either the left or right side of the main window.

4. Use Command+V or Edit ➤ Paste to paste the audio onto the new layer.

5. Holding down Command+Shift will turn your cursor into a Hand tool, which you can use to reposition the new layer anywhere within the sound file.

Figure 7.18 shows the new layer and the Layers panel.

FIGURE 7.18
A new layer and the
Layers panel

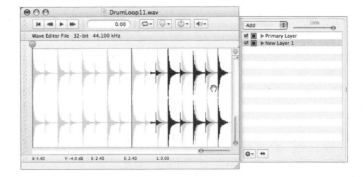

EFFECTS

You can use Audio Unit effects on your sound files. Effects are applied to individual layers. If you are working with multiple layers, make sure the layer you want to add the effect to is selected in the Layers panel.

To add an effect:

1. Select the layer you want to add an effect to.

2. Choose Layer ➤ Add Audio Unit to view a list of available Audio Unit folders.

3. Choose Apple ➤ AUDelay to open Apple's OS X Audio Unit delay effect.

4. Click the Play button in Wave Editor's Transport bar to hear the file with the added effect.

5. Adjust the effect's parameters or load a preset if there are any available from the preset menu in the top right corner of the plug-in interface.

6. To permanently add the effect, choose Layer ➤ Flatten Layer.

7. In the pop-up dialog that appears, choose between Retain Tail and Retain Current Length:

   ◆ Retain tail will elongate your file, for example, adding extra time for a delay or reverb effect to fade out.

   ◆ Retain current length will keep your file at the same length and is more appropriate when working with loop files.

For more information on Audio Units and other plug-ins, see Chapter 8.

Recording

Wave Editor can make single-track recordings through your hardware audio interface or your Mac's built-in recording line in. To record into Wave Editor:

1. View Wave Editor's recorder by selecting Window ➤ Recorder.

2. Click the microphone icon on the bottom left of the Recorder window to open the audio input preferences panel.

3. Select the audio input device from the drop-down menu. Assign audio tracks for mono or stereo recording, if necessary.

4. Next to the microphone icon is a button that looks like a stopwatch. Click this button to open Wave Editor threshold recording panel. Using these settings, you can have Wave Editor automatically begin recording when a certain volume level is reached and automatically stop recording when the sound drops below a predetermined volume level.

   Figure 7.19 shows the Recorder window with the Threshold Recording panel visible.

FIGURE 7.19

Wave Editor's Record window

5. Click the Start button to begin recording.

6. Once recording, begins the Start button becomes the Stop button. Click it again to end recording.

7. If desired, use the Stop/Start button to record more audio onto the same file.

8. Click the Done button to finish the recording process and automatically open the file in Wave Editor's standard editing window.

Keyboard Shortcuts

Wave Editor's keyboards shortcut menu appears on the lower right of the screen when you open the program. If you have closed this window you can reopen it by choosing Wave Editor ➤ Keyboard Shortcuts. Figure 7.20 shows the Keyboard Shortcuts window.

◆ Click the triangle next to any category to view the Wave Editor's functions and any already assigned shortcuts.

◆ Change or add a keyboard shortcut by double-clicking any function to open the keyboard shortcut dialog, shown in Figure 7.21.

FIGURE 7.20
The Keyboard Short-
cuts window

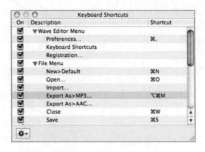

FIGURE 7.21
Add a new keyboard
shortcut.

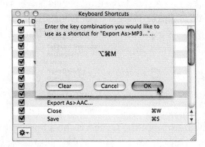

◆ Use your Apple keyboard to type in the keyboard shortcut you wish to assign to a particular function.

If you try and assign a keyboard shortcut that is already taken by another function, Wave Editor will display an error message telling you which function is already using that keyboard shortcut.

If you want to reassign a keyboard shortcut that is already in use, locate the function in the Keyboard Shortcut list and double-click to open it, then click the Clear button in the dialog box.

BIAS Peak

BIAS' Peak Pro 5 (http://www.bias-inc.com) is the most full-featured audio editing program for Mac OS X, and it has many features that make it more than just an audio editing program. Peak is also used as a sound design program for film and multimedia projects and is popular as a mastering and CD authoring program. Some of Peak's features include:

◆ Built-in effects, including the ImpulseVerb room simulator/reverb plug-in

◆ Support for Audio Unit and VST instruments and effects

◆ The ability to import and export a wide range of file types, including adjustable sample and bit rates

◆ Integration with hardware samplers

◆ Nondestructive and destructive editing

◆ Unlimited Undo/Redo

◆ Batch processing

◆ Support for QuickTime/DV video

The demo versions of Peak Pro and Peak LE work for 15 days. Both programs are also available as part of a Studio software bundle that includes BIAS' Deck multitrack recording program. Peak Pro costs $599, and Peak LE costs $129.

BIAS Peak Basics

Locate the folder MMA Audio\Bias Peak and copy it to your desktop or another location on your hard drive. Choose File ➢ Open and locate the file BPDrumOne.wav in the MMA Audio\Bias Peak folder. Then select the file in the Open File dialog box and click Open.

Peak has an interesting interface that's a bit different from many other audio programs. At the top of the screen is the Toolbar, which contains many of Peak's more frequently used functions. The Toolbar can be resized by selecting its lower right corner and dragging either down or to the right to reveal more available tool buttons. Tool buttons can be added or removed from the Toolbar by selecting Peak 5 ➢ Preferences and clicking the Shortcuts/Toolbar preferences.

You'll be working with the middle section of the Toolbar shown in Figure 7.22.

FIGURE 7.22

The middle of the Peak Toolbar

At the bottom of the screen is the Transport bar, which contains an LCD-style counter displaying the current location of the playhead in any selected audio file. Next to the counter are the Rewind, Stop, Start, Fast Forward, and Record buttons. Just off to the side of those buttons is the Use Loop in Playback button. On the right side of the Transport bar is a Volume display and slider that can raise or lower the volume of a selected audio file. The Transport bar can be resized by selecting its lower right corner with your mouse and dragging to the left or right. Figure 7.23 shows the Transport bar.

FIGURE 7.23

Peak's Transport bar

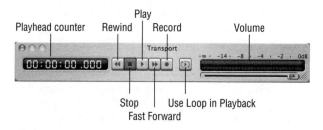

In the center of your screen is the Audio Document window. This displays the file you are currently working on or listening to in Peak.

Figure 7.24 shows the Audio Document window.

To play back the audio file, click the Play button in the Transport bar. To play back a file or region as a loop:

1. Click your mouse anywhere in the Audio window.

2. Highlight a section of the audio file or use the keyboard shortcut Command+A to select the entire file.

3. Click the Loop This Selection button in the Toolbar. (Don't confuse this button with the Use Loop in Playback button, which appears on the Transport bar.)

4. Click the Play button to play back the region or complete file as a loop.

FIGURE 7.24

Peak's Audio Document window

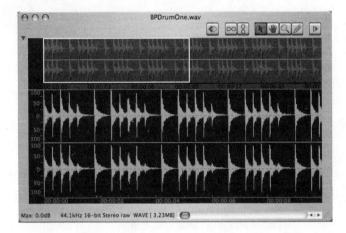

Editing with Peak

Peak contains many powerful audio editing features that can be used for anything from applying minor fixes to audio files to creating entirely new sounds from an existing file. Let's look at the options. Use File ➢ Open to locate and open the file PeakEdit1.wav in the MMA Audio\Bias Peak folder, then select the whole file (click your mouse anywhere in the Audio Document window and choose Edit ➢ Select All, or use the keyboard shortcut Command+A).

In the menu bar, take a look at the menus to see some of Peak's editing options:

Edit Menu Contains common editing parameters like Cut, Copy, and Paste as well as options for inserting silence and selecting sections of the audio file.

Action Menu Contains the viewing parameters as well as some looping functions and marker/region settings.

DSP Menu Contains Peak's effects and many audio processing options. Use the DSP menu to normalize, create panning, repair audio, and add reverb effects with the ImpulseVerb reverb plug-in.

To add the ImpulseVerb Reverb to an audio file:

1. Select the entire file or a section of audio.

2. Choose DSP ➢ ImpulseVerb.

3. Select a category from the Space drop-down menu.

4. Select a reverb space.

Figure 7.25 shows the ImpulseVerb with a selected space.

FIGURE 7.25

Peak's ImpulseVerb
reverb effect

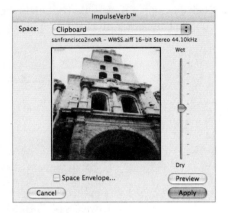

5. Set the amount of effect to add to your file with the Wet/Dry slider.

6. Preview the results with the Preview button. Click Apply to process the audio file.

Recording into BIAS Peak

You can create loops, sound effects, and other tracks by recording directly into Peak through your hardware audio interface or your Mac's built-in ⅛-inch audio in. Once you've made a recording you can use Peak's editing functions to alter the recording.

To create a new recording in Peak:

1. Select File ➤ New Mono Document. This creates a new, empty Peak file.

2. Click the Record Settings button in the Transport bar of the Peak Toolbar.

Figure 7.26 shows the Record Settings dialog box.

FIGURE 7.26

The Record Settings
dialog box

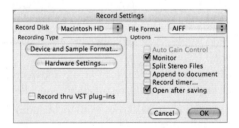

3. Select Record Disk from the drop-down menu at the top left of the dialog box. This is the disk where your audio file will be stored. You'll set a specific location for the file once the recording is complete.

4. Click the Hardware Settings button to open the CoreAudio Settings dialog. Select your input and output device. If you are using your Mac's built-in audio input, be sure to raise the Input Volume slider at the bottom of the CoreAudio dialog.

5. Click OK.

6. Click the Device and Sample Format button and set your track input settings and sample rate. For this recording, set Channels to Mono. The Sample Rate, Clock Source, and Bit Depth settings can be left as they are.

7. In the Options field of the Record Settings dialog box, make sure there are check marks next to Monitor and Open After Saving. Leave the other settings unchecked.

8. Click OK.

9. Click the Record button in the Transport bar to open the Record dialog box.

10. Click the Record button in the dialog box to begin recording.

You now have some idea of potential uses for the Peak program. Peak's editing and sound shaping abilities far exceed what I can cover in this short section. For more information on BIAS Peak Pro 5 and Peak LE 5 be sure to check out the BIAS website and included documentation.

Melodyne Cre8

The Melodyne applications from Celemony (http://www.celemony.com) are audio sequencing and editing programs that have their own unique methods of arranging and editing audio files. With Melodyne you can easily pitch-shift and time-stretch single notes and sections of audio files by selecting, clicking, and dragging. It's very much like MIDI editing, but with audio files. Melodyne can fix out-of-tune vocal or instrument performances or create entirely new melodies and performances from existing loops and tracks.

Some of Melodyne's editing functions are similar to the slicing techniques used in ReCycle and the RX2 format but with some notable differences, including more editable parameters and the ability to work with longer files such as a complete vocal track.

Melodyne is available in three versions:

Meldoyne Uno   A single-track audio editor that can be used as a stand-alone audio editor or in any host program that supports ReWire. $199.

Melodyne Cre8   An eight-track audio editor that can also create multipart harmonies and arrangements. Can be used as a standalone application, ReWire instrument or Audio Unit, VST, or RTAS plug-in. ReWire support. $369.

Melodyne Studio   A complete multitrack editing application that can be used as a standalone application, ReWire instrument or Audio Unit, VST, or RTAS plug-in. ReWire support. $699.

In this tutorial you will be working with Melodyne Cre8. The demo version works for 30 days. Saving and ReWire support are disabled. It also emits an occasional beep.

Setting Up Melodyne

Once you download and install Melodyne Cre8 or the demo version, do the following:

1. Start the program and choose an Audio Device in the setup assistant window that appears.

2. Select Melodyne ➢ Preferences to open the Preferences dialog.

3. Under the Recording tab, select or create a folder for unsaved arrangements.

4. Under the Plug-ins tab, activate your Audio Unit and VST plug-ins. Melodyne will scan your system for plug-ins. This may take some time if you have a large collection.

5. Select the MIDI tab and set your default input and output and other relevant MIDI information.

6. Close Melodyne's Preferences.

Working with Audio Files

Melodyne's arrangement and editing features are very intuitive and easy to begin using:

1. Make sure the folder MMA Audio\Melodyne has been copied to your desktop or another location on your hard drive.

2. Select File ➢ New Arrangement. This will open Melodyne's Arrange window.

3. Click the Track 1 box on the left side of the interface.

4. Choose File ➢ Import Audio File and locate the MMA Audio\Melodyne folder. Select the file MeloDrum1.wav and click the Open button.

5. Select Track 2 and load the file MeloBass1.wav in the same way.

Figure 7.27 shows the Melodyne interface and the two imported audio files.

FIGURE 7.27
The Melodyne interface

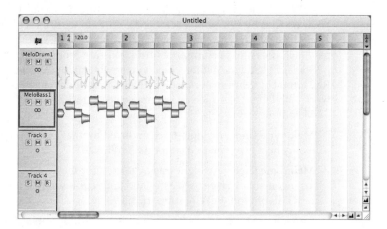

6. Double-click the bass track's header to open the Editor window, shown in Figure 7.28.

At the top left of the Editor window is a row of six buttons, Melodyne's Expert Tools. These are, from left to right:

Select tool Depending on where the cursor is placed over the note, makes different editing options/tools appear.

Edit Pitch Raises or lowers the selected note.

Edit Formant Raises or lowers formants. Formants are frequency bands within a particular sound. In Melodyne, formants are automatically raised and lowered along with pitch. Raising or lowering the formants independently can significantly alter a sound in interesting ways.

Edit Amplitude Raises and lowers the overall volume of the selected note.

FIGURE 7.28

The Editor window

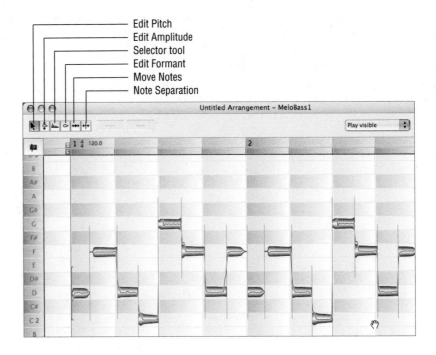

Move Notes Moves notes vertically in the Editor window.

Note Separation Edits the amount of space between notes in the Editor window.

Melodyne's Editor window will be familiar to anyone who has worked with Logic's Matrix Editor or created and edited a MIDI performance in Live. The difference here is that you are now working with actual audio files. Next, you'll use Melodyne's Edit window to rearrange the notes of the bass loop:

1. Choose the Edit Pitch tool and select any note in the Editor window. Drag the note up or down to change its pitch.

2. Press the spacebar to play the newly altered note.

3. Press 0 to return to the beginning of the loop and press the spacebar again to play the entire loop.

4. To hear the altered loop in the context of the arrangement, select Play Arrangement from the Play drop-down menu at the top right of the Editor window (labeled Play Visible in Figure 7.28).

5. Select the Edit Formant tool. The formants will be displayed as rectangles superimposed over the waveform in the editor window. Try drastically raising or lowering the formant of a note to hear the results.

6. Select the Edit Amplitude tool. As you can see, some of the waveforms in the Editor window are larger (louder) than others. Select any note with the Amplitude tool and drag up or down to increase or decrease the volume of the note.

This loop responds particularly well to editing. You can create an entirely new bass line that sounds relatively natural from the existing notes. Not all tracks will behave the same way in Melodyne. Try experimenting with some of the different loops contained in the MMA Audio\All Loops folder to get an idea of how Melodyne works with various instruments and types of performances.

The Melodyne Mixer

Melodyne Cre8 includes a very straightforward mixer called Mixer 8 that you can use to EQ tracks, add effects, and create Aux Sends. To view Melodyne's Mixer 8 eight-channel mixer, select Window ➢ Mixer. Figure 7.29 shows the Mixer window.

FIGURE 7.29
Melodyne Cre8's
Mixer window

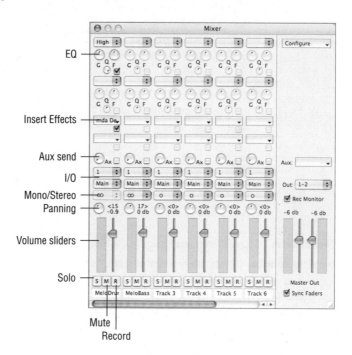

Each channel strip in the Mixer 8 mixer contains, from top to bottom:

EQ　Adds new EQs. Choose from High Shelf, Peak, or Low Shelf EQ from the drop-down menu at the top of the channel strip. Use the three knobs underneath the menu to adjust the gain, frequency, and EQ. You can add as many EQs as you want to any channel. Every time you add a new EQ, another will be created below it. You can also add EQ visually by selecting Show EQ Graph from the Configure menu at the top left of the Mixer window.

Insert Effects　Adds any of your VST or Audio Unit plug-in effects to your tracks.

Aux Send　Marked "Ax" on the Channel Strip, the Aux Send knob sends signal from any track to an aux track containing a VST, Audio Unit, or Melodyne effect. Configure an aux track by selecting an effect from the Aux drop-down menu on the right side of the Mixer 8.

I/O　Contains three drop-down menus: the top one determines the track's input, the middle determines the track's output, and the bottom selects whether the track will be mono or stereo.

Mono/Stereo　Indicates whether track is a mono or stereo track.

Panning　Controls the track's left and right panning.

Volume　Controls the track volume.

Solo, Mute, Record   These three buttons are the standard Solo, Mute, and Arm for Record buttons found on most DAW software.

Name   Allows you to rename the track in the channel strip's Name field.

With its combination of unique editing functions, multitracking capabilities, and ReWire support, Melodyne Cre8 is much more than an audio editor.

For the Mac user who is interested in taking advantage of Melodyne's editing functions but doesn't need the multitracking functionality, Melodyne Uno makes great and affordable alternative.

Rax

Rax is an Audio Unit "virtual rack" by Plasq Software (`http://www.plasq/rax.com`) that you can use to play your Audio Unit instruments and effects outside of a host program. With Rax you can:

◆ Play your Audio Unit instruments in a live setting without having to utilize a host program

◆ Create audio files for tracks and loops

◆ Create and recall different configurations of instruments and effects

◆ Easily try out different combinations of Audio Unit instruments and effects without a host program

Rax costs $49.95. The Rax demo version works for 30 days and is fully functional. When you start Rax for the first time, a demo library will be loaded. The included demo songs are MIDI files triggering assigned instruments created with OS X's built-in DLS Music device. You can play a demo song by selecting the MIDI file tab at the bottom left of the Rax window and clicking the Play button. Figure 7.30 shows what the Rax interface looks like when you first start the program.

FIGURE 7.30
The Rax interface

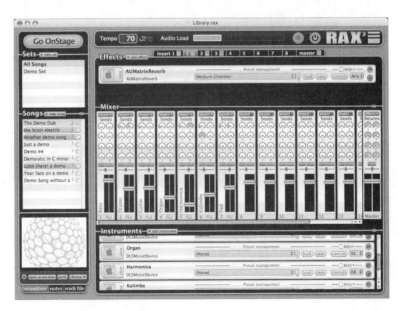

The left side of the window contains the program's set lists and song lists as well as the built-in visualizer in the bottom left corner. Most of the Rax interface is taken up by the Effects, Mixer, and Instrument sections, which I'll be focusing on in this section.

In order to use Rax, you'll need a virtual instrument. If you haven't already done so, check out the instructions for downloading and installing the Crystal synthesizer at the beginning of this chapter.

Setting Up Rax

Let's take a look at setting up Rax's audio, recording, and startup preferences:

1. Select Rax ➢ Preferences.

2. Select the General tab.

3. Deselect On Launch Open Most Recent Track.

4. For now, select Empty in the New Rack field. You can create a template rack later.

5. Under Audio, choose your default Audio Device and set the Recording Location folder for any audio files you will record with Rax.

6. Select the MIDI tab and put a check mark next to any MIDI input devices you plan to use.

7. Close Rax Preferences.

Playing Rax

Once you've set up Rax's preferences you're ready to begin adding and playing your Audio Unit instruments in the Rax interface. To get started:

1. Select File ➢ New Library to create a new, empty Rax library.

2. In the Instruments field at the bottom of the window, open the Add Instrument menu to select an instrument. If you have downloaded and installed the Crystal synthesizer, select Green Oak Software ➢ Crystal to add the Crystal synthesizer to the Rax song.

   Figure 7.31 shows the Crystal Synthesizer loaded as a Rax instrument.

FIGURE 7.31
The Crystal
Synthesizer
in Rax

3. Choose Preset 13 from the Preset Management menu.

4. On left side of the instrument in the rack is the Remote Editor button. Click this to view the Audio Unit instrument's interface.

In the center of the rack are the Preset Management controls. Here you can select available presets from the drop-down menu. You can also create new Rax presets clicking the Save button and load your presets by clicking the Load button.

You may notice that Crystal's included presets are listed in the menu by number but not by name. This will also be the case when using certain other Audio Unit instruments in Rax, though not always. You can view Crystal's presets by name by opening the instrument with the Remote Editor button.

Adding Effects

Effects can be added to tracks as inserts or send effects, or they can be added to the master track. At the top of the Rax window is the Effects rack, shown in Figure 7.32.

FIGURE 7.32
An empty Effects rack

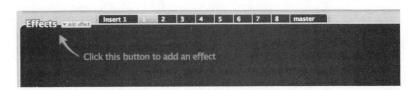

At the top of the Effects rack you'll see a row of buttons. These are used to decide which kind of effect (insert, send, or master track) you are adding to your Rax session.

INSERT EFFECTS

To add an effect as an insert:

1. Select the channel strip for the instrument you want to add the effect to.

2. Click the Insert button at the top of the channel strip.

3. Open the Add Effect menu at the top of the Effects rack and choose the Apple ➢ AUDelay plug-in. The AUDelay plug-in is now added to the Rax interface.

4. Click the Remote Editor button (labeled View on the left side of the Effects window) to open the AUDelay.

You'll notice that the AUDelay has a very different interface in Rax than it does in other programs. Rax has created its own interfaces for all of the Audio Unit effects that are bundled with OS X. Figure 7.33 shows the Rax interface for the AUDelay plug-in.

FIGURE 7.33
The Rax interface for
OS X's AUDelay plug-in

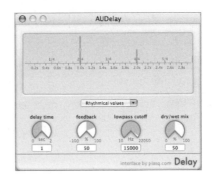

Using the insert method is the quickest way to add effects to a Rax track. With a plug-in like AUDelay, you can adjust how much of the effect to add to the track by using your mouse to raise and lower the Dry/Wet Mix knob on the AUDelay interface. However, not all plug-ins have an adjustable dry/wet or mix parameter. Those that are not adjustable can be added as send effects.

SEND EFFECTS

In Rax you can add up to eight different send effects in each session. To use send effects in Rax:

1. Select the button labeled 1 at the top of the Effects Rack window, shown in Figure 7.34.

FIGURE 7.34
The Send Effect 1
button

2. Open the Add Effect menu and select an effect.

3. Select a channel strip in the Mixer area and add the effect to your track by using your mouse to raise Send 1, as shown in Figure 7.35.

FIGURE 7.35
Raise Send 1 in
the Mixer

You can add multiple effects on a single send or configure up to eight different sends with single or multiple effects.

MASTER TRACK EFFECTS

You can add universal effects to Rax's master track as well. These are usually a compressor or a mastering EQ. To add a universal effect:

1. Click the Master button at the top right of the Effects rack.

2. Choose an effect from the Add Effects menu.

3. In the Effects area, click the View button to view the plug-ins remote editor and make any desired adjustments.

As with insert effects, levels for effects on the master track must be controlled within the plug-ins Remote Editor window.

Recording Rax

You can record Rax output as an AIFF file. That means you can open any recording you create in Rax in an Audio Editor or directly in your DAW host program.

To record Rax's output:

1. Select File ➤ New Song or File ➤ New Library to create a new Rax Song or Library and add any instruments and effects to the Rax interface.

2. Begin recording by using the keyboard shortcut Command+R, or click the Record button at the top of the Rax window.

3. Use your MIDI keyboard or controller to play the Rax instrument(s).

4. Stop recording by using the keyboard shortcut Command+R or clicking the Record button again.

All of your audio recordings will be located in the folder *yourusername*\Documents\Rax Recordings. You can access this folder through the Finder or by selecting Go ➤ My Recordings from the Rax menu bar.

I've gotten a lot of use out of Rax, especially as a tool for trying out virtual instruments. Rax has also garnered some well-deserved positive reviews. If the folks at Plasq would add ReWire support, this program could become indispensable.

VSTi Host

VSTi Host from Defective Records (http://www.defectiverecords.com/vstihost) is a very simple and inexpensive program that lets you use VST plug-in instruments and effects outside of a host program. It's also ReWire-compatible, so you can also use it to play VST instruments in some host DAW programs like Pro Tools that don't support the VST format.

VSTi Host's demo version emits periodic beeps but is otherwise fully functional.

Setting Up

Install VSTi Host by dragging the folder containing the program and documentation to your Applications folder.

In order to work with VSTi Host, you'll need to have at least one VST instrument on your system. If you've haven't already installed the Crystal synthesizer, please see the instructions at the beginning of this chapter. More freeware, shareware, and commercial VST instruments and plug-ins are covered in detail in Chapter 8.

When you start VSTi Host, it will automatically scan your system for any installed VSTs. If you have a large number of VST plug-ins on your system, VSTi Host may become overloaded and crash on startup. If you encounter this problem, you can work around it by temporarily moving some of your plug-ins out of the VST folder located at *yourharddrive*)\Library\Audio\Plug-ins\VST.

You can also use AudioFinder's Plug-in Manager window, covered earlier in this chapter, to disable some of your unused VSTs.

Figure 7.36 shows the VSTi Host interface.

FIGURE 7.36

The VSTi Host interface

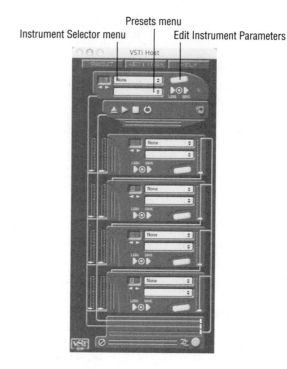

Presets menu

Instrument Selector menu   Edit Instrument Parameters

Your VST instruments will be available from the Instrument Selector menu in the top section of the interface. Effects are added in the bottom four sections. Follow these steps to prepare VSTi Host for loading and playing your VST instruments:

1. Start VSTi Host and click the Settings button at the top of the interface.

2. Select your MIDI input from the Device menu and (if necessary) select an input channel.

3. Select your preferred audio driver, input device, and input source from the Audio Options drop-down menus. To use VSTi Host as a ReWire instrument in Logic, GarageBand, or Pro Tools, select ad_wire as your Audio Driver.

4. Click Done to return to the main window.

Playing an Instrument in VSTi Host

Follow these steps to load and play a VST instrument in VSTi Host:

1. Choose Crystal.vst in the VST Instrument Selector drop-down at the top of the VSTi Host interface. If you have other VST instruments installed, they will also appear on the list.

2. Just below the VST Instrument Selector is the Preset list. Choose `Bigness MW` from the Vintage category.

3. Use your MIDI keyboard to play the Crystal synthesizer within the VSTi Host environment.

4. Just to the right of the VST Instrument Selector is the Edit Instrument Parameters button. Click this to open Crystal's interface and make any adjustments to the instrument.

Adding Effects: SupaPhaser

VSTi Host doesn't seem to like Pluggo effects, so in order to get an idea of how effects will work in this program you may need to download some other VSTs. There are lots of freeware and commercial VST plug-ins available, many of which are covered in Chapter 8. For this section I recommend downloading the donationware SupaPhaser plug-in from `http://bram.smartelectronix.com`. (Donationware means that if you like the plug-in and use it frequently you are asked to make a donation to the programmer.) SupaPhaser is a phaser plug-in with a fantastic interface and lots of presets to get you started.

Effects can be added in any of the four boxes that make up the bottom section of the VSTi Host interface:

1. Start VSTi Host and add the `Crystal.vst` instrument from the Instrument drop-down menu. Choose a preset like `Bigness MW` or `JP` that doesn't already have a lot of effects.

2. Choose the SupaPhaser from the first Select VST Effect drop-down menu.

3. Choose the preset `TheWall Mod` from the preset drop-down menu. Figure 7.37 shows VSTi Host with the Crystal synth and SupaPhaser.

FIGURE 7.37
Crystal and Supa-
Phaser in VSTi Host

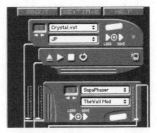

4. On the left side of each of the effects boxes are two faders. The fader on the far left (the red) sends the signal from the VST instrument to the VST effect. Raise this slider significantly.

5. At the bottom of the VST interface are three slider/faders: red, green and blue. The blue slider sends the effects to the mixer. Raise the blue slider significantly.

   The slider on the right side of the effects box determines how much of the effect's output goes to the mixer and how much goes directly to the next effect in the chain.

6. Use these three sliders to determine the levels of any effects you want to use within VSTi Host.

Recording

You can create samples, loops, and tracks by recording VSTi Host's output in standalone mode:

1. Click the Record AIFF File button on the bottom right of the VSTi Host window to begin recording.

2. Play the loaded instrument and effects.

3. Click the Record AIFF button again to stop recording.

4. Locate your recording in the folder `Applications\VSTi Host\RecordFiles`.

Note that it important the `RecordFiles` folder remain in the `VSTi Host` folder, or VSTi Host will not record.

Once you have recorded an AIFF file, you can open it in any audio editing program or DAW program.

VSTi Host and Pro Tools

Use VSTi Host and ReWire to play VST instruments in Pro Tools:

1. Open VSTi and select the Settings tab at the top of the interface.

2. Under MIDI options to choose VSTi Host.

3. Make sure the Audio Driver is set to `ad_rewire`.

4. Close VSTi Host.

5. Open a Pro Tools session and create a new stereo instrument track.

6. Add VSTi Host as a ReWire insert by selecting Multichannel Plug-in ➤ Instrument ➤ VSTi Host.

7. In the Instrument field, set the MIDI Output Selector to Predefined ➤ To VSTi Host 1 ➤ Channel-1.

8. Start VSTi Host.

9. Load the Crystal synthesizer or other VST instrument.

10. Add any VST effects.

11. Use your MIDI keyboard to play the instrument.

12. Record or create a MIDI performance in the Pro Tools instrument track.

VSTi Host may be a little difficult to get used to and can be occasionally unstable, but its ability to play VST instruments and effects outside of a host program and the included ReWire support make it a pretty good deal all around.

ReCycle

Propellerhead's ReCycle software was created to convert loops and samples into the RX2 format. Originally intended for use with the Dr. Rex Loop Player in Reason, the RX2 format is now supported by Pro Tools, Logic, and many virtual samplers. Where some programs work with loops though time-stretching and pitch-shifting, the RX2 format divides loops into individual slices that are then spaced apart or drawn closer together to adjust the tempo. The RX2 format allows for pitch-shifting of individual slices as well. Figure 7.38 shows a sliced loop file in ReCycle.

FIGURE 7.38

A sliced drum loop in ReCycle

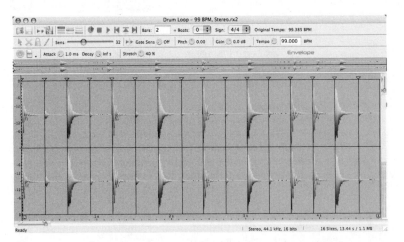

ReCycle's slicing method of working with loops can eliminate some of the sonic artifacts that are commonly present in other looping programs, especially when slowing down loops. ReCycle also includes processing effects and adjustable EQ parameters.

Converting loop files to RX2 from WAV or AIFF can also be very useful when working in Pro Tools and Logic. In these programs, RX2 files will be loaded as a series of individual slices allowing for greater control when looping or rearranging the slices that make up a loop. These methods are covered in detail in Chapter 10, "Apple Loops."

A demo version of ReCycle is available from http://www.propellerheads.se. While you can use the demo version to familiarize yourself with ReCycle, saving is disabled and you can only work with one of the five included loops.

Working with ReCycle

The main use for ReCycle is to create RX2 loops from either WAV or AIFF loops. To do this:

1. Open ReCycle, then choose File ➤ Open and use the Open Sound File dialog box to locate one of the following files:

    ◆ If you have the full version: open ReCyDrum.wav from the MMA Audio\ReCycle folder.

    ◆ If you are working with the demo version: Drum Loop – 99 BPM Stereo.

2. If you are working in the demo version, de-select View ➤ Show Grid to hide the Grid feature.

3. Adjust the Sensitivity slider (on the left side of the second row of tools) to choose the number of slices that your loop will contain. Higher sensitivity means more slices, lower sensitivity means less. The general rule of thumb with the Sensitivity slider is to try a give each beat a single slice, as in Figure 7.38.

4. Set the Bars, Beats, and Sign settings in the upper right corner of the ReCycle interface. These settings should reflect the original properties of the loop. In this case, the settings should be 2 bars and 0 beats at 4/4, as shown in Figure 7.39.

FIGURE 7.39
ReCycle's loop
property settings

5. Adjust the Tempo knob to set the tempo of the exported RX2 file. This is the tempo that your Dr. Rex Loop Player or DAW program will use as the loop's default tempo. To make the default playback tempo match the original loop tempo Command+click directly on the Tempo knob.

Since many loops are not created at precise tempos, you have a chance here to use these functions to set the loop tempo precisely. For example, if a loop's original tempo is 99.385, you can change the export tempo to 99.000. If you know the tempo of the session you are going to be using the file in, you can also change the loop tempo to match your session.

6. If you are using the full version, select Save As and choose RX2, then open your RX2 files in Reason or any other program that supports the RX2 format.

The Save As feature is disabled in the demo version of ReCycle. However, you can preview your changes by exporting the loop in other sound file formats, including WAV and AIFF files. To export loops from the ReCycle demo:

1. Select Process ➢ Export as One Sample.

2. Select File Export. Select WAV or AIFF from the Format drop-down menu.

3. Select a location and click the Save button.

Advanced Editing

ReCycle also included more advanced editing techniques that can alter loop files in more radical ways.
    At the top of the ReCycle window are the Open, Save, Toggle Export, and Export Sound File buttons. Next to these are three effects buttons. Clicking these buttons will open the Envelope Effect, Transient Shaper Effect, and Equalizer Effect toolbars.

FIGURE 7.40
ReCycle's task buttons

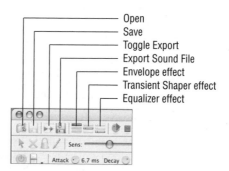

Figure 7.41 shows all three of ReCycle's Effects toolbars.

FIGURE 7.41
ReCycle's Effects
toolbars

THE ENVELOPE EFFECT

Follow these steps to begin working with the Envelope effect:

1. Open ReCycle, then choose File ➢ Open and use the Open Sound File dialog box to locate one of the following files:

   ◆ If you have the full version: `DrumLoop29.wav` from the `MMA Audio\ReCycle` folder.

   ◆ If you are working with the demo version: `Drum Loop - 99 BPM Stereo`.

2. In the demo version, deselect View ➢ Show Grid to get a clearer look at the file.

3. Click the Envelope Effect button to view the Envelope Effect parameters: Attack, Decay, and Stretch.

4. Make sure the Envelope Effect is turned on by clicking the Switch Effect On/Off button at the far left of the effect toolbar.

5. Try out the Envelope Effect presets by clicking the preset menu next to the On/Off switch.

   Attack   Adjusting the Attack setting changes what you hear at the beginning of each slice. A longer attack results in a rising sound. Having too long an attack setting will silence shorter slices.

   Decay   The Decay setting adjusts the length of each slice. Lower the decay significantly to create shorter, clipped sounds.

   Stretch   The Stretch knob will add more time or a "tail" to the end of the slices in your loop. This is useful if you're using ReCycle slow down a loop and want to lengthen the decay for a more natural sound.

TRANSIENT SHAPER EFFECT

The Transient Shaper effect is similar to a compressor and can be used to achieve compressor-like effects, evening out the sounds of your loop files and even achieving compressor-like distortion.

1. Click the Transient Shaper Effect button to view the effect's toolbar.

2. Make sure the effect switch is On.

3. Click the Play Loop button and, with the drum loop playing, try out the presets.

The Transient Shaper contains some standard compressor parameters:

Threshold   Sets the level at which the effect will start to work. Lower db means the effect will be applied at a lower volume level.

Amount   Sets how much of the effect is applied once the threshold is reached.

Attack   Sets how quickly the effect will be applied once the threshold is reached.

Release Determines how quickly the effect will stop being applied once the volume level drops below the threshold.

Gain Meter Shows the amount of effect being applied.

EQUALIZER

ReCycle's Equalizer is very straightforward. Basically a two-band EQ, ReCycle's Equalizer is suitable for quick, simple EQ tasks. The Equalizer section contains the following filters:

Lo Cut A high pass filter.

Lo Boosts or cuts lower range frequencies. Select a target frequency with the Lo knob then set the width of the selected frequency range with the Q knob. Finally increase or decrease the gain for the selected frequency with the G (gain) knob.

Hi Boosts or cuts higher range frequencies. Select a target frequency with the Hi knob then set the width of the selected frequency range with the Q knob. Finally increase or decrease the gain for the selected frequency with the G (gain) knob.

Hi Cut A low pass filter.

High and low pass filters, equalization types, and parameters are discussed in detail in Chapter 8.

Exporting

You can also use ReCycle to export the individual slices of a loop as individual samples in other formats. For example you can take an RX2 loop and export it or its slices in WAV, AIFF, SD II, or other formats. Using this feature you can create your own drum kits or sampled instruments from the slices that make up a loop.

To export the individual slices from a single loop:

1. If you're working with the full version, load any drum loop into ReCycle. If you are working with the demo version, load the file `Drum Loop - 99 BPM Stereo`.

2. Make sure that Process ➤ Export as One Sample is *deselected* (no check mark).

3. Select File ➤ Export.

4. From the Export dialog box, select a location for your samples and choose the appropriate file format for your exported slices. Make sure the format you are choosing is compatible with the host program or sampler you will be working in.

5. Load the slices as individual samples in your virtual sampler. For example, in Reason you would use the Browse Sample button on the Redrum Drum Computer to locate the individual samples.

ReCycle has other features that can help you create and adjust loops and samples. For more information on ReCycle's features, see the Propellerhead website and the program's included documentation.

Sample Manager

Audiofile Engineering's Sample Manager is an easy to use sample/loop editor and conversion and batch conversion utility. Like all of Audiofile Engineering's programs, it's built using the OS X programming environment Cocoa. This means that the program takes advantage of OS X's architecture at every level.

Sample Manager can convert any REX, WAV, or AIFF file to a WAV, AIFF, Apple Loop, Acid Loop, or Sound Designer II (SDII) file.

Sample Manager is available from `http://www.audiofile-engineering.com`. The fully functional demo version works for 15 days.

Let's start off by using a single audio file to take a look at some of the things you can do with Sample Manager:

1. Start Sample Manager.

2. Locate the file `AcousGtr1.wav` in the `MMA Audio\Sample Manager` folder and drag it directly onto Sample Manager's main window.

3. Select the file in the main window to view its waveform. Figure 7.42 shows the Sample Manager interface.

FIGURE 7.42

Sample Manager

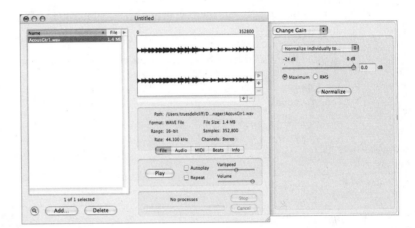

4. In the bottom right section of the Sample Manager window, put a check mark in the Repeat box so the file will play back as a continuous loop.

5. Click the Play/Stop button to hear the loop.

6. Click the Play/Stop button again to stop playback.

7. With the loop playing, adjust the Varispeed slider to hear the loop at different tempos. Command+click the Varispeed slider to return it to its default position.

Normalizing

Looking at the size of the waveform in the display window, you can see that the file is significantly quieter than it could be. Sample Manager includes a Normalizing function that can adjust the volume of any file to its maximum volume without distorting:

1. Select the `AcousGtr1.wav` file in Sample Manager's main window.

2. Select Change Gain from the Process panel's menu. (The Process panel is the section on the left or right side of the Sample Manager window that contains the various functions you can perform with the program. If the Process panel is not currently showing, access it by selecting View ▸ Process.)

3. Make sure the Gain slider is set to 0db.

4. Select the Maximum button.

5. Click the Normalize button.

Converting a File

Aside from the ability to imports various file types, Sample Manager also contains lots of options for converting and exporting files. Sample Manager can convert files to AIFF, WAV, and SDII formats, as well as create Apple Loops and Acid files. Sample Manager can also change the sample rate and bit range for any audio files.

Use Sample Manager to convert this WAV file into an Apple Loop:

1. Select and highlight the `AcousGtr1.wav` file in the Sample Manager window.

2. If the Process panel is not currently showing, access it by selecting View ➤ Process.

3. From the drop-down menu at the top of the Process panel, choose Convert.

Figure 7.43 shows the Convert options in the Process panel.

FIGURE 7.43
The Convert options
in the Process panel

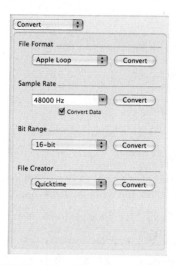

4. In the File Format field, you can choose from the various file formats. Select AIFF for this file. The other conversion options are Sample Rate, Bit Range, and File Creator:

Sample Rate   The most common sample rate is 44,100Hz. With Sample Manager, you can increase or decrease the sample rate of your audio files. This can be useful when converting files to match the sample rate of an existing session. You can also reduce the size of a sound file by decreasing the sample rate.

Bit Range   The most common bit range setting with a 44100Hz sample rate is 16-bit. Sample Manager lets you choose between 8-, 16-, 24- and 32-bit.

File Creator   The File Creator menu sets which program will become the default for opening your saved file. I chose QuickTime for this setting because (as we covered at the beginning of this chapter) it's a good program for previewing AIFF and WAV loops. You can use a different setting, if you prefer, to use any of the other programs on the list.

Sample Manager gives you three options for saving your files:

- Clicking any of the Convert buttons will convert the original file to the new format. This means the original file will no longer exist.

- Option+clicking any of the Convert buttons will save a copy of the file in the selected new format within the same folder as the original file.

- Command+Option+clicking any of the Convert buttons will allow you to save a copy of the file and choose or create the folder you'd like to save it in.

5. Command+Option+click the File Format Convert button and create a new folder named Converted Apple Loops to save your new file in.

6. Click the Convert button for each process you wish to apply to the file.

Adding Effects

You can also use Sample Manager to add Audio Unit effects to a sound file:

1. Select the `AcousGtr1.wav` file in the Sample Manager window.

2. Select Audio Units from the Process panel drop-down menu.

3. Click the Add button to open a list of folders containing your Audio Unit plug-ins. Choose Apple ➢ AUMatrixReverb to add Apple's built-in reverb plug-in.

4. The plug-in is now added to a list in the Process panel window. Double-click the plug-in's name on the list to open its interface.

5. Make any desired adjustments to the plug-in. In this case, reduce the dry/wet mix to 50 percent.

6. Click the Play button in the Sample Manager window to preview the loop with the added effect.

7. Click the Process button to save the loop with the added effect(s). You can use the same Option+click and Command+Option+click keyboard shortcuts to save copies of the file instead of altering the original file.

Batch Converting

One of my favorite uses for Sample Manager is to convert large groups of files at once. It's certainly not the only batch-converting program around, but its interface makes sense and the necessary features are easy to access. The ability to normalize all of the converted files in one click is a nice bonus as well. Use Sample Manager to convert a folder of REX files to the Apple Loop format:

1. Start the Sample Manger program.

2. Locate the `MMA Audio\REX Files` folder on the included DVD or your hard drive.

3. Drag the entire folder directly onto the Sample Manager window. All of the REX files in the folder will now appear on a list in the Sample Manager window.

4. Select all the files by choosing Edit ➢ Select All or by clicking any single file and then using the Command+A keyboard shortcut.

5. If the Process panel is not currently showing, access it by selecting View ➢ Process.

6. From the drop-down menu at the top of the Process panel, choose Convert.

7. In the File Format field, you can choose from the various file formats. Select Apple Loop.

8. Command+Option+click the Convert button and create a new folder named Converted Rex Files to save your new files in.

Some of Sample Manager's other functions include audio reversing, splitting stereo files into two mono files, and exporting as MP3. For more information on the included features be sure to read the online manual at Audiofile Engineering's website.

Sample Manager also makes a good companion to the other Audiofile program covered in this chapter, the audio editing program Wave Editor.

CREATING FADES

One of the most common problems that you'll come across when editing loop files and other audio files is abrupt endings and beginnings. Crossfading is fading the end of one audio file into the beginning of another. Crossfading is a built-in feature of almost all audio recording programs.

When you're working with loop files or exporting audio between programs, you'll find that some files that would otherwise flow perfectly will contain a slight pop at the beginning or end of the file. Or, you might find when linking two audio files together that there's an abrupt, noticeable transition. Many of these problems can be corrected by creating quick fades at the beginning, end, or both of an audio file.

All audio editing programs will include various options for creating fades and crossfades. I choose Sample Manager for this, because while it doesn't have a lot of advanced editing features, it does have a very handy fade in/fade out option that can be used quickly and easily when I need to create and save a fade. To create a fade in Sample Manager:

1. Locate the file SMBell.wav in the MMA Audio \Sample Manager folder and drag the file onto the Sample Manager window.

2. Put a check mark in the Play as Loop box and click the Play button to hear the loop.

3. As you can hear, this file has a distinct pop at the end. To clean up the pop, you'll create a quick fade at the end of the file. Select Fade from the Process panel drop-down menu.

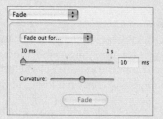

4. In the second drop-down menu you can select the fade parameters. Choose Fade Out For. In this case you're just cleaning up the very end of the file and you don't want to create a noticeable fade.

5. Set the Fade Out For slider at the minimum of 10ms.

6. Use the scroll bar and the plus (+) symbol at the bottom of the Waveform Display to zoom in on the end of the audio file.

7. Adjust the curvature of the fade with the Curvature slider. Since you just want to "fix" the very end of the file, you can slide the Curvature fader all the way to right.

8. Click the Fade button to process the file.

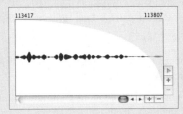

The usual keyboard shortcuts for creating duplicate files apply here. If you don't want to alter the original file, create a copy using the keyboard shortcuts. You can also use the Command+Z keyboard shortcut to undo any changes you make.

 Real World Scenario

CREATING SAMPLES WITH AN AUDIO EDITOR

No matter what DAW program or musical style you are working in, having a catalogue of your own samples can greatly enhance your music creation, writing, recording, and mixing abilities. Samples can be used in a wide variety of contexts. For example, you can create "standard" instruments such as keyboards, guitar, or drum kits; nonstandard instruments from sound effects and other recorded sources; or spoken word samples from movies, radio, and television. In fact, anything that you can record can become a virtual instrument— radio static, your sister yelling, a vacuum cleaner.

As I've covered already in Chapters 2 ("Reason"), 3 ("Ableton Live," and 5 ("Logic"), and as we will explore in even more detail in Chapter 9, "Virtual Instruments," the ability to create your own instruments is one of the primary functions of virtual samplers. What's really amazing about this technology is that there are no constraints.

In the "Audio Hijack/Audio Hijack Pro" section of this chapter, we looked at creating spoken word samples. Spoken word samples have been used in a musical context since the beginning of "experimental" music (check out Steve Reich's 1965 tape loop composition "It's Gonna Rain" for an early example). Industrial, hip-hop, and other forms of pop music have also extensively used spoken word samples from movies and television.

CREATE SAMPLES FROM AN ITUNES SONG

One way to get familiar with digital sampling techniques is to create your own sampled drum kit. This process has three basic steps: first, find a song that contains individual drum hits. Then, use an audio editor to separate and isolate each drum hit. Finally, save each hit as a WAV or AIFF file.

Check your iTunes or CD collection for any song with a drum solo or drum break to create a drum kit from. When looking for appropriate source material, keep in mind that it's not necessary to use completely isolated drum samples. You can use a file with hits that can't be separated (kick drum and hi-hat, for example).

This process will work with MP3 or AAC files, but wherever possible you will want to use WAV or AIFF files for better quality. If you have a version of the song on CD, set your iTunes program to automatically import WAV or AIFF format.

1. Select iTunes ➢ Preferences. Click the Advanced tab and then the Importing tab.

2. Choose AIFF Encoder or WAV Encoder from the Import Using drop-down menu.

3. Choose Automatic from the Setting drop-down menu.

4. Insert your audio CD into your CD drive.

5. A message may appear asking if you want to import the entire CD. If you don't want to import the entire CD in AIFF or WAV format, click No.

6. Control+click any song that you do want to import and select Convert Selection to WAV or Convert Selection to AIFF from the pop-up menu.

7. When conversion is finished, select your Music library in the upper left of the iTunes window and use the Search function on the upper right to locate your new WAV or AIFF file.

8. Once you've located the file in your iTunes collection, select it in the iTunes window and create a copy by dragging the file directly to your desktop

From here you can use any audio editing program to create individual samples. I prefer to work in such as Peak, Wave Editor, or Audacity—programs that were created specifically to edit audio. But you can also use your DAW's editing and exporting functionality. I'll use Audacity for this example.

To create your samples:

1. Start Audacity and choose File ➢ Open. Locate and open the WAV or AIFF file.

2. Use the Zoom tool to zoom in on the section containing the sounds you want to sample.

3. Use the Selection tool to select the specific area you want to sample, plus a bit of extra audio information before and after the specific section.

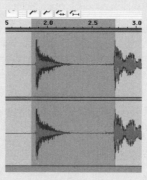

4. Create a new file from the selection.

Each audio editor or DAW accomplishes this differently. Some include a Create New File from Selection option. I've found that the fastest way to work in Audacity is with keyboard shortcuts:

◆ Command+C to copy the section of audio

◆ Command+N to create a new file

◆ Command+V to paste the audio into the new file

Once you've created a new file with your sample, you will want to edit the sample to make sure it starts and ends where you want it to.

5. In Audacity use the Zoom tool to zoom in on the beginning and end of the file and use the Selection tool to select the sections of audio you don't want to keep.

6. Use the keyboard shortcut Command+X to delete the unwanted pieces of audio.

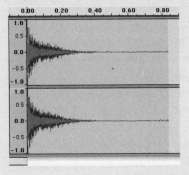

7. Once you've performed any necessary edits, export your samples as WAV files at a bit depth/sample rate of 16/44.1 for maximum compatibility with all virtual samplers.

REVERB AND FADES

One of the common problems you'll face with samples in general and with drum samples in particular, is that the file will end abruptly, resulting in an unnatural, clipped sound. For example, a "real" drum hit consists of the immediate sound of the stick hitting the drum and also the decaying sound that follows. This is especially true for cymbals.

When you are creating a sample from a recording that cuts off abruptly, try adding a reverb effect and creating a fade to give your sample a more realistic sound.

USING YOUR SAMPLES

These techniques can be used to create any kind of sample from any audio source. Once you've created the elements that will make up your drum kit or other sampler instruments, you can use virtual samplers and drum computers such as Reason's NN-XT and Redrum; Ableton Live's Impulse, Simpler or Sampler; Logic's EXS24 mkII; or the iDrum. Battery or Kontakt virtual samplers are covered in Chapter 9 and allow you to create and save drum kits and other virtual instruments.

The Bottom Line

Create and edit loops, samples, and other audio files with an audio editor   All DAW programs have audio editing functions built in to some extent. A dedicated, separate audio editor can have a number of uses including creating editing loops and samples, converting files, sound design, and mastering. Along with built-in recording functions, many audio editing program also contain more advanced editing features than those contained within your DAW program.

Master It   Use the freeware program Audacity to record and edit a sound file, add an effect, then export the file as an AIFF to use as a loop or sample in your DAW.

Use Audio Units and VST plug-ins outside of a host program   Programs like Rax and VSTi Host allow you to use Audio Units and VST virtual instruments and plug-ins outside of a host program. This includes the ability to play the instruments, add and configure effects, and record the output to your hard drive.

Master It   Use the Rax program to record a performance using the Crystal synthesizer and Apple's AUDelay Audio Unit plug-in.

Rax places your audio recording by default in the folder *yourusername*\Documents\Rax Recordings. You can change this by opening Rax's Audio Preferences tab and clicking the Recording Location Browse button to select a new location.

Batch convert audio files   Many audio editing programs contain file conversion functionality. One of the programs I've covered, Audiofile Engineering's Sample Manager, contains a quick and especially easy to use the batch conversion feature.

Master It   Keeping the original files in their current location, use the Sample Manager program to batch-convert the WAV files in the MMA Audio\WavFiles to Apple Loops in a new, separate folder.

Create a loop or sample from a DVD   With Audio Hijack or Audio Hijack Pro you can use any sound source on your computer to create loop and sample files. This includes songs in your iTunes library, streaming audio from the Internet, or the audio output of any program running on your Mac.

Master It   Use the Audio Hijack Pro program to capture a sound clip from a DVD in your Mac's DVD player.

Scan a hard drive or folder for all of its audio files   Iced Audio's AudioFinder program contains a number of features designed to help you organize all of the sound files on your computer system.

Master It   Use AudioFinder's Scanner tab to view all of the audio files in the MMA Audio folder. Locate the file SynBassArp1.wav then copy the file to a Bookmarked location.

Chapter 8

Plug-in Effects

In digital recording there are two main categories of plug-ins: plug-in effects, also known as plug-in processors, and plug-in virtual instruments. In this chapter we will cover plug-in effects and, in Chapter 9, "Virtual Instruments," we will cover plug-in virtual instruments.

When working in your DAW program, plug-in effects can be added to audio or MIDI tracks to change the sound in any number of ways. These can be drastic changes like a sweeping phaser effect or an intense delay, though plug-ins are also used to achieve more subtle effects such as adding a small amount of compression to a track to help it stand out in a mix or using a tube emulator plug-in to add "analog warmth" to a track. Plug-in effects can also be found in many audio editing programs and are frequently used on final mixes and in the mastering process. Not all plug-ins are used to alter sound; they can also be monitoring devices (like a virtual VU meter), instrument tuners and frequency analyzers.

There are a vast amount of plug-in effects available for OS X, covering a huge spectrum of functions and sonic possibilities. These plug-ins range in price from free to extremely expensive. Many plug-ins are also available in "bundles" as part of a group of effects, in some cases combined with virtual instruments.

In this chapter, you will learn to

◆ Install Audio Unit, VST, and RTAS plug-ins

◆ Use plug-ins in any DAW program

◆ Locate plug-ins on the Web

Plug-in Formats

In this chapter we'll be working with the three different plug-in formats that can be used with the host software covered in the first section of this book: Audio Units, VST, and RTAS. All three function in essentially the same way. Any differences in how each format works will generally have more to do with the DAW host program than the plug-in itself. Many plug-ins are available in multiple formats, which means that you can use them no matter which DAW software you are using. However, there are also a great number of plug-ins (often free or inexpensive) that are available in only one or two formats.

Audio Units (AU)

Audio Units are Apple's plug-in format. Many programs support the Audio Units format including GarageBand, Logic, and Live. Audio Units are also supported by some audio editing programs such as Audiofile's Wave Editor and Bias Peak.

OS X has a number of built-in Audio Unit effects and instruments that will automatically be accessible in any Audio Unit–capable host program. Audio Units can be plug-in effects or virtual instruments.

VST WRAPPERS

Before we get any further into the various available formats, I should mention that FXpansion (www.fxpansion.com) makes two wrapper programs that convert VST plug-ins to the RTAS and Audio Unit format. These are excellent utilities that make many of the format differences irrelevant.

However, occasionally a "wrapped" plug-in may lose some of its functionality or cause your DAW to crash. There are options within the wrapper programs to exclude problematic plug-ins if necessary.

If you are using a DAW that supports Audio Units or RTAS format but not VST, you may want to consider one of the FXpansion programs. The sheer number of free and inexpensive VST plug-ins available make the VST to AU or VST to RTAS wrapper a great investment.

Most commercial Audio Unit plug-ins have an installer program that places the necessary component files and presets in the appropriate locations. Many freeware Audio Units and some shareware and commercial Audio Units may require manual installation. In these cases you download a .component file that needs to placed in one of the following directories:

```
yourusername\Library\Audio\Plug-ins\Components
yourharddrive\Library\Audio\Plug-ins\Components
```

VST

VST stands for Virtual Studio Technology. The VST format was invented by the software company Steinberg, originally for use with its Cubase software. VST plug-ins exist for both Mac and PC and are used in multiple programs, making it the most common of all plug-in platforms. Unfortunately, PC-based VSTs cannot be used on Apple computers, although quite often the author of a VST plug-in will create both Mac and PC versions. VST plug-ins can be used in Cubase and Live and are also supported by other types of programs such as audio editors.

Most commercial VST plug-ins come with an installer program that places the necessary files in the appropriate locations. As with Audio Units, many free VST plug-ins and some shareware and commercial VSTs may require manual installation. In these cases, you download a VST file that needs to placed in one of the following directories:

```
yourusername\Library\Audio\Plug-ins\VST
yourharddrive\Library\Audio\Plug-ins\VST
```

RTAS (Real Time AudioSuite)

RTAS is the plug-in format created by Digidesign for use with their Pro Tools software. All versions of Pro Tools come with large collections of included RTAS plug-ins, many of which are covered in the "Included Plug-ins" section of Chapter 4, "Pro Tools." The more expensive Pro Tools HD systems also include the TDM plug-ins, which use Pro Tools HD's DSP cards for CPU power. I am going to focus on RTAS plug-ins only in this chapter because they can be used with every version of Pro Tools.

Almost all RTAS plug-ins come with an installer program. To install the few that don't, drag and drop the plug-in file here:

```
yourharddrive\Applications\Digidesign\Pro Tools\Plug-ins alias
```

QUICK INSTALLATION

Because I like to try out as many plug-ins as I possibly can, I added my Components and VST folders to the sidebar of the Finder window. This way when I open a DMG or ZIP file containing a new .component or VST file, I can just drag and drop directly in the appropriate folder. Conversely, if a particular plug-in is causing problems or if a demo version has expired it's a simple matter to locate the file and delete it.

Other Formats

Other plug-in formats used on Mac computers include MAS (Motu Audio System) for use with Mark of the Unicorn's Digital Performer DAW software, as well as Pro Tools' HTDM and Audio-Suite formats, which are discussed in Chapter 4.

Dongles and Keys

Some plug-in effects (as well as some virtual instruments and DAW programs) require an authorization key, sometimes known as a dongle. These devices are actually tiny USB-powered computers that contain digital licenses for your software. These licenses are for copyright protection, to prevent people from using illegal or "cracked" versions of software. Some software that requires an authorization key will work in demo mode for a limited time until it needs to be authorized. With some software it is occasionally possible to bypass the authorization key and register and authorize your software by mail or phone. Generally, however, if your software requires a dongle or key, you'll have to own or buy one.

The most common dongles and keys are as follows:

Pace iLok   The Pace iLok key (www.ilok.com) is used to authorize many Pro Tools plug-ins as well as Waves plug-ins and bundles and other software.

Steinberg/Syncrosoft Key   The Steinberg and Syncrosoft keys are interchangeable. The Steinberg key is used to authorize Steinberg products like Cubase, the HALion sampler, and Groove Agent. It is also used (when known as the Syncrosoft key) to authorize IK Multimedia products and Arturia synthesizers, among others.

Other programs, like Logic, will come with their own individual dongles that must be inserted into an available USB port in order to run the program.

An iLok is included with all versions of Pro Tools, and the Steinberg/Syncrosoft key is included with Cubase and many other Steinberg programs. Both the iLok and Steinberg/Syncrosoft key are also available from music retailers such as www.musiciansfriend.com and www.zzounds.com.

Using Plug-ins in Your DAW

Plug-in effects are generally used in one of two ways: as an insert on a single instrument or vocal track, or on an auxiliary or "aux" track in a send/return configuration, where the signal from multiple tracks can be routed in and out of a single track containing the effect. The second method is often used to conserve processor power, to save time, or to achieve uniform results (such as having the same kind of delay effect on multiple tracks).

While every DAW program will use plug-ins in essentially the same way, there will be some minor differences, mostly having to do with how the plug-in's interface appears in the host program and how presets are stored and recalled.

The following sections are brief tutorials on how to use third-party plug-ins in each of the DAW programs covered in this book.

In order to get the most out of these tutorials and examples, you need to have some third-party plug-in effects installed. If you haven't done so already, I recommend you download and install Pluggo Junior from www.cycling74.com/downloads/pluggo.

Pluggo Junior is a free suite of plug-ins in Audio Unit, VST, and RTAS format. Pluggo Junior and its parent program, Pluggo, are both covered later in this chapter in the section "Cycling '74."

PLUG-INS IN ABLETON LIVE

Along with its built-in plug-in effects, Ableton Live can also use third-party Audio Unit and VST effects. In order to use Audio Units and VSTs:

1. Open Live's Preferences and select the Plug-in tab.

2. Click the Use Audio Units button and the Use VST Plug-in System Folders button to turn these features on.

   If you have more VSTs installed than you need access to, you may want to create your own custom VST plug-in folder containing only the VST plug-ins you want to use in Live. If this is the case turn on Use VST Custom Folder and use the Browse button to locate your custom folder.

3. Close Live's Preferences.

4. Click the Plug-in Device Browser button to open the Device Browser shown in Figure 8.1. Within the Audio Units and VST folders there will usually be separate folders for each plug-in manufacturer, but in some cases VST plug-ins may appear at the top level of the Audio Units or VST folder.

5. Open the Audio Units folder, then open the Apple folder to view the included OS X Audio Unit plug-ins.

6. Select the AUMatrixReverb plug-in and drag it onto any track or to any empty section of the Clip/Device Drop area.

As with all Audio Unit or VST plug-ins in Live, the AUMatrixReverb window will automatically open when you add the plug-in to your track. You can use this window to choose presets or adjust the plug-in's parameters. You can also work with plug-ins within the Live environment.

One of Live's interesting features is that along with opening the plug-in's standard interface, Live also incorporates all of your third-party plug-ins into its own interface. To view your plug-in in Live's Track view, close the AUMatrixReverb window by clicking its top left corner. Then click the track header to view the plug-in at the bottom of the Live interface. Figure 8.2 shows the AUMatrixReverb in the Live Device Chain window.

FIGURE 8.1

Live's Plug-in Device Browser window

FIGURE 8.2

The AUMatrixReverb in Track view

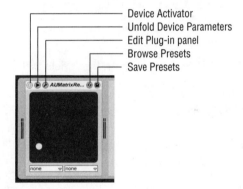

Every plug-in effect that you open as a Live device will have similar controls, which are, from left to right:

Device Activator   Turns the plug-in on and off.

Unfold Device Parameters   Opens the effect's adjustable parameters in the Device window.

Edit Plug-in Panel   Opens the plug-in's original interface window.

Browse Presets   Makes the Presets folder visible in the Browser window. It also links the device to the Device Browser so you can browse and automatically load presets by double-clicking them in the device browser.

Save Presets   Saves the current plug-in settings as a recallable preset.

VST plug-ins work in essentially the same way in Live with one minor difference. As you can see in Figure 8.3, a VST plug-in in Live's track view has a second row of buttons that contains the Load Preset or Bank and Save Preset or Bank buttons, as well as a Preset drop-down menu.

FIGURE 8.3
A VST plug-in in Live's
Track view

Load Preset or Bank

The blue hand icon, visible in Figure 8.3, indicates that the plug-in can be controlled by a connected MIDI device.

Essentially, third-party effects in Live are treated exactly like Live's included effects. In fact, you can group them with Live's included effects as part of a chain or rack. Any Live clips you create with Audio Unit or VST effects will function exactly the same way as Live clips created with Live's own plug-in effects.

LOGIC

Aside from its own very impressive collection of included plug-ins, Logic can also work with Audio Unit plug-ins. VST plug-ins can also be accessed in Logic through the use of FXpansion's VST to Audio Unit wrapper. To use third-party Audio Units in Logic:

1. Double-click any audio, audio instrument or other track in the Arrange window to open the Mixer window.

2. Click your mouse in the Insert field at the top of any channel strip as shown in Figure 8.4.

FIGURE 8.4
Insert a plug-in.

3. In the menu that appears, select your plug-in.

   All of your third-party Audio Unit effects will appear in the Mono or Mono ->Stereo submenu and will be organized by manufacturer. If you are using FXpansion's VST to AU wrapper, your VST plug-ins will appear in a submenu labeled VST.

   Figure 8.5 shows the Pluggo Junior Jet Plug-in in Logic.

FIGURE 8.5
The Jet plug-in
in Logic

When using third-party plug-ins in Logic, presets may be available from the Settings menu (the down arrow just below the Bypass button at the top left of the plug-in interface) or from a separate Presets menu on the top right of the plug-in interface. Any presets you create and save will appear in the Settings menu.

PRO TOOLS

Pro Tools uses its own TDM, AudioSuite, and RTAS plug-in formats. These formats are described in detail in Chapter 4. The most commonly used Pro Tools plug-in format is RTAS (Real Time AudioSuite), which works in every version of Pro Tools. VST plug-ins can also be accessed in Pro Tools by using FXpansion's VST to RTAS wrapper. VST instrument/plug-in effects combinations can also be accessed in Pro Tools by using the program VSTi Host with Propellerhead's ReWire protocol (see Chapter 7, "More Really Useful Software").

Most commercial plug-ins are available in RTAS format, but many freeware and shareware plug-ins are not. There are some free third-party RTAS plug-ins available, but by far the best free Pro Tools plug-ins are Digidesign's own, including the Bomb Factory plug-ins covered in Chapter 4. Digidesign is constantly releasing new free plug-ins and upgrades for all Pro Tools systems. Check their website (www.digidesign.com) regularly to make sure you have all of the latest free plug-ins.

To use a third-party RTAS plug-in in Pro Tools:

1. Make sure that Inserts View is visible by selecting View ➤ Edit Window ➤ Inserts or View ➤ Mix Window ➤ Inserts.

2. In the Inserts View, use an Insert Selector to choose a plug-in by type or manufacturer. For example, to load Pluggo's Chamberverb you would choose Plug-in ➤ Cycling '74 ➤ Chamberverb.

For most plug-ins, the first place to check for presets is the Librarian menu. Other plug-ins may contain preset lists in other locations. Wherever the included presets are located, saving new presets will generally create a new list in the Librarian menu.

Presets for the Chamberverb can be accessed from the View drop-down menu shown in Figure 8.6

ACCESSING PRESETS

Different third-party plug-ins may have their own unique menus for loading presets, though not always. For example, presets in the Chamberverb plug-in are accessed by clicking the View drop-down menu. Presets in Waves plug-ins (see the section "Plug-in Bundles") are accessed by clicking the Load button. Many third-party plug-ins will have presets available from the Librarian menu, just like Pro Tools' own RTAS effects.

Create your own presets for all third-party plug-ins by selecting Settings ➤ Save Settings As and then creating a new folder in the Save Settings dialog box.

Any presets you create this way will always appear in the Librarian menu.

FIGURE 8.6
The Chamberverb and
its Preset menu

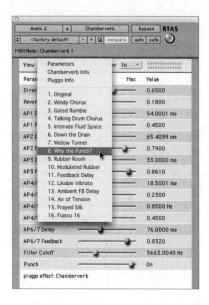

GARAGEBAND

Along with its included plug-ins, GarageBand uses Audio Unit plug-ins. Audio Unit effects can be added to any Real Instrument or Software Instrument track. VST plug-ins can also be accessed in GarageBand by using FXpansion's VST to Audio Unit wrapper.

To access third-party plug-in effects in GarageBand:

1. Double-click any track header to open the Track Info window.

2. Make sure the Details view is open (if it's not, click the Details view at the bottom of the Track Info window).

3. Use the first drop-down menu to add a plug-in in the first additional effect slot.

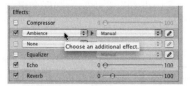

All of your available effects are divided into two lists. The top list is GarageBand's built-in effects and the bottom list is all of your available Audio Unit effects. These are considered additional effects because GarageBand's Echo and Reverb sliders at the bottom of the Effects section are available on every Real and Software Instrument track.

Once you have chosen an effect, you can access any included presets from the Presets drop-down menu to the right of the effects drop-down. Just to the right of the Presets menu is the Edit Preset button (with a pencil icon). Click the Edit Preset button to view the plug-in's interface, adjust parameters, and create your own presets. Figure 8.7 shows the Average Injector Pluggo plug-in as an Audio Unit in GarageBand.

FIGURE 8.7

The Average Injector
Pluggo in GarageBand

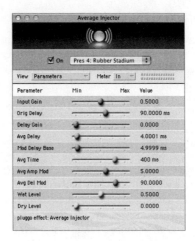

Finding Free Plug-ins

The World Wide Web is a fantastic resource for locating, downloading, and installing free plug-in effects. No matter what your primary DAW is, there are effects out there that you can access and use free of charge, or sometimes for a voluntary requested donation. Live users in particular have the benefit of being able to use both Audio Units and VSTs, which are the two most common formats for free plug-ins. Logic and GarageBand users can access all of the many free Audio Unit plug-ins. Pro Tools users have fewer options for free plug-ins, but many are available both from Digidesign and third-party manufactures. Pro Tools users can also take advantage of FXpansion's VST to RTAS program to install additional plug-ins.

These sites are some of the most complete for plug-ins:

www.macmusic.org   This site contains the most comprehensive list of free (and commercial) plug-in effects on the Internet. Click the Software tab and select the Plug-ins category or select a specific plug-in format. You can rearrange the list of plug-ins by clicking the Type link at the top of the list. This organizes the plug-ins into Commercial, Shareware, and Freeware categories. Click any plug-in to view a page with manufacturer information and a download link.

www.kvraudio.com   A comprehensive and continually updated list of music software and plug-ins for OS X and Windows, with a huge searchable database.

www.hitsquad.com   Click the Music Software link to browse software by category. Look for the Plug-ins-AU or Plug-ins-VST links.

www.google.com   Use Google to search for "free Audio Units," "free VST," "free RTAS," or other variations such as "Free Delay OS X" or "Free VST GarageBand." Get creative with your searches and you may come up with some interesting results.

www.bigbluelounge.com   Check out their Effects related forums for information on new and existing free plug-ins.

www.apple.com   Apple has an audio software download page at www.apple.com/downloads/macosx/audio. Not strictly plug-ins, but new free and demo version Audio Units appear there occasionally.

Types of Effects

The following sections discuss some of the most frequently used types of plug-in effects and the common parameters that make up each effect. Each section also contains a list of some of the currently available freeware, donationware, and commercial versions of each type of effect. What's covered in this chapter represents a good cross-section of available plug-ins for OS X. Many, many more are available, and the list grows every day.

DONATIONWARE

Some of the effects I cover in this chapter fall into the category of "donationware." What this means is that they are free to download and use and it's up to you to decide if and how much you'd like to pay for them. Donationware plug-ins are often some of the best of the "free" software that's available. A huge amount of work goes into creating a good plug-in, and I encourage you to make a donation of any amount if you enjoy and continue to use any of the donationware plug-ins covered in the section.

Delays

Delay effects are very popular and used in just about every recording in one form or another. Delays can be as subtle as an almost unnoticeable slapback effect, commonly used on vocal tracks. At the opposite end of the spectrum, a delay can be as prominent as the long echoing effects heard in reggae and dub style recordings and ambient music. Delays can also be manipulated in a number of ways, especially with automation, and used to create unique sounds and sound effects. While every DAW program comes with some kind of built-in delay effect, you can expand your sonic options with one or more of the many third-party delay effects available.

The first delay effects were created using tape machines. These experiments were later incorporated into tape-based delay effects, like Roland's Space Echo and Maestro's Echoplex units. These original tape-based delay effects created rich, analog sounds and became a staple of many dub producers like Lee "Scratch" Perry and King Tubby. These effects and other tape-based looping devices also found their way onto recordings by rock artists such as Pink Floyd in the 1970s, U2 in the 1980s, Jane's Addiction in the 1990s, and more recent recordings by Radiohead, along with many others. Delay effects are still heard prominently in most electronic music and continue to be a staple of recordings in almost every genre.

Delay effects can be used on any instrument or performance, though their most common applications are with guitars and vocals. Delay effects are also very useful in creating ambient sounds and synthesizer patches.

COMMON DELAY PARAMETERS

These are some of the parameters you'll commonly find on many delay effects:

Dry Sets the amount of dry, unprocessed signal that will be output from the plug-in.

Wet Sets the amount of delayed, effected output from the plug-in. Sometimes the Dry and Wet parameters will be incorporated in a single slider or fader.

Delay Time Sets the amount of time between each repetition.

Feedback Sets the length that a delay effect will continue. A very long feedback setting can create an infinite delay.

Sync Matches the delay effect to the tempo of the track. This can help keep things from getting too messy, especially on songs with multiple delay effects.

Filter/Cutoff Some delays will also include other parameters, such as a low or high pass filter, which can adjust the EQ settings of the delayed signal.

Using Delays

Because of delay effects' multiple uses and popularity, there are many different delays available, and many of them include interesting and sometimes unusual functionality. Let's take a look here at some of the free and commercial delay effects available for OS X audio applications.

GarageBand AUDelay

OS X comes with the included AUDelay (Audio Unit Delay) shown as a GarageBand plug-in in Figure 8.8. The AUDelay contains the basic parameters of a delay effect. Here's a brief introduction.

Figure 8.8
OS X's included
AUDelay effect

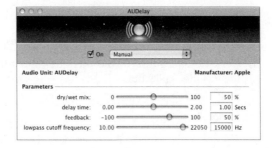

1. Adjust the Dry/Wet Mix slider to increase or decrease the amount of the delay effect from 0% to 100%.

2. Lengthen or shorten the delay time by milliseconds with the Delay Time slider.

3. Adjust the Feedback slider to increase or decrease the length of the delay. You'll notice here that –100% and 100% have the same effect.

4. The Lowpass Cutoff Frequency slider changes the sound of the effected (wet) signal. Raising the slider above the default 15000Hz will give the delay a brighter sound, lowering it will have the opposite effect.

Ohmforce OhmBoyz Delay

At the other end of the spectrum are more complicated delay effects like the Ohmforce OhmBoyz (AU, RTAS, VST, MAS), `www.ohmforce.com`. The price for this is $101 (demo available). Figure 8.9 shows the OhmBoyz delay in Pro Tools.

This is a fun and excellent-sounding but very complicated delay effect with lots of features. Be careful when installing this plug-in and make sure you choose Classic Skin. The other choice, Funky Skin, is a very busy interface that may be confusing if you are not already familiar with the plug-in.

OhmBoyz contains many of the effects associated with both analog and digital delays. The included banks of presets range from simple, rhythmic effects to the complex, exploding, sound-shifting effects associated with the original tape-based delay units. Try adding the OhmBoyz to any track containing a simple instrument performance or loop, or if possible, a track where you can play a live virtual piano or keyboard. Click any of the Presets buttons in the top right corner to try out the eight default presets.

To get more of an idea of some of the possibilities, follow these steps:

1. Click the Load button on the top right side of the interface to load banks of eight presets from the included collections.

2. Select the `Classic-Space.pbk` preset bank in the Load Preset Bank dialog box and click the Choose button.

3. These are all presets that are based on classic Tape Delay devices. Select each of the presets to see how a minor change to the Delay Level or Filter Resolution setting can have a dramatic effect on the sound.

For a more pronounced, strange effect load the Preset bank `experimental.pbk` and select preset number 5. You can use this preset to create analog style delay effects similar to those on Radiohead's *OK Computer* album. Try playing a long, sustained chord and letting it ring out. Be patient, as much of the effect will take place long after the chord has faded.

These effects represent a small taste of what's available with the OhmBoyz delay. Try out the remaining Preset banks.

To quickly create your own delay effects:

1. Add a new instance of the OhmBoyz plug-in to a new track in your DAW.

2. Adjust the main delay signal by moving the Delay knob in the lower left of the Delay Line #1 area.

3. The OhmBoyz has four separate delays in the areas labeled Tap #1 through Tap #4. Adjust the Level, Delay, and Balance knobs for Tap #1 and Tap #2. Be sure to select different delay times for each tap and use the Balance knobs to pan them in opposite directions.

FabFilter Timeless Delay

Another excellent, complicated delay plug-in effect is the FabFilter Timeless (Figure 8.10), which combines tape delay concepts with effects that are only possible in the digital realm. FabFilter Timeless is available from www.fabfilter.com for $129. A fully functioning 30-day demo version is available.

FIGURE 8.10

The FabFilter Timeless

While the Timeless interface is very complicated, you can get instructions, tips, and hints for each of the knobs and various parameters by selecting the Help button in the top right corner and selecting Show Interactive Help Hints from the pop-up menu. The Timeless comes with banks of presets. To get an idea of the possibilities, try adding the Timeless to a simple drum track or other sparse instrumental performance and use the arrows at the top of the plug-in window to scroll through the first set of presets in the Basic category.

What sets the FabFilter Timeless apart is its many adjustable, editable parameters that can create all kinds of sounds and effects that are unavailable to analog delay units. You can also use the Timeless to create modulation-based effects (which I'll cover in detail in the "Modulation Effects" section of this chapter).

WHICH DELAY?

Whether you need a complex delay effect or not depends on what kind of music you are recording or creating. For straight ahead rock, folk music, or jazz, you can probably accomplish much of what you need with your DAW's included delay effects or with simple, inexpensive, or freeware third-party delays. Sound designers or anyone creating music in any of the electronica/techno genres, psychedelic rock, dub/reggae and many other styles will benefit greatly from any of the delays covered in this section.

KING DUBBY

The King Dubby delay is one of my all-time favorite plug-ins. Unfortunately it's only available in Audio Unit format. The good news is it's a free plug-in and you can download it at www.lowcoders.net/kd.html.

The King Dubby is based on analog tape-delay effects, specifically the Roland Space Echo unit that was popular with Jamaican reggae and dub producers in the 1970s. If you are interested in creating dub or dub-influenced music or you just want to add a great sounding (and great looking) delay to your Audio Unit arsenal, check out the King Dubby ASAP.

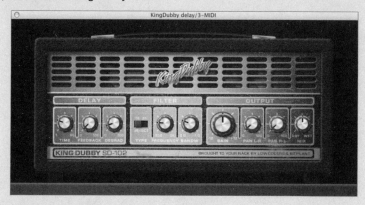

AVAILABLE DELAY PLUG-INS

The following is a list of some of the additional delay effects currently available for OS X.

Free Delay Plug-ins

    Cow Delay (AU) apulsoft.ch/freeports

    MDA Dub Delay (AU, VST) www.mda-vst.com

    Bouncy (AU, VST) www.smartelectronix.com

    Analog Delay (VST) mdsp.smartelectronix.com/classic (donationware)

    Delayifier (VST) www.greenoak.com/vst.html

    Meringue (AU, VST) www.collective.co.uk/expertsleepers

Commercial Delay Plug-ins

    Dub Station (AU, VST) www.audiodamage.com, $39

    RatShack Reverb Analog Delay (AU, VST) wwwaudiodamage.com, $34.99

    DelayPack (AU, VST, RTAS) www.codeoperator.com, $50

    EchoBoy (RTAS, TDM) www.soundtoys.com, $349

Compressors and Limiters

Compressors and limiters are frequently used plug-ins with a lot of possible applications. Both are used in the recording and mixing stage as well as in the mastering process. For information about using compressors and limiters in the mastering process see the "Mastering" section of Chapter 13, "Post-Production."

COMPRESSION

Compressors can be used on any instrument, especially those with wide dynamic range. Compression is commonly used on vocal tracks, drum tracks, bass tracks, and in the mastering process. Some engineers are even known to compress just about every track in a session to a greater or lesser degree, while others feel that overcompression is responsible for a lot of what's "wrong" with recording today. I'm going to avoid any controversy here and agree with everyone on both sides of the argument. What I mean is that, on the one hand, it's very easy to go overboard with compression, and too much compression can certainly suck the life out of a recording. On the other hand, compressors have a very interesting ability to bring out the overtones in a performance that can sometimes add musicality to an otherwise dull performance and help separate instruments in a mix.

Much of the second half of that statement refers to compression that is frequently associated with popular hardware compressors like Universal Audio's 1176LN, LA-2A, and LA-3A models and other vintage compressors made by manufacturers like Altec and Joemeek.

Digital compression, on the other hand, often has the reputation of being particularly harsh, cold, and unpleasant sounding. Compressors are often included in DAW software, sometimes in very basic form like GarageBand's compression slider and also as more complex plug-ins such as Pro Tools' included compressor plug-in. Along with the compressor plug-in that comes with your software, many of the classic compressors from years past have been recreated as plug-in effects, often with excellent results.

As the technology used to create digital compressor plug-ins improves, the line between the quality of hardware and software compressors has become blurrier. One of the main advantages to software compressor plug-ins is that you can buy one effect and use it on multiple tracks, whereas with most hardware compressors you need a dedicated unit for each track that you want to compress. The advantage that hardware compressors still have over their digital counterparts remains greater warmth and better-sounding harmonic distortion. If the option is available, you may want to try using both hardware and software compression on some of your tracks to compare and contrast sounds and to see which works best for your needs.

Basic Compressor Parameters

The following are some of the common parameters you'll find on most compressor plug-ins:

Threshold   Sets the volume level at which compression will begin to kick in. A lower threshold setting means the effect will begin to be applied at a lower volume level.

Ratio   Describes the amount of compression applied in relation to the amount that the signal increases. A lower ratio will result in less compression; a higher ratio will cause more compression. A ratio above 10:1 is generally considered "limiting."

Attack   Determines how quickly the compression effect will be applied when the volume threshold is reached.

Release   Determines how quickly the effect ends once the volume has fallen below the threshold level. The other end of the Attack spectrum.

Knee   Describes the amount of compression that is applied before the threshold is actually reached. A "soft knee" means that compression will be gradually applied as the signal gets closer to the threshold. A "hard knee" means no compression is applied until the threshold is reached.

RMS/Peak   Some compressors offer a choice between RMS and peak detection. Choosing the RMS setting means your compressor will use a mathematical equation to determine the average level of a signal and compress the signal accordingly. This is useful for evening out a performance, such as a vocal without too much dynamic range or a lead guitar. A compressor that is using peak detection is better suited to compressing sudden "spikes" in volume like a snare drum.

Limiting

While compressing and limiting are technically two different things, they are often confused and frequently used to accomplish similar, if not the same functions. Limiting is generally considered to be compression with a ratio of 10:1 or higher. Limiting is used in the mastering stage (covered in the "Mastering" section of Chapter 13) and is also frequently used in the mixing stage in pop music where high compression ratios are common, especially on drum tracks.

USING COMPRESSION

For an excellent, simple, and free compressor plug-in, check out the Blockfish (AU, VST) from www.digitalfishphones.com (Figure 8.11). Blockfish is part of a set of three free plug-ins (the other two are Spitfish, a de-esser, and Floorfish, an expander/gate plug-in).

FIGURE 8.11
The Blockfish
compressor

The Blockfish comes with nine presets covering a lot of what you might use a simple compressor plug-in for: rhythm guitar, vocals, drums, and bass. Try adding the Fat Drum Loop preset to any drum loop track for a huge, slightly overdriven sound. This setting is particularly excellent for adding life to GarageBand's Software Instrument drum loops or any snare drum track. You can easily create harsh, CB-style vocals by using the Blockfish preset Industrial Vocals.

The Blockfish is a simplified compressor. As you can see, the compression knob goes from 0 to "max," and the Attack, Release, and Threshold settings are all combined into one "response" knob.

Figure 8.12 shows the Waves Renaissance Compressor plug-in (AU, RTAS, VST, MAS, TDM), from www.waves.com. The Renaissance Compressor is available as part of one of Waves' plug-in collections (I'll cover Waves bundled plug-ins later) or as an individual plug-in for $200. The Renaissance contains all of the "classic" parameters of a hardware compressor: threshold, ratio, attack, release, and gain.

Pro Tools users have a couple of options that other DAW users don't have, All Pro Tools systems come with their own compressor plug-ins (as do Logic, Live, and GarageBand), but Pro Tools also includes a separate set of free Bomb Factory plug-ins with their software. Included with these plug-ins is the Bomb Factory BF76 Peak Limiter, shown in Figure 8.13.

The free Bomb Factory BF76 is based on the Universal Audio 1176LN, which I mentioned earlier as one of the premier hardware compressors.

FIGURE 8.12

The Renaissance
Compressor

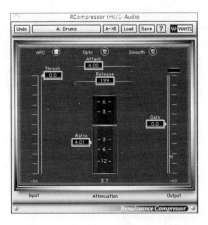

FIGURE 8.13

The BF76 Peak Limiter

While this plug-in is called a "limiter," its compression ratio begins at 4:1, below what is generally considered limiting. The BF76 comes with only two presets, one of which is very well-known in relation to the hardware version of the 1176: All Buttons In. The All Buttons In setting was discovered by recording engineers in the early 1980s who liked the overcompressed, radical sound created by pressing all of the 1176's buttons at once. Try adding the BF76 to your vocal tracks, drum overhead mics, and drum loops. Then experiment with the All Buttons In setting.

MULTIBAND COMPRESSION

Multiband compression is a combination of EQ and compression, allowing you to select certain frequencies in a performance or track and apply compression. Multiband EQ is frequently used in the mastering process, so you'll often find many mastering-related presets included with multiband compressor plug-ins.

Figure 8.14 shows Slim Slow Slider's freeware C3 Multi Band Compressor (AU, VST) plug-in, available from www.apulsoft.ch/freeports.

"RIGHT" COMPRESSION

Compression, like EQ, is a somewhat subjective art. What sounds "good" to one person may not sound right at all to another. More importantly what sounds good will vary from project to project and mix to mix. A super-compressed vocal or a lo-fi, trashy drum sound may be just right for one song and sound totally out of place in another. There are a few things that compression does exceedingly well: getting a vocal performance to fit in a mix, smoothing out a bass performance, and adding "life" to drum tracks (both real and virtual).

FIGURE 8.14
The C3 Multi Band
compressor

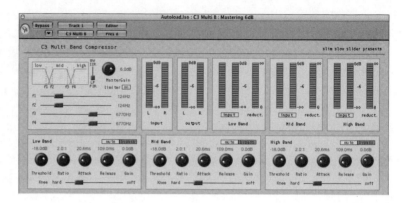

The following is a list of some basic compressor settings. For a plug-in like Blockfish or any other compressor with limited functionality, you can approximate the settings within the limited parameters. These are just some possible starting points; through time and experimentation you'll come up with settings that work for you and your music. Threshold settings (the point at which the compression actually starts to take place) will vary from track to track. I've made a few Threshold suggestions, but in general what settings you come up with will depend on your tracks and your ideas of what sounds good.

Electric Guitar   Distorted electric guitar is already heavily compressed, but adding a bit more from a compressor plug-in can sometimes bring out nice, unexpected overtones. Less distorted guitars (especially those with a wider dynamic range) and choppy performances (like funk, reggae, and Motown) can also benefit from added compression. Try starting off at 6:1 with a Soft Knee and a lower threshold (start at 0db and go lower from there).

Acoustic Guitar   Acoustic guitar can gain a lot from compression. Try starting with a medium ratio (around 5:1) and a low threshold. Increase the ratio depending on the performance and mix.

Bass   In most pop/rock genres, bass is one instrument that almost always gets some kind of compression. How much depends on the song and the recording, but 4:1 compression with a Hard Knee is usually a good place to start. You'll want to be careful with this, however, because a lot of compression will affect the lower frequencies of the bass signal.

Kick Drum   To work with a kick drum start at 3:1 with a fast attack and fast release. Raise the ratio and lower the threshold for a more pronounced effect. This is another place where you'll want to be careful not to overdo it. Too much compression on the kick drum can degrade the low end of your signal, causing a clipped kick drum sound.

Snare Drum   Try a 3:1 ratio with a fast attack as a starting point. Increase the ratio and lower the threshold for a more noticeable effect.

Overhead Cymbals   Try a 2:1 ratio for quieter mixes. Increase to taste for noisier mixes. By adding more compression on the overhead microphones you can sometimes get away with using less compression on other elements in a drum mix. Too much compression on your overheads can result in harsh-sounding cymbals.

Vocals   Try starting off with lighter compression, around 3:1. Increase depending on the singer's dynamic range. Try super-heavy compression to achieve CB radio–style vocals. You'll generally want a fast attack and slow release on vocals. If you have a compressor plug-in that emulates tube compression (like the PSP Vintage Warmer—see the link at the end of this section), you can add life to a vocal by using a heavy compression to add harmonic distortion to the vocal track. Try a 5:1 ratio with a semifast attack, medium release and a –20 setting for the threshold as a starting point.

Piano   Piano performances tend to have a very wide dynamic *and* musical range. This makes them hard to mix on two fronts. Notes and passages that may be clear at one spot of a mix can easily get lost in another. Try starting with a lower ratio like 3:1 or even 2:1 and a high threshold. Increase the ratio and lower the threshold as needed.

COMPRESSOR AND LIMITER PLUG-INS

The following is a list of some of the additional freeware and commercial plug-in compressor effects available for OS X.

Free Compressor Plug-ins

CamelPhatFree (VST)   www.camelaudio.com

MDSPCompressor (AU, VST)   www.mdsp.smartelectronix.com/classic

Bomb Factory BF-3A (RTAS)   www.digidesign.com

Commercial Compressor Plug-ins

CX1V (AU, VST)   www.anwida.com, $69

Limiting Amplifier LM-662   www.nomadfactory.com, $149

PSP Vintage Warmer   www.pspaudioware.com, $149

PSP Mastering Compressor   www.pspaudioware.com, $249

Digidesign Smack! (RTAS)   www.digidesign.com, $595

Mc2000 (RTAS,TDM, AudioSuite)   www.mcdsp.com, $495

Distortion/Gain

Sometimes referred to as saturation or overdrive, distortion is most commonly associated with guitars. Distortion in the analog realm is sometimes achieved by overdriving a signal by increasing the volume. In the digital world, however, increasing the volume to the point of distortion doesn't usually achieve very pleasing results. If you're at all familiar with digital distortion, you know what I'm talking about. If you are not I suggest you plug in a guitar or microphone to your most readily available software, turn things up "too loud" and record the results. To accomplish the right kind of distortion you'll need to use plug-ins that simulate a tube, tape, or other analog device being overdriven.

For guitars and basses there are many virtual amplifier plug-ins, like those covered in Chapter 9, which can achieve overdrive/distortion effects. What we're going to look at in this section are similar, sometimes more subtle and sometimes not, effects for instruments and tracks other than guitar. Many DAW programs include their own gain plug-ins. Live has the Saturator plug-in, Reason has the Scream 4 distortion (covered in Chapter 2, "Reason"), and Logic has included distortion and overdrive plug-ins.

Gain plug-ins are useful for adjusting the volume of your tracks and, as you'll see, sometimes contain other useful controls.

DISTORTION/GAIN PARAMETERS

Distortion and gain are pretty easy concepts to understand. The parameters you'll generally see on distortion and gain plug-ins are as follows:

Overdrive Generally associated with the sound of a tube-based amplifier being turned up to the point of distortion.

Gain An increase in volume. In the digital recording realm, gain should be closely monitored to avoid digital distortion.

Figure 8.15 shows the FreeG gain plug-in from Sonalksis.

FIGURE 8.15

The FreeG by Sonalksis

The FreeG is a gain plug-in, but it also contains some cool extras like a Phase flip button, panning, and trim features. FreeG allows you to get a closer look and greater control over any track in your mix. And of course, by raising the Volume slider and the Trim knob you can increase the volume of your track, dramatically if necessary.

The FreeG is available as a VST, RTAS, or Audio Unit plug-in. Though some of its features may already be present on the volume and panning sections of your DAW, it has unique features that make it useful in all programs. I especially like using it with Live because it gives me a Pro Tools–style fader in the Live environment.

Another free gain/distortion plug-in is the CamelCrusher (Figure 8.16) from Camel Audio (www.camelaudio.com). As far as gain plug-ins go, the CamelCrusher is the opposite of the FreeG. The names of some of the included presets (Annihilate, Destroyer, Turn it to 11) give you an idea of what this plug-in is about.

Using these kinds of plug-ins on digitally created or recorded tracks is a great way to bring a bit of realism to otherwise sterile digital sounding performances. There's certainly a lot you can do with virtual instruments and MIDI tracks to create more life-like performances, but sometimes a computer program or virtual instrument needs that extra push or analog-style warmth to make it sound more like music and less like machine-generated sound. Gain, distortion, and tube emulation plug-ins, used sparingly, can often be just what you need to make your tracks sound a lot better. You can even try adding a distortion or gain plug-in to your master track to give your entire mix a more "vintage" feel.

FIGURE 8.16
The CamelCrusher

DISTORTION/GAIN PLUG-INS

The following is a list of some of the additional distortion/gain effects currently available for OS X.

Free Distortion /Gain Plug-ins

RubyTube (VST)   www.silverspike.com

Fuzz+ (AU, VST)   www.audiodamage.com

Warp Drive (AU)   www.cs.camosun.bc.ca

Cyanide (AU, VST)   http://bram.smartelectronix.com

ColorTone Free (AU, VST, RTAS)   www.tritonedigital.com

Commercial Distortion /Gain Plug-ins

Trash (AU, VST, RTAS, MAS, HTDM)   www.izotope.com, $159

Predatohm (AU, RTAS, VST, MAS)   www.ohmforce.com, $79

Modulation Effects

Modulation-based effects work by creating a duplicate version of a sound, altering it slightly (or drastically) and playing the two back simultaneously. Some of the more common modulation-based effects are choruses, phasers, and flangers, all of which utilize similar but slightly different techniques to create their effects.

Other modulation-based effects include tremolo, vibrato, and wah-wah.

Modulation-based effects have been in use for many years now. Many of the earliest uses of modulation-based effects were pioneered by recording engineers in the 1960s and were created by recording two signals at the same time then playing them back while slowing down one of the signals very slightly. Early well-known uses of this kind of flanging effect appear on records like the Small Faces' "Itchycoo Park," the outro of Jimi Hendrix's "Bold As Love," and the drum track on Led Zeppelin's "Kashmir."

Since then phasers, flangers, and other modulation-based effects have become a part of just about every style of music, often used to varying degrees on guitars, vocals, and synthesizers, among many other applications.

MODULATION PARAMETERS

Some of the parameters you'll often see on modulation effects include:

Frequency/Rate/Speed   Controls the speed of the effect. Faster speeds result in quick, warbling effects. Slower speeds result in longer sweeping effects.

Depth   Controls the amount of the effect. A higher depth setting results in a more pronounced effect.

Delay   Controls the distance in time between the original signal and the duplicate signal.

Mix   Controls how much of the effects output is the original signal and how much is the processed signal.

LFO(Low Frequency Oscillator)   Creates effects ranging from a long sweeping sound to a rapid-fire warbling sound.

Shape   Describes the waveform; some modulation effects that contain LFOs will let you choose between different waveforms.

USING MODULATION PLUG-INS

Because of the similarities between the different modulation-based effects, you may find that it's possible to achieve one by using another, for example a flanger or phaser effect might have a chorus preset, and a flanger effect might contain a phasing preset.

Figure 8.17 shows the free Nomad Factory Nomad-Phaser plug-in.

FIGURE 8.17

The Nomad-Phaser

The Nomad Factory phaser is part of a suite of three free modulation plug-ins available from www.nomadfactory.com.

The Nomad Factory Free Bundle contains the Nomad-Phaser, Nomad-Sweeper, and Nomad-Tremolo. You can download the plug-ins by going to www.nomadfactory.com and clicking the Support tab, then clicking the Free Bundle Information link to download the plug-ins.

The Nomad-Phaser contains all the basic parameters of classic phaser effects. Try adding the plug-in to a clean electric or acoustic guitar loop or track and adjusting the parameters to create different types of phaser effects. Raise the depth, feedback, and color settings to create a more pronounced effect. Reducing the LFO rate will give you a more sweeping tone; raising the LFO will result in a faster, warbling sound. You can achieve interesting results using any phaser effect on vocals, drums, keyboards, or guitars.

One of my favorite modulation effects is the donationware SupaPhaser shown in Figure 8.18.

ALL AT ONCE

One way I like to get familiar with a new effect or plug-in is to use Live to quickly try it out on a bunch of different types of instruments at once. You can do this by creating a new Live set and then adding different types of loops to a single audio track, each in its own clip slot. Once you've added a drum loop, a guitar loop, a piano loop, and any other instrument (or even a vocal performance clip), add the new effect or plug-in to the track. Select one of the plug-in's presets and try out each clip. Select another preset and repeat the process.

This can give you a quick insight into which instruments might benefit (or not) from your new plug-in and which presets might be good starting points for your mixing and recording needs.

FIGURE 8.18

The SupaPhaser

I mentioned this plug-in briefly in Chapter 7 in the "VSTi Host" section. The SupaPhaser comes with a big collection of presets that cover many of the different kinds of effects you can create with a phaser. One of my favorite uses for the SupaPhaser is as a kind of virtual amplifier plug-in for clean electric guitar tracks and electric piano. The first preset, Preset 0 Bdj Simple Phaser, is great for simulating mid-'70s guitar and keyboard sounds.

Try adding the SupaPhaser to a virtual synthesizer track and selecting one of the more noticeable presets like Pres 6: The Wall Distorted cycle or Pres28 RCG Mental (Guitar). Use phaser or flanger effects on your synthesizer tracks in conjunction with delay effects to create excellent ambient tones and background noises.

Figure 8.19 shows the Anwida Soft Chorus effect, part of the Anwida Soft Modula Pack (AU, VST) of six modulation-based plug-ins available from www.anwida.com for $149.

FIGURE 8.19

The Anwida Soft
Chorus plug-in

Chorus effects are very similar to phasers. Like many modulation effects, the chorus effect is often associated with electric guitars, keyboards, and sometimes vocals. The results of the two effects are often quite similar, with phasers being known to add more colorations and sweep. Some well-known guitar players who make frequent use of chorus effects include Robert Smith of The Cure and Dave Navarro of Jane's Addiction and the Red Hot Chili Peppers.

The chorus effect has another useful application, but it's one that you should be careful with. Adding chorus to an out of tune or weak vocal track can sometimes make it sound better or even make it seem to be in tune. Unfortunately as a result, over-chorused vocal tracks have become a hallmark of many amateur home recordings. Try adding a small amount of chorus to a weak or out of tune vocal track as a last resort, if compression and delay effects aren't enough.

MODULATION EFFECTS

The following is a list of some of the other free and commercially available modulation plug-ins for OS X.

Free/Donationware Modulation Plug-ins

MonstaChorus (AU, VST) www.betabugsaudio.com

Phaser (AU, VST)(Donationware) www.collective.co.uk/expertsleepers

Chorusifier (VST) www.greenoak.com/vst.html

Phasifier (VST) www.greenoak.com/vst.html

Commercial Modulation Plug-ins

Metaflanger (VST, AU, RTAS) www.waves.com, $150

MobileOhm (AU, RTAS, VST, MAS) www.ohmforce.com, $101

PhaseTwo (AU, VST) www.audiodamage.com, $49

Reverbs

A basic reverb effect is usually the simulation of large or small room or concert halls or cathedrals. More complex reverb effects can also approximate metal tubes, echo chambers, open fields and just about any environment you'd like to recreate. A classic example of a "natural" reverb is the drum sound on the Led Zeppelin song "When The Levee Breaks," which was achieved by placing the drums at the bottom of a stairwell and two microphones at the top. Other popular forms of reverb include chamber reverbs that use a microphone and speaker to simulate echo, and plate reverbs that use a metal plate with an attached pickup to create the effect. Spring reverbs (frequently found in guitar amplifiers) are similar to plate reverbs but with a coiled spring used to create the sound instead of a plate.

Reverb plug-ins will often contain presets and other options used to simulate each of these different types of reverb.

There are similarities between delay and reverb plug-ins. For example, you might use either one to achieve a short delay effect like slapback or vocal doubling. Generally reverb effects are used for ambience, whether subtle or dramatic.

COMMON REVERB PARAMETERS

The following are some of the most frequently seen parameters associated with reverb plug-ins:

Room Size   Determines the size of the room that is being replicated. A higher setting will indicate a larger room, such as a cathedral or auditorium. Choose lower settings to replicate a vocal booth or closet.

Width   Indicates the width of the room.

Decay   Closely related to room size, decay controls the length of time it takes for your reverb to fade out.

Diffusion   Affects the early reflections of the reverb sound. Higher diffusion settings will result in a thicker sound. Be careful with this setting though—a high diffusion setting can sometimes cause muddiness.

Damping   Controls how much the "walls" absorb the sound. Lower or less damping will mean a longer, more noticeable effect.

EQ   Some reverbs will also contain EQ settings, which allow you to boost or remove certain frequencies in the effect.

USING REVERB

Reverb effects are most commonly used on guitars, vocals, and drums (snare drum in particular) but can be used on any instrument that needs to sound more "live." Reverb effects are also used extensively in sound design and movie production. As a result many sound editing programs like Bias Peak will contain their own reverb plug-ins, as will almost all DAW programs.

Figure 8.20 shows the free plug-in Black Water Reverb, a very basic reverb effect.

FIGURE 8.20

The Black Water Reverb

The Black Water Reverb is available as an Audio Unit and VST effect and can be downloaded from www.apulsoft.ch/freeports. To get a look at this basic effect:

1. Create a new session in your Audio Unit or VST-compatible host program.

2. Create an audio track and add one of the drum loops from your MMA Audio\Drum Loops folder on the included DVD.

3. Add the Black Water Reverb as an insert effect.

4. Increase and decrease the wet and dry signals to come up with a good mix of the two.

5. Increase the Room Size and Width settings for a bigger effect. The larger the room size and width are, the longer and more pronounced the effect will be.

6. Raise the Damp slider for a "tighter" sound.

Some virtual reverbs, such as Bias Peak's included ImpulseVerb and Audio Ease's Altiverb (Figure 8.21) contain acoustic models of specific rooms.

Acoustic modeling plug-ins are quite expensive and may be more reverb than you need, unless you have an unlimited budget or expect to be doing a lot of high-powered sound design. Altiverb is available from www.audioease.com and costs $595. A demo version with included acoustic modeling room simulations is available. With the Altiverb you can simulate many famous rooms, including churches, concert halls, and stadiums. What's more, you can virtually "place" yourself or any instrument performance at any location within these virtual environments. The method used to create these virtual is called *impulse response*. With impulse response, a room is acoustically "sampled" and mathematically recreated by the reverb effect. This kind of effect can be very useful for mixing orchestration, large ensembles (like big band groups) and surround 5.1 mixes, as well as movie or television sound design.

FIGURE 8.21
Audio Ease's Altiverb
plug-in

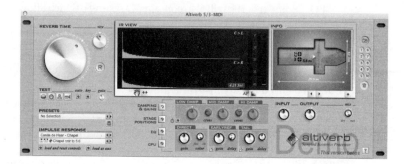

The problem with most of the reverb effects that are included with DAW programs is that they tend to be very harsh sounding (Logic's included reverbs being a notable exception), and the available free reverb plug-ins may or may not represent a dramatic enough improvement over your DAW's included effects. If you are looking for an effect that improves on your DAW's plug-ins but doesn't contain a lot of unnecessary high-end applications, a middle range plug-in effect like Waves' TrueVerb or Nomad Factory's BlueVerb DRV-2080 will definitely get the job done.

Figure 8.22 shows the BlueVerb DRV-2080.

Aesthetically speaking, the BlueVerb has a really nice interface and large, clearly marked knobs. The parameter knobs and separate EQ section give you detailed control over a number of aspects of the reverb effect. BlueVerb also includes a set of presets to get you started.

FIGURE 8.22
The BlueVerb
DRV-2080

OS X REVERB EFFECTS

The following is a list of some of the other freeware, donationware, and commercially available reverb plug-ins for OS X.

Free/Donationware Reverb Plug-ins

Ambience (AU, VST) magnus.smartelectronix.com (donationware)

DX Reverb Light (VST) www.anwida.com

Commercial Reverb Plug-ins

RaySpace (AU, VST) www.quikquak.com, $90

MasterVerb (VST/MAS/AU/RTAS) www.wavearts.com, $199.95

Arts Acoustic Reverb (AU, VST) www.artsacoustic.com, $189

True Verb (AU, VST RTAS) www.waves.com, $200

Reverence (AU, VST) www.audiodamage.com, $39.00

TL Space (RTAS, TDM) www.digidesign.com, $495–$995

EQs

EQ (short for equalization) is the process of manipulating frequencies of recorded instrument and vocal performances. Equalization techniques are very important in the recording the mixing process. Many engineers refer to the process of "carving" EQs—raising and lowering certain frequencies to place instruments in their proper place within the spectrum of available frequencies. EQ can also have a dramatic effect on the sound of an instrument.

EQ ranges are subjective, meaning that different people will have different ideas about what constitutes low, high, or middle ranges. This is a rough sketch to give you a general idea of frequency ranges:

- Low range: 20Hz to 800Hz

- Low midrange: 700Hz to 7KHz

- High midrange: 1K to 10 K

- High range: 5K to 20K

EQ PLUG-INS

There are essentially two kinds of EQ plug-ins: graphic and parametric. Sometimes you'll see a combination of the two ("paragraphic"). In this section we'll take a look at both types.

Graphic EQ

Graphic EQs are very straightforward. They have sliders or faders that adjust specific frequencies, or "bands." These controls are used to raise or lower a chosen frequency or frequency range. Graphic EQs are often available in 1-band, 4-band, and 10-band modes, but any configuration is possible. OS X includes the Audio Unit AUGraphicEQ, which you can use in any Audio Unit compatible host program. Figure 8.23 shows the AUGraphicEQ in 10-band mode.

FIGURE 8.23

OS X's AUGraphicEQ equalizer

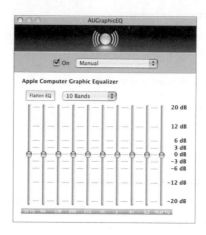

Parametric EQ

Parametric EQ is more complex and can perform more precise equalization of tracks. Parametric EQs generally contain one or more of the following controls:

Frequency   Allows you to choose the specific frequency that you wish to boost or reduce. Often a parametric EQ will contain multiple knobs for each frequency range.

Q   Lets you zoom in or zoom out of the specific frequency range. A lower, or tighter, Q setting will boost or reduce a specific frequency. Widening the Q setting will affect a larger frequency range.

Boost/Gain   Raises or lowers the selected frequency.

Figure 8.24 shows the Pro Tools 4-band EQ 3 equalizer.

As with many parametric EQ plug-ins, you can either use your mouse to adjust the EQ knobs or manually draw your EQ by selecting control points on the EQ graph.

FIGURE 8.24

The Pro Tools 4-band EQ 3 plug-in

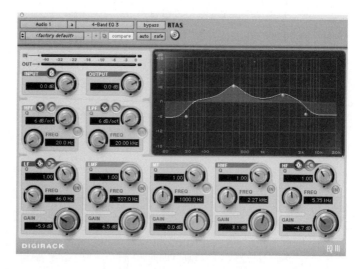

USING EQ

The "proper" use of EQ is an extremely subjective thing. There are many different possibilities and schools of thought about what sounds good and how to get there. It's also very important to remember that EQs are best used to enhance a well-recorded track, not to fix or create good sounds on their own.

One basic concept that works across the board is the idea of "carving" out EQ frequencies. This means choosing instruments that use similar frequencies and boosting or cutting one while either leaving the other alone or adjusting it in the opposite direction. For example, this technique is often used with bass guitar and kick drum tracks, which reside in similar frequency ranges. For a quick look at this technique, try opening or creating a session that contains an electric bass and kick drum track. On the bass track, use an EQ plug-in to locate and cut any frequency between 100Hz and 150Hz. Use an instance of the same EQ to boost the same frequency on your kick drum track.

Two other frequently competing sounds are vocals and guitar. You want to be careful when EQing vocal tracks; it's very easy to take the life out of a vocal track by overusing an EQ plug-in. Removing the midrange from a guitar can sometimes make room for a vocal track.

To quote engineer Scott Tusa:

> One analogy you can use is that mixing a song is like building a house. The bass is your foundation, kick drum is the pillars and beams, the guitar is the rooms and meat of it, and the vocals are the roof and paint.

> This is subjective, but one good golden rule is if there doesn't need to be low end or top end in a specific instrument, take it out. You'll notice how your mix goes from muddy to clear.

The following are some basic settings for EQing specific instruments. Keep in mind that these are just possible starting points and that every recording and every mix is different:

Electric Guitar Fatten up a thin-sounding guitar by boosting between 75Hz and 200Hz. Cut below 100Hz to remove more low-end noise and above 3.4KHz to remove high-end noise.

Acoustic Guitar Much of how you EQ an acoustic guitar will depend on how it was miked and recorded and how you want it to sound in your mix. Try cutting and boosting in the high midrange to add or remove brightness, depending on the mix and recording. In a denser mix you may want to try cutting the lows from an acoustic guitar, anything below 200Hz.

Bass The appropriate bass sound can vary widely from session to session. A basic tip: Cut below 30Hz to reduce low-end noise. You may also want to cut and boost specific frequencies in relation to the kick drum. Try looking for the right mids (around 150 to 200Hz) to boost or cut depending on the mix. Boost above 1KHz to add clarity.

Piano Boost the high end above 7KHz for more clarity. For more low-end try a slight boost between 100Hz and 400Hz—but be careful not to step on any bass instrument frequencies. In a denser mix you may want to try the opposite, cutting out low frequencies to clear up the overall sound.

Kick Drum Cut below 80Hz to eliminate rumble. Try boosting around the 5K level for more "punch." Try reducing some of the midrange frequencies to create room for other instruments if needed.

Snare Drum Cut below 150Hz to remove unneeded frequencies. Boosting in the 1KHz or 5KHz area can add some life to a dull snare.

Vocals Every singer's voice is different, and male and female singers may require different approaches as well. Male vocals often benefit from a slight boost in the high frequency range, while female vocals can often use some rolling off in the mid to high range. Add presence to a vocal performance by boosting around 3Hz to 4Hz. Try cutting some of the lows on backing vocal tracks to differentiate them from your lead tracks.

OS X EQ PLUG-INS

The following is a list of more EQ plug-ins available for OS X.

Free EQ Plug-ins

zEQ (AU) www.musicunfolding.com

NWEq (VST) www.wwaym.com

Linear Phase Graphical Equalizer (AU, VST) www.apulsoft.ch/freeports (donationware)

Commercial EQ Plug-ins

Q10 Paragraphic Equalizer (AU, VST, RTAS, MAS) www.waves.com, $150

Program Equalizer EQP-4 (AU, VST, RTAS) www.nomadfactory.com, $149

Frequalizer (AU,VST, RTAS) www.rogernicholsdigital.com, $249

AirEQ (AU, VST, RTAS) www.elisound.com, $269

DQ1 (AU, VST, RTAS) www.solalksis.com, $279

ValveTone '62 (AU, VST, RTAS) www.tritonedigital.com, $79 *requires Pluggo Runtime

Renaissance Equalizer (AU, VST, RTAS, TDM) www.waves.com, $200

URS A series, N Series, S Series (AU, RTAS, VST) www.ursplugins.com, $249

Filters

Filtering is related to EQ in that filter plug-ins isolate and eliminate or boost certain selected frequencies or frequency ranges. Filters are often found as part of an EQ plug-in or in virtual instruments such as synthesizers and samplers. In fact, many analog synthesizers like the Moog Modular and Korg MS-20 are known for the ability to use their filter banks as stand-alone effects processors. Their virtual counterparts also include plug-in effects that are used independently of their synthesizers.

FILTER PARAMETERS

The following are some of the parameters you'll find on filters and filtering-related plug-ins:

Low Pass Filter Cuts off high frequencies and allow low frequencies to "pass" through. A low pass filter can eliminate unnecessary frequencies on lower range instruments like kick drum and bass or unwanted high range harmonics on a synth track.

High Pass Filter The opposite of a low pass filter, a high pass filter cuts unwanted lower frequencies. High pass filters can clean up vocal tracks and eliminate unwanted low frequencies on guitars, pianos, or any instrument. High pass filter are also useful in eliminating unwanted background noise from tracks, such as a fan or street noise.

Band-pass Filter   Eliminates an entire range of frequencies.

Frequency/Cut-off   Determines the frequency that is cut or boosted.

LFO (Low Frequency Oscillator)   Determines the shape of the effect.

Some filter plug-ins are simply low pass, high pass, or band pass filters. In fact, OS X comes with Audio Unit versions of each one. Figure 8.25 shows the OS X's included low pass filter, AULowpass.

FIGURE 8.25

OS X's low pass filter Audio Unit

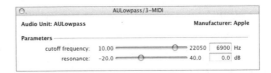

Filtering effects are very prominent in electronic music genres. Dance music in particular often features filtered synthesizers and drums, often during breakdowns (sections of a song where most of the instruments drop out). Through electronic music many filtering techniques have found their way onto pop recordings. For excellent examples of filtering techniques in popular music, check out any CDs produced by William Orbit, including Madonna's *Ray of Light* and the pop/rock band Blur's 1998 CD *13*.

To get an idea of some of the many ways you can use filtering, download the Volcano plug-in from FabFilter (`www.fabfilter.com`) shown in Figure 8.26.

FIGURE 8.26

The FabFilter Volcano

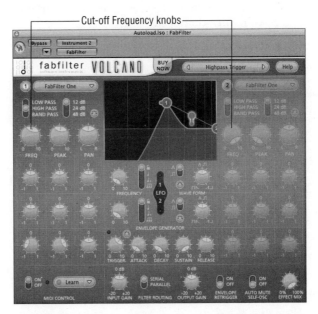

The following steps show one of the possible uses of a filter plug-in on a drum or synthesizer track:

1. Create a new session in your DAW and add the Volcano to a drum track and a synthesizer track. If you have the Apple Loops for GarageBand installed, try any of the club beats or the 80s dance synth loops. You can also use the MMA Apple Loops or WAV loops to try out the Volcano.

2. Use the Preset menu in the top right corner of the FabFilter to try out the different categories of effects. For well-known filtering effects, check out the presets Synth ➢ Stereo Sweeps and General ➢ Shifting Peaks.

3. Use the preset menu to select the preset FX ➢ Helicopter. With the drum loop or other track playing, raise and lower either of the Cut-off Frequency knobs to achieve a sweeping effect. Many of the filtering effects you hear on recordings involve movement of various parameters to achieve a sweeping effect. This is often accomplished by adjusting the Cut-off Frequency knob in real time as the song plays.

4. Capture this effect using whatever automation techniques are available in your DAW.

Volcano also includes a MIDI Learn automation feature, which you can use to assign a MIDI knob to a corresponding knob on the plug-in interface. Assigning a MIDI knob to the frequency or panning parameters is a great way to implement real-time filtering techniques. The MIDI Learn button is located at the bottom left of the Volcano interface. Try the following steps to use Volcano's MIDI learn function with your MIDI controller:

1. Make sure your MIDI keyboard is attached and powered.

2. On the Volcano, click the MIDI Learn button to turn it on. If the Volcano is receiving MIDI information from your keyboard, pressing any key or adjusting any knob will trigger the light next to the MIDI Learn button.

3. To assign a knob, adjust any parameter on the Volcano interface, then adjust any knob on your MIDI controller.

4. Deselect the MIDI learn button.

This technique will work on MIDI tracks in Live but not audio tracks.

Quick Filtering

If you're using Logic or Live, you can use OS X's included band pass filter to create quick, sweeping effects:

1. Create a new track in your DAW.

2. Add one of the '80s dance bass synth GarageBand loops or one of the MMA Audio synthesizer loops.

3. Add the AUBandPass as a plug-in or an insert (Audio Units ➢ Apple ➢ AUBandPass).

4. Set the bandwidth to around 4000 Cents to start (you can change this later to what sounds best to you).

5. Preview the effect by moving the Center frequency slider from left to right while playing back the loop.

6. In your DAW, set up automation. In Live, press the Record and Play buttons in the Transport bar to record automation. In Logic, select Write, Latch, or Touch from the track automation drop-down menu to activate automation.

OS X FILTER PLUG-INS

The following is a list of some of the additional filter effects currently available for OS X.

Free Filter Plug-ins

Crayon Filter (AU, VST)   www.betabugsaudio.com

Frohmage (AU, VST, RTAS, MAS)   www.ohmforce.com

Commercial Filter Plug-ins

PSP Nitro (AU, VST, RTAS)   www.pspaudioware.com, $149

907A Fixed Filter Bank (AU, VST)   www.audiodamage.com, $29

Filter (VST, RTAS, MAS)   www.antares.com, $199

FilterBank (RTAS, TDM)   www.mcdsp.com, $495

Filter Freak (RTAS, TDM)   www.soundtoys.com, $349

Filterscape (AU, VST)   www.u-he.com, $129

QuadFrohmage (AU, RTAS, VST, MAS)   www.ohmforce.com, $190

OFF THE WALL

Some plug-in effects don't easily fit into specific categories such as "this is a delay" or "this is a reverb." Some of the more creative plug-in programmers will occasionally make plug-ins that do strange and interesting things that fall out of the range of everyday "normal" sound processing. Some excellent examples of unusual plug-ins can be found in the Super Destroy FX collection.

Super Destroy FX (AU, VST) (destroyfx.smartelectronix.com). This is a collection of unusual plug-ins, most of which can do unexpected and sometimes distinctly unmusical things to your audio tracks. Look for the Audio Units link to download the AU versions of these plug-ins. If you want to hear what these plug-ins are capable of, there are before and after sound examples on the VST page. These are donationware and the creators ask that if you use them in a song that you let them know.

 **Real World Scenario**

DUB TECHNIQUES

Dub is a style of reggae music that was invented by Jamaican recording engineers in the late 1960s and early 1970s. Dub pioneers like Errol Thompson, Lee "Scratch" Perry, and King Tubby took backing tracks from existing reggae songs and produced instrumental tracks called "versions." These tracks would often be used as the B-side for a single, giving Jamaican DJs tracks over which they could improvise vocally or "toast" (Jamaican DJing and toasting had a huge influence on early rap and hip-hop). Eventually the production of these instrumental tracks became its own art form. It usually involved adding heavy sound effects to individual tracks and bringing various elements from the song in and out of the mix.

Of course, I've found these techniques to be useful when working in reggae-based projects. Over the last few years, however, I've noticed that the styles and uses of various effects developed by these early dub producers have been incorporated into music across many genres. Punk and post-punk bands such as PiL and The Clash released records that include many dub-styled and dub-influenced tracks. Trip-hop and down-tempo artists such as Massive Attack and Portishead frequently incorporate sound effects and echoes that can be directly traced to dub recordings. Other popular artists such as Sublime, Radiohead, and Nine Inch Nails have found new and interesting ways to use familiar dub tricks.

While quieter, more ambient tracks in particular can benefit from these techniques, I've found I can add these elements to just about any song in any genre that needs an extra creative push.

The two main elements of dub-style effects are delay and reverb. For a delay effect, wherever possible, you'll want to choose one that contains an EQ filter. By removing or adjusting certain frequencies, an EQ filter will allow you to create noticeable differences in the delayed, effected sound.

Here are my recommendations for delay plug-ins:

◆ If your DAW supports Audio Units, I recommend the King Dubby free delay plug-in covered in the "King Dubby" sidebar earlier in the chapter.

◆ For Logic users, the included Tape Delay plug-in is a great sounding effect. The Tape Delay is covered in the "Included Effects" section of Chapter 5, "Logic."

◆ In Pro Tools, you can use the included Medium Delay plug-in covered in the "Adding an Insert" section of Chapter 4 "Pro Tools."

◆ You can also use more interesting effects such as the FabFilter Timeless and OhmBoyz delays covered in the "Delays" section of this chapter.

For reverb effects, I recommend the following:

◆ In Live or GarageBand, download and install the Audio Unit or VST version of the donationware Ambience plug-in from www.smartelectronix.com.

◆ In Pro Tools, you can use the included D-Verb plug-in covered in the "Reverb Plug-ins" section of Chapter 4.

◆ In Logic, you can use any of the many excellent included reverb plug-ins covered in the "Included Plug-ins" section of Chapter 5.

◆ You can also use high-quality commercial reverb effects such as Nomad Factory's BlueVerb DRV-2080 or AudioEase's Altiverb, both covered in the "Reverbs" section of this chapter.

In each of the individual DAW chapters, we covered the process of creating sends and returns for effects (the exception being GarageBand, which does not include this kind of functionality). This is generally the best way to apply the same effects to multiple tracks simultaneously. If you prefer to add plug-ins as inserts on individual tracks, make sure you have enough processor resources to use multiple instances of effects.

Use your DAW's send functionality to send the signal from your basic tracks to the return tracks containing the effects. In dub music, the most frequently effected tracks are the drums (especially snare drum), guitar and keyboards, but any and every track is fair game.

1. Create two Return tracks (In Pro Tools they'll be called Aux tracks), one for a delay effect and one for a reverb effect. Every delay effect will have different parameters, but with many you can use the following settings as a starting point:

   ◆ Mix setting of 50 percent

   ◆ Delay setting of around 150ms

   ◆ Feedback of 65 percent

For reverb settings, choose large hall or room settings.

2. Create or access Sends for the tracks you want to add effects to.

3. Use the Sends faders or knobs to send a signal from the basic tracks to the effects track at different times during playback.

Try the following specific techniques on your tracks:

   ◆ Use a fader or knob to quickly add then remove an effect. For example, add a heavy reverb or delay effect to one snare hit at the beginning of a measure, then lower the knob or fader to silence the effect.

   ◆ Apply an effect to a track, then adjust different effect parameters in real-time. For example, add a delay effect to a track, then adjust the feedback setting to increase and decrease the delay.

   ◆ Use your DAW's automation functionality to record the movement of your Send knobs or faders.

   ◆ Use your DAW's plug-in automation functionality to record automation of your real-time adjustments.

Multi-effects Plug-ins

Some plug-ins include multiple effects in a single plug-in. These plug-ins may have multiple effects such as delay or reverb, or they may contain effects more commonly associated with basic recording functionality, such as Metric Halo's Channel Strip plug-in, shown in Figure 8.27, which combines gating, compression, and multiband equalization.

A multiple effect plug-in like this one can be very useful for quickly getting a track or tracks under control. For example, it may be necessary for a vocal track or a group of backing vocal tracks to be gated, compressed, and equalized. With all of these plug-ins in one place you can get the job done quickly. Create and save a preset to standardize your process, and you've just eliminated a big chunk of time from the mixing process. This may not be the most effective way to work in multiple sessions, but if you are mixing a group of songs from a single session that all contain similar elements you can use this method.

FIGURE 8.27

Metric Halo's Channel Strip multiple effect plug-in

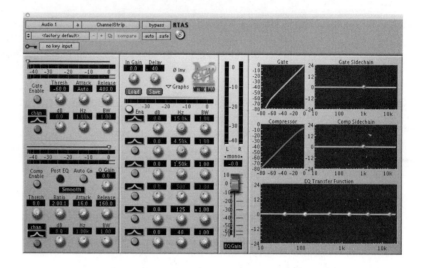

LUXONIX LFX-1310

Luxonix LFX-1310 (www.luxonix.com) is a free virtual multi-effects processor unit that works in any Audio Unit or VST host DAW program, including Logic, GarageBand, Live, Audacity, and Peak. The LFX-1310 contains 24 effects that can be used individually or in combinations of up to three at a time. LFX-1310 also comes with over 120 presets. Figure 8.28 shows the Luxonix LFX-1310.

FIGURE 8.28

The LFX-1310

Follow these steps to use the Luxonix LFX-1310 on a track or tracks in a recording or mixing session:

1. Add the Luxonix LFX-1310 to a session in your DAW program as an insert effect.

2. Click the Load button to load one of the presets. To clear the device choose preset 127, No Effect.

3. Create your own settings by turning effects on and off. Each effect has three on/off buttons marked 1, 2, and 3.

4. Select an effect by clicking the field next to the on/off switch.

5. Use the three knobs to adjust the effects parameters.

6. You can save any presets you create, but you'll have to overwrite an existing preset to do so.

The Luxonix is a great multi-effect unit. Its only real drawback is that there are only three knobs for each effect, so that effects that generally have more than three parameters aren't as adjustable as their individual counterparts might be.

OS X Multi-effects Plug-ins

The following is a list of some of the currently available multiple effects plug-ins for OS X.

Metric Halo Channel Strip (AU, VST, RTAS)   Expander/Gate/Compressor, EQ, www.mhlabs.com, $345

URS Classic Console Strip (AU, VST, RTAS)   Compressor/EQ, www.ursplugins.com, $499

CamelSpace (AU, VST)   Delay, reverb/filter/modulation, www.camelaudio.com, $85

CamelPhat3 (AU, VST)   Distortion/compressor/EQ, www.camelaudio.com, $85

TrackPlug (AU, VST, RTAS, MAS)   Gate/compressor/EQ, www.wavearts.com, $199

SFXMachine RT (AU, VST)   Multi-effects, www.sfxmachine.com, $75

SFXMAchine Pro (AU, VST)   Multi-effects, www.sfxmachine.com, $149.99

Channel G (RTAS, TDM, AudioSuite)   Gate/compressor/EQ, www.mcdsp.com, $995

Plug-in Bundles

Buying bundled plug-ins is a good way to insure quality and consistency and can be especially useful if you find that you like working with plug-ins from a specific company and are comfortable with their interface and functionality.

Nomad Factory

Nomad Factory produces four different plug-in bundles ranging in price from $200 to $500. Each of the Nomad Factory plug-ins and bundles are available as ten-day fully working demo versions from www.nomadfactory.com.

Download the Audio Unit, VST, or RTAS version of the bundle and run the installation program.

Authorization

Once you've installed the plug-ins, follow these instructions to authorize them:

1. Install the necessary Interlok (iLok) extensions. These are located in the installer folder.

2. Next, start the Authorizer application and copy the Challenge code.

3. Open the Read Me file and scroll to the bottom. The Read Me file contains two links, one for permanent registration and one for demo registration.

4. Choose which type of registration you want and copy the appropriate link into your Web browser.

5. Fill out any necessary information and generate a response code.

6. Paste the response code in the Authorizer application and click OK.

Liquid Bundle II

If I had to choose just one set of plug-ins within $100 to $200 price range, the Liquid Bundle II would be hard to beat. This bundle contains just about all of the plug-ins you'll ever need for basic recording and mixing. Each plug-in is both easy to use and contains many possibilities.

Make sure to download the separate Presets Installer as well.

The Liquid Bundle II contains the following plug-ins:

Liquid Compressor A very nice-sounding compressor plug-in with included side-chaining features.

Liquid Delays A very nice delay unit with a filter section and syncable filter modulation and tempo syncing. Also contains a drop-down menu at the bottom of the plug-in for arranging the order of the included filter, delay, and drive effects.

Liquid Gate A standard gating plug-in.

Liquid Mod A modulation plug-in that can create an entire range of modulation-based effects, from simple chorus and flange to unrecognizable warbling and other LFO modulated sounds.

Liquid Phase Based on classic analog phase units. This plug-in creates warm, thick sweeping effects.

Liquid Verb A reverb effect with all of the standard reverb parameters and some interesting unique functionality.

All of the Liquid II plug-ins have similar interfaces, which are both easy to read and to use. Parameters are generally divided into boxes and are adjusted by clicking and dragging within each box. A level meter is visible within each box giving you a visual representation of how much of any given parameter has been applied.

Figure 8.29 shows the Liquid Delays II plug-in in Pro Tools.

One of the best aspects of the Liquid Bundle II is that while the plug-ins contains some very advanced features, they are presented in a straightforward way. Try out some of the Liquid Delays II presets on any type of track. The Liquid Delays II, like all of the Liquid Bundle plug-ins, does a great job with its "standard" functionality but also contains extra features that can be used in all sorts of interesting and creative ways.

FIGURE 8.29

Nomad Factory's
Liquid Delays II
plug-in

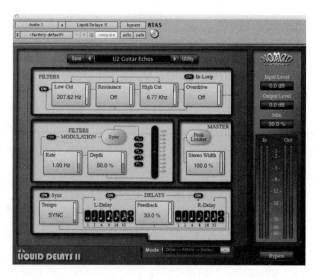

Check out the Filters and Modulation area of the Liquid Delays plug-in. These effects are similar to the King Dubby delay plug-in I mentioned earlier and a fairly common feature on more complex delay effects. Liquid Delays modulation effects are even more in-depth than most, allowing you to choose between different LFO shapes (see Chapter 9's "Virtual Synthesizer" section), then adjust the rate and depth of the effect. Scroll through the included presets to get an idea of the range of delay effects that are possible with the Liquid Delays plug-in.

Each of the Liquid Bundle II plug-ins comes with a great collection of included presets. If you want to create your own, presets are saved and recalled by clicking the Save button in the preset bar at the top of each plug-in window.

ANALOG SIGNATURE PACK

The Analog Signature Pack is a suite of three plug-ins:

Limiting Amplifier LM-662   A compressor, limiter, and tube emulator in one.

Program Equalizer EQP-4   An equalizer modeled on classic vintage analog EQ devices. Straightforward to use, yet capable of subtle or drastic equalization, depending on the needed effect.

Studio Channel SC-226   A combination EQ unit, compressor, and tube emulator. This multi-effect plug-in is similar to the Metric Halo Channel Strip and can enhance any vocal or instrument track or group of tracks quickly and dramatically.

These plug-ins are all modeled on vintage analog effects units. As a result, the knobs and buttons are large and intuitive. Both the LM-622 and the SC-226 contain a 12AX7 tube emulation, excellent for adding analog warmth and depth to any instrument or vocal track. Adding one or more of these plug-ins to your collection can go a long way toward creating better sounding tracks and final mixes.

The entire pack is available for $287, or you can purchase any individual plug-in for $149.

OTHER NOMAD FACTORY BUNDLES

Nomad Factory makes other bundles as well that may better suit your specific needs.

Blue Tubes Bundle (AU, VST, RTAS), $499   A suite of 16 plug-ins covering the complete range of audio processing effects needed for the recording and mixing process. Multiple versions of some plug-in effects are included for different applications. For example, there are multiple limiters, compressors, and equalizers, some good for mixing and others put to better use in the mastering process.

Essential Studio Suite Bundle (AU, VST, RTAS), $399   A collection of nine plug-ins, including a loudness maximizer, tube/tape simulation, and compression and EQ effects.

Waves

Waves offers a large number of choices for purchasing their products. You can buy plug-ins individually or in one of many different available bundles and configurations, depending on your budget, interests and needs.

Fully functioning 14-day demos of many Waves bundles and plug-ins are available at www.waves.com. It's a good idea to try out all the plug-ins you are interested in at once, because activating any single Waves demo will use up the trial period for all Waves demos.

The most complete package is the Diamond bundle, which contains over 40 plug-ins, including virtually every kind of signal processing effect, EQ, and compressor you'll ever need to record, mix, export, and master audio sessions.

For the smaller budget or more specific recording functionality, Waves also offers the Gold and Platinum bundles as well as the Musicians and Musicians II bundles. For information about exactly which plug-ins are contained in each bundle check out the Waves website.

The Waves plug-ins all have similar interfaces and standardized functionality. Figure 8.30 shows the Waves MetaFlanger plug-in.

FIGURE 8.30

The Waves MetaFlanger plug-in

Adjustments to the Waves plug-ins are made by clicking and dragging up or down, often inside the rectangular boxes that contain specific parameters.

Each Waves plug-in has a row of similar features across the top of the interface. On the far left is the Undo button, allowing you to erase the last adjustment you made to the plug-in.

The setup button (labeled A->B on Figure 8.30) lets you create two different settings and switch back and forth between them or load two presets at once for comparison. To use the A/B functionality, just make any adjustments you want to the selected plug-in, then click the Setup button. Create an entirely new set of adjustments, then click the Setup button again to switch between them.

Most of the Waves plug-ins come with included presets to get you started and to give you an idea of what each effect is capable of. Presets are accessed through the Load button at the top of the interface. Figure 8.31 shows the MetaFlanger's preset list.

Since the Waves plug-ins have their own preset functionality, independent of the DAW host program, you can save your own presets in the plug-in itself by clicking its Save button. You can also use your DAW's standard preset saving method if you prefer.

One of the best features of the Waves plug-ins is the question mark button on the top right of the interface. Clicking this button automatically opens a PDF file with instructions for using the specific plug-in. The instruction manuals are all well written and include in-depth descriptions of the plug-ins and their features.

FIGURE 8.31

The MetaFlanger plug-in Preset menu

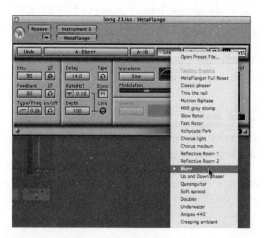

Cycling '74

Cycling '74 (`www.cycling74.com`) is a software company in San Francisco that creates a wide range of products, built in their own Max/MSP modular programming environment. With Max/MSP, programmers can create audio plug-ins and other software useful in various multimedia projects and formats. More information and a demo version of the Max/MSP programming environment are also available on the Cycling '74 website.

PLUGGO

For anyone making music on computers, Pluggo is one of the best deals around. Pluggo is a suite of over 100 plug-in effects and MIDI instruments produced by Cycling '74. "Pluggos," as these plug-ins are affectionately known, work as Audio Units, VSTs, or RTAS plug-ins. You can download and install a demo version of the entire Pluggo suite from `www.cycling74.com/products/Pluggo`. The demo version is fully functioning, but each Pluggo will emit a random, unpleasant noise from time to time.

The Pluggo package consists of over 20 synthesizers and dozens of effects, including both simple and complex plug-ins (sometimes at the same time). Many of the included plug-ins are based on standard effects such as delay or reverb but add an interesting or creative element to the effect or interface. For example, take a look at the Flange-o-tron Pluggo plug-in in Figure 8.32.

FIGURE 8.32

The Flange-o-tron Pluggo

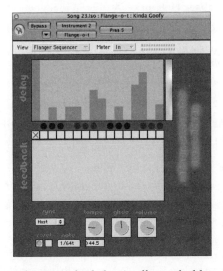

Like many Pluggos, the Flange-o-tron takes a standard plug-in effect and adds an unusual twist, creating a whole new range of possibilities along with the usual application. In this case, you can use the Tempo knob and the Note Value drop-down menu just below it to sync the flanger effect to your DAW host program, then adjust the flanger amount for each step. Like many Pluggos, the actual adjusting can be moved down manually by using your mouse to "draw" the delay time and delay feedback for each step. This kind of creative interactivity is a consistent feature in the Pluggo collection.

Many Pluggos come with presets that can be accessed by the standard preset menus in your DAW or via their own included preset menus.

Along with the plug-in effects, Pluggo contains virtual instruments such as the Bassline Synthesizer and the Analogue Drums drum sequencer. These instruments can be added to your Instrument tracks in Logic or Pro Tools, your Software Instrument tracks in GarageBand, or your MIDI tracks in Live. For more information on how to use virtual instruments in your DAW, see Chapter 9.

One of the more interesting features of Pluggo is that because it is created with Max/MSP, Pluggo users who work in that environment can create their own Pluggos, and owners of the Pluggo suite can download and install plug-ins created by other users as well. A number of free and commercially available plug-ins have been created in the Max/MSP environment that don't require ownership of Pluggo to work in your DAW.

These plug-ins do require you to install Pluggo Runtime, which a shell that allows you to use Max/MSP-developed plug-ins in your DAW. Pluggo Runtime is also available from the Cycling '74 website as a free download at www.cycling74.com/downloads/pluggo.

Third-party plug-ins that work with Pluggo Runtime include the free plug-ins available at www.audiooo.com/jp/freestuff/pluggo.html and commercial plug-ins like the Code Operator Delay Pack available at www.codeoperator.com/delaypack.htm.

PLUGGO JUNIOR

To give you an indication of some of Pluggo's possibilities, Cycling '74 has a free set of Pluggos called Pluggo Junior that shows off the range and quality of the Pluggo suite. Most of the Pluggo Junior plug-ins include presets to get you started. The plug-ins include:

Jet   A simple but powerful flange effect.

HF Ring Mod   A ring modulator that you can use to create dissonant sounds.

Feedback Network   A plug-in that generates both controllable and uncontrollable feedback.

Filter Taps   A combination filter/delay effect.

Generic Effect   An effect that allows you to combine vibrato/chorus/flange and delay in interesting ways.

Limi   A limiter plug-in for controlling dynamics.

Average Injector   An interesting chorus/phaser/delay effect.

Chamberverb   An easy-to-use reverb plug-in with some exceptionally complex features.

Nebula   A very interesting panning/tremolo effect.

Resonation   A combination filter and delay effect.

Resosweep   A combination filter/phaser effect.

Spectral Filter   A filter effect that allows you to choose which frequencies are filtered by drawing them with your mouse.

Download and install Pluggo Junior from the Cycling '74 website. Each Cycling '74 installer includes a very cool "cleaner" application that you can use to delete all of your old Cycling '74 product versions. If you have already installed the demo version of Pluggo (or any other Cycling '74 demo), I recommend running the cleaner before installing Pluggo Junior.

HIPNO

Hipno is a set of more than 40 strange and interesting plug-in effects and virtual instruments. Many of these use a colorful visual interface called the Hipnoscope to create audio effects and sounds in unique ways. Using the Hipno plug-ins can be a fun an interesting way to create new sounds and add some unexpected elements to your music.

Hipno costs $199, and you can download a fully functional demo version from www.cycling74.com/products/hipno.

Like the Pluggo demo, the Hipno demo version emits an occasional unpleasant beeping sound.

The plug-ins that come with Hipno are not at all like any other plug-in effects you may be used to. In fact, along with some plug-ins that have some familiar parameters, the Hipno collection contains a number of plug-in effects that operate in completely original ways. These effects are definitely not something you'd use in a conventional or straightforward recording or mix. The Hipno plug-ins are more appropriate for creating interesting, unexpected ambient sounds and experimental effects or for sound design, video, or soundtrack composition.

Once you download and install Hipno or the Hipno demo:

1. Create a new session in your DAW and add some kind of instrument or loop performance to an audio or MIDI track.

2. Locate the Hipno folder in your DAW and add the Amogwai plug-in as an insert to your track. Figure 8.33 shows the Amogwai plug-in.

FIGURE 8.33

The Amogwai plug-in

3. Use your mouse to move the cursor within the Hipnoscope window to alter the sound. On the left side of the plug-in are the sliders that adjust the plug-in parameters. These can be adjusted manually or will respond to the mouse movements within the Hipnoscope. On the far right of the plug-in window are the Snapshot buttons. The right row of buttons records the current settings as a snapshot, the left row of buttons recalls saved snapshots.

4. Click the Import button.

5. Locate the folder `Applications\Hipno\Hipno Extras\Hipnoscopes`.

6. Select a Hipnoscope and click Choose.

Not all Hipno plug-ins include the Hipnoscope, though many do. Hipno also includes a number of virtual instruments like the VTheremin (an odd plug-in even by Theremin standards) and SfylterSynth. There are also some Hipno plug-ins that are closer to "standard issue" effects or at least can create somewhat familiar sounds.

Try adding the Morphulescence plug-in to any drum loop track and choosing the Pulsation Three or Slow Morph presets.

Hipno makes a great candidate for the method I mentioned previously of adding a group of different types of loops to a Live track and trying each loop out with the effect and its various presets. This is also a good way to figure out pretty quickly whether a Hipno plug-in is going to be easier or more difficult to work with.

More from Cycling '74

Cycling '74 makes a number of products for various audio and video applications. Here's a list of their other available audio plug-ins and bundles.

Mode (AU, VST, RTAS) A set of plug-ins and modules. Less off-the-wall than the Hipno collection but still a very creative group of effects. Mode contains five "main" plug-ins and 18 "modules."

Upmix (AU, VST, RTAS) A set of plug-in for converting stereo mixes and creating six-channel mixes for film, DVD, and other surround formats.

Octirama (TDM) A mastering plug-in for working 5.1 surround sound on Pro Tools TDM systems.

MDA

MDA has free sets of Audio Unit and VST plug-ins available at www.mda-vst.com. Click the AU & VST Effects link at the top of the page.

The Audio Unit suite contains 14 effects including a delay, a ring modulator, dynamics effects, and a rotary speaker simulator. The VST bundle includes all of the Audio Unit plug-ins and adds a few more, including a flanger and a filter effect.

These free plug-ins are not much to look at as far their interfaces go, but they include some very interesting effects.

For example, try adding the RePsycho! plug-in to a drum track and adjusting the tuning and other parameters. The RePsycho! can lower the pitch of any track two octaves, while the other sliders adjust the sound in unexpected ways. Try mixing the lowered signal with the original.

Figure 8.34 shows the RePsycho! in Live.

FIGURE 8.34

The RePsycho! plug-in

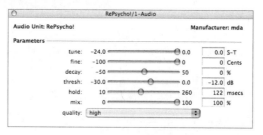

Another interesting effect in the MDA bundle is the Tracker plug-in. Tracker can be used as an EQ, a ring modulator, or to generate a tone, which can then be altered by the incoming audio from the track it's placed on. Add the Tracker as an insert or send effects to any audio track in your DAW, select a mode from the drop-down menu, adjust the sliders, and raise and lower the mix.

Finally, my favorite of the MDA free plug-ins is the Dub Delay, shown here in Logic (Figure 8.35).

FIGURE 8.35

The MDA Dub Delay plug-in

The Dub Delay is similar to the King Dubby. It has basic delay parameters like delay time, feedback, and mix with an LFO to create delay effects that shift and change as they trail off. Try adding the Dub Delay to a snare track (or any track with a tight, clipped instrument performance) with a short delay time (around 250ms). Raise the feedback, LFO depth, and rate settings to create an interesting dub effect.

More Bundles

Here is a partial list of some of the other plug-in effects bundles available for OS X. Most have demo versions available.

Wave Arts (AU, VST, RTAS, MAS), *www.wavearts.com*   Offers bundled versions of their mix-oriented plug-ins in two, three, and five plug-in configurations.

DUY (AU, VST, RTAS, TDM, MAS), *www.duy.net*   Has different types of bundles for their many products. Some bundles are specifically geared towards Pro Tools TDM users.

Pro Bundle (AU, VST, RTAS), *www.rogernicholsdigital.com*   Contains four plug-ins geared towards dynamics and EQ ($749).

URS (AU, VST, RTAS), *www.ursplugins.com*   Has collections of their excellent EQ and compressor plug-ins available in various configurations depending on your needs and budget.

Project Studio Bundle (RTAS, AudioSuite), *www.mcdsp.com*   One of a number of high-quality plug-in bundles for Pro Tools systems available from McDSP ($495).

The Bottom Line

Install Audio Unit, VST, and RTAS plug-ins   Most plug-ins come with an automatic installer program that puts the plug-in and accompanying presets into the necessary locations on your hard drive. Some plug-ins, especially many of the free or less expensive effects require manual installation.

Master It   Download and install any of the freeware Audio Unit and VST plug-ins from bram.smartelectronix.com or www.mda-vst.com.

Use plug-ins in any DAW program   Each DAW program works with plug-in effects in essentially the same way. However, there are some minor differences in how plug-ins are added to tracks.

Master It   Add a third-party delay plug-in effect as an insert effect on any track.

Locate free plug-ins on the Web   The World Wide Web is a great resource for locating free Audio Units, VST, and RTAS plug-in effects.

Master It   Use the Internet to locate, download, and install free effects plug-ins.

Chapter 9

Virtual Instruments

In this chapter I'll attempt to cover the vast and constantly expanding universe of virtual instrumentation. Virtual instruments are generally considered to be any plug-in that contains sounds that can be triggered by a MIDI keyboard or other controller or manually created MIDI sequence.

Virtual instruments interact in different ways in your DAW depending on the program's features and functionality. Quite often a virtual instrument may appear side by side with an effect plug-in or as part of a group of plug-ins that includes both effects and instruments (such as Pluggo).

There will also be some crossover in the instrument categories. For example, you can certainly use a virtual sampler (such as Kontakt from Native Instruments or Reason's NN-XT Advanced Sampler) to play sampled synthesizer sounds and sampled keyboard sounds and even to create virtual drum kits. By the same token, many virtual drum machines can be loaded with nondrum related sounds and used as a sampler. In some cases, a single virtual sampler may be everything you need to create your music. However, as impressive as many virtual samplers are, sometimes it's easier or more appropriate to work with a specific kind of virtual instrument.

Another area of crossover is the category of virtual amplification, frequently considered part of the plug-in effect category. Along with amplifier, cabinet, and microphone modeling, virtual amps often contain other plug-in effects like phasers, delays, and flangers. While virtual amplifiers can certainly be used as effect plug-ins, I've put them into the virtual instrument category because they are generally associated with specific instrumentation and also because (as you'll see) there's been a shift in focus recently toward including hardware components along with proprietary, stand-alone software for recording guitar.

In this chapter, you will learn to

◆ Use virtual instruments in your host DAW program

◆ Create basic presets and patches with virtual synthesizers

◆ Create drum loops with iDrum

◆ Create a drum performance in your DAW with a virtual drum machine

Plug-in Formats

While many virtual instruments work as stand-alone programs, most of what I will be covering are programs that work as plug-ins. Just like their counterpart plug-in effects, virtual instruments fall into the same plug-in formats (Audio Unit, RTAS, and VST), with the same uses and limitations. Many of the programs I am covering will be available in multiple formats, meaning that in whatever host program you choose as your main DAW, you will be able to use these virtual instruments as well. The information I covered in the "Plug-in Formats" section in Chapter 8, "Plug-ins," applies across the board to plug-in instruments as well.

FXpansion's VST to RTAS and VST to AU adapters, also covered in the Chapter 8's "Plug-in Formats" section, will work just as well with virtual instruments as they do with plug-in effects.

Using Virtual Instruments

Using virtual instruments is similar to using plug-in effects; in fact, they are often located side-by-side in your DAW's available plug-in lists. Some bundled software, such as Pluggo and Reaktor, contain both instruments and effects. Other virtual instruments, like those contained in Reason, are brought into your sessions via ReWire. This chapter covers a huge range of different types of virtual instruments. In some cases there may be specific detailed instructions that relate to a specific instrument or family of instruments. The following are basic tutorials on how to use virtual instruments in each of the DAW programs covered in the first section of this book.

NOTE TO PRO TOOLS USERS

Throughout this book I've tried to keep much of the focus on software that works in conjunction with multiple programs. Most of the commercially available programs covered in this chapter are available in RTAS format, but, as with plug-in effects, much of the freeware and shareware is not. If you want to try out some of these programs that are available only in Audio Unit or VST format I suggest (yet again) FXpansion's VST to RTAS wrapper or the VSTi Host program, which is covered in Chapter 7, "More Useful Software."

In Live

Live supports Audio Unit and VST virtual instruments. Live has its own unique way of dealing with virtual instruments, incorporating them as MIDI instruments into the Live interface as well as allowing you to work within the instrument's original interface.

USING AUDIO UNIT VIRTUAL INSTRUMENTS

To use Audio Unit instruments in Live:

1. Click the Plug-in Device Browser button to open the Browser.

2. Open the Audio Unit folder and select the manufacturer and plug-in, for example, Green Oak Software ➤ Crystal.

3. Drag the instrument from the Device Browser directly onto any MIDI track or empty space in the Clip/Device Drop area.

4. The instrument will open automatically, allowing you to view its interface.

5. Select the track that contains the virtual instrument and click the Arm Session Recording button at the bottom of the channel strip. If this section of the channel strip is not showing, select View ➤ Mixer from the Live menu bar.

6. Use your MIDI keyboard or your Apple keyboard to play the virtual instrument or use Live's Clip View to create a performance.

7. Live will add all virtual instruments to the MIDI Track view at the bottom of the Live interface. Figure 9.1 shows the freeware Crystal synthesizer in the MIDI Track view.

FIGURE 9.1

The Crystal synthesiz-
er in Live's Track view

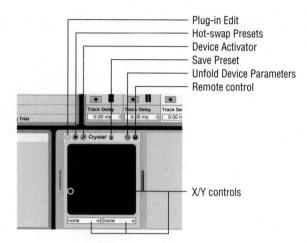

Plug-in Edit
Hot-swap Presets
Device Activator
Save Preset
Unfold Device Parameters
Remote control

X/Y controls

The buttons along the top of the Crystal synthesizer track are, from left to right:

Device Activator   Turns the instrument on and off.

Unfold Device Parameters   Opens a window to the right that contains all of the instruments editable parameters.

Edit Plug-in Panel   Opens the plug-in's interface.

Hot-swap Presets   Allows you to view any included presets. Presets will generally appear in a folder in the Plug-in Device Browser. Sometimes they will also be available in a drop-down menu in the MIDI Track view window.

Save Preset   Saves the current instrument settings as a recallable preset in the Device Browser.

Below the Device title bar are Live's Assignable X/Y controls. With some instruments you'll be able to assign parameters from the two drop-down menus at the bottom of the window and adjust them by using your mouse to move the yellow circle.

If there is a blue hand icon visible in the Device title bar, it indicates that the device can be remotely controlled.

USING VST VIRTUAL INSTRUMENTS

T o use VST instruments in Live, follow the same instructions as Audio Units, selecting your instrument from the VST folder in the Device Browser.

VST instruments have a slightly different interface in Live's Track view, with the preset menu visible within the plug-in window.

Figure 9.2 shows the Crystal synthesizer as a VST instrument in Live.

If an instrument is available as both an Audio Unit and a VSTi, use the VSTi version for access to presets within the Track view window.

In Pro Tools

Pro Tools supports RTAS virtual instruments. VST instruments can also be accessed through FXpansion's VST to RTAS wrapper.

FIGURE 9.2
The Crystal VST in
Live's Track view

Virtual Instruments in Pro Tools are added as inserts on instrument tracks:

1. Create a new stereo instrument track.

2. Make sure Instrument and Inserts view are showing. If they aren't, select View ➤ Mix Window or View ➤ Edit Window and put a check mark next to Instruments and Inserts.

3. Using Insert Selector One, choose Multi-channel Plug-in ➤ Instrument and choose your instrument from the list. Figure 9.3 shows the Plugsound Free virtual sampler as a virtual instrument in Pro Tools.

FIGURE 9.3
The Plugsound Free
sampler in Pro Tools

4. In the Instrument field, set your MIDI input to All or select a predefined input if necessary.

5. If you are using more than one virtual instrument in a session, make sure the appropriate instrument is selected in the MIDI output selector.

6. Use your MIDI keyboard or controller to play the virtual instrument, or use the Pencil tool to create a MIDI performance.

When you add a ReWire-compatible instrument or program to an instrument track, Pro Tools automatically opens a ReWire plug-in window. Use this window to select the instrument's output. This will almost always be Mix L/Mix R or Output 1 and 2.

To create an audio track out of a virtual instrument performance:

1. Create a stereo audio track.

2. In the I/O field set the output of the instrument track to Bus 1-2 (Stereo).

3. Set the input of the new audio track to Bus 1-2 (Stereo).

4. Arm the audio track for recording.

5. Record the output of the instrument track to the audio track.

In Logic

Logic supports Audio Unit Virtual Instruments. VST virtual instruments can be accessed by using FXpansion's VST to AU wrapper.

1. Start Logic and create a new session.

2. Select an audio instrument track in either the Arrange window or the Mixer window.

3. In the I/O field of the selected track's channel strip, select Stereo ➤ AU Instruments and choose a manufacturer and instrument.

   Figure 9.4 shows the freeware Buzzer2 synthesizer as a virtual instrument in Logic.

FIGURE 9.4

The Buzzer2 in Logic

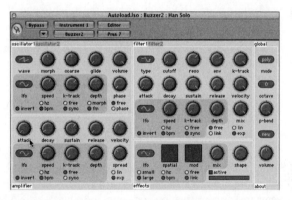

Included preset instruments will be accessed either from the Preset menu at the top of the plug-in interface or by using the specific instrument's preset/load parameters.

Selecting any single instrument track in Logic automatically arms it to receive MIDI information. Third-party virtual instruments in Logic will follow the same "rules" as Logic's included instruments.

In GarageBand

GarageBand supports Audio Unit virtual instruments. VST virtual instruments can be accessed by using FXpansion's VST to AU wrapper.

1. Start the GarageBand program and create a new music project.

2. Select Track ➤ New Track and create a new Software Instrument track.

3. Double-click the track header to open the Track Info window.

4. Open the Details view at the bottom of the Track Info window.

5. Click the Generator drop-down menu at the top of the Details view.

6. Select an instrument from the Audio Unit Modules list.

7. Click the Preset button to view the instrument's interface and any available presets and to edit and save any instrument settings. Figure 9.5 shows the freeware Ticky Clav virtual clavinet instrument in GarageBand.

FIGURE 9.5
The Ticky Clav in
GarageBand

8. Use your MIDI keyboard or controller to play the instrument or create a performance using GarageBand's Musical Typing or built-in keyboard.

Third-party virtual instruments operate in essentially the same ways as GarageBand's built-in instruments. You can even select an appropriate instrument category and save presets in the Track Info window.

Virtual Samplers

Most DAW programs come with some kind of built-in or add-on virtual sampler. Reason has the NN19 and NN-XT Samplers and Logic Express and Logic Pro have the EXS mkII and the EXS, respectively; Live 6 contains the drag-and-drop Simpler instrument and the new, more intricate (and cleverly named) Sampler sampler. These are all excellent virtual instruments that perform many of the same instrument creation and sound editing tasks that hardware samplers are used for.

Like many other virtual instruments, many software samplers have outgrown their hardware counterparts. Giant sample libraries, numerous effects, and new functions are now included with most commercial software samplers. In most cases, all of the original features are still in place, but more and more features are being added all the time.

In addition, many virtual samplers are becoming even more realistic sounding due to multi-layered sampling that captures not only the notes and tones of live instruments, but also—in the case of instruments such as the Vienna Strings sample library and Synthology's Ivory virtual piano—detailed sonic aspects like harmonics and string noises. Today's (and tomorrow's) virtual samplers are becoming even more interesting to work with and consistently opening up all sorts of new creative possibilities.

Limitations

As far as virtual instruments go, samplers have the advantage of having the ability to do just about everything. A sampler can play piano, keyboard, or synthesizer sounds or to create sound effects. You can also map out drum kits with individual drum sounds and trigger and playback loops.

While many samplers give you quite a range of options and control, when it comes to accessing libraries of sounds and then editing them and adding effects, they are not always the best choice.

Some virtual instruments benefit greatly by having software equivalents to specific hardware parameters, as you'll see when we examine some other virtual instrument categories. In some cases, as with electric guitars and wind instruments, samplers can require very intensive programming and still fall short when trying to create realistic performances.

Which Sampler Is the Best?

Every virtual sampler will have its advantages and disadvantages. One might be particularly good at multisampling or time-stretching, while another might be able to read and import more third-party file sample and patch formats, giving you access to a much wider selection of sample material. If you are already familiar with or already using a specific company's plug-ins or software, it may make sense to integrate a sampler they make into your work environment.

Some samplers are certainly more intuitive than others. Whether you need something simple to get the job done or you want to work with a more complex piece of software in order to have more options will impact your choice as well.

If you're not sure which sampler will best suit your needs, I suggest trying out the tutorials in this chapter along with the samplers that are included in the Reason program covered in Chapter 2, "Reason." If you are currently using Logic or Live, you may want to look into their included sampler instruments as well.

Sampler Formats and File Formats

When working with samplers, the question of which formats you can or should be using can sometimes be confusing. Many samplers work with their own proprietary sample format, which means you either have to buy samples in that format (usually from the company that makes the sampler) or use the sampler's import function to load samples from another collection.

The most commonly supported sampler formats are WAV and AIFF. This includes Acid files (a kind of WAV file) and Apple Loops (a kind of AIFF file). Just about every sampler on the market today supports the importing (and where applicable, exporting) of WAV and AIFF format samples. Other common formats include SDII (Sound Designer II), SF2 (Sound Fonts), and RX2 (ReCycled loops and samples).

Some formats like AKAI and EMU are not file formats but Hardware Library formats. These often come in the form of CD-ROMs and were originally designed for use with hardware samplers. Some virtual samplers, like Native Instruments' Kontakt, are capable of importing sample Hardware Library CD-ROMs.

There is also a difference between the sample or audio file format and the program or software file format. For example, the individual sounds used to create a multisampled piano in Reason's NN-XT may be WAV files, but the file you save will have the suffix SXT. This file doesn't contain the actual WAV files; it just points to them and contains the information about how to map them. SXT and similar files are sometimes called "patches" and in some cases can be used across different samplers.

Information about which formats your sampler is capable of importing and whether or not your sampler is capable of importing Hardware Library CD-ROMs is generally included on the manufacturer's website and in your software documentation.

In order to keep things simple and straightforward when buying sample CDs or DVDs or creating and exporting your own individual samples, it's a good idea, whenever possible, to work with the WAV or AIFF file format. This way if you end working in different environments or with different samplers you will be able to mix and match.

Basic Sampler Parameters

Every sampler will share certain parameters and functionality. Some will be "deeper" than others with more available effects or editing features, and the way the basic elements are implemented tends to vary from device to device. At their core, however, all virtual samplers perform essentially the same function, which is to create instruments and performances from sampled sounds.

Reason's NN-19 was one of the first full-featured virtual samplers to have many of the same features found in hardware samplers. You'll use the NN-19 Sampler to get a look at some of the most common virtual sampler parameters. If you don't own Reason, you can download a demo version of the program from `www.propellerheads.se`. For more information on using Reason, see Chapter 2.

Figure 9.6 shows the NN-19 interface.

FIGURE 9.6
Reason's NN-19

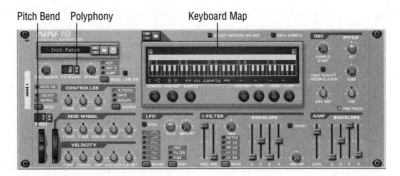

Let's look at some of the features of the NN-19.

Polyphonic and Monophonic settings   The NN-19 has an LED Polyphony control near the top left corner. Most virtual samplers will have some form of polyphony options that allow you to choose how many notes or samples can be played back simultaneously.

LFO   LFO stands for low frequency oscillation and can alter the sound of any sample or patch. LFOs generally have a Waveform selector that allows you to choose the shape of the LFO. Different LFOs will affect the sound of your sample in different ways. For example, a sine wave will rise and fall smoothly, while a square wave will have a drastic rise and drop-off. LFOs appear in virtual samplers and synthesizers in various uses. Among other things, LFOs can be used to create modulation-style effects like tremolo and phasing and to create panning effects.

Amp envelope   ADSR stands for Attack, Decay, Sustain and Release. The ADSR Amp envelope is used to adjust how a sample is played and how long and at what volume the note or sample is held.

Filter envelope   The Filter envelope applies a low pass, high pass, or band pass filter to the sample. Each of these settings represents a different frequency range and affects your sample in different ways. The ADSR envelope controls how the filter is applied. On the NN-19 in the Filter envelope section you can choose from different frequency ranges as well as adjust the ADSR properties of the filter.

Keyboard map   The Keyboard map maps notes, assigning a sample to specific keys or a specific range of keys. Assigning multiple samples to a single key or range of keys is called "multisampling."

Pitch Bend and Mod wheel   These parameters correspond to the Pitch Bend and Mod wheels found on most MIDI controller keyboards. The Pitch Bend wheel raises or slower the pitch of any note or chord in real time. The Mod wheel modifies the sound according to whatever parameters are assigned to it.

Two other common virtual sampler parameters not found on the NN-19 are:

Equalization   Many virtual sampler contain an EQ section where you can adjust the EQ settings for a sample or patch.

Effects   Many virtual samplers contain included effects. How those effects are accessed depends on the interface and architecture of the sampler.

How each sampler is "loaded" depends on the specific model. The NN-19 is very much like most virtual samplers in that it has two distinct ways of operating. You can load files that use the device's proprietary file format (in this case the NN-XT's format is SXT) using the Browse Patch button, or you can load REX, AIFF, or WAV files through the Browse Sample button located just above the Keyboard map.

Most virtual samplers also include the ability to load individual samples and then use them to create patches that are saved in the sampler's format.

SampleTank 2

IK Multimedia's SampleTank 2 sampler comes with over 6.5GB of samples and can also import WAV, AIFF, SDII, and AKAI formats. SampleTank 2 works as an Audio Unit, VST, or RTAS plug-in.

The full version of SampleTank (SampleTank 2 XL) is in the expensive price range and is available from `http://www.sampletank.com`. IK Multimedia also makes a moderately priced light version of SampleTank called SampleTank L that comes with 2GB of included samples.

SampleTank 2 is a full-featured virtual sampler. Along with all of the "standard" parameters I've covered, SampleTank also features many included audio effects and its own saving, patch creation, and multisampling functionality.

SAMPLETANK 2 FREE

If you'd like to try out SampleTank 2, IK Multimedia offers SampleTank 2 Free. More than just a demo version, SampleTank 2 Free is a close to fully functioning version of the program but with a few important limitations:

- You can only use the included SampleTank Free instruments.

- You can't import instruments or sounds.

- You can only use one instance of the program at a time in your DAW.

That said, SampleTank 2 Free is a great way to get familiar with SampleTank's effects and editing features and, even if you decide against buying the full version of the program, SampleTank 2 Free includes some great sounds, making it well worth adding to your virtual instrument collection.

You'll use SampleTank Free to take a look at how SampleTank implements some basic sampler parameters and functionality. To set it up, follow these steps:

1. Download and install the OS X version of SampleTank 2 Free from `http://www.sampletank.com`.

2. Download the presets from the same page. The presets will have to be downloaded individually.

3. Unzip all of the presets and move them to the folder `Applications\SampleTank 2 Free\ST2FreeInstruments`.

4. Start your DAW and add the SampleTank 2 Free as a virtual instrument plug-in.

5. The first time you use SampleTank 2 Free, the Registration Wizard will appear. If you have an active Internet connection, use the Register Online button to go to the SampleTank website and fill out the form, then check your e-mail for the authorization code.

Loading an Instrument

Once you've authorized SampleTank Free 2, you can start using the included sounds to create tracks and learn the SampleTank interface. Even with the limited number of included sounds as a starting point, the possibilities are pretty incredible.

If you've downloaded and installed the free SampleTank instruments, they will appear in a list near the center of the interface in the Browser window.

Figure 9.7 shows SampleTank 2 Free in Pro Tools.

FIGURE 9.7
SampleTank 2 Free

To start using SampleTank 2 Free:

1. Many of the free SampleTank instruments include more than one patch. Click the triangle next to the name of the instrument to view all of the included patches.

2. Double-click any patch to load it.

3. Use your MIDI keyboard or other controller to play the patch.

Try out more of the included patches. The Organ and Electric Piano sounds in particular are very realistic. The other free instruments include a couple of drum kits, some synthesizer sounds, and a collection of 90BPM loops that give you an indication of SampleTank's looping abilities.

Using Effects

SampleTank's built-in effects are among its best (and easiest to use) features. Figure 9.8 shows a close up of the Effects section of the SampleTank interface.

FIGURE 9.8
SampleTank's effects

To start using SampleTank's effects:

1. Open the HQ Free Piano instrument and select the Dynamic Piano patch. Looking at the Effects slots you can see that, aside from the default EQ/Compressor effect in the top slot, this patch contains Reverb Delay and Parametric EQ effects.

2. Select any effect to view its adjustable parameters to left of the Effects slots. As you select each effect, the available knobs change to reflect the parameters for each effect.

3. Add a new effect by selecting the one of the slots currently marked NO EFF and choosing an effect from the drop-down menu.

Effects can be turned on and off at any time by clicking the On button to the right of the effect slot.

LFO Settings

Like most virtual samplers, SampleTank contains the ability to create new sounds and effects using low frequency oscillators. In the Synth-Sampler section of the SampleTank interface shown in Figure 9.9, you'll find the LFO 1 and 2 buttons. Click the LFO 1 button to view the LFO parameters.

FIGURE 9.9
The LFO parameters
in the Synth-
Sampler field

The Wave knob on the far left is the waveform selector. As I covered in "Basic Sampler Parameters," the Waveform controls the basic shape of the LFO. Try returning to the Wave knob after you've adjusted some of the other parameters.

The Speed, Depth, and Level knobs are the most important for creating your basic settings. Try raising each of these significantly to get an idea of how the LFO setting can affect a sample. Among other things, LFO settings can create synthesizer-like sounds from any sample.

Try combining the LFO setting with effects for new, unique sounds.

Saving

The more complex User Preset saving and recalling functions, accessed on the right side of the SampleTank interface, are disabled in the free version of SampleTank. However, there is a way to save and recall the simple presets you create with the free instruments. To save, click the Save or Save As button at the top of the SampleTank interface. To recall your presets, click the Preset menu shown in Figure 9.10.

SampleTank 2 contains much more functionality than I can cover here. If you'd like to learn more, IK Multimedia has some free tutorials available on the SampleTank 2 Free download page. Look for the Tips & Tricks link, as well as the QuickTime video tutorials.

FIGURE 9.10
Recall presets from
the drop-down menu.

Kontakt

Kontakt is sampler program by Native Instruments. Like much of the Native Instruments software, it offers much more than just sampling. It may be more accurate to call Kontakt a sound manipulation tool.

One of Kontakt's best features is its ability to load samples and patches across multiple formats and devices, including just about every hardware *and* software format available and even some that are no longer available (if you've been holding on to that sound bank from your Unity DS-1 or some other discontinued software, this is the program for you). Kontakt will even import sample CDs that your computer can't read. A complete list of Kontakt-compatible file formats is available on the Native Instruments website.

Other advantages to using the Kontakt program include easy implementation of multisampling (combining multiple sounds into one sample) and an incredible array of effects and sound manipulation tools.

Kontakt can be used as a stand-alone program or as a virtual plug-in instrument with any program that supports Audio Unit, VST, or RTAS format. Kontakt is available from `http://www.native-instruments.com`. A 30-day demo version is available. The demo version will quit after 30 minutes of use and saving is disabled.

SETTING UP KONTAKT

When you first run Kontakt as a stand-alone program or as a plug-in virtual instrument, you'll see the Audio Setup window shown in Figure 9.11.

FIGURE 9.11
Kontakt's Audio Setup

You can reopen the Setup window at any time by selecting Setup ➢ Audio/MIDI. Check the default setting and make any necessary changes:

1. Select the Soundcard tab and choose your audio input and output devices.

2. Select the MIDI tab and turn any MIDI input and output devices on.

3. Click OK.

LOADING INSTRUMENTS

Kontakt's Browser window is located on the left side of the interface. This is where you browse for audio files, patches, and Multis (Kontakt's multiple instrument patches) to load in Kontakt. There are two ways to browse with the Browser window:

◆ Use the Files tab to locate files by location. Clicking the Files tab will display a list of all of your connected drives and main system folders. The Files tab conveniently includes the desktop as a starting point for browsing files.

◆ Use the Database tab. The Database tab lets you browse quickly through only relevant files.

To quickly view all of your available Kontakt Instruments:

1. Select the Database tab and click the Search button to open the Search window.

2. Select the Search for: Instruments tab.

3. Leave the filename and author fields empty.

4. Click the Search button. The Browser window will display a list of all of the available NKI-format Kontakt instruments. You can double-click or drag any NKI file directly onto Kontakt's workspace. For this example, use the Electric Piano instrument to get a look inside an NKI file.

5. Drag the Electric Piano.nki instrument from the Browser to the workspace.

6. Use your MIDI keyboard to play the Electric Piano instrument.

Figure 9.12 shows the Electric Piano instrument in the workspace.

FIGURE 9.12
The Electric Piano instrument

Edit Instrument

Remove Instrument

Show/Hide Details

On the right side of the instrument are the Solo and Mute buttons. Next to these are the Volume and Panning sliders and LCD-style Volume meter. On the far right, click the "X" button to remove the instrument and click the "+" or "−" button to view or hide the Tuning knob, output, MIDI, and polyphony information.

Click the Edit Instrument button (the wrench) at the top left corner to view the "insides" of the Kontakt instrument. Within each Kontakt instrument are a staggering number of possibilities. Figure 9.13 shows the Electric Piano instrument with the Edit Instruments button selected.

FIGURE 9.13
Instrument Edit mode

Solo
Mute
Panning
Volume

EFFECTS

At the bottom of the patch is the Insert Effects section. You can easily add up to eight insert effects in this section. This particular patch has three assigned effects: compressor, chorus, and delay. Select any effect to view its editable parameters.

You can add a new effect by clicking one of the empty Add Fx boxes and selecting an effect from the drop-down menu (Figure 9.14).

FIGURE 9.14
Kontakt's
Effects menu

IMPORTING SAMPLES

To get a look at all of the sample files on your system that are compatible with Kontakt, you may want to use the Rebuild Database function to scan your hard drive. This process can be a bit time consuming, but it's a good idea to do it at least once. Once it's done you'll have quick access to all of the WAV, AIFF, and other samples on your hard drive that can create instruments, patches, and multisamples in Kontakt. To scan your hard drive:

1. Select the Database View tab on the left side of the Kontakt interface.

2. Click the Rebuild DB tab.

3. Select the formats you'd like to have catalogued. You can choose the three Kontakt formats—Multis, Banks, and Instruments—as well as the Samples format, which will catalogue all of your Kontakt-compatible audio files.

4. Select the hard disk or network locations you want catalogued.

5. Click the Rebuild button.

You can now use the Database tab to browse and locate all of the samples on your computer:

1. Click the Search button.

2. Select the Samples tab.

3. Choose a filename or type. For example, try "Drum" to search for your drum-related samples or try keywords like "snare," "hihat," "piano," or "guitar" to be more specific.

CREATE A SINGLE SAMPLE INSTRUMENT

For the following exercises, make sure that you have copied the MMA Audio folder to your desktop. Creating a single sample instrument in Kontakt couldn't be much easier:

1. Use Kontakt's Browser window to locate the DropOne.wav file in MMA Audio Files\ Kontakt folder.

2. Drag the file from the browser window onto Kontakt's workspace.

3. Use your MIDI keyboard controller to play the instrument.

CREATE A MULTISAMPLE INSTRUMENT

In Chapter 4, "Pro Tools," we looked at creating a multisample with Ableton Live's optional Sampler instrument. Most virtual samplers have this functionality, but as you'll see here, how multisamples are created varies greatly from sampler to sampler. However, because the underlying concepts are essentially the same, If you take the time to learn how to create a multisample in one or two different sampler instruments the process becomes a bit more intuitive when you begin working with a new virtual sampler.

1. Delete the Electric Piano instrument by clicking the "X" in the top right corner.

2. Use Kontakt's Files Browser window to locate the folder MMA Audio\Kontakt\Multisample.

3. Drag the file PianoC1.wav onto Kontakt's workspace. You've created a single sample instrument.

4. Click the Edit Preset (wrench) button to view the "insides" of your new instrument.

5. Near the top of the Edit Preset window is a row of Editor buttons. Click the center button marked Mapping Editor. Figure 9.15 shows the Mapping Editor window.

FIGURE 9.15
The Mapping Editor window

When you create a new single sample instrument, the sample is automatically mapped across the entire key range. When creating a multisampled instrument, you'll want to reduce the key range depending on how many different samples will make up the total patch. In this case five notes will cover one octave each.

6. Click and drag from each end of the sample with your mouse to resize the key range. As you resize and move the key range you'll notice that one of the keys on the keyboard is shaded.

This is the Root key, the key that plays the original sample in its original state. What you want to do with this sample is set a one-octave range with the root key matching the sample's name (C1). Figure 9.16 show how this will look in the Kontakt Mapping Editor window.

FIGURE 9.16
A sample mapped to a one-octave range

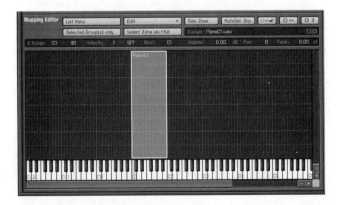

7. From here it's a very simple matter to drag each of the remaining samples onto the Mapping Editor and resize each sample's key range to cover one octave each beginning with the sample's root note. For example, map the sample PianoC3.wav to the key range C3–B3, the sample PianoC4.wav to the key range C4–B4, and so on. The final mapping is shown in Figure 9.17.

FIGURE 9.17
The finished multi-sample in the Mapping Editor

This kind of sample mapping can be used to create any kind of instrument. Multisampling at its most intricate is often used to create drum kits by assigning a different drum, cymbal, or percussion sample to each MIDI note.

IMPORTING PATCHES

Another one of Kontakt's features is its ability to import patches from other formats. To demonstrate this I've created a simple drum kit in Reason's NN-XT Advanced Sampler and saved it in the NN-XT's SXT format. Here's how to load a third-party sampler patch into the Kontakt player:

1. Click the Files tab at the top of the Browser.

2. Navigate to the MMA Audio Files\Kontakt\SXT folder.

3. Drag the file BadDrum.sxt directly onto the workspace.

4. Use your MIDI keyboard to trigger the sounds of the drum kit.

Using this method you can import sample patches from other virtual samplers, provided you have access to the actual audio files that make up the patch. For example, you won't be able to use this method with SXT files that were created using sounds contained in a ReFill, such as the Reason Factory Sound Bank. But you can load the BadDrum.sxt file into Kontakt because the WAV samples that make up the patch are located within the same folder as the patch file.

TAKE IT FURTHER

In this tutorial I've covered some of the basic functions contained in the Kontakt program. Even more than in most software there are many deeper levels of functionality available in Kontakt.

The only downside to Kontakt is that it is not a very intuitive program. Kontakt's complexity makes it a difficult tool to use for entry-level software users or someone just starting to learn about virtual sampling. If you have some experience with virtual or hardware sampling or just have the desire to learn and perform complex sampling and audio manipulation functions, Kontakt can keep you busy for a very long time.

Other Virtual Samplers

The following is a list of some of the other virtual samplers currently available for OS X.

Plugsound Pro (AU, VST, RTAS), `http://www.ultimatesoundbank.com` The full version of Ultimate Sound Bank's Plugsound Pro sampler comes with an 8GB core library of sounds and loops covering every instrument and genre imaginable. Plugsound also supports REX, Apple Loops, AIFF, and WAV files. The full version requires an iLok key.

HALion (AU, VST, stand-alone), `http://www.steinberg.com` Steinberg's HALion is available in three versions:

◆ HALion (full version, expensive)

◆ HALion Player (light version, moderately priced)

◆ HALion SE, which comes with the StudioCase II VST instruments collection

Yellow Tools Independence (VST, RTAS, AU, Stand-alone), `http://www.yellowtools.de` Independence is a fairly new, expensive product that comes with a huge 18GB sample library as well as its own mixing and sequencing interface. Independence also includes many effects and unique "humanizing" features for creating realistic performances.

MachFive (AU, VST, RTAS, MAS), `http://www.motu.com` MachFive comes with over 4GB of included samples, integrated effects, and the ability to import a huge range of third-party sample formats, including drag-and-drop importing and key mapping for quickly creating multisamples.

Virtual Synthesizers

Each of the DAW programs I've covered comes with its own options for virtual synthesizer instruments, sometimes built directly into the program. Reason has the Malström and SubTractor, GarageBand has its suite of synthesizers, Live has the Operator synthesizer, and Pro Tools now includes the Xpand! Synthesizer as well as Reason Adapted's included synths. The Logic program has the widest range of all, from the simple ES-1 to the highly complex Sculpture synth.

Still, no matter what program you are using there are many other exciting possibilities for adding new instruments to your synthesizer collection. There are dozens of currently available virtual synthesizers for OS X ranging in price from completely free to extremely expensive. One interesting feature of many of these instruments is that price is not always a good indication of value. As you'll see, there are some pretty incredible free and inexpensive virtual synthesizers out there.

Choosing the right synthesizer instrument can be difficult for other reasons as well. Many synths include great sounds and sonic possibilities but somehow don't fit in across genres or styles. Since so many are available, it's well worth the investment of time to download and check out a demo versions of a wide range of instruments. Any new synth will by virtue of its included sounds, unique architecture, and interface be a possible source of unique inspiration.

In this section, you'll get a look at the range of available virtual synthesizers including freeware, shareware, and commercially available programs. We'll also take a look at some virtual synthesizers that are based on classic analog models and some that are based on newer technologies only possible in the digital realm.

Using Virtual Synths

Many virtual synths will work as stand-alone programs, including built-in recording functions for saving the instruments output in AIFF or WAV format. Generally, however, you will want to use your virtual instruments in a host program.

While each virtual synthesizer has its unique functions, most synthesizers will act in similar ways within each host environment when used as plug-in virtual instruments.

SYNTHESIZER BASICS

Just as there are many different kinds of hardware synthesizers, there are now many different kinds of virtual synthesizers. Many virtual synthesizers are based on specific types of synthesis or synthesizer models. For example, the Native Instruments FM7 is based on FM synthesis, most commonly associated with the Yamaha DX7 synthesizer from the 1980s.

However, within the virtual environment some of the rules have begun to change significantly. While many virtual synthesizer models continue to emulate their hardware counterparts, now virtual synthesizers can also create their own forms of synthesis. Two excellent examples of this are Reason's Malström and Logic's Sculpture synths. The Malström is based on a combination of synthesis technologies including Graintable synthesis, which is a digital combination of Granular and Wavetable synthesis. Logic's Sculpture (see Chapter 5, "Logic") is based on an entirely new concept. The sound begins when a "string" is played by one of three built-in "objects" that generate different kinds of sounds. At the same time, something that both of these virtual synthesizers have in common is the appearance of concepts and parameters familiar to most, if not all synthesizers, hardware and virtual.

COMMON SYNTH PARAMETERS

Understanding a little bit about these common parameters will go a long way toward enhancing your overall experience, especially when creating and shaping your own sounds and patches.

Every synthesizer will have different parameters. The following is a list of some of the most common and what they do. Just about every synthesizer will have some variation of these parameters.

Oscillators

Oscillators generate the waveform sound that will make up the basic sound that is the starting point for creating sound in many synthesizers. Different types of waveforms are used to create different sounds. When creating sounds from scratch or altering existing sounds you will achieve different results depending on which kind of waveform is being used as the starting point.

The most common waveforms are as follows.

Sine   Sine waves usually produce a softer sound, associated with organ tones and smooth bass sounds.

Saw   Saw waves are harsher and tend to generate more mechanical-sounding tones.

Triangle   Represented by an up and down symbol, triangle waves sound similar to the sine wave but a bit sharper.

Square   Sonically, the square wave falls somewhere between the sine and saw waves.

Noise   Noise is just that: noisy. Noise waves can be used as a starting point for new sounds or added to existing sounds to create a harsher tone or effect.

These waveforms are often represented visually, such as the most common oscillator waveforms as shown here in the freeware Remedy synthesizer (`http://www.keytosound.com`).

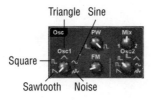

Many virtual synths use other types of sounds as their starting point. These can be anything from included sounds like vocals, organs, or other instruments to noise or any other random sound.

ADSR Envelopes

Envelopes are used to shape the sound of the waveform created by the oscillator. There are frequently multiple envelopes within a synthesizer, each controlling different parameters. The most common ADSR envelope is the Amp envelope, which often appears immediately after the oscillator and shapes the sound's volume characteristics using the ADSR parameters.

ADSR stands for Attack, Decay, Sustain, and Release. ADSR envelopes, sometimes with added parameters, are found in many synthesizers and virtual instruments, including most virtual samplers.

Attack   The amount of time from when the sound is triggered until it reaches its full volume. Short attacks produce an immediate sound; longer attacks can create swelling effects.

Decay   The amount of time it takes for a sound to diminish from its peak volume to the level it will hold at for the sustain parameter.

Sustain   The steady volume that the note will stay at until it is released.

Release   The amount of time it takes for the sound to fade when the note is no longer being played.

Filters

Most virtual synthesizers have some kind of filter section, usually containing choices between high pass, low pass, and band pass filters as well as the ability to adjust specific elements of the chosen filter. Some synthesizers include other types of filters, such as ring modulators and comb filters. Filters sometimes include an ADSR envelope or some variation of ADSR parameters. Figure 9.18 shows the Filter 1 section of Reason's SubTractor synthesizer.

FIGURE 9.18

The Filter 1 section of the SubTractor synthesizer

LFOs

An LFO is a low frequency oscillator. LFOs use waveforms to alter the sound being generated by an oscillator or sample in various ways, often creating tremolo, vibrato effects, or pitch variations. LFOs are generally made up of one of the common waveforms used in standard oscillators. Sometimes synthesizers or parameters within synthesizers will contain a fixed LFO, usually a sine wave or saw wave.

Figure 9.19 shows the LFO section of the Remedy synthesizer.

FIGURE 9.19

The Remedy's LFO section

Effects

Quite often what sets a sound or patch apart isn't just the sound created by the oscillators, envelopes, and filters. Effects play a large part in many synthesizer sounds. With many virtual synthesizers today, the effects are built into the software. In other cases, you'll alter the sound the after the fact with plug-in effects.

Effects commonly used with synthesizers include delays, reverbs, choruses, phasers, and other modulation effects.

Figure 9.20 shows the Effects section of IK Mutimedia's Sonik Synth.

FIGURE 9.20

Sonik Synth's
Effects section

SIMPLE SYNTHESIS

Figure 9.21 shows the Chip32 synthesizer as a virtual instrument in Logic.

FIGURE 9.21

The Chip 32 synth

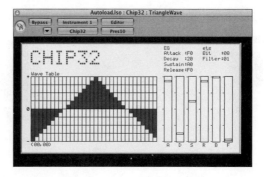

Chip32 is a freeware Audio Unit and VST synthesizer. It's available from www.apulsoft.ch/freeports and http://www.kvraudio.com/get/229.html.

The Chip32 is as simple as synthesis gets: an oscillator and an ADSR Amp envelope. Use your MIDI keyboard to play the default square waveform. Other waveforms can be accessed from your DAW's presets menu:

1. Download and install the VST or Audio Unit version of Chip32.

2. Start your host program and add the Chip32 to any MIDI or instrument track as a virtual instrument.

   The ADSR envelope controls the sound parameters.

3. Raise the Attack slider for a quicker attack.

4. Lower the Decay slider for a shorter decay.

5. Raise the Sustain slider for a longer sustain.

6. Lower the Release slider for a longer release time.

Chip32 also contains a simple bit rate adjuster and EQ filter. Playing with the Chip32 for a bit is a good way to get familiar with some of the basics of oscillator and Amp envelope sound manipulation.

ADDING MORE ELEMENTS

Let's use Reason's Malström instrument to get a look at how synthesizers use LFOs to shape sounds. If you don't own Reason you can download a demo version of the program from `http://www.propellerheads.se`. If you need instructions on the basic setup and operation of Reason, see Chapter 2.

As I mentioned earlier, the Malström is an example of a new kind of synthesis. However, the Malström also uses very familiar parameters and techniques to shape its sounds. The Mod sections of the Malström use LFOs to alter the initial waveform of the synth and create new sounds.

1. Start Reason or the Reason demo.

2. Make sure your MIDI controller is attached and powered up.

3. Create a Mixer 14:2 and a Malström synth.

4. Use your MIDI keyboard to play a single note. If you don't have a MIDI keyboard, use Reason's Key Lane to create a single long note. Figure 9.22 shows the Mod A section of the Malström interface.

FIGURE 9.22
Malström's Mod A
(LFO) section

This section uses an LFO to alter the sound of the notes generated by the Malström. To hear the effect, adjust the Pitch or Shift knob, then play or trigger another note. The Mod A section's default LFO waveform is a sine wave. By clicking the up and down arrows next to the sine wave, you can scroll through a large selection of different waveforms. Each waveform will have a noticeably different effect on the sound.

5. Click the Sync button to synchronize the LFO's effect with the session's current tempo.

6. Adjust the speed of the LFO with the Rate button.

Digital Synthesizers

The instruments in this section incorporate some of the common synthesizer parameters from the world of hardware synths and then add features previously unavailable outside of the digital realm to create something entirely new.

CREATING SYNTHESIZER PATCHES

Every hardware or virtual synthesizer will contain its own unique set of parameters. Those parameters are often organized in very different ways, depending on the instrument. The elements that make a synthesizer unique are things like the "base" sounds that each patch starts with, how the filtering sections and LFOs sound, what elements the instrument contains, and the quality of the effects.

However, there is a general "formula" for creating synth sounds and patches from scratch with virtual synth instruments. This formula is:

Oscillator ➢ Filter(s) ➢ Mod/LFO ➢ Effects

The oscillator creates the original sound; the filter or filters, LFO/modulators, and effects then shape the sound.

Not every instrument will follow this routing exactly, and many virtual synths contain multiple oscillators, filters, and effects that can be combined and creatively routed to create intricate patches.

BASIC PATCH CREATION WITH BLUE

We'll use Rob Papen's Blue synthesizer to get a look at basic patch creation with virtual synthesizers. I've chosen this synth as an introduction to creating patches because it contains the elements that most virtual synths have, laid out in a very systematic, sensible way.

Blue is moderately priced and available in AU, VST, RTAS, and stand-alone formats from `http://www.robpapen.com/synths/blue`. A demo version is available that emits white noise at random intervals and has its saving functions disabled. Figure 9.23 shows the Blue interface in Pro Tools.

FIGURE 9.23

The Blue interface

The top row contains six oscillators labeled A through F. You can use one or more oscillators at any time. Turn any oscillator on or off by clicking its letter in the top left corner. Just below the oscillators are Filters A and B. Click either filter's Type menu to see that Blue contains the standard High Pass, Low Pass, and Band Pass options as well as a Ring Modulator and Comb Filter options.

Below the filters are a series of tabs for accessing Blue's "deeper" functionality. Let's use Blue to create a simple synth patch:

1. Select the Presets tab to view the Presets window, as shown in Figure 9.23.

2. Click the Clear button at the bottom of the Presets window to create a new empty patch.

3. Make sure Oscillator A is turned on. As with many virtual synths, Blue's default oscillator is a sine wave.

4. Click on the Oscillator type field (labeled Sine in Figure 9.23) to view the different oscillator choices shown in Figure 9.24.

FIGURE 9.24

The Oscillator menu

5. Select the Saw oscillator type from the Analogue category.

   The next step is to choose a destination for the sound. In Blue's case you can choose to send the signal to one or both of the filters or directly to the effects.

6. Click the Dest box and select Filter A.

7. In Filter A's type menu you can choose the type of filter you want to apply to the sound. Select 12db LP (low pass). Raise the Freq, Env, and Dist knobs to adjust the sound.

8. In the Filter A Destination box, make sure FX A is selected.

9. Click the FX tab to view the Effects window.

10. Click the FX A box in the Effects window, then select an effect from the FX A drop-down menu.

    Figure 9.25 shows the Stereo Delay parameters in the Effects Window.

11. Adjust the effect parameters.

At this point you can save your patch either in the virtual synthesizer you are working in or using your DAW's built-in preset functionality.

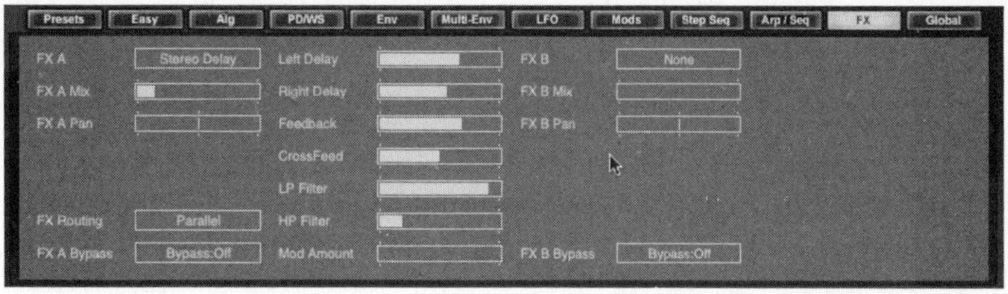

FIGURE 9.25

The Stereo Delay
effects parameters

ADD MORE VOICES

With the Blue and other virtual synths you also have the option of adding more oscillators to your patch
to make a more complex or interesting sound. In Blue you can click the Oscillator B button, select a
waveform, and route the signal either to Filter A or B or directly to the effects.

Whenever you are working with a new virtual synth, you can look for these parameters as a starting
point to investigation the instruments functionality. How easily a synth or other virtual instruments
implements its basic functions is often a good indication of how easy or difficult it will be to access and
work with its more involved features.

ABSYNTH

Absynth's strengths are its combination of rich, ambient, and techno style sounds and its complex
editing functions. A quick browse through Absynth's presets will reveal a wide range of sounds and
sonic sculpting possibilities, with a definite focus on long sweeping pads and heavily effected sounds.
Like all of Native Instruments' products, Absynth stands out with its clear sounds and deep editing
capabilities. Absynth is on the expensive side. It's available in AU, VST, RTAS, and stand-alone
formats. A 30-day limited demo version of is available from http://www.native-instruments.com.

You'll use Absynth to take a look at how another virtual instrument will implement the same
standard synthesizer parameters you set in the Blue in a different environment and create very
different results.

Load Absynth into your host program or use it as a stand-alone instrument. Figure 9.26 shows
the main window of the Absynth synthesizer.

FIGURE 9.26

The Absynth
synthesizer

In the middle of the window you can try out some of Absynth's included presets. Let's take a look inside of Absynth by creating a new sound from scratch:

1. At the top of the Absynth window, choose File ≻ New.

2. Use your MIDI keyboard to play the blank instrument. This sound, a single sine wave, is a very common default for many virtual synthesizers.

3. Click the Patch tab at the top of the Absynth window. Figure 9.27 shows the Patch window.

FIGURE 9.27
Absynth's Patch window

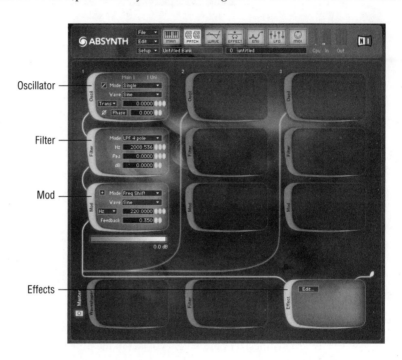

Oscillator

Filter

Mod

Effects

The patch window contains 12 boxes:

Three Oscillators   Use any one, two, or three oscillators individually or simultaneously to create a sound.

Three Filters   Each oscillator has its own filter.

Three Mods (LFOs)   Each filter has its own Mod section for applying ring modulation or frequency shifting.

Master Section   Use the Master section to shape and add effects to the combined output of all three oscillators, filters, and/or mods.

Activate any parameter by clicking the name field on the left side of its box.

4. In the Oscillator 1 box, click the Wave field and select Factory from the drop-down menu to view a list of available Waveforms. Select a waveform to load it into the oscillator.

Many of these are standard waveforms found in many virtual and hardware synths. The list also contains some variations specific to the Absynth.

5. Play your MIDI keyboard to preview the sound of the waveform.

6. After trying out some of the other waveforms select Triangle.

7. Just below Oscillator 1, turn the filter on by clicking the left side of the Filter box.

8. Choose any setting from the Mode drop-down menu.

9. On the right of each parameter box, you'll see hexagon shapes. These indicate an adjustable parameter. Click any hexagon and drag up or down to adjust a selected parameter.

   If you want to create a more complex patch, take the time here to add another Oscillator or two and make any Filter/Mod adjustments.

10. Click the Effect tab at the top of the Absynth interface to view the effects window. Here you can choose from five different categories of ambient/delay effects.

11. Turn the effect on by clicking the On button.

12. Click Echoes to add the Echoes effect and use your mouse to adjust the effect parameters displayed in the center of the window.

   Figure 9.28 shows the Effects window.

FIGURE 9.28
The Effects window

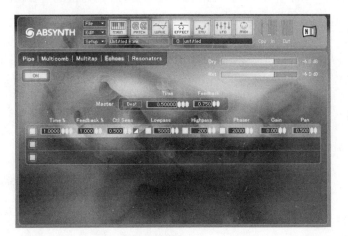

13. Save your patch by selecting Save or Save As from the File menu at the top of the Absynth interface.

Absynth is a very good example of a synthesizer that contains all of the usual suspects as far as parameters and routing goes, but because of the combination of included effects, the way the interface is set up, and other factors, it lends itself to creating certain types of sounds. Absynth has many more intricate editing, sound, and patch creation features. For the user looking to create patches and sounds in a variety of styles, Absynth may not be the best choice. But if you are looking for the ability to create ambient sounds with lots of customizable features, Absynth is hard to beat.

For more information on Absynth, the Native Instruments website has a great tutorial video, further exploring the synth and its functionality.

OTHER NATIVE INSTRUMENTS VIRTUAL SYNTHS

Native Instruments offers several other types of virtual synthesizers, including:

FM8   A virtual recreation of FM synthesizers from the 1980s, updated digitally for the 21st century. FM8 is on the expensive side.

Massive   Appropriately named, the expensive Massive synth contains a huge number of presets and editable parameters.

Pro 53   Based on a classic analog synthesizer, the Pro 53 gives you access to a wide range of vintage synth sounds. It's less expensive than the FM8 and Massive.

CRYSTAL

Crystal is a freeware virtual synthesizer that works as a VST and an Audio Unit virtual instrument. It's available from `http://www.greenoak.com/crystal`. Crystal comes with over one hundred presets and has expansion sets available as well. Many Crystal users also create and share their own banks of presets. Crystal is an excellent-sounding virtual synthesizer. Its presets tend to be geared toward ambient and techno sounds, but Crystal is capable of much more, especially if you take the time to install the expansion sets. Many Crystal users consider it their favorite virtual synthesizer, commercial or freeware.

Installing and Using Crystal

Installation of the Crystal synthesizer is simple. Download the `Crystal.dmg` file, open it, and run the installer. Once you've installed Crystal, you can add it as a virtual instrument plug-in in your host program.

We'll start off by using the included sounds and presets to get familiar with Crystal's interface and basic functionality. Figure 9.29 shows Crystal as a virtual instrument in GarageBand.

FIGURE 9.29
The Crystal synthesizer

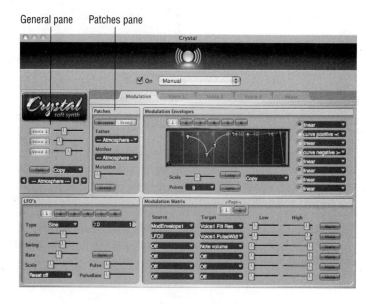

1. Start your host program and locate the Crystal instrument. Depending on your host program, the synthesizer may be located within a folder named `Green Oak Software`.

2. Add Crystal as a virtual instrument plug-in. Crystal's presets will either be available in your host program's standard location, or you can access them in Crystal's interface. The presets are located in the General pane at the top left of the interface in the field currently labeled Atmosphere.

3. Click the downward pointing triangle next to the Preset field to view a list of available presets.

4. Use your MIDI keyboard controller to play the Crystal synthesizer, or create a performance in your host program's MIDI editor.

Expanding Crystal's Sounds and Presets

Crystal's included sounds and presets are great. But if you are using Crystal a lot you may want to check out some of the expansion sets. Many of the user-created sets are quite good, and adding the Sound Fonts expansion packs opens up entirely new worlds of possibility.

There are more patches for Crystal available at `http://www.greenoak.com/crystal/patches.html`.

To make these patches available in Crystal:

1. Download any of the available FXB files. I recommend downloading all of them at once.

2. Create a folder named `CrystalPatchBanks` and place all of the FXB files in the folder.

3. Place the `CrystalPatchBanks` folder in your *username*`\Library\Preferences` folder.

4. Start your host program and add Crystal as a virtual instrument plug-in.

5. Banks and patches are accessed in the Patches pane located just to the right of the General pane. Click the Browse button and select a bank from the Banks drop-down menu and a patch from the Patches drop-down menu.

Breeding Presets

Crystal has an interesting function that allows you to combine elements of two different presets and create a new sound. This is a neat way to come up with unique original sounds and create your own presets.

1. Click the Breed tab at the top of the Patches pane and select any two presets from the Father and Mother drop-down menus.

2. Adjust the Mutation slider, raising the slider to add more randomness to the new patch.

3. Click the Breed button at the bottom of the Patches pane.

A new and different patch is created every time you click the Breed button. If you want to keep any of the patches you come up, with use your DAW's Save Preset functionality.

Expanding Crystal's Instruments

You can further expand the Crystal by downloading and installing a 20MB set of instruments from the Green Oak website at http://www.greenoak.com/crystal/download.html. Downloading this set will greatly enhance your options for creating original patches and your ability to play user created patches that utilize the included instruments.

1. Scroll down to New Features in 2.4 and click the link to download the Sample ROM.

2. Unzip the sample ROM.

3. Place the CrystalSoundFonts folder in your *username*\Library\Preferences folder.

4. Restart your host program and add the Crystal synthesizer as a virtual instrument plug-in.

Creating Patches

For a look at the new instruments:

1. Select any bank and choose any patch named Unused.

2. Click the Voice 1 tab at the top of the Crystal interface.

   Figure 9.30 shows the Voice 1 window in default mode.

FIGURE 9.30
Crystal's Voice 1
window

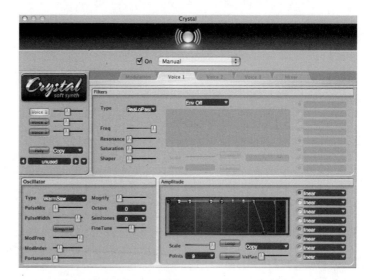

3. Click the Type box in the Oscillator section to view the available oscillator choices.

4. Choose any oscillator type. If you've installed the 20MB sample ROM, you'll have an extra category named Sound Fonts. Use any of these as a starting point to create unique patches and sounds in Crystal.

Crystal's Amplitude envelope is a great example of a familiar parameter being implemented in a unique way:

◆ Using the Points box you can select anywhere from four to nine control points that you can adjust manually with your mouse or set with the drop-down menus on the far right of the Amplitude pane.

- There's also a drop-down menu with nine amplitude presets.

- The Loop button loops the amplitude settings, repeating the effect that your control points have on the sound in a continuous loop.

- The Sync button syncs the amplitude setting to the current tempo of your DAW.

The Filter pane is set up similarly to the Amplitude pane. Turn the Filter pane on by select Env On from the drop-down menu in the center of the pane.

Select a filter type from the Type menu. Choose one of the nine presets or use the points box to choose anywhere from four to nine control points and adjust them manually or by using the drop-down menus on the far right of the Filters pane (Figure 9.31).

FIGURE 9.31
Crystal's Filter
controls

Activate Voice 2 and 3 in the General pane, then use the Voice 2 and Voice 3 windows to create multiple voice patches. When you've created a sound you want to keep, use your DAW's patch saving functionality to save a recallable patch.

Take It Further

Crystal documentation and user groups contain even more resources for expanding Crystal and further exploring the synth's functionality.

"Vintage" Virtual Synths

I have to admit a personal bias here—this category contains some of my favorite instruments of all time, virtual or otherwise. Anyone who has spent any time with vintage hardware synthesizers can tell you about the many difficulties that go along with these excellent instruments. Very expensive, hard to move around, hard to repair, and frequently out of tune, vintage hardware synthesizers can be simultaneously intensely rewarding and intensely frustrating.

Fortunately (or maybe unfortunately depending on your worldview), the people who develop these sorts of things seem to have a hard time leaving well enough alone. Aside from fixing some common problems (none of these instruments go out of tune—unless you want them to), without exception the digital versions of these synthesizers have added functionality, such as included effects, arpeggiators, and of course, the ability to save and recall your settings easily as presets and patches.

MINIMONSTA:MELOHMAN

The Minimonsta:Melohman is a recreation of the 1970s Minimoog designed by the great Robert Moog. Probably the first synthesizer to be used widely by popular musicians, the Minimoog can be heard on recordings by electronic music pioneers like Kraftwerk and Devo, classic rock albums by

Pink Floyd, ELO, and Rush and on funk records by Stevie Wonder and George Clinton. Modern-day recording artists like The Rentals and Coldplay still make use of the Minimoog.

The Minimonsta:Melohman is moderately priced and available in AU, VST, RTAS, and stand-alone versions from www.gforcesoftware.com. A fully functional demo version is available. After 30 hours of use the demo version will emit more and more background noise.

Start using the Minimonsta:Melohman by inserting it on any MIDI or instrument track in your DAW program. Figure 9.32 shows the Minimonsta:Melohman in Pro Tools.

FIGURE 9.32

The Minimonsta Minimoog

In the center of the Minimonsta is a faithful recreation of the Minimoog's hardware interface. All of the original knobs, buttons, and parameters are visible and fully functional.

The Minimonsta:Melohman does add some elements that were not included in the original Minimoog. At the top of the interface the Minimonsta:Melohman has included LFO modulation and MIDI control, bringing the instrument into the realm of digital synths.

Just above the keyboard are the Minimonsta's patch management fields. On the right you can load, save, and access patch banks. In the left you can select, load, and save specific patches. Click the Scrn Max button to view the complete list of included preset banks (Figure 9.33).

FIGURE 9.33

The Minimonsta's preset banks

Select any preset bank and click the Scrn Max button again to close the list.

Each bank has up to 12 patches use the buttons on the Patch Manager to select specific patches. You can save patches either within the Minimonsta:Melohman interface or by using your DAW's built-in preset saving functionality.

ARTURIA ANALOG FACTORY

Arturia (`http://www.arturia.com`) makes a number of synths based on classic analog models. These include:

- ◆ Minimoog V (another digital take on the classic Minimoog synthesizer)

- ◆ Moog Modular V

- ◆ CS-80V

- ◆ ARP 2600

The Analog Factory synth combines presets from all of these instruments in one package. The Analog Factory is moderately priced and works as both a stand-alone instrument and as an Audio Unit, RTAS, or VST plug-in.

The Analog Factory is made up of two connected screens. The top screen contains the Preset Browser, and the bottom screen contains the keyboard and editing knobs and sliders. You can view either screen individually or both simultaneously. Decide which view you want to use by clicking one of the three view buttons in the top right corner of the instrument's interface.

Figure 9.34 shows the Analog Factory's Browser window.

FIGURE 9.34

Analog Factory's Browser window

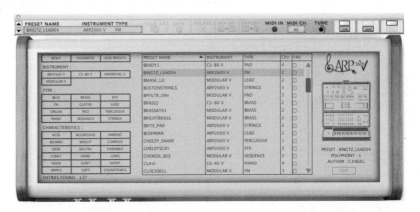

The Browser is as straightforward as these things get. On the left side of the window you browse patches by selecting a specific model or multiple models, then selecting the type of instrument(s) and finally the characteristics you are looking for. Presets that match your choices will be displayed in a list in the center of the Browser window.

Add any preset to your Favorites category by putting a check mark in the Fav box.

The bottom half of the Analog Factory contains its keyboard and editing features. Use your mouse to preview notes and adjust the Pitch and Mod wheels. The parameter knobs across the top of the keyboard adjust different parameters depending on which preset you have loaded. Place your mouse over any knob to see what parameter you are editing.

Figure 9.35 shows the keyboard and parameters.

FIGURE 9.35
The Analog Factory's
keyboard and parameter knobs

If you want a straightforward virtual instrument with quick access to a wide range of vintage synthesizer sounds at a reasonable price, the Analog Factory is a very good choice.

KORG LEGACY COLLECTION

The Korg Legacy Collection is a bundle of three synthesizers, each one representing a different decade of Korg synths. The collection comes in AU, VST, RTAS, and stand-alone formats.

MS-20   A digital recreation of one of the most enduring synthesizers from the 1970s.

Polysix   A 1980s Korg synth originally popular for its combination of great sounds and affordability, the digital version contains all of the original features and more.

Wavestation   Korg's 1990s-era synthesizer with numerous functions including a joystick.

Also included is the Legacy Cell, which allows you to link the PolySix and MS-20 to take advantage of both synthesizers and their effects in a single unit. One of the coolest features about this collection is that it also contains a hardware control surface for the MS-20 based on its original hardware interface.

The MS-20

The MS-20 was introduced in 1978 and has been in use consistently since then, finding its way into a variety of popular music styles; it's still used today by many electronic artists, such as William Orbit and Aphex Twin. The MS-20 also remains popular for its use as an effects processor. In fact, the digital version of the MS-20 includes a separate plug-in for using the MS-20 effects.

Figure 9.36 shows the Korg Legacy Collection's digital take on the MS-20.

With its complex routing, manual wiring, and many adjustable parameters, the MS-20 is not the best choice for beginners looking to create their own sounds from scratch. However, combined with the included hardware interface as a part of the Korg Legacy collection, it makes an incredible learning tool, giving you hands-on, real-world access to the functionality of a vintage hardware synthesizer.

As with most of the virtual synths I'm covering in this chapter, you can spend vast amounts of time just playing with the included presets. Presets on the MS-20 are accessed by clicking the Preset arrows at the bottom left of the interface. You can edit the synthesizer's parameters in the main window by moving your mouse over any of the parameter knobs to see the parameter and its current setting.

FIGURE 9.36
The Korg MS-20

Click the Edit button on the lower right of the interface to view the parameters close up.

If you've installed the Korg Legacy collection or the demo version you'll have a second plug-in available called MS-20FX. This plug-in can be added to any audio or virtual instrument track to use the MS-20 as an effects processor.

The Polysix

Based on a popular synth from the 1980s, the virtual Polysix is another favorite of mine. Its operation is fairly simple, the presets are quite good, and the synth itself seems incapable of generating anything but thick, precise synthesizer sounds. The Polysix makes great lead lines and bass tracks across electronic and rock music genres.

Figure 9.37 shows the Polysix.

One cool feature of the Polysix is its easy to use editing functions. Just click the Edit button on the lower right side of the screen to get an up-close view of the Polysix's editable parameters. Holding your mouse over any knob displays its current setting. Adjust any knob or series of knobs to alter the current patch. To return a parameter to its default state Command+click the knob.

FIGURE 9.37
The Polysix

The Polysix has a very simple built-in Arpeggiator for creating quick melodies. Figure 9.38 shows the Arpeggiator section of the Polysix Edit window.

FIGURE 9.38
The Polysix
UC Arpeggiator

More Virtual Synthesizers for OS X

It would be impossible to catalogue all of the synthesizers available for OS X. This section contains brief descriptions of some of the better free synthesizers and a list of commercial synthesizers.

Free Synthesizers

Automat (AU), http://www.kvraudio.com/get/1552.html   A freeware three-oscillator Audio Unit synth, its operation is very simple. At the top right of the Automat's interface are three randomization buttons that can be used to create new sounds. The right button creates minor variations to the current settings, the center button increases the randomness, and the left creates an entirely new sound.

Buzzer2 (AU), http://www.kvraudio.com/get/1020.html   An extremely cool freeware synthesizer with many editable parameters. Buzzer2 also has a randomizer button for creating totally original sounds. Be careful with the randomizer—if you create a sound you like be sure to save it as a preset, unless you've got a few thousand years to spare trying to keep clicking the random button.

Da Hornet (AU, VST), http://www.apulsoft.ch/freeports   Based on the vintage WASP synth Da Hornet, a great module for creating vintage sci-fi sounds and old horror movie effects.

Remedy (AU, VST), http://www.keytosound.com   A very simple synthesizer that contains the all of the basic parameters that make up most virtual synths. Using Remedy is a great way to familiarize yourself with synth basics and patch creation.

Orca (VST), http://www.fxpansion.com   Free to all registered members of the FXpansion website. You don't have to own any of their products—just go to their site and register. Orca has a unique interface and can create a surprisingly large range of sounds with what at first seems to be a limited set of parameters. Orca also comes with a large collection of presets. Creating and saving your own sounds is very easy as well.

COMMERCIAL SYNTHESIZERS

Following are some of the commercial virtual synthesizers available for OS X, arranged roughly in order of price. Almost all of these synthesizers have available demo versions.

- Inexpensive
  - FabFilter One (AU, VST), http://www.fabfilter.com
  - FabFilter Twin (AU, VST), http://www.fabfilter.com
  - Ultra Analog Session (AU, VST, RTAS), http://www.applied-acoustics.com

- ◆ Moderate
  - ◆ Base Line (AU, VST), `http://www.audiorealism.se`
  - ◆ Ravity(S), (AU, VST), `http://www.luxonix.com`
  - ◆ Bass Station (AU, VST), `http://www.novationmusic.com`
  - ◆ Zebra (AU, VST), `http://www.u-he.com`
  - ◆ Cameleon 5000 (AU, VST, RTAS), `http://www.camelaudio.com`
  - ◆ Albino (AU, VST, RTAS), `http://www.linplug.com`
  - ◆ Ultra Analog VA-1 (AU, VST, RTAS), `http://www.applied-acoustics.com`
  - ◆ Base Line Pro (AU, VST), `http://www.audiorealism.se`
  - ◆ V-station (AU, VST), `http://www.novationmusic.com`
  - ◆ TimewARP 2600 (AU, RTAS), `http://www.timewarp2600.com`
  - ◆ MX4 (AU, VST, RTAS, MAS), `http://www.motu.com`
- ◆ Expensive
  - ◆ Tassman 4 (AU, VST, RTAS), `http://www.applied-acoustics.com`
  - ◆ SonikSynth (AU, VST, RTAS), `http://www.soniksynth.com`

Virtual Keyboards

Separate from the world of virtual synthesizers is the virtual keyboard. These are programs that mimic the functions and sounds of keyboard instruments like organs and pianos. While it is certainly possible to achieve excellent-sounding piano and organ tracks using a sampler, programs devoted specifically to virtual piano or organ instruments will generally combine intricately multisampled instruments with other modeling technologies to achieve an even greater level of realism than the sound sets available for samplers. By being devoted to re-creating a specific type of instrument, many virtual keyboards can also offer precise recreations of vintage instruments and their original hardware.

Even more than most instruments, acoustic pianos, electric pianos, and organs pose a number of challenges for the songwriter, smaller studio owner, or home studio environment. For many people the size and weight of these instruments alone puts them out of the running as potential studio gear.

As with many instruments, virtual keyboards in particular will benefit greatly from the use of a weighted MIDI keyboard when recording tracks. For more about MIDI keyboards, see Chapter 11, "MIDI."

Virtual Pianos

Many engineers will tell you that piano is one of the more difficult instruments to capture correctly. The proper microphone placement, recording, and mixing of a piano can be a real challenge, especially in conjunction with a band or large ensemble. Some of the problems lie in the large range of keys that need to be recorded and the variations in intensity throughout a performance. A virtual piano can come in handy if you want to capture a high-quality performance without the difficulties of real-world recording.

PIANOTEQ

Pianoteq is an excellent example of what's possible with a virtual piano instrument. The instrument is available from www.pianoteq.com as a 45-day working demo with eight "silent" keys. It comes in AU and VST versions.

Pianoteq starts with a default piano sound that is pretty good on its own. What's especially cool about Pianoteq is that contained within its small, simple interface are a number of adjustable parameters to help your piano performances sit better within a mix or stand out on their own. Figure 9.39 shows the Pianoteq interface with all of the editable parameters showing.

FIGURE 9.39
Pianoteq

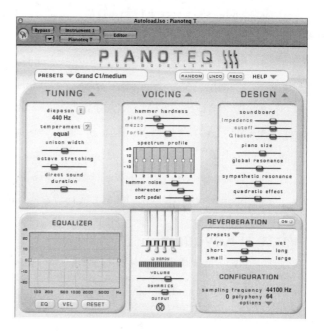

Add Pianoteq to a MIDI or instrument track in any VST or Audio Unit–compatible host. Use your MIDI keyboard controller to record a performance. I recommend using the default piano sound to create your performance, then utilizing all of the available parameters in the Pianoteq interface to adjust the sound to fit in with your mix. You can also apply effects from your DAW or third-party effects if you are more comfortable using those.

Pianoteq comes with a small number of presets, accessible from the Presets menu in the top left corner of the interface.

You can adjust any preset or the default Grand C1/Medium piano by moving any of the sliders or using your mouse to create and move edit points on the equalizer on the lower left side of the interface.

You can Command+click any slider to return it to its default position. One of the coolest features of Pianoteq is that if you hold your mouse over any slider or parameter, a window appears telling you what the parameter does, often in detail. The windows also sometimes offer suggestions for when and how you might want to make certain adjustments.

With all of its adjustable parameters, the Pianoteq plug-in is capable of creating an incredible range of piano and strange piano-like sounds. You can get some idea of the possibilities by using the Random button at the top of the interface to generate completely new sounds by randomly altering the Pianoteq's settings.

OTHER VIRTUAL PIANOS

Here are some of the other virtual piano instruments currently available for OS X:

- MDA Piano (VST), http://www.vst-mda.com (free)

- The Grand (AU, VST), http://www.steinberg.com

- Synthology Ivory (AU, VST, RTAS, stand-alone), http://www.synthogy.com

- Akoustik Piano (AU, VST, RTAS, stand-alone), http://www.native-instruments.com

Virtual Organs

Organs are another instrument that can be difficult to record. While some models are easier to move around than others, few people have regular access to the entire range of organ instruments, especially the church and theater pipe organs and some of the more expensive vintage instruments. And even if you have an organ or two at your disposal, you may run into other problems, such as dealing with repairs and maintenance. Virtual organ instruments can be a good solution to these problems.

B4 II

The Native Instruments virtual organ B4 II is all of the organs you could ever want in one extremely easy to work with package. Figure 9.40 shows the B4 II interface in Pro Tools.

FIGURE 9.40
The B4 II interface

The B4 II is one of the most realistic-sounding in-depth virtual instruments around. Based on the Hammond B3 organ as a starting point, the B4 II also includes Vox and Farfisa sounds as well as a harmonium. The presets contained in the B4 include some of the most famous and recognizable organ sounds around. A preset's name will often provide a clue as to its sound. With settings like "Stevie," "Preston!" and "No B4 No Cry," you should be able to easily find the tone you're looking for and discover some unexpected, new sounds along the way.

You can certainly use nothing but the included presets and have a world of great sounds at your disposal. But, if you decide that you want make your patches, the process is pretty straightforward and there are a lot of parameters to work with.

Click the Organ button to get a look "inside" the B4.

Figure 9.41 shows the B4's Organ window.

FIGURE 9.41
The B4's Organ
window

In the top left panel you can make adjustments to the Organ and Pedal Bass settings. In the center panel you can adjust the volume, overdrive the virtual tube, and do basic EQing. In the top right panel you can choose the kind of cabinet you want to simulate and make microphone settings. The bottom panel contains the organ's drawbars and vibrato settings. These parameters can all be adjusted to create variations on any of the included presets. You can also click the Expert button to view even more editable parameters.

To save your changes, click the Preset button, locate the File Operation section in the bottom right corner of the B4 interface, and click the Save button.

B4 XPRESS

The B4 Xpress is a fantastic deal for users who want an inexpensive, simple but great-sounding organ instrument. The B4 Xpress is part of the moderately priced Xpress Keyboards package from http://www.native-instruments.com. It comes in AU, VST, and stand-alone versions. The Xpress Keyboards package also includes "light" versions of the Pro-53 and FM7 synthesizers.

Like the B4 II, the B4 Xpress is based on the Hammond B3 and contains some very familiar-sounding presets based on organ sounds from well-known songs. The B4 Xpress is much simpler in its design and limits you to a smaller number of editable parameters. Even without all of the bells and whistles, the sound quality and realism of the B4 II are definitely there, just in a more compact and affordable package.

Electric Pianos

Used frequently in jazz (especially prominent on fusion records like *Bitches Brew*–era Miles Davis), R&B (Ray Charles's "What'd I Say"), and pop music (Billy Joel's "Just The Way You Are"), the various Fender Rhodes models and the Wurlitzer A200 are enduring keyboard sounds that are instantly recognizable.

LOUNGE LIZARD

Let's take a look at the Lounge Lizard, moderately priced and available in AU, VST, RTAS, and stand-alone versions from `http://www.applied-acoustics.com`. An inexpensive "light" version called Lounge Lizard Session is also available. Demo versions of both products have saving disabled, intermittent silences, and will stop working after 20 minutes of continuous use.

The Lounge Lizard EP-3 contains faithful recreations of the famous Fender and Wurlitzer sounds as well as built-in modulation and reverb effects. Figure 9.42 shows the Lounge Lizard EP-3.

FIGURE 9.42
The Lounge Lizard EP-3

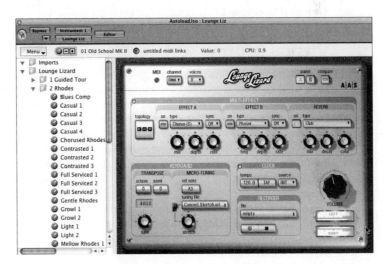

The Lounge Lizard's sounds are very realistic and the parameters are easy to adjust. There are two different views, accessed by clicking the Panel buttons at the top right of the interface.

In the center of the Panel A view are the Lounge Lizard's effects. You can use this section to apply modulation, delay, and reverb effects to the current instrument settings. There's an interesting feature here called the Topology button, located just to the left of Effect A. Click the Topology button and drag up or down to rearrange the order and routing of the effects.

Panel B contains basic sound parameters for the EP-3. In the top row you can adjust the Mallet, Fork, and Pickup parameters to create vastly different sounds and tones. The bottom section of Panel B contains more tone control in the Damper and EQ sections. The Tremolo control panel is my favorite thing about the EP-3. You can use the Tremolo settings to create some great sounds, and the Lounge Lizard gives you pretty intricate control over the Tremolo parameters, including stereo panning and a Sync function to match the BPM of your current session.

OTHER VIRTUAL ELECTRIC PIANOS

Here are some more electric piano virtual instruments available for OS X.

- ◆ Elektrik Piano (AU, RTAS, VST) is a top-of-the-line model available from `http://www.native-instruments.com`.

- ◆ Velvet (RTAS) is a moderately priced model from `http://www.digidesign.com`.

- ◆ MDA ePiano (VST) is free. You can download it at `http://www.mda-vst.com`.

Virtual Drums

Depending on whom you are talking to in the music-making world, the drum machine, virtual or otherwise, is either a godsend or a curse. There's no doubt that drum machines have changed the way we create and listen to music. The drum machine introduced entirely new sounds into popular (and unpopular) music. Many sounds, like those produced by the 808 and 909 drum machines, at one time may have been considered futuristic or unnatural but are now considered vintage and possibly even outdated. Entire genres such as industrial music, hip-hop, and all of the various permutations of electronic dance music would certainly not exist as we know them today without the use of drum machines.

For the most part virtual drum machines have followed that same patterns as all of the other virtual instruments and programs I've covered. The progression went from early software that was difficult to use and lacking in advanced features to more useful programs with better and better sound quality. Finally, we have today's wide range of choices and options, from the very simple to the extremely complicated.

Probably the single most difficult aspect of virtual drums, especially for the nondrummer, is drum programming. Even basic drum programming can be quite intimidating for the inexperienced user. Creating complex, changing rhythmic performances can be nearly impossible.

Fortunately, there are other options available today for the digital musician. Loops are frequently the tool of choice for creating drum tracks. A major advantage to loop-based drum tracks is that you can take real, human performances and add them to your sessions. A disadvantage to this is that no drum loops you buy or download will be created with your songs in mind. However, with a world of choices for loop libraries and more and more control over the editing process, it's very possible to create great tracks with loops.

Another option that seems to be gaining ground is the virtual drummer. Programs like FXpansion's BFD and Digidesign's Strike are taking drum programming out of the equation altogether and providing you with already created, yet highly customizable performances.

Ultimately the virtual drum machine/drummer/looping program or collection you decide on should depend on what you hope to accomplish. For demos or simple percussion tracks you might not need much more than a basic drum module (see iDrum, covered in this chapter). To create more involved tracks, you may want to investigate more complex programs with deeper programming options and the ability to create more realistic-sounding performances.

Using a Virtual Drum Machine in Your DAW

Every drum machine and every DAW has its own idiosyncrasies and specific functionality. However, there are some similarities within each program that I can cover up front. The following are the general instructions for creating a virtual drum performance in each of the DAW programs I've covered.

With a MIDI keyboard:

1. Add the instrument as a plug-in on any virtual or instrument track.

2. Create a click track or activate your DAW's click function.

3. Make sure your virtual drum instrument is receiving MIDI information. This will vary from DAW to DAW but usually involves arming the track for recording.

4. Use your MIDI keyboard to figure out which notes correspond to which drum samples. Generally virtual drum kits drum will start at C1 with the kick drum, then D1 with the snare and so on. This is not a hard and fast rule, however.

5. Begin recording.

Once you've created a virtual drum performance you can use your DAW's MIDI abilities to fix your performance as needed.

To edit or draw a MIDI performance with a virtual drum machine:

◆ In Live, use the Clip View, just as you would with the Impulse drum sampler.

◆ In Pro Tools, you can draw the MIDI notes with the Pencil tool right on the instrument track.

◆ In Logic, use the Pencil tool in the Matrix Edit window.

◆ In GarageBand, Control+click with your mouse in the Track Editor window.

A third option is to combine these techniques, recording a performance in real time, then fixing it using your DAW's editing and quantizing MIDI functions. This functionality is covered in the specific chapters relating to your DAW and in Chapter 11.

Not only can these techniques be used with virtual drum machines, you can also use the same methods to create drum performances with virtual drum kits included or loaded into your virtual sampler.

iDrum

iZotope's iDrum program is a virtual drum sampler and sequencer. iDrum is inexpensive and is available from www.izotope.com. It works as an AU or RTAS plug-in or as a stand-alone program.

A 10-day fully functional demo version is available as well.

Some of iDrum's advantages include its low price, its very easy to use interface, and its ability to quickly import WAV or AIFF files from any source to create your own drum kits.

GETTING TO KNOW IDRUM

Once you've downloaded and installed the iDrum program you can add it to a session in your DAW program as a virtual instrument plug-in, or you can use iDrum as a stand-alone program to create drum loops and sequences. We'll start off by using the program on its own to get familiar with its basic functions.

1. Locate the iDrum program in your `Applications` folder and start the program.

    Figure 9.43 shows the iDrum interface.

FIGURE 9.43

The iDrum interface

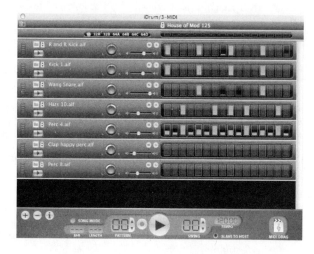

The iDrum interface will be somewhat familiar to GarageBand users. Each individual drum track is set up to look very much like the individual track headers in GarageBand, with the same look and feel for the panning, volume, mute, and solo parameters.

2. When iDrum starts it loads its default song. Press the Play button at the bottom of the interface to hear the default song.

3. With the default song playing, use the scroll arrows at the very top center of the window (next to the House of Mod 125 label on Figure 9.43) to hear the included kits and preview songs.

As you can tell from the included drum kits and preview songs, iDrum is capable of some pretty complex drum programming. However, my one major complaint about iDrum is that they don't make it easy to "turn off" the included drum kits and preset patterns. Like many people I prefer to start my sessions with a blank slate. In the following sections, we'll take a look at creating and saving your own drum kits and patterns.

BASIC PROGRAMMING

Now we'll take a look at creating a basic beat with iDrum.

1. Choose File ➢ New to create a new iDrum session.

2. Click the file folder icon in the upper left corner of the iDrum window and select Clear Entire Pattern from the pop-up menu.

iDrum is a very basic pattern sequencer. Patterns are created by clicking in any of the empty steps to fill them in. Once you've added a note in the step sequencer, you can adjust its velocity by clicking the note and using your mouse to drag up or down. The ability to adjust the velocity of each hit goes a very long way toward creating more realistic performances.

3. Use your mouse to add steps on any track in the pattern sequencer.

4. Press the Play button to begin playback.

Once you've created a pattern in the step sequencer you can:

◆ Export the pattern as a drum loop by clicking the file folder icon and selecting Bounce Pattern to AIFF.

◆ Select File ➤ Save As to save the file as a recallable iDrum song.

◆ Use the loop as the basis of a new song in Song mode.

CREATING A NEW KIT

Here's how to use iDrum to create your own custom kits.

1. Select File ➤ New to create a new iDrum session.

2. Hold down the Control key on your Apple keyboard and select any channel.

3. Choose Delete Selected Channel from the pop-up menu.

4. Delete all of the remaining channels in the iDrum session.

5. Click the File menu icon in the top left of the iDrum window and choose Insert New Channel from the pop-up menu.

6. Use the dialog box to locate the folder MMA Audio\iDrum and select the KickOne.wav sample.

7. Select Load.

8. Follow steps 5 through 7 to load the SnareOne.aif and HihatOne.aif files.

9. Now try programming a simple beat to try it out and set any panning or volume levels. Make sure you clear all of the patterns before you save the iDrum kit in the next steps. Any patterns you leave in place when you save the kit will reappear every time you open the kit.

10. Choose File ➤ Save As and select Copy Samples to iDrum Kit in the Save iDrum File dialog box.

11. Save the .idrum file to the folder *username*\Library\Application Support\iDrum\Kits.

To make your new kit the default kit, locate the *username*\Library\Application Support\ iDrum\Kits folder on your hard drive and delete the file default.idrum. Save your new file as default.idrum.

MAKING LOOPS WITH IDRUM

One of the most useful things you can do with iDrum is to create drum loops to use in your songs and recording sessions. Drum loops created in iDrum can be used for individual parts or sections of songs. You can also program and export multiple loops at once to use as a complete drum tracks for your songs.

1. Start iDrum in stand-alone mode.

2. Create a new iDrum session using a kit with a blank pattern or select a kit and choose Clear Pattern from the File menu.

3. Program a simple or complicated beat.

4. Click the file folder icon on the top left of the iDrum interface and choose Bounce Pattern to AIFF.

You can now drag and drop your drum loop onto any audio track in your DAW, edit it with any of the editing software covered in Chapter 7, or convert it to an Apple Loop using the Apple Loops utility covered in Chapter 10, "Apple Loops."

Unlike many virtual instruments, you can also export loop files from iDrum when it's in use as a virtual instrument plug-in as well.

MIDI MAPPING

Mapping iDrum to your MIDI keyboard controller or to specific MIDI notes in your DAW is very easy. I'm assuming that you have created a new default kit with the included samples or your own samples. You can use this method to map any of the included kits as well.

1. Insert iDrum as a virtual instrument on any MIDI or instrument track.

2. Select the kick drum channel and click the "I" button on the lower left side of the iDrum interface to open the Editing panel shown in Figure 9.44.

FIGURE 9.44
The iDrum
Editing panel

3. If you have a MIDI keyboard, make sure your connections are in place and that the iDrum track is receiving MIDI information.

4. Click the Auto-Map button.

5. Play any note on your MIDI keyboard. The note will now be automatically assigned to trigger the kick drum channel.

6. Repeat these same steps, assigning notes to the rest of the channels in your iDrum kit.

You can now use you MIDI keyboard to "play" the iDrum instrument. Try setting up a click track in your DAW and playing along. For more information on MIDI and your DAW, see Chapter 11.

If you don't have a MIDI keyboard or you prefer to "draw" your performances, you can assign a specific channel to a corresponding MIDI note in your DAW's sequencer window. Mapping the notes of your kit close together can make drawing MIDI sequences easier. For example:

◆ Assign your kick drum channel to the note C1 by selecting MIDI Note 36.

◆ Assign the snare drum channel to the note D1 by selecting MIDI note 38.

◆ Assign the hi-hat to E1 by selecting note 40.

Continue to assign notes until you've mapped out your entire kit. You can then use your DAW's instrument or MIDI tracks to draw the drum performance.

MIDI DRAG

Another way to work with iDrum is use the MIDI drag feature to create sequences. To use the MIDI drag:

1. Add iDrum to any instrument or MIDI track in your DAW host program.

2. Create a new pattern or use one the default patterns.

3. Select the MIDI drag button on the lower right of the iDrum interface.

4. Click and drag directly onto your instrument track.

5. Before you play back the MIDI file be sure to select Clear Entire Pattern from the iDrum File menu. Otherwise you'll be triggering the notes in iDrum's sequencer and your DAW at the same time, which will create a washy-sounding performance.

Each program will work with this functionality in slightly different ways. For example, In Live's Session View you can drag the MIDI file directly onto any Clip Slot. In GarageBand you'll have to drag each MIDI file to a blank space on the Timeline and create a new track, then drag the MIDI sequence onto the track containing the iDrum instrument.

Battery

For even more control over your virtual drum sounds and performances, check out the Native Instruments Battery drum sampler. Battery goes above and beyond the basics of a simple drum machine and contains lots of editing features and intricate control over your drum sounds. Battery is moderately priced and available from http://www.native-instruments.com. It comes in AU, VST, RTAS, and stand-alone versions.

Like its cousin the Kontakt sampler, Battery can import an incredible range of file formats, so compatibility with any drum units or sample libraries you may have used in the past will be seamless. Battery also contains loop editing and playback, which means you can load Apple Loops, REX files and Acid/WAV loops directly into the Battery interface for editing and playback.

BATTERY BASICS

Battery comes with a 12GB collection of included drum kits and samples. These sounds range from jazz to rock to electronica and also include orchestral kits and other types of percussion. Battery can be further expanded by importing AIFF and WAV files, as well as EXS24, AKAI, and other sample, patch, and sound file formats.

When you start Battery for the first time you'll see the Audio/MIDI setup window that is familiar to you if you've installed any of the Native Instruments virtual instruments I've covered. Use the Audio and MIDI windows to set the output and MIDI settings for Battery in stand-alone mode.

LOADING AND PLAYING A DRUM KIT

The fastest way to use Battery is to load one of the included drum kits.

Figure 9.45 shows the Best of FM7 demo kit in the Battery interface.

FIGURE 9.45
Battery's interface

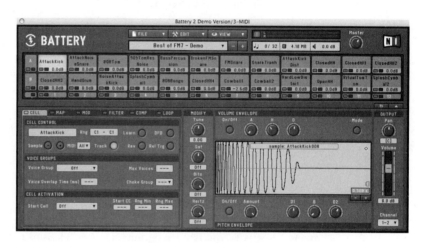

If you have a MIDI keyboard you can use it to play the different samples. You can also click any cell (the gray boxes with names like AttackKick and HandDrum) to preview the notes.

CREATING YOUR OWN DRUM KITS

Creating your own drum kit is one area in which Battery really combines simplicity for the basics with access to more complex functionality.

1. Start Battery as a stand-alone program.

2. Locate the folder MMA Audio\Battery on your hard drive.

3. Select a single file or multiple files and drag and drop the file(s) directly onto the Battery workspace.

   Each individual sample will be assigned to its own cell. You can rearrange the order of the cells by clicking and dragging with your mouse.

   Figure 9.46 shows the samples in each individual cell. You can view the properties for any individual cell by hovering over the cell with your mouse.

FIGURE 9.46
The new kit in the Battery workspace

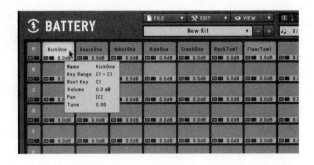

4. Select any cell and click View ➢ Cell Settings to view the individual cell's properties (Figure 9.47).

FIGURE 9.47
The Cell Settings window

5. Use the output section on the far right to adjust the volume and panning for the selected cell.

You can also create kits out of the included sample library, rearrange existing kits, and create hybrid kits from Battery's samples and samples from another source. You can create and save kits while using Battery as a plug-in virtual instrument as well as in stand-alone mode.

USING BATTERY IN YOUR DAW

As with most virtual instruments, you can create a performance in one of two ways: use your MIDI keyboard to play the instrument in real time, or create a performance using your DAW's MIDI note drawing functionality.

To get started:

1. Add Battery as a virtual instrument plug-in on any Instrument or MIDI track in your DAW host program.

2. Load one of the included kits or create your own.

3. Make sure your track is receiving MIDI information from your controller keyboard. This will vary from DAW to DAW but is usually determined by arming your track for recording.

Each drum sample in your kit corresponds to a specific MIDI note, which you can determine by holding your mouse over the sample's cell and viewing the cell's info pop-up window, as shown in Figure 9.48.

FIGURE 9.48
The cell info pop-up

From here you can follow the "Using a Virtual Drum Machine in Your DAW" instructions from the beginning of this section to create drum performances with Battery.

 **Real World Scenario**

CREATING A COMPLETE DEMO TRACK WITH IDRUM

For the musician who writes and demos his or her own original songs, creating drum tracks is probably the single biggest obstacle in the demo process. This can be especially frustrating considering how easy it's become to work with other real and virtual instruments. With a little work, a simple, inexpensive condenser microphone can capture high quality guitar and vocal performances. Many DAWs already include excellent sounding virtual samplers and synthesizers. Even guitar and bass tracks can be recorded directly into the simplest GarageBand session with high-quality results.

However, drum tracks are generally more complicated, especially for the musician (like myself) who doesn't have percussion or drumming experience. Drum loops and programs like BFD that contain MIDI drum performances can go a long way toward creating a good backing track. But, as I mentioned earlier, these kinds of tracks are not created with your song in mind. For the best results, you'll want to create your own drum tracks around your songs.

CREATE A CLICK TRACK

The first thing to do is figure out the tempo of your song. If your DAW contains a Tap Tempo feature (like the Tap Tempo button in Live), you can use your mouse to determine the tempo of your session. Otherwise, use your DAW's tempo adjustment functionality to raise and lower the session tempo.

Once you've established a tempo for your session, add a click track or activate your DAW's built-in click, then use your DAW's recording functionality to record your basic tracks.

ADD INSTRUMENTATION

At this stage, it's up to you to decide how complete you want to make your song or what instrumentation you want to include. For now, I recommend keeping it fairly simple and recording only the main elements. For example, a piano and vocal track or guitar and vocal track will be enough to start with. If you prefer more instrumentation, try adding a bass track since the bass and drum tracks will often influence each other.

PROGRAM THE DRUMS

Once your song is outlined and the basic arrangement is in place, you can begin to program the drums.

Add the iDrum to any empty Instrument or MIDI track in your DAW. You can use the included iDrum kits to create your track, but you will probably want to create your own kits, especially for rock or pop music. See the section "iDrum" in this chapter for information on creating your own drum kit.

At this point you'll want to take advantage of your DAW's looping functionality. If you have recorded your performance to a click track, you'll be able to play back sections of the song as loops. This functionality is covered in each of the DAW chapters and in Chapter 10, "Apple Loops."

We'll use Logic for this example.

Create a cycle region of the first four bars of the first verse. With the cycle region playing, start adding notes to the iDrum. First kick drum, then snare drum, then hi-hat. Basically, what you are able to do here is create an intricate drum performance based on this particular section of your song.

One of iDrum's coolest functions is the ability to create slight variations on the velocity of each drum hit by clicking and dragging inside the note.

By adding minor variations on the all of the drum hits, you can create a more human-sounding performance.

ADD THE DRUM TRACK TO YOUR SONG

Once you've created a loop that matches up with this section of the song, select the MIDI Drag button at the bottom left of the iDrum window and drag the MIDI sequence directly onto your DAW.

Before you play back the sequence, make sure to choose Clear Entire Pattern from iDrum's file menu. Otherwise the notes will be triggered twice: once by iDrum and once by your DAW.

From here, you can copy and paste your first drum pattern, or you can create a loop or cycle region of the next section of your song and create a new drum pattern. Every time you create a new drum pattern, it's a simple matter to use the MIDI drag function to add it to your MIDI or Instrument track, then move on to the next part of your song. At the very least, you'll probably want different patterns for your verse and chorus. For more intricate songs, you can create as many variations as you need.

Once you've created a drum track for your entire song, you can use your DAW's MIDI editing features to further edit or adjust your drum track.

Virtual Drummers

As I mentioned at the beginning of this chapter, an exciting and fairly recent development in the world of virtual instrumentation in the virtual drummer plug-in. These programs—such as Spectrasonic's Stylus and FXpansion's BFD drum module—all follow essentially the same concept. Sampled drum kits and percussion sounds and instruments are used to create lifelike performances that can be sequenced to follow your other instruments' performances. Each in its own way, these programs bring to your sessions the randomness and imperfection that makes a performance "human." They also offer exceptional control over the specific sounds that make up a drum performance, including detailed mixing capabilities.

BFD

BFD from FXpansion is one of the most popular virtual drum units available. BFD's strength is its ability to bring lifelike, realistic acoustic drum performances into the virtual environment. BFD offers an incredible range of control over the sounds that make up their virtual drum kits and comes with an expandable library of performances that covers a range of genres. BFD is relatively expensive. It's available from http://www.fxpansion.com. BFD works as an Audio Unit, RTAS, or VST plug-in and can also be used as a ReWire instrument. There is a demo version of BFD available at www.fxpansion.com. You must be using OS X 10.4 or higher to install and use the BFD demo.

Start BFD in stand-alone mode to get a look at some of its basic functions.

Figure 9.49 shows the BFD interface.

FIGURE 9.49
BFD

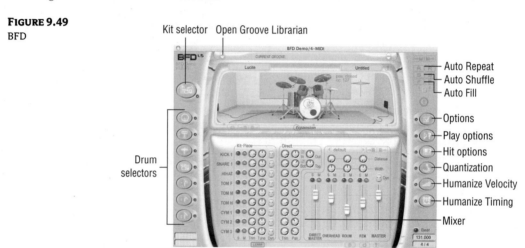

The Groove Librarian

There are multiple ways to use BFD; we'll take a quick look here at one of them. Click the Groove Librarian button in the top left of the interface.

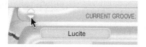

The Groove Librarian contains multiple drum performances in a variety of categories. Figure 9.50 shows the Grooves menu and the Fills menu.

FIGURE 9.50
The Groove Librarian

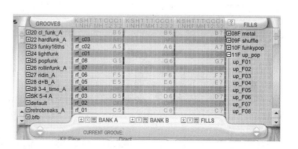

Preview a drum performance in the Groove Library by placing your mouse over the file in the Groove Library window. Click the green button that pops up to trigger the file.

On the left side of the Groove Librarian is a list of available grooves. These are groups of drum performances that can be sequenced to make up a complete track. Select any category by name with your mouse, then click and drag the category onto Bank A to view the included performances. Each category will have up to 12 performances. You can also drag a second set of grooves onto Bank B to have access to a wider selection.

On the right side of the Groove Librarian are the Fills collections. These correspond to the Grooves and can be dragged onto the Fills bank and previewed just like the grooves.

The Mixer

Before you take a look at the mixer, you need to get a beat playing so you have something to mix. At the top right of the BFD interface are the Auto Repeat, Auto Shuffle, and Auto Fill buttons for Bank A, Bank B, and the Fills bank.

Click the Auto Repeat button for Bank A, then select and trigger any drum performance in Bank A.

The performance will now loop itself until you click the red Stop button in the Groove Librarian window. (It replaced the green Start button as soon as you triggered the loop.)

At the bottom of the BFD interface is the mixing section of the BFD instrument. In the Kit Piece and Direct sections, you can control the volume and panning for each individual drum. This can be very useful, especially if you have specific ideas about how you want your drum performances to sound.

One of my favorite BFD features is section containing the five sliders on the right side of the interface.

The Direct Master slider controls the overall volume of the direct microphones. These are the microphones placed right up against the drums. The Overhead, Room, and PZM sliders are a big part of how BFD creates realistic drum sounds. These are flat condenser microphones that are taped or stuck to a floor, wall, or other surface. They are used in drum recording to pick up the sound of the room or environment where the recording is taking place. Many sampled drum kits include room sounds, and in many cases you can also create the illusion of "live" recording with reverb effects and panning, but it's still very difficult to take all of these elements and create a realistic performance and recording with a sampler or virtual drum machine.

BFD makes the process much easier. Essentially, what BFD contains is a meticulous virtual recreation of a really well-recorded drum session. The advantage here is that you can come up with great drum sounds for your sessions before you even start, then adjust, alter, and remix them as you go along, right up to your final mix.

With one of the performances from the Groove Librarian playing, try raising and lowering each slider to get an idea of what each one adds to the overall sound of the drums.

BFD in Your DAW

Once you've familiarized yourself with BFD's basic functionality, you can begin using the program as a plug-in in your DAW.

BFD can be used as a simple drum machine instrument, just like iDrum, Battery, or Ableton Live's Impulse drum machine (Chapter 3, "Ableton Live").

You'll find that with BFD (as with many virtual drum programs that can be triggered by MIDI information), the kit will start at C1 with the kick drum, moving up through the snare, hi-hats, and so on. You can use your MIDI keyboard to trigger the sounds of the kit and record performances in real time or draw a MIDI performance, as I covered in "Using a Virtual Drum Machine in Your DAW" at the beginning of this section.

However, one of the things that separates BFD from the standard virtual drum machine is the ability to use BFD's Groove Librarian in conjunction with your host programs sequencing ability. If you look closely at the Groove Librarian window you'll see that each drum performance in Bank A is assigned a MIDI note.

You can use these notes in your host program to sequence a series of drum performances into a complete song:

1. Add BFD to your host program on a MIDI or instrument track.

2. Click the Play Options button on the right side of the BFD interface to view the Play Options menu (Figure 9.51).

FIGURE 9.51
Set BFD's Play
Options.

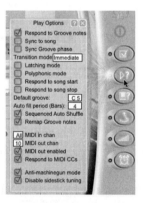

3. Make sure these boxes are *not* selected: Sync to Song, Latching Mode, Polyphonic Mode, Respond to Song Start, and Respond to Song Stop

   With any of these selected BFD will not play back correctly with your DAW.

4. Use BFD to create a performance as you would any virtual instrument. This is very similar to the method you would use to draw single notes, but instead of using your MIDI track to trigger single hits you'll use it trigger an entire groove.

One important thing to be aware of: The notes in the Groove Library actually correspond to notes two octaves lower on your MIDI keyboard and DAW, so C5 in the Groove Library will be triggered by C3 on your controller or in your DAW.

Figure 9.52 shows a four-measure sequence in Live.

FIGURE 9.52

A four-measure sequence in Live

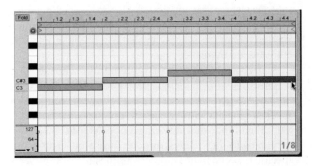

As Figure 9.52 shows, you'll want to drag your MIDI notes for the entire length of each measure. You can also create stop and starts by drawing your MIDI notes for shorter amounts of time.

By using performances from the Fills section of the Groove Librarian window you can create more rhythmic variation. These fills will be mapped out two octaves higher than the Bank A grooves.

BFD has lots more built-in functionality and is also expandable with collections and kits ranging from electronic to world music and beyond. FXpansion's website has videos and tutorials with more information about BFD and their other products as well.

MORE VIRTUAL DRUM PROGRAMS

The following are other virtual drum programs available for OS X. All are moderately priced.

- Addictive Drums (AU, VST, RTAS), `http://www.xlnaudio.com`

- Stylus (AU, VST, RTAS), `http://www.spectrasonics.net`

- Strike (RTAS), `http://www.digidesign.com`

- Groove Agent (AU, VST, ReWire), `http://www.steinberg.com`

Virtual Amplifiers

The world of virtual amplification has gotten a lot more interesting in the last few years with the increase in availability and popularity of hardware components added to software-based amplification programs. As a result not only are virtual amplifiers becoming more common in the recording studio, but many guitar players are finding it easier to plug their axes into a laptop and access the many presets and self-made patches in a system like Logic's Guitar Amp Pro and Native Instruments' Guitar Rig.

Many rock artists like Queens of the Stone Age, Weezer, and Aerosmith are incorporating virtual amplification into their live and recorded performances.

How Virtual Amps Work

Virtual amplifiers generally mimic the way "real world" amplification and recording setups work but with some minor differences. In the real world you'd probably choose your amp first, then add effects, then bring it down to the recording studio and decide how you want to place microphones around it to get the desired recording. Once your recording is complete you can make adjustments with EQ, compression, reverb, and other effects, but for the most part the core elements of your recording are set in stone. With virtual amps you're more likely to start with a preset combination of amps, microphones, and effects; deal with microphone placement (modeling); and then add and subtract elements at any time during the recording or mixing process. This kind of flexibility can be a good thing, allowing you to significantly alter your guitar sounds at any time during the process. Having too many choices can also be a problem, especially when multiple musicians with multiple opinions are involved.

Many virtual amps come with multiple choices for amplifier configuration including combo amps (everything in a single unit) and "stacks," which separate the speaker cabinet form the amplifier head. Stacks are customizable, allowing you to choose different types of amp heads and speaker cabinets to achieve different tones. Often for trademark reasons, the actual names of the amplifier brands that are being replicated cannot be used. These brand names are often replaced by euphemisms, nicknames, or other indicators. You'll also find that included presets often reference specific players, bands, and sometimes recordings with names like "Edge-y," "Jimi-fied," and "Bring the Hammett Down." If you'd like to approximate the guitar setup used by a specific player, you may want to check out your virtual amps preset list to see if there's already a preset with the artist's name on it.

Microphone modeling is used to approximate the different sounds achieved by using different kinds of microphones and placing them in different locations in relation to the amp's speakers. The most common choices you will have are dynamic or condenser microphone and centered or off-axis microphone placement:

◆ Dynamic microphones are used for close miking.

◆ Condenser microphones can be used for close or distant miking and are often placed at to distance to create roomier, ambient sounds.

◆ Centered means placing the microphone directly in front of the speaker cone for a clearer more precise sound.

◆ Off-axis means placing the microphone away from the center of the speaker cone, creating a different, sometimes less harsh tone.

Effects are basically plug-ins within a plug-in. One of the great things about working with virtual amps is the ability to try out endless different effect configurations without having to buy a huge collection of expensive effects pedals. However, keep in mind when you're setting out to become a virtual Billy Corgan that the same order of effects rules that work in the analog world will apply in the digital world as well. As with any recording "rules," these were certainly made to be broken in the name of experimentation, but generally when working with guitar effects you can achieve good results by placing them in the following order:

◆ Distortion

◆ Modulation effects like phaser and flanger

◆ Compression/limiting

◆ EQ

◆ Delays and reverbs

Some virtual amplifiers will set the order of effects in such a way that it can't be changed. Other will let you customize the settings in any way you like.

Setting Up a Virtual Amplifier in Your DAW

Virtual amplifiers will be used in much the same way that plug-in effects are used: you'll add them to your tracks as inserted effects. Some virtual amplification software will have its own software that is added to your sessions through the use of ReWire.

COMMON PROBLEMS WITH VIRTUAL AMPLIFICATION

Probably the biggest difficulty with virtual amplification is the problem of creating realistic, natural-sounding guitar tracks with digital tools. Amplifier, room, and microphone modeling has certainly come a long way in the last decade, but there's some question (certainly in my mind) as to whether or not any software program will ever be able to truly simulate the combination of a Gibson or Fender guitar being played through a vintage amplifier in a big room, recorded through well-placed microphones and tube pre-amps into an analog tape machine.

That's a lot to expect from a bunch of 1s and 0s.

Another common complaint about virtual amp software is that the presets and amplifier configurations are either not what they claim to be or just don't sound very good. A lot of this has to do with the fact that there are so many different guitar/pickup/setup configurations. A preset that sounded great when it was created by a guy playing a Telecaster with a hot-wired, single coil pickup is going to sound very different when you plug in your Les Paul with Classic '57 humbuckers or your seven-string Steve Vai model Ibanez with active pickups.

What I'm getting at here is that what you get out of your virtual amplification software (and hardware) will greatly depend both on what you are expecting and the time and energy you are willing to invest in creating the sounds you want. You can create some great sounds, but if replicating analog guitar recordings is your goal, you are probably better off investing in the ability to record live guitars.

IN LIVE

To use virtual amplification plug-ins in Ableton Live:

1. Locate the manufactures folder (Native Instruments, Waves, and so on) in the Plug-in Device Browser window.

2. Drag the amp you want to use from the Plug-in Device Browser onto an audio track or create a new audio track by dragging the plug-in onto any empty space in the Clip/Device Drop area.

3. Select your input from the drop-down menu and arm the track for recording.

4. Select a preset or create your own amp configuration.

IN PRO TOOLS

To use virtual amplification plug-ins in Pro Tools:

1. Create a new mono or stereo audio track.

2. Add the virtual amplifier as an insert.

3. Arm the track for recording in order to preview the sound.

4. Select a preset or create your own amp configuration.

You can also add virtual amplification in Pro Tools by adding the plug-in as an insert on any instrument or aux track. In all versions of Pro Tool 7, virtual amplifiers will generally be located in the Plug-in ➤ Instrument directory.

IN LOGIC

To use virtual amplification plug-ins in Logic Pro or Logic Express:

1. Select any audio track.

2. Make sure your guitar or bass is routed to the track.

3. Add your virtual amplifier as a plug-in insert on the track.

4. Arm the track for recording to preview the sound.

5. Select a preset or create an amplifier configuration.

IN GARAGEBAND

To use virtual amplification plug-ins in GarageBand:

1. Select Track ➢ New Track and create a new Real Instrument track.

2. Double-click the track header to open the Track Info window.

3. Open Details view at the bottom of the Track Info window.

4. Click the first Effects drop-down menu.

5. Choose your virtual amp from the list.

6. Click the Edit Preset button to view the instrument, load patches, or edit the instrument.

Virtual Amp Options

Virtual amplifiers come in a variety of packages. The simpler programs can be as easy to use as plugging them into your tracks and pressing Record. The more complicated programs can involve setting up complex amplifier and effects routings. In this next section you'll get a look at both ends of the virtual amplifier spectrum.

GUITAR COMBOS

One very cool option for guitar players who don't need all the bells and whistles of more complicated virtual amplifier software is the Native Instruments Guitar Combos software. Each Guitar Combos amp replicates the sound of a well-known amplifier. The Twang Combo is based on the Fender Twin (country, jazz), the Plexi Combo are based on the Marshall JMP50 (loud rock, metal), and the AC Box Combo is based on the Vox AC30 (pop, rock). They all work as either as stand-alones or as plug-ins in your VST, RTAS, and Audio Unit programs.

The inexpensive Guitar Combos are available from http://www.native-instruments.com. Thirty-day demo versions with a thirty-minute time limit and saving disabled are available for download.

Figure 9.53 shows the Twang Combo.

The Guitar Combos are extremely easy to use. Just add the amplifier as an insert effect, arm your track for recording, and start playing. The included presets are all listed right on the front of the speaker grille interface and are also available from the large drop-down menu on the left just above the speaker grille. Click any preset name to load and play it. You can create your own tones from scratch by selecting an unused preset number. You can easily modify an existing preset and save the new version by clicking the Save As button. Each combo has an included instrument tuner on the right side of the interface, just above the speaker grille. Next to the tuner is a button you can use to resize the plug-in by hiding the speaker grille and preset list.

FIGURE 9.53

The Twang Combo

If you are looking for a great-sounding, simple way to replicate one or two popular amp models, the Guitar Combos make a good choice. If you want more tone and effects options, you can also use the Guitar Combos in tandem with any third-party or DAW effects you have in your collection.

GUITAR RIG 2

The Native Instruments Guitar Rig 2 is one of the most complete guitar interfaces available. The Amplifier selection includes virtual recreations of Marshall, Fender, Mesa, and Vox amplifiers. The amp collection is augmented by a huge selection of speaker cabinets in just about every conceivable size and shape. Guitar Rig's microphone selection also goes well beyond much of the competition with virtual versions of many well-known dynamic and condenser models. Guitar Rig also contains a huge collection of virtual effects, from modern to vintage. In addition to the amp, cabinet, effects, and microphone selection, Guitar Rig adds other useful components including a tuner, metronome, and a built-in recording device.

Guitar Rig is available from `http://www.native-instruments.com` in two versions, either as software only (moderately priced) or with an included foot controller (expensive). It works as an AU, VST, or RTAS plug-in or as a stand-alone program. A 30-day demo version with a 30-minute time limit and saving disabled is available for download.

Using Guitar Rig

Add Guitar Rig as an insert effect to any audio track in your DAW, then arm the track for recording.

Figure 9.54 shows the Guitar Rig interface.

The Guitar Rig interface is divided into two sections. The right side of the interface contains the all of the elements that make up the current amplifier preset including the amplifier, cabinet, microphones, and any include effects. Near the top is a section marked Control Center. In the Control Center filed you can choose presets and show or hide the tape decks, tuner, and metronome elements in the current preset configuration. Just to the left of the control center is the Show/Hide Left Frame button, which you can use to resize the Guitar Rig interface. On the left side of the interface you can select and manage presets, create your own amplifier setups, and set the parameters for the Guitar Rig hardware controller.

FIGURE 9.54
Guitar Rig

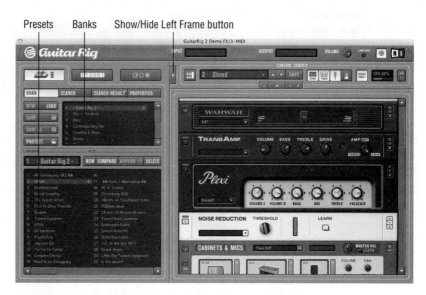

Once you've got a signal going, I recommend trying out some of the presets. You can select from one of the 14 preset banks, then choose a preset from the list. As you try out new presets, check out the various amp/speaker cabinet/effects configurations as they appear on the left side of the interface. You'll have to use the scroll bar on the far right to see all of the included components. In most cases you'll see a pretty intricate configuration of elements.

Create Your Own Amplifiers

To create a new amplifier with Guitar Rig:

1. Click the New button at the top of the Presets field. If you are working with the demo version you'll get a pop-up that says "You cannot save presets." Ignore this for now.

2. Hide the tape decks and tuner by clicking the Show/Hide Tape Deck buttons in the Control Center field.

3. Click the Show All Available Component button. Figure 9.55 shows the Available Components window.

   The Available Components window contains eight tabs. Each tab contains one of the elements that makes up a virtual amplifier configuration in Guitar Rig.

4. Double-click any Amp model to add it to your preset. Select an amp setting preset from the drop-down menu on the left side of the amp head or use your mouse to adjust the settings manually.

   When you add an amp model to your preset, Guitar Rig will automatically create what it thinks is the best speaker cabinet/microphone configuration. You can keep the default setting or change it by using the Cabinets & Mics drop-down menu to choose a different configuration. You can also use the scroll buttons next to each element to choose a new cabinet, microphone position, or microphone type. Figure 9.56 shows Guitar Rig's Plexi amp and default cabinet/microphone configuration.

FIGURE 9.55
The Plexi amp and default cabinet/microphone configuration

FIGURE 9.55
The Plexi amp and default cabinet/microphone configuration

The next five tabs in the Components window contain Guitar Rig's effect and audio processing components.

FIGURE 9.56
The Components window

1. Click any tab to view the available effects. Double-click any effect to add it to your new preset.

2. Return to the Manage Presets and Banks view and (assuming you're not using the demo version) select Save to overwrite the current preset or Save As to create a new preset.

With such a vast number of possibilities for creating amp setups, you are pretty much guaranteed to find the tone you are looking for if you have the time and inclination to get there. Guitar Rig's extras, including the tape decks and the Loop Machine component, add even more levels of creative possibility as well.

AMPLITUBE 2

AmpliTube 2 is another virtual amplifier with an awesome range of possibilities. With virtual representations of all of the world's most popular amplifiers, cabinets, and effects units, AmpliTube 2 also lets you get "under the hood" to construct your own amplifiers by mixing and matching preamps, EQs, and power amps from different sources to create your own original hybrid amplifiers.

Combined with 21 virtual stomp boxes and 11 virtual rack effects, AmpliTube 2 puts virtually unlimited sound sculpting at your fingertips. The moderately priced Amplitube 2 is available from http://www.amplitube.com. There's a fully functioning demo version available that's good for 30 starts or 10 days and requires a Syncrosoft USB key. AmpliTube 2 is available in AU, VST, RTAS, and stand-alone formats.

I like Amplitube 2 for its natural guitar sounds. As I mentioned earlier, one of the biggest difficulties in using virtual amplification is coming up with realistic guitar tones that don't sound overly processed or unnaturally digital. Amplitube 2 really delivers on that front.

Creating a Realistic Amp Sound

As a way to get familiar with Amplitube 2, I'll walk you through the process I used to create what I think is one of the best virtual amplifier tones I've heard. If you're looking for a different sort of tone you can follow these same instructions substituting the amplifiers, microphones, and effects with your choices.

1. Add AmpliTube 2 to any audio track in your DAW. Figure 9.57 shows the Amplitube 2 plug-in.

    Clicking the Preset selector at the top of the Amplitube 2 window opens up a menu with a list of preset groups; within each group are lists of categories and presets in various styles and configurations. We're going to start with a basic amplifier configuration.

FIGURE 9.57
The Amplitube 2
virtual amp plug-in

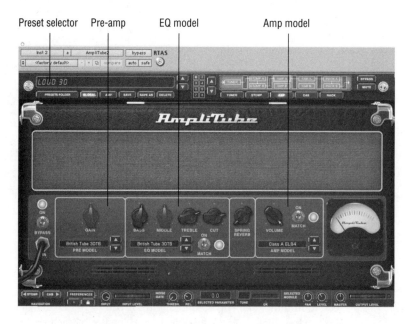

2. Use the Preset menu to select Pure Amps ➤ British Tube 30B ➤ Loud 30. This is the amplifier shown in Figure 9.57.

   The three main fields on the face of the amplifier are Pre Model (pre-amp), EQ Model, and Amp Model. These are three components that make up a hardware amplifier. With Amplitube 2 you can use the arrow buttons in each field to mix and match different components, taking a pre-amp from one source, an EQ from another, and an Amp Model from yet another.

3. At the bottom left of the interface are the navigation buttons. Click the Cab button to see the cabinet and microphone settings.

4. The Speaker Model and Mic Model fields (Figure 9.58) both have arrow buttons you can use to mix and match speaker configurations and microphone settings. Amplitube 2 contains virtual representations of many of the most commonly used microphones for guitar recording.

FIGURE 9.58
Amplitube 2's Speaker and Microphone modeling

5. Click the Rack navigation button to view the virtual Rack window.

6. Select any of the four available racks and click the field marked Empty to view the available rack effects. Add the rack effect EQ & Dynamics ➤ Tube Compressor.

7. Click the Tuner navigation button to view the included tuner.

8. Click the Stomp navigation button to view the Stomp Box window. This very similar to the Rack window but geared more toward effects commonly associated with foot pedals.

9. Add any stomp effects by clicking an empty slot and selecting an effect from the pop-up menu. I particularly like the pedals that are approximate recreations of vintage effects like the Fuzz Age, the Phazer10, and the EchoMan delay pedal (Figure 9.59).

10. Click the Amp navigation button to go back to the original amp interface.

11. Click the Save As button to store your new preset for future use.

Endless Possibilities

Right next to the presets field at the top of the interface there are eight small numbered buttons.

FIGURE 9.59
Amplitube 2's vintage
effects pedals

Each of these buttons represents a different configuration and routing of Amplitube 2's available amplifiers and stomp boxes. Just to the right of the eight buttons you can actually see the routing change as you click each button.

Combine these routing possibilities with all of Amplitube 2's amp wiring, cabinet choices, and rack and stomp box effects and you can see that Amplitube 2 has a pretty incredible range of possible configurations.

Line 6

Line 6 makes a range of products geared toward the guitar player. Originally a hardware amplifier manufacturer, Line 6 introduced the popular Pod guitar interface in 1997. The Pod became popular with home studio guitarists because of its faithful recreation of a large number of guitar tones in a portable package. Both the original and rack-mounted versions of the Pod also found their way into many live guitar rigs, in some cases replacing hardware amplifiers altogether.

Line 6 guitar-based digital products include:

◆ Guitarport

◆ TonePort

◆ GearBox

◆ RiffTracker

◆ Riffworks

While Line 6's guitars and amplifiers are definitely geared toward a more professional clientele, their software products and hardware interfaces seem to be aimed directly at the guitar-focused amateur home studio owner. If guitar is your primary (or only) instrument, then the Line 6 series is worth checking out.

More Virtual Amps

The following are some of the other virtual amplifier plug-ins available for OS X.

Waves GTR (AU, VST, RTAS, TDM), `http://www.waves.com`   A top-of-the-line virtual amplifier plug-in suite from Waves that comes with 10 virtual amplifiers, 23 virtual effects, and a hardware interface.

Nomad Factory Rock Amp Legends (AU, VST, RTAS), `http://www.nomadfactory.com` Nomad Factory, working with former Aerosmith guitarist Jimmy Crespo, created a moderately priced virtual amp plug-in that falls somewhere between the simple straightforward Guitar Combos and the more complicated programs like Amplitube 2 and Guitar Rig.

AmpliTube SVX (AU, VST, RTAS, stand-alone), `http://www.amplitube.com`   Demo version: 30 starts or 10 days, requires Syncrosoft USB key. Although it's on the expensive side, for many bass players, especially in the hard rock genres, Ampeg represents the best of the bass amp manufacturers. AmpliTube SVX puts an Ampeg bass rig inside your DAW.

AmpliTube Live/LE (AU, VST, RTAS, stand-alone) `http://www.amplitube.com`   The inexpensive AmpliTube LE is included with all versions of Pro Tools Basic; instructions for using AmpliTube LE are in Chapter 4.

Virtual Instrument Bundles

Like plug-in effects bundles, virtual instrument bundles can be an excellent way to acquire a collection of compatible instruments at a good price. Virtual instrument packages can be light versions of a company's more expensive instruments or full versions of multiple programs sold in quantity at a discount rate.

Reaktor

While at its core Reaktor contains a modular synth program, there are so many other features and ways of working within the Reaktor environment that it goes well beyond the limits of being just a synthesizer. Although on the expensive side, Reaktor comes with over 60 instruments and plug-ins, including synthesizers, drum machines, and audio effects. Each module or component can be used within Reaktor in conjunction with other Reaktor components or on its own as a plug-in virtual instrument or effect. What's even more amazing is that within the Reaktor environment you can reverse engineer any module. Reaktor's manipulability can lead to all kinds of creative possibilities, and many Reaktor users create and share their own instruments. The full version of Reaktor is available from `http://www.native-instruments.com` or your local retailer or online store.

Komplete

Komplete is the most comprehensive (and therefore the most expensive) software package available from Native Instruments. It's 12 of NI's most popular software titles bundled together. Komplete includes:

◆ Reaktor 5: Modular sound design studio

◆ Absynth 4 Synthesizer

◆ Guitar Rig 2: Virtual guitar amp

- Kontakt 2: Sampler

- Battery 3: Drum sampler

- Akoustik Piano: Four virtual pianos

- Elektrik Piano: Four electric pianos

- B4 II: Virtual organ

- FM-8: FM synthesizer

- Pro 53: Analog synth emulation

- Vocator: Vocoder effect

- NI Spektral Delay: Delay effect

Pluggo and Hipno

The Pluggo and Hipno plug-in suites (both covered in Chapter 8) also contain a number of synthesizers, drum samplers, and other instruments that can be used in any Audio Unit, VST, or RTAS-compatible host program.

Pluggo and Hipno are moderately priced and are available in downloaded and packaged versions from `http://www.cycling74.com`.

Steinberg Studio Case II

Studio Case II is a combination of Steinberg's Cubase SE DAW software and SE (light versions) of many of Steinberg's VST virtual instrument plug-ins. Studio Case II includes:

- Groove Agent SE

- Virtual Bassist SE

- Virtual Guitarist SE

- The Grand SE virtual piano

- Halion SE virtual sampler

Studio Case II is a good introduction to Steinberg's virtual instruments. All of the included instruments are upgradeable to their full versions at a discounted price. Studio Case II is available from `http://www.steinberg.net`.

All of the included VST instruments can be used in any DAW program that supports VST plug-ins.

The Bottom Line

Use virtual instruments in your host DAW program DAW sequencer programs like Live, Logic, GarageBand, and Pro Tools can take advantage of third-party virtual instruments to create musical performances. Each program handles virtual instrumentation in similar ways, but there are some variations from program to program.

Master It Add a virtual synthesizer or keyboard instrument to a track in your DAW and create a simple performance.

Create basic patches and presets with virtual synthesizers   Every virtual synthesizer comes with its own set of included presets, but understanding how synthesizers generate sounds and knowing how to create your own patches gives you much greater control over the creative process.

Master It   Use Rob Papen's Blue synthesizer to create a simple patch with an oscillator, low pass filter, and an effect. You can download Blue or the Blue demo from `http://www.robpapen.com`.

Create drum loops with iDrum   Izotope's iDrum program is the perfect tool for quickly creating simple or complex drum loops. You can export your iDrum loops and save them for use in future projects, or you can string together a series of loops to create an entire backing track.

Master It   Create and export a simple drum loop with iDrum.

Create a drum performance in your DAW with a virtual drum machine   Virtual drum machines like Izotope's iDrum and Native Instruments' Battery can create complete drum tracks in your DAW host program.

Master It   Use any virtual drum machine as a plug-in virtual instrument to create a simple drum performance in your DAW.

Chapter 10

Apple Loops

While repetition has long been incorporated into many different styles of music, looping is a fairly new innovation. Looping was first used in early electronic music, such as the experimental Music Concrete in the 1950s and then by early electronic composers like Steve Reich. Some of the early loop-based experiments were accomplished by splicing audio tape and creating a "closed loop" with a tape machine. Experimental and ambient musicians like Brian Eno and Robert Fripp experimented with a variety of tape-based looping techniques in the 1970s and 80s.

In the 1980s, digital sampling began to mimic many of the same effects created by tape loops. Around the same time hip-hop DJs began developing scratching techniques with vinyl records to create repeated rhythmic patterns. Meanwhile, in the recording studio, sections of popular disco songs were looped and then used as the background for early rap hits.

When Sonic Foundry introduced its Acid program (now owned by Sony Media) in 1999, the looping process changed dramatically. Looping functions, which had previously been the result of laborious work with a hardware sampler or tape machine, could now be accomplished quickly and seamlessly by a computer in mere seconds.

Unfortunately Mac users weren't able to get in on the action right away. After patiently waiting (or in my case, impatiently and painfully trying to run Acid with Virtual PC), Bitshift Audio introduced the Phazer looping program in 2001. While Phazer served a valuable role, it never quite caught on with Mac users. Ableton Live (see Chapter 3, "Ableton Live") did catch on, however, bringing time-stretching and pitch-shifting solidly to the Mac users digital music palette. This was followed by Apple including similar looping functions within GarageBand and Logic. Looping in general and Apple Loops in particular are now an indispensable part of many Mac-based studios, regardless of genre or professional capacity.

In this chapter, you will learn to:

◆ Convert any WAV or AIFF file into an Apple Loop

◆ Batch Convert WAV or AIFF files into Apple Loops

◆ Create new Apple Loops in any DAW program

◆ Export loops from any DAW program

What Apple Loops Are

The term *Apple Loops* specifically refers to a loop format created by Apple and originally used with its Soundtrack program, which is included with Final Cut Video editing software. Soundtrack allows nonmusicians to create musical accompaniment for video projects. Apple Loops were then incorporated into the GarageBand program, introduced with iLife '04 in 2004.

There are two different types of Apple Loops: Software Instrument loops and Real Instrument loops. Software Instrument loops are basically MIDI files that also contain other information that tells the host program to load and play a specific software instrument and specific effects. Software Instrument loops can be used in GarageBand, Logic Express, and Logic Pro. They can also be used in other programs like Pro Tools and Ableton Live, though they will automatically be converted to standard AIFF files when they are imported.

Real Instrument loops are sound files made up of a specific performance, usually of a single instrument.

Both Software Instrument and Real Instrument Apple Loops contain extra information known as metadata. This information tells the host program (such as GarageBand or Logic) how to play back and categorize the file. Most Apple Loops contain the following metadata:

- Tempo

- Transients (where to divide the loop)

- Time signature

- Key/scale type

- Genre

- Instrument

- Descriptors

You can use this included metadata to locate Apple Loop files in GarageBand or Logic's Loop Browser.

Since Apple Loops are essentially AIFF files, they can be imported or added to any DAW program or session. In Ableton Live for example, Apple Loops will be treated exactly the same as WAV loops or any other audio file.

Other Loop Formats

Just as Apple Loops can be used in programs like Live and Pro Tools, non-Apple Loops can also be used in Apple's GarageBand and Logic programs.

Most audio loops will be in either AIFF or WAV format, and either format can be used in just about any looping program, regardless of operating system. For example, Sony Media's PC-based Acid program uses Acid Loops, which are WAV files encoded with their own kind of metadata. Acid can also play back Apple Loops and any other AIFF files.

REX Loops

REX Loops are created in Propellerhead's ReCycle program for use in Reason's Dr. Rex Loop Player. Because of the flexibility and popularity of REX loops, more and more programs (including Pro Tools and Logic) are adding the ability to recognize and play back .rx2 (REX) files. For programs that don't recognize REX files, you can use software like AudioFinder or Sample Manager (both covered in Chapter 7, "More Really Useful Software") to convert REX files to AIFF or WAV.

Acid Loops

The Acid Loops format was created for use in Sony Media's looping audio program Acid. They are essentially the PC equivalent of Apple Loops. Like Apple Loops, Acid Loops contain metadata that allows the Acid program to read them. The process of turning WAV files into Acid Loops is called Acidizing and is done in the Sony Media program Sound Forge. Acidized Loops can be used just like Apple Loops in GarageBand, Logic, and Live.

Acid Loops can be especially useful in Pro Tools, where many (though not all) Acidized files can be imported automatically at the current session's tempo by dragging and dropping from the Finder directly onto the Timeline.

Buying Loops

There is a vast market out there for loops and, as a result, you may have a hard time deciding which loop libraries you would like to buy. Sites like `http://www.iCompositions.com` and `http://www .sonymediasoftware.com` have free loops from a variety of loop libraries that you can try, as do many websites with loop libraries for sale. Even if they don't offer actual samples, many sites have MP3 or streaming audio versions of their products.

From personal experience, I can tell you that it is a good idea to avoid buying any loop collections based solely on descriptions or even user reviews. One person's idea of "good-sounding" loops may vary greatly from another person's. Very often loops that are entirely appropriate for one genre or style can be totally useless in a different setting.

While it's not necessary to buy only Apple Loop libraries if you are using GarageBand or Logic, it's a good idea to look for them first, as they will be easier to catalog and locate in those program's Loop Browser utilities. While many excellent libraries are only available in a single format, it is rapidly becoming standard procedure for many companies to offer multiple formats in order to appeal to the widest possible audience.

Here are some basic buying guidelines for purchasing loop libraries.

Whenever possible, buy 24-bit loops   All currently available Apple computers are capable of playing back 24-bit loops, the highest quality available. This doesn't mean you should never buy 16-bit loops; they'll be just fine for all of your projects. But if 24-bit is available, go for it.

Ableton Live users   Purchase either Apple Loops or Acidized WAV files. Either format will work equally well in Live.

Logic users   Your first choice should be Apple Loops. You can also use Acidized WAV format loops in your Logic sessions. Logic also includes support for REX files, but they aren't as easy to use as Apple Loops and Acid Loops. You can also buy Acidized loop libraries and batch convert them with the Apple Loops Utility, which I'll cover later in this chapter.

GarageBand users   Whenever possible, use Apple Loops. GarageBand does include support for Acidized WAV files, and many of them will work. However, you may have a hard time locating some Acid files with the Loop Browser. It's possible to buy a library of Acidized WAV files and batch convert them with the Apple Loops Utility.

Pro Tools users   At this time, REX format loops may be your best bet when working in Pro Tools. I much prefer working with Acidized WAV files, but because of their inconsistencies they are not always the best choice. As of this writing, Apple Loops are not supported by Pro Tools and will import only as regular audio files.

Read the License

The vast majority of loop collections you purchase will be royalty free. This means that when you purchase the collection you are allowed to use all the loops contained in the collection for whatever music projects you like. This includes work you are paid for, such as commercially released songs and movie and television soundtrack work. (The usual exception is that you can't resell the loops as part of a collection.) In fact, once you have become familiar with some of the more popular loop libraries, it's not at all uncommon to begin hearing familiar loops on television shows and radio broadcasts.

Generally, the license included with the loop collection will grant you all of the aforementioned rights. In some cases a distinction is made about using an unaltered loop by itself as a commercially available work.

However—and this is extremely important—not all loop library manufacturers have the same licenses. In fact, I was very surprised a couple of years ago to find that I had just paid a fairly substantial amount of money for a loop library that specifically denied owners the right to use their loops in any commercial works without notifying and crediting the company that created the library. Needless to say, those loops don't show up in any of my projects.

For this reason it is a very good idea to read any included licenses very carefully and to keep your loop collections as organized as possible.

ORGANIZING LOOP COLLECTIONS

Organizing my loop collections used to be a real problem for me and sometimes still is. I've tried a number of methods: organizing by style, instrument, and so on. I've found that the best method for me is to keep the folders organized by manufacturer. When I need to access a specific style or instrument I can use AudioFinder (see Chapter 7) to perform my searches.

Free Loops

The Internet is a great resource for collections of free loops. These generally fall into two different categories:

Previews of larger collections   These are loops made available by companies or individuals who are selling larger collections of loops. This is a great way to get a feel for a particular loop library or the style and quality of the loops created by a specific company. It's very important to remember that in many of these cases the included loops are not royalty free. If you decide to use them in a commercially available song you are well advised to actually buy the collection. That way you are granted the appropriate license as well.

Genuinely free loops   These are loops that are created and uploaded by kind souls, possibly with too much time on their hands (just kidding), or by companies that are offering free loops to drive traffic to their site(s). My experience with genuinely free loops is that you get what you pay for, which is to say, not so much.

Apple Loops Utility

The Apple Loops Utility is a free program that you can use to create Apple Loops by adding metadata to AIFF loop files. It's especially useful as a final step in the loop creation process. It can also be set up to automatically convert WAV files to Apple Loops, either one at a time or through its batch conversion process.

RESOURCES FOR FREE AND COMMERCIAL LOOPS

The following sites are resources for loops in a variety of formats. Some sites have free downloads, including previews of larger collections.

◆ Beta Monkey Drums, `http://www.betamonkeymusic.com`

◆ Apple's Jam Packs, `http://www.apple.com/jampacks`

◆ Samples4, `http://www.samples4.com`

◆ Mac Idol, `http://www.macidol.com`

◆ Zero G, `http://www.zero-g.co.uk`

◆ Big Fish Audio, `http://www.bigfishaudio.com`

◆ iCompositions, `http://www.icompositions.com`

◆ Acid Planet, `http://www.acidplanet.com`

◆ Sony Media Software, `http://www.sonymediasoftware.com`

◆ Drums On Demand, `http://www.drumsondemand.com`

There are also a number of free loops and samples available under what's known as Creative Commons licenses. You can learn more about Creative Commons and locate download loops and samples from their website `creativecommons.org`.

You can download the Apple Loops Utility as part of the Apple Loops SDK Developer Kit from `http://developer.apple.com/sdk/`. Scroll about halfway down the page to download the Apple Loops SDK file.

Let's use the Apple Loops Utility to get a close look at the metadata that makes up an Apple Loop:

1. Once the program is downloaded and installed, locate the program in your `Applications` folder and double-click the icon to start it.

2. When the Apple Loops Utility starts, it immediately opens the Search window so you can load a file. Use this window to locate the folder `MMA Audio\Apple Loops Utility\Apple Loops`, which is part of this book's companion DVD.

3. Select the file `AppleLoop14.aif` and click Open.

4. If the Assets window is not showing, make it visible by clicking the Assets button in lower left corner.

   You can also open files in the Apple Loops Utility by manually dragging and dropping them onto the Assets window.

5. In the main window of the Apple Loops Utility shown in Figure 10.1, you can see all of the fields already populated with the metadata that make this an Apple Loop.

FIGURE 10.1

The Apple
Loops Utility

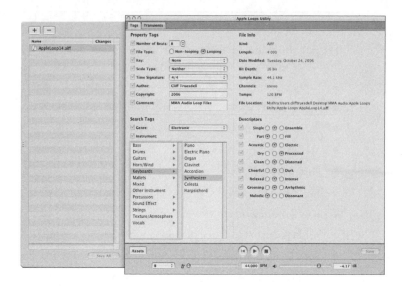

Inside View of an Apple Loop

The Apple Loops Utility's main window gives you access to all of the metadata that makes an AIFF file into an Apple Loop. Much of this information can also be added to or edited in the various fields. We'll take a closer look here at each section and how the included metadata affects the organization and playback of each Apple Loop.

Property Tags The Property tags gives the loop's musical information, such as key and time signature. You can also see other information such as the loop creator's name, copyright information, or any comments.

ONE-SHOTS AND LOOPS

Probably the single most important piece of information about an Apple Loop is the file type, near the top of the Property Tags list. This is where you decide whether the file is a loop or not. By selecting Non-looping, you create a "one-shot," which is a sound file that will be played once at its original tempo. One-shots are useful when creating samples from individual instrument "hits" like a snare drum hit or a piano note. Another common one-shot is a spoken word sample from a movie or television show.

File Info The File Info section tells you what kind of file you are currently working with (WAV or AIFF), along with its bit depth and sample rate, the tempo, and whether or not the file is mono or stereo. At the bottom of the File Info section is information about the location of the currently selected file. None of the information in this field can be changed with the Apple Loops Utility.

Search Tags In the Search Tags section you'll select the loop's genre (or a close approximation) and the instrument category and specific instrument type, where applicable.

Descriptors The Descriptors section further categorizes your Apple Loops. GarageBand and Logic use your selections in this section to organize your loops in their respective Loop Browsers.

At the bottom of the window is the Transport bar, which contains the very basic controls Rewind, Play, and Stop. At the very bottom of the interface are the Tempo and Volume sliders. These sliders can be used to preview tempo and volume changes to your files but have no effect on the actual Apple Loop file.

Converting an AIFF File to an Apple Loop

Converting an AIFF file to an Apple Loop in the Apple Loops Utility is as simple as opening the file, changing any parameter, and clicking the Save button. However, to get the most out of your Apple Loops, you will probably want to change more than a single setting. Generally speaking, as a bare minimum for every Apple Loop you'll want to:

◆ Make sure Looping is selected in the File Type field.

◆ Choose a genre.

◆ Select the appropriate instrument category and instrument.

◆ Select at least one descriptor.

For your own original loops you will also want to include your name or organization in the Author field, any copyright information in the Copyright field, and other information, such as a website URL, in the Comments field.

Adjusting Transients

Click the Transients tab to view the Transients window shown in Figure 10.2.

FIGURE 10.2
The Transients
window

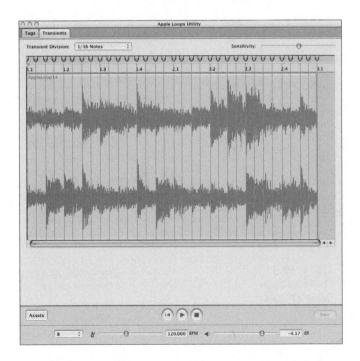

Transients are similar to slices in REX files. They are the points at which your host program will divide the loop for time-stretching and contracting. How the loop plays back when time-stretched or contracted will depend on how the transients are set.

The Apple Loops Utility usually does a pretty good job of setting transients by default. To get an idea of how the transient settings affect an Apple Loop:

1. Drag the file `AppleLoop15.AIFF` from the `MMA Audio\Apple Loops Utility\Apple Loops` folder directly onto the Assets window.

2. Select the file in the Assets window.

3. Click the Transients tab.

   The transients for this file have been automatically set at $\frac{1}{16}$. Basically, the Apple Loops Utility has detected each note change and used that to assign a transient.

4. Adjust the Tempo slider to play back the `AppleLoop15.aiff` file at its default tempo of 120BPM.

5. Use the Tempo slider to raise the play back tempo to 120BPM.

6. Select 1/64 from the Transient Division drop-down menu. Playing back the loop with too many transients will cause a warbling, out-of-phase tone at both increased and decreased tempos.

7. Select 1/2 from the Transient Division drop-down menu and play the loop back at 120BPM. As you can hear, playing the loop back with not enough transients causes sections of the loop to fall out of time.

If a loop is not sounding as good as you think it should, sometimes adjusting the transients will do the trick. If you're going to do this, however, it's a good idea to work on a copy of the file and not the original. It's very possible to make unfixable changes in the Apple Loops Utility.

Setting Preferences

The Apple Loops Utility does not have many adjustable preferences. There are a couple of important changes you can make to how the program works, though. To change the program's startup and saving preferences:

1. Choose Apple Loops Utility ➤ Preferences.

2. If you don't want the Open File dialog widow to appear automatically every time you start the program, you can uncheck the Show Open Panel On Launch box.

3. To automatically convert any WAV files to AIFF format select Close WAV and Edit AIFF.

4. Figure 10.3 shows the Apple Loops Utility's Preferences window.

FIGURE 10.3
The Apple Loops Utility's Preferences window

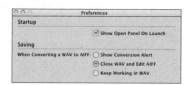

Converting WAV Files to Apple Loops

Using WAV files (both Acidized and non-Acidized) in Logic and GarageBand can be hit or miss when it comes to adding and locating the files in those program's Loop Browsers, taking advantage of the included metadata to find and organize the loops or quickly accessing automatic looping functionality. The Apple Loops Utility eliminates these and other problems by letting you convert single or multiple WAV files into the Apple Loops format quickly and easily. To convert a single WAV file to an Apple Loop:

1. Start the Apple Loops Utility and locate the folder `MMA Audio\Apple Loops\WAV Loops`.

2. Open the file `DrumLoop97.wav`.

3. Click the Play button to listen to the loop.

4. In the Property Tags section, set the File Type option to Looping.

5. Fill in the appropriate metadata. For example, in the section select Drums ➤ Drum Kit.

6. Make sure that the Apple Loops Utility's preferences are set to Close WAV and Edit AIFF.

7. Click the Save button in the lower right corner.

8. Open the `MMA Audio\Apple Loops\WAV Loops` folder on your hard drive. The Apple Loops Utility automatically created a folder named `Converted to AIFF` within the `WAV Loops` folder. The new folder contains your new Apple Loop.

Batch Conversion

You can also use the Apple Loops Utility to convert multiple files at once:

1. Make sure all the files you want to convert are collected into a single folder.

2. Open the Apple Loops Utility and click the Cancel button on the automatic file-opening dialog.

3. Open the Assets drawer by clicking the Assets button on the lower left corner.

4. Drag the folder `MMA Audio\Apple Loops\WAV Loops` directly onto the Assets drawer.

5. Click any loop in the Assets window the use the keyboard shortcut Command+A to select all of the loops at once. Figure 10.4 shows all of the WAV loops selected in the Assets window.

6. In the Property Tags section, make sure that there's a check mark next to File Type and that Looping is selected.

7. Fill in any other metadata that's relevant to all of the Apple Loops.

8. Click the Save All button at the bottom of the Assets window.

9. All of your new Apple Loops will be located in the `MMA Audio\Apple Loops\WAV Loops\Converted to AIFF` folder.

FIGURE 10.4
Select all of the WAV
loops in the Assets
window.

CONVERTING REX FILES TO APPLE LOOPS

The Apple Loops Utility won't recognize or open REX files, so in order to convert them to Apple Loops you'll have to use another program to convert them to WAV or AIFF format first. I prefer Audiofile's Sample Manager (covered in Chapter 7) for this kind of batch conversion because it's very easy to use and doesn't involve too many steps. You can use Sample Manager to convert REX files directly into the Apple Loops format; however, you can't use the program to add the metadata that allows Logic and GarageBand to categorize and organize the files. It's always a good idea to use the Apple Loops Utility as a final step whenever you're creating Apple Loops.

Other programs that can export REX files as AIFF or WAV format include ReCycle, AudioFinder, and Wave Editor.

Changing Tempos

With the Tempo slider the Apple Loops Utility can preview incremental adjustments to loops, but these changes will not be saved to the Apple Loop file. However, you can use the Number of Beats option in the Property Tags section to double or halve the default tempo of a loop file:

1. Locate the file Drumloop67.aif in the MMA Audio\Apple Loops Utility\Apple Loops folder.

2. Select the file in the Finder window, then Option+drag (or use the Command+D keyboard shortcut) to create a copy.

3. Start the Apple Loops Utility and open the *copy* of the file.

4. In the Property Tags section, change the Number of Beats field from 8 to 4. This will double the default playback speed of the loop when it's added to a session in Logic or GarageBand.

To halve the default playback speed, change the number of beats from 8 to 16.

Where to Go from Here

The Apple Loops Utility is an indispensable tool for anyone working with GarageBand or Logic, but anyone working with loops on an Apple computer can benefit from using this program regardless of your primary DAW. In combination with a program like Sample Manager, Audacity, or AudioFinder, the Apple Loops Utility can be used to create Apple Loops from just about any file format or sound source you can imagine.

In the rest of this chapter I'll focus on using and creating Apple Loops, as well as loops in other formats, in each of the DAW programs covered in this book.

Using and Creating Loops with Reason

Using loops in Reason generally means using the Dr. Rex Loop Player. In Chapter 2, "Reason," I covered the basic operation of the Dr. Rex Loop Player, including using it in conjunction with the Reason Sequencer to create original loops from existing REX files. Also, in Chapter 7, I covered the basics of creating Dr. REX loops with the ReCycle program.

Since the basics are covered elsewhere, I'll use this section to focus on some other ways to incorporate loops into your Reason sessions.

Converting Loops in the Redrum

While Reason doesn't have the ability to time-stretch and pitch-shift WAV and AIFF files, it's still possible to incorporate these kinds of files into your Reason Songs. Because of its simple and easy to automate interface, I like to use the Redrum Drum Computer to trigger WAV or AIFF loops. We'll add a WAV file to a Reason song with the Redrum Drum Computer (the procedure also works with an AIFF file):

1. Create a new Reason song with a Mixer 14:2 and a Redrum Drum Computer.

2. Select Channel Strip 1's Browse Sample button on the Redrum (Figure 10.5) and locate the file MMA Audio\Reason\Loops\RSNone86bpm.wav.

At this point it's helpful to know the loop file's BPM (beats per minute) in order to match the song's tempo with the tempo of the loop. In this case the name of loop contains the relevant information. While this may not always be the case, quite often your WAV, AIFF, Acid, or Apple Loops are organized by tempo. For example, a group of drum loops may reside a folder named 90BPM. If you are unable to determine the BPM by folder name or file name, you can open the file in a program like Sample Manager or the Apple Loops Utility to get a look at the file's default BPM setting.

FIGURE 10.5
Channel 1's Browse
Sample button

Since you know this file's BPM, set the session tempo accordingly to match the loop file.

1. Use your mouse to lower the tempo of the session in the Transport bar to 86BPM.

2. Click the first step in the Redrum step sequencer.

3. Click the Run button to play back the loop.

   As you may be able to tell from the volume increase and the phase problems, this loop is actually twice as long as the 16 beats that make up the current Redrum settings. This means you'll want to reduce the length of the beat by half. To do this:

4. Select the Drum 1 Decay/Gate button (located just to the right of the Length knob) and switch it to Mode:1. (Mode:0, the default, is the gradual decay. You want a sharp cutoff.) The setting is shown in Figure 10.6.

FIGURE 10.6
Select the cutoff mode

5. Next, use the Length knob to adjust the length of the loop. For this loop, choose 87. The setting you choose for other loops will vary depending on the loop file and its default BPM.

6. You can also create interesting stop/start effects by reducing the length value below 87. To adjust the Length knob in single increments hold down the Shift key while using your mouse to raise or lower the length amount.

If this seems like an awful lot of work to add a single drum loop to a session—it is. But this method really comes in handy when you've got a particularly excellent drum loop that isn't available in REX format or if you don't have ReCycle available to convert your loop. For example, one of the best-sounding Drum Loop ReFills I own contains only WAV files. Since it's not possible to export WAV files from ReFills, this solution is the simplest way to add these loops to a Reason song.

Playing Loops in the NN-XT

The NN-XT is another one of the Reason instruments that can be used to load and play back WAV and AIFF samples and loops. In Chapter 2 I covered the process of creating a new multisample by combining different sounds. You can also use similar mapping techniques to load and trigger single or multiple loop files in the NN-XT.

LOADING AND PLAYING A SINGLE LOOP

First you'll load a single loop file and play it back in the NN-XT:

1. Create a new Reason song with a Mixer 14:2 and an NN-XT Advanced Sampler.

2. Open the Remote Editor window by clicking the triangle in the lower left corner of the NN-XT interface.

3. Click the Load Sample button and locate the MMA Audio\Reason folder.

4. Select the RSNone86bpm.wav file and click OK.

5. Make sure the NN-XT is selected in the Reason Sequencer window and that it's armed to receive MIDI information. Figure 10.7 shows the drum loop in the Remote Editor window.

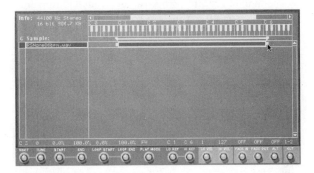

FIGURE 10.7
A WAV drum loop
in the NN-XT
Remote Editor

You can now use your MIDI keyboard to trigger the drum loop. The NN-XT will automatically map the loop so that middle C (C3) will play the loop back at its default tempo. One very interesting thing here is that triggering the note at C4, an octave higher, will play the loop at exactly twice the default tempo. Triggering the note at C2, an octave lower, will play the loop back at exactly half tempo.

Since you know the tempo of this loop (86BPM), you can adjust the Reason song tempo to match. Using the Sequencer window you can either record a MIDI event each time you want to trigger the drum loop, or you can draw a MIDI event in the Key Lane.

LOADING AND PLAYING MULTIPLE LOOPS

Another option with the NN-XT is to load multiple drum loops and trigger them individually throughout an arrangement. Here you'll be using many of the same concepts covered in the "Using the NN-XT Advanced Sampler" section of Chapter 2, but with a slightly different focus.

1. Start by reducing the key range of the original drum loop. Do this by selecting one end of the key range with your mouse and clicking and dragging inward until the entire key range is only one note, C3.

You can also resize the key range for any sample or loop by using the Lo Key and Hi Key knobs at the bottom of the Remote Editor window.

2. Click the blank area inside the Remote Editor window to deselect the current sample.

3. Use the Load sample button to load the file RSNtwo86bpm.wav.

4. Use your mouse or the Lo and Hi Key knobs to reduce the loop's key range to the single note D3.

   Here you will also need to change the sample's root key. The root key sets the MIDI note that will trigger the sample at its original tempo and pitch. The Root Key knob is located at the bottom left of the Remote Editor sample window.

5. Use the root key to set the second loop's root note as D3.

6. Load the loop RSNthree86bpm.wav.

7. Set the key range and root key to E3. Figure 10.8 shows the complete multisample in the Remote Editor.

FIGURE 10.8
The complete
multisample

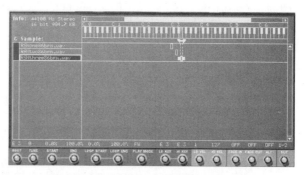

You can now use your MIDI keyboard to trigger the samples and record and arrangement. You can also use the Reason sequencer to draw arrangement with the Pencil tool in the Key Lane editor.

SAVING A SELF-CONTAINED PATCH

Save the patch for future use by clicking the NN-XT's Save Patch button. You can also save the loops within your Reason song by choosing File ➤ Self-Contain Settings and putting a check mark next to each loop file. Figure 10.9 shows the Self-Contain Settings dialog box.

Whenever possible, self-containing your Reason songs is a good idea. A self-contained Reason song can save you a lot of headaches if your original loop files get lost or moved or if you want to open your Reason session on another computer.

FIGURE 10.9

The Self-Contain
Settings dialog

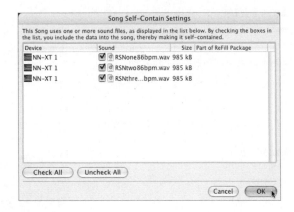

Creating Loops in Reason

Because of its built-in looping playback and exporting features, Reason is an excellent tool for creating loops for use in other programs. Once you have a working knowledge of Reason's basic functions, you have at your disposal an amazing loop creation machine.

WORKING WITH DRUM LOOPS IN REDRUM

Reason's Redrum Drum Computer is pretty hard to beat when it comes to creating drum loops. For starters you have immediate access to all of the included Redrum kits in the Reason Factory Sound Bank. There are also tons of ReFills available with Redrum patches for everything from classic drum machines to ethnic percussion to any number of complete drum kits for rock, jazz, or other styles of music.

Creating a Basic Loop

Start with a very basic configuration for creating drum loops:

1. Create a new Reason song.

2. Add a Mixer 14:2 and a Redrum Drum Computer.

3. Click the Browse Patch button and load one of the included Redrum kits from the Reason Factory Sound Bank or use a kit from another ReFill.

4. Program a simple (or complex) beat.

5. Turn looping on and set the loop to start at measure 1 and end at measure 3 as shown in Figure 10.10.

FIGURE 10.10

Set the loop parameters in Reason

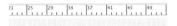

Mixing it Up

Once you have the basics down you can start to combine Redrum's features with Reason's effects. Here are some quick suggestions for creating more interesting drum loops. Start by following the steps in "Creating a Basic Loop," earlier in this section, and then follow these steps:

1. Select the Mixer 14:2 and add a DDL-Digital Delay Line and an RV7000 Advanced Reverb.

   At the top of each channel strip in the Redrum are two knobs marked S1 and S2 (Figure 10.11). These are effects sends for each individual sample.

FIGURE 10.11
The Redrum
effects sends

2. Use the S1 Send to add delay to your hi-hat or snare sample to create more intricate rhythms.

3. Use the S2 Send to add reverb to the snare (or any other drum sample).

4. Use the Dynamics Selector on the right side of the Redrum interface to create harder or softer "hits" in the step sequencer.

5. Select the Mixer 14:2 and add a Scream 4 Distortion unit.

6. Use the aux sends on the Mixer 14:2 to try out some of the different distortion effects on your drum loops.

MORE THAN JUST DRUM LOOPS

You are not limited to just creating drum loops with the Redrum. You can also load, loop, and adjust any WAV or AIFF loop or sample in the Redrum and create interesting and unusual loops. In addition, you can use the Browse Sample button on any Redrum Channel to load individual slices from any REX file.

EXPORTING A LOOP

The following are the standard instruction for exporting any loops from Reason:

1. Turn looping on and set the beginning and end of the loop to match the area you want to export.

2. Select File ➤ Export Loop as Audio File.

3. In the Export Loop as Audio File dialog box, choose a name and location for the file.

4. In the Format drop-down menu, choose Audio IFF File (AIFF) or WAV.

5. In the Export Audio Settings dialog box, set the Sample Rate to 41000Hz. This can affect how the loop is played back in your DAW program.

6. For maximum compatibility with other programs, choose a bit depth of 16.

If you have used any 24-bit AIFF or WAV files as samples in your Reason session, you'll want to select the Dither option when exporting 16-bit files. For more information on this feature see the "Dithering" section in Chapter 13, "Post Production."

Figure 10.12 shows the Export Audio Settings window.

FIGURE 10.12

The Export Audio
Setting window

CREATING INSTRUMENT LOOPS

Using Redrum is just scratching the surface of the loop creation possibilities in Reason. You can also create and export loops with any of Reason's other included instruments. Here's a quick example of how to create a simple synth bass line with the Malström Synth and the Matrix Patter Sequencer.

1. Create a new Reason song.

2. Add a Mixer 14:2 and a Malström Graintable Synth.

3. Select the Malström in the Reason window and create a Matrix Pattern Sequencer.

4. Adjust the Malström's settings or use the Browse Patch button to choose and load a patch.

5. Use the Matrix Pattern Sequencer to create a simple (or complicated) one-measure pattern, as in Figure 10.13.

FIGURE 10.13

The Matrix and
the Malström

6. Turn Looping on in the Transport bar and follow the instructions in the previous section, "Exporting a Loop," to save the instrument loop.

You can use the Matrix Pattern Sequencer to quickly create melody lines and bass lines with any Reason instrument.

Turning a MIDI Performance into a Loop

Reason's sampler devices and effects can be used to create complex and interesting performances. In this example, you'll use Reason's NN-XT sampler and Delay effect to create and export multiple loops.

1. Create a new Reason song with a Mixer 14:2 and an NN-XT Advanced Sampler.

2. Select the Mixer in the Reason window and create a DDL-1 Digital Delay line.

3. Use the NN-XT's Browse Patch button to load any instrument from the Reason Factory Sound Bank or Orkester ReFills.

4. Raise Channel Strip 1's Aux Send 1 button to add the delay effect.

5. Activate the click track in the Transport bar.

6. Make sure the NN-XT is selected in the Sequencer window and armed to receive MIDI input.

7. Turn looping off in the Transport bar.

8. Click the Record button on the Transport bar, then click the Play button to begin recording.

9. Use your MIDI keyboard to create a performance.

10. Click the Stop button to end recording.

11. Deactivate the click track and listen back to your performance. If you want, use the Key Lane to quantize and/or edit your performance.

12. Choose a section to export as a loop by setting the loop's start and end points in the Transport bar. Figure 10.14 shows measures 6 and 7 of a performance selected for exporting as a loop.

FIGURE 10.14
Export a section of a performance as a loop.

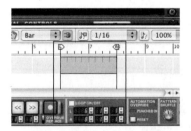

13. Export the loop following the instructions in the "Exporting a Loop" section earlier in the chapter.

Maintaining Consistent Volume Levels in Loops

When you are creating loops in Reason, it's a good idea to get in the habit of exporting files with a consistent volume level. You can always raise and lower the volume of the loop later on in whatever

DAW program you are working in, but an audio file that's too loud can distort, and one that's too quiet can easily get lost in a mix. The Apple Loops Utility can come in handy as a way to make sure your files are being exported in a consistent manner:

1. Open the file in the Apple Loops Utility.

2. Click the Transients tab to view the waveforms.

This is a good place to check and see if the file is at a good volume. At the perfect volume the waveform's highest peaks should come close to the top of the window. However, if you are seeing the kind of flat lines shown in Figure 10.15, your files will contain digital distortion.

FIGURE 10.15

A distorted audio file in the Apple Loops Utility

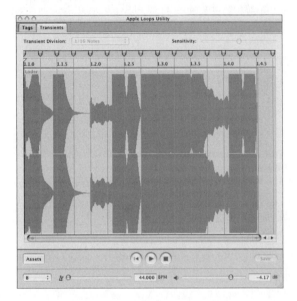

If the file is too loud or too quiet:

1. Return to the original Reason session and raise or lower the volume of the Instrument track in the Mixer 14:2.

2. If this doesn't give you enough of a boost, raise the output volume of the Mixer 14:2.

If you still need more volume try using the MClass Maximizer to increase the volume:

1. In the Reason window, select the instrument you want to make louder, for example a Redrum Drum Computer.

2. Choose Create ➤ MClass Maximizer. Take a look at the track's channel strip in the Mixer 14:2—the track is now named MAXIMIZER 1.

3. Raise the input gain and output gain incrementally until your track is sufficiently loud. Keep an eye on the Master Level fader in the Mixer 14:2 shown in Figure 10.16.

FIGURE 10.16
The Master Level fader in Reason

When creating loops (and other Reason songs), the master volume on the Mixer 14:2 can go into the orange zone should rarely or never hit the red zone. If you are hearing any distortion it could be coming from any number of places in your Reason song. Check the following:

◆ The master volume on the Mixer 14:2

◆ The track volume on its assigned channel strip

◆ The input and output gain on the MClass Maximizer

◆ The individual channel strips on the Redrum Drum Computer, each of which has its own level and velocity adjustments

A little bit of trial and error early on will establish the final output level you are most comfortable with. If necessary you can always use an Audio Editor like Wave Editor or Bias Peak to normalize (make louder) your loop files. Removing digital distortion, however, is not an option, so the most important thing to remember is to avoid creating files that are too loud.

WORKING WITH YOUR EXPORTED LOOPS

Once you've exported your Reason loops:

◆ To achieve a consistent volume level with all of your files, use a program like Sample Manager to normalize your loops.

◆ Use the ReCycle Program to convert your loops to REX files.

◆ Use the Apple Loops Utility to add metadata and turn your loops into Apple Loops.

◆ Add your new loop to the Loop Browser in Logic or GarageBand by launching either of those programs and dragging your loops directly onto their Loop Browser.

◆ To create a separate directory within either program's Loop Browser, place all your loops in a new folder and drag the entire folder onto the Loop Browser.

Using and Creating Loops in Live

Aside from having some of the best features available for manipulating existing AIFF and WAV loops, Ableton Live also contains a wealth of tools and instruments for creating original loops for use in Live and other programs. Since I covered many of Live's basic looping functions in Chapter 3, here I'll focus on some of Live's more advanced functions.

Warp Modes

Most programs that perform time-stretching and looping functions treat all loops in the same way, which is a shame because all loops are not created equal. A drum loop and a lead guitar loop, for example, will contain very different kinds of sonic information and respond differently to being pitch-shifted or time-stretched. One of the things that sets Live apart is that it contains five different modes for working with different types of loops. This means that Live applies different, more appropriate algorithms to different kinds of loops, creating better-sounding shifted or stretched loops.

Choose the appropriate mode for any audio loop from the Warp Mode drop-down menu in the sample box shown in Figure 10.17:

FIGURE 10.17

The Warp Mode menu

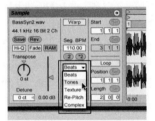

Beats   Beats mode should be your first choice for working with drum loops and other rhythmic patterns.

Tones   The Tones Warp mode is good for single instrument loops—a piano, vocal, bass, or any clearly articulated melody line.

Texture   Use Texture mode for complex sounds like multi-instrument/melody loops.

Re-Pitch   Re-pitch mode will lower or raise the pitch of the loop along with the session tempo.

Complex   Complex mode is used for entire songs and multipart loops.

REVERSE LOOPS

One quick way to come up with new and interesting sounds is to add reversed loops to your sessions. Near the top of the Samples Box is the Rev button. Click it to create a reversed version of any selected audio loop or clip.

Loop Editing

Live's Sample Display can edit loops and clips. These are some of my favorite functions in Live—having the ability to use sections of loop or clip, to start and end a loop at any point, and to discard unwanted regions. Let's try it out with a simple drum loop:

1. Use one of the file browsers to locate the folder `MMA Audio\Ableton Live\Loops`.

2. Drag the file `DrumLoop7.wav` to any audio track clip slot.

   Figure 10.18 shows the Sample Display.

FIGURE 10.18

The Sample Display

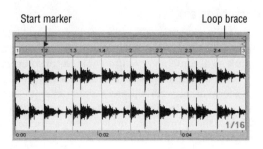

At the top of the Sample Display is the Loop brace. The Loop brace determines the length of the loop. Only the area selected inside of the Loop brace will play back.

3. Resize the Loop area by moving your mouse to the beginning or end of the Loop brace and clicking and dragging.

4. Just below the Loop brace on the left side of the Sample Display is the Start marker. Drag the Start marker to determine where playback will begin when the loop or clip is launched.

Figure 10.19 shows a loop that has been edited in the Sample Display.

FIGURE 10.19

An edited loop in the Sample Display

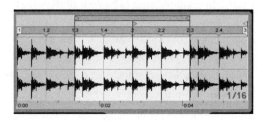

Only the middle section of this loop (the part included within the Loop brace) will play back. When the clip is launched, playback will begin at the center of the loop, where the Start marker has been placed.

Once you have performed edits in the Sample Display, you can save your loop as a clip with the included edits or export the file as a new AIFF or WAV loop.

Exporting as AIFF or WAV

Once you have a clip you'd like to export and/or save in WAV or AIFF format, follow these steps:

1. Select File ➤ Render to Disk or press Command+Shift+R. Figure 10.20 shows the Render to Disk dialog box.

2. Set the length of the loop. For loop files this will generally be 1, 2, 4, or 8 bars.

3. Turn Normalize on and Render as Loop on.

4. Select the output you would like to render. This can be the Master or any single track.

5. Choose the file type you'd like to export. For Apple Loops choose AIFF.

6. Select Bit Depth and Sample Rate.

   For maximum compatibility with other software, choose 16-bit and 44100Hz. If you know for certain that you will be using the loop with software that can handle a higher bit rate/ sample rate, you can select those settings instead.

7. If you plan to use your loop with Live, turn on Create Analysis File. This will slightly increase the speed at which Live loads your loop file.

8. If you'd like to save your file in mono, turn the Convert to Mono button on.

9. Click OK and select a location for your new loop file.

Once you've completed these steps you can open the file with the Apple Loops Utility and add the necessary metadata to turn your loop into an Apple Loop.

Creating Loops with Live's MIDI Instruments

New in Live 6 is a group of Rack Instruments that take advantage of Live's new instrument and effect grouping functionality. These Rack Instruments can be an excellent starting point for creating MIDI and audio loops.

Creating a Simple Loop

You'll start off by creating a simple loop and then you'll use some of Live's more interesting effects to create random and unexpected results.

1. Use the Device Browser to open the `Instruments` folder.

2. Open the `Instruments Rack` folder and take a look at the different categories.

3. Open the Keys Category and drag the Eclectric Piano instrument onto any available MIDI track.

4. Double-click the MIDI track's first clip slot to create an empty clip.

5. Use your mouse to create a simple pattern in the Note Editor like the one shown in Figure 10.21.

FIGURE 10.21
A simple pattern in
the Note Editor

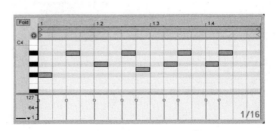

This is loop creation at its most basic in Live.

6. From here you can follow the instructions in the previous section, "Exporting as AIFF or WAV." Then open the exported file in the Apple Loops Utility and create an Apple Loop.

You can use this simple method to create loops with any of Live's instruments, including the Impulse Drum machine, the Operator synth, and the Sampler or Simpler sampler instruments.

A slightly more complicated version of this method is to use the MIDI recording techniques covered in Chapter 3 to create a longer performance and then use the Loop brace to select any 1-, 2-, 4-, or 8-measure section to save as a clip or export as a loop.

SWAPPING SOUNDS AND EFFECTS

Instead of stopping here though, to make things more interesting let's use Live's audio and MIDI effects to explore some other possibilities:

1. First, make sure you've created a melody with multiple notes.

2. Double-click the track header (the top of the track in the Session View window) to view the track's devices in the Track view.

3. Use the Device Browser to open the Audio Effects ➤ Beat Repeat folder.

4. Select the Airpusher preset and drag it directly onto the Track View window.

   Figure 10.22 shows the Eclectric Piano and the Beat Repeat audio effect in the Track View window.

FIGURE 10.22
Electric Piano and
Beat Repeat

5. Launch the clip to hear the audio effect.

In the top right corner of every Live instrument and plug-in is a button that contains two arrows pointing in opposite directions. This is the Hot-Swap Preset button.

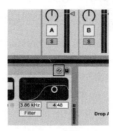

This little button opens up many worlds of possibility when creating loops in Live. You can instantly:

◆ Switch between instrument presets with the Impulse, Operator, Simple, Sampler, or the Rack Instruments.

◆ Change out any audio effect or preset for another.

◆ Change out any MIDI effect or preset for another.

◆ To try out the Hot-Swap button:

1. Launch the Eclectric Piano clip.

2. Click the Hot-Swap button on the upper right corner of the Beat Repeat effect in the Track View.

3. Double-click any of the other Beat Repeat presets to switch them out with the Airpusher.

4. Open any effect category and double-click any preset to try it out. I suggest trying the more noticeable effects like the filter delay and the flanger.

5. Click the Hot-Swap button on the Eclectric Piano instrument.

6. Double-click any of the Rack Instruments in the device browser to switch them with the Eclectric Piano.

Swapping out instruments and effects is a great way to get unexpected results from existing clips and loops. Once you find something you like, it's a simple matter to follow the exporting instructions and save any loops as AIFF or WAV files. Use the Apple Loops Utility as the final step in creating new Apple Loops with Live.

Using and Creating Loops with Pro Tools

While it has always been possible to work with loops in Pro Tools, recent versions continue to become more and more loop-friendly. The current versions of Pro Tools now allow you to drag and drop loop files in a variety of formats directly onto a Pro Tools session. In some cases you can even use loops to determine the Tempo setting of your newly created sessions.

Taking advantage of Pro Tools' Grid mode and working with loops can save time in a number of ways. Using a "good" section of an erratic drum performance or copying and pasting a MIDI performance are two popular ways to use looping to your advantage in Pro Tools.

Setting Up

As with much of Chapter 4, "Pro Tools," we'll be working in Grid mode in Pro Tools' Edit window for this chapter. Use the Grid Mode buttons on the upper left of the Edit window to make sure your sessions are set to Absolute Grid. Use the Grid Value pop-up to set the grid value to ⅛ notes and Bars:Beats as shown in Figure 10.23.

Finally, in the menu bar, choose Options ➤ Loop Playback. With this option selected any region you highlight with the Selector tool will play back as a loop.

FIGURE 10.23
The Grid Value menu

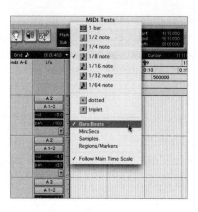

The Time Compression/Expansion Tool

The toolbar includes a second, hidden tool for expanding and contracting audio regions. To view and access the Time Compression/Expansion tool, click the Trim tool and select the TCE tool from the pop-up menu as shown in Figure 10.24.

FIGURE 10.24
The Time
Compression/
Expansion tool

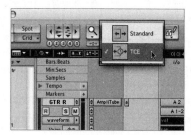

To get an idea of how the Time Compression/Expansion tool works, drag and drop any audio file from the `MMA Audio\All Loops\Apple Loops` folder onto a Pro Tools session.

1. Choose the Time Compression/Expansion tool from the Pro Tools toolbar.

2. Select the end of the file in the Timeline, then click and drag to the right to expand (elongate) the file.

3. Listen back to the results.

4. Use the Undo keyboard shortcut (Command+Z) to return the file to its original state.

5. Select the end of the file again, and this time use the Time Compression/Expansion tool to contract (shorten) the file.

6. Listen back to the results.

As you've probably noticed, more often than not the Time Compression/Expansion tool creates sonic artifacts that give the file a wavering, unsteady quality. Because of this the Time Compression/Expansion tool is best used to create small changes in files. For example, if you have a loop that you wish to add to a session that is extremely close in tempo but not exact, using the TCE tool may be an option. The TCE tool can also fix slightly out of time regions. For more intensive compression and expansion functions, however, it's not necessarily the right tool for the job.

Drag and Drop Rex Loops

Pro Tools now includes support for REX or .rx2 files. These files can be added to your sessions by importing them (see "Using Import Audio to Add Loops to a Session," later in this chapter) or by dragging and dropping them directly onto the Pro Tools Edit window. Because of the way REX files load (as individual "hits" comprising a complete loop), you have more control over time-stretching functionality. To add a REX file to a Pro Tools session:

1. Create a new Pro Tools session but don't create any tracks.

2. Copy the folder `MMA Audio\Rex Files` from the book's companion DVD to your desktop or another location on your hard drive.

3. Drag the REX loop `DrumLoop11.rx2` from the folder directly onto the Pro Tools Timeline.

4. A pop-up window appears, asking if you want to "Import original tempo from file?" Click Import. This will automatically change the Pro Tools session to match the tempo of the REX file.

Figure 10.25 shows the new track with the REX file.

FIGURE 10.25

A REX loop in
Pro Tools

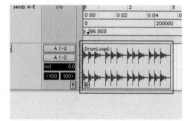

One of the really cool features here is that each individual slice has been imported into your Pro Tools session. This means that you can alter the tempo of the session and the REX file will expand or contract to match the current tempo. Try changing the tempo of this session to 120BPM and then speeding it up to 200BPM.

This option to match the session tempo to a REX file only works at the start of a session when the first file you import is a REX file. If you drag and drop a REX file into a session with tracks already created, your REX loop automatically conforms to the session's current tempo.

You can also drag and drop individual slices from REX files onto tracks. Make sure that the Regions view is showing by clicking the double arrow on the bottom right corner of the Pro Tools window. Figure 10.26 shows the Regions window with the individual REX slices.

FIGURE 10.26

The Regions list with
individual REX slices

Select any single REX slice and drag it directly on or onto a blank area of the Pro Tools window to create a new track. Drag multiple REX slices onto a track to create your own rhythms and patterns from individual REX slices.

The complete REX loops are located at the bottom of the Regions list. You can also drag and drop the complete RX files onto new or existing tracks.

COPY AND PASTE OR DUPLICATE?

Pro Tools' copy and paste functions are slightly different from those of many other DAW programs. As with most programs you can use the keyboard shortcut Command+C to copy a region or loop, but in order to paste it you'll need to use the Selector to choose a location first. Once you've chosen a new location (anywhere on any track) you can use the Paste keyboard shortcut (Command+V) to paste the selected audio. For each instance you'll have to use the Selector tool to choose another location.

To create a duplicate of a selected region or regions, use the keyboard shortcut Command+D. This will place a new copy immediately following the end point of the selected region. You can use the Command+D keyboard shortcut to quickly create multiple copies of a selected region or regions.

Acid Loops in Pro Tools

Loops that have been optimized for use in Sony's Acid looping program will often act in the same way that REX files do when added to a Pro Tools session, loading as individual slices and conforming to the current session tempo. Unfortunately this can be a hit or miss proposition, and not all Acidized WAV loops will work this way. I've used a number of loop libraries that contain Acidized files that don't conform to Pro Tools tempos when added via the drag and drop or importing method. To make matters even more confusing, there are a number of Acidized loops available that you can use to set the tempo at the start of a session (with the Import Loop Tempo function) but that will not conform to the session tempo when added later. Much of this seems to be related to how the files were created and when. Acidized loops from more recent Sony-produced loop libraries will be more likely to work smoothly in your Pro Tools sessions. Whenever possible download demo or sample files from any loop library you intend to purchase and try them out in Pro Tools before making your final purchase.

Apple Loops and Pro Tools

As of this writing Pro Tools does not offer the same support for Apple Loops that it does for REX and WAV loops. Apple Loops will function in exactly the same way as AIFF files and non-Acidized WAV loops.

You can still add Apple Loops, AIFF files, and non-Acidized WAV files to a Pro Tools session by dragging and dropping directly onto a track or an empty space on the Timeline. But these files will not automatically adjust themselves to the session tempo or import as slices.

If you want to use Apple Loops in your Pro Tools sessions you can:

♦ Drag and drop them directly into your sessions and use the Time Compression/Expansion tool.

♦ Work with them in Ableton Live or another loop-based program through ReWire.

♦ Convert your Apple Loops to REX or to the Acidized WAV format using programs like ReCycle (REX Format) and Sony's Sound Forge (Acidized WAV format, PC only).

Using Import Audio to Add Loops to a Session

You can also use the Import Audio window to add loops to a session. This has a couple of advantages in that you can preview the loops before adding them and you can add multiple files at once to your sessions. To use this method:

1. Choose File ➢ Import ➢ Audio to Track to open the Import Audio Window.

2. Navigate to a folder containing a loop or loops you'd like to import.

3. Select the loop (Shift+click to select multiple files) to add it to the regions in Current File list on the bottom left of the Import Audio window.

4. If you have selected a single loop, you can use the Play and Stop buttons to listen to the file.

5. Click the Convert button to add the file(s) to the regions to Import list. Figure 10.27 shows the Import Audio dialog box.

FIGURE 10.27

The Import Audio dialog box

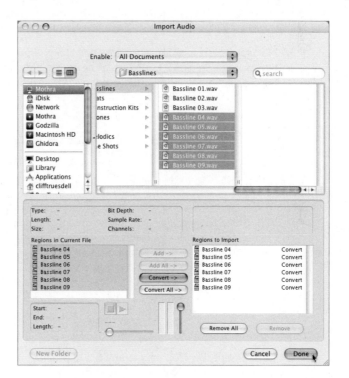

6. Click Done.

7. Choose a location for your converted audio files. By default Pro Tools will select the Audio Files folder it created when you started your session. Pro Tools will automatically create a new track for each loop you import.

If you want to import loops without automatically creating a track for each one, choose File ➢ Import ➢ Audio to regions List. You can then choose whichever loops you want to add by selecting them in the Regions list and dragging and dropping them onto the Timeline.

AUTOMATIC CONVERSION

Using this method will convert your REX or Acidized WAV files to audio files in whatever format (WAV, AIFF, or SDII) your current session is using. In order to import your REX or Acidized WAV files as individual slices, drag them into your session.

Using the Workspace

Pro Tools' built-in Workspace is another way to preview and add loops to your sessions. This tool has some interesting features as well some advantages and disadvantages:

1. Open the Workspace by selecting Window ➤ Workspace or using the keyboard shortcut Option+; (semicolon). If you're opening the Workspace for the first time, you will see your hard drive and any external or internal drives currently attached to your system.

2. To navigate the Workspace open a drive either by clicking the triangle to the left and viewing the drive's contents or by double-clicking any drive to open it in a new Workspace window.

3. Navigate to any location where you have loops stored. If you do not currently have any loop libraries, use the WAV Loops or Apple Loops folder from the MMA Audio\All Loops folder. Figure 10.28 shows the contents of the MMA Audio folder in the Workspace.

FIGURE 10.28

The Pro Tools Work-space window

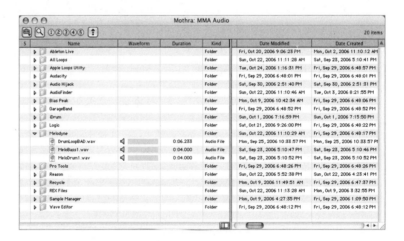

4. Click the speaker icon next to any file to preview it. Drag and drop any file from the workspace directly onto your Pro Tools Edit window to add it to your session.

Creating Loops in Pro Tools

Pro Tools works very well as a loop creation tool because of its simple, easy to use recording abilities, its effects, and its quick, easy editing functions. The included MIDI-controlled instruments like Xpand, Reason Adapted, and SampleTank LE also make excellent looping tools. The following examples can be used to make loops for use in your Pro Tools sessions, for use in other DAW programs, or for your own loop library.

CREATING AUDIO LOOPS

First we'll take a look at creating loops with audio instruments. For this example I used an electric guitar and the included Amplitube LE virtual amplifier, but you can use any instrument or instrument/effect combination.

The first step in creating an audio loop in Pro Tools is to record a performance:

1. Create a new Pro Tools session.

2. Add a mono audio track and a Mono aux input.

3. Option+click the Volume indicator on the aux input and add a click track from the Instrument category.

4. Make sure your chosen instrument and audio interface are properly connected.

5. Choose the correct input for your audio track.

6. Arm the track for recording to make sure you are getting signal.

7. Add any effects or virtual amplification.

8. Record your performance.

9. Mute the aux input click track.

    At this point you will want to listen back to your recording and perform any editing that you need to do. If necessary, change to Slip mode to perform more precise editing functions.

10. Use the Selector tool select the loop area.

11. Make sure Options ➤ Loop Playback is selected and press the spacebar to begin playback.

Once you've recorded a performance, separate out the part you want to use as a loop. Take a look at Figure 10.29.

In Figure 10.29 I used the Selector tool to select exactly two bars. I then used the keyboard shortcut Command+E to separate the selected area as its own region.

When you create loops this way, they will often contain a slight pop at the beginning and/or end. This pop is very common when creating loops and can be fixed by performing a simple cross-fade at the beginning and end of the loop.

To cross-fade in Pro Tools:

1. Just below the Trim, Selector, and Grabber tools is the Smart tool. Choose it.

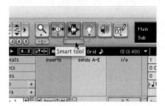

The Smart Tool makes use of multiple tools at once, depending on where you place your cursor on any region or track.

FIGURE 10.29

Separating the loop

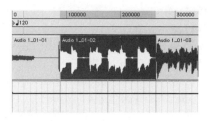

2. Place your cursor at the top left or right side of any region to access the Fade tool.

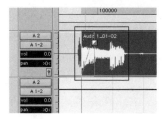

The Fade tool can create long or short fades at the beginning or end of audio regions. Here we want to create a very quick fade:

3. Select the Slip Mode button to change from Grid to Slip mode.

4. With the Smart tool selected, place the cursor at the top left of the region, then click and drag to create a quick fade.

5. Move your cursor to the other side of the region and create a corresponding fade at the end of the file.

Creating fades takes a little getting used to. Generally when working with loops you want to create extremely short fades. You can use the Trim tool to lengthen or shorten fades created with the Smart tool or use the Undo keyboard shortcut (Command+Z) to return the region to its original state.

EXPORTING AN AUDIO LOOP

When you are ready to export your loop:

1. Use the Selector tool to select only the region you want to export.

2. Choose File ➤ Bounce to ➤ Disk. Figure 10.30 shows the Bounce dialog box.

3. Select the File Type (WAV or AIFF).

4. Select the Stereo Interleaved format.

5. Select the Resolution and Sample Rate.

6. Select Convert After Bounce.

7. Click the Bounce button.

8. Name the file and select a location.

9. Click the Save button.

FIGURE 10.30

The Bounce to Disk
dialog box

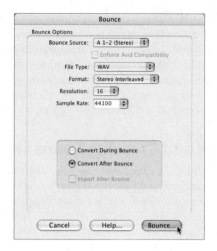

CREATING MIDI LOOPS

Since many of the tools and keyboard shortcuts for audio files work the same for MIDI files, you'll find that many of the same rules apply as well. Using MIDI instruments to create loop performances in Pro Tools has some distinct advantages. You have much more flexibility and control, and your loops can be recreated and edited easily, if necessary.

For more detailed information about using MIDI with Pro Tools see the "MIDI and Pro Tools" section of Chapter 11, "MIDI."

We'll use the Xpand! Synth to create and export a MIDI loop in Pro Tools:

1. Create a new Pro Tools session.

2. Create a new stereo Instrument track.

3. Make sure that the Instruments and Inserts views are showing.

4. Add the Xpand! synth as an insert (Multi-channel Plug-in ≻ Instrument ≻ Xpand!).

5. From the Xpand!'s Librarian menu, select 13 Acoustic Piano ≻ 01 Natural Grand Piano.

6. Use the Pencil tool to create a simple MIDI performance as shown in Figure 10.31.

Use the Selector tool to select and highlight the two-measure loop and click the Play button in the Transport bar to listen to the loop. You can edit and rearrange the loop while it playing back:

◆ Use the Bounce to Disk function to export the loop as an audio file.

◆ Use the Copy (Command+C) and Paste (Command+V) or Duplicate (Command+D) keyboard shortcuts to make copies of the loop.

FIGURE 10.31

Create a two-measure
MIDI performance
with the Pencil tool.

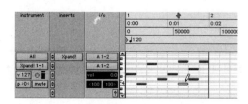

Take It Further

All of the tutorials in this section make use of specific instruments and presets (like the piano setting on the Xpand!). You can take all of these concepts and apply them to any real or virtual (MIDI) instrument you have at your disposal. Try adding any of Pro Tools' RTAS effects to your real or virtual Instrument tracks for even more variations.

Once you create and export a loop file, you can also open, edit, and/or convert your loops with programs such as ReCycle, AudioFinder, and of course, the Apple Loops Utility.

Using and Creating Loops with Logic

Logic's built-in Loop Browser functions almost exactly like GarageBand's, so if you are at all familiar with looping in GarageBand you'll be very comfortable with the looping in Logic. Like GarageBand, Logic makes use of both kinds of Apple Loops, Real Instrument loops and Software Instrument loops. Logic also contains support for Acid loops and REX files.

Whether you are using Apple Loops, loops for Acid, creating your own loops from live instrumental performances, or using Logic's built-in Software Instruments and MIDI instruments, Logic is a great program for using and creating loops.

Using Loops in Logic

In Chapter 5, "Logic," I covered the basics of working with and editing Real and Software Instrument loops in your Logic sessions. Let's take a look at some of the other ways that you can work with loops in Logic:

1. Locate the folder `MMA Audio\Logic\Loops`.

2. Drag and drop the file `OrganicOne.aif` onto any Instrument track. In the upper left corner of the Arrange window what used to be the MIDI Thru Box becomes the Region Parameters box, shown in Figure 10.32.

FIGURE 10.32

The Region
Parameters box

3. Put a check mark in the Loop box in the Region Parameters box to loop the file for the length of the entire song.

4. With the loop playing back, try clicking and dragging the Transpose number to raise and lower the pitch of the loop.

This is the equivalent of the Region Pitch slider in GarageBand or the Pitch knob in Live. Using the Transpose function you can add loops to your sessions that may not be in the correct pitch and then adjust them to match the current song key.

You can also use the Transpose function to create new performances from existing loops:

1. Create a duplicate of the OrganicOne.aif Apple Loop by holding down the Option key, selecting the loop and dragging. Figure 10.33 shows the Apple Loop copied in the Arrange window.

FIGURE 10.33
Option+dragging
to copy a loop

2. Create an eight-measure cycle region and press the spacebar to begin playback.

3. Select the second region (the copy) and use the Region Parameters box to transpose the loop down three steps (–3).

4. Select the Glue tool from the Arrange window toolbar.

5. Hold down the Shift key and click both regions with the Glue tool to create a single consolidated region.

You can use these kinds of editing techniques to create new loops or fix sections of existing loops. Try using the scissors to split a loop into two regions, transpose one of the regions, then use the Glue tool to rejoin them.

Splitting, copying, and transposing will also work with Real Instrument loops and nonlooped WAV and AIFF files.

Creating Apple Loops in Logic

As I've mentioned, there are two kinds of Apple Loops: Real Instrument and Software Instrument. Software Instrument Apple Loops can be created in GarageBand and Logic and shared between the two programs. When you open Software Instruments in other programs such as Pro Tools or Ableton Live, they will be automatically converted to the equivalent of Real Instrument loops.

To create Software Instrument Apple Loops in Logic:

1. Create a new Logic Project.

2. Double-click any Instrument track to open the Track Mixer window.

3. In the channel strip's Input field choose Stereo ➤ Logic ➤ GarageBand Instruments.

4. Select any GarageBand instrument.

5. Create a MIDI performance with your MIDI keyboard, the Caps Lock keyboard, or the Matrix Edit window.

6. Create a cycle region to preview the loop.

7. Use the Matrix Edit window or any of Logic's other MIDI editing functions to fix any inconsistencies in the file.

8. Use the Arrow tool to select the region in the Arrange window.

9. Select Region ➢ Add to Apple Loops Library from the Arrange window's File menu.

10. Name the new loop and choose the appropriate metadata information. Be sure to choose a genre; otherwise the loop may not appear in the Browser. Figure 10.34 shows the Add Region to Apple Loops Library window.

FIGURE 10.34

The Add Region to Apple Loops library window

By adding your loop to the Loop Browser in Logic you will also be automatically adding it to the Loop Browser in GarageBand. I suggest giving your loop a distinctive name (other than the obvious Drum Loop 1 or Piano Loop 12) so that you can easily use Spotlight or OS X's search function to locate the loop outside of Logic or GarageBand.

Loops added to the Logic/GarageBand Loop Browser will be located either at the root level of your hard disk or in your user folder at the following location:

```
Library/Audio/Apple Loops/User Loops/SingleFiles
```

You can quickly convert your Software Instrument Apple Loops to Real Instrument loops by dragging them from the Loop Browser onto any audio track.

Creating Real Instrument Loops

The process for creating Real Instrument Apple Loops in Logic is very similar to the process for creating Software Instrument loops, but with a "real" instrument plugged into your audio interface:

1. Create a new Logic project.

2. Make sure your instruments and audio interface are properly connected.

3. Select an audio track and make sure the track's input corresponds with your audio interface.

4. Select any plug-in effects or virtual amplification.

5. Arm the track for recording.

6. Click the Record button on the Transport bar to begin recording after a four-beat count-off.

7. Record a vocal or instrumental performance.

8. Use Logic's Editing tools to create a 1-, 2-, 4-, or 8-measure loop (You can use any increments you want, but these are the most common for loops). Figure 10.35 shows the Scissors tool being used to separate a two-measure region.

FIGURE 10.35
Use the Scissors tool to create a new region.

9. Create a cycle region to preview the loop.

10. Select the region in the Arrange window and choose Region ➤ Add to Apple Loops Library from the Arrange window's menu.

11. Fill in the appropriate information in the Add Region to Loop Library dialog box.

Click and Export

Another interesting function contained in Logic is Export Region as Audio File. This function allows you to quickly create loops in WAV, AIFF, or SDII format for use in other programs. To use the Click and Export functions:

1. Use the Arrow tool to select the region.

2. Select File ➤ Export ➤ Region as Audio File.

3. Name the file and select a location and format.

EXPORTING LOOPS IN LOGIC EXPRESS

Logic Express doesn't contain the Export Region as Audio File option. However, you can use this procedure to get the same results:

1. Solo the track containing the region you wish to export.

2. Select the region in the Arrange window.

3. Choose File ➤ Bounce from the Logic Express File menu.

4. In the Bounce dialog box, make sure the start position and end position match your selected region.

5. Select a file format and location.

6. Name the new exported region.

Importing WAV and AIFF Files

In Logic, dragging and dropping a WAV file or an AIFF that's not an Apple Loop file will not always result in an automatic loop, though many WAV files that have been "Acidized" to work with Sony's Acid looping program will automatically conform to your current Logic session's tempo. If you add a WAV or AIFF file to a Logic session and it does not conform to the current tempo settings, try opening the file in the Apple Loops Utility, converting it to an Apple Loop and then reintroducing it to your Logic session.

Normalizing a Loop in the Sample Editor

Many imported WAV or AIFF loops contain drastically different volume levels. Conversely, when exporting a region as loop you may want to have consistent volume levels as well. To normalize your audio regions and loop files in the Sample Editor:

1. Use the Arrow tool to select a Real Instrument loop or any region on an audio track in the Arrange window.

2. Double-click the region or loop to open the Sample Editor, shown in Figure 10.36.

FIGURE 10.36
The Sample Editor

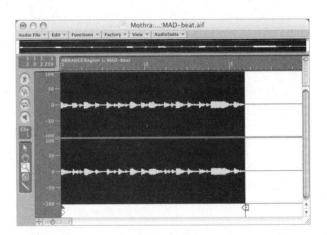

3. Select Functions ➤ Normalize from the Sample Editor menus.

4. Click the Process button in the Normalize pop-up dialog.

Cross-fading in the Sample Editor

To eliminate the pesky pops and clicks that often go along with creating your own Real Instrument loops, you can use the Sample Editor to perform quick and easy cross-fades:

1. Double-click a loop or region to open the Sample Editor.

2. Use the Zoom tool to zoom in on the beginning of the loop.

3. Use the Arrow tool to select a small section at the very beginning of the loop.

4. Select Functions ➤ Fade In.

5. Use the Zoom tool to zoom in on the end of the loop.

6. Use the Arrow tool to select a small section at the very end of the loop. Select Functions ➤ Fade Out.

7. Play the loop back. If you hear a noticeable drop-out in the sound at the beginning or end of the loop, go back and create a quicker fade-in and/or fade-out.

Take It Further

Logic really is the ultimate Apple Loop program, for both using and creating Real and Software Instrument loops. Using the techniques I've covered here as a starting point and in conjunction with all of Logic's instruments and plug-ins, you can pretty quickly create an arsenal of Apple Loops for use in Logic and any other DAW program.

Using and Creating Loops with GarageBand

GarageBand is a very loop-oriented program, so I covered many of its looping functions in the "GarageBand Basics" section of Chapter 6, "GarageBand." Here I'll discuss some of the more advanced editing possibilities for working with existing loops and creating new ones from scratch.

Editing Software Loops

One distinct advantage to working with software loops is the ability to edit them extensively and come up with otherwise unexpected results. We'll start by working with a string section loop.

1. Create a new GarageBand session and open the Loop Browser.

2. Select the Strings loop category and add the loop 70s Ballad Strings 02 to the Timeline.

3. Create a two-measure cycle region the same length as the loop and click the Play button to hear the changes you'll be making as you edit the loop.

4. Double-click the loop in the Timeline to open the Track Editor, shown in Figure 10.37.

FIGURE 10.37
The strings loop in
the Track Editor

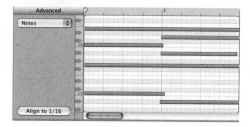

5. Click individual notes or select groups of notes and move them around in the Track Editor to edit the loop. If necessary, use the Zoom slider on the bottom left of the Track Editor to zoom in on the loop to make editing easier.

6. Add notes to the loop by holding down the Command key and clicking anywhere in the Track Editor window.

7. Move your mouse to the end of any MIDI event, then click and drag to lengthen or shorten MIDI notes.

Pitch Shifting

Use the Region Pitch slider on the left side of the Track Editor to raise or lower pitch of the loop. Try these steps to create a new, longer loop using GarageBand's Pitch-shifting and Join functions:

1. Change the cycle region from two measures to four measures.

2. Select the loop in the Timeline, then hold down the Option key.

3. While holding down the Option key, drag the loop to the right to create a copy of the loop.

4. Double-click the new region in the Timeline.

5. Use the Region Pitch slider to raise or lower the pitch of the selected region (try smaller numbers at first).

   If you want, create a new continuous loop from the two regions. Hold down the Shift key and select both regions in the Timeline, then select Edit ➤ Join.

Adding Individual Loops to the Loop Browser

To add a newly edited or newly created loop to the Loop Browser, select the loop in the Timeline and choose Edit ➤ Add to Loop Library.

A dialog box will appear allowing you rename the loop and to add much of the same metadata as you would with the Apple Loops Utility. Give the loop a new name, then choose the appropriate Instrument Descriptors and Mood Descriptors. Finally click the Create button at the bottom of the window. Figure 10.38 shows the Add to Loop Library window.

FIGURE 10.38

The Add to Loop Library window

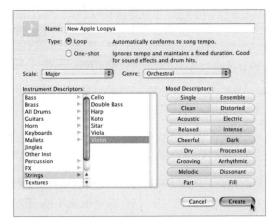

Adding Loop Libraries to the Loop Browser

If you have downloaded or purchased any third-party loop libraries, you can add the entire collection at one time to GarageBand:

1. Locate the folder you'd like to add on your hard drive (if you don't have any third-party loops of your own, you can use the Apple Loops folder from the included DVD).

2. The name of the folder is what GarageBand will use to organize it, so make sure it's something simple and descriptive. If you've downloaded a free loop library, you may need to change the name of the folder from `Free Loops` to something else.

3. Drag the folder onto the GarageBand Loop Browser.

4. In the dialog box that appears, choose Move to Loops Folder as shown in Figure 10.39.

FIGURE 10.39

Add the loops to your Apple Loops folder.

At the top of the Loop browser is a drop-down menu that allows you to choose which library is being browsed. To view the contents of your new folder:

◆ Select Show All to browse from your entire collection.

◆ Select My Loops to browse only loops you have added.

◆ Select GarageBand to view only the loops that you installed with iLife.

◆ Select an individual library from the bottom of the list.

Editing Real Instrument Loops

Real Instrument loops have their advantages as well. Generally, they will be less synthetic sounding (unless they are synth loops). Real Instrument drum loops in particular can add a much needed realism to sessions. Let's use one of GarageBand's excellent-sounding included acoustic guitar loops:

1. Create a new GarageBand Music project.

2. Use the loop Browser to locate the loop `Acoustic Picking 11`.

3. Drag the loop onto the Timeline and place it at the beginning of the session.

4. Create a two-measure cycle region.

5. Listen to the entire loop.

6. Double-click the loop in the Timeline to open the Track Editor, shown in Figure 10.40.

7. Move your cursor to the bottom right corner of the waveform in the Track Editor. The cursor will turn into a line with a straight arrow, also shown in Figure 10.40.

8. Click and drag backward to shorten the loop by half.

9. Move your cursor to the top of the waveform in the Track Editor. The cursor will turn into a line with a curved arrow (the same tool you use in the Timeline). Click and drag to repeat the edited loop.

FIGURE 10.40
A Real Instrument loop in the Track Editor

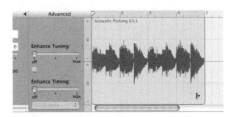

You can use the editing techniques covered in Chapter 6 to create new Real Instrument loops from existing loops. You can also use the same Pitch-Shifting and Join functions you used with Software Instrument loops to create new loops from existing Real Instrument Apple Loops.

Creating Loops in GarageBand

GarageBand and Logic are the only two programs that can create Software Instrument Apple Loops, and this is one area where GarageBand has a bit of an advantage over Logic. When you create an Apple Loop in Logic for use in GarageBand, you can't use any of Logic's included effects. If you do, the loop won't open correctly in GarageBand (you'll get a message asking if you want to convert the loop to a Real Instrument loop, which you should if you want it to include the effects). However, working the opposite way is not a problem. Any loops you create in GarageBand (provided you use only GarageBand's effects) will open seamlessly in Logic.

To create a Software Instrument Apple Loop:

1. Select Track ➢ New Track and create a new Software Instrument track.

2. Double-click the track header to open the Track Info dialog box.

3. Select any GarageBand instrument category and instrument.

4. Use your MIDI keyboard or the Musical Typing keyboard to play the instrument.

5. Add any of GarageBand's effects to the instrument.

6. Make sure your track is armed for recording.

7. Click the Record button in GarageBand's Transport bar to begin recording.

   Once you have recorded a performance you can perform any necessary edits in the Track Editor:

8. Create a cycle region to make sure your performance works as a loop.

9. Select the loop in the GarageBand Timeline and choose Edit ➢ Add To Loop Library.

In the Add Loops to Loop Library dialog box, be sure to choose the correct instrument and as many descriptors as possible. It's also very important to choose a genre from the Genre drop-down menu, otherwise your new loop might not show up in the Loop Browser. If the exact genre is not available, choose the closest or the Other Genre category.

Creating a Real Instrument Apple Loop

Real Instrument Apple Loops are created in much the same way as Software Instrument loops:

1. Make sure your instrument and audio interface are properly connected.

2. Select Track ➤ New Track and create a new Real Instrument track.

3. Double-click the track header to open the Track View window.

4. Select an Input and turn Input Monitoring on (Figure 10.41).

FIGURE 10.41
Turn Input
Monitoring on.

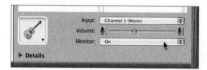

5. Add any effects or virtual amplification.

6. Arm the track for recording.

7. Click the Record button to begin recording.

8. Use the Track Editor to edit the performance if necessary.

9. Select Edit ➤ Add To Loop Library and fill out the appropriate metadata.

CONVERTING SOFTWARE INSTRUMENT LOOPS

Software Instrument loops can be converted to Real Instrument loops by dragging them from the Loop Browser directly onto any empty Real Instrument track. You can also automatically convert all the Software Instrument loops added to a session by clicking the Loops tab in GarageBand's Preferences and selecting the Adding Loops to Timeline: Convert to Real Instrument option.

Exporting Loops to iTunes

You can also create Real Instrument Apple Loops by exporting your GarageBand tracks directly to iTunes; this creates a 16-bit 44100hz AIFF file and saves it to an iTunes playlist.
To export the loop:

1. Solo the track that contains the loop you want to export.

2. Create a cycle region the length of the loop you want to export.

3. Select Share ➤ Send Song to iTunes.

4. The loop will automatically be added to your iTunes library.

You can now drag the loop from the iTunes window directly onto your desktop. Open the loop in the Apple Loops Utility to add metadata and convert the file to an Apple Loop.

 **Real World Scenario**

CREATING A LOOP LIBRARY

Along with creating your own Apple Loops for use in your songs and music projects, all of these loop creating ideas and concepts can be put to another use as well—creating your own loop library. Having a collection of free loops can get people to visit your website and check out your music, you can share them with your friends and collaborators or you can sell them through your website, eBay or other outlets.

The first thing you need to decide is what kinds of loops you plan to make and how they will be organized. For example, will they be Synth Loops? Drum Loops? Will they be a combination of different instruments? Will there be multiple styles of music represented? Other ways to organize loop collection include song sets (the elements that make up a song or drum track) loops sets (the elements that make up a specific loop) and Beats Per Minute.

You don't necessarily have to decide how you want things organized before you start, but it's a good idea to get the organizational element out of the way early, especially if you plan on creating a lot of files. Once you do have an organizational idea in mind, create a main "catch-all" folder and then subfolders for each subcategory.

As we've covered, you can use both Logic and GarageBand to create both Software Instrument and Real Instrument Apple Loops. I like working in GarageBand when creating Software Instrument loops because I like being able to use all of GarageBand's included effects. If you use Logic's included effects when creating Software Instrument loops GarageBand wont be able to read them and they'll have to be converted to Real Instruments. Logic users, however, can open your GarageBand created loops with no difficulty.

For creating Real Instrument loops I prefer to work in Logic because of the ability to quickly open any loop files in the Sample Editor and Normalize them.

When creating Software Instrument Apple Loops in Logic or GarageBand the final step will be using either program's "Add to Loop Library" function. You can then locate the actual Apple Loop file on your hard drive at one of the following locations

 Your Username/Library/Audio/AppleLoops/User Loops/Single Files

 Your Hard Drive/Library/Audio/AppleLoops/User Loops/Single Files

Once you've located the file, create a copy in the appropriate folder.

For Real Instrument Loops I use the "Export Region as Audio File" function in Logic and the "Send to iTunes" function in GarageBand, then use the Apple Loops Utility to convert the files to Apple Loops.

I've found that the following method is one of the most effective ways to quickly produce a large number of consistently good, interesting loops:

1. Create Software Instrument loops using Logic's virtual instruments *and* effects, then add the loops to Logic's Loop Browser.

2. Locate the loops in the Loop Browser, then drag them to an Audio track to convert them to Real Instrument loops.

3. Open the loop in the Sample Editor and use the Normalize function.

4. Either use the "Export Region as Audio File" function or add the Real Instrument loop to the Loop Browser.

As we've seen you can also use other DAW programs to create Real Instrument Apple Loops. The following is a basic outline of the steps you can take to create consistent loops. I prefer to use Audiofile's Sample Manager for batch conversion, normalization and quick editing, but there are other programs that can perform these functions as well.

1. Export the loop from your DAW program as a 16-bit, 44100hz AIFF or WAV file.

2. Once you have a group of files, open them all at once in Sample Manager or another program that supports batch conversion.

3. Normalize all the files.

4. Listen back to each file. If there are any "pops" or "clicks" at the beginning or end of any file, use your program's cross-fading functions to fix them.

5. Open the files in the Apple Loops Utility and convert them to Apple Loops.

You may want to use the Apple Loops Utility twice for each file. The first time you can open all of your new files at once and add the metadata that is appropriate for all of your Apple Loops, such as File Creator, Copyright info, etc. The second time open the files individually to choose Search Tags and Descriptors.

TAKE IT FROM ANYWHERE

Loop files can also come from sessions you've already created. Try going through your original songs and isolating specific sections, such as a drum track or guitar track. Two-, four-, and eight-measure sections of many songs will often make excellent loops.

I asked producer and engineer Mark Pistel (see the full interview in Chapter 4, "Pro Tools") about the various sources of different files on the *Electronic Point Blank* loop collection he created for Sonic Foundry.

Mark Pistel: "Around that time I was doing a lot of dance re-mixes for Cleopatra [Records, a Dance/ Industrial record label]. They would license all of these weird songs from the 60s and 70s and I was hired to make this stuff sound 'clubby' for the dance clubs. So some of those loops come from recycled stuff from those sessions. I would open up a session and take a 4 or 8 bar loop of whatever I had—whether it was synth, blip, or a breakbeat I had made—then export that as a loop file."

Another source for new loops is the Apple Loops, REX loops, or WAV loops that you already have on your system. You can use your DAW's plug-in effects and audio processes such as reversing and pitch-shifting to create totally new sounds from existing loops.

The Bottom Line

Convert any WAV or AIFF file into an Apple Loop   Using Apple's free Apple Loops Utility you can convert any WAV or AIFF file into an Apple Loop by including metadata that tells programs like GarageBand and Logic how to play and catalogue the file.

Master It   Use the Apple Loops utility to convert any WAV file to an Apple Loop.

Batch Convert WAV or AIFF files into Apple Loops   You can also use Apple Loops Utility to convert multiple files at once from any folder or loop library CD. This can be especially useful if you want to buy a loop collection that is only available in the WAV or Acidized format and convert it to the Apple Loops format.

Master It   Convert a large or small collection of WAV files into Apple Loops then add them to the Loop Browser in Logic or GarageBand.

Create new Apple Loops with any DAW program   Any DAW program that can export audio (and that's all of them) can create Apple Loops in conjunction with the Apple Loops Utility. Some programs, such as GarageBand and Logic, can create Apple Loops on their own that can then be accessed for use in other programs by locating them on your hard drive.

Master It   Use GarageBand to create a new Software Instrument Apple Loop and add it to the Loop Browser.

Export Apple Loops from any program   Each DAW program has its own method and options for exporting audio files. The settings you choose when exporting your files will determine their sound quality and their compatibility with other programs.

Master It   Export an AIFF file or Apple Loop from your DAW program to your desktop folder.

Chapter 11

MIDI

MIDI stands for Musical Instrument Digital Interface; it was originally created to allow two synthesizers to communicate with each other. Early in its history (way back in 1980), MIDI was decided upon as an industry-wide protocol for connecting synthesizers. Over the years MIDI has found its way into a number of uses including lighting, video games, and of course, computer-based music programs.

The relationship between MIDI and computer music dates back to the mid-1980s. In fact, well before computers could record directly onto a hard disk, they were being used as MIDI controllers. Almost all of today's music-related applications make some use of MIDI information and many include both very simple and extremely advanced MIDI processes. Aside from the obvious uses, such as using a MIDI keyboard to trigger a piano, keyboard, or other virtual instrument, MIDI information can control automation and many other features in programs like Reason and Pro Tools.

As recently as a few years ago it seemed as if there were two kinds of people who created music with computers: those who used MIDI and those who did not. Many people were confused by the technology or associated MIDI with poor sound quality and overly mechanical performances, while others were frustrated by the complicated processes of hooking up MIDI instruments and interfaces. All of these "problems" are rapidly fading into history as MIDI implementation becomes easier and easier with every advance in digital recording technology.

In this chapter you will learn to:

◆ Open MIDI files in any DAW

◆ Control Reason with a MIDI keyboard

◆ Use MIDI to "play" Ableton Live

◆ Quantize a performance in any DAW program

Getting Started

In the dark days before OS X, the process of setting up a MIDI keyboard or other MIDI interfaces involved installing specific drivers for your MIDI interface, installing Opcode's OMS (Open Music System) software, then getting all of your gear routed and working with your DAW. While this may not sound too complicated, the process almost invariably involved much confusion, lengthy trouble-shooting sessions, and frequent headaches.

Much of this difficulty is now ancient history. Working with MIDI in OS X has become incredibly simple. Many MIDI devices still come with drivers on CD or DVD that you need to install, but true plug-and-play devices are becoming more and more common every day. The proliferation of USB-connected MIDI devices and the use of virtual MIDI instruments have also significantly simplified the process of creating music on your Mac.

Today many entry-level software musicians are using MIDI with increasing frequency. In fact, many users of programs like GarageBand may not even be aware that when they create a Software Instrument track or add an Apple Loop to their session they are utilizing MIDI technology. It's entirely possible to use programs like GarageBand or Ableton Live with MIDI technology to create performances, sound clips, and loops without having any real understanding of how MIDI works or what it does.

However, while it's certainly possible to create music with your Mac with very limited knowledge of MIDI, the more you know the more you can take advantage of the MIDI capabilities included in today's DAW programs.

In order to get the most out of this chapter you should have some kind of MIDI keyboard controller connected either via USB or through a MIDI interface. If you're not sure exactly what that means, read on....

MIDI Basics

Probably the most common misconception about MIDI (other than that it's difficult to use) is that it transmits musical notes. MIDI data is just that: data. The way MIDI "plays" musical notes is this: a MIDI controller (a keyboard or other control surface) creates a signal or MIDI message that then triggers a sound module, such as a synthesizer, a drum machine, or a virtual instrument. The instrument, not the MIDI signal, contains the actual sound. A MIDI message or signal can contain lots of information telling your instrument not just what to play but how to play it. Aside from information about specific notes, note length, and velocity, a MIDI message can also contain information telling an instrument to apply an effect, modulate the pitch of a note, and much more.

MIDI messages can contain other, nonmusical kinds of information as well, including things like timing, song selection, and patch selection. Further on in this chapter I'll talk about how MIDI can be used to control just about every aspect of the recording and playback process. For example, in many DAW programs MIDI controls track panning, effects, automation, and even stopping and starting playback and recording.

The following are some of the terms and concepts associated with MIDI that are used frequently in conjunction with MIDI and digital recording.

SOUND MODULE

A sound module is anything that actually creates sounds. Sound modules can be hardware, like a synthesizer or a drum machine. They can also be software such as one of Reason's synthesizers, a Logic or GarageBand instrument, or any other virtual instrument.

SEQUENCERS

The term *sequencer* can refer to different types of devices. Originally MIDI sequencers were separate hardware devices that you programmed to create arrangements (sequences) with your MIDI-controlled sound modules. Today's most commonly used MIDI sequencer is actually your DAW software. There are still hardware sequencers available and in use. Some companies still producing hardware sequencers include Korg (the devices in the Electribe series all work as both synths and sequencers), Yamaha, and Roland. There are also keyboard sequencers such as the Korg Triton and the Yamaha PSRE303 that contain keyboard, synth, and sampler functionality along with built-in MIDI sequencing.

MIDI CONTROLLER

A MIDI controller can be any device that creates MIDI messages and sends them to a sequencer, sound module, or both. The most common type of MIDI controller is the MIDI keyboard. Other types of controllers include percussion-style pads, used to trigger MIDI events such as drum hits or samples, and mixer-style control surfaces, which function like analog mixing boards and can control the mixing functions of your DAW software.

MIDI CHANNELS

Your MIDI keyboard or other controller will have 16 channels with which to send information in or through your MIDI devices. This is only part of the MIDI information available on most MIDI controllers, but it is the most basic. Each MIDI channel can be assigned to a different instrument or MIDI track in your DAW. Frequently your DAW program's default setting will accept information from all of your MIDI controller's channels, meaning you won't have to change any settings on your MIDI controller to get it to work. However, learning to switch MIDI channels on your MIDI controller is a good place to begin learning more advanced MIDI techniques.

MIDI OUT, IN, AND THRU

All of your MIDI devices will have between one and three MIDI ports depending on the type of device and its functionality:

MIDI Out The MIDI output on your MIDI controller or MIDI interface. From here, MIDI messages are transmitted to whatever MIDI devices, hardware, or software you have connected to your controller.

MIDI In Where your MIDI instrument, device, or interface receives MIDI information. For example, a MIDI controller will send a MIDI signal from its MIDI Out, and the signal will then trigger a sampler or other device via the device's MIDI In.

MIDI Thru Many MIDI keyboards and interfaces contain a MIDI Thru port. MIDI Thru ports are used for sending MIDI signals to multiple devices from a single controller or trigger. Let's say you have a MIDI controller and you want to use it to trigger two synthesizers simultaneously. You will send the MIDI signal from the first device (controller) to the first synth. Instead of using the MIDI Out on the first synth, you use the MIDI Thru port and connect that to the second synth's MIDI In. This way the signal travels both "in" and "thru" the first synthesizer.

GENERAL MIDI (GM)

General MIDI (GM) refers to the sound set developed in 1999 to so that there would be a standard set of sounds when sharing MIDI files between MIDI devices. Your Mac contains the QuickTime Music Synthesizer, which has its own GM sound bank. These are the sounds you hear when you download a MIDI file from the Internet and open it with QuickTime or in your web browser. There have been updates and expansions made to General MIDI, but the basic core remains the same.

The General MIDI Sound Set consists of 16 banks of 8 instruments apiece:

1–8 Piano	49–56 Ensemble	89–96 Synth Pad
9–16 Chromatic Percussion	57–64 Brass	97–104 Synth Effects
17–24 Organ	65–72 Reed	105–112 Ethnic
25–32 Guitar	73–80 Pipe	113–120 Percussive
33–40 Bass	81–88 Synth Lead	121–128 Sound Effects
41–48 Strings		

You can access the QuickTime Music Synthesizer's General MIDI sound bank with your MIDI keyboard and the included OS X's Audio Unit instrument the DLS (Downloadable Sounds) Music Device.

The DLS Music Device will be located with all of your Audio Unit instruments in whichever DAW you are using. Add the DLS Music device to any MIDI track in Logic, Live, GarageBand, Rax, or any program that supports Audio Units. The default sound bank for the DLS Music Device is the QuickTime Music Synthesizer. The different sounds contained in the QuickTime Music Synthesizer are accessed by a signal sent from your MIDI device. This signal is called a *program change*. You'll need to consult your MIDI keyboard's manual for instructions on creating a program change with your specific device.

Once you've learned how, you can create a program change to try out any of the 128 included instruments in the QuickTime Music Synthesizer's sound bank.

QUANTIZATION

Quantization is used to adjust the timing of a MIDI performance. A very common use for quantization is to fix a drum or other instrument performance created with a MIDI controller or keyboard. For example, when you create a drum track, chances are your individual drum sounds may not line up perfectly with the timing of the song. Using your DAW's quantization functions you can line up the performance exactly. Figure 11.1 shows an imperfect drum performance in Live; Figure 11.2 shows the same performance after quantization.

FIGURE 11.1
An imperfect drum
performance

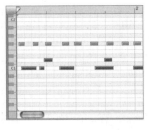

FIGURE 11.2
A quantized drum
performance

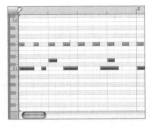

It's very easy to go overboard with quantization. A performance that's too perfect can sound forced or mechanical. Many DAW programs also include various "groove" functions, which are a kind of reverse quantization. Live's Groove adjuster and Reason's Groove knob are good examples of this. Logic, Pro Tools, and other programs also include "Groove Mapping" which can create humanized performances with MIDI information. Using some of Logic's more advanced functionality you can even create Groove templates from audio performances and apply them to MIDI tracks.

Using MIDI

At its most basic MIDI is used to trigger notes (sometimes referred to as events). For example, let's say you have a MIDI keyboard attached to your computer running a music program. You play a middle C on your keyboard and the same note is triggered on your computer. This is a simple exchange of MIDI information.

Many of today's DAW programs are set up specifically to receive both musical and nonmusical MIDI information. Any time you see a knob or slider in your DAW that goes from 0 to 127, it means that the parameter is set up to be controlled by MIDI information.

With OS X, using MIDI with your DAW software or any MIDI music program should be as simple as installing any necessary drivers and then plugging your device in. Many programs will allow you to specify a specific brand and model to facilitate a smoother relationship between your software and hardware. See the chapter of this book about your DAW software or see your MIDI hardware and software's included documentation for more information.

MIDI Keyboards and Interfaces

Generally, when I refer to MIDI controllers in this book I am referring to "standard" MIDI keyboards. This means a MIDI instrument with between 25 and 88 piano-style keys. Almost all MIDI keyboards also include knobs and/or sliders for controlling MIDI data. There are, however, many different kinds of MIDI-related devices. In this section I'll cover some basic information you'll need to know in order to make a decision about buying a MIDI keyboard. I'll also cover other types of controllers, mixers, and MIDI interfaces.

Choosing a MIDI Keyboard

MIDI keyboard controllers come in many different sizes, functionalities, and costs. When choosing a MIDI keyboard you'll want to take into consideration your specific needs, such as portability and MIDI functionality and compatibility with your primary recording software.

The least expensive MIDI Keyboard available today is probably the no-frills Evolution 37-key eKeys. The eKeys has no knobs or faders—no functionality beyond the ability to trigger MIDI notes. If you are an absolute beginner or have no intention of using MIDI for anything other than simply creating a musical performance, the eKeys may be a good choice.

At the opposite end of the spectrum are keyboards like the Keystation Pro (www.m-audio.com). The Keystation Pro has 88 weighted keys (to simulate playing a real piano or organ) and lots of functionality, including sliders, knobs, buttons, and wheels that can create complex MIDI messages and control just about every aspect of any virtual instrument or DAW program.

In between the two extremes, there are many models in the $100 to $300 range that will more than get the job done for the beginner, intermediate, or even expert user. For the intermediate MIDI user/keyboard player, there are a number of 49-key and 61-key MIDI controllers that are both affordable and contain good functionality. If this is your interest and skill level, check out models like the Edirol PCRM80 or the more fully featured M-Audio Axiom 61.

BENEFITS OF EXTRA FEATURES

The advantage to having a MIDI controller with multiple adjustable faders and knobs is being able to go beyond the ability to control simple MIDI note information. As you'll see later on in this chapter, all DAW programs have lots of other types of built-in MIDI functionality that you can access with your keyboard controller. In some cases having a single set of eight faders or knobs can open up lots of creative possibilities you may not have been aware of. If you are just starting to investigate the world of MIDI, as a rule of thumb you might want to consider buying a MIDI controller or other device that's got a bit more functionality than you think you need. As you investigate the available possibilities, you may be glad to have greater access to some of your DAW's less well-known features.

Some of the companies that have a wide range of MIDI keyboard controllers available include M-Audio, Korg, Edirol, and Alesis. To get an idea of some of the available brands and models, try searching for the term "MIDI Controller" on www.zZounds.com or www.musiciansfriend.com.

PORTABILITY

For a mobile or laptop-based studio, keyboards such as the M-Audio O2, Axiom 25, and Alesis Photon X25 are perfect. These models are not much bigger than a laptop and fit easily into a travel bag. Unfortunately, there's only so much functionality that you can fit in a small keyboard. When working with a program like Reason or Logic you may find that you quickly run out of the knobs and slider you want to create complex automation and mixes.

SYNTHESIZERS

I should take a moment here to mention another possibility: the synthesizer/MIDI keyboard combination. Most synthesizers available today include MIDI ports (In, Out, and often Thru as well) and can double as MIDI controllers for your DAW software and virtual instruments. If you already own a hardware synthesizer you may not need to invest in a separate MIDI keyboard controller, though you may still want one for portability and USB plug-and-play functionality.

Other Types of Controllers

While the most common type of MIDI controller is the MIDI keyboard, there are other types of controllers that may suit your specific needs or open up other creative possibilities.

PADS

Controller pads are great option for creating drum performances, "playing" live, and triggering loops. The M-Audio Trigger Finger and Frontier's Tranzport are both frequently used in conjunction with Ableton Live. Any of the following models will work with your DAW software. All cost about the same except for the Akai MPD 16.

- Akai MPD 16 MIDI Pad control surface (this model is less expensive than the others listed)
- Alesis Control Pad
- M-Audio Trigger Finger
- Korg Pad Control USB
- Frontier Tranzport

Aside from expensive electronic drum kits like Roland's V-Drums, MIDI controller pads are far and away the best choice for creating genuinely human-sounding drum performances. If you already have some drumming knowledge, ability, and skill, with a little practice and the right virtual drum kit you can create very realistic drum tracks. You can also find bundled software/control surface packages. For example, Native Instrument's Battery drum sequencer is available bundled with the M-Audio Trigger Finger, and Ableton Live is available with the Tranzport.

MIDI MIXERS

There's another group of MIDI devices available that you can use to control the mixing parameters of your DAW. In some cases these can be devices built specifically to work with your software, such as iControl for GarageBand, or one of the Pro Tools control surfaces, like the D-Control or Digi 002.

For a combination of price, functionality, and instant compatibility with most OS X music software, the Evolution UC-33e is a good choice. It comes with 30 preset configurations to give you immediate control of a wide range of software including Reason, Live, and Logic. Unlike some other models however, the UC-33e does not have an automated fader that will move in concert with your DAW's recorded automation.

Other MIDI controlled mixers include:

- ◆ Moderately priced:
    - ◆ Behringer BCF2000, www.behringer.com
    - ◆ PreSonus Faderport Single Fader DAW Controller, www.presonus.com
- ◆ Top-of-the-line:
    - ◆ Mackie Control Universal, www.mackie.com

While any MIDI-controlled mixer can be set up to work with any DAW program, for maximum compatibility you should check your software's preferences to make sure that your DAW supports the specific make and model before you buy any USB or FireWire mixer device. You can find a list of devices supported by your DAW by using the appropriate following steps.

In Live

1. Open Preferences.
2. Select MIDI/Sync.
3. Click the Control Surface drop-down menu to view the control surfaces that Live supports.

In Reason

1. Open Reason's Preferences.
2. Select Control Surfaces and Keyboards.
3. Click the Add button.
4. Look at the Manufacturer and Model menus.

In Logic

1. Choose Logic Pro/Express ➢ Preferences ➢ Start Logic Setup Assistant.
2. When you get to the MIDI Devices window click the Add button.
3. Look at the Manufacturer and Model lists.

In Pro Tools

Since Digidesign manufactures their own interfaces and mixers, Pro Tools doesn't include a list of third-party controllers that will work with the software. Check the documentation for any control surface you are interested in to see if it will be compatible with whatever version of Pro Tools you are working with.

In GarageBand

Since GarageBand's MIDI functionality is essentially plug and play, there's not much control over which MIDI interfaces you can use. The iControl is the only control surface specifically made for GarageBand. There's a free utility you can use called GarageRemote that lets you control Garage-Band with any MIDI controller that has assignable buttons. GarageRemote is available from: www.muratnkonar.com/otherstuff/garageremote.

NOT ON THE LIST?

In almost all cases control surfaces, MIDI keyboard, and MIDI interfaces that do not appear on your DAW software's lists will still work with your DAW, as long as they are supported by OS X. However, you'll often have an easier time working with an interface that is officially supported by your DAW. Troubleshooting and other various issues that arise are often easier to resolve when working with hardware and software that are known to be compatible.

MIDI INTERFACES

As we've discussed, many MIDI keyboards will plug directly into a USB port, and many audio interfaces also contain built-in MIDI ports. It often makes sense to combine your audio and MIDI in one interface, especially if your MIDI needs are not too complicated. For users who are dealing mostly with internal, virtual MIDI instruments, a separate MIDI interface will most likely not be necessary.

However, if you have multiple external MIDI devices (including controllers and MIDI-controlled hardware sound modules) and/or your audio interface doesn't include MIDI ports, you may need purchase a separate MIDI interface. MIDI interfaces run the gamut from very simple to extremely complicated. At the less expensive end of the spectrum are single In/Out interfaces like the Edirol UM-1EX and the M-Audio Uno. On the more expensive side are complex MIDI interfaces like Mark of the Unicorn's MIDI Timepiece AV, which includes eight MIDI Ins and Outs, synchronization, and compatibility with every conceivable audio and visual format and machine and many other features. Many interfaces that fall between these two extremes are also available. The following is a list of some of the companies currently manufacturing OS X compatible MIDI interfaces:

- M-Audio, http://www.m-audio.com
- Mark of the Unicorn, http://www.motu.com
- E-Mu, http://www.emu.com
- Edirol, http://www.edirol.com

Playing and Creating MIDI Files

A standard MIDI file has the suffix MID and can contain a long or short single performance, from a single instrument loop to a complete track to multiple performances, such as a complete song. There are three different types of standard MIDI files:

◆ Format 0: a single-track MIDI file

◆ Format 1: a multitrack MIDI file

◆ Format 2: can store multiple independent MIDI sequences

Just about all of the MIDI files you open, create, or work with will be Format 0 or Format 1.

There are a number of MIDI file websites that have large collections of complete MIDI songs. These files are freely available for download and can be used for fun, such as karaoke, or educational purposes, such as learning to play a specific song. MIDI files can also be used to share data such as drum patterns or chord progressions between DAW programs. Commercial drum loop MIDI files are less common than they used to be but are still available

Each DAW has its strengths and weaknesses when it comes to playing and creating MIDI files. The simplest way to get a quick look at how your DAW handles MIDI files is to download any MIDI song from `http://www.mididb.com` or `http://www.freemidi.org` and drop the file directly onto your DAW program.

WHY USE MIDI FILES?

MIDI files have one distinct advantage over every other kind of music-related file format: their size. MIDI files are tiny compared most other sound file types. A complete song containing seven or eight tracks of MIDI information including drum tracks, chord progressions, and lead lines can often come in around 50 to 100KB. A drum loop MIDI file may be under 10KB. Compare this to an MP3 or AAC file (10 times larger) or an AIFF or WAV file (up to 100 times larger), and you can see why MIDI files and files that are based on MIDI information (like Software Instrument Apple Loops) are still frequently used for transmitting music and music-related data.

GARAGEBAND

GarageBand in particular is set up to open MIDI files as complete songs and in many cases will automatically assign what it thinks are the most appropriate instruments to each individual MIDI track. This puts GarageBand at the head of the class when it comes to opening and playing MIDI files. If a track that you open in GarageBand isn't automatically assigned the correct instrument, it's a very simple matter to open the Track Info window and assign a better instrument. To play a MIDI file in GarageBand:

1. Create a new GarageBand music project.

2. Download any MIDI song file from `http://www.mididb.com` or `http://www.freemidi.org`.

3. Drag the MIDI file directly onto the GarageBand Timeline.

4. Press Play to play back the MIDI song.

Unfortunately (and somewhat inexplicably), GarageBand does not include the ability to export MIDI files. For the truly adventurous there is a freeware Audio Unit plug-in called midiO that can be used to send MIDI signals out of GarageBand and into another MIDI host; it's available at `http://home.comcast.net/~retroware`.

LOGIC

True to form, Logic has many different options for importing and playing MIDI files. Quickly playing a MIDI file in Logic is not as easy as in GarageBand but is still a fairly straightforward drag-and-drop proposition. Where Logic really stands above most other programs is in its ability to create and export complex MIDI files.

To quickly open a MIDI file in Logic:

1. Create a new Logic session.

2. Locate the folder `MMA Audio\MIDI` on this book's companion DVD.

3. Drag the file `MIDISong1.mid` directly onto the first instrument track in Logic. Logic will divide the MIDI file into multiple tracks. Figure 11.3 shows the MIDI file opened in Logic.

FIGURE 11.3

Opening a MIDI file in Logic

From here you can assign the appropriate instrument to each MIDI track. To create MIDI files in Logic:

1. Create a new Logic session.

2. Select any instrument track and add a virtual instrument.

3. Create a MIDI performance with your MIDI controller or the Caps Lock keyboard.

4. Create as many MIDI performances as you want on multiple tracks.

5. Shift+click to select all of the tracks you want to include in your MIDI file.

6. From the menu bar, select File ➤ Export ➤ Selection as MIDI File.

7. Choose a name and location for your MIDI file.

Your MIDI tracks will be named according to the instruments they were created using. This way when you or someone else opens them on another computer or in another program, they will know which instruments to assign to each track.

ABLETON LIVE

Live can export single tracks and clips as one-track MIDI files. Live can also open MIDI files that you drag directly onto the Arrange or Session View windows. You can also open MIDI files via the File Browser.

To export a MIDI file:

1. Select any MIDI clip or track in the Session or Arrange view.

2. Choose File ➢ Export MIDI Clip.

3. Select a location to save your file.

To import a MIDI file you can drag and drop the entire file onto Live's Session or Arrange view, or use the following method to import individual tracks via the File Browser:

1. Use the Live File Browser to locate the folder MMA Audio\MIDI.

2. Click the triangle next to MIDISong1.mid to view each individual track. Figure 11.4 shows a MIDI file in the File Browser.

FIGURE 11.4

A MIDI file in the
File Browser

3. Select an individual track and drag it to an open MIDI clip slot, track, or blank spot on the Clip/Device Drop area.

4. Assign a Live or third-party virtual instrument or drum kit to each MIDI track.

REASON

Importing an exporting MIDI files in Reason is relatively straightforward. It can definitely come in handy if you want to create MIDI performances in other programs or incorporate MIDI-based drum sequences into your Reason songs. You'll use the same MIDISong1.mid file to look at the importing process in Reason.

1. Create a new Reason song and add a Mixer 14:2.

2. Select File ➢ Import MIDI File.

3. Use the MIDI File Browser window to locate the folder MMA Audio\MIDI, select the MIDISong1.mid file, and click Open.

   Reason will open your MIDI file as a series of separate tracks with no instruments assigned. For each track you'll have to create and assign an instrument.

4. For the drum track, create an NN-XT Advanced Sampler. (The reason I'm having you use the NN-XT for your drum track and not the Redrum is because you can safely assume MIDI drum files are created using standardized MIDI procedures. For example, whatever drum

kit you assign to the drum track, you can be fairly sure that the kick drum will be triggered by the note C1 and that the snare drum will be triggered by the note D1 and so on. Because the Redrum uses a total of only ten notes, it doesn't always follow the same MIDI note/sample assigning system.)

5. Use the Browse Patch button to locate the folder `Reason Factory Sound Bank\NN-XT Sampler Patches\Drums and Percussion\Drums and Kits`.

6. Select any of the NN-XT drum kits.

7. Select the Drums Ch1 track in the sequencer window and use the drop-down menu to assign the drum track to the NN-XT 1 instrument (Figure 11.5).

FIGURE 11.5
Assign the drum
track to the NN-XT
1 instrument.

8. Use this same method to create bass, guitar, and piano NN-XT instruments and assign them to each sequencer track.

Exporting MIDI files from Reason is as simple as selecting File ➤ Export as MIDI File. This exports your entire song as a MIDI file, there's no option for exporting a single track.

PRO TOOLS

There are multiple options available for importing and exporting MIDI files in Pro Tools. For importing MIDI files, I like to use the Import MIDI to Regions List, which doesn't create automatic tracks but allows you to assign the instruments yourself by dragging the MIDI information directly to open instrument tracks.

1. Create a new Pro Tools session.

2. Choose File ➤ Import ➤ MIDI to Region List.

3. Locate the folder `MMA Audio\MIDI` and select the file `MIDIsong1.mid`.

4. Select All Documents from the Enable drop-down menu at the top of the dialog box.

5. Click Open. All of the MIDI file's tracks will appear in the Regions list on the right side of the Edit window (Figure 11.6).

FIGURE 11.6
MIDI tracks in the
Regions list

6. Create a new stereo instrument track.

7. Drag the Drums-01 track directly onto the new instrument track.

8. Add the Xpand! Synthesizer as an insert on the instrument track.

9. Use the Xpand!'s Librarian menu to load one of the drum kits from the Preset folder 26 Drums.

10. Click the Play button to hear the drum track.

11. Create new instrument tracks for each of the MIDI tracks and use the Xpand! or any other virtual instrument to create the appropriate instrument for the MIDI performance.

12. To export MIDI files from Pro Tools:

13. Select File ➤ Export ➤ MIDI.

14. Select File Format 0 (for a single-track file) or 1 (for a multitrack file) from the Export dialog box.

15. Choose a location for your MIDI file.

MIDI and Reason

MIDI, in one form or another, is right at the heart of just about every aspect of the Reason program. Whether you are using the Matrix pattern sequencer, an external keyboard, or your mouse to draw automation in the Controller Lane, you are triggering, adjusting, and manipulating MIDI information. When composing in Reason you can take advantage of this by mapping various functions to your MIDI keyboard. This allows you "play" Reason as if it were itself an instrument.

You can use MIDI mapping to control just about all of the parameters of Reasons instruments and effects. You can also use MIDI mapping to assign the faders and knobs of the Mixer 14:2 to corresponding faders and knobs on a MIDI hardware control surface mixing device. In addition, you can use the faders and knobs included on some MIDI keyboards to simulate a hardware mixing board.

Setting Up a Control Surface or Keyboard

If you haven't set up a default master keyboard yet:

1. Make sure your MIDI interface(s) are connected and all the necessary drivers are installed.

2. Open Reason's preferences and select the Control Surfaces and Keyboards tab.

3. Click the Auto-detect Surfaces button.

   Reason will now automatically detect your control surface or keyboard. If you have more than one MIDI device connected, select which device you want to use as your master (main) keyboard. Figure 11.7 shows the Control Surfaces and Keyboards Preferences panel.

4. If Reason does not automatically detect your control surface or keyboard, click the Add button.

5. Select your control surface or keyboard's manufacturer from the drop-down menu. If the manufacturer is not on the list, select Other.

6. Select the model or type of controller from the second drop-down menu, depending on what the list displays.

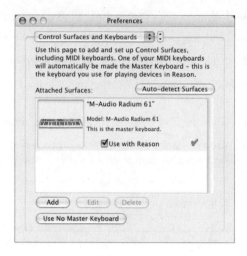

7. If necessary, type a name for your MIDI interface in the Name field.

8. Select a MIDI input.

Reason is now ready to work with your MIDI control surface or Keyboard.

Automatic MIDI Mapping

Reason has automatic MIDI mapping in place for any interface that appears on its list of automatically detected surfaces. Those that do not appear on the list will follow a predetermined set of
MIDI mapped features.

To try out the automatic MIDI mapping feature in Reason:

1. Create a new Reason Song.

2. Choose Create ➤ Mixer 14:2.

3. Choose Create ➤ Sequencer Track.

4. Assign the new sequencer track to the Mixer by selecting Mixer 1 from the output drop-
   down menu as shown in Figure 11.8.

FIGURE 11.8
Assigning the new
sequencer track

5. Select the track in the Sequencer window and name it Mixer 1.

6. Click the keyboard icon to arm the track to receive MIDI information.

7. Try out the various knobs, faders, and keys on your MIDI interface to see which knobs, faders, and buttons they correspond to in the Mixer 14:2.

Using this method you can familiarize yourself with the correspondences between MIDI parameters for your keyboard and each of Reason's instruments and effects. You can use your MIDI interface to control any Reason instrument. To do this, add a new instrument to the Reason song, select the instrument in the Sequencer window and arm it to receive MIDI information.

To use MIDI mapping with additional mixers and effects in your Reason song:

1. Add an effect or another mixer to the Reason song.

2. Create a sequencer track for the effect or mixer.

3. Assign the sequencer track to the new effect or mixer.

4. Select the new sequencer track in the Sequencer window and arm it to receive MIDI information.

Only mixers and effects require a new sequencer track in order to receive MIDI information. With Reason's instruments all you have to do is select the instrument in the Sequencer window and arm it to receive MIDI information.

AUTOMATION

To record automation with your MIDI interface, click the Record button and the Play button in the Transport bar. Use your MIDI interface to adjust any faders and knobs while recording. Stop recording and play back the Reason song. Your automated faders and knobs will be highlighted.

Erase automation by Control+clicking in the highlighted area and selecting Clear Automation from the pop-up menu.

REMOTE OVERRIDE

Reason's Remote Override function can be used to create your own MIDI mapping on all of Reason's instruments and effects. This is especially useful if you have a limited number of MIDI controls on your MIDI controller and would like to assign them to specific functions. Any Remote Override settings you create will only affect the current song, so any changes you make will not remain in place in any new sessions you create. However, as a workaround you can create a template session with your Remote Override settings and assign it as the default Reason session.

To use Remote Override:

1. Create a new session.

2. Add a Mixer 14:2 and an NNXT Advanced Sampler.

3. Select Options ➤ Remote Override Edit Mode. The entire Reason interface appears slightly grayed out. All of the assignable MIDI parameters have arrows or highlighted knobs, as shown in Figure 11.9.

FIGURE 11.9
The Remote Override
Edit mode

The yellow knobs signify that the parameter is already mapped to a knob or slider on your MIDI controller. In Remote Override mode, any of these can be re-assigned to another MIDI knob or slider. The blue arrows mean that the parameter is available to be mapped if you want it to be. Taking a look at the Remote Override mode is also a great way to get familiar with which of Reason's parameters can be controlled by MIDI and assigned automation.

4. Double-click any of the arrows or knobs so that it changes to a revolving lightning bolt.

5. Adjust any knob, fader, or slider on your MIDI interface to automatically assign it to the corresponding function in Reason.

6. Once you have assigned your customized MIDI mapping, deselect Remote Override Edit Mode in the Options menu to return to the normal Reason interface.

You do not have to create a sequencer track for the mixers or effects in Remote Override Edit Mode.

KEYBOARD MAPPING MODE

Similar to the Remote Override function is Reason's Keyboard Control. Keyboard control lets you assign letters and numbers from your Apple keyboard to functions in Reason. To set up keyboard control:

1. Select Options ➢ Enable Keyboard Control.

2. Select Options ➢ Keyboard Control Edit Mode.

3. Any assignable parameter will be marked with a yellow arrow. Double-click any arrow to activate it, then press any key on your Apple Keyboard to assign it to the button or knob.

The Keyboard Mapping mode can be useful if you don't have a MIDI controller or want to improvise a Reason mix on a laptop in a live setting.

Manually Working with MIDI

Reason contains a huge number of editable parameters for all of its instruments and tracks. Many of these may not be obvious at first, but by investigating the various sequencer views you'll find more and more ways to create automation and access new sounds and ideas by adjusting various MIDI-controlled parameters. Let's take a look at the Controller Lane to see some of what's available to work with:

1. Create a new Reason song.

2. Add a Mixer 14:2 and a Redrum drum computer to the Reason song.

3. Select the Redrum in the Sequencer window and click the Edit/Arrange Mode button to view the Edit mode.

4. Deselect any currently showing lanes.

5. Click the Show Controller Lane button to view the controller lanes that you will select in the next step.

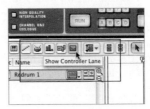

6. Click the Controllers button to view the Controllers drop-down menu, as shown in Figure 11.10.

FIGURE 11.10

The Controllers drop-down menu

As you can see from this list, there are a huge number of available parameters that can be automated. Many of these can, of course, be automated by assigning their functions to your MIDI keyboard. However, in some cases it may be easier to work manually with your mouse.

7. Select Drum 1 Mute from the list.

8. Select Drum 1 Send Amount from further down the same list.

9. Select the Pencil tool and use it to draw automation in each of the controller lanes. Figure 11.11 shows the manually drawn automation.

As you can see, there are two different types of automation here. The Mute automation gives you two choices, off or on. The send amount can be increased or decreased incrementally.

FIGURE 11.11

Manual automation in the controller lanes

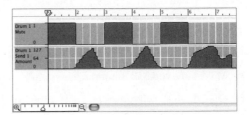

As soon as you draw automation for any selected parameter, the corresponding knob or slider on the device will be highlighted, just as it would if you created the automation with your mouse or MIDI controller.

Quantizing in Reason

Once you've created a performance in Reason with your MIDI keyboard (see Chapter 2, "Reason" for basic instructions) you may find that you want to change or fix some of the timing aspects without necessarily re-recording the entire performance. This is where quantization can be very useful. Quantizing your manually created drum and other instrument tracks can go a long way toward getting your Reason songs and tracks sounding tighter and cleaner. Reason makes quantizing any instrument performance very simple:

1. Use the Arrow tool to select the notes or region you want to quantize.

2. Select the quantization value from the Quantize Value drop-down menu (Figure 11.12).

FIGURE 11.12
The Quantize Value menu and Quantize Notes button

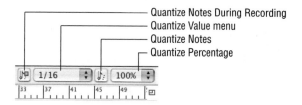

Quantize Notes During Recording
Quantize Value menu
Quantize Notes
Quantize Percentage

3. Click the Quantize Notes button (also shown in Figure 11.12).

You may want to try different levels of quantization (½, ¼, ⅛, and so on) before deciding on the right amount. You can always use the Undo command (Command+Z) to return to the unquantized performance. You can also create different types of rhythms by selecting a value from the Quantize Percentage drop-down menu just to the right of the Quantize Notes button.

To the left of the Quantize Value drop-down menu is the Quantize Notes During Recording button. Click this button to automatically quantize your performance during the recording process.

MIDI and Ableton Live

Live's basic MIDI functions are fairly straightforward. As I covered in Chapter 3, "Ableton Live," MIDI is used in Live to create clips and loops. You can also use MIDI to create different kinds of automation and to trigger events such as the launching of scenes and loops as well as starting and stopping events. This is a frequently used method for "playing" Ableton Live in a live performance or DJ situation. I'll use a standard MIDI keyboard in this example, but you can use any MIDI controller to trigger Live. In fact, you can buy controllers like the M-Audio Trigger Finger and the Frontier Tranzport at a discount bundled rate along with the newest version of Live.

MIDI Mapping in Live

To set up basic MIDI mapping in a Live session:

1. Make sure you MIDI interface is connected and all of the necessary drivers are installed.

2. Open Live's preferences and select the MIDI/Sync Tab.

3. In the Control Surface drop-down menu, locate and choose your MIDI controller.

4. Select your MIDI input and output. Figure 11.13 shows the Control Surface, Input, and Output settings.

FIGURE 11.13
Control Surface,
Input, and Output
settings

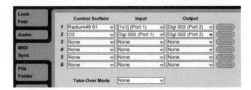

5. In the Input section make sure the Track, Sync, and Remote buttons for your preferred MIDI device are set to On.

Figure 11.14 shows the MIDI/Sync settings Input section.

FIGURE 11.14
The MIDI/Sync
Input settings

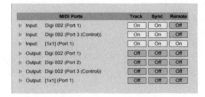

1. Close Live's preferences.

Activate MIDI mapping by clicking the MIDI Map Mode Switch in the upper right corner of the Live window.

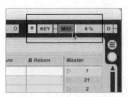

Clicking the MIDI Map Mode Switch will highlight all of the assignable parameters in Live.

Live's unique layout and assignable MIDI mapping sets up a number of interesting possibilities. Aside from the usual suspects such as panning, muting, and soloing, there are some more interesting possibilities available as well. For example, you can assign a keyboard key or controller pad to the Tap Tempo parameter, or you can assign any of your MIDI controller's knobs to adjust the tempo of your session, allowing you to speed up or slow down playback in real time.

Which configuration you ultimately decide on will depend on your own style of working. The following is a basic tutorial in setting up a simple MIDI map for arranging and live performance:

1. Open the file `MMA Audio Files\Ableton Live\Sets\MasterOne.als`.

2. Click the MIDI Map Mode Switch.

3. Select Scene 1 in the master track.

4. Press the C3 key on your MIDI keyboard. Playing a note on your MIDI keyboard sends a MIDI message to Live. Live "sees" the message and automatically assigns the note to the selected scene.

5. Select Scene 2 in the master track.

6. Press the D3 key on your MIDI keyboard.

7. Select Scene 3 in the master track.

8. Press the E3 key on your MIDI keyboard.

9. Select the Stop Clips button.

10. Press F4 on your MIDI keyboard.

11. Click the MIDI Map Mode Switch again to leave MIDI mapping mode.

Figure 11.15 shows the MIDI mapping on the master track.

FIGURE 11.15

MIDI mapping on the
master track

The three scenes are now linked to the three keys on your MIDI keyboard. Use C3 to trigger playback of Scene 1, then use the other assigned keys to play the other scenes. Press the F4 key to stop playback.

To create and save an arrangement:

1. Click the Stop button in Live's Transport bar twice to make sure the Live session is at zero.

2. Click the Record button to arm Live for recording.

3. Launch any scene to begin recording.

4. Create an arrangement "on-the-fly" by launching scenes.

5. Click the Stop button to stop recording.

You can now switch to the Arrange View window and play back your new arrangement.

KEY MAPPING

All of the Live functions that can be assigned to a MIDI controller can also be assigned to keys on your Apple keyboard using Live's Key Map mode. Use the Key Map Mode Switch just to the left of the MIDI Map Mode switch to turn key mapping on and off.

CREATIVE MIDI MAPPING

To see even more assignable parameters, add clips and effects to your Live session then select Clip View and Track View. As you can see, you can even assign a MIDI control to transpose a clip or adjust its default playback start position. The point here is that there's not much that Live's programmers have left "uncontrollable."

Let's use the MasterOne.als file from the previous example to assign some knobs or faders from your MIDI controller to some of Live's more interesting parameters:

1. Make sure the MasterOne.als file is open with the MIDI mapping you set up earlier in this section.

2. Make sure MIDI Mapping mode is deselected.

3. Select the clip DrumLoop3 in Scene 3. The clip and its properties should now be visible in Clip view.

4. Click the MIDI Map Mode Switch to activate MIDI mapping.

5. Select the Track Pan knob in Track 2's Mixer section. Select any knob or slider on your MIDI controller and adjust it slightly. Just as it does when you play a MIDI note on the keyboard, adjusting a slider or knob sends a MIDI signal to Live. Live "sees" the message and automatically assigns the knob or slider to the selected parameter.

6. Select the Transpose button in the Clip View window.

7. Select any knob or slider on your MIDI controller and adjust it slightly to assign it to the Transpose knob.

8. Deselect the MIDI Map Mode switch.

You're now ready to "play" your session and make real-time changes to the drum clip during playback. Use the C3, D3, or E3 notes to launch any scene and begin playback. During playback, use the first assigned knob or slider to adjust the track panning.

In order to use the assigned knob or slider to transpose the drum loop, you'll have to select the clip in the Clip view, then adjust the parameter. By assigning a knob to the Transpose function, you can transpose any clip in the session by selecting in the clip slot and adjusting the assigned knob or slider. Be careful with this, though: it's very easy to make a sonic mess out of an arrangement by adjusting the pitch of a track or two. It's also important to remember here that you are not changing the pitch of the track, only the selected clip. If you have multiple instances of the same clip on your track you can return things to normal by selecting and launching an unchanged clip.

CONTROLLING EFFECTS

Using MIDI mapping to add and remove effects on a Return track is another way to add an improvisational element to your mixes and live performances.

1. Reopen the MasterOne.als Live set you used earlier in this section.

2. Use the Live Device Browser to locate the Audio Effect Ping Pong Delay, select the Ping Preset, and drag it to the A Return track.

3. Select View ➤ Sends.

4. Double-click the A Return track header in order to view the Ping Pong Delay effect in Track view.

5. Click the MIDI Map Mode switch.

6. Select the Send A knob for Track 1 and assign it to a knob or slider on your MIDI controller.

7. Do the same for Send A on Tracks 2 and 3.

8. In the center of the Ping Pong Delay are eight Mode buttons, which can be used to switch between different types of delay effects. Assign a MIDI knob or slider here so you can use it to switch among the eight modes. Figure 11.16 shows this section of the Ping Pong Delay.

FIGURE 11.16
Ping Pong Delay
Mode buttons

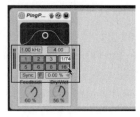

9. Deselect the MIDI Map Mode switch.

10. Launch Scene 3 and use your assigned MIDI controls to add the Ping Pong Delay effect by raising the sends on each track. Use the control you assigned to the Ping Pong Delay to switch between different types of delay effects.

Whether your interest is live performance or creating arrangements on the fly, the more you experiment with MIDI mapping and Live, the more you'll want to have access to as many parameters as possible. If you don't already have a separate MIDI mixer style control surface, once you start playing with Live's MIDI mapping you may want to take a second look at acquiring one.

MIDI Velocity and Clips

Adjusting the velocity of each note in a musical performance or each hit in a drum performance can go a long way toward humanizing your Live MIDI clips. You can adjust the velocity for each individual MIDI note in a clip at the bottom of the Clip view.

1. Select any Impulse kit and drag it to an empty MIDI track.

2. Create a new clip by double-clicking in any empty clip slot.

3. Create a simple kick/snare drum pattern.

4. Select any note, then click and drag its Velocity slider.

Figure 11.17 shows the velocity being adjusted on a snare drum hit.

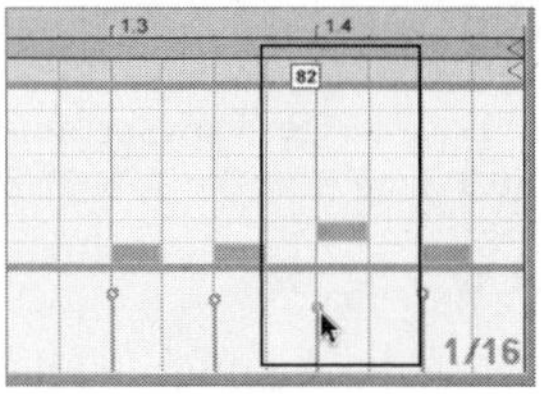

FIGURE 11.17
Adjusting the velocity
on a single MIDI note

As you raise or lower the velocity of the selected note the new velocity appears in a small box at the top of the Clip view, also shown in Figure 11.17.

You can also use your mouse to select and raise or lower multiple notes simultaneously. Making even minor adjustments, especially to a snare drum, can go a long way towards creating more realistic-sounding performances.

Quantizing in Live

Live gives you the option of either quantizing your performance as it's happening or after recording.

To activate Record Quantization:

1. Select Edit ➤ Record Quantization.

2. Choose a note value from the list.

Once you're finished recording, turn off Record Quantization by selecting No Quantization from the top of the list.

To quantize after recording:

1. Use your mouse to select a note or group of notes in the Note Editor.

2. Choose Edit ➤ Quantize.

3. Select a quantization amount from the Quantize To drop-down menu, then click OK.

Figure 11.18 shows the Quantization dialog box.

FIGURE 11.18
The Quantization
dialog box

MIDI and Pro Tools

I've covered some of the basic MIDI functions in Chapter 4, "Pro Tools." Pro Tools contains a number of complex MIDI functions that you can access easily. For this first example I'll use the included Xpand! software synth to create and edit a MIDI performance. If you have the full version of Reason, you can use Reason instead of Xpand! if you prefer.

Creating a MIDI Performance

Using MIDI instruments in Pro Tools used to require two separate tracks, an aux input for the instrument and a MIDI track for the recorded MIDI information. Pro Tools 7 introduced a new feature, instrument tracks, which makes the process much simpler.

1. Create a new Pro Tools session and name it MIDI Instrument. Save the session to your Pro Tools session folder.

2. Choose Track ➤ New and create a stereo instrument track and a mono aux input.

3. Make sure the Instruments and Inserts fields are showing, as is in Figure 11.19. If they are not currently visible, use the View ➤ Edit Window function to put a check mark next to both fields.

FIGURE 11.19
Make sure the Instru-
ments and Inserts
fields are both
showing.

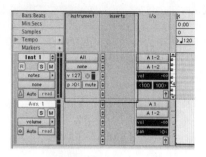

4. In the Audio Volume field you'll see what looks like a "minus infinity" symbol. This means the track is silent. To raise the volume to zero you can Option+click the Volume field, or use the pop-up Volume slider. Raise the volume to zero (0db) for both tracks.

5. Select the aux input and add a click instrument.

6. On the instrument track, select Insert A and from the pop-up window choose Multi-channel Plug-in ➢ Instrument ➢ Xpand! (stereo).

7. In the Xpand! window, select the Librarian menu and load the instrument 13 Acoustic Piano ➢ Natural Grand Piano.

8. In the Instrument field, use the MIDI input selector to choose the MIDI input you want to use.

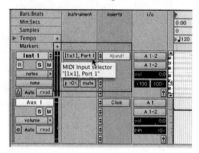

9. Arm the instrument track for recording and then use the keyboard shortcut Command+space-bar to begin recording.

10. Record a performance using your MIDI keyboard to play the Xpand! Instrument. Figure 11.20 shows a MIDI performance on your instrument track.

FIGURE 11.20
A MIDI performance
on the instrument
track

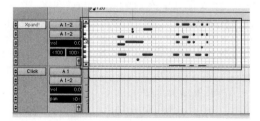

CREATING A MIDI PERFORMANCE WITHOUT A MIDI KEYBOARD

If you don't have a MIDI controller or keyboard, you can create a performance by using the Pencil tool to draw notes in the track window

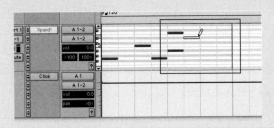

Humanizing Your Performance

There are two ways to achieve quantization in Pro Tools: during the recording process (in Pro Tools, this functionality is called input quantization) or after (grid / groove quantization). Quantizing during the recording process has the advantage of allowing you to create "perfect" performances without having to play perfectly. The downside is that some of the natural humanness of your performance may be lost. In addition, choosing too high a quantization value can create an incorrect-sounding performance. It's a good idea to experiment a bit with your Pro Tools quantization settings, wherever you choose to quantize your performance.

INPUT QUANTIZE

To set up Input Quantization:

1. Select Event ➢ MIDI ➢ Input Quantize.

2. Put a check mark in the Enable Input Quantize box at the top of the dialog box.

3. Select which parameters you want to quantize. I generally choose Attacks and Preserve Note Duration. Figure 11.21 shows the Input Quantize dialog box.

FIGURE 11.21
Input Quantize
settings.

4. In the Quantize Grid field choose your note duration. This setting will depend on the type of performance you are intending to create. A simple drum performance will probably benefit from using ⅛-note or 1⁄16-note settings. For a more complicated, intricate performance, choose a higher note value. If you expect to use dotted notes or triplets, be sure to choose these options.

5. Create a performance.

GRID/GROOVE QUANTIZE

For "after the fact" quantization:

1. Use either the Grabber tool or the Selector tool to highlight the notes you want to quantize.

2. Choose Event ➤ MIDI ➤ Grid/Groove Quantize.

3. Select which parameters you wish to quantize.

4. Select a note value or groove style.

5. Click the Apply button.

The main advantage to quantizing after you record is greater control over the final results. If you are not happy with your quantization, you can easily Undo (Command+Z) and try a lesser or higher value.

VELOCITY

The MIDI Operations dialog box has another view that comes in handy when trying to tame an inconsistent performance. The Change Velocity dialog can be used to smooth a performance that contains drastic dynamic shifts.

First let's take a look at the Velocity view of a MIDI performance. This is done by clicking the Track View selector in the track header.

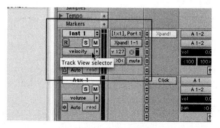

Figure 11.22 shows the Velocity view in the Timeline. As you can see, there's a pretty wide dynamic range to this performance. Sometimes that's a good thing, but on this occasion you want to create a smoother, more consistent performance.

FIGURE 11.22

The Velocity view in the Timeline

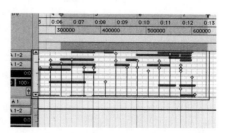

You can correct the velocity easily by selecting the Free Hand Pencil tool and clicking and dragging across all of the MIDI notes in the performance.

MIDI Editing in Pro Tools

Pro Tools editing tools have similar and, in some cases, exactly the same functions in MIDI editing that they do in audio editing (see Chapter 4). You can zoom in and out of MIDI performances, tracks, and the Timeline; change the length of notes; and select and move notes, tracks, and regions.

The Pencil tool is the most useful tool in MIDI editing. You can use it to create and edit your MIDI performance. If you click and hold down the Pencil Tool button you will see a drop-down menu of different types of curves. Figure 11.23 shows all of the available Pencil tools.

FIGURE 11.23
The Pencil tools

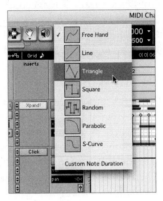

Free Hand   Use the Free Hand Pencil tool to create unconstrained MIDI edit points and velocity changes.

Line   Use the Line Pencil tool to create straight line MIDI edits, including volume swells and fade outs. You can also use the Line Pencil tool to even out velocity.

Triangle   The Triangle Pencil tool creates edits in an up-and-down pattern. Figure 11.24 shows the results of clicking and dragging with the Triangle Pencil in the Velocity view.

FIGURE 11.24
Using the Triangle
Pencil tool on a MIDI
performance.

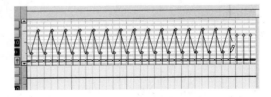

Square   Similar to the Triangle Pencil, the Square Pencil creates edit points along a repeating rectangular pattern.

Try each of the Pencil tools out in your MIDI performance to get an idea of how they each work. MIDI editing in Pro Tools follows many of the same rules as audio editing. As you learn more skills and try out Pro Tools editing functions in both formats, you'll find that quite often you'll be simultaneously increasing your knowledge in both areas.

You can easily group your MIDI performances for quick editing, moving, copying, and pasting. Use the Selector tool to select all of the notes of your performance or a section of your performance, then choose Region ➤ Group. You can now use the Grabber to easily move your new MIDI group.

MIDI and Logic

As I mentioned in Chapter 5, "Logic," one of Logic's big selling points is the intricacy of its MIDI functions—and this is also one of the things that keeps the new user away from Logic Pro. In a book of this size I can only scratch the surface of what is possible with MIDI in Logic, but at the very least I can try to demystify it a bit.

I covered the process of creating and looping a MIDI performance in Chapter 5. Here we'll take look at some of Logic's more advanced MIDI editing capabilities.

Logic has multiple MIDI editors; some have been a part of the program through many versions and some are newer additions. Which MIDI editor you choose will depend on your preferred method of operation and what kinds of MIDI editing you hope to accomplish.

The Matrix Edit Window

I covered the basic functionality of the Matrix Edit window in Chapter 5. But, as I'm sure you've figured out, the Matrix Edit window has a lot more to it than just creating and moving notes around.

There are two ways to quantize a performance in Logic's Matrix Edit window. You can use the Quantize button or the Quantize tool. To use this tutorial, locate the MMA Audio\Logic\Loops folder and drag the Software Instrument Apple Loop file ImpLoop26.aif onto any open instrument track. Then double-click the file in the Arrange window to open the Matrix Edit window.

To use the Quantize button:

1. Use the Arrow tool to select the first group of notes.

2. With the notes highlighted, click and hold the Quantize button just below the Matrix Edit toolbar (Figure 11.25).

FIGURE 11.25
The Matrix Edit window Quantize button

Clicking the Quantize button opens the Quantize pop-up menu. Here you can choose from a list of values to quantize any selected notes. In this case choosing any note value for $\frac{1}{1}$ note to $\frac{1}{12}$ note will line the selected notes up at the beginning of the loop. Choosing $\frac{1}{16}$ note will move the notes to the closest $\frac{1}{16}$-note value.

Another option for quantizing in the Matrix Edit window is the Quantize tool, third from the bottom in the Matrix Edit Tool bar.

To use the Quantize tool:

1. Select the Quantize tool in the Matrix Edit toolbar.

2. Click and hold a single note or "lasso" a group of notes, then click and hold any one of them.

3. Choose a quantize value from the pop-up menu.

The Event List

Logic's Event List window is exactly what the name suggests: a list of all of the MIDI events in a selected region. What makes it interesting is that you can use the Event List to preview, edit, and rearrange MIDI events. Sometimes this can actually be faster than working in the Matrix Editor, especially for editing groups of notes.

To take a look at the Event List:

1. Create a new Logic session.

2. Select the first instrument track and create an ES P Polyphonic Synth.

3. Use the Pencil tool to create a new region on the selected instrument track in the Arrange window.

4. Double-click the new region to open the Matrix Edit window.

5. Use the Pencil tool to create four notes anywhere in the Matrix Edit window.

6. Select Windows ➤ Event List.

7. Figure 11.26 shows the Event List window.

FIGURE 11.26

The Event List window

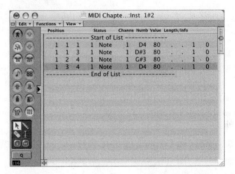

Arrange the currently open Logic windows so that the Matrix Edit window and the Event List window are side by side. As you can see, the Event List contains four events—one for each MIDI note you've created in the Matrix Edit window

Select any note in the Matrix Edit window and move it. You will see the corresponding note information change in the Event List.

Select a note in the Event List. Click any of the numbers in the Position field and drag up or down. Any changes you make on the Event List will be reflected in the Matrix Edit window. Click and drag in the field labeled Numb to raise and lower the selected MIDI note.

The Hyper Edit Window

In the Hyper Edit window you can perform a number of frequently used MIDI parameter editing functions.

BASICS OF THE HYPER EDIT WINDOW

To get a look at the Hyper Edit window:

1. Create a new Logic Session

2. Use the Loop Browser to locate the Software Instrument loop Classic Rock Piano 01.

3. Drag the loop from the Loop Browser to any empty instrument track and place the loop at the beginning of the Timeline.

4. Select the loop in the Timeline and choose Windows ➢ Hyper Edit.

5. To the left of the Hyper Edit Timeline are the various parameters you can edit with the Hyper Edit window. Select the Pan parameter and click and draw across the Pan grid as shown in Figure 11.27.

FIGURE 11.27

Creating panning changes in the Hyper Edit Window

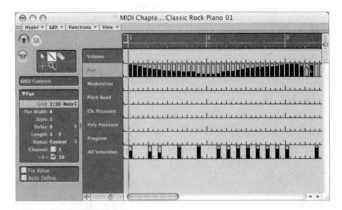

Once you've created the events in the Hyper Edit window you can use your mouse to change the panning by clicking in the grid and drawing across the events. Figure 11.27 shows the mouse being used to create a sweeping, back and forth panning effect.

Using the click and drag method, you can create events and edit them for all of the Hyper Edit window's parameters.

PROGRAMMING DRUMS IN THE HYPER EDIT WINDOW

The Hyper Edit window's grid format, combined with the ability to quickly adjust the velocity of each note, is also very useful for creating drum patterns. Here's how:

1. Create a new Logic Project.

2. Double-click the first instrument track to open the Track Mixer.

3. In the channel strip's Input field, choose Stereo ➢ Logic ➢ GarageBand Instruments ➢ Drum Kits.

4. Return to the Arrange window and use the Pencil tool to create a two-bar region.

5. Create a matching two-bar cycle region at the top of the Arrange Window Timeline.

6. Use the Arrow tool to select the region in the Timeline.

7. Select Windows ➢ Hyper Edit from Logic's File menu.

8. From the Hyper menu at the top left of the Hyper Edit window, choose Create GM Drum Set (Figure 11.28).

FIGURE 11.28
Create a GM
Drum Set.

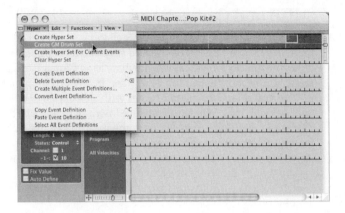

The parameters of the Hyper Edit window are now replaced with drum sounds, and the Hyper Edit grid can be used to trigger individual drum hits and create patterns, loops, and complete drum tracks.

9. Select the Pencil tool from the Hyper Edit Tool bar.

10. Locate the Kick 1 grid and click with the Pencil tool to create events on the first beat of each measure.

11. Locate the SD 1 (Snare Drum 1) grid and create snare events.

12. 12. Locate the Closed HH (hi-hat) grid and create hi-hat events. Figure 11.29 shows a simple kick/snare/hi-hat pattern in the Hyper Edit window.

FIGURE 11.29
A simple drum
pattern in the Hyper
Edit window

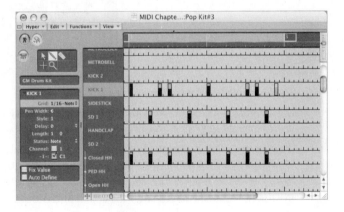

13. Press the spacebar to begin playback of the cycle region.

14. Select any event in the Hyper Edit window and click and drag up or down to raise or lower the velocity of the event.

The Hyper Edit window isn't limited to creating drum performances, but its layout and ability to quickly create GM Drum Sets make it a perfect tool for quick drum programming and looping.

MIDI and GarageBand

One of the coolest things about GarageBand is that it introduces the user to a number of MIDI functions in very simple, straightforward ways. As a result, sometimes without realizing it, anyone who takes the time to become an intermediate level GarageBand user becomes familiar with some of the basic MIDI concepts that can be applied in any program that uses MIDI.

Foe example, GarageBand comes with a stockpile of both Software and Real Instrument loops and Apple Loops. What are Software Instrument loops? They're MIDI performances that trigger GarageBand's built-in virtual instruments. You can use GarageBand's Track Editor window to open any GarageBand Software Instrument loop and alter it to suit your session by performing some basic MIDI editing tasks. While this is certainly not as complex as the MIDI editing you can do in Logic or Pro Tools, it's still in the same family.

Let's open up a Software Instrument Apple Loop and take a look at some of GarageBand's MIDI editing functions:

1. Start GarageBand and create a new music project.

2. Open the Loop Browser and add the Loop 70s Ballad Piano 03 to your session.

3. Press C on your keyboard and create a two-measure cycle region.

4. Double-click the loop in the window to open the Track Editor.

5. In the Tracks Editor's Advanced field, select the Advanced drop-down menu to view the editable MIDI parameters shown in Figure 11.30.

FIGURE 11.30
The Advanced
drop-down menu

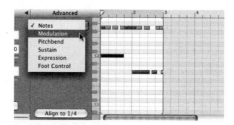

The available MIDI parameters are as follows:

Modulation Adding modulation can give your MIDI tracks a wavering sound. It's especially useful in making synthesizer lines stand out in a mix.

Expression This is essentially volume control, but it also affects the attack or initial force of a MIDI note. Adding control points that raise and lower the expression creates dynamics. Used lightly, it can be a good way to give your MIDI performance a more "human" feel.

Pitchbend Pitchbend will alter the actual pitch of a note or range of notes.

Sustain This is the length of time a note sounds. For example, a note or chord played on a guitar that rings out is "sustaining." Adding sustain can give your tracks a more relaxed feel. You also can use it to create a "larger" sound, because multiple sustained notes blend into each other. In GarageBand, Track Editor sustain is either on or off.

Foot Control The Foot Control parameter can control the information from an external device such as a sustain pedal.

MIDI information is edited in the Track Edit window by creating control points using your mouse and the Command key.

1. Select the Modulation parameter from the Advanced menu and Command+click anywhere in the Track Editor Timeline to create a control point.

2. Command+click to create more control points.

3. Use you mouse to move the control points around in the Track Editor.

4. To remove a control point, select it with your mouse and press the Delete key.

Figure 11.31 shows Modulation editing with control points in the Track Editor.

FIGURE 11.31

Modulation control points in the Track Editor

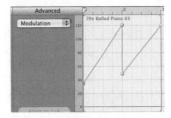

Velocity

You can also control the note velocity for individual notes in a GarageBand Software instrument track or loop.

1. Select Notes from the Advanced drop-down menu to return to the default Notes view.

2. Use your mouse to select any single note in the Track Editor Timeline.

3. Raise or lower the note's velocity using the Note Velocity slider in the Regions field on the left side of the Track Editor (Figure 11.32).

FIGURE 11.32

The Note Velocity slider

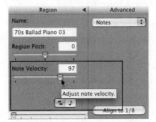

You can also select, raise, and lower the velocity of multiple notes at once with the Note Velocity slider.

Quantizing in GarageBand

GargaeBand's Track Editor has a very basic quantizing feature. Like many GarageBand functions, they don't confuse you with fancy recording terminology. Quantizing in GarageBand is done by using the Align button at the bottom of the Advanced field in the Track Editor (Figure 11.33).

FIGURE 11.33

The Align button in
the Track Edit window

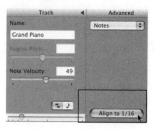

1. Select any Software Instrument track and use your MIDI keyboard or the Musical Typing keyboard to record a MIDI performance.

2. Double-click the performance in the Timeline to open the Track Edit window.

3. Use your mouse to select any note or multiple notes in the Track Edit window.

4. Quantize the notes by clicking the Align to button.

5. You can increase and decrease the quantization value by raising and lowering the Zoom slider at the bottom left of the Track Edit window.

GarageBand's simple, straightforward handling of MIDI has its advantages and disadvantages, sometimes simultaneously. For example, when you plug in or activate any MIDI device, GarageBand recognizes it instantly and lets you know with a pop-up that says, "The number of MIDI inputs has changed." The downside of how MIDI is handled in GarageBand is apparent when you look at GarageBand's Preferences, specifically the (lack of) MIDI Preferences, which consist of a MIDI Status field that lets you know how many MIDI inputs are currently active and a default MIDI velocity slider.

The good news is that Apple consistently upgrades and adds features to GarageBand with every new release, so it's very likely that future versions of the program will be even more MIDI-functional.

 Real World Scenario

USING MIDI TO PLAY YOUR DAW LIVE

More musicians are using MacBooks, PowerBooks, and iBooks in place of samplers and bulky keyboards for live gigs. I recently started using Ableton Live for performing live in order to add audio and spoken word samples from different sources and simultaneously have quick access to multiple keyboard sounds. What would have previously required multiple devices can now be done by loading and mapping out a single Live session.

THE SETUP

The setup I use is pretty simple: an iBook G4 with Live 6. My external MIDI device is an M-Audio 02 25-key USB MIDI controller. For most gigs I can go directly from the iBook's ⅛-inch line-out to the PA system, as long there are decent monitors. In situations without good monitoring or PA options, I run the iBook directly into a Peavey keyboard amp.

PREPARING THE SAMPLES

The first audio track of my Live session contains all of my spoken word samples and sound effects. Since these come from a variety of sources, I use AudioFile's Sample Manager program (covered in detail in Chapter 7, "More Useful Software) to convert them all to the same sample rate and bit depth (see Chapter 13, "Post Production," for more information on sample rates and bit depth). I also used Sample Manager's Normalize function on all of the samples so they all play back at similar volume.

Since I don't want my samples to loop and I want them to play at their original speed, I select each clip in the clip slot and turn Warping off in the Clip view. That sets up the samples to play back as one-shots.

THE INSTRUMENTS

My instrumentation needs are pretty simple. I created two MIDI tracks, each with a different keyboard sound—one using SampleTank Free's organ sound and one using the Pianoteq virtual piano.

Using free and "light" versions of programs is a good idea with live performance—not to save money, but because overloading your DAW can crash your sessions. Free versions and light versions tend to use less of your system's resources and reload faster in the event of a crash.

MIDI MAPPING

The key to making all of this work is Live's MIDI mapping functionality. Each sample is assigned to a note on my MIDI keyboard. For example, pressing the note C1 will trigger a movie sound clip or a sound effect.

To set up MIDI mapping in Live:

1. Click the MIDI Map Mode switch, select the first sample on Track 1, and assign it to a key on the MIDI keyboard controller.

Once this is done, every time you press the assigned key, the sample will play.

2. Assign a different key to each sample.

3. It's also a good idea to assign a keyboard note to one of the Clip Stop buttons, in case you trigger the wrong sample at the wrong time by mistake.

KEY MAPPING

Key mapping is exactly the same as MIDI mapping, but instead of assigning a function to your MIDI keyboard controller, it assigns functions to your Apple keyboard.

In order to play a Live MIDI instrument the track has to be armed for recording. In order to quickly turn a track on or off, you can use key mapping to assign a keyboard letter or number to the Arm for Recording button of each track.

1. Turn on key mapping by selecting the Key Map Mode switch right next to the MIDI Map Mode switch.

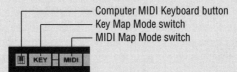

2. Click the Computer MIDI Keyboard button next to the Key Map Mode switch to turn off your Apple keyboard's ability to trigger notes on your MIDI virtual instruments.

Computer MIDI Keyboard button
Key Map Mode switch
MIDI Map Mode switch

3. Click the Arm Session Recording button for one of your MIDI instrument tracks and assign a letter on your Apple keyboard. Assign a different letter to the Arm Recording Session button for any tracks in your session that contain virtual instruments.

I assign the letters *z* and *x* to my instruments because they are easy to remember and to locate on the Apple keyboard.

4. Deselect the Key Map Mode switch.

Keep in mind that assigning keyboard notes to trigger samples means you can't use those notes to play the keyboard sounds. This isn't an issue for me because all of my keyboard parts are in a specific range. If you need access to all of your keys, you can assign your samples to other parts of your MIDI controller. For example, you could assign your Live samples to be triggered by moving a fader or a knob on your MIDI controller.

PLAYING LIVE

Like any new instrument or piece of equipment, once all of your keyboards and samples are in place it takes a little bit of practice to get used to switching between functions and triggering samples. You may find that not all virtual instruments that record well will sound good in live performance. For the best results, try creating multiple Live sessions and experimenting in rehearsal with different virtual instruments.

Other possible ways to use MIDI and your DAW for live performance:

◆ Create a Reason session with multiple instruments and samples. Use your mouse to switch between instruments.

◆ Create a GarageBand session with multiple tracks, each containing a different Software Instrument. Use your mouse or trackpad to switch between instruments.

◆ Create a Logic session with multiple tracks, each with a different instrument. Use your mouse or trackpad to switch between instruments.

The Bottom Line

Open MIDI Files in any DAW   MIDI files have many uses in your DAW programs. Among other things they offer a way to exchange a lot of information in a very small package. The process of importing and opening MIDI files is different for each DAW program.

Master It   Open the MIDI file MIDISong1.mid in your DAW program and assign instruments to each track.

Control Reason with a MIDI control surface or keyboard. Almost every instrument, effect, automation parameter, knob, button, and fader in Reason can be controlled by MIDI information coming from an external MIDI control surface or keyboard.

Master It Use your control surface or keyboard's default MIDI mapping combined with the Remote Override to control different parameters on a single channel on the Mixer 14:2.

Use MIDI to "play" Ableton Live Ableton Live is another program that can be controlled extensively by an external MIDI device. Using Live's MIDI mapping you can play Live as an improvisational instrument or create and record complex mixes of your Live songs.

Master It Use your MIDI control surface or keyboard to improvise an arrangement with the Live set `MasterOne.als`.

Quantize a performance in any DAW Quantization can create more consistent performances from any MIDI track

Master It Create a "live" drum performance in your DAW with your MIDI controller or virtual keyboard, then fix the performance with ⅛-note quantization.

Chapter 12

The Laptop Studio

FireWire and USB peripherals, faster processor speeds, and larger hard drives have brought the world of laptop recording firmly into the twenty-first century. Having a laptop studio is an excellent way to work on the road or in your neighborhood coffee shop. You can also use a laptop to record bands in any environment, including live performances. For composers working on soundtracks for film or television, a laptop makes the perfect solution for working on the go and for bringing your work directly to a client.

More and more artists are exploring the use of laptop computers for both live performance and studio recordings. Laptop artists range from electronic-based musicians like Moby and Kid 606 to former Byrds singer Roger McGuinn, who has made numerous folk-based recordings on his portable laptop studio using a couple of microphones and very basic DAW programs.

In this chapter you will learn to:

◆ Choose the right gear for your needs

◆ Record directly into your laptop without a hardware interface

◆ Record a drum kit with a limited number of microphones

Getting Started

The basic elements that make up your laptop studio will be:

◆ A laptop

◆ A DAW program

◆ An audio/MIDI interface

◆ A MIDI controller

Other peripherals that you may or may not need include microphones, studio monitors, headphones, and an external mixer.

At least one microphone will be necessary if you intend to record vocals or acoustic instruments. You'll need more if you are recording live multi-instrument bands. To record bands or multiple performers you will either need an interface with multiple inputs or an external mixer, but you may not need a MIDI controller. If you are planning on using your laptop as a complete "in-the-box" studio, you probably won't need an external mixer.

As far as headphones and studio monitors go, these decisions will be impacted by how you plan to create your final mixes. Many laptop engineers (especially those recording live bands in a mobile recording environment) use headphones for the recording process and then bring the session to a desktop-based studio for final mixes.

These elements will be different depending on what your needs and goals are. We'll look at each of them in detail in the "Other Peripherals" section of this chapter.

The first two items on the list—the computer and the DAW software—are far and away the most important. Whatever kind of music you intend to create, compose, or record you'll need to make these decisions first.

The interface or controller is dependent on what your goals, music style, and plan are. If you don't intend to record audio tracks at all, you can skip the audio interface and invest in a MIDI interface or a plug-and-play MIDI controller. If you have no use for MIDI, you may want to buy an audio-only hardware interface.

Portable or Stationary?

One of the main reasons for building a studio around a laptop is for mobility—to have the ability to work, travel, and create music with your laptop both locally and long range. In the past, when laptops were significantly less powerful than their desktop counterparts, this may have been the only reason for building a laptop studio. Today, it's possible to create a fully functioning studio around a Mac laptop that competes quite well with desktop models.

If you intend to build a studio that will be entirely stationary, your options are somewhat different than if you need a "studio on the go." If you are planning on mostly staying at home with your laptop you may want to invest in a larger MIDI keyboard and an audio interface with more I/O capabilities, or you may want to buy more MIDI sound modules and other external gear.

It's also possible to have it both ways. OS X makes it very easy to switch between multiple audio and MIDI interfaces and devices. If you have the budget for it, you can easily create two versions of your laptop studio, one for at-home use and one for taking outside or on the road.

Much of the following assumes the need for portability; however, you can use this information just as easily to research and create a stationary studio as well.

The Right Laptop

The right laptop for your mobile studio is, of course, the most laptop you can afford. Apple makes it pretty easy to put together a customized system for your recording needs.

Here are some important factors to keep in mind:

RAM Crucially important in any digital recording system, RAM is even more important in the laptop environment. How much RAM you have will dictate your track count, available plug-ins, and overall performance. If you can afford it, be sure to get the maximum amount of RAM possible for your laptop.

Hard Drive Speed Apple now offers multiple choices for hard drives. When you are configuring your laptop, make sure you are getting the fastest available hard drive for it.

Hard Drive Size Hard drive size is another crucial element that you have a lot of control over. Whenever possible I definitely encourage recording to an external hard drive. But in many cases this will not be possible or convenient with a laptop. Getting the largest possible hard drive will give you lots of room to maneuver when recording long sessions with multiple takes. Another benefit for the in-the-box musician will be the ability to store lots of loops, samples, Reason ReFills, or other files you need to access for your music. With the current Mac laptops, the largest hard drives available are not the fastest. In this case I recommend choosing speed over size.

If you have to choose between the model with fastest processor and the biggest display versus the lower-end Mac that you can customize, it often makes sense to go with the less expensive model, provided there's not a huge gap in processor speeds. You'll be better off with a slightly slower processor if it means you can afford more RAM and a larger, faster hard drive.

AppleCare for the Laptop

If you've been on the fence about purchasing AppleCare, building a laptop studio should tip your decision to the affirmative. Laptops have come a long way over the years, but they are still occasionally unreliable and prone to crashing, generally at the worst possible time. If you intend to use your laptop as your main studio, it's going to be really important to have things up and running as close to 100 percent of the time as possible. Having AppleCare means that any problems your Mac encounters can be resolved quickly at no extra cost, especially if you are anywhere near an Apple Store or an Apple Certified repair shop.

AppleCare for your laptop is moderately priced and adds two years onto your warranty (for a total of three years) and extends your phone support option from 90 days to three years. AppleCare can be purchased at any time during you first year of ownership.

The Right Software for Your Laptop Studio

We've discussed the pros and cons of the various DAW programs available for Macs at different points in this book. Here we'll take another quick look at each one, keeping in mind that the laptop musician/engineer may face specific challenges and have different goals and needs than the desktop studio owner.

Reason   Reason can be a great choice as a standalone program for the electronic music producer who intends to work primarily in the digital realm. Combine a Mac laptop, Reason, and a MIDI keyboard to create a simple setup with lots of possibilities. Reason also makes better use of your computer's CPU and RAM than just about any program out there, so even an older laptop with limited resources can achieve great results with Reason. Although Reason is aimed at the electronic music market, its incredible range of instruments, sounds, and sequencing possibilities make it an excellent adjunct to any DAW recording software and any style of music. The shortcoming for many laptop owners is that Reason doesn't record audio tracks. For that you'll need to look at a separate DAW program.

Ableton Live   Ableton Live is the program of choice for laptop musicians and DJs whose focus is live performing or a combination of composition and live performance. Live can also be used for more traditional multitracking and recording by working in the Arrange View. Live's support for both VST and Audio Unit plug-ins and instruments also make it extremely expandable. Ableton Live 6 now includes support for QuickTime video, which opens up the door to using it as a tool for soundtrack composition. For electronic musicians and DJs, a laptop studio with the combination of Live and Reason makes an excellent choice. Ableton Live is also being used more and more in conjunction with programs like Logic and Pro Tools for its ability to quickly add loop-related elements and other sequences to your music projects.

Pro Tools LE   One distinct advantage of using Pro Tools LE is the included Pro Tools hardware interface. A hardware/software package generally means less setup hassle and instant compatibility between the two elements. Every current version of Pro Tools is compatible with the other current versions, meaning you can record a session using Pro Tools M-Powered, overdub on another system using Pro Tool LE, and do your final mixes in a studio using Pro Tools HD.

> ### MBOX 2 PRO
>
> The FireWire-powered Pro Tools Mbox 2 Pro hardware interface, which is bundled with Pro Tools LE, is an excellent choice for mobile recording. With its compact size, choice of two XLR or ¼-inch inputs, and built-in MIDI in and out, the Mbox 2 Pro makes a perfect, complete mobile interface. Along with the included Pro Tools LE software, the Mbox 2 Pro will also work as an audio and MIDI interface for other DAW software, including Logic, Live, and GarageBand. The Mbox 2 Pro Factory bundle contains the hardware interface, Pro Tools LE 7 software, and a variety of third-party plug-in instruments and effects.

Pro Tools M-Powered   Digidesign also recently introduced Pro Tools M-Powered, which will work in conjunction with many M-Audio FireWire and USB interfaces. The M-Audio/M-Powered combination is in many ways perfect for laptop recording. This "lighter" version of Pro Tools uses less processor power, and M-Audio's interfaces are generally compact and mobile. This combination is also a great choice for solo musicians who want to add the ability to record instruments to their studio setup. With one of the less expensive M-Audio interfaces (like the Transit), you can easily add the ability to record 24-bit/96kHz stereo audio tracks to your laptop sessions.

Logic   If you are going to be using one program only, Logic (either Pro or Express) may be the best choice for simultaneously running an audio- and MIDI-based laptop studio. If you intend to work mostly in the digital environment, Logic contains so many of its own instruments and plug-ins that it eliminates much of the need for third-party software. With a simple, portable MIDI controller, you can create entire orchestrations, simulate a "live" band, or create just about any musical configuration imaginable. For more complex audio-based recording sessions, you'll have plenty of power and tracks (depending on your chosen audio interface). Another advantage to Logic is that as long as you have the included dongle you can install and run the program on multiple machines. This allows you to work with your mobile setup and a stationary setup without having to own two versions of the software.

GarageBand   For the budget studio, hobbyist, or quick demo, GarageBand is a great solution. GarageBand can be used in conjunction with any audio or MIDI interface. As I pointed out in the Chapter 6, "GarageBand," GarageBand's simplicity cuts both ways. While it's very easy to use, the lack of advanced features make GarageBand somewhat less desirable for higher-end recording. M-Audio's iControl is a MIDI-controlled mixer for GarageBand (covered in Chapter 11, "MIDI"). The combination of iControl, GarageBand, and a laptop is one possibility for creating an easy to use, inexpensive portable studio.

Audio and MIDI Interfaces

Aside from the laptop itself, the interface you choose may be the most important decision you make. Audio interfaces range all the way from inexpensive, simple devices like the Griffin iMic (http://www.griffintechnology.com) to high-end multiple input audio interfaces like the M-Audio FireWire 1814 (http://www.m-audio.com).

If you are planning on recording groups of musicians you will need, at the very least, the ability to record in stereo (using an external mixer to mix your tracks to stereo), though you may want to acquire a more complex interface like the Digi 002 or the FireWire 1814. If portability is your main focus, check out devices like the M-Audio Transit or Fast Track USB. Many companies offer a complete range of devices with 1, 2, 4, 8 or more inputs.

Some of the companies that make audio interfaces for OS X Macs:

◆ M-Audio, `http://www.m-audio.com`

◆ Digidesign, `http://www.digidesign.com`

◆ PreSonus, `http://www.presonus.com`

◆ Mark of the Unicorn, `http://www.motu.com`

◆ Mackie, `http://www.mackie.com`

Tips for Buying the Best Interface

Some things to consider when buying an audio interface follow.

Do as much research as you can   Every interface worth owning will have positive reviews by fans and long-term users and other statements about the product online. Check out sites like `http://www.harmony-central.com`, as well as commercial sites like Amazon and `http://www.musiciansfriend.com`, to see what other people are saying about a specific product. You may also want to check the website for your DAW software and look for forum postings and user groups discussing what hardware is best to use with your DAW.

Make sure the model is current and from a company that's still doing good business   Of course there's no way to tell who's going to be in business next year, but having the ability to upgrade your interface's drivers along with your operating system in the future may mean the difference between owning an audio interface or a very expensive paperweight.

Download the latest drivers before installing   Technology changes so fast these days, it's quite possible that during the time your interface was shipped to the store/online supplier you bought it from the included drivers became obsolete. Installing obsolete drivers can lead to crashes and other problems. For example, the drivers that your audio interface needs to run on OS X Panther may not work at all with OS X Tiger. Whenever possible, look for and download the current drivers from the companies website *before* you hook up your interface.

Use the right connections   Many audio interfaces have either a ¼-inch jack (or jacks) or an XLR connection or connections. If you're primarily going to be recording a guitar or other instrument directly in to your laptop, a ¼-inch jack will be all you need. For vocals or other kinds of microphone-based recordings, you want to have access to XLR inputs. Of course, it's quite possible to use adapters to convert the signal from either type of connector, but adapters tend to degrade and compromise your signal.

To MIDI or Not to MIDI

Many audio interfaces also include MIDI In, Out, and/or Thru functionality as well. If you intend to use external MIDI devices like synths and sound modules, you may want to consider an audio interface that contains MIDI ports.

For a laptop studio it generally does not make sense to have a separate MIDI interface; however, there are certainly possible studio configuration that may require one. If this is the case, refer to the "MIDI Interfaces" section of Chapter 11.

For maximum portability, you may want to consider buying a USB-powered MIDI controller (see Chapter 11). Mobile MIDI controllers are frequently inexpensive and hassle free. Quite often the device will be as simple to use as plugging it in to any available USB port.

CONTROL SURFACES

Having an external mixer/control surface is another possibility to consider for laptop recording. If you expect to be working exclusively on a laptop, the mixing process can get fairly tedious using the trackpad. Many laptop users are perfectly happy hooking up a mouse to do their mixing and recording tasks, while others would never consider working without an external MIDI control surface for panning, volume adjustments, and other mix-related functions.

There is also hardware available that combines the ability to record with the ability to control your DAW program remotely. The Pro Tools Digi 002, Tascam FW 1884, and M-Audio Project Mix are all examples of combination control surface/audio interfaces.

See the "MIDI Keyboards and Interfaces" section of Chapter 11 for more information on MIDI-based control surfaces.

Other Peripherals

The things that make your recording experience good, bad, or unmanageable will often have as much to do with your peripherals as your main gear. Some things you may need include the following.

Headphones

It's pretty likely that at some point in your laptop recording career you're going to need a set of headphones. Whether you need to monitor or listen back to a live/mobile recording or to get some work done in a moving vehicle, you'll probably find yourself in any number of situations where you won't be able to set up or listen to speakers. Your usual studio headphones may get the job done. Just make sure they are in good shape, though you may not want to bring your most expensive out on the road with you.

Wherever possible you'll want to use over-the-ear headphones for your music-making needs.

Moderately Priced Headphones   The following is a list of moderately priced headphones. Any of these models will be suitable for audio recording or laptop composition.

- Sony MDR-7506 (highly recommended)
- Sony MDR-V600
- Sennheiser HD-280
- Direct Sound Extreme Isolation
- Audio Technica ATH-M40fs

Top-of-the-Line Headphones   If you have a larger budget at your disposal you may want to check out some of the more expensive headphone models currently available:

- Beyerdynamic DT-770 Pro 80
- Bose QuietComfort 2 and 3 (noise-canceling headphones)
- Sony MDR-7509HD

Something else you might consider are iPod-style earbuds, though they are certainly not optimal for mixing purposes. On the other hand, the chances that you will be mixing in the back of a moving car, train, or plane are pretty slim. For a combination of portability, convenience, and quality when working on the go, noise-canceling earbuds are an option.

Headphone Splitters

If you need to have the ability for more than one person to monitor audio output at the same time, you can get a very simple headphone splitter. A headphone splitter will be a ⅛- or ¼-inch jack that splits the output signal to two ⅛- or ¼-inch signals. Griffin (www.griffintechnology.com) makes a neat little headphone splitter called SmartShare that includes individual volume controls.

Cables

If you are using a hardware audio interface, your cabling and microphone connections will be standard ¼-inch or XLR connections, depending on your interface. For users who want to record directly into their laptop's ⅛-inch line-in jack there are some new options available. In the past, connecting a guitar or microphone to your laptop's line-in jack involved a series of adapters. Now Griffin (http://www.griffintechnology.com) has come up with the GarageBand Microphone Cable (XLR to ⅛-inch) and the GarageBand Guitar Cable (¼-inch to ⅛-inch). These cables are not just for use with GarageBand, they can be used to record audio into any DAW program on your laptop or desktop.

If you prefer, you can still create your own connections using guitar and microphone cables in conjunction with adapters available from your local electronics store.

RECORDING DIRECTLY INTO YOUR LAPTOP

Most Mac laptops have an ⅛-inch line-in that can be used to record audio directly into your DAW.

1. Open your System Preferences and select the Sound Preferences icon.

2. Make sure Audio Line-in Port is selected and the Input Volume slider is raised.

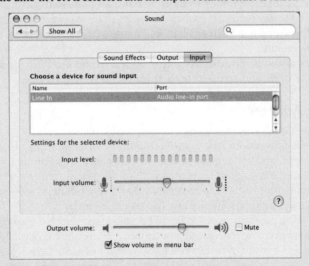

3. If you have or have had an audio interface connected to your laptop, you may need to open your DAW's preferences and change your Audio Input setting to Built-in Audio.

One of the newest developments for laptop (and desktop) recording is the ¼-inch-to-USB cable. Both StealthPlug by IK Multimedia (`http://www.stealthplug.com`) and Lightsnake by SoundTech (`http://www.soundtech.com`) give you the ability to plug your guitar, bass, or any other instrument with a ¼-inch output directly into your laptop. These are essentially "sound cards in a cable" and make an excellent choice for high-quality recording directly into your virtual amplification and/or DAW software.

SoundTech has also created a microphone (XLR) to USB cable that will be available soon.

Speakers

If you do intend to do any mixing, or you want to get a break from ear-fatigue-inducing headphones, you may want to invest in some portable speakers. This a tough one because there are generally pretty big differences between studio monitors and speakers that are sold for consumer listening purposes. Specifically, studio monitors will have a much greater frequency range, especially when it comes to bass or lower-end frequencies.

For portable speakers I recommend any of the various Altec Lansing InMotion models. These portable speakers all contain a dock for your iPod but can just as easily be connected to your laptop. I wouldn't recommend doing final mixes on these, except in a pinch. For monitoring, playback, and rough mixing, any of the InMotion models will get the job done.

Information on the complete line of Altec Lansing portable speakers can be found at `http://www.alteclansing.com`.

Storage and Backup

I have two giant collections of loops and Reason ReFills. Either one will take up enough room on my laptop's hard drive to severely compromise my ability to record. In order to have access to my loop and ReFill collections I've tried carrying DVD-Rs with multiple collections and copying the files I need to my hard drive when necessary. This works, but a much better solution I've found are bus-powered hard drives like those made by SmartDisk (`www.smartdisk.com`) and LaCie (`www.lacie.com`).

Bus-powered drives are available in both USB and FireWire models. Prices start at around $80 for a 40GB drive and go up from there for larger storage devices.

Power Adapters

If you are doing a lot of touring or traveling by plane, car, or van, you might look into getting adapters to power your Mac in these situations. Finding the right adapter to use your Mac laptop on a plane or land vehicle can be difficult and confusing. For my iBook G4, I ultimately found an adapter from Kensington that came with multiple connectors and worked for both planes and "cigarette lighter" outlets in motor vehicles. Unfortunately, reviews and information on Mac laptop power adapters are not always easy to come by.

Part of the problem seems to be that Apple insists on changing the power requirements and adapters for every new generation of laptop, making any car or plane adapters obsolete with every new Mac. As a result, whether you have a newer or older laptop, there are options available, but you might have to look pretty hard for them. Try bringing your laptop into your local Apple Store or Apple retailer and seeing what they have in stock or can order for you.

You can also try searching on your particular model with the words "car adapter" or "power adapter" on Google, Amazon, the Apple Store website, or your preferred electronics retail website.

APPLE WORLD TRAVEL ADAPTER KIT

For the international traveler, Apple's World Travel Adapter kit is available from your local Apple retailer or Apple's online store. This kit is a set of six AC plugs that will allow you to charge your iPod, iBook, PowerBook, or MacBook just about anywhere in the world, including Europe, Australia, Japan, and China.

Microphones

There are essentially two main types of microphones used in recording:

Dynamic   Dynamic microphones are used for miking things up close. The most common dynamic microphone is the Shure SM57. Dynamic microphones can be used on any amplified instrument, any part of a drum kit, or any instrument that requires a closely placed microphone.

Condenser   Condenser microphones can be used in close proximity to the instrument or amplifier being recorded but are also capable of picking up sounds from a distance or even an entire room. Large-diaphragm condenser microphones are used for vocals, instruments, and room sounds. Small-diaphragm condenser microphones are noticeably smaller in size and are particularly good for drum overheads, percussion instruments, and acoustic guitars.

Most condenser microphones require phantom power. Phantom power is a tiny electrical signal generated by your mixing board or your audio interface in order to power your condenser microphones.

Over the last decade or so a number of factors have led to the increasing availability of excellent, inexpensive microphones. This is especially true in the condenser microphone arena. Models like the MXL-990 (www.mxlmics.com) and the Rode NT1A (www.rode.com) have put very high quality condenser microphones well within the reach of the average home studio owner.

If you are planning on recording bands or "live" drums, keyboards, bass and/or guitar your microphone collection should consist of at least:

- One or more Shure SM57s. These can be used on electric guitar, snare drum, and just about anything else if needed. The SM57 is a mainstay in recording studios from home and project studios to some of the biggest professional studios in the world.

- A large-diaphragm condenser microphone for recording vocals and other instruments. Check out the previously mentioned MXL and Rode microphones, as well as more expensive models from companies like Audio Technica, Neumann, and AKG.

- A matching pair of small-diaphragm condenser microphones for drum overheads or stereo room miking. Some choices for matching small-diaphragm condensers include the Rode NT 5, Behringer C2, and Samson C02.

- A good low-end response microphone for kick drum or bass instruments. Popular (and relatively inexpensive) microphones for recording kick drum and bass include the Shure Beta 52A and AKG D112.

As I mentioned earlier in relation to audio and MIDI interfaces, it's a good idea to research a particular microphone before you buy it. You can find user and industry reviews of specific microphones at http://www.harmony-central.com as well as commercial sites like Amazon.com and http://www.musiciansfriend.com.

Microphone prices tend to fluctuate, and it's not at all that uncommon to find expensive microphones at huge discounts. Keep an eye on your favorite retail sites and your local musical equipment retailer as well as recording forums and magazine ads. Most engineers have added at least one or two great microphones to their collection through a special sale or a great one-time deal.

Mixers

Having an external mixing board may be necessary, especially if your hardware audio interface has a limited number of inputs. Mixers can range from simple and cheap, like the Behringer UB802 Eurorack 8-input mixer (`http://www.behringer.com`), to 24- or 48-channel mixing consoles for thousands of dollars. For laptop recording you'll probably want something in between those two extremes. Check out devices like the Mackie 1202-VLZ Pro (`http://www.mackie.com`). These are moderately priced, solid, good-sounding portable mixers.

Another option you might consider is a USB mixer such as the Alesis MultiMix 8USB (`http://www.alesis.com`). The MultiMix is moderately priced and can record directly into your DAW via one of your laptop's USB ports.

Laptop Recording

Your laptop can be used for any number of different types of recording sessions. In the following sections I'll cover some basic techniques for recording bands and individuals in a mobile environment.

Since the reasons for recording a live band with a laptop are generally either recording a live club or concert performance or capturing a band in the practice studio or other nonrecording studio environment, you will be faced with a series of challenges particular to those environments. Other factors that come into play have to do with the style of music being recorded and the overall volume level and instrumentation.

Creating Isolation

If you are working in a larger room and have the ability to move your players around, you can get pretty good isolation by facing amplifiers away from each other, asking the band to play at a slightly lower volume than usual, or tracking one or two instruments at a time. Much of this depends on whether or not the players are comfortable and able to perform well under these conditions. Recording "live" with everyone playing together may cause some mixing difficulties later (see "Using the Bleed"), but it may also be the best way to get the best performance. In an environment such as a rehearsal facility, where outside noise is an issue, recording live and loud can actually resolve some problems simply by drowning out the competition.

Using the Bleed

Bleed is what happens when a microphone that's being used to record one instrument unintentionally picks up the sound of a different instrument. Bleed can be a very good thing or a very bad thing, depending on what's picked up, how aware you are of it and how you deal with it.

You can't control bleed exactly, but it's an important part of the "live" sound of many great recordings. Some classic examples of bleed include everything Phil Spector recorded, most Motown sessions, and many songs in the Beatles' catalogue. The process of severely isolating every single instrument to control the sound of a recording only started coming into use as more tracks were added to the recording process. This can certainly be a good thing, allowing recording engineers more control over a mix, but the downside is that too much control can create sterile, lifeless recordings.

Experimenting a bit with bleed can lead to much better-sounding recordings. How useful it is will depend greatly on the quality of the musicians, however, as microphones pick up mistakes just as clearly (if not more so) than good performances.

Recording Drums

Recording drums in close quarters with limited microphones can be a challenge. If you have the inputs and microphones available, you can take advantage of standard microphone techniques, which generally involve placing one or two microphones on each drum. However, in a more limited situation with a bit of patience you can achieve a great sound using the following configuration (a good drummer playing a well-tuned drum kit won't hurt either):

- A stereo pair of small-diaphragm condenser microphones as overheads

- A dynamic microphone with good low-end response on the kick drum

- A dynamic microphone on the snare drum

SUBMIXES

Using an external mixer to create submixes is a good way to maximize a limited number of tracks. For example, you can use the 4 four-microphone configuration I just described on a drum kit and run all four microphones into your external mixer. Create your mix in the mixer and send the result in stereo to your audio interface. This way you can combine 4 four different microphone signals into two tracks. Submixes can also be a combination of instruments, like multiple guitars or drums and bass, mixed down to one or two tracks.

Recording Vocals

Recording vocals on a mobile session can be tricky. Quite often when recording a band in a rehearsal space or in a live setting the vocal performance can be one of the hardest to capture correctly. Vocals tend to have two major problems: imperfect performances and "bleed" (vocals from the PA system bleeding into other microphones).

ISOLATION

Whenever you can, you'll want to isolate the vocalist as completely as possible (this will generally make the drummer very happy as well). In some cases this may mean putting the vocalist in the hallway, a closet, or even the bathroom. Use whatever is available.

GATING

Most DAWs will include a gate plug-in that can eliminate the background noise that a vocal microphone picks up when a singer is not singing. A gate plug-in will mute a track until a certain volume level is reached, for example, when a singer starts singing directly into a microphone. When the volume hits a certain level, the gate will allow signal to flow through, just like a physical gate that opens and closes. When the volume level drops (the singer stops), the gate will close, eliminating all of the extra noise that the singer's microphone may be picking up.

IS IT LIVE OR...?

Many "live" albums (especially those produced by hard rock bands in the '70s) are not really completely "live" but a combination of live performance and studio overdubs. If you listen closely to many of these records you can often hear "ghost" vocal track where the original vocals have been reduced in volume and replaced by a studio track or overdub. The combination of the two tracks sometimes produces a doubling effect that actually enhances the vocal.

If your singer is "close but not quite" with his live performance, you may be able to use the original track or vocal bleed in conjunction with a new track to get a good vocal sound.

DOUBLING

Doubling is a frequently used recording technique. It's exactly what it sounds like: a vocal or instrument is recorded and then a matching performance is recorded on top of the original. Vocal doubling has long been a staple of the pop and rock music recording process. For examples of vocal doubling, listen closely to early Beatles songs like "Can't Buy Me Love" and "Eight Days A Week." You can also hear some excellent examples of vocal and instrumental doubling on Elliott Smith's *XO* and the Beach Boys' classic *Pet Sounds*.

Many instruments as well as vocal performances can benefit greatly from being doubled. Acoustic or electric guitars are frequently doubled and panned to opposite sides of a mix. Horns, lead guitar lines, and many other kinds of performances are often doubled to create a richer sound.

In the laptop environment, doubling can be especially useful if you need to fix up a weak or poorly recorded instrument or vocal track.

Recording Electric Guitars

For recording live guitars in a smaller environment, you'll want to use close miking techniques. This means putting the microphone extremely close to the amplifier's speaker. Exactly where to place the microphone in relation to the speaker cone is a matter of personal preference. Some engineers prefer the sound of the microphone being placed directly in the center of the cone, some suggest off to the side a bit. The location of the microphone and distance from the speaker may also depend on the specific amplifier and session. In a particularly loud session you may want to move the microphone closer for less bleed, while the opposite may be true for a quieter session.

VIRTUAL AMPLIFIERS

The virtual amplifiers we l covered in Chapter 9, "Virtual Instruments," can be an excellent tool for laptop recording. In situations where you have limited microphones or isolation, one possible solution may be to record guitar directly into your DAW through virtual amplifier plug-ins.

You can also use virtual amplification plug-ins to experiment and familiarize yourself with the effect that different kinds of microphone placement will have on the sound of your electric guitar tracks.

Recording Acoustic Guitars

Wherever possible you'll want to use a condenser microphone on acoustic guitars in order to pick up the full spectrum of sounds. If this is not possible—for example, if you are recording an acoustic guitar playing with a loud drummer—you may want to consider adding the acoustic guitar later as an overdub. Acoustic guitars can be recorded with either dynamic or condenser microphones, though condensers tend to sound fuller. Try placing either type of microphone a few inches away from the twelfth fret of the guitar as a starting point and then move your microphone around to hear some of the possibilities.

For recording singer/songwriters, try using a dynamic microphone on the guitar and a condenser microphone on the vocals, then mixing the two tracks together to take advantage of the microphone bleed.

CLICK TRACKS

Click tracks are generally a matter of preference for individual bands, musicians, and engineers. There are two basic schools of thought: "Click tracks are how it's done—all the pros use click tracks," or "Click tracks create mechanical, uninteresting performances."

I believe that the click track has its place and that some performances don't benefit from it, while others do. Often it depends on the players, style, and situation. I am more inclined to use a click track in a band recording situation these days because I've found it helps greatly in the overdubbing process when musicians have a steady beat to follow. Also, if a session requires any kind of looping, a click track makes the looping process much easier.

If you are only able to provide a single click track, it's generally the drummer who gets it, since they have the greatest control over the overall tempo of the song.

Recording Bass

Recording bass is a fairly straightforward proposition. If you have limited available inputs you can save space and hassle by recording bass directly into your recording setup, possibly using virtual amplification, though this is not always necessary. If you are able to record multiple signals, the best results are often achieved with a combination of direct signal and a microphone placed in front of the bass amp. Any dynamic microphone can be used to record a bass amp, but if possible it's best to use a microphone with better low-end response such as the Shure Beta 52A or AKG D112.

Using Overdubs

Overdubbing is possibly your best weapon in a laptop recording session. If you can reduce the number of musicians on your original track (for example, by recording just the drums and rhythm guitar or drums and bass), you have much greater control over the rest of the process. Fewer instruments and musicians recording at once means fewer chances for mistakes, better track isolation, and less risk of your laptop overloading and crashing. The trade-off here is often sacrificing the "vibe" generated when musicians are playing together. As a result this may not be the way to go in every situation, especially when you're recording groups that do a lot of improvisation.

Much of the success or failure of this technique this will depend on the session's drummer. If a drummer can play as if he's being accompanied by the entire band, you can often use this as a foundation to build a complete song by overdubbing the rest of the musician's performances.

Whether you record basic tracks as individuals or as a complete group, overdubbing is often a part of the process. When fixing tracks (mistakes, missed notes, and so on), it's best to try and accomplish as much overdubbing as possible in the environment you recorded the basic tracks in, using the setup and microphone configurations already in place from your basic tracks. This will ensure better sonic consistency in your tracks.

For new or additional performances, it may make sense to take your session to another location, possibly another studio or a room with greater isolation, better working conditions, or access to various instruments. This kind of mobility is one of the great advantages of a laptop studio and should be taken advantage of whenever possible.

Headphone Mixes

Headphone mixes are the individual mixes you give to the musicians in a recording session. Headphone mixes can be especially tricky in a laptop session and in some cases impossible. If your audio interface is equipped with multiple outputs, these can be used to create individual mixes. The really important factor here is often getting a vocalist in the headphone mix so the players have a structure to follow.

If you find yourself with a limited number of headphone mixes available, it's a good idea to give the mix to the drummer, if possible with a guide vocal track and/or a click track.

Since you'll probably be working in a smaller, closer-together environment you may find that for basic tracking, headphone mixes aren't always needed for many, or any, of the players.

Creative Editing

One way to take advantage of your DAW's digital editing abilities is to simply chop out or mute the unneeded sections of a noisy track. Figure 12.1 shows a vocal track that was recorded live with a band. I've used Pro Tools editing and muting functions to silence the track when the singing stops.

FIGURE 12.1
An edited vocal track
in Pro Tools

 Real World Scenario

A SIMPLE LAPTOP STUDIO

This configuration is one I started to use when I wanted to create a simple, cheap and quickly mobile laptop configuration, partially inspired by an article I read on Roger McGuinn's simple but effective recording set-up. The results were very surprising and considerably better than I expected. If you already own a laptop and don't want to break the bank, you can use this setup to make pretty high-quality audio recordings for under $100.

This setup can be used to record complete sessions with singer/songwriters and also works for quick one-microphone preproduction with bands.

The tools are these:

◆ A Griffin iMic adapter

◆ A Sony ECM-DS70P minicondenser microphone

◆ Headphones (iPod headphones or other earbuds will work just fine)

◆ GarageBand

THE GRIFFIN iMIC

The Griffin iMic is a useful little USB audio input for Macs that don't have an audio line in. It works as a very simple stereo recording interface and also includes connectors and downloadable software that can quickly be used to convert your vinyl records to CD or MP3. Once you plug the iMic in, your iBook or Mac-Book will automatically detect its presence and add it to the list of available audio inputs. The disadvantage to the iMic is that it can be a little noisy, sometimes creating a bit of static crackling on your tracks.

If your Mac laptop already has a line in (as many do), you can use that to plug your microphone in directly, without the iMic.

THE ECM-DS70P

The Sony ECM-DS70P is an inexpensive "plug-in powered" condenser microphone. Unlike most condenser microphones, the ECM-DS70P will work without phantom power. This means you can get all of the qualities of a condenser microphone without needing a pre-amp or phantom power to use it. The ECM-DS70P records in stereo and can make astonishingly good recordings in the right environment.

Other similar products in the same general price range include the Sony ECM-DS30P and the Aiwa CM-P11 and CM-TS22 models. Try searching Google or your favorite retail site for "stereo condenser microphone."

The main thing you need to watch out for with the ECM-DS70P (or any condenser microphone in this situation) is overloading the microphone and distorting the signal. Whenever possible you'll want to do as much level checking as you can before you begin actual recording.

RECORDING

As I mentioned, recording with the iMic is as simple as plugging it in. Open your System Preferences, click the Sound Preferences, and change the default device for sound input to iMic USB audio system. Then:

1. Start GarageBand and create a new Music Project.

2. Set GarageBand's sound preferences: Open GarageBand's Preferences and click the Audio tab. If you're using the iMic, select iMic USB Audio System from the Audio Input drop-down menu. Otherwise select Built-in Audio.

3. Plug your headphones in to your Mac's Line-out jack.

4. Choose Track ➢ New Track

5. Select Real Instrument in the New Track dialog box, then click the Create button.

6. In the Track Info window, use the Monitor drop-down menu to turn monitoring on.

7. The Sony ECM-DS70P microphone is capable of recording in mono or stereo. You can choose which kind of track you'd like to record by using the Track Info window to select Channel 1 (mono), Channel 2 (mono), or Channel 1 & 2 (stereo).

8. Arm the track for recording by clicking the Enable Recording button on the track header.

9. Record your first instrument or vocal track,

Now that you have recorded a single track, you can use the same method to overdub more tracks.

To allow more than one person to the session's audio output you can use a headphone splitter like the Griffin SmartShare mentioned earlier in the "Headphone Splitters" section of this chapter.

In-the-Box Composition

A lot of what I've covered in this chapter applies to the laptop engineer who wants to record external music, such as live bands and singer/songwriters. Another popular reason for creating a laptop studio is to have a self-contained mobile composition tool. With today's virtual instruments and a portable MIDI controller, a laptop-based musician can write, compose, and arrange music anywhere at any time. Feeling stuck and uninspired at home? Take your laptop to a cafe or park and compose outside. I've used my laptop studio to create music in airports (not *for* airports—that's Brian Eno), moving vehicles, subway trains (not recommended), restaurants (always popular with your date), and, of course, hotel rooms.

There are a few recurring challenges with creating music entirely on a laptop, but these can often be turned into advantages or at least accommodated with the right tools.

MIDI Programming

If you work with MIDI a lot in your home studio, you probably have a MIDI keyboard with 61 or 88 keys. When you're working with a full-sized MIDI keyboard it's easy to create piano passages or string sections or even to program complex drum patterns. Working away from home you may find yourself limited to a smaller, portable MIDI keyboard (25 keys, usually), or you might have no MIDI controller at all.

Working with a small MIDI keyboard can be frustrating if you're trying to create the same kinds of performances you would on a larger keyboard. Sure, it's possible to use multiple "passes" and overdubbing techniques to create complex chord forms, but I've found that in these situations you're better off refocusing your attention toward creating melody lines, bass lines, or simple three-note chord forms.

Working without a MIDI keyboard can also be a great opportunity to familiarize yourself with your DAW's deeper MIDI editing functions, most of which can be accessed and adjusted with your trackpad or mouse.

Work with Loops

Working on the road is a great time to investigate your loop collection or any free or preview libraries you may have downloaded. Since most of the "work" involved with loop-based composition consists of pointing, clicking, dragging, and dropping, it's something you can do anywhere, even in the back of a moving vehicle. Because of its looping functionality, Ableton Live is one of my favorite programs for traveling, but Logic and GarageBand can work for this as well. Copy a few collections of loops to a DVD-R or directly to your laptop's hard drive and spend some time investigating the folders and files you may have missed when you were looking for that specific drum loop or synth sound.

Lack of "Real" Instruments

As a guitar player, I've found that one of the most difficult aspects of working without external recording abilities has been the lack of quality distorted electric guitar sounds. It seems that most of the people who create guitar sample libraries aren't clear on the concept of what a "real" distorted electric guitar sounds like. I've found an interesting way to work around this, and though it doesn't always sound perfect, it improves on a problem I've stressed over for a while. Most of the electric guitar samples I've come across tend to be overprocessed and unrealistic. Acoustic guitars samples, on the other hand, tend to be better recorded, often exceptionally well. The workaround

I found is that by taking a good-sounding acoustic guitar patch and playing it through a virtual amplifier with the right settings, I can create pretty realistic lead guitar lines. What's more, the sounds that don't work as guitar lines are often interesting and useful in other ways. This kind of strategy brings to mind the phrase "necessity is the mother of invention."

The point I'm trying to make here is that experimentation and creative thinking can lead to all sorts of interesting and unexpected results. The very few limitations that are still left in laptop composition and recording can often be used to your advantage.

Real World Scenario

THE FREAK ACCIDENT

One of my main motivations for building a laptop studio was to have the ability to take my system down to any rehearsal space and record preproduction, demos, or even, eventually, complete albums for bands in their rehearsal environment.

A lot of the inspiration for this came from my friend Ralph Spight. Ralph's been recording and touring for over 20 years as a member of progressive punk bands such as Victim's Family, the Hellworms, and most recently as a solo artist. A few years ago Ralph bought a Digi 001 Pro Tools system and began recording in his rehearsal space, which eventually morphed into Nerve Center Recording Studio, where he's since recorded a number of bands and solo artists.

The majority of Ralph's 2005 CD *The Freak Accident* (Alternative Tentacles) was recorded by Ralph (with some help from me) at Nerve Center, mostly using a Digi 001/G3 system that's considerably less powerful than the laptop systems available today. Ralph's recordings of his own music and of his clients are great examples of the possibilities available on seemingly limited systems.

Ralph and I talked about the equipment and techniques he used to make the *Freak Accident* CD and how some of the limitations of a small studio can be turned into advantages.

MICROPHONES

CT: Your recordings really demonstrate how to get great sounds with a small microphone collection. What was in your microphone collection for this CD?

RS: I bought one of those Audix mic packs—the F-series. There's an F12 for the kick drum, three F10s [dynamic mics], and two F15s [for overheads]; it's like a $300 set of mics. Along the way I bought a Beta 52a for kick drum, and I like to throw that on the bass a lot as well. The Swiss Army knife that I had for the *Freak Accident* CD was an AKG 4000 large-diaphragm condenser mic. I threw that on everything. It can handle high SPL [Sound Pressure Levels] so I can throw it in front of a guitar cabinet, drum kit, whatever.

RE-AMPING

Re-amping is the process of taking a recorded signal and running it out of your DAW through an amplifier or PA system and recording the results. Re-amplification can enhance dull sounding tracks or create the illusion of space.

RS: Here's the other Swiss Army knife on the *Freak Accident* CD—my VOX AC15 reissue [guitar amplifier]. With a nice-sounding amplifier with good reverb and tremolo, you can do anything. The organ sounds were the usually the stock sounds out of my Alesis [QS6 keyboard]. Basically what I did with a lot of the organ sounds was just pump them out of the output of the 001 and into the AC15.

A lot of this has to do with the fact that I'm a guitar player. I think like that. I think "Okay, I can put this through a distortion pedal, I can put this through an amp."

It's also about creating "air" in a production. With keyboards I think that's really important. Because the temptation with keyboards is, y'know, plug it in direct, you know what you're going to get. You've got the levels right there, it's gonna sit, it's gonna be stereo, it can be fine. But that's not always the best thing for a mix. It's not always the most interesting thing for a mix. Sometimes you'd rather that it sounded terrible…that could be a hook…Really the timbre of things is what really sets them apart. I think tonality really determines how a sound fits in a mix.

DEALING WITH NOISE

CT: How do you deal with the sound of other bands around you?

RS: A lot of times, particularly with vocals, you can edit around that. I run into that a lot and it's a drag. I'm working on a project, it comes time to do vocals, and all of a sudden I've got bands playing all around me. It's definitely a problem. That's one place where Pro Tools' Edit functions really come in handy. Say you're doing vocals with somebody and you've got loud bass guitar going in the next room and you're picking some up. You just have to cut around it (with EQ) or use your automated mutes. Unless it's, like, cacophonously loud, you can work around it.

A lot of this depends on your goal. We all want good sounding recordings, the best bang for your buck. But in the real world, I'm in a studio complex where there's like a hundred loud bands playing, and they're all there for the same reason I am. I need to be able to make a lot of noise, I need to be able to stack two Marshalls on top of each other and mic 'em all up and play LOUD. But the thing is when you've got a small recording studio, the first thing you see is a lot of singer/songwriters and that can be problematic because a lot of your bread and butter work really comes from quiet music, one person with a guitar who's going to come in and spend a hundred dollars for a recording.

MAKING DECISIONS

RS: Because I was working on an old computer, I really had to measure out my RAM usage. So plug-ins became problematic. I have the Waves Gold bundle [covered in Chapter 8, "Plug-ins"], and I use the Pro Tools Compressor plug-in a lot. I end up using the Audio Suite plug-ins more than the RTAS plug-ins.

But this is something that ended up working in my favor, I think. That's the thing about having a lot of power that can be problematic. You tend to not commit to things. That's something I feel pretty strongly about and one of the reasons I avoid using MIDI too much.

The more I can commit to a sound, the more I don't have to think about it again. If everything is up to, "Well, I can change that later," then decisions sometimes don't get made. I'll check out, like, a small slice of Amplitube on a bass passage and say, "Okay, I like that tone," create it as an Audio Suite file, make sure it's all good, and I'm done.

Now I've got it down to, "Here's a good sound, I like it, it works well in this mix—let's do it."

The Bottom Line

Choose the right gear for your needs   Your laptop-based studio must be created with your specific needs in mind. Whether you are you are planning on recording live bands, primarily using your laptop for composition, or working while traveling, the combination of hardware and software should be customized to your situation.

Master It   Build a laptop studio that's right for your needs.

Record directly into your laptop without a hardware interface   Most Mac laptops have an ⅛-inch line-in jack that can be used to record directly in to your DAW.

Master It   Record a vocal or Instrument track directly into your DAW.

Record a drum kit with a limited number of microphones   Having a small microphone collection doesn't mean you have to settle for inferior-sounding recordings. With some practice and experimentation you can get good results from a few well-placed microphones.

Master It   Record a drum track with only four microphones.

Chapter 13

Post Production

Before the advent of digital recording and digital distribution, the final stages of a music project generally followed one path. At the end of the recording and mixing process your final mixes would be sent to a mastering studio on tape, DAT, CD, or in another format. The mastering studio would create a "master" copy that would be the template for duplication at the vinyl or CD duplication plant.

This is still the way it's done today by many studios and musicians, especially at the commercial/professional level. But, as with many of the subjects I've covered in this book, the new technologies of the last decade or so have changed things quite a bit and opened up many new options. The proliferation of smaller studios and home-based digital recording, combined with the availability of mastering and CD authoring software, have made it possible for the studio engineer, the self-recording musician, and the home studio owner to master, sequence, and even duplicate their own CDs.

The other new development that has impacted the mastering and duplication process is online digital distribution. Much of today's music is available both on CD and in digital format. However, in a growing number of situations, artists today bypass the entire CD duplication process, instead exporting files and converting them to MP3 or AAC format for digital distribution through iTunes, an artist's website, or promotional sites like MP3.com or MySpace.com or in community music sites like iCompositions.com, where GarageBand users can share their songs with each other.

In this chapter, you will learn to

◆ Use a limiter plug-in to increase the volume of your final mixes

◆ Export CD-ready files from your DAW

◆ Create high-quality MP3 and AAC files with iTunes

File Formats

In other chapters I covered the file formats used in creating samples, loops, and tracks. Here, we'll take a look at file formats used in the mix-down, mastering, CD authoring, and digital distribution process.

Over the years there have been many file types introduced in the digital recording world, but only a handful have actually caught on and remained in popular usage. Every once in a while a new format shows up that catches on (the AAC format used by Apple's iTunes store being the most recent), but the history of digital recording and distribution is full of formats that never quite made the cut—though some, like the Ogg Vorbis format (http://www.vorbis.com), remain popular with a handful of diehard users.

Let's take a closer look at the most common file formats used in audio recording, CD Authoring and digital distribution:

WAV The WAV file type (sometimes WAVE) is actually an abbreviation of the word "waveform." The WAV format was developed by Microsoft and IBM to store audio on computers and is based on Pulse Code Modulation (PCM). PCM is a method of converting analog sound to digital form and is used in digital audio recording formats as well as in creating audio CDs. PCM is an uncompressed format, which means that while the files may be large they also contain high-quality, detailed information, making the WAV format perfect for professional audio applications.

AIFF AIFF stands for Audio Interchange File Format and was developed by Apple for storing audio files on Apple computers. As a result, AIFF files are commonly associated with digital recording on Apple computers, though today WAV and AIFF files are essentially interchangeable. Like WAV files, AIFF files are uncompressed PCM files, making them another perfect format for digital audio recording. All DAWs offer the option to export files as either WAV or AIFF; the one you choose is purely a matter of personal preference.

MP3 MP3 was the first popular format for creating audio libraries on home computers and sharing and distributing audio files on the Internet. MP3 is a form of data compression that eliminates frequencies that the human ear can't hear. This creates smaller files. Most MP3 encoders give you the ability to create MP3 files of varying size and sound quality. The most common MP3 file is encoded at 128Kbps, or 128,000 bits per second. As with anything related to digital audio, the more bits per second the better quality the audio will be. As a result, encoding your MP3 files at 160Kbps or 192Kbps (two very common settings) can greatly improve the quality and sound of your MP3 files. We'll cover this more detail in the "Converting Files in iTunes" section of this chapter.

AAC AAC stands for Advanced Audio Coding. The AAC format is used by Apple to sell music from their iTunes store. The iTunes program can easily convert your CDs, AIFF, and WAV files to the AAC format. The main advantage to the AAC format is that it sounds better than MP3 at smaller file sizes. An AAC file encoded at 128Kbps sounds comparable to an MP3 file encoded at 160Kbps. Some of the disadvantages of AAC include the fact that not every digital audio music player (this includes hardware and software) supports the format. Apple, iTunes, and other elements in the music industry like the AAC format for another reason as well: it's much easier to include file and copyright protection with built-in limitations, such as how many times the file can be copied or converted.

Mastering

Mastering is the final step or series of steps in just about every commercial recording. The mastering process typically involves making sure that the volume levels and overall sound of the songs on a CD are consistent and of the best possible sonic quality. The mastering process is also where decisions about the space between songs on a CD are made. Sometimes mastering includes the creation of fade-outs at the end of songs or cross-fades, where one song blends into the next. Once the levels, sequencing, and spacing are set, a "master" CD is then created that will then be duplicated by a CD manufacturer. The mastering process generally involves the use of compression, limiting, and EQ. We'll look at this process in more detail in the "Mastering Yourself" section of this chapter.

If you can afford it, mastering is best handled by a professional whose only involvement in the project is at the mastering stage. Having a fresh set of ears at the final stage of a project can be a great benefit. What's more, mastering is a very specific art and often involves the use of special, sometimes very expensive tools to achieve the best results.

Mastering studios are not hard to find. Check out `http://www.tapeop.com` or try using Google to search for "mastering studio" and the name of your city or town.

Mastering, like many things related to music and recording, is a subjective art. What sounds good to one mastering engineer may not sound good to another, and what works well for some genres may not be appropriate for others. My point is that you should try to find a mastering engineer or studio that has experience with your specific style of music. Mastering studios tend to be just like other recording studios in that they will work across a variety of styles and genres but may excel in a particular area. Check the mastering studio's client list (generally found on their website if they have one) and see if they've worked with artists or bands in your genre. If you like the sound of a specific CD by a local band or artist, check the credits to see who mastered the disc or ask them where they got it mastered.

Keep in mind that a good mastering job can really enhance a good recording. A bad or inappropriate mastering job can do the opposite.

MASTERING OR PREMASTERING?

These two terms are often confused. What we are referring to as "the mastering process" is sometimes called premastering by professionals. The final step in the process—the creation of the actual final master CD, also known as a "glass master"—will take place at the CD manufacturing plant. However, for most people these days the terms mastering and premastering refer to the same thing.

As with many other aspects of digital recording, the lines have become blurred a bit concerning the mastering process. Now that more artists are recording and producing themselves, more small studios are involved in aspects of recording that were previously the exclusive domain of high-paid professionals, and more formats and avenues for distribution and promotion are available, the mastering process can potentially involve a number of different scenarios. For example:

◆ You can write, record, and master your entire CD yourself and send it to a CD duplication plant to create your CDs.

◆ You can write, record, and sequence your CD (place tracks in their final order) and send it to a professional mastering studio (in any number of formats including CD-R or WAV files) for mastering. The mastering studio then sends you (or your record label or CD duplicators) the mastered CD.

◆ You can bypass the CD format altogether and create MP3 or AAC files for downloading from your website or a promotional site like MySpace or MP3.com.

◆ You can create your own master CD and duplicate it on your home system for sale or demo purposes.

Mastering Yourself

Mastering software is available in both plug-in and stand-alone formats. If you decide to do your own mastering or are interested in mastering other people's music, you'll want to invest in one or more of the mastering programs or plug-ins available for OS X. Because the mastering process is really a series of separate processes (creating consistent sounds and CD authoring being the two basic components), you'll have a number of choices to make regarding how you want to build your

---

SENDING YOUR FILES OUT

Some mastering houses will have a preferred format for delivering your files for mastering, but many will accept files in a variety of formats including data CD with WAV or AIFF files or even an audio CD. Be sure to check with them for specific instructions about the best possible format. Just because a mastering studio will accept a certain format doesn't mean it's the best for getting the job done right.

---

mastering setup. One option is to collect the best versions of the various plug-ins you'll need—a compressor, a limiter, and in some cases, a reverb. Another option is to buy a suite of mastering plug-ins like the Waves Mastering bundle (`http://www.waves.com`) or IK Multimedia's T-RackS, which I'll cover in the next section. Finally, if you are serious about mastering at a professional level, you will want to look into investing in the combination of hardware and high-end mastering software that you will find in many of today's professional mastering studios.

Once we've looked at the components that make up the sonic end of mastering, I'll cover the exporting and CD authoring processes.

Using T-RackS

IK Multimedia's T-RackS mastering software is available in two versions, a stand-alone and a plug-in version. The T-RackS 24 stand-alone version is moderately priced and can import your WAV, AIFF, or SDII files for mastering. If you know a bit about the mastering process the stand-alone may be a good choice. If you're just starting out, I recommend the plug-in version, as it contains a lot of excellent presets you can use to learn the functions and abilities of each device. The plug-in version is somewhat more expensive, but it will work in any AU, VST, or RTAS host program. Both versions of T-RackS include the following:

◆ Equalizer

◆ Tube compressor

◆ Multiband limiter

◆ Soft clipper

Fully functioning ten-day demo of both versions of the T-RackS mastering suite are available from `http://www.t-racks.com`.

The stand-alone version groups all of the devices in a single connected unit. Along with the four individual plug-ins, the plug-in version of T-RackS also includes a 4-1 "gold sounding" plug-in that groups all of the T-RackS devices in one unit. The various devices that make up both the gold sounding plug-in and the stand-alone version of T-RackS can be configured in any order using the Patch buttons.

We'll use the individual components and included presets of the T-RackS to get a look at the different elements that will be used to master a typical track in a mastering session. Once you've installed T-RackS or the T-RackS demo, open a track or session in your DAW. For the following instructions you can use a simple piece of music. If possible, choose something with both loud and quiet sections (dynamic range).

In a pinch, if you don't have a track of your own, you can import a track from your CD collection into your DAW. Use iTunes to convert the file to WAV or AIFF format. A track from your CD collection will obviously already be mastered, but you can still get an idea of the effect that many of the devices will have on a completed song.

The T-RackS Equalizer

The mastering EQ has the potential to be the most drastic, noticeable effect you'll use to process your final mixes. Remember that part of your goal is to create compatible sound files, songs that flow together and sound like they belong on the same CD. This means that you're going to want to use your mastering EQ to clean up any major differences between tracks. For example, if some tracks have much more low end than others, you can use your mastering EQ to find the middle ground, removing low end from some tracks while adding lower frequencies to other tracks.

Figure 13.1 shows the T-RackS EQ.

Figure 13.1

The T-RackS EQ

Use the preset menu to try out presets like Dull Mix?, More Vocal, and More Warmth to get an idea of how a mastering EQ can change the overall sound of a mix.

Tube Compressor

Next in the T-RackS chain is the Tube Compressor. One goal of the compressor in mastering is to even out the loud and quiet passages of a song, creating a consistent volume level from start to finish. If you (or the artist/band you are mastering) are specifically looking to retain dramatic quiet/loud dynamics, you'll want to go easy on the tube compression.

Figure 13.2 shows the T-RackS Tube Compressor.

The T-RackS Tube Compressor can also add analog-style warmth or "punch" to the sound, just as compression is often used on individual instruments in your sessions. The T-RackS Tube Compressor also includes a Stereo Enhancement knob that can increase or decrease the perceived stereo field of a recording.

Figure 13.2

The T-RackS Tube Compressor

You'll notice that unlike other compressor plug-ins, there's no threshold setting on the Tube Compressor. The amount of compression in this plug-in is raised and lowered by adjusting the Input Drive knob.

Add the Tube Compressor to your track and try out some of the presets like Vintage Tape and Mastering Tube 1 to get an idea of how this plug-in can enhance the overall sound of your tracks.

LIMITER

As I covered in Chapter 8, "Plug-ins," limiting is a kind of drastic compression, usually with a minimum compression ratio of 10:1. The limiter and the compressor perform similar functions in mastering. In general though, compression is used for subtler purposes and sonic flavoring. Limiting is often much more about "how loud can we make this track?" One of the most common settings for limiting plug-ins is the "Brick Wall" setting, meaning that no matter how hard your limiter is pushed, the volume never goes over the set "limit."

The limiter is a double-edged sword. It can certainly make your mixes louder and help your tracks stand out, but too much limiting can also take the life out of a track.

You can use the T-RackS Multiband Limiter to increase the overall volume of your mixes by reducing unwanted volume peaks and raising the overall volume of the track.

Figure 13.3 shows the T-RackS Multiband Limiter.

FIGURE 13.3

The T-RackS Multi-band Limiter

Try out some of the included presets like Extra Loud Master and Super loud lim to get an idea of how limiters can increase overall volume.

Use the Input Drive knob to increase the amount or overall volume of the track. Use the Output knob to set the maximum volume. The main thing you want to watch for is that your master track stays out of the red zone on the sound meter. If the track sounds like it's distorting, try lowering the Input Drive and raising (increasing) the Release Time knob. The T-RackS limiter is multiband, meaning it contains separate controls for the low end, midrange and high end of the frequency spectrum. Each of the frequency ranges has its own threshold knob. Lower the threshold settings for each band to increase the amount of limiting.

Other limiter plug-ins may have slightly different names for these parameters, but generally speaking the key to limiting is this: for more limiting, use higher Input levels, lower Threshold settings, and faster Attack/Release times. For subtler limiting, reduce the Input and Threshold levels and raise the Attack/Release time.

Figures 13.4 and 13.5 show the waveform of the same section of a song before and after limiting.

FIGURE 13.4
A sound file before limiting

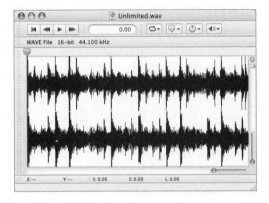

FIGURE 13.5
The same file after limiting

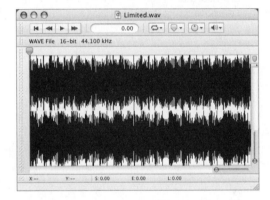

SOFT CLIPPER

Figure 13.6 shows the T-RackS Soft Clipper.

The Soft Clipper will be the last link in your mastering chain. It can keep your final output close to 0dB (the maximum volume you'll want your masters at) without going over. The Soft Clipper is similar to the limiter but applies a less noticeable (softer) form of peak reduction. The Gain knob adjusts how much signal goes in to the Soft Clipper. With the Shape knob you can apply settings from soft nonclipping (all the way to the left) and hard, full-on clipping (all the way to the right). As with the limiter, use the output knob to set the maximum volume of your overall mix.

FIGURE 13.6
The T-RackS Soft Clipper

Mastering Plug-ins

Some of the currently available mastering plug-ins and plug-in suites for OS X include:

♦ L2007 (RTAS, TDM) is inexpensive and available from `http://www.masseyplugins.com`.

♦ FinalPlug 5 (AU, VST, RTAS, MAS) is moderately priced and available from `http://www.wavearts.com`.

♦ Ozone (AU, VST, RTAS, MAS, HTDM) is moderately priced and available from `http://www.izotope.com`.

♦ PSP MasterPack (AU, VST, RTAS) is expensive and available from `http://www.pspaudioware.com`.

♦ ML4000 (RTAS, TDM) is expensive and available from `http://www.mcdsp.com`.

♦ Essential Studio Suite (AU, VST, RTAS) is expensive and available from `http://www.nomadfactory.com`.

♦ Waves Masters Bundles (AU, VST, RTAS) is top-of-the-line and available from `http://www.waves.com`.

♦ URS (AU, VST, RTAS, TDM) URS produces a wide range of high quality EQ, compressor, and limiter plug-ins from inexpensive on up. Prepackaged and customized bundles are also available from `http://www.ursplugins.com`.

Dithering

Dithering is one of the more complicated digital audio concepts to understand but is very important to the mastering and exporting process. I'll break it down into a few main points:

♦ All audio CDs contain sample rates of 44,100 samples per second (44.1KHz) and a bit depth of 16 bits per sample.

♦ Many digital recording sessions take place at higher sample rates and bit depths. Higher sample and bit settings allow for better quality recording. The higher the Sample/Bit settings are, the more digital information is being recorded. More information means a more faithfully replicated, higher quality sound.

♦ No matter what sample rate/bit depth you record at, to create a CD all of your sessions must be reduced to a sample rate/bit depth of 44,100 samples per second and 16 bits per sample.

♦ Reducing sample rate and bit depth creates unwanted sonic artifacts, sounds that degrade the overall quality of your recordings.

This is where dithering comes in. When you convert audio from a higher sample rate/bit depth (also known as "down-sampling") to 44.1/16 for the CD format, the "extra" digital information that gets eliminated results in unpleasant noise. This is sometimes noticeable, sometimes not. It can become especially pronounced in quiet passages and fade-outs at the end of songs.

Dithering actually adds a small amount of imperceptible noise to the session. The dithering noise combines with and cancels out the unwanted noise created in the down-sampling process.

Many CD authoring programs, especially those that are Red Book–compatible (see the CD Authoring section of this chapter), include automatic dithering. This means you can export your audio files at the same sample rate and bit depth as your sessions and let your CD authoring software do the rest. Depending on your software, however, this kind of automatic dithering may not always achieve the best results. Programs like Pro Tools and Logic contain built-in dithering options. In Pro Tools you can add the included Digidesign dithering plug-in as an insert on your master track by using any insert selector to choose Multi-channel Plug-in ➢ Digidesign ➢ Dither (stereo). In Logic, dithering options are included in the exporting window.

Another possibility is to add a plug-in that contains dithering functionality to your session's master track. Mastering plug-ins such as WaveArts FinalPlug 5 (http://www.wavearts.com) or Izotope's Ozone plug-in (http://www.izotope.com) contain adjustable parameters that give you precise control over your dithering options along with limiting, compression, EQ, and other mastering-related functionality.

Figure 13.7 shows the WaveArts FinalPlug 5 in a Pro Tools session.

FIGURE 13.7
WaveArts FinalPlug 5

On the right side of the plug-in is the Truncate/Dither section. Clicking the Shape button at the top right allows you to choose from a list of 12 different dithering presets.

Exporting Sessions from Your DAW

This section covers the procedures for exporting CD-ready WAV files from the DAW programs I've covered in this book.

These instructions assume one of the following scenarios:

◆ Your sessions are taking place at the bit depth/sample rate of 16/44.1.

◆ You have taken the necessary steps to dither your recordings.

If you are going to be sending your songs to a mastering engineer, it's better not to down-sample and dither. The mastering engineer will most likely have much better algorithms for dithering and will take care of that. If this is the case, you should follow the exporting instructions detailed in the next section for each DAW program, substituting your session's current bit depth/sample rate for the CD authoring standard of 16/44.1.

SAMPLE RATES AND BIT DEPTHS

Sample rate refers to the number of times per second that a sound is being "sampled" or duplicated. The standard CD sample rate of 44.1KHz was chosen because humans can only hear frequencies up to 20KHz or 20,000Hz, and the generally accepted rule is that a sampling rate should be twice as high as the highest frequency you want to record.

Where sample rates determine the highest frequency that can be captured, bit depth controls the total dynamic range of the recorded audio. A higher bit depth means greater dynamic range. The two settings do not have to be connected. For example, with many DAWs it's possible to record or export files at with a sample rate of 44.1 and a bit depth of 24 or other configurations. Generally, however, the two settings are linked, and you are more likely to see configurations like 16/44.1 and 24/96.

No Peaking

When you are exporting tracks from your DAW for mastering or CD authoring, you'll want to make sure that your audio is not peaking. This may not always be discernable by listening. Tracks can often be "in the red" and still sound good with no noticeable distortion. For the best results from your final masters, keep an eye on the Master Volume slider, master track, or output tracks of your DAW, and make sure that your tracks are as loud as they can be without actually going into the red zone on your master track LED.

Exporting in Reason

Once you've created your final mix and arrangement in Reason's Sequencer window, here's how to export your song:

1. Scroll to the end of the song and locate the Song End marker.

2. Drag the Song End marker to the end of the last measure of the song.

3. In the menu bar, select File ➤ Export Song as Audio File.

4. Name the file and select a location.

5. Select Windows WAVE File or Audio IFF File from the Format drop-down menu.

6. Click the Save button.

7. Select 44100Hz from the Sample Rate drop-down menu.

8. Select 16 from the Bit Depth menu.

9. Put a check mark in the Dither box.

10. Click Export.

Exporting in Live

Once you've used Live's Arrangement view to create your final arrangement, here's how to export your song:

1. Use the Loop/Punch-Recording Region selector to select the entire arrangement or the section you want to export (Figure 13.8).

FIGURE 13.8

Select the entire arrangement in Live's Arrangement view.

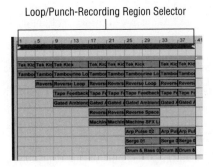

Loop/Punch-Recording Region Selector

2. From the menu bar, select File ➤ Render to Disk.

3. Select Master from the Rendered Track drop-down menu.

4. Set the Normalize option to Off.

5. Set the Render As Loop option to Off.

6. Choose AIFF or WAV from the File Type drop-down menu.

7. Set the Bit Depth to 16 and Sample Rate to 44100.

8. Set Create Analysis File and Convert to Mono to Off.

9. Check the selected time range at the bottom of the Render to Disk window to make sure it is correct.

10. Click OK, then select a location for the rendered file.

Figure 13.9 shows Live's Render to Disk dialog box.

FIGURE 13.9

Live's Render to Disk dialog box

Exporting in Pro Tools

Once you've created your final mix in Pro Tools and checked the Master Track for peaking, here's how to export your song:

1. Use the Selector tool to select the entire mix or the region that you want to export.

2. From the menu bar, select File ≻ Bounce To ≻ Disk.

3. Choose A 1-2 Stereo from the Bounce Source drop-down menu (this assumes that you haven't made any significant changes to your output routing configuration).

4. Select WAV from the File Type drop-down menu.

5. Select Stereo Interleaved from the Format drop-down menu.

6. Set Resolution to 16. (Resolution is another term for bit rate.)

7. Set Sample Rate to 44100.

8. Select Convert After Bounce.

9. Click Bounce and choose a location for your file.

Figure 13.10 shows Pro Tools' Bounce dialog box.

FIGURE 13.10

Pro Tools' Bounce dialog box

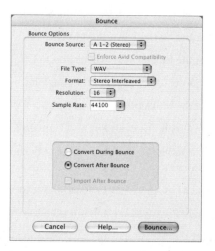

Whenever possible, it's a good idea to bounce your sessions to a different drive than the one the session currently resides on. Having Pro Tools read from and write to the same drive simultaneously can cause your bounces to fail.

Exporting in Logic

Once you've created a complete song in Logic, you will want to export or "bounce" the final mix to burn a CD, convert to MP3 or AAC, or send it off for mastering. To do this, you use the Master Fader and Main Outputs.

In the Autoload song we've created for this session, the Master Fader is not currently visible. To make the Main outputs and/or the Master Fader visible:

1. Open the Track Mixer.

2. Click the Global button on the left side of the Track Mixer to see all of the available tracks in this session, including the Master Fader.

3. Scroll to the right to view the Output 1-2 channel strip and the Master Fader.

4. Double-click the tracks Bus 1 and Bus 2 to make them visible in the Arrange and Track Mixer windows.

5. Deselect the Global button.

   Your Output and Master Fader tracks will be visible in the Track Mixer window on the right side of the "console."

6. Click the Bounce button at the bottom of the Out 1-2 track, or from the menu bar select File ➤ Bounce.

7. In the Bounce Output dialog box shown in Figure 13.11, choose a destination for your bounced mix(es).

FIGURE 13.11

The Bounce Output 1-2 dialog box

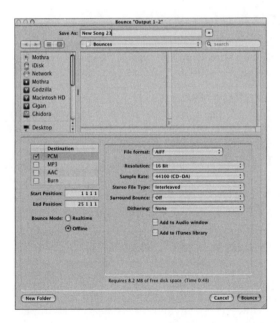

Logic lets you create multiple file types at once. The Destination box on the left side of the Bounce Dialog box contains four choices: PCM, MP3, AAC, and Burn (which will immediately burn an audio CD of your session).

8. For most mixes you want to choose the PCM export option. PCM includes AIFF, WAV, and Sound Designer II files. Select PCM in the Destination box and choose the file format, resolution, and other settings.

Logic Express users have the same export options with one difference—you can't export in multiple formats at once.

Exporting in GarageBand

GarageBand offers very limited options for exporting files. You basically have two choices: exporting directly to iTunes or saving your file as a podcast. Saving your file as a podcast automatically converts the file to AAC format, with settings based on your choice of quality in GarageBand's Export Preferences.

To create a CD-ready 16/44.1 AIFF file, select Share ➤ Send Song to iTunes.

GarageBand will create a mix-down of your song and send it to iTunes. iTunes will automatically open and add your song to your GarageBand playlist.

FIGURE 13.12
Choosing Send Song to iTunes will create a CD-ready AIFF file.

CD Authoring

Creating a CD of your music can be very easy. If your Mac has CD burning capabilities, then creating a CD for sharing music with your friends or passing out demos to band members is as simple as creating a playlist in iTunes and burning it to disk. To do this:

1. Start iTunes.

2. Create a new playlist by selecting File ➤ New Playlist.

3. Name your new playlist.

4. Drag your AIFF or WAV files directly onto the Playlist window.

5. Insert a blank disc into your disc drive.

6. Click the Burn Disc button on the lower right side of the iTunes window.

However, for anything else, especially for duplication or any professional purposes, you'll need to go a step further and make sure you are creating Red Book–compliant CDs, which I'll cover in the next section.

Red Book Standard

Red Book refers to the actual color of the color-coded books that contain the various specifications for audio CD authoring. These specifications were originally agreed upon by Sony and Phillips in 1980 and later accepted by the Digital Audio Disc Committee as the standard for creating commercially available CD-DA (Compact Disc-Digital Audio) discs. Every CD you buy at a music store or online is created to meet the Red Book standards.

Some of the specifications for creating Red Book–compliant CDs include:

◆ A sample rate/bit depth of 44.1/16.

◆ Maximum playing time is 78 minutes.

◆ Minimum time limit for a track is four seconds.

◆ Maximum number of tracks is 99.

◆ International Standard Recording Codes (ISRC) can be included.

◆ Red Book discs must be created using Track At Once or TAO (as opposed to Disc-At-Once, or DAO, which creates an entire disc from a single image).

ISRC NUMBERS

ISRC stands for International Standard Recording Code. ISRC is a unique number that is assigned to every track on a commercially released recording. ISRC codes are a series of 12 characters (letters and numbers) that represent the country of origin, registrant information, year of release, and specific track number. You should have your own three-digit ISRC (registrant) number if you are a record label or an artist who is planning to release your own commercially available recordings. You can find more information and apply for a registrant number (it's free) at http://www.riaa.com/issues/audio/isrc_faq.asp.

If you are mastering a CD for a record label or independent artist, ask them if they have been issued an ISRC number so you can include this information where applicable.

If you are creating your own CDs either for mastering, duplication, or distribution, Red Book–compliance is extremely important.

The main reason for this is that all commercially available CD players will play Red Book–compliant CDs, but the same cannot be said for non-Red Book–compliant CDs. Almost anyone who has burned their own compilation discs or has passed out copies of homemade band demos has had the experience of being unable to play certain CDs in certain CD players. This is usually because the CD player (often the more expensive units) can't read non-Red Book–compliant CDs.

Something else to consider: If you are creating your own master CD and it's not Red Book–compliant, when you have it duplicated the copies will not be Red Book-compliant either.

More and more commercially available CD players and home computers will read a wide range of CDs, but on higher-end CD players, such as those used by radio stations, theaters, or professional DJs, it's quite possible that your non-Red Book–compliant discs won't be playable.

Creating a Red Book–Compliant CD with XO Wave

When choosing your CD authoring software it's very important that it be Red Book–compliant. If it is, it will almost certainly say so in the product's specs. If you are having a hard time figuring out from a company's website or product information whether your CD authoring software is Red Book–compliant, it probably isn't.

XO Wave is a Red Book–compliant CD authoring program available in two versions, XO Wave Free and the inexpensive XO Wave Pro. Both versions are available from http://www.xowave.com.

XO Wave has a number of features including multitrack recording, video support, and built-in audio effects. For our purposes, we'll take a look at creating a Red Book–compliant CD with XO Wave Free.

CD-TEXT

CD-Text is an extension of the Red Book standard. CD-Text files are text files created in the mastering process that are included in your final CD. CD-Text information is stored in an otherwise unused section of your CD and generally contains the album name, artist, and track listing information. This information can be read by CD-Text–enabled CD players, which include most hardware and software devices.

The CDs you create with XO Wave Free will be Red Book–compliant in that they will be readable in all CD players, but they will not include IRSC codes and CD-Text information. In order to include the IRSC codes and CD-Text features used in creating professional-quality master CDs, you'll have to upgrade to XO Wave Pro. However, you can include this information (as you will in the following section) in master CDs you create with XO Wave Free and access it later if you decide to upgrade to XO Wave Pro.

Once you've downloaded and installed XO Wave Free:

1. Make sure all of the songs you want to include on your CD are in a single folder on your hard drive.

   For this first CD I suggest using only three songs. Once you know your way around XO Wave you can create longer CDs.

2. Start the XO Wave program.

3. In the Select Task dialog box, choose Create New CD Mastering Session.

4. After reading the introduction, click the Next button to create your session.

5. Use the Select Output File button on the Create Session page to name your CD and choose a location for the folder that will contain all of the necessary files. Then click Next.

   The next window that appears is the Select Source Files and Set Up Session dialog box.

6. Click the Add Multiple Files button and use the dialog box to locate the folder containing the songs you'd like to include on your CD. You can select multiple files by Command+clicking in the dialog box.

7. If you already know the order in which you want to arrange your files, use the Move Up and Move Down buttons to create the appropriate order.

8. Make sure Pad CD Track Markers is selected. This starts your tracks a tiny amount before the actual audio starts and prevents skipping in CD players.

9. Use the drop-down menu to select the amount of silence between tracks. I recommend 2.0 seconds.

10. Choose your Create Volume Automation settings from the drop-down menu.

    ◆ If you have already done extensive mastering work on each track and created masters with equal volume levels, you may want to select Don't Create Volume Automation

♦ Otherwise, the Equalize Average Loudness of Each Track setting will create a CD with compatible volume levels on each track.

♦ Selecting Add Extra Volume for Automation will allow you to control the overall volume of the session without affecting the individual track volume automation.

♦ The Determine Automation Values Fast setting speeds up the process used to determine the volume levels. Unchecking this box will cause XO Wave to take a longer time to set up your session but may create better automation results.

11. Click Next. XO Wave's main window (Figure 13.13) appears.

FIGURE 13.13

XO Wave's main window

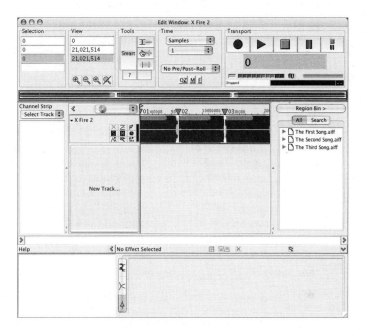

12. Select Windows ➢ Session Metadata and fill in as much information as you can for the CD. Don't worry if there's a lot of information here that you don't know, but it's a good idea to at least fill out the Album Name, Artist, and Genre.

13. Click OK to close the Session Metadata window.

14. Select a track in the Region Bin and Control+click to view the metadata for the individual track.

15. Fill out as much information as you can for each track, at the very least the track's name and artist information.

XO Wave also contains a number of editing features you can use to apply effects, fades, and cross-fades and to make other adjustments to your tracks. For more information on these features, consult the help files on the XO Wave website.

Once you've added your session and track metadata you are ready to create a master CD.

To create your CD Master:

1. Select File ➤ Burn CD ➤ Create CD Master.

2. Read the introduction information and click Next.

3. Name the CD master and click Next.

4. Leave the Setup CD Master settings as they are. Click Next.

5. Make sure the Burn CD When Done Creating Master setting is selected.

6. Insert a blank CD into your CD burner or drive.

7. Click Done.

8. Use the Burn CD from Master dialog box to select your CD burner. Make sure all of the available options are checked and click Next.

9. Click Done! to burn your disc.

Toast with Jam

One of the easier to use Red Book–compliant CD authoring programs for OS X is Roxio's Toast with Jam. Toast is a very popular burning software for OS X, but by itself Toast does will not create Red Book–compliant CDs. For that you'll need to get the version that comes with Jam. This can be a bit confusing, as of this writing the current version of Toast is 7, but the most recent version to also contain Jam is 6. Toast with Jam 6 is moderately priced and available from http://www.roxio.com. There is no demo version.

Jam makes the process of creating Red Book CDs very easy. There are advanced functions for creating cross-fades and more intricate editing features, but for our purposes we'll focus on creating a basic master CD for duplication or distribution using Jam's default settings.

1. Once you've installed Toast with Jam, start the Jam program from your Applications folder.

2. Make sure the AIFF or WAV files you want to add to the disc are located in a single folder.

3. Drag your 16/44.1 AIFF or WAV files directly onto the Jam window. Jam also includes automatic dithering if you want to drag and drop files with higher bit depth/sample rates.

4. Rearrange the track order by selecting any track and dragging up and down. Figure 13.14 shows the Jam interface.

5. The CP (Digital Copy Prohibited) and PE (pre-emphasis) buttons can be selected or deselected. These settings refer to features that are obsolete but are still required as options to create Red Book–standard CDs.

6. If you want to include ISRC numbers for your tracks, click the ISRC field for each track and input the appropriate number.

7. Select Disc ➤ Mastering Info and fill out the Disc Title, Artist information, and so on.

8. Highlight one track at a time in the Jam window and select Disc ➤ CD-TEXT Info to fill out Disc and Track information for each song. You'll only need to fill out the Disc information for the first song—each song after that will fill in the Disc information automatically.

9. To maximize the volume for each track or reduce the volume of any tracks that are too loud, highlight any track and select Disc ➤ Normalize Selection.

FIGURE 13.14
The Jam interface

10. When your disc is ready to burn, select Recorder ➤ Record.

11. Click the Advanced tab and select TAO (Track At Once) from the Auto Write Mode field.

12. Click Record.

It's a good idea to create a backup copy of your Master Disc as a disc image. This way if there are small (or large) errors in your master disc you can open the disc image file, fix the problem(s), and burn a new copy. To save a disc image Select File ➤ Save As Disc Image.

Other Red Book–Compliant CD Authoring Software for OS X

The following is a list of other commercially available software that will create CDs in compliance with Red Book specifications:

◆ Inexpensive authoring software

    ◆ **Discribe** from http://www.charismac.com

    ◆ **Bias Peak LE 5** from http://www.bias.com

◆ Expensive authoring software

    ◆ **Bias Peak Pro 5** from http://www.bias.com

    ◆ **Sonic Studio PreMaster CD** from http://www.sonicstudio.com

Using iTunes to Create MP3 and AAC Files

Originally a fairly straightforward digital jukebox, Apple's free iTunes software has become a lot more. Among iTunes' most useful features are its audio conversion functions. If you've ever ripped songs from your CD collection to your iTunes collection, you are already somewhat familiar with this functionality.

WHY DOESN'T MY DAW EXPORT TO MP3?

Considering all of the complex audio recording, processing, and mixing tasks your DAW can perform, many people wonder why so many music programs do not contain the option to export as MP3—or, as in the case of Pro Tools, why the user must pay extra for the MP3 export option.

The answer may vary from DAW to DAW, but one possible reason is that MP3 technology is not free. Companies that want to include the ability to create and export MP3 files as a part of their software must pay a licensing fee.

Converting Files in iTunes

If your DAW doesn't allow you to export directly to MP3 or AAC format, iTunes can take care of all of your MP3 and AAC conversion needs. iTunes can convert audio files to and from AIFF and WAV formats as well.

The custom conversion options in iTunes let you choose a number of different settings for your MP3 files. The default setting of Good Quality (128Kbps) is the standard that most MP3 files are encoded at. Using this setting creates files of decent quality, small enough to be stored and shared relatively easily by Internet users with smaller hard drives and slower download connections. It's a safe bet that every MP3 or digital audio player in existence will play MP3 files encoded at 128Kbps.

However, as larger hard drives and faster connections become more common, many people now encode their MP3 files at higher bit rates for increased quality. In fact, the difference between an MP3 file encoded at 128Kbps and one encoded at 160 (or 192) Kbps can be quite dramatic—the higher bit rate can make the music much nicer to listen to. This slight adjustment can eliminate common MP3 deficiencies such as the "washy" sound associated with some MP3 files.

Another option for increasing the sound quality of your MP3 files is to use Variable Bit Rate (VBR) encoding. The idea behind VBR is that the bit rate varies from section to section of the song. Parts of the song that require a high bit rate (because they have a wider dynamic range) get it, while other sections (quieter parts, silences) use a lower bit rate.

Some older MP3 players and software may not play VBR-encoded MP3 files, but this problem is getting rarer as technologies and MP3 players are updated.

For creating great quality MP3 files with iTunes I recommend the settings shown in Figure 13.15.

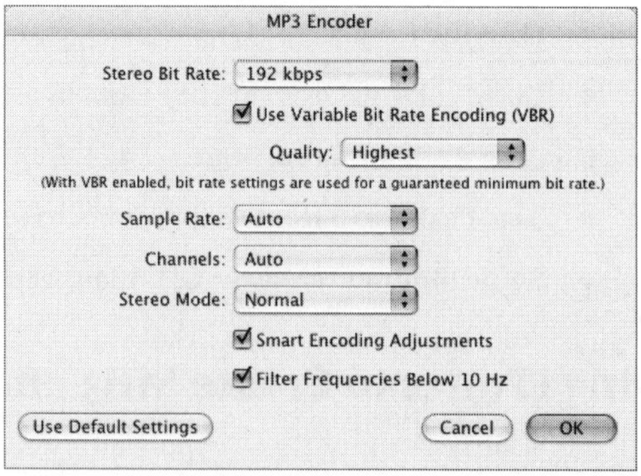

FIGURE 13.15
iTunes settings for
high quality MP3 files

You may also want to create a second copy of each file with VBR deselected for listeners with older systems and software.

Use the following instructions to create high-quality MP3 files:

1. First you'll have to set up iTunes Importing preferences. Select iTunes ➤ Preferences and click the Advanced button.

2. Select the Importing tab.

3. Select MP3 Encoder from the Import Using drop-down menu.

4. Create your own settings by choosing Custom from the Setting drop-down menu and making the selections you want.

5. Click OK to return to the Preferences window.

6. Click OK to close iTunes Preferences.

7. Select File ➤ New Playlist to create a playlist.

8. Drag your AIFF or WAV file directly onto the playlist in the iTunes window.

9. Select the file in the iTunes window and choose Advanced ➤ Convert selection to MP3.

Unfortunately there's currently no option for automatically adding the converted file to the current playlist. To locate the file, select your Music library and use the Search box at the top left. If you're aren't sure which file is your original and which is the MP3, select the file in the iTunes window and use the keyboard shortcut Command+I to view the file's information.

You can create a copy of your new MP3 file by selecting it in the iTunes window and dragging the file directly onto your desktop or another location.

To create AAC files, follow steps 1–3, then choose AAC Encoder from the Import Using drop-down menu. For high quality AAC files, I recommend encoding at 160Kbps and using the VBR option.

Adding Metadata

You can use iTunes to add metadata to your files. This is similar to the metadata I covered in Chapter 10, "Apple Loops," that turns AIFF files into Apple Loops. The metadata that's included in MP3 and AAC files gives listeners information about the track, including artist information and song titles. In many cases only the basic information you add with iTunes will be visible in other MP3 players, but it's really all you'll need. If most of your listeners will be using iTunes or an iPod, you can include a lot more information, including lyrics, artwork, and URLs.

Figure 13.16 shows iTunes' Song Info window.

When you upload your files to file-sharing sites like MP3.com and MySpace, they'll be re-encoded with information you provide during the uploading process.

Gracenote

You may have noticed that when you insert a CD into your computer and open it in iTunes, iTunes will automatically recognize the CD and provide you with Artist and Track Listing information.

For CDs you are opening in iTunes for the first time, this only works if you are online. What's happening is that iTunes is accessing the Gracenote database. Gracenote is a constantly expanding database of CD artist and track listing information.

Gracenote uses a variety of information to figure out which CD you've put in to your CD player.

FIGURE 13.16

The iTunes Song
Info window

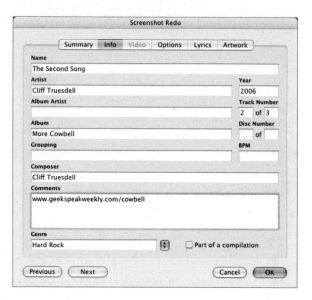

FIGURE 13.16

The iTunes Song
Info window

You can use iTunes to submit your original CD information to the Gracenote database so that
when someone plays a copy of your CD in iTunes application or another Gracenote-enabled CD
player or application, your correct artist and track listing information will show up. To add your
CD to the Gracenote database:

1. Insert your CD into your Mac's CD drive.

2. When the CD opens in iTunes, use the Command+I shortcut to access the Info window and
   make sure the metadata you want to make available (such as Artist name, Album name, and
   Track information for each track) is filled in.

3. Select the disc in your iTunes devices and choose Advanced ➤ Submit CD Track names.
   Make sure all of the appropriate fields are filled out in the CD Info window shown in
   Figure 13.17

4. Click OK to submit your CD information to the Gracenote database.

FIGURE 13.17

The Gracenote CD
Info window

Digital Distribution

For professional, amateur, major label, and independent artists alike, the Internet has dramatically changed the way musicians interact with their audiences. E-mail lists, band sites, fan sites, promotional sites, message boards, file-sharing networks…all of these options are available to artists at every level. To paraphrase a statement I heard recently: "The Internet is great because anyone can upload and share their music with the world, but the problem with the Internet is that anyone can upload and share their music with the world."

The upshot of all this is that the Internet can be an amazing free or cheap resource to promote, sell, and expose your music to a potentially vast audience, but it's easy for your music to get lost in the shuffle. Definitely take advantage of the opportunities that are available. But keep in mind that there's still no substitute for high-quality recordings and hard-working musicians who perform live, often, and well.

Mostly Free, Do-It-Yourself Services

MySpace (`http://www.myspace.com`**)**   Probably the single best free promotional tool available today. MySpace was originally a social networking site, but the brains behind the website noticed early on that bands were creating their own profile pages. MySpace adapted pretty quickly, allowing musicians to create customized band profiles with a built-in MP3 player. You can upload up to four songs at a time and use the blogging features to keep your fans up to date with your news and upcoming gig information. While many artists still have both, some bands are starting to abandon the traditional website in favor of a MySpace page.

MP3.com (`http://www.mp3.com`**)**   Back with a new format and a website geared toward users and artists alike. Bands and solo musicians can create their own artist pages and upload up to 100MB of songs. But there's one glitch at MP3.com that I hope they work out: If your band already has a commercial release, MP3.com may have already created a page for you that you can't access and change.

Pure Volume (`http://www.purevolume.com`**)**   Similar to MP3.com—allows both fans and musicians to create accounts. Musicians and bands can upload songs and bios and create a profile (similar to MySpace.com). Pure Volume also offers an inexpensive Pro level account with extra services and features.

Other free websites where you can upload and share your music include:

◆   `http://www.iCompositions.com`

◆   `http://www.macband.com`

◆   `http://www.myjonesmusic.com`

◆   `http://www.creativecommons.org`

iTunes

A lot of independent artists wonder about how to get their songs on the iTunes Music Store. This process is both easier and harder than you'd think. Many artists assume that the iTunes model is similar to that of MP3.com or other music sites where an artist can upload and promote their music just by signing up. Unfortunately, this is not the case. If you are an independent artist or record label you can contact Apple/iTunes directly by going to the Artists and Labels page (`http://www.apple.com/itunes/musicmarketing`) and clicking the Online Application link. It usually takes quite a while to get a response and it's quite possible the response will be negative.

CD Baby

A quicker and surer way to get your songs on iTunes is to use the online CD retailer CD Baby (http://www.cdbaby.com). For a low one-time set-up charge and a percentage commission on sales, CD Baby will sell your CDs online and also make your songs available through on iTunes, eMusic, Napster, and other digital distribution services. Signing up with CD Baby is as easy as filling out a few very simple forms on their website and sending them five copies of your CD.

IODA

Another excellent service is IODA, the Independent Online Distribution Alliance. IODA works with independent artists and labels and will get your original music on iTunes, eMusic, Rhapsody, Napster, and so on. IODA generally deals directly with independent labels. If you are an independent label or self-released artist with multiple CD releases, contact IODA directly through their website http://www.iodaalliance.com.

Other Sites

Other websites offering online distribution and other promotional services include:

◆ Nimbit (http://www.nimbit.com)

◆ Massive Music (http://www.massivemusicamerica.com)

◆ Reap and Sow (http://www.reapandsow.com)

 **Real World Scenario**

DELIVERING YOUR TRACK FOR MASTERING

Once your sessions are tracked and mixed, it's time to make decisions about the final mastering. If you are planning on sending your files out to a mastering engineer, there are a number of things to consider including file types, sample rate, bit depth, delivery format, and more.

As a studio owner, record label owner, producer and recording engineer, Nate Perry has worked on many recording projects in a variety of different capacities. I talked with Nate to get the lowdown on some of the things every musician and recording engineer should know about exporting and delivering final mixes for the mastering process.

Thanks to Mike Wells (http://www.mikewellsmastering.com) for his input on the questions and answers in this interview.

GET IN TOUCH

CT: "So your mixes are done. What happens next?"

NP: "The number one rule here is contact your mastering engineer and talk to them about what they want. You're going to want to know what file types are supported [by their mastering software], although WAV or AIFF will work just about anywhere. You'll want to talk to them about what sample rate and bit depth they want to work at and how they would like to receive the files. Really, the best option is to call your mastering engineer and say, 'How would you like to receive this stuff?'

"I've delivered projects to different mastering engineers in all kinds of formats. For example, there are some really high quality mastering engineers who don't work at 24/96 [a very common sample rate and bit depth setting for newer DAWs]. Just because someone doesn't do that, I wouldn't judge their mastering ability. Some of these guys will drop stuff down to 48 or 44.1 right off the bat. You may even encounter a mastering engineer who says, 'I can't even open this at 24/96—you need to give this to me at 16/44.1 or 24/48.' So it's really good to know this stuff ahead of time.

"If they need you to do this [convert to a lower sample rate and/or bit depth], you can easily do it ahead of time when you bounce to disk [export from your DAW]. But generally speaking, the mastering engineer is going to have a higher quality sample rate conversion program than whatever platform you're using."

Split Mono vs. Stereo

"Another thing you'll want to ask you mastering engineer about is split mono versus stereo. Basically, this is a host issue, and it depends on the program they're using. Some mastering programs prefer stereo interleaved, some prefer split mono [these are both exporting options in Logic and Pro Tools]. This isn't a quality issue, though, it's a time issue. If you give your mastering engineer one format and he needs the other, you'll be paying him to convert the files, which you could have just as easily done yourself. So if you're in a situation where the mastering engineer hasn't yet been decided on, if you really want to be prepared, you can provide both split mono and stereo interleaved."

Compression and EQ

CT: "What about using compression and EQ on your master track?"

NP: "If you're doing any compression or EQ on the master track, that may be okay. This is a preference issue and you'll get a variety of answers, but most mastering engineers will tell you that if you are going to EQ or compress your stereo mix, don't go to town on it. Go easy. Because if you do really slam something, that will limit what they can do. On the other hand, a lot of mixes can really benefit from some light compression on the stereo master track."

Mac to PC

"Occasionally you'll encounter difficulties with programs—Logic in particular—when the mastering is taking place on a PC. You may want to create both AIFF and WAV versions if this is a possibility. It's also a good idea to keep your filenames under 31 characters in case files are going to be transferred across different operating systems, especially on older computers."

Delivery

CT: "What's the best format for delivering your AIFF or WAV files?"

NP: "The media that's ideal for delivering to a mastering engineer is DVD-R in UDF format. That generally works across the board. You can also use UDF formatting on CD-R, but if you're doing a lot of mixes at high sample rates, you'll probably run out of space on a CD-R. At the same time, if you run into a mastering engineer who doesn't have a DVD [player], you'll have to ask them what will work best for them. I've definitely delivered mixes in all kinds of formats."

To Fade or Not to Fade?

CT: "Should the recording engineer do song fades as part of the final mixes or let the mastering engineer handle that?"

NP: "As far as fades go, it really depends on whether you're going to attend the mastering session or not. Basically, if you're going to be at the mastering session it's best to not do your own fades [beforehand]. The mastering engineer is going to have better gear to create higher resolution fades; their software is going to be better. If there's any analog gear in the [mastering] chain, that's also going to play a role in how the fades turn out. So if you create them ahead of time you're going to limit what the engineer can do and there's going to be new variables that you might not have considered as well that will come up in the mastering session. So if you can be there, you can tell the engineer what you want and do it there.

"On the other hand, if you aren't going to be there for whatever reason, the next best thing is to create a mock-up CD. This is an audio CD, not data, where you actually create the fades and the sequence [song order] and give it to them as guide.

"You can even do that if you are going to be there. If you know what you want, it'll always be to your benefit to have everything mapped out. You can bring in a mock-up as a guide, make your decisions ahead of time, and then it's just a matter of replicating that in the mastering studio."

The Bottom Line

Use a limiter plug-in to increase the volume of your final mixes   The mastering process traditionally contains a number of steps, including EQ compression and limiting. Limiting in particular can help your tracks stand out, raising the overall volume of the track by lowering the loudest peaks.

Master It   Use a limiter plug-in to raise the overall volume of one of your mixes.

Export CD-ready files from your DAW   Every DAW contains the ability to export files in AIFF or WAV form in order to create audio CDs. The best way to do this is to export your sessions at the standard 16/44.1 bit depth and sample rate used to create audio CDs.

Master It   Export a 16-bit 44.1Hz AIFF or WAV file from your DAW.

Create high-quality MP3 and AAC files with iTunes   Aside from being a digital jukebox and audio and video store, iTunes can also create high-quality MP3 files for uploading to your personal, band, or promotional website.

Master It   Create a 192Kbps MP3 file with Variable Bit Rate Encoding.

Appendix A

The Bottom Line

Each of The Bottom Line sections in the chapters suggest exercises to deepen skills and understanding. Sometimes there is only one possible solution, but often you are encouraged to use your skills and creativity to create something that builds on what you know and lets you explore one of many possible solutions.

Chapter 1: Optimizing Your System

Set your computer's preferences for optimal performance   Setting up your system's preferences correctly can serve two functions: it saves processor resources for your audio software and makes your interactions with OS X smoother when working in your DAW program.

Master It   Use System Preferences to turn off the screen saver, then resize and automatically and hide the dock when it's not in use.

Master It Solution   Follow these steps to set your preferences.

1. Open System Preferences from the Apple menu.

2. Select the Desktop & Screen Saver preferences.

3. Select the Screen Saver tab.

4. Move the Start Screen Saver slider all the way to the right.

5. Select Dock preferences.

6. Drag the Dock Size slider to the left to reduce the Dock size.

7. Select the Automatically Hide and Show the Dock check box.

Disable the Dashboard utility   Dashboard widgets can be fun and useful, but they can also drain your computer's resources by running in the background or connecting to the Internet when you're in the middle of some other task.

Master It   Use the Disable Dashboard utility to turn Dashboard off.

Master It Solution   Here's how you can turn the Dashboard off.

1. Download the Enable and Disable Dashboard utility from www.natal.be.

2. Put the Enable and Disable buttons on the desktop or in your Applications folder.

3. Click the Disable Dashboard button to turn Dashboard off.

4. Click the Enable Dashboard button to turn Dashboard on again.

Format and partition a hard drive   Installing a new FireWire or USB hard drive is usually as simple as plugging it in. To optimize it for audio recording you may need to reformat it. You can also partition your drive for multiple uses.

> **Master It**   Recreate the steps you would take to reformat or partition a hard drive (don't *actually* reformat or partition your hard drive unless you mean to).
>
> **Master It Solution**   Here are the steps you will follow to reformat a hard drive.
>
> 1. Start the Disk Utility (`Applications/Utilities/Disk Utility`).
>
> 2. Select the disk you want to format from the list on the left side of the window.
>
> 3. To erase and reformat: click the Erase tab.
>
> 4. From the Volume Format drop-down menu, select Mac OS Extended (Journaled).
>
> 5. Name your hard drive.
>
> 6. Click the Erase button to reformat the hard drive.

To partition a hard drive:

> 1. Start the Disk Utility.
>
> 2. Select the disk you want to partition from the list on the left side of the window.
>
> 3. Click the Partition tab.
>
> 4. Select the number of partitions you'd like to create from the Volume Scheme drop-down menu.
>
> 5. Select each partition and name it in the Volume Information field.
>
> 6. For each partition, choose Mac OS Extended (Journaled) as the format.
>
> 7. Click the Partition button.

Run OS X maintenance scripts   OS X performs regular maintenance of your computer at regular intervals. This maintenance can help to prevent crashes and keep your system running at its best. Many of these scripts run at times when your computer may be turned off. To work around this, you can download and install a maintenance program to run these scripts manually.

> **Master It**   Download and install the OnyX program and use it to run all of the OS X maintenance scripts.
>
> **Master It Solution**   Follow these steps to use the OnyX program on your OS X Mac.
>
> 1. Download and install the OnyX program from `www.macupdate.com/info.php/id/11582`.
>
> 2. Start OnyX.
>
> 3. Click the Maintenance tab.
>
> 4. In the Run Maintenance Scripts field, select the Daily, Weekly, and Monthly check boxes.
>
> 5. Click the Execute button.

Chapter 2: Reason

Create a new Reason song with a mixer, instruments, and effects   Reason songs can be made up of any configuration of instruments and effects. What instruments make up a particular session and in what order they appear will depend on how you prefer to work and the type of music you are creating, among other factors. The following is one possible template for working in Reason. Using the Tab key to toggle between front and back view of the Reason interface is a good way to begin creating your own routing configurations.

Master It   Create a new Reason song with a Mixer 14:2 and one each of Reason's instruments. Also include an RV7000 Advanced Reverb and a Scream 4 Distortion Unit as Send effects. Minimize the mixer and all of the instruments and effects.

Master It Solution   Use these steps to create your Reason song.

1. Create a new Reason song. Select Create ➤ Mixer 14:2.

2. Next, choose Create SubTractor Analog Synthesizer.

3. Create one each of the instruments below the SubTractor in the Create menu.

4. Select the Mixer 14:2 in the Rack view.

5. Choose Create ➤ RV7000 Advanced Reverb.

6. With the RV7000 selected, choose Create ➤ Scream 4 Distortion Unit.

7. Option+click the small upside-down triangle in the upper left corner of any of the Reason instruments or effects to minimize all of the Racks modules.

Edit loops in the Dr. Rex Loop Player   Reason's Dr. Rex Loop Player can load and play back any file in the REX format. The most commonly used file in the Dr. Rex is the drum loop, though any instrument loop file can be converted to the RX2 format using Propellerhead's ReCycle program.

Master It   Open a drum loop in the Dr. Rex Loop Player and raise its overall pitch by one octave except for the first slice: lower that to one octave below the original pitch and pan it hard left.

Master It Solution   Here is how you can use this method for editing loops in the Dr. Rex Loop Player.

1. Create a new Reason song and add a Dr. Rex Loop Player.

2. Use the Browse Loop button to locate and load any REX drum loop.

3. Click the Preview button on the Dr. Rex Loop Player to hear the loop in its current state.

4. Located to the right of the Preview and To Track button is the Osc Pitch section of the Dr. Rex. Use the Oct (octave) knob in this section to adjust the overall pitch of the loop by clicking and dragging with your mouse to raise the knob one click from Oct:4 to Oct:5.

5. Beneath the Osc Pitch section at the bottom of the Dr. Rex interface are the five knobs used to edit individual slices. Use the Select Slice knob to select the first slice in the loop.

6. Use the Pitch knob to lower the pitch of the slice to −24 (two octaves below the current pitch, on below the original).

7. Use the Set Slice Pan knob to pan the first slice to −64 (hard left).

Add effects as inserts and sends   Reason's included effects can be used to enhance an instrument track, to help out in a mix, or to create completely new sounds from instrument performances.

Master It   Create a Reason song with two Dr. Rex drum loops. Add reverb to both Dr. Rex Loop Players as a Send effect. Add a delay to the second Dr. Rex only as an Insert effect.

Master It Solution   Follow these steps to utilize effects in a Reason song.

1. Create a new Reason song.

2. Add a Mixer 14:2 from the Create menu.

3. Choose Create ➢ Dr. Rex Loop Player.

4. Create a second Dr. Rex Loop Player.

5. Use the Browse Loop button on both Dr. Rex Loop Players to browse and load drum loops.

6. Select and highlight the Mixer 14:2 in the Rack window. Choose Create RV7000 Advanced Reverb.

7. Use the RV7000's Browse Preset button to locate and load a preset from the Reason Factory Sound Bank.

8. On the Mixer 14:2, raise the Aux 1 knob on channels 1 and 2.

9. Select and highlight the second Dr. Rex Loop Player in the Rack window.

10. Choose Create DDL-1 Digital Delay Line.

11. Adjust the Wet/Dry knob on the DDL-1 to raise and lower the amount of delay effect added to the drum track.

Create and save your own patches with the Malström Synthesizer   The Malström Graintable Synthesizer, like all the Reason instruments, comes with a large collection of included presets. More presets are available from many commercially available ReFills as well. The real fun with Malström, though, is investigating all of the possibilities it contains for creating your own sounds and saving them as original, recallable patches.

Master It   Use both of Malström's Oscillators and the Mod A LFO to create and save an original patch.

Master It Solution   Follow these instructions to work with Malström's features.

1. Create a new Reason song. Choose Create ➢ Mixer 14:2.

2. Choose Create ➢ Malström Graintable Synthesizer.

3. Select a base sound from the Oscillator One's Graintable menu.

4. Make adjustments to Oscillator One's motion, index, or pitch-shifting parameters and/or adjustments to the ADSR Envelope.

5. Turn on Oscillator B by clicking its On/Off button.

6. Choose a graintable and adjust any desired parameters.

7. Select an LFO waveform in the upper left corner of Mod A.

8. Adjust at least one of the pitch, index, or shift parameters.

9. Raise or lower the Rate knob to adjust the tempo of the LFO cycle.

10. Turn Mod A's Sync button on to sync the modulation to the current session tempo, or click the One-Shot button to cycle through the LFO only once.

11. Click the Save Patch button to save your new Malström patch.

Create Automation on a Reason Mixer 14:2   Reason's Automation features can be used to introduce effects, adjust various parameters, silence a specific part or instrument, and much more. On the Reason Mixer, automation is especially useful for final mixes, raising and lowering tracks, and adding and reducing effects.

Master It   Create volume automation on channel 1 of a Mixer 14:2.

Master It Solution   Create automation by following these steps.

1. Create a new Reason song. Choose Create ➢ Mixer 14:2.

2. Choose Create ➢ Sequencer Track.

3. In the Sequencer window, select Mixer 1 from the sequencer track's drop-down menu. Rename the Sequencer track `Mixer 1`.

4. Select the Mixer 1 track in the Sequencer window to arm it for recording.

5. Click the Stop button in the Transport bar to make sure the playhead is at the beginning of the session.

6. Click the Record button in the Transport bar to prepare for recording.

7. Click the Play button to begin recording automation.

8. Raise and lower the Volume slider on channel 1 of the Mixer 14:2.

9. Click the Stop button to end recording.

10. Click the Stop button again to return the playhead to the beginning of the session.

11. Play back your automation. The volume fader or any other automated parameter will have an outline around it.

12. To remove automation, Control+click anywhere inside the automation outline and select Clear Automation from the pop-up menu.

Chapter 3: Ableton Live

Create MIDI performances in Live   Live's built-in instruments, the Impulse Drum kit and Simpler virtual sampler, can be used to create loops or entire tracks by using your MIDI keyboard or manually creating a performance in the Note Editor.

Master It   Create a basic MIDI loop using one of Live's Simpler virtual sampler presets.

Master It Solution   Use these steps to create a simple loop.

1. Create a new Live Set.

2. Use the Live Device Browser to open Instruments/Simpler and, from any instrument category, select a preset instrument.

3. Drag the instrument from the Browser window to any empty MIDI track or empty spot on the Clip/Device Drop Area.

4. Double-click any empty clip slot in the MIDI track to create a blank clip.

With your new blank clip you have multiple choices for creating a MIDI performance. You can:

◆ Create a MIDI performance in the Note Editor.

◆ Arm the track for recording, click the Clip Launch button, and use loop recording and your MIDI keyboard to create a performance.

◆ Use your computer's keyboard in place of a MIDI keyboard to create a performance.

Use Live's included instruments and effects to create clips   Live's audio and/or MIDI playback and editing functions can be combined with the program's built-in effects to create recallable clips.

Master It   Create and save a reusable MIDI clip with an Impulse drum sequencer kit and a ping-pong delay effect preset.

Master It Solution   Follow these steps to create a MIDI Clip.

1. Create a new Live Set and save it to the desktop or another location.

2. Use the Live Device Browser to open the Impulse Drum Sequencer in the Instruments folder.

3. Select a preset kit from either the Acoustic or the Electronic folder.

4. Drag the kit from the Browser directly onto any empty MIDI track or a blank spot on the Clip/Device Drop Area.

5. Double-click any empty clip slot to create an empty clip and open the MIDI Note Editor.

6. Use your mouse to create a drum performance in the Note Editor window.

7. Press the Launch Clip button to hear your loop.

8. Use the Live Device Browser to open the Audio Effects folder, then open the Ping Pong Delay effect folder and select any preset.

9. Add the effect by dragging the preset directly on the clip slot in the MIDI track.

10. Use the File Browser to open the folder Live created when you saved your new set.

11. Drag the Impulse/Ping Pong Delay clip from the clip slot directly onto the Project folder.

12. Select File ➢ Collect All and Save to keep all related audio files in the Project folder.

Edit Audio loops in Live's audio Clip View   Live's ability to time-stretch, adjust, and edit audio loop files is one of its most useful features. Most of this editing takes place in Live's Clip View at the bottom of the Live interface.

Master It   Add an audio loop file to a Live set; adjust its pitch, volume, and panning; and save it as a clip.

Master It Solution   Edit your audio loop with these steps.

1. Create a new Live Set and save it to the desktop or another location.

2. Use one of the Live File Browsers to locate any audio loop. If you don't have any other audio loops, you can use the `MMA Audio Files/All Loops` folder from the included DVD.

3. Drag the loop from the File Browser to any empty audio track clip slot or any blank spot on the Clip/Device Drop Area.

4. Double-click the loop in the clip slot to open the Clip View at the bottom of the Live interface.

5. Display the Sample Box and Envelopes Box by clicking the Show/Hide Sample Box and Show/Hide Envelopes Box buttons in the lower left corner.

6. In the Sample Box, use the Transposition knob to adjust the loop's pitch and the Volume slider to raise or lower the loops volume.

7. Click the Pan button in the Envelopes Box to view the Breakpoint Envelope in the Note Editor.

8. Create breakpoints and use them to adjust the track's panning.

9. Use the File Browser to open the folder Live created when you saved your new set.

10. Select the clip in the clip slot and drag it to the Project folder.

11. Select File ➢ Collect All and Save to copy the original audio file to the Project folder.

Edit MIDI clips in Live's MIDI Clip View   The MIDI Clip View is similar to the audio clip view, with a few significant differences having to do with functions that are specific to each format.

Master It   Create a MIDI loop with Simpler, then pitch shift the second half of the loop using the Note Editor and Envelopes Box.

Master It Solution   Follow these instructions to create and edit a MIDI clip.

1. Use the Live Device Browser to open the Simpler instrument.

2. Drag one of the preset instruments to any available MIDI track.

3. Double-click any clip slot to create an empty clip.

4. Create a MIDI performance in the Note Editor.

5. Click the Launch Clip button to hear your clip.

6. Click the Pitch Bend button in the Envelope Box.

7. Create two breakpoints on the Breakpoints Envelope. Use the second breakpoint to raise or lower the pitch of the loop.

Use Live and Reason together in a ReWire session   With Propellerhead's ReWire protocol, you can use Reason and Live together. Combining the two programs allows you to take advantage of Live's audio recording and looping functions and Reason's samplers, synthesizers, and effects in a single session.

Master It   Create a new Live set and Reason song with a Mixer 14:2 and a Dr. Rex Loop Player. Route Reason's output to a single stereo track in Live. Add some Live clips, then save the project in a single folder.

Master It Solution   Use Reason and Live together by creating and combining sessions using the following steps.

1. Create a new Live Set.

2. Add a Live clip from the Live Library (or from any audio loop) or create a MIDI clip with the Simpler or Impulse.

3. Start Reason.

4. Create a new Reason Song and add a Mixer 14:2 and a Dr. Rex Loop Player.

5. Use the Dr. Rex's Browse Loop button to load a RX2 file from the Reason Factory Sound Bank

6. Click the Dr. Rex's Preview Loop button (you shouldn't hear any audio yet).

7. Select an empty audio track in Live.

8. Make sure that the Live audio track's I/O section is showing. If not, use the keyboard shortcut Command+Option+I.

9. In the Live interface, select the first unused audio track.

10. Under Audio From at the top of the I/O section, choose Reason.

11. In the Input Channel menu below Audio From choose 1/2: Mix L,Mix R. You should hear audio from Reason.

12. Create arrangements in Reason and Live.

Chapter 4: Pro Tools

Create and save a new Pro Tools session   Every time you start a new Pro Tools session, decisions will have to be made about location, file format, and settings and the types of track to be included. These decisions will impact the rest of the session in various ways and will also play a part in determining compatibility with other Pro Tools systems, should you end up working on a session in multiple studios.

Master It   Create a new Pro Tools session with the WAV file format, containing a mono audio track, a stereo instrument track, one mono *and* one stereo aux input, and a master Fader track.

Master It Solution

1. Launch Pro Tools and choose File ➢ New Session.

2. In the New Session dialog box choose an audio File Type, Sample Rate, and Bit Depth.

3. Select a location to save your new session.

4. Click Save.

5. Select Track ➢ New to open the New Track window.

6. Click the "+" sign on the far right of the New Track window four times to create a total of five tracks.

7. Use the drop-down menus to select the appropriate track types.

8. Select File ➤ Save.

Add plug-in effects to Pro Tools tracks   Pro Tools includes a wide range of plug-in effects, which will be used in some capacity in almost every recording session.

Master It   Add Pro Tools' RTAS Medium Delay and D-Verb plug-ins to a mono audio track.

Master It Solution   Here is how to add insert effects in Pro Tools.

1. Create a new Pro Tools session or open an existing session with at least one mono audio track.

2. Use Insert Selector A to locate Plug-in ➤ Delay ➤ Medium Delay II.

3. Adjust the Mix slider to include the original signal and the delay effect, or choose a preset form the Librarian menu.

4. Use Insert Selector B to add the D-Verb located at Plug-in ➤ Reverb ➤ D-Verb (mono).

Process audio with AudioSuite plug-ins   Pro Tools AudioSuite plug-ins can make permanent changes to your audio tracks.

Master It   Process an audio track with Pro Tools' Multi-tap delay AudioSuite effect.

Master It Solution   Use these steps to process your track.

1. Select any Pro Tools Track containing audio.

2. Use the Selector or Grabber tool to choose a section of audio. Select AudioSuite ➤ Delay ➤ Multi-Tap Delay.

3. Adjust the settings or choose a preset from the Librarian menu. Press the Preview button to preview the effect.

4. Press the Process button to apply the effect.

Create volume automation on a Pro Tools track   Pro Tools has a number of automation features built in to the program. Automation can adjust volume levels, panning, many of the parameters of any plug-in effects or virtual instruments, and more.

Master It   Use the Pencil tool and the Grabber tool to create and adjust volume automation on a Pro Tools audio track with breakpoints.

Master It Solution   Follow these steps to use the the Pencil tool and the Grabber tool.

1. Create a new Pro Tools session or open an existing session with at least one audio track.

2. Select an audio track to automate and choose Volume from the Track View selector.

3. Select the Pencil tool from the toolbar.

4. Use the Pencil tool to create breakpoints along the Volume graph line in the Track window.

5. Select the Grabber tool and use it to adjust the breakpoints.

Use Pro Tools as a ReWire master with Reason.   Using Propellerhead's ReWire protocol allows you to sync two DAW programs together, taking advantage of the strengths and features of each program. Host programs like Pro Tools can control all the output and functionality of slave programs like Propellerhead's Reason. Since all versions of Pro Tools come with Reason Adapted for Digidesign, every Pro Tools user can take advantage of this excellent feature.

Master It   Add Reason or Reason Adapted for Digidesign to a Pro Tools session as a ReWire slave.

Master It Solution   Use the following method to combine Reason and Pro Tools.

1. Create a new Pro Tools session.

2. Select Track ➤ New and add a new stereo instrument track.

3. Option+click the track's Volume indicator to raise the track volume.

4. Make sure that Instrument view and Inserts view are visible.

5. Add Reason or Reason Adapted for Digidesign on Insert Selector A.

6. Open a Reason song or create a new Reason song.

7. Add instruments and/or effects in Reason.

8. Use Pro Tools to start, stop, loop, and control the tempo or Reason.

Chapter 5: Logic

Create an Autoload session   Creating an Autoload session saves time, simplifies your Logic experience and can be used to automatically create your own customized Logic session by default whenever you start the program.

Master It   Use the Logic Setup Assistant to set up Logic, then create your own Autoload template.

Master It Solution

1. If you already have an Autoload song, locate it and delete it. It will be located in the folder *yourusername*\Library\Application Support\ Logic\Song Templates.

2. Choose Preferences ➤ Logic Pro/Express ➤ Initialize All Except Key Commands.

3. Choose Preferences ➤ Logic Pro/Express ➤ Start Logic Setup Assistant.

4. When you get to the Core Audio Mixer Setup page, choose the maximum number of audio tracks, audio bus channels, and audio instruments you might need.

5. Select the maximum number of audio inputs you intend to use.

6. Select the maximum number of audio outputs you intend to use.

7. When Logic starts, delete any unwanted tracks and make any adjustments you wish to save as part of your template.

8. Select File ➤ Save As Template from Logic's File menu.

9. Save the file as Autoload.

Any new sessions you create will automatically use your Autoload song as the default template.

Use Logic's Loop Browser   Logic's built-in Loop Browser gives you quick access to all of your Real Instrument and Software Instrument Apple Loops.

Master It   Use the Loop Browser to add a Real Instrument and Software Instrument loop to a Logic session, then convert a Software Instrument to a Real Instrument.

Master It Solution   Follow these steps to access the Loop Browser.

1. Select Audio ➢ Loop Browser to open the Loop Browser.

2. Select an instrument, genre, or mood category.

3. Click and drag a Software Instrument loop (green icon) from the Loop Browser directly onto any instrument track.

4. Click and drag a Real Instrument loop (blue icon) from the Loop Browser directly onto any audio track.

5. Convert a Software Instrument loop to a Real Instrument loop by dragging it from the Loop Browser onto any audio track.

Use Logic's Arrange window editing tools   Logic's Arrange window contains a palette of editing tools that you can use to edit audio and MIDI tracks. The edit tools can fix major or minor problems in your audio or MIDI recordings or create entirely new performances out of existing tracks and loops.

Master It   Use the Arrange window edit tools to cut an Apple Loop, audio, or audio performance into three separate regions. Mute one of the regions. Drag one of the regions to a new track and loop it.

Master It Solution   Edit your audio using the following method.

1. Record an audio performance or use the Loop Browser to add an Apple Loop to the Timeline.

2. Use the Magnify tool to zoom in on the track in the Timeline.

3. Select the Scissors tool.

4. Use the Scissors tool to create three separate regions.

5. Select the Mute tool and click one of the regions to mute it.

6. Select the Arrow tool and use it to move one of the remaining regions to a new track.

7. Move the Arrow tool to the end of the region, then click and drag to loop the region.

Create MIDI performances with Logic's virtual instruments   Logic's collection of virtual instruments includes keyboards, drum modules, synthesizers, and the all-purpose EXS24 sampler. Using these instruments, you can create single tracks, multiple tracks, or complete performances.

Master It   Add an ES1 synthesizer to your Logic song and use the Caps Lock keyboard to create and record a simple MIDI performance.

Master It Solution   Use these steps to work with a synthesizer in your Logic session.

1. Create a new Logic Session.

2. Double-click any instrument track to open the Track Mixer.

3. In the I/O field of the selected instrument track, choose Stereo ≻ Logic ≻ ES1.

4. Choose a preset from the ES1's preset menu.

5. Press the Caps Lock key to view the Caps Lock keyboard.

6. Close the Track Mixer.

7. Make sure the instrument track containing the ES1 is selected in the Arrange window.

8. Click the Record button on the Transport bar to begin recording after a four beat count-off.

9. Press the 0 key on your numeric keypad to return to the beginning of the session.

10. Press the spacebar to play back your performance.

"ReWire" Logic with Reason and Ableton Live   Using Propellerhead's ReWire to connect Ableton Live and/or Reason to Logic has gotten easier with each successive Logic update.

Master It   Create a new Logic session using a Dr. Rex Loop Player in Reason as a drum track.

Master It Solution   Follow these steps to add Reason or Live to a Logic session.

1. Create a new Logic Project.

2. Select an empty instrument track in the Arrange window.

3. If the Objects Parameters Box is minimized, click the triangle on the left side of the box to open it.

4. Rename the track "Reason" in the Object Parameters box.

5. In the Object Parameters box, select Channel ≻ ReWire Stereo ≻ Reason ≻ RW: Mix L/R.

6. Start Reason and create a Mixer 14:2 and a Dr. Rex Loop Player.

7. Use the Browse Loop button on the Dr. Rex Loop Player to load any REX loop from the Reason Factory Sound Bank and click the Preview button on the Dr. Rex.

8. Use the To Track button on the Dr. Rex to send the drum loop to the Reason Sequencer.

9. Start playback in either Logic or Reason.

Chapter 6: GarageBand

Use GarageBand's Musical Typing keyboard   GarageBand's built-in keyboard and Musical Typing features make it possible to use your computer's keyboard to create music quickly without attaching a MIDI controller. The Musical Typing keyboard can be especially useful on a laptop if you are traveling or unable to hook up your MIDI devices for any reason.

Master It   Use the Musical Typing keyboard to create a performance with one of the GarageBand synthesizers.

Master It Solution   Here are the steps you will use to access and use the Musical Typing keyboard.

1. Start GarageBand and create a new music project.

2. Double-click the default Piano track to open the Track Info window.

3. Select any of the synth categories from the left side of the Track Info window.

4. Select a preset from the category you've chosen.

5. Select Window ➢ Musical Typing to view the Musical Typing keyboard.

6. Use the designated alphabet keys on your computer's keyboard to try out the preset.

7. Make sure the correct track is armed for recording. Press the Record button to begin recording.

8. Click the Play button to end recording.

Locate specific kinds of loops and add them to a session   GarageBand's Loop Browser organizes loops by various attributes such as instrument type, genre, and other keywords. The Loop Browser also contains a section where you can view information about the selected loops such as key and original tempo.

Master It   Create a four-measure cycle region, then add a Real Instrument drum loop and a Software Instrument bass loop. Finally, locate a Real or Software Instrument guitar loop that fits musically with the other loops.

Master It Solution   Use these steps to locate and add loops in a GarageBand session.

1. Create a new GarageBand music project.

2. Press "C" to create a cycle region.

3. If necessary, lengthen or shorten the cycle region to four measures.

4. Open the Loop Browser by selecting Control ➢ Show Loop Browser or using the keyboard shortcut Command+L.

5. Click the All Drums selector button in the Loop Browser window to view all of your available drum loops.

6. Select any Real Instrument drum loop (Real Instruments are represented by a blue icon) to preview it.

7. Add the loop to your session by dragging it from the Loop Browser directly onto the GarageBand Timeline.

8. Place the loop at the beginning of the session.

9. Place your mouse at the end of the loop so the cursor changes to a curved arrow. Click and drag the loop to fill out the entire four-measure cycle region.

10. Click the Reset button at the top left of the Loop Browser.

11. Click the Bass keyword button and locate a bass loop that's compatible with the drum loop. Note its tempo and key on the right side of the Browser window.

12. Click the Loop Browser reset button again.

13. Choose the guitar category and select a loop that matches the tempo and key of the first two loops.

Create a drum track using GarageBand's Software Instruments   GarageBand's Software Instruments include drum kits, basses, pianos and organs, and a large collection of different types of synthesizers. All of the included instruments can be used to create loops and complete tracks.

Master It   Create a drum loop using your MIDI keyboard and one of GarageBand's included virtual drum kits. Then use the Editor window to fix any mistakes or inconsistencies.

Master It Solution   Here's how to create a drum loop in GarageBand.

1. Create a new GarageBand music project. Double-click the default Piano track's track header to open the Track Info window.

2. Select the Drum Kits instrument category on the left side of the Track Info window to view a list of available kits.

3. Select any of the kits on the list to automatically replace the default piano instrument with a drum kit.

4. To use your MIDI keyboard to play the drum kit, locate the corresponding keys on your MIDI keyboard. The kick drum is often at C1.

5. Create a cycle region to enable Loop Recording.

6. Turn the metronome on or off by selecting Control ➤ Metronome.

7. Click the Record button to begin recording.

8. Click the Play button to stop recording.

9. Double-click the recorded file in the Timeline to open the Track Editor.

10. Select and move notes around in the Track Editor.

Add effects to a GarageBand track   GarageBand's built-in effects, OS X's built-in Audio Unit effects, and any third-party Audio Unit plug-in effects are all accessible from the Track Info window and can be added to any Real or Software Instrument track.

Master It   Create a new track with any loop from the Loop Browser and add two plug-in effects.

Master It Solution   Use these steps to add effects to a GarageBand track.

1. Create a new GarageBand music project.

2. Open the Loop Browser and drag any loop file on the GarageBand Timeline.

3. Double-click the track header to open the Track Info window.

4. If the track details are not currently showing, click the Show Details triangle at the bottom left of the Track Info window.

5. Choose effects from the first and second effects drop-down menus in the Track Info window.

6. Choose effects presets from the second drop-down menu, or edit the effects parameters by clicking the Edit Preset button.

Export a GarageBand song to iTunes   GarageBand automatically mixes your songs down into the iTunes program. From there you can add metadata, burn CDs, or convert songs into other formats.

Master It   Create a song on GarageBand using loops or loops and your own audio recordings, then export it to iTunes.

Master It Solution   Follow these steps to export your GarageBand songs to iTunes.

1. Create a new GarageBand music project.

2. Add loops from the Loop Browser and/or record tracks using your audio interface.

3. Select Share ➤ Send Song to iTunes.

Chapter 7: More Useful Software

Create and edit loops, samples, and other audio files with an audio editor   All DAW programs have audio editing functions built in to some extent. A dedicated, separate audio editor can have a number of uses including creating editing loops and samples, converting files, sound design, and mastering. Along with built-in recording functions, many audio editing program also contain more advanced editing features than those contained within your DAW program.

Master It   Use the freeware program Audacity to record and edit a sound file, add an effect, then export the file as an AIFF to use as a loop or sample in your DAW.

Master It Solution   Follow these steps to use the Audacity program as an audio editor.

1. Launch Audacity.

2. Make sure the instrument or microphone you are using to record is properly connected.

3. Check Audacity's Preferences (Audacity ➤ Preferences ➤ Audio I/O) to make sure Audacity is ready to receive a signal from your audio interface.

4. Click the red Record button at the top of the Audacity window to begin recording.

5. Click the yellow Stop button to end recording.

6. Use any of Audacity's editing tools to edit the recording. For example, use the Selection tool to highlight and delete a section of the file.

7. Use the Selection tool to select all or some of the audio file, then choose an effect from the Effect menu.

8. Choose File ➤ Export as AIFF.

If Audacity's File menu does not show Export as AIFF as one of the export options, then you'll have to change Audacity's default exporting file format. To do this:

1. Choose File ➤ Audacity ➤ Preferences.

2. Click the File Formats tab.

3. In the Uncompressed Export Format field, select Apple/SGI 16-bit PCM.

Use Audio Units and VST plug-ins outside of a host program   Programs like Rax and VSTi Host allow you to use Audio Units and VST virtual instruments and plug-ins outside of a host program. This includes the ability to play the instruments, add and configure effects, and record the output to your hard drive.

Master It Use the Rax program to record a performance using the Crystal synthesizer and Apple's AUDelay Audio Unit plug-in.

Master It Solution Create your performance by following these steps.

1. Launch the Rax program.

2. Create a new song, new set, or new library.

3. Open Rax's preferences and select the MIDI tab. Make sure your MIDI controller is activated to work with Rax.

4. In the Instruments field at the bottom of the Rax interface, use the Add Instruments menu to add the Crystal synthesizer.

5. Choose a preset from the Presets menu or click the Remote Editor button to view the Crystal interface.

6. At the top of the Effects field, click the Insert 1 button.

7. Click the Add Effect button and use the Add Effect menu to choose Apple ➢ AUDelay to add OS X's built-in Audio Unit delay effect.

8. Use your MIDI keyboard to play the instrument/effect combination.

9. Click the Record button to begin recording the audio output of your Rax session.

10. Click the Record button a second time to end recording.

11. Locate your audio recording.

Rax places your audio recording by default in the folder *yourusername*\Documents\Rax Recordings. You can change this by opening Rax's Audio Preferences tab and clicking the Recording Location Browse button to select a new location.

Batch convert audio files Many audio editing programs contain file conversion functionality. One of the programs I've covered, Audiofile Engineering's Sample Manager, contains a quick and especially easy to use the batch conversion feature.

Master It Keeping the original files in their current location, use the Sample Manager program to batch-convert the WAV files in the MMA Audio\WavFiles to Apple Loops in a new, separate folder.

Master It Solution Use these steps to batch convert audio files with Sample Manager.

1. Launch Sample Manager. Locate the folder MMA Audio\WavFiles.

2. Drag the folder onto the Sample Manager window.

3. Choose Convert from the drop-down menu at the top of the Process panel.

4. From the File Format drop-down menu, select Apple Loop.

5. Use the keyboard shortcut Command+A to select all the audio files at once.

6. Hold down the Command+Option+Shift, then click the File Format Convert button.

7. Use the Choose Destination Directory dialog box to choose or create a folder for the converted files.

8. Click Choose.

Sample Manager will copy and convert all of the selected files and place the newly created copies in whichever folder you have designated in step 7.

Create a loop or sample from a DVD With Audio Hijack or Audio Hijack Pro you can use any sound source on your computer to create loop and sample files. This includes songs in your iTunes library, streaming audio from the Internet or the audio output of any program running on your Mac.

Master It Use the Audio Hijack Pro program to capture a sound clip from a DVD in your Mac's DVD player.

Master It Solution Here is how to use Audio Hijack Pro to record audio.

Before you begin, make sure that Instant Hijack is installed. This "extra" feature allows Audio Hijack Pro to grab audio from a program without asking you to restart it. If you have not already installed Instant Hijack, do the following:

1. Launch Audio Hijack Pro. Select Audio Hijack Pro ➤ Install Extras.

2. Select the Instant Hijack tab.

3. Click the Install button.

4. When installation is complete restart your computer.

You are now ready to begin sampling with Audio Hijack Pro:

1. Select a DVD that you'd like to sample.

2. Insert the DVD in your DVD drive and locate the section or scene you would like to use.

3. Select Video ➤ Half Size from the DVD player menu so you'll have room on the screen to view both the DVD player and Audio Hijack Pro.

4. Launch Audio Hijack Pro.

5. Select DVD Player from the component list.

6. Click the Hijack button.

7. Click the Record button. Audio Hijack Pro will not actually begin recording until you begin playing the DVD Player.

8. Click the Play button on the DVD player.

9. Once you've recorded the section you want, press the DVD player's Stop button.

10. Deselect the Record and Hijack buttons in Audio Hijack Pro.

11. Locate and play back the new recording by clicking Recording Bin at the top of the Components window.

12. Use the Reveal in Finder button to locate your new audio file. Drag it directly into your DAW program or copy it to a new location where you'll have easy access to it for future use.

Scan a hard drive or folder for all of its audio files   Iced Audio's AudioFinder program contains a number of features designed to help you organize all of the sound files on your computer system.

Master It   Use AudioFinder's Scanner tab to view all of the audio files in the MMA Audio folder. Locate the file SynBassArp1.wav then copy the file to a Bookmarked location.

Master It Solution   Follow these steps to scan and copy a file with AudioFinder.

1. Launch AudioFinder.

2. Locate your desktop in the Browser window. The file path will be Users*your username*\Desktop.

3. Add your desktop to your AudioFinder Bookmarks by clicking the Bookmark button on the top left of the AudioFinder window and selecting Add Selection to Organizer Bookmarks from the drop-down menu.

4. Use the Browser window to locate the MMA Audio folder.

5. If it's on your desktop the file path will be Users*your username*\Desktop\MMA Audio.

6. Click the Scanner tab at the top of the AudioFinder interface.

7. On the left side of the Scanner window, Live Scan From Browser should be selected by default.

8. Type **SynBass** into the Search field at the top of the Scanner window.

9. Click the Search button.

10. Select the file SynBassArp1.wav in the Scanner window.

11. Click the Bookmarks icon in the Organizer section on the bottom right of the AudioFinder window.

Chapter 8: Plug-in Effects

Install Audio Unit, VST, and RTAS plug-ins   Most plug-ins come with an automatic installer program that puts the plug-in and accompanying presets into the necessary locations on your hard drive. Some plug-ins, especially many of the free or less expensive effects require manual installation.

Master It   Download and install any of the freeware Audio Unit and VST plug-ins from bram.smartelectronix.com or www.mda-vst.com.

Master It Solution   Install your plug-ins to any of the following locations.

Audio Units should be placed in either of the following:

yourusername\Library\Audio\Plug-ins\Components
yourharddrive\Library\Audio\Plug-ins\Components

VST plug-ins should be placed in either of the following:

yourusername\Library\Audio\Plug-ins\VST
yourharddrive\Library\Audio\Plug-ins\VST

RTAS plug-ins that require manual installation are extremely rare. RTAS plug-ins should be placed in:

yourharddrive\Applications\Digidesign\Pro Tools\Plug-ins alias

Use plug-ins in any DAW program   Each DAW program works with plug-in effects in essentially the same way. However, there are some minor differences in how plug-ins are added to tracks.

Master It   Add a third-party delay plug-in effect as an insert effect on any track.

Master It Solution   Here are instructions for adding delay effects in each of the DAW programs we've covered.

In Live:

1. Use the Live Plug-in Device browser to locate the Audio Unit or VST plug-in folder.

2. Select the manufacturer's folder and specific plug-in you want to use.

3. Drag the plug-in directly onto any audio or MIDI track.

In Pro Tools:

1. Select any track and click Insert Selector A.

2. Navigate to the Delay effect category or to a specific manufacturer.

3. Select your plug-in from the list. Pro Tools will automatically add the effect to the track.

In Logic:

1. Select a track in either the Arrange window or Mixer window.

2. Click your mouse in the Insert field at the top of any channel strip.

3. In the menu that appears, depending on the type of track or plug-in, select Mono⊳ Audio Units, Stereo ⊳ Audio Units, or Mono -> Stereo ⊳ Audio Units.

In GarageBand:

1. Double-click any track header to open the Track Info window.

2. Make sure the Details view is open (if it's not, click the Details view at the bottom of the Track Info window.

3. Use the first drop-down menu to add a plug-in in the first additional effect slot.

Locate free plug-ins on the Web   The World Wide Web is a great resource for locating free Audio Units, VST, and RTAS plug-in effects.

Master It   Use the Internet to locate, download, and install free effects plug-ins.

Master It Solution   Follow these steps to locate free plug-ins.

1. Go to www.macmusic.org's software page.

2. Locate the Plug-ins link.

3. Select a plug-in format that your DAW uses.

4. Click the Type link to organize by commercial, free, and so on.

5. Select a plug-in and follow the necessary links to download it.

You can also check sites like www.kvraudio.com, www.bigbluelounge.com, and www.hitsquad.com, as well as performing Web searches on www.google.com, for more free plug-in resources.

Chapter 9: Virtual instruments

Use virtual instruments in your host DAW program   DAW sequencer programs like Live, Logic, GarageBand, and Pro Tools can take advantage of third-party virtual instruments to create musical performances. Each program handles virtual instrumentation in similar ways, but there are some variations from program to program.

Master It   Add a virtual synthesizer or keyboard instrument to a track in your DAW and create a simple performance.

Master It Solution   Use these steps to add and use a virtual instrument in your DAW.

In Live:

1. Create a new Live set.

2. Use the Plug-in Device Browser to locate a virtual instrument.

3. Drag the instrument from the Browser directly onto any empty MIDI track.

4. Do one of the following:

◆ Double-click any empty clip slot and create a performance with your mouse.

or

◆ Arm the track for recording then click any Clip Slot Record button to begin recording.

In Pro Tools:

1. Create a new Pro Tools session.

2. Create a new stereo instrument track.

3. Select View Mix/Edit Window and put a check mark next to Instruments and Inserts.

4. Using Insert Selector One, choose Multi-channel Plug-in ➤ Instrument and choose your instrument from the list.

5. Do one of the following:

◆ Use your mouse to draw a MIDI performance on the instrument track.

or

◆ Set your MIDI input to All or select a predefined input.

In Logic:

1. Create a new Logic session.

2. Select and click any instrument track to open the Track Mixer window.

3. In the I/O field of the selected track's channel strip, select Stereo ➤ AU Instruments and choose a *manufacturer* ➤ *instrument*.

4. Use your MIDI keyboard to record a performance or create a performance in the Matrix Edit window.

In GarageBand:

1. Create a new GarageBand music project.

2. Select Track ➤ New Track and create a new Software Instrument track.

3. Double-click the track header to open the Track Info window.

4. Open Details view at the bottom of the Track Info window.

5. Click the Generator drop-down menu at the top of the Details view.

6. Select an instrument from the Audio Unit Modules list.

7. Click the preset button to view the instrument's interface.

8. Use your MIDI keyboard, the Musical Typing keyboard, or the Track Editor window to create a performance.

Create basic patches and presets with virtual synthesizers   Every virtual synthesizer comes with its own set of included presets, but understanding how synthesizers generate sounds and knowing how to create your own patches gives you much greater control over the creative process.

Master It   Use Rob Papen's Blue synthesizer to create a simple patch with an oscillator, low pass filter, and an effect. You can download Blue or the Blue demo from www.robpapen.com.

Master It Solution   Follow these steps to work with the Blue synthesizer.

1. Add Blue to an Instrument or MIDI track in you DAW program.

2. Select the Clear button at the bottom of the Presets view.

3. Choose an Waveform from the Oscillator A menu.

4. Select Filter A from the Destination menu.

5. Select one of the low pass filters from the Type menu and use the knobs in the Filter section to make any desired adjustments.

6. Choose FX A from the Filter A Destination menu.

7. Click the FX button to view the Effects window.

8. Select an effect from the FX A menu.

9. Save the patch either in the Blue interface (click the Save button on the lower right side of the Presets window) or using your DAW's preset saving functionality.

Create drum loops with iDrum   Izotope's iDrum program is the perfect tool for quickly creating simple or complex drum loops. You can export your iDrum loops and save them for use in future projects, or you can string together a series of loops to create an entire backing track.

Master It   Create and export a simple drum loop with iDrum.

Master It Solution   Use this method to create and export a drum loop.

1. Start iDrum in stand-alone mode.

2. Create a new iDrum session using a kit with a blank pattern or select a kit and choose Clear Pattern from the File menu.

3. Program a simple or complicated beat.

4. Select Export as AIFF from the File menu.

Create a drum performance in your DAW with a virtual drum machine   Virtual drum machines like Izotope's iDrum and Native Instruments' Battery can create complete drum tracks in your DAW host program.

Master It   Use any virtual drum machine as a plug-in virtual instrument to create a simple drum performance in your DAW.

Master It Solution   Follow these instructions to create a drum performance.

1. Add the instrument as a plug-in on any virtual or instrument track. Wherever possible use a stereo track.

2. Create a click track or activate your DAW's Click function.

3. Arm the track for recording and make sure your virtual drum instrument is receiving MIDI information.

4. Use your MIDI keyboard to figure out which notes correspond to which drum samples.

5. Begin recording. Once you've created a virtual drum performance you can use your DAW's MIDI quantizing or editing functionality to fix your performance as needed.

6. To edit or draw a MIDI performance with a virtual drum machine.

◆ In Live, use the Clip View, just as you would with the Impulse drum sampler.

◆ In Pro Pools, draw the MIDI notes with the Pencil tool right onto the instrument track.

◆ In Logic, use the Pencil tool in the Matrix Edit window.

◆ In GarageBand, create MIDI notes by Control+clicking with your mouse in the Track Editor window.

Chapter 10: Apple Loops

Convert any WAV or AIFF file into an Apple Loop   Using Apple's free Apple Loops Utility you can convert any WAV or AIFF file into an Apple Loop by including metadata that tells programs like GarageBand and Logic how to play and catalogue the file.

Master It   Use the Apple Loops utility to convert any WAV file to an Apple Loop.

Master It Solution   Use these steps to create an Apple Loop.

1. Download and install the Apple Loops SDK from `developer.apple.com/sdk`.

2. Start the Apple Loops Utility.

3. Use the dialog box to locate and open a WAV file *or* click the Cancel button and drag and drop a file from your hard drive onto the Assets window.

4. Select Looping in the File Type field.

5. Fill in any other appropriate metadata.

6. Click either the Save or the Save All button to convert the file to an Apple Loop.

7. Your new Apple Loop will be located in a folder named Converted to AIFF in the same directory as the original WAV file.

Batch Convert WAV or AIFF files into Apple Loops   You can also use Apple Loops Utility to convert multiple files at once from any folder or loop library CD. This can be especially useful if you want to buy a loop collection that is only available in the WAV or Acidized format and convert it to the Apple Loops format.

Master It   Convert a large or small collection of WAV files into Apple Loops then add them to the Loop Browser in Logic or GarageBand.

Master It Solution   Follow these steps to batch convert Apple Loops.

1. Start the Apple Loops Utility.

2. Click the Cancel button on the Open File dialog box.

3. Locate the folder containing the files you want to convert.

4. Drag the folder directly onto the Assets window.

5. Select Looping in the File Type field.

6. Select any appropriate metadata in the Search or Descriptor Tags fields.

7. Click the Save or Save All button to convert your files.

Your new Apple Loops will be located in a new folder named `Converted to AIFF` inside the folder containing your original WAV files. You can add them to your Logic or GarageBand loop collection by dragging the `Converted to AIFF` folder directly onto the Loop Browser in either program.

Create new Apple Loops with any DAW program   Any DAW program that can export audio (and that's all of them) can create Apple Loops in conjunction with the Apple Loops Utility. Some programs, such as GarageBand and Logic, can create Apple Loops on their own that can then be access for use in other programs by locating them on your hard drive.

Master It   Use GarageBand to create a new Software Instrument Apple Loop and add it to the Loop Browser.

Master It Solution   Here's how to use GarageBand to create a new Apple Loop.

1. Create a new GarageBand Music Project.

2. Double-click the default piano track's track header to open the Track Info window.

3. Choose an instrument category and instrument.

4. Arm the track for recording.

5. Click the Record button to begin recording.

6. Use your MIDI keyboard or the Musical Typing keyboard to create a performance.

7. Use the Track Editor to edit the performance if necessary.

8. If necessary use the Split Track (Command+T) function to create a 1-, 2-, 4-, or 8-measure loop.

9. Select Edit ➢ Add To Loop Library.

10. Name the loop and select the appropriate metadata.

Your loop can now be accessed in either GarageBand's or Logic's Loop Browser. You can also locate the Apple Loop file in the folder *(yourharddisk) or (Yourusername)*\Library\Audio\ Apple Loops\User Loops\Single Files in order to use it in another program.

Export Apple Loops from any program   Each DAW program has its own method and options for exporting audio files. The settings you choose when exporting your files will determine their sound quality and their compatibility with other programs.

Master It   Export an AIFF file or Apple Loop from your DAW program to your desktop folder.

Master It Solution   You can create new loops in each DAW using one of the following methods.

In Reason:

1. Turn the Loop On/Off button to On.

2. Set the loop length to 1, 2, 4, or 8 measures.

3. Select File ➤ Export Loop As Audio File.

4. Choose a name, location, and format in the Export Loop As Audio File dialog box.

5. Choose a Sample Rate and Bit Depth in the Audio Export Settings window.

6. Open the file with the Apple Loops Utility to convert it to an Apple Loop.

In Live:

1. Select File ➤ Render to disk.

2. Set the length of the loop file.

3. Choose the output to render (either the Master track or an individual track).

4. Turn Normalization on.

5. Turn Render as Loop on.

6. Select the File Type, Sample Rate, and Bit Depth.

7. Click OK.

8. In the Save Audio File As dialog box, name the file and save it to the desktop folder.

9. Open the file with the Apple Loops Utility to convert it to an Apple Loop.

In Pro Tools:

1. Solo the track you want to export.

2. Use the Selector tool to select the region you want to export.

3. Choose File ➤ Bounce To ➤ Disk.

4. Select AIFF as the file type.

5. Select Stereo Interleaved.

6. Set the bit resolution and sample rate.

7. Chose Convert After Bounce.

8. Click the Bounce button

9. In the Save Bounce As dialog box, name the file and save it to the desktop.

In Logic Pro, save the loop to the Loop Browser:

1. Select the region you want to save as a loop.

2. Add the loop to the Loop Library by selecting Region ➤ Add to Loop Library from the Arrange window File menu.

3. Name the file and choose the appropriate metadata.

4. Click the Create button.

To export the loop:

1. Select File ➤ Export ➤ Region as Audio file from Logic's file menu.

2. Name the file and choose the format and bit depth.

3. Save the file to your desktop.

In Logic Express:

1. Add the loop to the Loop Library by selecting Region ➤ Add to Loop Library.

2. Name the loop and choose the appropriate metadata.

3. Use OS X's Finder to locate the file and drag it to your desktop folder.

To export the loop:

1. Select the region.

In GarageBand:

1. Select the loop in the GarageBand Timeline.

2. Add the loop to the Loop Browser by selecting Edit ➤ Add to Loop Library.

3. Name the loop and fill in the appropriate metadata.

4. Click Create.

5. Use OS X's Finder to locate the file and drag it to your desktop folder.

To export the loop to iTunes:

1. Solo the track.

2. Create a cycle region the length of the loop you want to export.

3. Select Share ➤ Send Song to iTunes.

4. The loop will automatically be added to your iTunes library.

5. Drag the loop directly from the iTunes window to your desktop.

6. Open the file with the Apple Loops Utility to convert it to an Apple Loop.

Chapter 11: MIDI

Open MIDI Files in any DAW MIDI files have many uses in your DAW programs. Among other things they offer a way to exchange a lot of information in a very small package. The process of importing and opening MIDI files is different for each DAW program.

Master It Open the MIDI file `MIDISong1.mid` in your DAW program and assign instruments to each track.

Master It Solution Here are instructions for opening MIDI files in each of the DAW programs we've covered.

In Reason:

1. Create a new Reason song.

2. Add a Mixer 14:2.

3. Choose File ➢ Import MIDI File.

4. Create Reason instruments and assign them to each individual MIDI track.

In Live:

1. Create a new Live set.

2. Use the Live File Browser to locate the MIDI file.

3. Click the triangle next to the file name to view the file's individual MIDI tracks.

4. Drag individual tracks or the entire file onto any blank space in the Clip/Device Drop area.

5. Assign Live or third-party virtual instruments to the new MIDI tracks.

In Pro Tools:

1. Create a new Pro Tools session.

2. Choose File ➢ Import ➢ MIDI to Regions List.

3. Create stereo instrument tracks for each MIDI track.

4. Assign a virtual instrument to each track.

In Logic:

1. Create a new Logic session.

2. Drag the MIDI file directly onto the first available instrument track.

3. Assign Logic's or any third-party virtual instruments to each track.

In GarageBand:

1. Drag any MIDI file directly onto the GarageBand Timeline.

2. Double-click any track header to open the Track Info window and assign a different MIDI instrument to the track if you don't want to use the instruments that GarageBand automatically assigns.

Control Reason with a MIDI control surface or keyboard.   Almost every instrument, effect, automation parameter, knob, button, and fader in Reason can be controlled by MIDI information coming from an external MIDI control surface or keyboard.

Master It   Use your control surface or keyboard's default MIDI mapping combined with the Remote Override to control different parameters on a single channel on the Mixer 14:2.

Master It Solution   Here's how to control Reason with an external MIDI device.

1. Make sure your MIDI controller is powered up, properly connected, and recognized in Reason's preferences.

2. Create a new session and add a Mixer 14:2.

3. Choose Create ➢ Sequencer Track.

4. Use the new sequencer track's drop-down menu to assign the sequencer track to the Mixer 14:2 (named Mixer 1 in the drop-down menu).

5. Select Options ➢ Remote Override Edit Mode to see which of the Mixer 14:2's parameters are already mapped to knobs or sliders on your MIDI controller.

6. Unmapped parameters will be represented by a blue arrow. Double-click any unmapped parameter on the Mixer 14:2. The blue arrow will change to a revolving lightning bolt, indicating that the parameter can now be assigned to a knob or slider on your MIDI controller.

7. Adjust any knob or slider on your MIDI controller to assign that knob or slider to the selected parameter.

Use MIDI to "play" Ableton Live   Ableton Live is another program that can be controlled extensively by an external MIDI device. Using Live's MIDI mapping you can play Live as an improvisational instrument or create and record complex mixes of your Live songs.

Master It   Use your MIDI control surface or keyboard to improvise an arrangement with the Live set `MasterOne.als`.

Master It Solution   Follow these steps to work with MIDI and Ableton Live.

1. Locate the folder `MMA Audio\Ableton Live\Sets` and open the file `MasterOne.als`.

2. Click the MIDI Map Mode switch

3. Assign MIDI keys or buttons to Scenes 1, 2, and 3 as well as the Stop Clips button.

4. Deselect the MIDI Map Mode switch.

5. Click the Stop button in the Transport bar.

6. Click the Record button in the Transport bar to prepare Live for recording.

7. Use your MIDI keyboard or control surface to launch any scene.

8. Create an arrangement by switching between scenes.

9. Click the Stop button to end recording.

10. Press the Stop button a second time to return to the beginning of the arrangement.

11. Switch to Arrange view to view and further edit your arrangement.

12. Press the spacebar or click the Play button to hear your arrangement.

Quantize a performance in any DAW   Quantization can create more consistent performances from any MIDI track

Master It   Create a "live" drum performance in your DAW with your MIDI controller or virtual keyboard, then fix the performance with ⅛-note quantization.

Master It Solution   Use these steps to quantize performances in each of the DAW programs we've covered.

In Reason:

1. Create a new Reason song.

2. Add a Mixer 14:2 and a Redrum Drum Computer.

3. Select the Redrum in the Sequencer window and arm the track to receive MIDI information

4. Turn on Reason's click track.

5. Click the Record button in the Transport bar.

6. Click the Play button to begin recording.

7. Use your MIDI keyboard or pad control surface to create a drum performance.

8. Click the Stop button to end recording.

9. Use the Pencil tool to select all of the notes in your performance.

10. Select 1/8 from the Quantize drop-down menu in the Sequencer window.

11. Click the Quantize Notes button.

In Live:

1. Create a new Live set.

2. Add any Impulse drum kit.

3. Use your MIDI keyboard or turn on Live's Computer MIDI keyboard function to create a simple drum performance.

4. Use your mouse to select a single note or a group of notes.

5. Select Edit ➢ Quantize.

6. Select a Quantize value from the Quantize To drop-down menu.

7. Click OK.

In Pro Tools:

1. Create a new Pro Tools session.

2. Create a Stereo instrument track with an Xpand! Synth or any other virtual instrument.

3. Create an aux input click track.

4. Use your MIDI keyboard to create a MIDI performance.

5. Use the Hand tool or the Selector tool to choose a note or group of notes.

6. Choose Event ➢ MIDI ➢ Grid/Groove Quantize.

7. Select a quantization value from the drop-down menu.

8. Click Apply.

In Logic:

1. Create a new Logic session.

2. Create a MIDI performance on an instrument track with any virtual instrument.

3. Double-click the region containing the MIDI performance to open the Matrix Edit window.

4. Select the Quantize tool the select a single note or "lasso" a group of notes.

5. Click one of the highlighted notes and select a quantization value from the pop-up menu.

Or, after step 3, continue with these steps:

1. Select a single note or "lasso" a group of notes.

2. Click the Quantize button just below the toolbar.

3. Select a quantize value from the pop-up menu.

In GarageBand:

1. Create a new GarageBand music project.

2. Create a MIDI performance on any Software Instrument track with your MIDI keyboard or the Musical Typing keyboard.

3. Double-click the performance in the Timeline to open the Track Edit window.

4. Select any note or group of notes.

5. Click the Align To button at the bottom of the Advanced field.

6. Adjust the View slider on the bottom left of the Track Editor window to raise or lower the quantization value.

Chapter 12: The Laptop Studio

Choose the right gear for your needs   Your laptop-based studio must be created with your specific needs in mind. Whether you are you are planning on recording live bands, primarily using your laptop for composition, or working while traveling, the combination of hardware and software should be customized to your situation.

Master It   Build a laptop studio that's right for your needs.

Master It Solution   Follow these steps to put together a laptop studio.

1. Choose a laptop with the best combination of RAM, hard drive size, and speed you can afford.

2. Choose the best DAW software for your particular recording or composition work.

3. For external recording, research and select a hardware audio or audio/MIDI interface.

4. For MIDI recording, research and select a portable MIDI keyboard.

5. Depending on your goals, research and select some or all of the following: an external mixer, headphones, speakers, audio cables, power adapters, and microphones.

Record directly into your laptop without a hardware interface   Most Mac laptops have an ⅛-inch line-in jack that can be used to record directly in to your DAW.

Master It   Record a vocal or Instrument track directly into your DAW.

Master It Solution   Use these steps to record into your laptop.

1. Open your System Preferences and select the Sound button.

2. Make sure Audio Line-in port is selected and that the Input Volume slider is raised.

3. Connect an instrument or microphone with a ¼-inch to ⅛-inch cable, an XLR to ⅛-inch cable, or a ¼-inch to USB cable.

4. Use your DAW's recording functionality to record your tracks.

Record a drum kit with a limited number of microphones   Having a small microphone collection doesn't mean you have to settle for inferior sounding recordings. With some practice and experimentation you can get good results from a few well-placed microphones.

Master It   Record a drum track with only four microphones.

Master It Solution   Use this method to record with limited microphones.

Use two matching small-diaphragm condenser mics for your overheads and a single dynamic microphone, such as an SM57, on the snare drum. If possible, use a dynamic microphone with good low-end response, such as a Shure Beta 52A or AKG D112, on the kick drum; if not, use an SM57 or other dynamic microphone. If your audio interface has only one or two inputs, you can use an external mixing board to create a submix and send the signal from the mixing board to your audio interface.

Chapter 13: Post Production

Use a limiter plug-in to increase the volume of your final mixes   The mastering process traditionally contains a number of steps, including EQ compression and limiting. Limiting in particular can help your tracks stand out, raising the overall volume of the track by lowering the loudest peaks.

Master It   Use a limiter pug-in to raise the overall volume of one of your mixes.

Master It Solution   Follow these instructions to use a limiter plug-in.

Add T-RackS Limiter or another limiter plug-in to the Master Track on any session in your DAW.

For drastic limiting use:

◆ High input levels (controlled by the Input Drive knob on the T-RackS limiter)

◆ Lower threshold settings (on the T-RackS Limiter use the three knobs on the top left marked "THR")

◆ Faster attack/release times (using T-RackS Release Time knob)

For subtler limiting, reduce the input and threshold levels and raise the attack/release time. Different limiter plug-ins may have slightly different parameter names and configurations.

Export CD-ready files from your DAW   Every DAW contains the ability to export files in AIFF or WAV form in order to create audio CDs. The best way to do this is to export your sessions at the standard 16/44.1 bit depth and sample rate used to create audio CDs.

Master It   Export a 16-bit 44.1Hz AIFF or WAV file from your DAW.

Master It Solution   Use these steps to export audio files from each of the DAW programs we've covered.

In Reason:

1. Scroll to the end of the song in the Sequencer window and locate the Song End marker.

2. Drag the Song End marker to the end of the last measure of the song.

3. Select File ➢ Export Song as Audio File from Reason's File menu.

4. Name the file and select a location.

5. Select Windows WAV File or Audio IFF File from the Format drop-down menu.

6. Click the Save button.

7. Select 44100Hz from the Sample Rate drop-down menu.

8. Select 16 from the Bit Depth menu.

9. Put a check mark in the Dither box.

10. Click Export.

In Live:

1. Use the loop/Punch-Recording Region selector to select the entire arrangement or the section you want to export.

2. Select File ➢ Render to Disk from Live's File menu.

3. Select Master from the Rendered Track drop-down menu.

4. Turn the Normalize option to On.

5. Turn the Render As Loop option to Off.

6. Choose WAV from the File Type drop-down menu.

7. Set the Bit Depth to 16 and Sample Rate to 44100.

8. Create Analysis file should be Off.

9. Convert to Mono should be Off.

10. Make sure the selected time range is correct.

11. Click OK, then select a location for the rendered file.

In Pro Tools:

1. Use the Selector tool to select the entire mix or the region that you want to export.

2. Select File ➤ Bounce To ➤ Disk from Pro Tools' File menu.

3. Choose A 1-2 Stereo from the Bounce Source drop-down menu (this assumes that you haven't made any significant changes to your output routing configuration).

4. Select WAV from the File Type drop-down menu.

5. Select Stereo Interleaved from the Format drop-down menu.

6. Set the Bit Resolution to 16.

7. Set the Sample Rate to 44100.

8. Choose a Conversion Quality of Best.

9. Select Convert After Bounce.

10. Click Bounce and choose a location for your file.

In Logic:

1. Open the Track Mixer.

2. Click the Global button on the left side of the Track Mixer to see all of the available tracks in this session, including the Master Fader.

3. Scroll to the right to view the Output 1-2 channel strip and the Master Fader.

4. Double-click the tracks Bus 1 and Bus 2 to make them visible in the Arrange and Track Mixer windows.

5. Deselect the Global button. Your Output and Master Fader tracks will be visible in the Track Mixer window on the right side of the "console."

6. Click the Bounce button at the bottom of the Out 1-2 track, or from the menu bar select File ➤ Bounce.

7. In the Bounce Output dialog box, choose a destination for your bounced mix(es).

8. For most mixes you want to choose the PCM export option. PCM includes AIFF, WAV, and Sound Designer II files. Select PCM in the Destination Box and choose the file format, resolution, and other settings.

In GarageBand:

Select Share ➤ Send Song to iTunes. GarageBand will create a mix-down of your song and send it to iTunes. iTunes will automatically open and add your song to your GarageBand playlist.

Create high-quality MP3 and AAC files with iTunes   Aside from being a digital jukebox and audio and video store, iTunes can also create high-quality MP3 files for uploading to your personal, band, or promotional website.

   Master It   Create a 192Kbps MP3 file with Variable Bit Rate Encoding.

Master It Solution   Follow these steps to encode your MP3 files.

1. Set up iTunes' Importing preferences by selecting iTunes ➢ Preferences and clicking the Advanced button.

2. Select the Importing tab.

3. Select MP3 Encoder from the Import Using drop-down menu.

4. Create your own settings by choosing Custom and filling out the following settings in the MP3 Encoder window:

5. Stereo Bit Rate: 192Kbps

6. Use Variable Bit Rate Encoding: Yes

7. Quality: Highest

8. Sample Rate: Auto

9. Channels: Auto

10. Stereo Mode: Normal

11. Smart Encoding Adjustments: Yes

12. Filter Frequencies Below 10Hz: Yes

13. Click OK to return to the Preferences window.

14. Click OK to close iTunes Preferences.

15. Select File ➢ New Playlist to create a Playlist.

16. Drag your AIFF or WAV file directly onto the playlist in the iTunes window.

17. Select the file in the iTunes window and choose Advanced ➢ Convert selection to MP3.

Use the Search function to locate your new MP3 file. You can create a copy by selecting the file in the iTunes window and dragging and dropping it onto your desktop.

Index

Wiley Publishing, Inc.
End-User License Agreement